the student's companion to social policy

edited by

pete alcock,
angus erskine
margaret may

 BLACKWELL
Publishers

 SPA

First published 1998

Blackwell Publishers Ltd
108 Cowley Road
Oxford OX4 1JF
UK

Blackwell Publishers Inc.
350 Main Street
Malden, Massachusetts 02148
USA

British Library Cataloguing in Publication Data

A CIP catalogue record for this book is available from the
British Library.

Library of Congress Cataloging in Publication Data

The student's companion to social policy / edited by Pete Alcock,
    Angus Erskine, and Margaret May.
        p.   cm.
    The authors are members of the Social Policy Association.
    Includes index.
    ISBN 0–631–20239–0. — ISBN 0–631–20240–4 (pbk.)
    1. Great Britain—Social policy.   2. Public welfare—Great Britain.   3. Social policy—Study and teaching.   I. Alcock, Peter, 1951– .   II. Erskine, Angus.   III. May, Margaret.
    IV. Social Policy Association (Great Britain)
    HN390.S78 1997   97–10142
    361.6'1'0941—dc21   CIP

Typeset in 9 on 11 pt Palatino
by Graphicraft Typesetters Ltd., Hong Kong
Printed in Great Britain by T.J. International Limited, Padstow, Cornwall

This book is printed on acid-free paper

contents

Contributors   vi
Preface   xiii
Acknowledgements   xiv

Introduction   1

Part I What Is Social Policy?   5
  I.1   The Discipline of Social Policy   7
        Pete Alcock
  I.2   The Approaches and Methods of Social Policy   14
        Angus Erskine
  I.3   The Role of Comparative Study   20
        Margaret May

Part II Values and Perspectives   27
Key Concepts   29
  II.1   Social Needs, Social Problems and Social Welfare   31
        Nick Manning
  II.2   Equality, Rights and Social Justice   37
        Peter Taylor-Gooby
  II.3   Efficiency, Equity and Choice   43
        Carol Propper
  II.4   Altruism, Reciprocity and Obligation   49
        Hilary Land
Key Perspectives   55
  II.5   The Neo-liberal Perspective   57
        David G. Green
  II.6   The Conservative Tradition of Social Welfare   64
        Robert Pinker
  II.7   The Social Democratic Perspective   71
        Michael Sullivan
  II.8   The Socialist Perspective   78
        Norman Ginsburg
  II.9   Feminist Perspectives   85
        Jane Lewis

II.10 'Race' and Social Welfare 91
Waqar Ahmad and Gary Craig
II.11 The Green Perspective 98
Michael Cahill
The Social Policy Context 105
II.12 Social Policy and Economic Policy 107
Ian Gough
II.13 Social Policy: Culture and Nationhood 115
Fiona Williams
II.14 Social Policy and Family Policy 121
Jane Millar
II.15 Social Policy in a Shrinking World 128
Bob Deacon
II.16 Social Policy and the Political Process 136
Michael Hill

Part III The Production, Organization and Consumption of Welfare 143
The Production of Welfare 145
III.1 State Welfare 147
Norman Johnson
III.2 Private Welfare 154
Edward Brunsdon
III.3 The Voluntary Sector 161
Nicholas Deakin
III.4 The Informal Sector 169
Clare Ungerson
The Organization of Welfare 175
III.5 Managing and Delivering Welfare 177
John Clarke
III.6 Central–Local Relations 184
Allan Cochrane
III.7 Social Policy within the United Kingdom 191
Richard Parry
III.8 European and Supranational Dimensions 199
Linda Hantrais
The Consumption of Welfare 205
III.9 Paying for Welfare 207
Howard Glennerster
III.10 Principles of Welfare 214
Ruth Lister
III.11 The Distribution of Welfare 221
John Hills

Part IV Issues in Social Policy 231
Social Policy and Particular Groups 233
IV.1 Children 235
Christine Hallett
IV.2 Young People 242
Bob Coles

IV.3 Older People 249
Alan Walker

IV.4 Disabled People 257
Mike Oliver

IV.5 Lone Parents 263
Jonathan Bradshaw

Service-based Issues 271

IV.6 Income Protection and Social Security 273
John Ditch

IV.7 Employment 280
Alan Deacon

IV.8 Health Care 286
Judith Allsop

IV.9 Education 293
Miriam David

IV.10 Housing 299
Alan Murie

IV.11 The Personal Social Services and Community Care 306
John Baldock

Part V Resources 313

Studying Social Policy 315

V.1 Doing Projects in Social Policy 317
Hartley Dean

V.2 Fieldwork Placements and the Social Policy Curriculum 323
Duncan Scott

Learning Resources 333

V.3 A Guide to the Literature 335
Robert M. Page

V.4 Data Sources in the UK: National, Central and Local Government 344
Fran Wasoff

V.5 Other Sources of UK Data 354
Fran Bennett

V.6 European and International Data Sources 361
Deborah Mabbett

V.7 The Role of Computers in Social Policy 368
Millsom Henry

Part VI Careers in Social Policy 375

VI.1 Careers and Social Policy Graduates in the UK 377
Eithne McLaughlin

VI.2 Postgraduate and Further Training Opportunities 388
Francesca Peroni

Glossary of Key Terms 395
Appendix: the Social Policy Association (SPA) 404
Name Index 405
Subject Index 408

CONtRiBUtORS

Waqar Ahmad is Senior Lecturer and Head of the Ethnicity and Social Policy Research Unit, University of Bradford. His teaching and research interests include ethnicity in relation to chronic illness and family-based care. He has written on 'race' and health, and 'race' and community care.

Pete Alcock is Professor of Social Policy at Sheffield Hallam University. He teaches on British social policy and poverty and anti-poverty policy. His research work includes local anti-poverty activity, the development of welfare rights work, and social security and unemployment. He has written books and articles on British social policy, poverty and anti-poverty policy, and social security reform.

Judith Allsop is Professor of Health Policy at South Bank University, where she teaches courses in health policy and the sociology of health and illness. Her research interests are in: health and health behaviour; UK and comparative health policies, particularly primary care and user involvement; the professions and regulation, complaints and disputing. She has written widely on aspects of UK health policy, complaints in health care settings and the regulation of medical work.

John Baldock is Reader in Social Policy at the University of Kent at Canterbury, where he teaches a course on the personal social services. He has published widely on social care issues and has carried out research into the provision of care to older people in the United Kingdom and in other parts of the European Union. He is particularly interested in home care and the development of the mixed economy of care.

Fran Bennett is a former director of the Child Poverty Action Group. She is currently self-employed as a policy analyst and researcher, working on social policy issues, in particular social security and poverty. She also writes the Digest in the *Journal of Social Policy*.

Jonathan Bradshaw is Professor of Social Policy at the University of York. His main research interests are in poverty and living standards, family policy, social security policy and comparative social policy. He is currently undertaking a national survey of fathers living apart from their children and a study of the impact of rising poverty among children.

Edward Brunsdon is a Principal Lecturer in Social Policy at London Guildhall University, where he teaches courses on the political economy of welfare, British social policy, comparative social policy and the assessment of welfare policies and practices. His current research interests are private welfare and comparative social policy, and he has published in the areas of private welfare and Swedish welfare.

Michael Cahill is Principal Lecturer in Social Policy at the University of Brighton. His main teaching areas are new social policy, history of social policy and transport policy. His research interests include children's travel and health and social problems of older English migrants in Spain. He has written on new social policy, older people, children and green social policy.

John Clarke works in the Faculty of Social Sciences at the Open University, where he is involved in the development and presentation of courses in social policy. He has research interests in the politics and ideologies of social welfare. He has published widely in these areas and is currently researching the impact of new managerialism in the restructuring of welfare.

Alan Cochrane is Senior Lecturer in Urban Studies in the Faculty of Social Sciences at the Open University, of which he is currently Dean and where he contributes to a wide range of teaching, particularly in urban policy and local government. His current research interests include issues of urban policy, local government restructuring and the rise of new mangerialism, focusing particularly on comparative social policy and the impact of globalization. He has written extensively on these areas and urban/social policy more generally.

Bob Coles is Senior Lecturer in Social Policy at the University of York. He has a long-standing research interest in youth issues. He is currently reviewing youth policies in European Union countries.

Gary Craig is Professor of Social Policy and Head of the Policy Studies Research Centre at the University of Humberside. He is editor of the *Community Development Journal*. He researches in the fields of social security, poverty and anti-poverty work, community care, community development and 'race'. He has written recently on community development, anti-poverty policy and child support.

Miriam David is Professor and Director of the Social Sciences Research Centre in the School of Education, Politics and Social Sciences and Head of Research at South Bank University. Her main teaching interests are in the area of women's studies. She is co-editor with Dr Dulcie Groves of *The Journal of Social Policy* and an executive editor of *The British Journal of Sociology of Education*. She researches and writes on families, gender, education and social policy.

Alan Deacon is Professor of Social Policy and Dean of the Faculty of Economics and Social Studies at the University of Leeds. His principal research and teaching interests are the twentieth-century history of social policy, social security and moral debates in welfare. He was editor of the *Journal of Social Policy* from 1986 to 1991.

Bob Deacon is Director of the International Social Policy Research Unit at Leeds Metropolitan University and Professor of Social Policy. He now researches and writes on the impact of globalization on social policy, having previously written on the social policy of Eastern Europe and the Soviet Union. He has acted as a consultant for international organizations and has advised governments on the future of their social policies.

Nicholas Deakin is Professor of Social Policy and Administration at Birmingham University, where he teaches on a wide range of social policy courses. His research interests include inner city issues, new towns, race relations and voluntary organizations. He has written extensively on these areas and, recently, chaired the NCVO's Independent Commission on the Future of the Voluntary Sector.

Hartley Dean is Reader in Social Policy at the University of Luton. His research interests are in the fields of poverty, social security, welfare rights and redress. He has conducted research that has involved especially vulnerable and marginalized members of society.

John Ditch is Professor and Head of Social Policy at the University of York. His research has included comparative studies of child support and social assistance, the impacts of changes in circumstances on benefit administration and the needs of first time applicants for benefit. He is Coordinator of the European Observatory of National Family Policies.

Angus Erskine is Senior Lecturer in Social Policy in the Department of Applied Social Science, University of Stirling. His research and teaching interests are in the fields of poverty, social security and unemployment.

Norman Ginsburg is Professor of Social Policy and Administration at the University of North London. His teaching and research interests cover the impact of social policy on class, race and gender divisions, with particular emphasis on housing, social security and family policies and cross-national analysis of welfare regimes. He has written books on capital and social policy and comparative social policy analysis.

Howard Glennerster is Professor of Social Administration at the London School of Economics, where he contributes to a wide range of social policy courses. His research has covered most aspects of the finance of social services, public expenditure controls, health service reforms, the finance of education and the history of social policy. He has published extensively in these areas, as well as advising on social policy.

Ian Gough is Professor of Social Policy at the University of Bath, following a long period at the University of Manchester. His teaching and research interests include economic and social policy and comparative policy analysis. He has written on the political economy of the welfare state, competition between welfare states and theories of human need.

David Green is the Director of the Health and Welfare Unit at the Institute of Economic Affairs. He was formerly a Labour councillor in Newcastle upon Tyne and a Research Fellow at the Australian National University. He has written books on mutual aid, the medical establishment, civil society and community politics and the development of the New Right.

Christine Hallett is Professor of Social Policy and Director of the Social Work Research Centre at the University of Stirling. She has published in the fields of child welfare, child protection and women and social policy. She is currently directing studies of the Children's Hearing system and of children's negotiation strategies and pathways to welfare.

Linda Hantrais holds a chair in the Department of European Studies and is Director of the European Research Centre at Loughborough University. Her main research interests are in cross-national comparative research theory, methodology and practice, with particular reference to public policy in Europe. She has written extensively on these areas and social and family policies in Europe.

Millsom Henry is the Deputy Director of SocInfo, the CTI Centre for Sociology, Politics and Social Policy based at the University of Stirling. Her research interests are in the areas of gender, ethnicity, culture and new technologies.

Michael Hill is Professor of Social Policy at the University of Newcastle upon Tyne. He has held academic posts at Reading, Bristol and Oxford and before these was a civil servant in social security administration. He was a local councillor in Reading (1966–9) and a member of the Council on Tribunals (1991–7). He has written a number of books on social policy and on the policy-making process.

John Hills is Reader in Economics and Social Policy at the London School of Economics, where he is also Co-Director of the Welfare State Programme. His research interests include social policy research methods, the economics of public finance, income distribution, social security, housing finance, taxation and the welfare state as a whole. He has published widely in these areas and also acts as Programme Advisor on Income and Wealth to the Joseph Rowntree Foundation.

Norman Johnson is Professor of Social Policy at the University of Portsmouth, where he teaches on a wide range of social policy courses. His main current research interests are comparative social policy and mixed economies of welfare. He has published widely in these areas and in social policy more generally, and is currently working on a comparative study of mixed economies of welfare.

Hilary Land is Professor of Family Policy and Child Welfare in the School for Policy Studies at the University of Bristol. Her teaching and research interests include analyses of the relationship between families and the state, particularly from feminist perspectives, the development of social security policies and employment policies in both comparative and historical contexts. Current research includes policies towards lone parents since 1945 and transitions from childhood to adulthood and 'independence'.

Jane Lewis is Professor of History at Oxford, where she is a fellow of All Souls College and Director of the Wellcome Unit for the History of Medicine. She was formerly at the LSE. She is the author of many books and articles in the areas of community care, the role of the voluntary sector, the history of social policy, and women and social policy.

Ruth Lister is Professor of Social Policy at Loughborough University, where she teaches on a wide range of social policy courses. Her main research interests are poverty and income maintenance, women and social policy and feminist perspectives. She has published widely in these areas and in social policy more generally.

Eithne McLaughlin is Professor of Social Policy at the Queen's University, Belfast, where she contributes to a wide range of social policy courses. Her main research interests, on which she has published widely, are in the areas of social security, employment policies and citizenship.

Deborah Mabbett convenes Brunel University's MA in Public and Social Administration, and lectures on social security and political economy. Her research includes comparative studies of social security in several EU countries, the USA and Australia. She also works on problems of the economic transition in the former Soviet Union, and has written a historical analysis of the political economy of Sweden and New Zealand.

Nick Manning is Professor of Social Policy and Sociology, and Head of the School of Social Studies, University of Nottingham. His recent research has been on Eastern Europe, and he is currently directing a study of unemployment and the labour market in Moscow, St Petersburg and Voronezh. He has written books on health care, social problems and comparative social policy.

Margaret May is a Principal Lecturer in Social Policy at London Guildhall University where she teaches courses on comparative social policy, the political economy of welfare, British social policy and the assessment of welfare policies and practices. Her current research interests are private welfare and comparative social policy and she has published in the areas of private welfare and Swedish welfare.

Jane Millar is Professor of Social Policy at the University of Bath. Her research interests are in the areas of social security, family and labour market. She is the UK represent-ative on the European Commission Observatory on National Family Policies and is currently involved in research projects on definitions of family obligations and on low pay and poverty. She teaches on family and gender, comparative social security policy and research methods.

Alan Murie is Professor of Urban and Regional Studies and Director of the Centre for Urban and Regional Studies at the University of Birmingham. He was previously Professor of Planning and Housing at Heriot-Watt University and has held visiting Professorships at the Universities of Amsterdam and Utrecht. He was editor of *Housing Studies* between 1984 and 1996, has acted as specialist advisor to the House of Commons Environment Committee and has published widely on housing and social policy.

Mike Oliver is Professor of Disability Studies, University of Greenwich. He has par-ticipated in major policy reviews in education, health and social services and published numerous books and articles on disability and other social policy issues over the past 15 years. He is Chair of the Research Advisory Group of the British Council of Disabled People and Executive Editor of *Disability and Society*.

Robert Page is Lecturer in Social Policy and Administration at the University of Nottingham. He has written on stigma and altruism. His main interest is in the theory and practice of socialist social policy.

Richard Parry is Senior Lecturer in Social Policy at the University of Edinburgh, where he teaches on a range of social policy courses. His main research interests are European social policy, Scottish government and privatization. He has published widely in these areas and is currently researching the Treasury's role in British social policy.

Francesca Peroni is a Lecturer in Social Policy at the University of Exeter, where she teaches on the sociology and politics of health and welfare, housing and education policy. Her publications include studies of the Citizen's Charter and chronic illness, and she is currently researching the social construction of choice and its impact on the policy agenda.

Robert Pinker is Emeritus Professor of Social Administration at the LSE and is a member of the Press Complaints Commission. His teaching and research interests lie in the fields of social welfare theory, military welfare and self-regulatory institutions. He has written on social theory and social policy and the role of social work in an enterprise society.

Carol Propper is Professor of Economics of Public Policy in the Department of Economics and School for Policy Studies at the University of Bristol. Her current research interests include the economics of the NHS quasi-market, equity in the delivery of health care and the dynamics of poverty. She publishes widely in both economics and social policy journals and books.

Duncan Scott is Senior Lecturer in Social Policy at the University of Manchester. He has taught at all levels of education and developed and taught an undergraduate course linked to fieldwork placements over more than twenty years. He has also coordinated and co-authored an audio-visual training pack related to fieldwork.

Michael Sullivan is the Acting Head of Social Policy at the University of Wales at Swansea. His teaching and research interests include British social policy and the history and politics of social policy. He has written a number of books on politics, ideology and social policy and the development of social policy in Britain.

Peter Taylor-Gooby is Professor of Social Policy at the University of Kent and Director of the ESRC Programme on Economic Beliefs and Behaviour. His main teaching and research interests lie in three areas: social policy in EU member countries; public opinion and social policy; and the development of a more humane welfare system in the UK. He has written on social change and social welfare, markets and managers, European welfare and the dependency culture.

Clare Ungerson is Professor of Social Policy at the University of Southampton, where she teaches courses on gender and social policy, informal care, reproductive policies and social protection, and social problems and social policy. Since the early 1980s she has conducted research, within a feminist perspective, in informal care and the general relationship between women and social policy, in both Britain and other parts of Europe. She has published widely in these areas and in social policy more generally, and is currently working on the marketization of community care and its impact on carers and users.

Alan Walker is Professor of Social Policy at the University of Sheffield. His research and teaching interests span a wide field in sociology, social policy and social gerontology. He has researched and published extensively on community care, the family care of older people, intergenerational relations, poverty and social exclusion, ageing and the labour market, social planning, disability and European social policy.

Fran Wasoff is Senior Lecturer and Head of Department, Department of Social Policy, University of Edinburgh. Her research interests are in the areas of family policy, gender and social policy, family law and social policy and socio-legal studies. She teaches research methods, gender and social policy, housing policy, family research and social policy and law and social policy.

Fiona Williams is Professor of Social Policy at the University of Leeds. She has written widely on social divisions and social policy. Her current research and teaching interests include: gender, race and class in comparative social policy; social theory, social change and social policy; and new approaches to thinking about welfare states and their futures.

preface

Social policy has become an increasingly popular subject in recent years. In part this probably reflects the normal growth of what only began to be taught in higher education in the UK as an independent subject in the 1950s and 1960s. But it is also the result of the much increased visibility of the subject as the present and future of the welfare state, its core topic for teaching and research, has become a constant issue of national debate.

The Social Policy Association (SPA) was established over thirty years ago to bring together teachers, researchers, practitioners and students to support the development of the study of social policy and administration. Its object is to encourage teaching, research and scholarship in this broad-based and multi-disciplinary subject, and its contributions include establishing the *Journal of Social Policy* and publishing the *Social Policy Review*. As student resources have become increasingly stretched and the cost of publications greater, the Association has become particularly aware of the need for an up-to-date, authoritative and concise handbook which could be made available at a reasonable cost.

The *Student's Companion* is based upon a close, as well as formal, collaboration between the SPA and Blackwell. The Association took the initiative in the production of the book and appointed the editors to act on its behalf to bring it to fruition. The contributors to the volume are members of the SPA and comprise leading academics and researchers in the subject throughout the UK. Their work provides a comprehensive and stimulating insight into the range of ideas and issues in social policy which students will encounter in their studies.

The Social Policy Association is pleased to join with Blackwell in presenting this first *Student's Companion to Social Policy* and is confident that it will meet the needs and expectations of all those who use it. The whole volume is designed as a handbook and guide to the subject of social policy. We shall be particularly glad to hear from you, its readers, on the use that you have been able to make of it.

Adrian Sinfield
President, Social Policy Association

acknowledgements

The authors and publishers gratefully acknowledge the following for permission to reproduce copyright material:

John Hills and the Joseph Rowntree Foundation for figures II.12.1, II.12.2 and II.12.3; Manchester University Settlement for figure V.2.2; Routledge, the authors and the artist for figure V.2.3; The Institute for Employment Studies for figure VI.1.1.

The publishers apologize for any errors or omissions in the above list and would be grateful to be notified of any corrections that should be incorporated in the next edition or reprint of this book.

INtRODUCtION

This *Students' Companion to Social Policy* is a resource book that will be of practical use to students of social policy throughout their undergraduate study. It aims to acquaint students with the study of social policy by covering some of the main themes and issues explored in it at undergraduate level in the UK. Readers are introduced to current theoretical and ideological debates. Each chapter includes a short guide to further reading which points to some of the literature that pursues the issues addressed in the chapter in more depth. The *Companion* should be of value to students studying social policy on its own, as part of another undergraduate programme (for instance, sociology, politics or applied social science) or as part of a professional course in a related field (for instance, social work or nursing).

The contributors to this book are scholars and teachers in the forefront of social policy studies in the UK, and were selected on the basis that their expertise in their particular areas would provide readers with an authoritative introduction to a range of thinking and scholarship. Because this publication has been prepared as a handbook and guide, rather than as a single text which focuses on one or two main themes, readers may wish to read the book from cover to cover. But, for most, it is more likely to be used as a source of reference for consultation. The chapters can be read in any order, separately or in groups.

Part I introduces students to the scope and structure of the subject – and its (inter)relationship with other disciplines. There is no agreement among those who teach and research in social policy about the exact boundaries of the subject, or, indeed, whether social policy is best described as a discipline or a field of study. The editors, in writing these chapters, provide their own different views of the nature of social policy.

Part II provides readers with a guide to the theoretical and ideological context of the study of social policy. Key concepts are addressed and explained, and students are introduced to the central themes which provide the intellectual foundations to debates about the focus and aims of the subject. This section then situates the debates about policy development within the changing economic, demographic and political structures in which policies are developed and implemented.

Part III focuses on the provision and delivery of social policies. The different providers of welfare are examined by looking at the four main sectors of welfare, setting these in the context of a brief examination of the ways in which welfare is produced and the split between providers, purchasers and consumers. The different geographical organization of welfare within the UK is explained, as well as the role of the supranational agencies, such as the European Union. The delivery of welfare is also explored by focusing on the access to, and use of, welfare by consumers, including examining the different constructions of the consumer adopted within debates about social policies. Finally, this section looks at the uneven consumption of welfare across different social classes and groups.

Part IV looks at the way welfare services are organized, and analysed. Welfare is frequently perceived by non-specialists as being focused upon particular social groups, notably those deemed to be in need of policy intervention or assistance. Some of these groups are examined and the range of services available to them discussed. However, social policy analysts do not generally conceive of welfare as being organized around client groups, but rather as providing a range of services for the population at large – from which a wide range of needs, from all social groups, will be met. This is a distinction which is sometimes confused with the debate over universalism and selectivity in welfare, which is explained in Part II. The main services which dominate much academic analysis of social policy are discussed separately in this fourth section.

Part V serves a more practical function for students of social policy. It focuses upon the resources that can be drawn upon while studying. Different modes of teaching and learning are examined, drawing attention in particular to the role of new forms of learning and assessment, and to the central place now occupied by the use of computers and electronically stored data. In this section a more general overview and guide to published material in the social policy field and summaries of the main sources of statistical and research data which students of social policy may use are provided.

Part VI also focuses upon practical issues for students of social policy. It deals with the further study of the discipline beyond undergraduate level and the use of social policy in the pursuit of a range of both specialist and non-specialist careers. The contributions to this section are likely to be of interest to the prospective student of social policy, as well as providing advice and suggestions to current undergraduates. Finally, there is a glossary of terms frequently used in social policy, which was drafted by Margaret May and developed further by the three editors.

The authors of the articles in this book have been asked by the editors to conform to a consistent style of referencing. We asked contributors not to refer to additional sources in their text apart from those contained in their guide to further reading. This may be confusing for an undergraduate student who submits an essay. This style has been followed here because we wanted to produce a book which was of a manageable size. The attention of readers is drawn to chapter V.3, by Robert Page, where he follows normal academic conventions in terms of referencing. This is the model that should more usually be adopted by students when preparing their assignments.

As editors we are very grateful for the work put into this volume by the contributors. We set out to produce a collection written by some of the most distinguished teachers and lecturers in social policy and we asked them to write in as accessible a way as possible while introducing complex issues in a short space. Authors in social policy are no different from other authors: some write sharply and clearly, others are more difficult to follow and pack difficult ideas together. This collection reflects the range of styles of writing and the range of ideological and political positions students of social policy are likely to encounter. We hope that it will encourage readers to investigate further and read more widely.

We were successful in persuading our authors to contribute because this volume has been prepared with the support and backing of the Social Policy Association, which brings together academics in social policy. While we, as editors, made the difficult and contentious decisions about what should be left out of this collection, what should be included and who should be asked to write, the SPA's support was essential in inveigling our contributors to take part. We hope that what we have produced is worthy of the backing of the SPA and will be of value to the social policy community as a whole. Any shortcomings in this collection are, however, our responsibility.

part 1
what is social policy?

I.1

tHe DISCIPLINe of sociaL poLICY
pete aLcock

WHAT IS IN A DISCIPLINE?

Social policy is a discipline within the social sciences. It is quite different to other social science disciplines such as sociology, economics and politics because, as discussed by Erskine in Chapter I.2, it is based upon a distinct empirical focus – the support of well-being through social action. However, as Erskine also discusses, social policy draws on the methods used and the understanding developed within these other disciplines. Thus, although it is on the one hand an academic discipline – to be studied and developed in its own right – it is also an interdisciplinary field – drawing on and developing links with other cognate disciplines at every stage and overlapping at times with these in terms of both empirical foci and methods of analysis. To put this another way, the boundaries between social policy and other social science disciplines are porous, and shifting; and students and practitioners of social policy may also be working in these other disciplines or cooperating closely with others who do.

The term social policy is not only used to refer to an academic discipline and its study, however; it is also used to refer to social action in the real world. Social policy is the term used to describe actions aimed at promoting well-being; it is also the term used to denote the academic study of such actions. This may seem a bit confusing at

first – whereas sociology students study *society*, social policy students study *social policy* – but it is a confusion which we all soon learn to live with.

This confusion is also true of the discipline versus interdisciplinary field debate referred to above. Social policy is a discipline which operates and develops through interdisciplinary collaboration. This may seem odd in principle; but it is not a problem in practice. Thus students studying social policy may well find themselves in the same departments, or on the same degree programmes, as others studying different disciplines such as sociology, or even pursuing professional education and training; for instance, in social work. These students will learn much from each other and will often learn together; but they are not all doing the same thing. Similarly, those engaged in social policy research often work alongside economists or statisticians, but the *focus* of investigation is on the explanation or evaluation of policy – not on economic models or data analysis.

Some of these links and overlaps with cognate disciplines, and some of the implications of these for the study of social policy, are explored in more detail in Part II, where we examine the values and the perspectives which underlie the discipline. We will not discuss them any further here, therefore; rather we will move on to look at the development of social policy as a discipline, for it has a particularly interesting history, involving even a change of name from *social administration* to *social policy*.

THE DEVELOPMENT OF SOCIAL POLICY

The development of social policy can be traced back at least a hundred years to the end of the nineteenth century. This is because it is closely linked to the establishment and development of the *Fabian Society* and to the influence of Fabian politics on policy development in Britain. The aim of the Fabian Society was to press for the introduction of social protection through the state to combat the social problems which, it argued, had developed in Britain's capitalist economic structure. This pressure was also linked to the establishment and growth of the Labour Party, which Fabians saw as a political vehicle for the achievement of policy innovation and reform. The early development of Fabian social policy drew on new research evidence emerging from the work of people like Booth and Rowntree, who had undertaken studies of the extent and depth of poverty in Britain at the end of the nineteenth century, and had concluded that it was both serious and widespread. Booth and Rowntree's work suggested that policy intervention through the state was needed, the Fabians took this up to argue that it should be done and the new Labour Party provided a potential base for securing the political power to implement it.

In fact, of course, it was some time before the Labour Party did achieve political power in Britain, and important reforms were introduced before this by the Liberal governments of the early twentieth century. One of the catalysts for this were the reports of a Royal Commission on the *Poor Laws* (the mainstay of nineteenth-century welfare policy) in 1909. There were two reports from the commission because different factions within it could not agree:

- a *Minority* Report, produced by prominent Fabians Sydney and Beatrice Webb;
- a *Majority* Report, dominated by Bernard and Helen Bosanquet, leading figures in the Charity Organisation Society (COS), a body coordinating voluntary action to relieve poverty.

Both, however, did advocate policy reform, and since then policy initiatives supported directly or indirectly by the state have become more and more widespread.

What is particularly significant for our purposes about the policy commitments of the Webbs and the Bosanquets, however, is that they did not encompass only the promotion of social policy, but extended to a commitment to the study and evaluation of policy as it developed. The most important vehicle for which was the establishment of the London School of Economics (LSE) by the Webbs and the incorporation within it of the COS's School of Sociology to form a new Department of Social Sciences and Administration in 1912. This was the first, and most important, base for the discipline of social policy. Its first new lecturer was Clement Attlee (later Prime Minister in the reforming Labour government after the Second World War); and later members included Beveridge (architect of the modern social security system), Tawney (who developed a theoretical case for policy reform) and T. H. Marshall (whose idea of 'social citizenship' has been used by many as a theoretical basis for the discipline).

The LSE has continued since then to provide a leading base for the study and evaluation of social policy. After the Second World War it was the base for Titmuss (the first Professor of Social Administration in the 1950s) and Townsend (who revitalized research into poverty and inequality in the 1960s and became a critic of the limitations of the post-war welfare state). Some of the contributors to this *Companion* come from the LSE's current Department of Social Policy and

Administration or from its research centres; but the study of social policy has extended much further than this over the past eighty years or so. Social policy is now studied in most universities in Britain (Townsend later worked in Essex and Bristol), and much more widely in schools and colleges too. There are also major research centres in a number of these universities and others operating independently to provide specialist services in particular fields.

What is more, as we shall see shortly, this wider development of teaching and research has promoted debate and controversy over the aims and methods of study and over the direction of, and priorities for, research and policy reform – and this has provided a challenge to the dominant role of Fabianism within social policy.

- Much of the early teaching of social policy was geared to the training of social workers and others to act as providers within existing welfare services – it was focused upon *how* to administer welfare, rather than upon *what* welfare should be administered.
- Much of the early research work concentrated on measuring poverty and other social problems in order to provide evidence of the need for policy intervention – it was focused upon *measurement* of social need, rather than upon *definition* of need or *debate* about the appropriateness of seeking to respond to it.

These broader questions have become much more important as the discipline has expanded and developed in the latter half of the twentieth century. However, in the middle of the century such questions seemed to a large extent to be answered by the introduction of a 'welfare state' by the Labour government of 1945–51. At this stage the debate about the direction of reform appeared to have been won conclusively by the Fabian supporters of state welfare, and the focus of the discipline upon the training of state welfare workers and the empirical measurement

of new welfare needs appeared to have been established as the orthodoxy for all.

THE WELFARE STATE AND THE WELFARE CONSENSUS

The most important development in social policy during the twentieth century, and the most important feature of it for academic study, has been the creation of the 'welfare state' in the years immediately following the Second World War. In fact, of course, the depiction of these reforms as a 'welfare state' is to some extent a controversial and contested analysis. It begs questions about what we mean by this and why these particular reforms should be seen as achieving it; and these questions are matters of significant debate and disagreement. Nevertheless, the post-war welfare state thesis has been widely promulgated – and for important and obvious reasons.

Part of the reason for the electoral success of the Labour government in 1945 was its manifesto commitment to introduce state provision to meet major welfare needs – and to do this on a comprehensive basis, replacing the piecemeal and partial provision which had been developed in the earlier part of the century. This message had been prefigured in Beveridge's famous report on the need for comprehensive social security reform, published in 1942 and included in Labour's manifesto promises. Beveridge had written about the *Five Giant Social Evils* which had undermined British society before the war: ignorance, disease, idleness, squalor and want. He argued that it was in the interests of all citizens to remove these evils from British society, and it was the duty of the state, as the representative body of all citizens, to act to do this.

In the years following the war, comprehensive state provision to combat each was introduced:

- free education up to age 15, to combat ignorance;

- a national health service (NHS) free at the point of use, to combat disease;
- state commitment to securing full employment, to combat idleness;
- public housing for all citizens to rent, to combat squalor;
- national insurance benefits for all in need, to combat want.

All of these required the development of major state services for citizens and they resulted in a major extension of state responsibility – and state expenditure.

Many of the reforms were the product of the post-war Labour government; but despite their Fabian roots they were not supported only by Labour. Indeed, the state education plans had been introduced by a Conservative member of the coalition government (R. A. Butler) in 1944, and the Conservative governments of the 1950s supported the spirit of the reforms and maintained their basic structure. This cross-party consensus on state welfare was so strong that it even acquired an acronym – *Butskellism*, comprised of the names of the Labour Chancellor (Gaitskell) and his Conservative successor (Butler).

For Fabian social policy, therefore, the post-war welfare state could be seen as the culmination of academic and political influence on government, and after this analysis and debate focused more on the problems of how to administer and improve existing state welfare than on the question of whether these were appropriate mechanisms for the social promotion of well-being. However, this narrow Fabian focus within post-war social policy did not last for long. It was soon under challenge from other perspectives which queried both the success and the desirability of state welfare.

THEORETICAL PLURALISM

In the 1960s and after the focus of social policy began to move beyond the narrow confines of Fabian welfare statism. This was symbolized most dramatically in a change of name from *social administration* (associated with analysing the operation of existing welfare services) to *social policy* (associated with questioning the policy base of welfare provision) in 1987. More generally, however, academic and political debate began to embrace a wider range of conflicting perspectives, which challenged the orthodoxy of Fabianism and moved the discipline towards a more open theoretical pluralism.

The new left

The predominant focus of Fabianism on the success and desirability of state welfare was challenged in the 1960s and 1970s by critics on the left. Drawing on Marxist analysis of capitalist society, they argued that welfare services had not replaced the exploitative relationships of the labour market; and that, although they had provided benefits for the poor and the working class, these services had also helped to support future capitalist development by providing a secure base for the market economy to operate. Unlike the Fabian socialists of the early twentieth century, these new left critics did not necessarily see the further expansion of the existing state welfare base of social policy as resolving this dilemma; rather they argued that policy changes would be needed in the economic structure of the capital and labour markets if well-being was to be promoted successfully for all. For the new left, therefore, state welfare was a double-edged sword which could not alone provide adequate welfare for all.

The new right

In the 1970s and 1980s rather different criticisms of state welfare began to appear from the right of the political spectrum. Right-wing proponents of free market capitalism, most notably Hayek, had been critical of the creation of the welfare state in the 1940s, but had at the time been a marginal voice in academic and political debate. In the 1970s, as the advent of economic recession revealed the limitations of state welfare, they became both more vocal and more widely supported – especially after the move to the right of the Conservative Party following the election of Margaret Thatcher as leader in 1975. The essence of the new right critique is that the development of extensive state welfare services is incompatible with the maintenance of a successful market economy, and that this problem will get worse as welfare expands to meet more and more social needs. Therefore, social needs must be met in other ways and state welfare withdrawn or removed – as was attempted to some extent by the Thatcherite governments of the 1980s. For the new right, therefore, the desirability of state welfare itself is called into question.

The new radicals

The failings and limitations of state welfare also came under challenge in the late twentieth century from perspectives outside of the traditional left/right political spectrum. Most significant here has been the challenge of feminism and its analysis of the unequal treatment of men and women in the development and delivery of welfare services. As feminists point out, the provision of welfare is 'gendered'. Other critical perspectives have also challenged traditional analysis of state welfare and have suggested that different and more radical questions should be addressed in the study and development of social policy. Anti-racists have pointed out that some welfare services can reinforce social divisions within society; disability campaigners have suggested that some social needs can be systematically ignored; and more generally environmentalists have argued that existing services are in any case predicated upon economic trends which cannot be sustained over the longer term.

These new radical voices vary widely, and sometimes are mutually conflicting; and, though they challenge state welfare, they are also critical of the new left and the new right, as can be seen in more detail in some of the chapters in Part II. Taken together, however, the effect of all of these new (or not-so-new) theories has been to challenge the Fabian support for state welfare which had previously been at the heart of social policy debate, and to replace this with a theoretical and ideological pluralism, in which questions of *whether* or *why* to pursue state welfare have become more important than questions of *how* or *when*.

GEOGRAPHICAL BOUNDARIES

Another challenge to the focus on state welfare in social policy has come from critics who have argued that a concentration on the national services of the early post-war period has ignored the importance of the local base of much welfare provision in Britain, and the impact of international and supranational pressures on policy development within the country.

The central/local divide in the development and delivery of social policy has always been a feature of the policy agenda, and even in reforms of the 1940s responsibility for major welfare services such as education and housing remained largely in local hands. More recently, however, the appropriate balance between central and local control of services has become an important focus of research and analysis within the discipline – and has also become a site of political debate and conflict, as discussed in chapter III.6. This is a conflict which cannot easily be resolved and there are arguments on both sides of the central/local debate; but it is a debate which must be addressed by all serious students of social policy.

The impact of international forces on policy development and debate in Britain is also a long-standing issue. However, the international context of British social policy has been altered significantly over the past two decades since Britain's entry into the

European Union (EU). The supranational powers of the EU directly affect the policy agenda within Britain, as discussed in more detail in chapter III.8; and they mean that policy analysis can no longer be contained within the political confines of one member state. However, the international influences on social policy in Britain, and in other countries, extend beyond the formal powers of the EU and include many of the global forces and institutions discussed in chapter II.15.

Thus the broadening boundaries of social policy debate and development mean that the policy parameters of nation states are determined in part at least by the decisions and actions of others outside them. And this means that the study of social policy must recognize and respond to this international policy order too. It is for these reasons, among others, that comparative analysis has become an essential feature of the curriculum within social policy, and this is discussed by May in chapter I.3.

The Future of Social Policy

The discipline of social policy therefore has developed from its Fabian roots at the LSE and its support for the welfare state reforms of the early post-war years to embrace a wide range of diverse – and conflicting – theoretical debates about both the value and the success of public welfare provision and a wider conceptualization of the policy context as the product of local and global action as well as national politics. Social policy is now characterized by theoretical and geographical pluralism. It is also characterized by 'welfare pluralism': the recognition, as discussed in the chapters in Part III, that state provision is only one feature of a broader mixture of differing forms and levels of welfare service.

We could perhaps capture these new pluralisms within social policy as the product of a shift in focus within the discipline from the *welfare state* to the *welfare mix* – and this is a shift which is likely to develop further as the twentieth century draws to a close. Like all academic disciplines, and all social forces, social policy is dynamic, and changes in the past will continue to restructure our agenda for study in the future. Looking to this future this may mean social policy:

- moving further beyond state-based welfare, to focus not only upon public services but also upon partnerships between the state and other providers of welfare and well-being and on the role of the state as a subsidizer and a regulator of the actions of others;
- moving further beyond the provider culture, to focus not only upon questions of who provides welfare services but also on examination of who benefits from these and how access to such benefits is determined, or prevented;
- moving further beyond provision through redistribution, to focus not only upon the consumption of welfare services but also upon how policy interventions can influence the production and initial distribution of wealth and power within society.

These changes will accentuate further the overlap and the collaboration between social policy and other disciplines such as sociology, economics, politics and law. As I said at the beginning of this chapter, however, it is just such interdisciplinary flexibility which has always been a central feature of the study of social policy – that this is likely to continue and to grow is a sign of academic vitality and strength.

Guide to Further Reading

There are no textbooks dealing with the history and development of the discipline of social policy – it is perhaps too boring a topic for a whole book. However, Bulmer, M., Lewis, J. and Piachaud, D. (eds) (1989) *The Goals of Social Policy*. London: Unwin Hyman, is a review and history of the social policy work of the London School of Economics (LSE). The LSE remains the leading institution in the field and this collection provides a valuable insight into how the discipline has developed there. The work of the LSE's modern 'founding father', Richard Titmuss, also provides an illuminating guide to early post Second World War debates within the field. The best collection here is Titmuss, R. (1958) *Essays on 'the Welfare State'*. London: Unwin.

More recently, however, a number of authors have sought to provide introductory guides to the discipline. The most well established is Hill, M. (1997) *Understanding Social Policy*, 5th edn. Oxford: Blackwell, which provides a service-based review of welfare policy. Alcock, P. (1996) *Social Policy in Britain: Themes and Issues*. Basingstoke: Macmillan, takes a broader approach identifying key questions of structure, context and issues. Spicker, P. (1995) *Social Policy: Themes and Approaches*. Hemel Hempstead: Harvester/Wheatsheaf, adopts a more theoretical approach based on explanation, organization and research.

Alternative and critical introductions are also now available. Two which may be of particular interest to students are: Cahill, M. (1994) *New Social Policy*. Oxford: Blackwell, which approaches policy issues from the perspective of citizen's lives, focusing on issues such as shopping, working or travelling; and Williams, F. (1989) *Social Policy: a Critical Introduction*. Cambridge: Polity Press, which points out the way in which much traditional writing within the discipline has underemphasized the important issues of gender and 'race'.

the approaches and methods of social policy

angus erskine

INTRODUCTION

Social policy is studied and taught in universities and colleges, as well as being an area of practice. This is to point to a distinction, which is frequently confusing for students of social policy, between social policy as a field of study and social policy as a set of policies adopted by organizations to achieve social purposes. The connection to practice is what is central to social policy, but that can create a further difficulty for students when they first come across the subject. Social policy analysts direct their attention to improving conditions. The problem with this is that there is no one scientific way of agreeing what is 'better'. The answer relies upon a value judgement. For example, some people argue that it is better for children to be brought up by biological parents who are married. Others argue that it is better for a child to be loved by his or her parent(s) than to live in a household in which the parents are fighting. Despite the attempts to 'measure' the outcomes of these alternatives, by looking at school performance, truancy or juvenile delinquency, neither case can be proved or disproved in a scientific way. The dispute is really about what a 'good' family and upbringing is, and this is a normative view. Ultimately the debate cannot be resolved because it is based upon values, not upon facts.

In social policy, there is another tension, that between analysis and practice. To an extent, they involve different skills and approaches. Analysis requires scepticism, while practice requires conviction. Those who study social policies have to ask questions about evidence. While social policy cannot claim to be a science, it draws its legitimacy as a subject on its ability to draw upon the methods of a number of social sciences and apply these in a rigorous and disciplined way to understand the field in which we are interested. But social policy also involves beliefs and taking sides about issues which social science cannot resolve. As chapters II.1 to II.13 illustrate, social policy involves understanding a range of philosophical and political perspectives.

Alcock refers in chapter I.1 to social policy as a discipline, but this is contested. Some people see social policy as a sub-branch of sociology. Sociology is interested in the relationships between social groups and individuals and in understanding how they work; and in many universities social policy is taught in the same department as sociology. But social policy makes a claim to be more than just a branch of sociology. Social policy is different, because while there is a set of areas which all social policy analysts would agree that they find of common interest, there is no one discipline to which they turn in examining them. Social policy analysts share a common concern with a particular field of study – social well-being. Within the subject, there are a diversity of approaches and methods. It is this which makes it difficult to understand what social policy is. Social policy draws upon the methods and theories used in sociology, statistics, management science, history, law, economics, political science, philosophy, geography and social psychology to help to explore well-being. It does not make a claim to having any unique set of methods, concepts, theories or insights. Unlike Alcock in chapter I.1, I would describe it as a multidisciplinary field of study rather than a discipline.

SOCIAL ISSUES

Within social policy there are a number of different starting points which authors and researchers take in developing the subject. One starting point to the study of social policy is exploring current social issues. For example, the demographic structure (the age profile) of the population is changing. People are living longer in most advanced capitalist countries and they are having fewer children. This rise in life expectancy, accompanied by a lower birth rate, is also taking place while the structure of households and families is changing. More people are living on their own, particularly young people and single elderly people; the former as a result of increasing affluence and the latter as people outlive their spouses for more years. At the same time, there is a growth in the number of what are called consensual unions (people living together and not being married) and an increasing number of divorces leading to more lone parent households. These trends in demography and in the social structure of the family are a starting point to consider the future consequences for social policies.

These trends are social, in that while they are experienced by individuals as personal, they are shared between groups of individuals. Longevity is not just a consequence of personal good health but of societal changes in diet, living and working conditions, and health care. Divorce is not just a consequence of the breakdown of a relationship between two individuals, but takes place within a socially determined context of norms and laws. These trends are social issues. For example, social policy cannot ignore that future health care planning requires paying attention to the growing number of elderly people in the population. Housing policy (see chapter IV.10) needs to respond to the different housing needs which come about as a result of the different size and form of households which are developing.

These issues interact with developing social policies. For example, the quality and quantity of care for people in the community (as opposed to care in institutions like hospitals, which was the predominant model in the post-war years) is affected by the social trends which are taking place. An issues-based approach to social policy requires an assessment of the relative future importance of these social trends. For example, many commentators argue that there will be a crisis in the funding of the state pension in the early part of the next century, whereas others point out that this is not necessarily the case (see chapter III.11). An issues-based approach seeks to identify the central, relevant trends and examine their consequences for social policies.

To explore the impact of these social issues, we can draw upon a range of methods from other disciplines: demography, public sector economics, social psychology and law. Demography, the study of patterns of births and deaths, provides us with the context. Statistics may provide us with techniques that can help us to predict. Public sector economics helps to analyse the likely pressure points on government finances. Social psychology and sociology provide an understanding of the structure and content of care and needs. A knowledge of law helps to analyse the legislative framework within which policy is implemented.

SOCIAL PROBLEMS

Another related approach is a 'social problem' focus on social policy. Many students are attracted to social policy because they hope it will help to resolve social problems. They want to study social policy, so that decisions can be made on a rational basis which will improve policies and overcome the difficulties that people face in their life. This is part of a long tradition in social policy research (although it has been criticized because it fails to question how far problems are constructed by dominant groups rather than being externally existing facts). A social problem approach looks for solutions. The work of early social policy analysts like Seebohm Rowntree was devoted to studying the problem of poverty and the measures necessary to overcome poverty. More recently, social policy has become interested in exploring other social problems, such as homelessness, long-term unemployment, AIDS, juvenile crime or the growth in lone parenthood.

In all Western European countries, long-term unemployment has now become an issue of growing concern. During the past twenty years, each slow down in European economies has been accompanied by ever rising levels of unemployment, and the proportion of the unemployed who have been unemployed for more than twelve months has been growing. This problem has been explained in a variety of ways.

- Some suggest it is a result of the development of new technologies, particularly those associated with new information technologies such as computing and telecommunication.
- Others identify the problem as having its roots in the characteristics of the people who are unemployed for a long period of time: either they lack enterprise because they have been brought up to expect that they will be employed by one employer for life or they do not have skills which can be transferred into other jobs.
- Others explain the problem in terms of economics. As a result of the speed of communication across the globe, the world is being drawn together into a single economic entity and long-term unemployment reflects the inability of the economies of Western Europe to compete effectively with the developing and growing economies in other parts of the world, particularly what have been called the 'Asian tigers' of South Eastern Asia.
- Others explain the problem as a result of the institutional structures that surround unemployment, which make people unwilling or unable to accept the changes that are taking place in a post-industrial society in which paid work has a different role in people's lifecourse. Therefore people who are unemployed should be encouraged to think about their lives in different ways.
- Another set of institutional explanations focuses upon the ways in which the structure of the benefits system interacts with paid employment, creating an unemployment trap for those who are unemployed, in which they are better off unemployed and living off state unemployment benefits rather than taking a low paid job.

These sorts of explanations all derive from a focus on unemployment as a social problem.

Investigation of social policies to deal with long-term unemployment, for instance, can draw on a range of methods. We might want to know about how unemployment has been tackled in the past, and this would involve investigating historical documents. A knowledge of labour markets and their analysis and the market for particular skills could be brought to bear to help understand the reasons for the trends, and would involve methods drawn from economics. We might investigate who are the unemployed, their employment history, how they became unemployed and their attitudes towards paid work. The problem of long-term unemployment can be approached from a number of different angles. Each provides part of an understanding of the nature of the problem.

SOCIAL GROUPS

Another approach to social policy is that which focuses upon the needs of different particular social groups, such as elderly people, children, homeless people or unemployed people. For example, while long-term unemployment may be approached as a social problem, equally it might be approached by looking at the needs of people who are long-term unemployed. A needs-based approach starts by looking at what happens to those who become unemployed and how unemployment affects their lives. Social policy analysts want to know how unemployed people's lives are changed by unemployment, how people who are unemployed experience it and what they identify as their needs – the impact of unemployment upon their lives. They would also be interested in how policies directed towards the unemployed in different countries meet their needs (or do not). For example, are the long-term unemployed socially isolated, facing financial hardship or being reintegrated into new employment more in one country than another?

SOCIAL SERVICES

In Britain, however, the most common and traditional approach to social policy is that which concentrates upon the big five social services. Education, health care, housing, personal social services and social security are the starting point of this approach to social policy. Social policy is concerned

with how these services are organized and administered, how they perform and whom they benefit. This original approach taken by social administration reflected the importance of state institutions in the development of social provision in Britain over the past century. This focus of study was upon what governments do and how the policies pursued in the broad areas of social services affect the social divisions of class, (and more recently) gender and ethnicity and the contribution they make in promoting the well-being of different social groups. To analyse these social policies requires knowledge of legislation, organization and politics. It brings to its analysis methods developed in a range of other disciplines.

SOCIAL POLICIES IN PEOPLE'S LIVES

In contrast to this traditional social administration approach, there is a new approach to social policy developing which argues that social policy should be understood differently. Instead of looking at the range of ways in which social services (in their widest definition) are produced, we should be looking at how people live, experience and consume a range of goods and services that go together to contribute to their welfare. What this approach contributes to the debate about the nature of social policy is a view of the subject in terms of how it connects to people's lives. It adds to our understanding of the nature of social policy because whereas most of the previously discussed approaches are to an extent detached from people's experiences and lives, it understands how social policies are integrated in the lived experience of individuals and groups.

In the past, social policy authors have tended to look at what happens to 'them', because, in the past, social policy has not been studied by those who are in a position to experience the conditions which people face. Therefore the issues are posed differently from the way in which they would be if they were informed by experience. A new concern with identity and experience has been developing in social policy which suggests that those who have direct experience have a crucial understanding of what is happening. Therefore women provide the basic understanding of the position of women in relation to social policies. Disabled people provide an essential insight into the study of policies for disabled people. Unemployment cannot be understood without listening to the voice of the unemployed. This view has an important political message for social policy analysts – the importance of listening to direct experience. Many students of social policy have important experiences which can help to illuminate their studies, but to help others to understand the issues being examined, these experiences have to be reflected upon in a systematic way. The immediate, intimate or experiential has to be structured in such a way as to provide an account which contains elements of the general and which can illuminate events for those who have no similar experience.

What Is Social Policy?

Explanations of what social policy is frequently focus upon its breadth and diversity and illustrate how wide an area of study it is and the range of disciplines upon which it calls in its analysis. This can lead a student to wonder whether social policy is not about everything and about nothing. There are a number of different starting points to studying social policy: social issues, social problems, social groups and social services. Social policy uses methods of inquiry drawn from a range of disciplines and it is more than the sum of the part of a number of different approaches taken in social policy and administration. But what holds it all together?

- First, there is an interest in the welfare of individuals and social groups. But 'welfare' is an essentially contested concept and one lesson from the history of social policy is that there is not any one agreed view of what constitutes it. Traditional Fabian approaches, the new right, greens and the diversity of feminist approaches are all concerned with the same issue, but the major differences between them lie in what they identify as being the constituents of 'welfare' and the appropriate routes towards it.
- Second, there is an interest in not just a philosophy or theory of welfare but an analysis of policies and their impact. Evaluating social policies according to specific criteria is the business of social policy academics, but different views of welfare give rise to assessments and analyses based upon different criteria, such as effectiveness, efficiency, equity, opportunity, liberation, autonomy or sustainability.
- Third, there is a concern with how policies are institutionally organized and implemented. This is because any evaluative analysis requires an understanding of the structures of organizations and the way in which those structures impinge both upon those who work within them and upon the consumers of their services. This involves examining not only state services but also personal and informal care and private providers of welfare services.
- Fourth, there is an examination of the components which construct 'welfare'. That is why social policy is concerned with looking at new areas and expanding its range of interests away from a focus just on state welfare services.

The study of social policy is concerned with those aspects of public policies, market operations, personal consumption and interpersonal relationships that contribute to, or detract from, the well-being or welfare of individuals or groups. Social policy explores the social, political, ideological and institutional context within which welfare is produced, distributed and consumed. It seeks to provide an account of the processes which contribute to or detract from welfare, and it does this within a normative framework which involves debating moral and political issues about the nature of the desired outcomes. This definition of social policy has two important components: the concern with welfare and a recognition of the normative and contested nature of social policy. It is the latter which distinguishes social policy from other social science subjects and makes it exciting.

GUIDE TO FURTHER READING

Much of the reading suggested for the previous chapter provides a useful starting point to looking at some of the different approaches to the subject of social policy. In particular, the five general introductions referred to provide contrasting approaches to the study of social policy: Hill, M. (1997) *Understanding Social Policy*, 5th edn. Oxford: Blackwell; Alcock, P. (1996) *Social Policy in Britain: Themes and Issues*. Basingstoke: Macmillan; Spicker, P. (1995) *Social Policy: Themes and Approaches*. Hemel Hempstead: Harvester/Wheatsheaf; Cahill, M. (1994) *New Social Policy*. Oxford: Blackwell; and Williams F. (1989) *Social Policy: a Critical Introduction*. Cambridge: Polity Press.

Other examples of different approaches to social policy which start from different types of analysis and different interests are: Oppenheim, C. and Harker, L. (1996) *Poverty: the Facts*. London: CPAG; Deakin, N. (1994) *The Politics of Welfare: Continuities and Change*, rev. edn. London: Harvester Wheatsheaf; Gladstone, D. (1995) *British Social Welfare: Past, Present and Future*. London: UCL Press; Glennerster, H. (1997) *Paying for Welfare: towards 2000*. London: Prentice Hall.

1.3

tHe ROLe of comparative stuDy
margaret may

The study of welfare provision is not based only on description or analysis of policies and practices. It inevitably involves some form of comparison between current practice and past or alternative ways of meeting need or improving existing policies. Such comparisons may not always be explicit, and the value bases may vary, but they are central to a discipline geared to evaluating welfare arrangements. This chapter focuses on the ways in which policy analysts have attempted to compare and contrast provision in different societies. It considers the aims of comparative study, the types of questions most commonly asked, the special demands such inquiry places on students and researchers alike, and the key areas of current debate.

It is important to recognize first, however, that comparative cross-national study is a relatively recent development, especially in the United Kingdom, where it was for long impeded by a widespread belief in the superiority of the Beveridge settlement. It has also been constrained by the locus of social policy as an academic discipline. In the United States and Canada, for instance, social policy is based primarily in social work departments, with a corresponding emphasis on professional practice. Elsewhere, apart from some separate provision in Australia, New Zealand, Hong Kong and the Republic of Ireland, it is located in political science, economics, sociology, public administration,

law, management studies or combinations of these. This diverse base has oriented comparative research in particular ways in different institutions, adding to the complexity of cross-national study. Whatever the setting, however, early studies, like social policy research generally, tended to focus on statutory welfare, particularly in Western industrialized societies. This preoccupation still frames comparative study. But over the past two decades a number of factors have inspired a growing interest in welfare systems in other parts of the world and comparative social policy has emerged as a key area of study.

WHY COMPARATIVE SOCIAL POLICY?

One starting point for comparative analysis was the observation that in the decades after the Second World War many countries, especially those of the industrialized West, experienced a massive expansion in publicly financed and delivered welfare. This was underpinned, as reports such as those of Marsh in Canada, Van Rhijn in the Netherlands, Laroque in France and Beveridge in Britain showed, by a widespread belief in the state's duty and capacity to care for its citizens. Funding methods and forms of provision, however, varied considerably, as did the scale of state involvement. One stimulus to comparative analysis, then, has been that of charting and explaining common trends and accounting for national differences.

A second, more pragmatic, impetus has come from reformers anxious to expand or improve provision and 'learn' from the experience (and 'mistakes') of others. Indeed, the fact that countries develop different responses to ostensibly similar problems has been projected as offering a sort of natural experimental basis on which to build. As will be seen, though, policy importation tends to be highly selective, often serving simply to legitimate desired change, with reformers from across the political spectrum deploying comparative ammunition to substantiate or disprove their particular prescriptions. Given the potential political and economic costs of innovation, governments too have long recognized the benefits of considering programmes developed elsewhere.

Policy 'borrowing' along these lines has a long pedigree. But since the early 1980s it has gained a new resonance as advanced industrial capitalist societies have become aware of the manifold implications of an increasingly globalized economy (discussed in chapter II.15). The extent to which economic change is undermining the autonomy of nation states is hotly debated, but it is clear that social policy, like other areas of government activity, has been subject to a number of common pressures. In many countries the combination of economic recession, high unemployment and changing work and family patterns with new political formations, rising consumer expectations and demographic fears has inspired a reassessment of the welfare settlements of the 1940s. While the pace and nature of restructuring has varied, there is considerable commonality in the types of policy changes adopted and it is clear that many governments have engaged in some form of comparative exercise, if only to leaven domestic debate.

Within Europe, including the UK, interest in comparative study has been further fuelled by the expansion of the European Union and the apparent demise of communism. Whatever the state of opinion in Britain, social policy here, as in other member states, is increasingly conditioned by pan-Union concerns. These are likely to increase in significance as the European Commission's interest in the 'social dimension' gathers pace (discussed in chapter III.8) and cross-European lobbying and networking by voluntary organizations and other pressures groups accelerates. The prospects for 'convergence' are debatable, but the growing inter-dependency of social provision is not confined to the Union. East European countries, while drawing on advice from other governments, are heavily dependent on the policies promoted by various supranational agencies. As Deacon argues (chapter II.15), these are also influencing developments elsewhere.

Welfare production has also started to internationalize in other ways. The deregulation of national markets in financial services means pensions, health insurance and mortgages in many advanced industrial societies may well be provided by local subsidiaries of multinational conglomerates. Similar trends can be discerned in welfare data processing, social security and housing. In Britain, for example, the French enterprise Générale des eaux not only owns part of the water industry but has contracts to manage housing, leisure and other public services. British social insurers are meanwhile trading in Europe and American companies are entering South Asian welfare markets. Equally significantly, global communication systems are not only bringing welfare advertising to a wider audience but enabling individuals to make their own policy comparisons.

These developments and the broader trends subsumed in the term 'globalization' present new challenges to comparative study. The growth of supranational agencies and the cross-national activities of governments in themselves constitute a

new focus for policy analysis. The welter
of statistics they routinely produce also
demand careful appraisal, as do the many
proposals to transplant provisions from
one society to another. Welfare restructuring in North America, Australia, New
Zealand and much of Europe since the
1980s has involved remarkably similar
shifts in the forms and role of state of
welfare. Different countries appear to have
experienced a resurgence of 'neo-liberal'
policy prescriptions and a weakening of
the forms of class solidarity and social
concerns which underpinned post-war welfare state building. This raises questions
about not only the nature and processes
of policy diffusion, but also the extent to
which national policy-making is structured by broad global trends, as against
more localized factors, and the sustainability of inherited welfare formations.

Approaches to Comparative Social Policy

Comparative social policy thus centres on
the complex task of examining the welfare order in different countries, identifying
commonalties and differences, explaining these and considering possible future
developments. More pragmatically it is
concerned with improving provision in
one country through drawing on the
experience of others and assessing the
implications of different systems for individuals and the wider society.

In addressing these over-arching concerns, analysts have tended to operate
at different levels of abstraction. Some
have undertaken the necessary ground-
work of providing country-specific studies, detailing the range and type of
policies and delivery systems but tending
to leave direct comparative assessments
to the reader. Others, while adopting a
more strictly comparative approach, vary
in their focus. Some, especially those undertaking government-sponsored studies

or concerned to inform policy-making,
concentrate on comparing programmes,
usually in countries with broadly similar socio-economic and political structures. Others adopt a similar 'micro' or
'single issue' approach but start from
other points on the social policy compass, focusing on provisions for specific
users, responses to particular 'problems'
or policy processes. Whatever the starting point, these 'micro' studies potentially
involve comparing a number of inter-
related elements:

- the extent and nature of the 'need'/
  'problem';
- the range of provision;
- the overall welfare context;
- policy-making processes;
- the aims of a particular programme(s)/
  service(s)/benefit(s);
- its origins and development over time;
- entitlement criteria;
- the provider structure (statutory/non-
  statutory);
- the resource structure;
- the administrative structure;
- delivery/allocation processes;
- the regulatory structure;
- the 'efficacy' of current provision;
- pressures for change;
- policy proposals.

A third group of analysts have developed a more 'macro' approach, attempting to characterize and compare 'whole
systems' across a range of societies and
often over time as well. This involves capturing the essence of a country's response
to social need through considering:

- the general welfare milieu;
- policy-making 'styles';
- the key forms of welfare 'input' or
  'effort';
- the predominant processes of welfare
  allocation;
- the predominant patterns of welfare
  production;
- the main welfare output(s);
- the major welfare outcome(s).

RESEARCH DILEMMAS

As later chapters show, exploring these issues within one's home country is far from straightforward. Cross-national study is even more problematic. 'Social needs', for instance, are highly contested. Benefit systems and welfare services may have several, possibly conflicting, aims, not all explicated in legislation or government statements, and which have to be 'read' from other sources. The purpose of one scheme may only be clear in the context of the overall patterning of welfare in a particular country. Providers may be governmental, non-statutory or 'mixed'. Establishing the resource structure involves analysing not only funding arrangements (national or local taxation, compulsory or private insurance, charging schemes or combinations of these), but staffing profiles and, in many instances, the role of non-paid carers or other helpers. Comparing administrative structures entails not only mapping formal organizational arrangements but comprehending management styles and the more informal processes of service delivery. Evaluating the efficacy of provision, whether in terms of take-up relative to 'need', enhanced individual well-being, decreased inequality, cost-effectiveness or other possible criteria, is a highly value-laden and difficult process.

Such problems are even more pronounced when one is trying to compare 'whole systems'. In many ways the methods used here are no different to those deployed in intranational studies and demand similar methodological sensitivity. But comparative study confronts additional issues. The well documented limitations of official statistics, for instance, are compounded by differing national conventions which may pre-empt direct comparison. The sources, the categories and format used may vary; records for some programmes may not have been kept; there may be gaps in coverage, changes in definitions (as with unemployment statistics in Britain) or in the methods of collecting and classifying data. Considerable effort has been invested in constructing harmonized cross-national data-sets (discussed in chapter V.6). But these still reflect governmental priorities rather than those of other stakeholders, and may conceal different conceptions of need or provision (Hantrais and Mangen, 1996). Nevertheless, the availability of such data combined with the manifold difficulties and cost of conducting alternative quantitative or more qualitative studies has made comparative study particularly reliant on official sources.

The issues, however, are not only a matter of accessing valid sources but of research reliability and the difficulties of a researcher of whatever nationality being able to undertake research according to the same investigative rules as a researcher from another country. Social policy analysts are not 'culture-free' in either their interpretations or their research remit. Indeed, one salutary feature of comparative research is the discovery that the burning issues in one country may not be so significant elsewhere. Moreover, as any tourist knows, superficially similar terms can carry very different meanings and informal customs are easily misread. Traversing such cultural and linguistic frontiers demands considerable methodological caution, especially in the contested arena of social policy. But the intrinsic difficulties of comparative inquiry should not mask the many policy insights gleaned through cross-national study and debate.

STUDYING WELFARE REGIMES

One major contribution has been the development of classificatory frameworks specifying the key features of different kinds of welfare systems. Although differing typologies can be found in the literature, until recently the most influential were variants on that advanced by the American writers Wilenski and Lebeaux in *Industrial Society and Social Welfare*. Writing in the wake of the post-war settlements (1958), they distinguished two 'models of welfare', the 'residual', based on the principles of economic individualism and free enterprise, and the 'institutional', based on the notions of security, equality and humanitarianism. These two 'models' characterized both the historical development of social policy (which they saw as a gradual evolution from residualism) and the patterning of welfare in particular countries. In the first 'needs' were met primarily through the market or the family. The state provided an emergency 'safety net' when these 'normal' supports broke down. Public welfare was, accordingly, highly selective, with low means-tested benefits, and widely perceived as stigmatizing. In contrast, the institutional model embraced universal, rights-based, non-stigmatizing state welfare as a 'normal' function of industrial society. In the UK, Titmuss similarly distinguished a 'residual' from an 'institutional-redistributive model', exemplified by the Unites States and Scandinavia respectively. To these he added a third, ideal type, the 'industrial-achievement model' typified by West Germany, in which state welfare functions as an adjunct to the economy and needs are correspondingly met on the basis of work performance and status.

These and similar ideal-type taxonomies formed the implicit template for other forms of macro analysis, especially in English-speaking countries. These have involved developing ways of plotting a country's welfare prowess, comparing quantitative aggregate data relating to the timing and coverage of national legislation and welfare expenditures. Equating high social spending with extensive welfarism, many studies similarly distinguished the welfare commitment exhibited in Scandinavia with that of the United States and fed into attempts to identify the pressures leading to increased welfare spending in Western states and variations between them.

Initially, purposive or teleological explanations tended to prevail, with state welfare perceived as safeguarding individuals against the shocks of industrial change and the vagaries of the market. From this evolutionary perspective welfare statism appeared as the concomitant of industrialization, urbanization and demographic change. Such theorizing was increasingly contested by Marxist-inspired analysts who highlighted statutory welfare's role in maintaining labour discipline, productivity and social stability, and, from the 1970s, by researchers drawing on other perspectives and focused more on theorizing cross-national variations. Many studies emphasized the correspondence between the spread of universal public welfare and the strength of social democratic or labour movements. Some, however, have highlighted the role of other political groupings and controversy has been further fuelled by research on the input of state bureaucracies and related institutional arrangements. This intense cross-national debate is now shifting again, stimulated by the restructuring of state welfare in many countries and growing concern about its future.

In trying to make sense of the changing pattern of welfare both within and between countries, a number of writers have developed new classificatory schemes, the most powerful being that of the Danish analyst G. Esping-Andersen. His seminal work, *The Three Worlds of Welfare Capitalism* (1990), develops a welfare state taxonomy based not only on differences in the scale, scope and entitlements of public provision in capitalist countries, but on differences in policy-making styles and processes and underlying patterns of class formation and political structures. It rests on a conception of state welfare as sustaining social citizenship along two related dimensions. The first he terms 'decommodification'; that is, the extent to which the state frees individuals from the operation of market forces and enables its citizens to lead a socially acceptable life independent of the labour market. Second, it involves the state in promoting equality and social integration. Recognizing that the traditional gauge of welfare commitment, high social expenditure, often obscures these distributional issues, Esping-Andersen devised 'decommodification' indices to measure the accessibility, coverage and performance of social security schemes in eighteen OECD states. His analysis leads him to distinguish three ideal type 'welfare regimes'.

- *Social-democratic regimes*, typified by Scandinavian countries, where the pressure of a broad coalition of left-wing labour organizations and small farmers secured a state committed to full employment and generous universalist welfare benefits, incorporating both middle and working class interests and with a strong redistributive element.
- *Conservative/corporatist regimes*, typified by Germany, France and Austria, where occupationally segregated benefits were introduced by conservative-dominated governments to secure both working class adherence and middle class support.
- *Liberal welfare regimes*, typified by the United States and Anglo-Saxon countries, where in the absence of stable cross-class alliances, state welfare has mainly operated on selective lines as a residual safety net for the poor.

New Directions

As with any ideal-type framework, some countries fit these constructs more easily than others, but Esping-Andersen concludes that different regimes appear to be moving along different trajectories. While contributing significantly to our understanding of differences between welfare states, Esping-Andersen's work has also attracted considerable criticism, reinvigorating debate on the gestation of welfare systems and their potential for change. Equally salient for this chapter is the extent to which his study has heightened awareness of crucial lacuna in comparative research generally and inspired a new wave of cross-national analysis. Like most of its predecessors, Esping-Andersen's typology has a narrow geographical and statist focus and to its critics neglects other variants in welfare provision. Some researchers have argued that other 'types', such as the 'Mediterranean rim' or the 'fourth world' of Australasian labourism, should be added. The place of the emergent welfare systems of Eastern Europe or the very different forms of welfare provision in Pacific rim countries and other parts of the world is more problematic. But the parameters of future debate are already discernible, with theorists questioning whether taxonomies based on welfare capitalism can be modified or whether different approaches with different explanatory models are needed.

This debate has highlighted other weaknesses in traditional comparative study, particularly the long-standing absorption with statutory welfare and the marginalization of social divisions other than class. As comparative analysts are well aware, these emphases partly stem from their reliance on aggregate statistical information produced by governments and international agencies and the resultant use of income transfer schemes as the proxy for a state's 'welfarism'. Cross-national data on other programmes, in contrast, are less accessible and in the case of social care services rarely available. Yet as current research is beginning to show, a different international picture can emerge if these or other services such as housing are used as a measure of welfare activity, particularly when non-statutory provision is taken into account.

Welfare programmes have been primarily assessed in terms of their impact on social class differences, with minimal reference to cross-national variations in terms of gender, ethnicity or other variables. As feminists have demonstrated, the concentration on state benefit schemes masked the extent to which, irrespective of 'regime type', public welfare is contingent on private, gendered provision. To understand fully the dynamics and impact of different welfare systems, it is contended that comparative study should extend its focus on state-market modifications and explore family issues and cross-national variations in the construction of gender roles and caring responsibilities. For some this means adapting Esping-Andersen's typology to incorporate gender issues; for others a radical retheorizing of comparative analysis is necessary.

More generally it also implies the construction of new types of data sets and the development of new kinds of cross-national research. Experimentation on both these fronts is already under way in the form, for instance, of panel studies and constructions of 'typical users'. Researchers are now engaged in a wealth of micro studies exploring the neglected areas of fiscal, private, voluntary and informal welfare cross-nationally. Such studies are beginning to inform broader theorizing on how different societies meet individual and social needs and the future of state provision. Attempts to engender comparative analysis and compare the experiences of different ethnic minorities are producing new insights, as are studies of welfare arrangements in 'non-Western' societies. Both micro and macro studies are also in various ways feeding into policy debate at both national and international levels. To participate fully in the many debates, however, a clear awareness of the range of issues confronting social policy analysts is necessary. It is to these that the rest of this *Companion* is devoted.

GUIDE TO FURTHER READING

Esping-Andersen, G. (ed.) (1996) *Welfare States in Transition*. London: Sage, provides a wide-raging review of current issues in comparative analysis and surveys current developments in a number of Western and other industrial societies. A more European focus is provided by George, V. and Taylor-Gooby, P. (eds) (1996) *European Welfare Policy: Squaring the Circle*. London: Macmillan, while Hill, M. (1996) *Social Policy: a Comparative Analysis*. Hemel Hempstead: Prentice-Hall, considers British social policy within a broad comparative framework. Sainsbury, D. (ed.) (1996) *Gender, Equality and Welfare States*. Cambridge: Cambridge University Press, considers variations in women's experiences of welfare states. The many methodological issues faced in comparative study are explored in greater detail by the contributors to Hantrais, L. and Mangen, S. (eds) (1996) *Cross-national Research Methods in the Social Sciences*. London/New York: Pinter. Recent responses to these and the range of issues raised by user- or service-specific comparative analyses are well illustrated by Bradshaw J. et al. (1993) A comparative study of child support in fifteen countries. *Journal of European Social Policy*, 3(4), and Wall, A. (ed.) (1996) *Health Care Systems in Liberal Democracies*. London: Routledge.

part II
values and perspectives

key concepts

social needs, social problems and social welfare

nick manning

The study of social policy focuses on the way in which social welfare is organized to meet the needs of individuals and groups, for health care, shelter, food, clothing and so on. It is also concerned with the way in which social problems are recognized and dealt with. In this chapter I will examine the growth and structure of social welfare provision; introduce some basic definitions of need; review the debates that have developed about this concept; and examine the way it is used in practice. I will also discuss ideas about social problems; the way these are related to needs and to social welfare provision; and the considerable debates about this.

What Is Social Welfare?

Social welfare refers to the various social arrangements that exist to meet the needs of individuals and groups in society, and to tackle social problems. Our use of the term social policy in modern times implies that social welfare means government welfare. This is not at all the case. Welfare for most people is still provided through other social mechanisms than the state. There are three main types: family and friends; the market; and non-governmental organizations (NGOs) such as voluntary organizations, mutual associations and charities. Social policy as an area of study is concerned with the way in which all

> **Box II.1.1** Types of social welfare institution
>
> - Family
> - Market
> - NGOs (non-governmental organizations)
> - The welfare state

these institutions affect the welfare of individuals and groups, as is taken up in more detail in some of the chapters in part III.

Social policy is a branch of social science. From this point of view, the basic conditions for the existence and survival of individual people are necessarily social. No individual, however resourceful, could survive for long in isolation. Human beings, in contrast to many other animals, are not capable of mediating directly with nature without mechanisms of cooperation and a division of labour between individuals. This is illustrated well by the long period of dependence that children need for them to become adults. The family, then, may be taken as the archetypal social welfare institution, both in fact and as an ideal. Markets, governments and NGOs are by comparison modern developments.

Families not only meet a whole variety of social needs at various stages of our lives, but they are at the same time the object themselves of government and academic concern. Of course families come in different shapes and sizes, as is discussed in chapter II.14. With the lengthening of life expectancy, the steady rise in the rate of marriage dissolution and the consequent growth of sole parenthood, the classic family form of two parents and dependent children has now become a minority structure within the overall mix of households. Nevertheless, over time the majority of people will at some point experience this pattern as children, and in turn as parents themselves.

Taking a historical view, however, the modern family provides less welfare than it did two hundred years ago. Hospitals, schools, shops, workplaces, transport and leisure facilities have developed to fulfil a variety of functions that mean that social welfare provision has become a more complex and mixed system than it used to be. Much of this change occurred in the nineteenth century, when hospitals, schools, shops and factories came to prominence. Two rival mechanisms underlay these changes: the market and NGOs. The market developed in two senses relevant to social welfare. The first sense is the market in labour as individual workers shifted increasingly from agriculture towards industrial wage labour. The vicissitudes of this means of livelihood threw up new insecurities whenever the availability of, or ability to, work stopped. The second sense is the market in goods and services, such as food, clothes and medical care, that accompanied these changes, and through which families increasingly met their various needs rather than through self-provisioning. Inability to pay could have disastrous consequences for a range of needs of family members.

Alongside the market, and very often in response to its failures to provide either adequately waged work or adequately priced goods and services, NGOs developed. However, this was not always for humanitarian reasons. On the one hand,

for example, mutual associations such as friendly societies were indeed designed for the mutual benefit of members when social needs arose. On the other hand, however, the settlement house movement for the 'improvement' of working class lives was also motivated by fear that upper middle class organizers had about the consequencies of poverty lifestyles, such as the spread of disease, for all social classes. In addition, there were also concerns about the costs of market failure, not to individual victims, but to those who might have to pick up the pieces. For example, in the later part of the nineteenth century the provison of education was motivated by the employment needs of industrialists, and the provision of agreed compensation for industrial accidents was designed to avoid more expensive court proceedings.

For a while the market and NGOs enjoyed considerable independence from the attentions of government, but there was a growing concern by the end of the nineteenth century to regulate their activities. In the twentieth century regulation led on to the provision of financial support and eventually to state provision of welfare services. Motives for this were again mixed. Genuine humanitarian concern for the meeting of social needs coexisted with the fear of social problems threatening the wider social order, and the realization that the costs of social reproduction (both the biological production of children for the future workforce and the daily replenishment of the capacity for work) might be better organized by the state. The climax of this process was the establishment of the British welfare state by the Labour government of the 1940s.

All of these institutions of social welfare – family, market, state and NGO – continue to coexist, but with regular changes in their functions and scope – most recently under the impact of eighteen years of Conservative government. State regulation has been strengthened in these recent years, while privatization and market mechanisms have been encouraged to the point where social welfare can increasingly be thought of as a consumption good. Nevertheless, the level of state expenditure on social welfare has remained at about 25 per cent of gross national product (GNP), albeit covering a steadily changing mix in favour of social security and health services, and away from education and housing.

Box II.1.2 Needs, wants and preferences

- Needs
    felt need
    expertly defined need
    comparative need
- Wants
- Preferences

WHAT ARE SOCIAL NEEDS?

While I have suggested that there were mixed motives for organizing social welfare institutions, the meeting of social needs remains their central concern. We must therefore review the definition of this crucial concept. A useful starting point is to distinguish needs from two related notions: wants and preferences. There are two important senses in which wants and needs differ. First, wants are more inclusive: we may want things that we do not need; indeed, marketing experts make great efforts to persuade us to do so. Second, we may need things which we do not want, through either ignorance or our dislike of them. Medical intervention can often be of this type. Both of these distinctions suggest that needs are more basic or essential to us than wants.

Preferences, a concept frequently used in economic analyses, differ from needs and wants in the sense that they are revealed only when we make choices, usually in the act of buying goods or services as consumers. The argument here is that it is difficult to know what people really need or want unless they act in some way to try to secure for themselves the things in question. This action component has its limits, however, for of course wants cannot be revealed in the market if we do not have the money to pay for things, and needs cannot be revealed by individuals where they are not aware of them, or there are no services to meet them. Needs, then, may well have to be discovered by those other than the individual concerned.

We should also make a distinction between needs and social needs. Needs (and problems and welfare) are 'social' in the sense that they are not concerned merely with, for example, individual causes and experiences of illness and poverty, but also with the amount and distribution of illness and poverty in different social groups; the reasons for this that arise out of the shared conditions of life for those social groups; and the social structures and processes through which they might be ameliorated. For example, it is only necessary to vaccinate a proportion of the population to stop the spread of infectious disease. In this case, the population can be seen to have a need, but any specific individual may not necessarily feel, or be defined by others as, in need. Waiting in line for an injection, we may have all felt this way as children!

These considerations enable us to make some simple classification of types of need. First are those needs which we are aware of ourselves, felt needs. These are obvious when we feel ill, or have an accident. The second type of needs are those defined for us by others, usually experts or professionals, such as doctors or teachers, but also importantly by family and friends. The third type of need is partly an extension of the second, to focus on needs as revealed, perhaps in surveys, in comparison with other people in the same social group. Here individuals can be said to be in comparative need because others have something that they do not.

An important aspect of needs, shared by all three types, has given rise to many debates in social policy. This is the question of how needs can be measured, particularly when we move away from the obvious examples such as major medical emergencies. The classic case is that of poverty. How much income do we need? One approach, drawing on the second type of need as defined by experts, is to think about the basic essentials, such as food, clothing and shelter, to work out the amount of money needed to buy the cheapest minimal provision of these and to define anyone with less as poor, or in need. However, any close study of the way in which poor people live reveals that the notion of 'basic essentials' or 'cheapest minimal provision' varies with the way of life of the particular family and community in which an individual lives. Is television an essential? Is meat eating essential? What cultural prescriptions about dress codes are essential?

An alternative approach is to use the first type of need, and merely to ask poor people what they feel they need. However, where this has been done, it seems that poor people often adjust to their circumstances and feel less in need than they 'ought' to, especially if they are older people; while others can feel poor where they 'ought' not to. Finally, we could merely define as poor those people with less than others as in the third type of need, comparative need; for example, by ranking incomes and identifying, say, the bottom 10 per cent as poor.

This problem of measurement has resulted in an oscillation in social policy debates between those who favour an objective interpretation of what is 'basic' or 'essential' – for example, in terms of the ability of an individual to remain alive, and to retain the capacity to act as a 'person' in society (Doyal and Gough, 1985) – and those who argue that needs are really more subjectively defined by individuals themselves, experts, government agencies and others who provide

services designed to meet needs (Piachaud, 1981).

WHAT IS A SOCIAL PROBLEM?

Social welfare institutions are also concerned with social problems, which are related to, but not the same as, social needs. For example, as C. Wright Mills famously observed, one person suffering from unemployment may be in acute need, but it is only when unemployment becomes a more widely shared experience in a community that there may be said to be a social problem. Social problems, then, are to be distinguished from individual need.

A further distinction should be made between the mere existence of a shared set of social misfortunes in a community, whether or not they have been defined as needs, and three further elements of a social problem: the extent to which they are perceived; the judgements made about them and the values they threaten; and the actions recommended to deal with them. Needs can exist whether or not they are known about by anyone. Social problems cannot. They exist within the public domain rather than private experience. The perceptions, judgements and recommended actions are in the broadest sense of the term part of the political process of a society or community.

Perceptions of social problems can occur through the eyes of experts or the general public. In the case of experts, social

---

Box II.1.3 Social problems: conditions, perceptions, judgements, solutions

Social problems
• social conditions
• perceptions
• judgements
• solutions

problems are typically defined in relatively objective terms such as the incidence of divorce, where the rate of change is a crucial issue (usually upwards!). However, since many social issues are less amenable to objective measurement (for example, the effects of family neglect on children), experts can differ widely in their claims about the objective state of a social problem. In these cases the general public, community groups, pressure groups and so on may have widely varied views, such that a social problem is more subjectively defined. Social problems, in the extreme version of this view, become merely 'what people think they are'. Since most of our experience of and knowledge about social issues is indirect, the mass media are an important influence not only on our knowledge of social issues, but also on the way in which they are framed, judged and dealt with.

Perceptions are heavily influenced by judgements about the kinds of values felt to be under threat. This brings us to the heart of defining a social problem, since it is the sense that something is wrong that motivates any attempt to put things right. There are two aspects of this that we have to consider. First is the issue of whose values are threatened. Some issues command widespread consensus; for example, that threats to life are unacceptable. The judgement that the spread of disease such as AIDS is a social problem from this point of view is relatively uncontested. Other issues, however, may be the site of sharp value conflict; for example, the relevance of people's sexuality to family life in various ways.

However, a second important aspect of value judgements in definitions of social problems can sharply modify the effects of these value concerns. This is the issue of who is to blame for the problem. In the case of AIDS, what might have been an ordinary medical issue was transformed in this regard by very sharp dissensus over the judgements of blame made about gay men, and therefore about the nature,

status and solution of the problem. Where problems are the site of value conflict, or blame is attributed, we can speak of contested or open social problems, the solutions to which are far from clear. Where consensus and lack of blame are typical we can think of social problems as closed or uncontested.

The solutions proffered to social problems have an intimate connection to perceptions and judgements made about them. Indeed, it has been argued that often the solution may indeed tend to determine these other aspects. An example of this process was the development in the 1970s of a social problem of hyperactivity among children, at a time when a drug treatment to calm them down became available. Certainly the ways in which a problem is perceived and judged strongly affect the kind of solution suggested. The running battle between the former Conservative government and the poverty lobby over the level and distribution of poverty illustrates this clearly. Both used conventional statistical analysis to try to demonstrate the presence or absence of poverty, and the two sides took very different positions over who should take the moral responsibility for the problem. The former government's solution, to create jobs through the enforced flexibilization of employment conditions, was the cause of the problem from the point of view of the poverty lobby.

A further interesting aspect of the former government's approach to solving social problems illustrates the subjective perception and definition of social problems, which in earlier years was used by progressive commentators to attack official or expert opinions (for example, patriarchal elements of medical opinion). This is the fact that such a strategy can be turned round to deny the existence of a problem, and therefore the need to do anything about it. Certainly the official suppression of the word 'poverty' in government policy debates in favour of 'low incomes' helped to obscure the growth of inequality.

Conclusion

Social welfare institutions have evolved in their current form alongside the development of industrial society. While they are chiefly oriented to meeting social needs and tackling social problems, this has not been the only motive. Both the German chancellor, Bismarck, and Winston Churchill argued in favour of social welfare institutions as a buttress against the attractions of socialist ideas.

Social needs and social problems are subject to contested definitions. In both cases a major debate concerns the relative weight to be given to objective or subjective definitions. Can needs and problems be scientifically measured in some absolute sense, or are they inescapably subject to the relative social circumstances of both those in need and the particular interests of the definers?

These points lead us back to the nature of social policy as a subject. The word 'policy' implies that it is a part of the political processes and institutions of modern society, and that social needs, social problems and social welfare are similarly political.

Guide to Further Reading

On social welfare institutions

Thane, P. (ed.) (1978) *The Origins of British Social Policy*. London: Croom Helm. This book provides a left-wing account of the struggle between different social welfare institutions to influence social policy in the late nineteenth and early twentieth centuries.

Hay, J. R. (1975) *The Origins of the Liberal Welfare Reforms 1906–1914*. London: Macmillan. This short book gives a very clear account of the variety of different reasons for the rapid development of state welfare in the early twentieth century.

Green, D. G. (1993) *Reinventing Civil Society*. London: Institute of Economic Affairs. This book argues from a right-wing perspective that the state has eroded other effective forms of social welfare institution.

On social needs

Bradshaw, J. (1972) The concept of social need. *New Society*, 30 March. This article was a milestone statement about different types of social need.

Piachaud, D. (1981) Peter Townsend and the Holy Grail. *New Society*, 10 September. This article presents a strong argument for the impossibility of finding an objective definition of need.

Doyal, L. and Gough, I. (1985) A theory of human needs. *Critical Social Policy*, 10, 6–38. This work represents a cogent argument for returning to an objective basis for the definition of needs.

On social problems

Manning, N. P. (ed.) (1985) *Social Problems and Welfare Ideology*. Aldershot: Gower. This book offers a detailed review of the theory of social problems, together with a range of case studies.

Rubington, E. and Weinberg, M. S. (1989) *The Study of Social Problems*, 4th edn. Oxford: Oxford University Press. This book presents a detailed analysis of six different models of social problems.

II.2

equaLity, Rights anD sociaL justice
peter tayLoR-gooby

'Equality', 'rights' and 'social justice' have been prominent among the rallying cries of those who call for radical reform in social policy, whether in terms of a Hayekian condemnation of the shameful perversion of a tax and spend policy based on an appeal to social justice (George and Page, 1995, p. 22), or the expansionary claims of those who link social justice to social investment (Commission on Social Justice, 1994, pp. 17–22). Since the concepts have been interpreted in different ways and used as ideological slogans by different groups at different times, we are faced with two main tasks in this chapter: understanding the root meanings attached to these terms, and tracing changes in the way in which they are used over time.

Meanings and Definitions

Equality

In mathematics, equality refers to a relationship whereby two distinguishable elements have equal value. Note that claims about equality for elements that are the same in every respect are uninteresting – if they are completely identical you cannot distinguish them. Similarly, no serious reformers who use a language of equality have argued for social uniformity, although detractors sometimes wish to treat them

as if they do. The egalitarian claim of welfare reformers has been that different groups should be treated as of equal value in social policy. In practice this has led to demands for equality in entitlement to benefits and services, in treatment by welfare authorities and in participation in decision-making. The main issues arise in two areas. First there is a problem in setting limits to the range of egalitarianism. Views on the scope of equality will depend on theories about what influences people's behaviour. The view, associated with neo-classical economic theory, that people are inclined to maximize their individual utility implies that egalitarianism may undermine work incentives and kill the goose that lays the golden egg. If being a victim of inequality gets you welfare benefits, why bother to be anything else? The view that individuals are more influenced by their social relations and by norms of behaviour suggests that the impact of equalizing policies will depend much more on the social framework within which they operate (Dean and Taylor-Gooby, 1992, chapter 3).

The second point concerns the practical rather than the moral scope of inequality. Many policy-makers have distinguished between 'equality of outcome' and 'equality of opportunity'. Policies directed at the former must aim to put people in positions of equal value, while those seeking the latter are more modest. The objective is simply to give individuals an equal starting point in an unequal society. Egalitarianism in this sense is entirely compatible with wide divergences in people's life-chances. Since few would describe the capitalist societies in which welfare states have flourished as equal in outcome, the main practical application of egalitarianism has been in the area of equal opportunities. The notion is immediately relevant to education and training, and to policies in relation to the acknowledged social divisions of sex, disability and ethnicity.

Different groups have struggled to ensure that particular divisions are recognized as meriting equal opportunity intervention. Issues of sexuality, of age, of disability, of region, of linguistic facility and sometimes even of social class are discussed as areas where equal opportunities policies should apply, and these struggles are traced elsewhere in this book (see George and Page, 1995, chapters 8, 9 and 18).

Rights

Right is essentially a juristic concept referring to the legitimacy of an individual's claims. In the context of social policy the question is whether claims to social benefits and services should be backed by state force, so that social rights become an element in citizenship in the modern state. In a celebrated analysis, T. H. Marshall distinguished civil, political and social rights originating at different periods and based on individual status in relation to the legal, political and social system (George and Page, 1995, chapter 6; see also Taylor-Gooby, 1991, pp. 190–200). Many commentators have pointed out that different patterns of rights have evolved at different speeds in different countries, as the chapter on comparative social policy shows. Developments in the UK indicate a gradual shift from residence-based rights towards an exclusionary notion of citizenship based on hereditary rights.

Weber, the prominent social theorist, pointed out that the development of the modern state and its framework of social individuation and categorization made possible the establishment of a precise and formal structure of social rights. This is one of the achievements of modern civilization. At the same time, the process of categorization also subordinates the individual to a structure of authority that enforces obligations as a member of society – the individual becomes a 'mere cog in the machine', victim of the 'iron cage of bureaucracy'.

The conflict between individual rights and state authority has been one of the central themes of modern literature from Kafka to the *X-Files*. In relation to welfare, governments have sought to impose obligations to pay taxes and to conform to particular norms in relation to work, sexuality, household and family transfers of income, child care, retirement and residence. The welfare components of the modern state apparatus can be particularly powerful in enforcing desired patterns of behaviour. In the UK, child support policies have been designed to enforce transfers between separated parents, recent changes to social security are intended to regulate job-seeking behaviour and in some cases area of residence, and employers are required to administer sick pay at a minimal level. Social rights, far from being a simple reflection of social progress, are two-edged.

Claims in the welfare area can be legitimated as rights in a number of ways. In practice, ideas about need and ideas about desert are most important. *Need-based* arguments tend to maintain that a class of human needs can be identified, which provides the justification for an obligation on government to ensure that these are met, at least as well as the society at its current stage of development is able to meet them. Although there are a number of problems in this approach, not least in establishing a bed-rock of human needs that is secure against relativist reduction (a position recently defended vigorously by Doyal and Gough, 1991, chapters 1 to 3), the human needs approach has offered some of the most profound bases for the legitimation of welfare as an ineluctable duty of government (see, for example, Plant, 1991, chapter 5).

Desert-based claims are essentially founded on the view that some quality or activity of a particular group imposes a requirement on society to provide them with certain services as a matter of obligation. Examples of such arguments are claims that motherhood or contribution through work or in war are deserving of social support, and that the obligation to provide it should come home to the state. Such claims are typically linked to functional or reciprocal arguments or are part and parcel of a normative system.

Functional arguments suggest that some activity is essential for the maintenance of society and that therefore the obligation is owed to those who carry it out. It is difficult to specify such activities in a society subject to rapid change in the way ours is. Social theorists such as the American writer Parsons tend to identify them at the highest abstract level ('authority', 'production', 'reproduction', 'communication'; see Doyal and Gough, 1991, chapter 5). The disadvantage with such generality is that abstract categories can be applied to a very wide range of activities. These arguments tend to parallel at a social level the issues raised in earlier discussions of individual obligation.

One result is that arguments about 'desert' are typically linked to normative systems. In our society the principal ethics involved are the family ethic, with its attendant claims about the gender division of labour, the spheres of childhood and adulthood, appropriate forms of sexuality and the work ethic, and the implied legitimacy of the market (Taylor-Gooby, 1991, chapter 8). These ethics are subject to modification. Traditional norms of family child care seem detachable from a strict gender division of spheres of home and paid employment. In relation to work, the boundaries between the life stage where

maintenance should depend on work or property and periods appropriate to retirement and education/training appear to have a certain malleability. Ideas about the desert of particular groups are of considerable importance in relation to social rights and the way in which they are put into practice: for example,

- entitlement to social insurance benefits based on work records is more secure and less subject to official harassment than entitlement on means-tested benefit based on need;
- support services designed to help those caring for frail elderly people are sometimes rationed by status and access to employment of the carer and receipt of them is influenced by gender and age;
- allocation of social housing of particular quality may involve the grading of tenants as appropriate to particular estates.

Social justice

Social justice is concerned with who ought to get what. Resource allocation in most welfare states is dominated by market systems which rest on the idea that goods are property to be owned, valued, bought and sold, and on normative systems of distribution closely linked to kin relationship. Arguments about rights and about equality have provided a basis for claims about justice which often cross-cut market and kin allocation. The most important arguments developed in recent years have been those of Nozick and Rawls, and these illustrate the way in which individualistic and social approaches to social justice may be developed.

- Nozick essentially argues that the core of just claims is labour – people have a right to what they have 'mixed their labour with', i.e. improved by their work. As a matter of strict justice, it is a violation of individuals' autonomy to appropriate or redistribute the goods that people have gained through their work, although individuals may as a matter of charity choose to surrender property to those they view as needy and deserving (Plant, 1991, pp. 210–13).

- Rawls's approach rests on the notion of a 'veil of ignorance'. The central idea is that just arrangements are those which people would agree on if they did not know what position in society they themselves would come to occupy, if they had no vested interests themselves (Plant, 1991, pp. 99–107). He goes on to argue that it is in principle possible to 'second guess' the kinds of choices about the allocation of goods (and bads) that individuals would arrive at under these circumstances. Unable to be certain that they would not end up in the worst possible position in an unequal and exploited society, they would tend to legislate for a social order in which only those inequalities existed which improved the position of the worst off; for example, by raising living standards throughout the community.

Both approaches have been extensively discussed and criticized. The first rests on a particular individualism in relation to labour which is not compelling. Production in modern society involves the interlinked labour of many people. The correct allocation of credit for work is highly controversial and is carried out in practice mainly through market institutions. The impact of a Nozickian approach, linking just distribution to work, may be to legitimate the market and to undermine any justification for welfare interventions. The Rawlsian approach is attractive in that it rests on negotiation free from the biases that social position – class, gender, tenure, age, employment opportunities, state of health and so on – in the welfare sphere generates in the real politics of social policy. However, there are severe problems in deciding *a priori* what allocation of benefits and services people who were abstracted from their social circumstances would agree.

There is nothing irrational in favouring a grossly unequal world and hoping to come out as a winner; or, if one felt more charitable, in supporting the highest average standard of living, providing the worst off are not too hard hit. It is difficult to devise approaches to social justice which both take seriously the autonomy of individual citizens and lay down the definitive policies a society must follow if it is to be labelled just – to put the seal of social justice on particular welfare arrangements.

THE CONCEPTS AS IDEOLOGY

Equality

In the post-war decades of confident welfare expansion the advancement of equality – in the sense of equality of opportunity – was often used to justify policy, particularly in relation to educational reform. Crosland's influential book *The Future of Socialism* (see George and Page, 1995, pp. 131–2, 144) argued that technical and economic change squared the circle. Meritocracy was both rational and just. Wilson as Labour leader succeeded in developing a political ideology based on this approach, which united traditionalists and modernizers among party supporters by arguing that both class struggle and class privilege were outdated by the requirement to get the best people in the right positions. Equality of outcome has never been seriously advanced as a dominant policy goal by the main left currents in British politics.

The remaking of Conservative policy associated with the charismatic leadership of Mrs Thatcher from the mid-1970s resulted in a vigorous commitment to free market principles and to a traditional family ethic. Egalitarianism had no place in this doctrine. Equal opportunity policies become a corrupt and unfashionable 'political correctness'. Reappraisal on the left after four successive election defeats led first to the programme of the Commission on Social Justice (1994, p. 1), which depreciated egalitarians as backward-looking 'levellers' and defined justice in terms of 'the need to spread opportunities and life chances as widely as possible', and more recently to the conception of a 'Stakeholders' Britain' in which equality of opportunity again plays a clear role but in which there is also a strong emphasis on individual responsibility to contribute to society.

In short, the right in politics prioritizes rights, derived from market and family, over claims based on considerations of equality. The left has regarded equality as important, but as only one policy objective among several. The commitment is increasingly to equality of opportunity (with an obligation to group opportunities) and to the linking of welfare to social contribution.

Rights

Individual rights are closely linked to notions of social justice. Equality has been one of the principal foundations of rights claims in social policy debate. The other major foundation has been the notion of desert. In policy debate, ideas about desert, linked to work and family ethics, have become increasingly important, so that rules of entitlement to benefit are drawn more stringently, the mechanisms for ensuring that able-bodied people are pursuing employment have been strengthened and obligations to maintain children after the end of a relationship have been codified (Dean and Taylor-Gooby, 1992, chapter 3). Much of this policy reform has also been concerned to reduce state spending, in line with the general emphasis on property rights which requires collective spending decisions to be justified against a stricter criterion than is applied to individual spending.

The emphasis on desert is a central pillar of right-wing approaches to welfare. However, recent arguments about stakeholding

on the left have also been concerned to emphasize individual contributions as part of a move towards more active policies. These are characterized by concern to expand opportunity and also to give due weight to individual responsibility for outcomes, rather than simply provide maintenance as in the passive receipt of benefits.

Social justice

Developments in relation to social justice follow largely from the above. The key shift is towards a more active notion of how social entitlements should be structured, in keeping with the move away from an egalitarian approach and towards one influenced by meritocracy or by ideas about property- and family-linked desert.

CONCLUSION

Debates about equality, rights and social justice have become both broader and narrower. On the one hand, struggles for the recognition of the rights of a wider range of groups, based on evidence of unjustified inequalities, have extended the range of social policy intervention. On the other, ideological pressure justifying allocation on market and family-ethic principles is stronger than it has been for half a century. Such an approach requires the state to step back a pace. Welfare interventionism is spread thin.

Social policy at the millennium is overshadowed by concerns about the impact of population ageing, technological un- or sub-employment, growing international competition, tax revolt, the weakening of kinship care networks and general distrust of big government and the future sustainability of Western welfare states. The climate of policy-making is one of retrenchment. Under these circumstances it is hardly surprising that conceptual debates turn away from a highly interventionist concern with the promotion of equality of outcome to an interest in the nourishment of existing structures of rights and obligations or the extension of more equal opportunities within the broad framework of such a system. It is interesting that these new directions are widely understood as more active policies in contrast to a previous regime of passivity, on the grounds that they expect and require individuals to act, whereas traditional welfare states allocated benefits and services to groups in need of them. It is as if the retreat of government and the imposition of extra responsibilities on the individual is to be understood as greater activity and involvement on the part of the state. Citizenship is increasingly what you do – not what you get.

GUIDE TO FURTHER READING

The best (and most clearly written) guide to the main currents in contemporary political philosophy in relation to the issues discussed above is Plant (1991), especially chapters 3 to 7. Doyal and Gough (1991) provide an analysis of need as a basis for rights in chapters 4 to 7. Dean and Taylor-Gooby (1992) review the political debate about work, family ethic and welfare entitlement. George and Page (1995) provide succinct accounts of the views of major policy commentators and critics. Taylor-Gooby (1991), chapters 7 and 8, discusses competing notions of citizenship and develops the argument that any desert-based view must include assumptions about social context. Spicker (1988, chapters 1 to 5) provides an introductory review of the main concepts. The Commission on Social Justice (1994) devised a policy framework designed to be feasible in twenty-first century Britain on the basis of a left-leaning meritocratic theory of social justice.

Commission on Social Justice (1994) *Social Justice: Strategies for National Renewal*. London: Vintage.

Doyal, L. and Gough, I. (1991) *A Theory of Human Need*. London: Macmillan.

George, V. and Page, R. (eds) (1995) *Modern Thinkers on Welfare*. Hemel Hempstead: Prentice Hall/Harvester Wheatsheaf.

Dean, H. and Taylor-Gooby, P. (1992) *Dependency Culture: the Explosion of a Myth*. Hemel Hempstead: Harvester Wheatsheaf.

Plant, R. (1991) *Modern Political Thought*. Oxford: Blackwell.

Spicker, P. (1988) *Principles of Social Welfare*. London: Routledge.

Taylor-Gooby, P. (1991) *Social Change, Social Welfare and Social Science*. Hemel Hempstead: Harvester Wheatsheaf.

efficiency, equity and choice

carol propper

Economic ideas and concepts are widely used in public policy. The domain of social policy is no exception: 'effective' and 'efficient' are adjectives frequently cited by politicians and policy-makers as goals for the welfare state and those responsible for delivering such services. Yet the ideas of economics are considerably more than 1990s buzz words. Economic analysis provides a framework which can be – and is – used to analyse questions about behaviour as diverse as worker participation in unions, the relative welfare of nations, the tendency of bureaucracies to grow or the behaviour of politicians. In addition, terms such as efficiency and effectiveness have rather more precise meaning within economics than when used by politicians or policy-makers. Economists see efficiency, equity and (sometimes) choice as ends: and ends which may be achieved through a number of possible means. These means include the market, the state and a mixed economy. This chapter presents these key economic concepts and illustrates their applicability to social policy.

Scarcity and Choice

Economic analysis begins from a single fact: we cannot have everything we want. We live in a world of scarcity. One way of seeing this scarcity is to notice that no one can afford all the things he or she would really like. This is obvious in the case of the homeless, but it applies equally to the carer who works part time and would like to have more time to devote either to her work or to the person she cares for, or to the rich rock star who goes on giving concerts in order to buy yet one more Caribbean island. It equally applies to governments who have a larger budget than an individual but can never spend as much on health services or education as the voters would wish.

Faced with scarcity, be it of money or time, people must make choices. To make a choice, we balance the benefits of having more of something against the costs of having less of something else. Because resources are finite, in making choices we face costs. Whatever we choose to do, we could have done something else. So, for example, the carer with limited time can choose between working more or looking after the person she cares for. Or a society which invests in building roads uses up time and material that could be devoted to providing hospital facilities. Economists use the term 'opportunity cost' to emphasize that making choices in the face of scarcity implies a cost. The opportunity cost of any action is the best alternative forgone. So if building a hospital is viewed by society as the next best thing to building a road, the cost of building a hospital is the opportunity cost of building a road.

In many situations the price paid for the use of a resource is the opportunity cost. So if a road costs £1 million to build, then if the materials and labour used in road construction would be paid the same amount were they used in construction of something else, £1 million is its opportunity cost. But market prices do not always measure opportunity costs and nor are all opportunity costs faced by an individual the result of their own choices. For example, when you can't get on to a bus in the rush hour, you bear the cost of the choices made by all the other people on the bus. This is not a price that is quoted by the market and nor it is one that the others on the bus take into account when choosing to get on the bus.

EFFICIENCY

Efficiency has a specific meaning within economics and in this section we will outline what this meaning is and how it relates to the behaviour of individuals. When deciding how much of a good or service should be produced we need to take into account that having the good or service gives rise to both benefits and costs, and how the benefits and the costs vary with the amount that is produced. In general, benefits are desirable and costs are to be avoided. Given this, it would seem sensible to choose that amount of the good at which the gap between benefits and costs is largest. When society has selected this amount of the good and allocated resources of production accordingly, economists say that this is the efficient level of output of this good, or alternatively that there is an efficient allocation of resources in production of this good.

In determining the level of output which is efficient, we need to take into account both the benefits from the good and the opportunity costs of producing it. As an example we consider the consumption and production of something simple – a foodstuff, ice cream. But the analytical framework can be equally applied to hospitals, schools, social work services and nuclear submarines.

Benefits of consumption

We would expect the benefits from eating ice cream to vary according to the amount eaten. In general, for someone who likes ice cream we would expect the total benefit to rise the more is eaten. However, this total benefit may not rise proportionately with each mouthful consumed. Let us consider the first spoonful. If the eater is really hungry the first spoonful will give considerable satisfaction. But as the amount eaten is increased the satisfaction derived from each additional spoonful will begin to fall. By and large, we would expect to find that the benefit derived from each additional spoonful falls the more has been consumed. If we define the last spoonful as the marginal spoonful, we can say that the marginal benefit falls as the quantity of ice cream eaten increases. Either you become full, or because variety is nice, you would rather eat something else.

This analysis can be applied to society as a whole. Defining society's benefits as the sum of the benefits received by all individuals from ice cream, we can add up across all individuals to get the total social benefit. Similarly, we can add up each person's marginal benefit at each amount of ice cream eaten to get the marginal social benefit. This is the increase in total social benefit as we increase society's consumption by one unit. We assume that we can add up the benefits received by different people. Often we can do this easily because benefits are measured in a single unit, say pounds. But in some cases there may be measurement problems: for example, when it is hard to value a good, or when £1 is worth much more to one person than another.

Both the total social benefit and the marginal social benefit can be drawn on a graph. Figure II.3.1 shows the total social benefit from ice cream consumption. The

Figure II.3.1   Total benefits and costs of ice cream consumption.

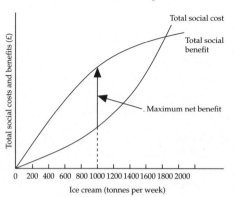

Figure II.3.2   Marginal benefits and costs of ice cream consumption.

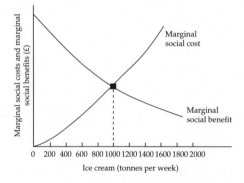

Costs of production

To determine the efficient level of production and consumption of ice cream we also need to consider the costs of production. Typically, the more of a good that is produced the more costly it is to produce. So total costs increase with production. However, what is required to establish efficiency is the cost of producing an extra unit of output, known as the marginal cost. Studies of production generally show that there is a level of production beyond which it becomes increasingly costly to expand output. This could be for all sorts of reasons: firms may have to pay overtime or use less productive machinery, or the costs of coordinating production or delivery rise as the amount of good produced rises. In other words, the marginal cost of production increases as output increases.

Assuming that ice cream production has the same pattern, we can add up the total costs of production across all producers. This will be the total social cost. We can also add up all the marginal costs to obtain the marginal social cost for each unit of output. The total social cost of figure II.3.1 shows the way that total social cost rises with output of ice cream. The corresponding marginal social cost of production is shown in figure II.3.2.

The efficient level of output

We can use the information on how social benefits and social costs of ice cream consumption and production vary with output to identify that level of output at which the difference between total social benefits and total social costs (net social benefit) is at a maximum. This is the efficient level of output. From figure II.3.1 we can identify this as at 1000 tonnes per week. Looking at figure II.3.2 we can see that this is the point at which marginal social benefits equal marginal social costs. This is no coincidence. As long as the marginal social cost is below the marginal social benefit,

amount of ice cream consumed is on the horizontal axis and the benefit from this in pounds is on the vertical axis. Total social benefit rises as consumption increases, but it rises at a falling rate. It rises at a falling rate precisely because the marginal social benefit of consumption falls as more ice cream is eaten.

Figure II.3.2 shows this marginal social benefit of ice cream consumption. The total amount consumed is on the horizontal axis and is measured in the same units as in figure II.3.1. On the vertical axis we show the value in pounds of the marginal benefit. The marginal benefit curve slopes downwards from left to right, showing that the marginal social benefit falls as consumption of ice cream increases.

society will gain by producing and consuming more ice cream. Conversely, if the marginal social benefit is below the marginal social cost, society would do better by putting its resources to other uses and consuming and producing less ice cream. Only when the marginal social benefit is equal to the marginal social cost will it be impossible to increase net social benefits.

The analysis of the efficient amount of ice cream output is relevant to all goods and services. So we can define the socially efficient output of hospitals, home helps, education or cars in exactly the same way. We may have more problem in measuring the benefits and costs, but the principle remains the same: the socially efficient amount of the good or service is produced at the point where the marginal cost and benefit are equal.

An efficient level of production is thus a desirable end: if all goods are produced in their efficient quantities then net social benefit cannot be increased by reallocating resources. Conversely, if the level of production is not efficient, then net social benefits can be increased by producing more (or less) of one good and less (or more) of at least one other. Given that resources are always finite, efficiency is thus an important social objective.

Efficiency and effectiveness

Although efficiency and effectiveness are often used synonymously by policymakers, they are different. Effectiveness means producing something in the best possible way technically, and is sometimes called technical efficiency. We can check whether a production is technically efficient by seeing whether, given the current technology, more output could be produced from the present inputs. As an example consider the delivery of meals on wheels by one person with one van. One service might visit houses by order of number. If all the even houses are on one side of the street and all the odd numbers on the other, this will mean crossing the

road between each delivery. This is likely to be less technically efficient than delivering meals to all the odd numbered houses and then to all the even ones.

Efficiency goes further than (and encompasses) effectiveness. To know whether a production process is efficient we must first check that it is effective. Then we have to see whether its current technology produces the output in a cheaper way than the alternatives. This requires looking at the prices of inputs, whereas effectiveness does not. So in our example it may be that once costs are taken into account, it might be found that it is better to change the amount spent, and so to employ two people and one van. Then we must check that consumers cannot make themselves better off by choosing to buy other goods. Finally, we must check that all the costs and benefits involved have been taken into account. (Technically, this is known as checking that there are no external costs and benefits. In the bus example given above, there were external costs – those imposed by bus users on others.)

So before we can say that something is efficient we must first ensure that it is effective; hence the drive toward effectiveness in the use of scarce medical resources, for example. However, just because a production method is effective, it does not mean it is efficient. We need to know the costs and the benefits of the service and of alternatives to know that. At present, for many areas of social policy, we are only at the stage of establishing effectiveness and not efficiency.

EFFICIENCY VERSUS OTHER GOALS

Equity

Even though efficiency is a desirable end it is not the only one. An efficient outcome is not necessarily a fair or equitable one. An efficient output is one for which the sum of all individuals' marginal valuations equals the marginal social costs of production. But each individual's valuation of a good or service – and so the sum of these valuations – will depend on the resources he or she has. So the efficient level of production will be defined in relation to the existing distribution of resources. If initial resources are distributed in a way that is judged as unfair, there is no reason why an efficient allocation of those resources should be fair.

An example may make this clearer. Suppose there are only two members of society, Ms A and Ms B. Given their initial resources, their likes and dislikes and the production methods available to them, the efficient level of production of ice cream is four tubs per week. These tubs could all go to Ms A, or all to Ms B, or they could share them equally. Each of these divisions of the total production is possible, but not all will be judged as fair or equitable. On the other hand, if each received only one tub, this allocation might be judged as fair, but it is not efficient. It is not efficient because we know that the efficient level of production is four tubs. If only two tubs were produced, net social benefit would be increased by producing more and in so doing we could make both Ms A and Ms B better off.

There are many possible definitions of equity or fairness – for example, minimum standards or equal distribution for all – but we do not discuss them here. The points to note are: first, that efficiency is not the same as fairness; second, that there is often trade-off between the two (a fair allocation may be one which is not efficient); third, that efficiency embodies a value judgement just as definitions of fairness do. The value judgement underlying the definition of efficiency is that some distribution of income (often the existing one) is legitimate.

Choice

Choice is often seen as an important goal by economists. By making choices, individuals can indicate their valuations of goods and services. If valuations are known then the production of those services which have greater net (marginal) value will be increased and the production of others decreased, and so the outcome will be more efficient. Choice is often linked to competition: competition is one means by which individuals can exercise choices. To see this, consider the case where there is no competition in the supply of goods and services because there is only one supplier. In this case individuals cannot choose the good they prefer as there is only one on offer.

Of course, there are costs to making choices – individuals have to decide which product they prefer and this will mean finding out about each possible option. In some circumstances it could be the case that very small differences between goods do not merit the costs of trying to choose between them. However, in general, more choice is judged to be better than less.

In the field of social policy, where choice has often been limited, increasing choice – and the allied goal of increasing responsiveness of suppliers to users' wishes – is viewed as an important goal. From an economics perspective this is viewed as a move in the right direction. However, this does not mean that the benefits of increasing choice necessarily outweigh the costs. This will depend on the particular service.

THE MEANS OF DELIVERING EFFICIENCY AND CHOICE

All societies have had methods of trying to get the most out of limited resources. In large-scale societies, two dominant mechanisms of allocation have been used. These are allocation by the government and allocation by the market. Under the former system (often called command economies), planning and administration are used to decide what and how goods should be produced, and to whom they should be allocated. Under the latter, allocation decisions are made by the ostensibly un-coordinated decisions of large numbers of individuals and private firms.

Markets are seen as desirable by economists since – in the absence of market failure – they will lead to an efficient allocation of resources without the need for co-ordination mechanisms and the costs of planning. In practice, of course, not all decisions in a market system are made by individuals, and not all ownership is private. Government has a large role in all market economies. However, the market mechanism currently has dominance. In social welfare the ideas of choice and competition have been introduced into systems where previously allocation was by means of administrative decision. In health care, education, social care and social rented housing in the UK (and elsewhere), competition in supply has been introduced as a means of increasing choice, responsiveness and efficiency. Services which were previously delivered by government monopoly have been opened up to competition – some from within the public sector, some from outside. It remains to be seen whether the precise institutional arrangements that have emerged bring the promised gains. Nevertheless, if choice and efficiency are important goals, market mechanisms may have their uses in welfare services as in other parts of the economy.

SUMMARY

The key points of this chapter are:

- Economics provides a framework to analyse the production and use of welfare services.
- Economic analysis begins from the assumption of scarcity – we cannot have everything we want. So people and society must make choices.
- The appropriate cost of these choices to society is the opportunity cost – the resources forgone if the choice is made.
- Economic efficiency means making the most of scarce resources. Economic efficiency occurs when the opportunity cost of using resources in a particular activity is equal to the sum of everyone's marginal benefits from that activity.
- Efficiency is not the only goal. Other goals include fairness and choice. These goals may clash with efficiency.
- Economists see markets as one way of delivering efficiency and choice in social and welfare services.

NOTE

The first two sections of this chapter draw heavily on Le Grand et al. (1992). I am grateful to both my two co-authors for use of this material.

GUIDE TO FURTHER READING

Le Grand, J., Propper, C. and Robinson, R. (1992) *The Economics of Social Problems*, 3rd edn. London: Macmillan, provides an economic analysis of social policy concerns and assumes no previous knowledge of economics. A more advanced textbook, designed for those already studying economics, is Barr, N. (1993) *The Economics of the Welfare State*, 2nd edn. London: Weidenfeld and Nicholson. Barr, N. and Whynes, D. (eds) (1993) *Current Issues in the Economics of Welfare*. London: Macmillan, contains essays useful for the study of social policy, but requires some knowledge of economics.

altruism, reciprocity and obligation
hilary land

Human Nature

Resources in societies, whether in the form of cash, kind or services, are claimed by and distributed to individuals and households within a variety of institutions. The family, broadly or narrowly defined, is important in all societies as a system for allocating resources between the young and old as well as between men and women. In market economies, in addition to the market itself, there may be state welfare systems alongside voluntary societies, charities and churches. The relative importance of each of these systems varies over time and between countries. For example, in England charities and voluntary societies play a much smaller role now than in the nineteenth century or than today in Italy or the Netherlands. The principles underlying the distribution of resources in each of these systems are often different because some claims are based on 'desert', others on 'need' – both highly contested concepts. Some principles are enshrined in law as obligations, which one person owes another and which the courts can enforce and punish those who fail to honour them; for example, the obligation that parents maintain their children. These also change over time and differ between countries. In the UK, for example, until 1948 grandparents could be obliged in law to maintain their grandchildren. That is still the case in Germany.

Others are less well defined and are in part the product of a society's history and culture, or what the sociologist John O'Neill calls 'rituals of reciprocity that celebrate exchanges between society, nature and God, involving a covenant between them as a model of all other civic reciprocities between individuals, neighbours, families, communities and the state'.

The assumptions about human nature on which these principles and practices are based also differ. Some assume that individuals are motivated primarily by self-interest and selfishness, others by altruism and concern for others. Adam Smith, one of the founding fathers of political economy in the early nineteenth century, recognized both but is more often quoted in support of the former view, particularly by those on the right of the political spectrum. He wrote:

It is not from the benevolence of the butcher, the brewer or the baker that we expect our dinner, but from their regard to their own interest. We address ourselves, not to their humanity but to their self-love, and never talk to them of our necessities but of their advantage.

However, he did recognize that not all human activity could be interpreted in this way. In a less well known quote he wrote:

How selfish so-ever man may be supposed, there are evidently some principles in his nature, which interest him to the fortune of others, and render their happiness necessary to him, though he derives nothing from it except the pleasure of seeing it.

In the words of a twentieth-century economist, David Collard, this means that:

altruism implies externalities in consumption. The happiness of one individual is a function not only of the volume of goods and services consumed by himself but also of certain goods and services consumed by others. Thus many people would be distressed to know that the sick were, for financial reasons, receiving very inadequate attention.

Adam Smith also recognized altruism to be particularly important within the family, for 'they are naturally and usually the persons upon whose happiness or misery his conduct must have the greatest influence'. However, by and large, political economy placed the family outside of its domain (it is no accident that the male pronoun is used in the above quotes) and concentrated instead on developing models of human society comprising solitary and independent individuals acting rationally and freely making contracts in pursuit of their own self-interest. As the philosopher Mary Midgley has pointed out, this model derives from seventeenth-century physics, in which the ultimate building blocks of matter were conceptualized as hard, impenetrable atoms. It is a model, she writes, in which 'all significant moral relations between individuals are the symmetrical ones expressed by contract'. However, there are other ways of thinking about human behaviour and human relationships:

If, on the other hand, we use a biological or 'organic' model, we can talk also of a variety of asymmetrical relations found within a whole. Leaves relate not only to other leaves but to fruit, twigs, branches and the whole tree. People appear not only as individuals, but as members of their groups, families, tribes, species, ecosystems and biospheres and have moral relations, as parts, to these various wholes.

In this model people are not independent but interdependent, and relationships cannot be specified with reference to a contract.

FAMILY RELATIONS

Family relationships have always been perceived to be different from those of the market place and not subject in the same way to rational calculation. Reciprocity between men and women or between parents and children are informed by love or altruism rather than narrow self-interest. Many economists treat the family or household as a 'black box' and have developed models which assume a household can be treated as if it were an individual – a male individual – with identifiable interests or 'joint utilities', to use the jargon. Gary Becker is one of a minority of economists who has shown an interest in the family and in altruism, arguing that:

families in all societies, including modern market oriented societies, have been responsible for a sizeable part of economic activity – half or more – for they have produced much of the consumption, education, health and other human capital of the members. If I am correct that altruism dominates family behaviour, perhaps to the same extent as selfishness dominates market transactions, then altruism is much more important in economic life than is commonly understood.

However, he accepts women's willingness to invest in the 'human capital' of their husbands and children rather than in their own, using a rather circular argument, namely that since on average they enter marriage with less education, training and marketable experience (i.e. less human capital) than their partners, it is rational from the point of view of maximizing the family's interest for them to use their time and effort in this way. Families invest less in the human capital of their daughters than their sons because they are expected to devote at least part of their adulthood to marriage and children and so the cycle is repeated. This changes, however, with improved opportunities for girls or if marriage becomes more risky. As Nancy Folbre, a feminist economist, has recently argued:

As long as male individualism is counterbalanced by female altruism, as long as rational economic man is taken care of by irrational altruistic women, families play a particularly important (and unfair) role. But when women gain the freedom to act more like men, pursuing their rational self interest, the price of caring labour goes up.

Hilary Rose and I have argued that because many social policies are still based on taken-for-granted assumptions about women's willingness and availability to care for other members of their families, so much so that it is only remarkable when it does not happen, women's altruism within the family is more accurately described as 'compulsory'. Women who do not care for their children, their partners or other relatives needing care may well find their access to resources such as housing substantially reduced. Moreover, it is argued that, in contrast to commodities sold in the market, payment for care within the family destroys the value of the care itself. For example, foster parents receive expenses, not a salary, unless the child they are looking after is especially difficult in some way. The caring professions, such as nursing, have historically been badly paid because nurses, it was argued, should be attracted by a sense of vocation rather than by the size of the salary. The same argument has never been applied to doctors.

FAMILY OBLIGATIONS

Janet Finch's and Jennifer Mason's research on family obligations has looked at how the meaning of responsibility or obligation is understood and put into practice in families. They challenge the concept of 'fixed obligations' associated with a genealogical link and argue that 'in reality the responsibilities which people feel and acknowledge towards their relatives have more complex and more individual roots'. Obligations between spouses may be more fixed in character (although we know less about obligations cohabitees feel towards each other), but those between parents and

adult children can be very variable. They argue for seeing responsibilities as commitments which are built up between specific individuals over time, perhaps over many years. This is done

through contact, shared activities and particularly through each giving the other help as it is needed. This process of reciprocity – accepting help and then giving something in return – is the engine which drives the process of developing commitments. Although people do not work with a simplistic balance sheet, reciprocal help given and received over time is a crucial factor in understanding how family relationships operate.

These commitments between the generations can survive divorce. They warn policy-makers against defining and attempting to enforce obligations which are not consistent with the ways in which families practise and understand these obligations. The controversy surrounding the implementation of the Child Support Act 1991 is a good example of how, by shifting the obligation to maintain children and their mothers from the legitimate or social father to the biological father, the government is ignoring deeply held beliefs about family responsibilities. As a result it is not working as well as the government intended, and absent fathers have not paid as much maintenance as was hoped.

COLLECTIVE OBLIGATIONS

The relationship of state welfare policies to both the market and the family has always been the subject of debate. Some have argued that the development of market economies has damaged the family and the capacity to support its members. As Alva Myrdal wrote in an influential book over fifty years ago, when many Western industrialized nations were debating the future of their state welfare systems: 'Changes in the economic structure of society weakens the family as an institution. Unproductive age groups have no assured place in the new economic order of individualistic money making in nation-wide competitive markets.' Social welfare provision, or what she calls 'collective devices', were therefore necessary to sub-stitute for the security once provided by families. Richard Titmuss, writing in the 1950s and 1960s, had a similar view of social welfare as a mechanism for com-pensating individuals and families who were damaged by economic growth. Those who benefited from a thriving and expand-ing economy had an obligation to share those benefits with the less fortunate. For him, state welfare policies were also mechanisms for extending altruism beyond the family:

The ways in which society organises and structures its social institutions – and particularly its health and welfare systems – can encourage or discourage the altruism in man; such systems can foster integration or alienation, they can allow for 'the theme of the gift' – of generosity towards strangers to spread among and between social groups and generations.

He studied blood donors in the NHS as an example of a willingness to give to strangers – moreover, strangers never encountered. However, he found that their willingness to give did stem from a sense of obligation to a wider society and con-fidence in the behaviour of future unknown strangers, who in their turn would give their blood should others, including them-selves, ever need it. (It is interesting that the recent NHS practice of selling blood products abroad has reduced the willing-ness of some to donate their blood.)

William Beveridge, regarded as one of the principal architects of the British post-war welfare state, proposed a social insur-ance system which was based on a clear contract between employers, employees and the state. He was also very clear about the pattern of obligations between hus-bands and wives, and between parents and children. Embedded in his social insurance and social assistance scheme were rules to ensure that men's obligations to take paid work in order to support their families and women's obligations to provide domestic services for their husband and children were carried over from earlier social security systems. In the last resort prison faced men who refused work and failed to support their families. However, he too wanted to encourage altruism within the wider society. This he called 'a sense of Divine Vocation' (although he was careful to point out that he had not been brought up in any particular faith). By this he meant 'that in the daily life of each of us there should be something done, not by instinct, but more and more consciously without thought of reward, whether it is part of our paid work or not. There should be something that is spending ourselves, not getting anything.' Unlike many social policy analysts at the time – or since – he noticed that 'serving, exhausting oneself without thought of personal reward – isn't that what most women do most of their lives in peace or war?'

Others have been rather more sceptical of developing what Robert Pinker subse-quently called 'the altruistic potentialities of ordinary citizens' and took a harder look at the evidence for this. He concluded that:

The welfare institutions of a society symbolise an unstable compromise between compassion and indif-ference, between altruism and self-interest. If men were predominantly altruistic, compulsory forms of social service would not be necessary; and if men were exclusively self-regarding such compulsion would be impossible ... The spirit of altruism, far from being a natural flowering of human nature, must be seen as the product of the rigorous discipline of injunction to self-denial and the repression of the grosser form of self-love.

Jose Harris, William Beveridge's bio-grapher, has also more recently urged historians to investigate 'if, for good or ill, particular welfare policies do encourage particular types of economic, moral or civic behaviour'.

Peter Baldwin has posed the question the other way around in his examination of the social bases of the welfare state in five European countries. He asks why and how solidaristic social policies ever occur:

'Why have the fortunate ever agreed to institutionalise aid for the worse off except to the degree necessary to prevent unrest or still the naggings of conscience?' He rejects the economists' explanation derived from their ability 'to reduce even apparently genuine altruism to rationally motivated self interest ... [so that] ... much of what appears to be redistribution is in fact merely insurance'. True, there are economic efficiencies to be won from altruistic behaviour but, that being so, why then would anyone oppose mutually beneficial arrangements? In any case, 'individuals may be economically rational, but groups and classes – the actors in politics – must recognise and develop their stake in reciprocal exchanges before they can be realised'. He also rejects a simple appeal to altruistic sentiments so that social policy is understood as an expression of altruism generalized to wider society. Rather, he concludes that:

Solidarity – the group's decision to allocate resource by need – is only misleadingly analogous to altruism. An individual sentiment, altruism is generally confined to narrow circles of like-minded. Solidarity, in those few instances where it has been realised, has been the outcome of a generalised and reciprocal self-interest. Not ethics, but politics explain it.

His meticulous examination of the development of social insurance systems led him to the conclusion that an analysis of the role played by the middle classes is essential for understanding Western European welfare states.

SELF-RELIANCE AND SELF-PROTECTION

The debates about social welfare in the UK during the 1980s and 1990s have been dominated by those who believe that state welfare provision undermines both the efficient working of the economic market and obligations within the family. This has been coupled with a view that only the

poor need state welfare provision – the middle classes and the wealthy can look after themselves. Peter Baldwin's analysis of the history of state welfare provision seems correct, for the role of state welfare systems in distributing resources in society has been eroded in the past twenty years as the middle classes seek more services in the private sector. Before she became Prime Minister, Margaret Thatcher had written:

The sense of being self-reliant, of playing a role within the family, or owning one's property, of paying one's way, are all part of the spiritual ballast which maintains responsible citizenship and a solid foundation from which people look round to see what more they can do for others and for themselves.

Taxation was seen to be not only damaging to enterprise but also a way of 'buying your way out of your obligations to society', to use the words of a Home Secretary, and therefore undesirable. Margaret Thatcher herself asserted that 'there is no such thing as society'. So, by definition, state welfare policies could neither foster, nor be fostered by, altruism and reciprocity beyond the family.

This view of society comprising self-seeking, individualistic people has been strengthened by the rise of sociobiology. Eugenics, which underpinned the belief in the naturalness of inequalities and hierarchies in the first half of this century, was influential in the social policy debates of the time in Britain and the United States. Sociobiology is now providing a similar ideological basis for undermining the arguments for a universalistic welfare state. From the early 1970s its proponents have been arguing that prime among the traits inherent in our nature is selfishness. Richard Dawkins claims that everything organisms do is done out of self-interest, because 'selfish genes' exist only to replenish themselves: 'They are in you and me; they created us, body and mind, and their preservation is the ultimate rationale for our existence.' In this model women's greater commitment to child rearing follows from the belief that women and men must adopt different strategies to maximize opportunities to spread their genes into future generations. Altruism is explained away.

What passes for co-operation turns out to be a mixture of opportunism and exploitation. The impulses that lead one animal to sacrifice himself for another turn out to have their ultimate rationale in gaining advantage over a third, and acts for the good of the 'society' turn out to be performed for the detriment of the rest ... Scratch an 'altruist' and watch a 'hypocrite' bleed,

wrote a more extreme advocate of this position. Sociobiology is being challenged within the biological sciences but genetic determinism and genetic reductionism do serve to turn attention away from the environmental and structural causes of inequalities, fail to recognize the interdependence of individuals within society or of societies across the globe and so support the view that a minimal welfare state is not only desirable but all that is possible. There are parallels here with nineteenth-century political economy and debates about the role of the national state in relation to the market economy. Robert Pinker described the study of social welfare as 'a study of human nature in a political context'. Central to this are the concepts of altruism, reciprocity and obligation. To understand their full meaning, students of social policy have to draw on economics, philosophy, history and biology as well as politics, sociology and social policy.

GUIDE TO FURTHER READING

Titmuss R. M. (1971) *The Gift Relationship*. London: Allen and Unwin, has remained an important contribution to the social policy literature on altruism and reciprocity and includes his empirical study of blood donors.

Pinker, R. (1971) *Social Theory and Social Policy*. London: Heinemann, reviews some of the key concepts used in social policy analysis and has also stood the test of time.

Land, H. and Rose, H. (1985) Compulsory altruism for some or an altruistic society for all? In P. Bean, J. Ferris and D. Whynes (eds), *In Defence of Welfare*. London: Tavistock, reviews a number of social policies and exposes the extent to which women's altruism underpins the policies analytic.

Finch, J. and Mason, J. (1995) *Negotiating Family Responsibilities*. London: Routledge, reports on a study which researched the processes by which family members actually meet – or do not meet – the obligations between them.

Collard, D. (1978) *Altruism and the Economy*. Oxford: Oxford University Press, discusses altruism and its relevance to economic and social analysis from an economist's point of view.

Folbre, N. (1994) *Who Pays for the Kids?* London: Routledge, gives an economist's perspectives on the costs – in time and care as well as in money – of bringing up children and examines the very different distribution of the obligations to meet these costs between men and women.

O'Neill, J. (1994) *The Missing Child in Liberal Theory*. Toronto: University of Toronto Press, argues for a renewal of the social contract between the generations and criticizes a political economy which emphasizes individualism and ignores social responsibility.

Midgley, M. (1985) *Evaluation as Religion*. London: Methuen, gives a philosopher's perspective on these concepts and provides an excellent critique of sociobiology.

key perspectives

II.5

the neo-liberal perspective

david g. green

The task of this chapter is to explain neo-liberalism as an *intellectual tradition* as distinct from the *public policies* pursued by the Thatcher and Reagan governments. These policies reflected a variety of intellectual influences, of which neo-liberalism was only one.

The Neo-liberal Understanding of History

Let me begin with a rather brisk survey of the interpretation of history to which neo-liberals typically subscribe. They see themselves as the heirs of a long historical struggle for freedom. For much of human history, rulers were able to do more or less whatever they wished, but in Europe during the Middle Ages limits were gradually placed on royal power. Acton (1907, p. 39) assesses the achievement of the Middle Ages in these terms:

the principle that no tax was lawful that was not granted by the class that paid it . . . was recognised . . . Slavery was almost everywhere extinct; and absolute power was deemed more intolerable and more criminal than slavery. The right of insurrection was not only admitted but defined, as a duty sanctioned by religion.

Despite its inclination to favour absolute authority, leaders of the medieval Catholic Church commonly bestowed religious legitimacy on secular rulers only on condition that they acknowledged a force superior to their own, usually by means of an oath of fidelity which gave them limited authority, to be enjoyed only during good behaviour and in accordance with the law of the land. Consequently, during the Middle Ages, rivalry between church and state had helped to limit the power of governments.

However, under the impact of the Reformation in the sixteenth and seventeenth centuries, the clergy, having fought slavery and despotism, began to side with absolute monarchy to keep Protestantism at bay. As Acton (1907, p. 44) remarked, instead of emancipating nations, religion 'had become an excuse for the criminal art of despots'.

Campaigns for what today might be called 'religious cleansing' were conducted. In 1685 Louis XIV (1643–1715) had ordered all French Protestants to renounce their religion on pain of death. He enjoyed the right of arbitrary arrest and exile and openly asserted that kings were 'no more bound by the terms of a treaty than by the words of a compliment; and that there is nothing in the possession of their subjects which they may not lawfully take from them' (Acton, 1907, p. 48.) Protestant monarchs were equally quick to use force to achieve their ends.

In France tyranny was to survive until the nineteenth century, but in England the efforts of Charles I to emulate French kings led to bloody revolution in the 1640s, as ordinary people sought freedom of worship without fear of persecution and the opportunity to improve their lives without the imposition of arbitrary taxes or controls.

It was in this age, when the cause of liberty had suffered reverses at the hands of tyrants, that modern liberalism had its origins. Seventeenth-century liberals felt that they were restoring liberties stolen by absolutist rulers and turned their minds to discovery of the shared laws and morals under which Catholic and Protestant alike could live in peace, despite disagreement. They sought a common core of laws conceived for the most part as the pure word of God, unadulterated by the all-too human interpretations of any given religion.

William Blackstone, whose *Commentaries on the Laws of England* became the most influential legal guide on both sides of the Atlantic, believed that law was based on the will of God who had provided us with two kinds of law: 'revealed law' and the 'law of nature'. Revealed law, as expressed in the scriptures, was of 'infinitely more authority' because it was 'expressly declared so to be by God himself', whereas the law of nature was 'only what, by the assistance of human reason, we imagine that law to be' (Blackstone, 1765, vol. 1, p. 42).

Liberty was understood as living under the protection of the law, not at the mercy of arbitrary rulers. The purpose of law, said Blackstone (1765, vol. 1, p. 53), was to ensure: that every man may know what to look upon as his own, what as another's; what absolute and what relative duties are required at his hands; what is to be esteemed honest, dishonest, or indifferent; what degree every man retains of his natural liberty; what he has given up as the price of the benefits of society.' After the reverses of the sixteenth and seventeenth centuries, the eighteenth and nineteenth centuries brought further progress towards liberty and wherever freedom reigned it brought extension of the franchise and unparalleled prosperity.

Then, the twentieth century saw the rise of new tyrannies in the extreme form of German and Italian fascism and Russian communism, accompanied in Western countries by a renewed faith in the capacity of rulers to govern the lives of subjects for their own good. Western socialists often expressed their ultimate aims in terms that Stalin could have accepted, but they renounced terror and were democratic, displaying a willingness to be voted out of office and refrain from violence against liberal opponents.

During the first half of the twentieth century, liberals were slow to see the dangers of creeping collectivism, but during and just after the Second World War they began to warn that Western countries were slowly surrendering their liberties without noticing. It is no coincidence that the most active in warning of the dangers of burgeoning state power had experienced fascism at first hand. Popper had left Nazi-dominated Austria in 1937 before writing *The Open Society and Its Enemies*, and Hayek had encountered the rise of fascism in Austria before leaving for the London School of Economics in 1931. In 1947 Hayek and others had founded an international academic society – the Mont Pelerin Society – to improve understanding of liberty through public discussion. In Britain, Hayek's initiative led eventually to the foundation of the Institute of Economic Affairs in the mid-1950s.

THE IDEAL OF LIBERTY: A RE-STATEMENT

Against the backdrop of this all-too-hasty survey of the ebbing and flowing of freedom since the Middle Ages, let me try to restate the ideal of liberty in modern terms. Michael Oakeshott (1975) distinguished between two rival models of modern society: 'corporate association' and 'civil association'. Each represents a different approach to understanding the relationship between the individual and the collectivity. There are three questions:

- What are people like?
- How are people united?
- What should the government do?

Initially, I will consider the answers typically given to these questions by collectivists, or adherents of 'corporate association'. A common strategy is to state the collectivist approach positively and then to employ a false contrast to caricature the opposing view.

1 What are people like? The corporatist view is that human nature is moulded by outside forces, including environmental and social influences, and the economic structure. They often deploy a false contrast. The only alternative view, they say, is that individuals are autonomous bundles of wants or preferences – not 'social' at all.

2 How are people united? The corporatist view is that we are united in pursuit of a common purpose, part of a team under leadership. The false contrast they make is to claim that the only alternative is 'isolated individualism' – that people have no concern for others, and no sense of unity.

3 What should the government do? According to corporatists, it should give leadership by managing and directing lives. Again, a false contrast is deployed: the only alternative aspiration is said to be 'no government', or *laissez-faire*.

The civil associate answers each question in a different way.

1 What are people like? They are not the product of outside forces. They are bearers of responsibility, carriers of a moral compass, capable of facing moral dilemmas, self-management, learning from mistakes and self-improvement.

2 How are we united? A society should not be conceived as a collectivity of followers under leadership, but the alternative is not isolated individualism. There is a sense of community, but not that of leaders and followers. Individuals are united by their free acceptance of the obligation not to exempt themselves from the rules, their willingness to do their bit to uphold a mutually respectful moral framework and acknowledgement that everyone has a chance to succeed.

3 What should the government do? The government's task is not to direct and manage people, but to create and uphold the framework of law that allows the exercise of responsibility, and to provide some services. *Laissez-faire* is not the ideal. The government has important duties, but they are limited.

Civil association is the tradition of liberty embodied in Locke, Smith, Hume, Burke, Tocqueville, Acton and Hayek. It is not *laissez-faire*, isolated individualism, or naked market forces. Nor is it 'negative freedom'. On the contrary, classical liberals were concerned not only to limit government, but also to devise and uphold a constitution that made it possible for people to put their talents to positive use. But how does this claim square with the common perception that neo-liberals celebrate the naked pursuit of self-interest?

ADAM SMITH AND SELFISHNESS

Some critics (such as Haworth, 1994, p. 6) identify Adam Smith as the arch-exponent of a society based on the pursuit of self-interest, in which the invisible hand will 'magically' sort everything out.

To understand Smith's theory of the human condition it is necessary to know *The Theory of Moral Sentiments* as well as *The Wealth of Nations*. The most important human quality, in Smith's view, was the inclination to seek the approval of others, which meant that the greatest happiness came from acting in a manner that brought praise and the greatest misery from blame. This tendency rested on 'sympathy', an emotion described in the opening sentence of *The Theory of Moral Sentiments*: 'How selfish soever man may be supposed, there are evidently some principles in his nature, which interest him in the fortune of others, and render their happiness necessary to him, though he derives nothing from it, except the pleasure of seeing it' (Smith, 1976, p. 48).

Smith believed that we can achieve much by pursuing our legitimate self-interest through mutual adjustment to others, but that we should also seek to do right according to our sense of duty. According to Christian teaching, he said, the sense of duty should be the 'ruling and the governing' principle of our conduct: 'to feel much for others, and little for ourselves, that to restrain our selfish, and to indulge our benevolent, affections, constitutes the perfection of human nature; and can alone produce among mankind that harmony of sentiments and passions in which consists their whole grace and propriety' (Smith, 1976, pp. 71–2). Thus, Smith did emphasize the importance of harnessing self-interest, but for him self-interest was not enough. We have a duty to pursue our objectives unselfishly.

MODERN NEO-LIBERALS

Some core beliefs are shared by all neo-liberals.

1 Neo-liberals favour a competitive market economy and oppose an economic system planned and directed by the state.
2 They contend that a market economy is an essential bulwark of democracy because, by dispersing property ownership, it prevents the concentration of power in the hands of the few.
3 Neo-liberals subscribe to the rule of law, that is the doctrine that the powers of governments should be limited by a higher constitutional law and that the

exercise of power should be based on predictable laws rather than discretionary commands.
4 Implicit in the third, they contend that there is a higher morality to which governments are subject and which in extreme cases may justify rebellion against tyrannical rulers.

However, as acceptance of the value of a competitive market economy has spread, so neo-liberals have turned their attention to other elements of a free society, not least the moral underpinnings. This departure has highlighted some differences of view. Two traditions may be discerned: 'hard-boiled economism' and 'liberty rightly understood'. There are two fundamental philosophical disputes. The first is about how best to understand human nature: on the one hand are those neo-liberals (mostly economists) who see people as 'rational utility maximizers', and on the other are those who find this approach too narrow, insisting that people are, above all, moral agents who constantly face the burden of choice between right and wrong, good and bad. This dispute is closely related to a second, namely about how best to understand the community to which we belong. One view is that it is a unity brought about by bargainers seeking mutually acceptable arrangements, a state of affairs considered to be in the common good because such bargaining leads to outcomes beneficial for all. This claim is also challenged as too narrow, despite containing much truth. The rival view asserts that the bond of unity essential to a free society is not the 'accidental' outcome of bargaining, but rests upon a conscious effort to uphold a liberal way of living – a culture – across the generations.

The tradition of 'hard-boiled economism' sees an economy as a self-balancing system which ensures the efficient allocation of resources. One of the weaknesses of this view, exemplified in the work of Becker (1976), is that economic investigators see themselves as 'outside the society looking in'. But such methods of understanding tend to see people as reacting to stimuli, and to play down their inner motivations and perceptions. When applied to public policy, this behaviourist approach can have serious limitations, not least because it is a mentality that appeals to centralizers of all parties who want to use economic incentives to achieve their objectives. This 'system design' approach influenced the Thatcherite health reforms, but the mere introduction of prices and tendering does not provide what a fully competitive market can offer, let alone restore the institutions necessary for liberty.

As Hayek taught, competition is valuable as a 'discovery procedure' and can only be understood as part of a wider philosophy which acknowledges how the free use of personal initiative under law helps to overcome human fallibility and to encourage progress. Competition and free entry into the market allow consumers to discover who can do a better job in three senses. First, prices tend to settle at that point which cannot be beaten by anyone else, at least for the time being. Second, products or services tend to be developed only if consumers want them. Many people are free to try their hand at predicting what consumers will want and from their efforts we learn who produces the best ideas. It is not obvious in advance. Third, the people and organizations offering their services depend on consumers' decisions. At any given moment, some suppliers may be advancing their case despite a lack of customers but, in time, the competitive process filters out the unwanted producers.

From the standpoint of 'liberty rightly understood', the NHS reforms also lacked a moral dimension which should have led to the privatization of hospitals. The rational utility maximizers also advocate privatization of hospitals, but in the form of for-profit corporations in order to maximize 'efficient allocation'. The alternative tradition urges privatization in the form of voluntary hospitals, to restore civil society and encourage the rebuilding of an ethos of mutual service. Before their nationalization in 1948, the voluntary hospitals were the backbone of the acute hospital service and relied entirely on private finance. Above all, they were focal points for local people of goodwill, providing means whereby people could show their mutual concern by donating blood, visiting lonely patients and giving money.

'Liberty rightly understood' emphasizes that each person is a custodian of his or her character and a custodian of the culture which shapes personal virtues. People are not seen as having 'given' preferences which they seek to fulfil, but as leading lives of thinking, learning and choosing. It is exemplified in Martin Luther King's 'I have a dream' speech, delivered in August 1963 in Washington, DC: 'I have a dream that my four little children will one day live in a nation where they will not be judged by the color of their skin but by the content of their character. I have a dream today!' He did not say, they will live in a nation where they will be able to fulfil themselves, or achieve as much as their talent allows, let alone to maximize their return on capital. He referred only to character – their moral achievement. The task of each person is to use his or her talents for the greater good, to uphold the values worth preserving and to pass them on from generation to generation.

The conflict between rational utility maximizers and adherents of 'liberty rightly understood' can also be found in social security. The former tend to favour the 'treat 'em mean and keep 'em keen' approach to social security reform, based on low benefits and avoidance of moral judgement. Friedman and Friedman's (1980) negative income tax is an example of such a scheme: they advocate a single payment to simplify an over-complex tax–benefit system and avoid administrative discretion.

The counter view concentrates on the character of the person being helped, with the intention of trying to enhance the chances of each person for making the most of his or her abilities. Its focus is on helping individuals to acquire the skills and virtues they need for self-support. Instead of relying on material incentives alone, it urges a combination of a state minimum with the additional support of charities and mutual aid associations because they attend also to character and are better able to appeal to people's strengths, not their weaknesses, by devising personalized schemes to help them back on their feet.

CONCLUSION

During the 1970s and 1980s the collectivist economic planning of the post-war years was abandoned in favour of competitive markets. Few wish to exhume economic planning, but a market economy is only one element in a free society.

Neo-liberals historically did not make a sharp distinction between economic questions and other issues. They sought a society based on a democratic political system that recognized the value of open discussion and accountability; the rule of law (rules for living that applied equally to all and were not subject to arbitrary interpretation); and recognition that government had important but limited duties.

Underlying these beliefs was mistrust of unfettered authority and confidence in the potential for progress through learning and experience. Classical liberals pictured a society, not comprising individuals with established preferences, but made up of people learning as they went along – discovering new things about themselves, measuring up to the expectations of others, doing good and being of service.

Participants in a market economy may be guided by a narrow, self-centred materialism or they may be influenced by a more generous ethos based on strong family life and a commitment to serving others. Adam Smith understood that self-interest, enlightened or otherwise, was not enough and that justice and benevolence were no less indispensable elements of a free society. For this reason, many of the free-market intellectuals who in the 1980s were concerned about monetary policy, fiscal constraint and privatization have moved on to talk of civil society, mediating structures and social capital.

GUIDE TO FURTHER READING

Lord Acton's two short essays 'The history of freedom in antiquity' and 'The history of freedom in Christianity' continue to be excellent introductions. For a discussion of the Mont Pelerin Society see Max Hartwell's *The History of the Mont Pelerin Society* (Indianapolis: Liberty Fund, 1995). Michael Novak's *The Spirit of Democratic Capitalism* (London: ILA Health and Welfare Unit, 1991) provides a good introduction to the moral dimension of capitalism. Hayek's *The Constitution of Liberty* (London: Routledge and Kegan Paul, 1976) and Arthur Seldon's *Capitalism* provide clear statements of the essential principles of a free society and the implications for social policy. My own *Community without Politics* (London: ILA Health and Welfare Unit, 1996) discusses some of the tensions within neo-liberal thought and outlines a neo-liberal approach to social security reform. Jerry Z. Muller's *Adam Smith in His Time and Ours* (New York: Free Press, 1993) is a very readable and up-to-date appraisal of Adam Smith.

Acton, J. (1907) The history of freedom in Christianity. In *The History of Freedom and Other Essays*. London: Macmillan, pp. 30–60.
Becker, G. S. (1976) *The Economic Approach to Human Behavior*. Chicago: University of Chicago Press.

Blackstone, W. (1765) *Commentaries on the Laws of England* (4 volume facsimile, 1979). Chicago: University of Chicago Press.

Friedman, M. and Friedman, R. (1980) *Free to Choose*. London: Secker & Warburg, p. 119.

Haworth, A. (1994) *Anti-libertarianism: Markets, Philosophy and Myth*. London: Routledge.

Oakeshott, M. (1975) *On Human Conduct*. Oxford: Clarendon Press.

Smith, A. (1976) *The Theory of Moral Sentiments*. Indianapolis: Liberty Fund.

tHe conservative tradition of social welfare

robert pinker

Conservatism and the Enlightenment

Conservatism is as much an attitude of mind as the doctrine of a political party. It is a generic way of looking at the world, of conceptualizing society and responding to social change. True conservatives know in their hearts that all political and economic theories are subject to a law of diminishing marginal utility. They are as sceptical of the free play of market forces as they are of state regulation, which sets them apart from both neo-liberals on the one hand and socialists on the other. They look on compromise as the invisible hand that reconciles equally important but frequently conflicting imperatives. Extreme reluctance to compromise turns conservatives into reactionaries, just as an excessive disposition to temporize destroys the delicate balance between scepticism and conviction that made them conservatives in the first place.

The scholars of the Enlightenment laid the foundations of the modern social sciences and opened a new era in the application of scientific methods to the analysis and solution of social problems. They challenged the traditional institutions of political and religious authority and delineated new kinds of relationship between the state, civil society and individuals in a spirit of optimism regarding the possibilities of social progress. Enlightenment scholarship was characterized by a belief in the powers of human reason to enhance human well-being and in the abstract principle of natural law individualism. The guiding tenets of the French Revolution – liberty, equality and fraternity – were inspired by some of the most powerful traditions of Enlightenment thought.

By the start of the nineteenth century, however, an intellectual reaction against Enlightenment thought was becoming more overt, widespread and influential. This development was inspired by a number of conservative thinkers who were opposed to the ideals and objectives of the French Revolution, and wished to restore the old, pre-revolutionary order. There were also a number of early socialists who had supported many of the revolutionary ideals, but were deeply disillusioned with the political, social and economic outcomes. Although these intellectual movements were separated by fundamental political differences, their leading thinkers shared a common belief in the virtues of an organic model of society and an aversion to what they saw as the rampant individualism of the new social orders which were emerging in Western Europe and North America.

Throughout the eighteenth century, most of the help given to the poor and needy had always been provided through the informal networks of social care based on the family, local community, church and workplace, and these networks were to survive the Industrial Revolution, the triumph of political economy and the rise of the modern administrative state. In the structure and functioning of these informal networks we can identify two major traditions of welfare, the first of which had always derived its authority and effectiveness from the paternalistic values of a hierarchical social order in which the high-born and wealthy discharged their welfare responsibilities to the low-born and poor. The second tradition of welfare took its character from the egalitarian and fraternal values which held together the countless forms of mutual aid through which the poor discharged their responsibilities to each other, as kinsfolk, neighbours and fellow workers. The dictates of rationality and reason played little part in the moral dynamics of either of these informal traditions of welfare, and the idea of the state as an involved and benevolent partner was looked on with general suspicion and doubt.

The Conservative approach to social welfare starts not from the formulation of abstract principles, but from the reality of established social institutions such as the family, community, class, religion, private property and government. It expresses a preference for order and continuity and a spirit of deference to the past rather than an assumption that change is necessary because existing institutions are deficient or that progress has more to offer than does the status quo. A second characteristic of Conservative political and social thought is its veneration for society as such, and its organic view of social institutions. When Mrs Thatcher remarked that there was no such thing as society, she was expressing a profoundly un-Conservative sentiment.

In essence, we can say that the central tenets of traditional English Conservative thought were the commitment to an organic model of society and a respect for responsibilities, rights and liberties grounded not in abstract notions of natural rights or contract, but in the traditions and moralities embedded in established institutions. Allied to these beliefs was a hostility towards the encroachments of the central government into local affairs and a natural suspicion of free-market liberalism. While believing in minimal government, Conservatives rejected the distinctions drawn in Enlightenment thought and liberal political economy between the state and civil society.

THE EVOLUTION OF MODERN CONSERVATISM

Historically, the British Conservative, or Tory, political tradition dates from the Restoration of 1660. The term 'Tory' was first used in the Exclusion crisis of 1679–81 but, after the Hanoverian succession of 1714, the Tories were left in more or less permanent opposition to the Whigs, upholding the established Church, opposing high taxes and foreign wars and defending rural interests. The Whigs grew from the political factions which opposed James II's succession to the throne, and supported the Glorious Revolution of 1688–9 and the establishment of the supremacy of Parliament. Yet there were throughout the eighteenth century many Conservatives who came to accept and defend the Glorious Revolution and to see it as a restoration and reaffirmation of 'ancient rights'.

Edmund Burke is generally considered to be the founding father of modern Conservatism, although for the greater part of his life he was a leading Whig politician. 'Politics', Burke argued, 'ought to be adjusted, not to human reasoning, but to human nature; of which the reason is but a part and by no means the greatest part.' Certainly there was a place for reason in politics but it should be exercised under the guidance of precedent and what Burke called 'prejudice'; that is, opinions which have stood the test of time. He thought that in political life, the arts of government and reform should not 'be taught *a priori*' because abstract principles took insufficient account of the complexities of human nature and society. 'The pretended rights of these theorists are all extremes; and in proportion as they are metaphysically true, they are morally and politically false. The rights of men are in a sort of *middle*, incapable of definition, but not impossible to be discerned ... Political reason is a computing principle, adding, subtracting, multiplying and dividing, morally and not metaphysically, or mathematically, true moral dimensions.' I give this quotation in full because it seems to me that it summarizes the essence of Conservative political philosophy.

Burke was not opposed to constitutional and social reform, arguing that 'A state without the means of some change is without the means of its conservation. In the interests of order and continuity it was, however, vitally important to strike the right balance between 'the two principles of conservation and correction'. He described the sentiments which create the moral framework of a nation in developmental terms: 'To be attached to the subdivision, to love the little platoon we belong to in society, is the first principle (the germ, as it were) of public affections. It is the first link in the series by which we proceed towards a love to our country and to mankind.'

From the early nineteenth century onwards close normative affinities developed between the doctrines of political economy, utilitarianism and British liberal thought. By contrast, Conservative political philosophy remained closely identified with an organic ideal of social organization and the defence of traditional institutions against the attacks of social critics and innovators. Romantic Conservatives like Samuel Coleridge, Tory radicals like William Oastler and William Wilberforce and maverick populists like William Cobbett shared a common detestation of the theories propounded by Bentham, Ricardo and Malthus.

These Conservatives acknowledged that the old traditions of paternalist concern had been eroded in many parts of the country. They denounced the new Poor Law because they believed that its introduction would further undermine the traditional framework of obligations and entitlements on which British society had always been based. In their opinion the transition from status to contract as the basis of political obligations in the newly emergent market economy was destroying the organic bonds of social life and degrading the poor to the status of either rootless wage-earners or paupers.

Much of the subsequent history of Victorian Conservatism can be seen as a gradual process of coming to terms with the realities of industrial and urban change and reconciling as far as possible the old values of order, hierarchy and paternalism with the new values of competition and possessive individualism. Under Peel's administration the Corn Laws were finally repealed, and a long overdue start was made on fiscal and administrative reform. Disraeli's vision of 'one nation' sought to reaffirm the ideal of an organic model of society held together by traditional bonds of patriotic sentiment but strengthened by new solidaristic doctrines and objectives, including the extension of representative democracy through the enfranchisement of the respectable working class, a programme of popular welfare reforms and the inculcation of a sense of imperial mission in the British people.

In brief, some important changes were taking place within the Conservative political tradition. The party that had once opposed the growth of empire became the party of empire, and the old values of patriotism became overlaid with a new doctrine of imperialism. In the 1890s Joseph Chamberlain set out to make the Conservatives the leading party of social reform. In his Tariff Reform League he tried to link the objectives of imperial preference and social reform together in one programme. Chamberlain hoped that the revenue raised from tariffs on non-imperial imports could be used to finance a radical programme of free education and universal old-age pensions. The League was founded in 1903 but it did not long survive the Liberal election victory of 1905.

CONSERVATISM AND SOCIAL REFORM

By the end of the nineteenth century, British Conservatism had come to terms with market capitalism. Its own paternalist tradition of collectivism lived on but it was now complemented by a defence of industrialism *and* a limited measure of state intervention in social welfare. It had become a tradition of thought that was as much opposed to liberal individualism as it was to socialist collectivism. Writing in 1947, the young Quintin Hogg, a leading Conservative thinker later to become Lord Hailsham, indicted liberalism as the 'body of doctrine aimed at reducing the authority of the state to a minimum'. It was, he went on to argue, 'the Tory Party which took its stand in the nineteenth century against the principles of *laissez-faire* liberalism' and supported the idea of state regulation in some spheres of economic activity. Conservatism, he argued, stood for the ideals of economic democracy, the extension of property ownership and the diffusion of political power.

Nevertheless, the Conservative Party spent most of the first two decades of the twentieth century in standing against the rise of liberal collectivism. It opposed most of the social reforms introduced by the liberals from 1905 to the outbreak of the First World War. It should, however, be noted that when the Conservatives were in office during the inter-war years they left the basic structure of these new provisions intact. In some sectors of social service they imposed cuts and in others they introduced new benefits, notably with regard to widows, orphans and old age pensions. It was a Conservative administration that replaced the Poor Law with Public Assistance in 1929 and opened the

way for local authorities to develop their own hospital services. In many respects the Conservatives were more successful than the liberals in reconciling the conflicts between individualism and collectivism that beset both parties during the inter-war years.

It was, however, during this period that a minority of Conservative politicians began to campaign for more radical collectivist policies. In 1938 Harold Macmillan – then a young and dissident backbencher – published his classic exposition of the case for Tory collectivism, *The Middle Way*. Ritschel describes this work as 'essentially a conservative vision of a business commonwealth, nominally subservient to parliamentary authority, but in practice free to determine the course of economic development'. *The Middle Way* set out 'a spirited defence of private enterprise and a corporatist style economy' managed on Keynesian lines. It commended a substantial degree of subsidy for state-owned public utilities, policies of full employment with minimum wage legislation, and a major extension of the statutory social services.

If a Labour backbencher were to publish such a book today it would cause almost as much embarrassment and shock to the Labour Party leadership as it caused to the Conservative establishment in the late 1930s. At the time, Macmillan and his supporters were largely ignored. Like the neo-liberal Conservatives of the 1950s and 1960s, they had to wait for nearly two decades before their policy proposals were to be taken seriously and implemented.

During the Second World War the Conservative Party was both collectivist and anti-collectivist in its approach to social reform. It committed itself to supporting policies of full employment, educational reform and the introduction of family allowances. It opposed many of the key proposals of the Beveridge Report and went on to suffer a humiliating electoral defeat in 1945 as a consequence. Quintin Hogg had anticipated this defeat in 1943 when he wrote an 'open letter' to his party. He asked his colleagues: 'are we being progressive enough in our attitude to reform . . . are we being quite true to our traditions as a national party?' He went on to argue that if the Conservatives continued to oppose the Beveridge plan they would end up not only 'dead but damned'.

In the event the Conservatives were damned but not left for dead. During their years in opposition they began a radical reappraisal of their approach to social policy issues. Some of the younger Conservatives, notably Enoch Powell, Ian MacLeod and Angus Maude, were invited by the Conservative Political Centre to write a monograph on the future of the social services. Their proposals were published in 1950 under the title *One Nation* and were endorsed at the Party's Annual Conference of that year.

Although the *One Nation* group were critical of some aspects of the newly established post-war welfare state, notably with regard to what they considered to be its undue reliance on universalism, they recommended a higher rate of public sector home building, support for the National Health Service, the maintenance of full employment and closer cooperation with the trade unions.

Much has been written about the extent to which the years between 1951 and 1979 can be described as a period of post-war consensus between the major political parties regarding the future of the welfare state. When the Conservatives were returned to office in 1951 they did not dismantle the institutional framework of the post-war settlement. In many respects they extended it. Macmillan himself played a major role, first as Minister of Housing and later as Prime Minister, in defending and extending the institutions of the British welfare state. Yet it was during this period that neo-liberal Conservative scholars and politicians started to mount their critique of collectivist welfare and to extend their influence throughout the rank-and-file as well as the top echelons of the Conservative Party.

CONSERVATISM AND THE CHALLENGE OF NEO-LIBERALISM

When Edward Heath took office in 1970 he dallied briefly with some of the free-market policies of the neo-liberal 'new right', but soon abandoned these approaches in the face of rising unemployment. After Margaret Thatcher became leader of the Conservatives in 1976, the tide of influential opinion in the party turned sharply against all forms of collectivism and the neo-liberal theories of the 'new right' moved into their ascendancy.

The ensuing battle for the 'soul of the Conservative Party' is described in retrospect by Ian Gilmour, who was to become one of its first casualties. Only two years before Margaret Thatcher became Prime Minister in 1979, Gilmour felt able to claim in his book *Inside Right: a Study of Conservatism* that the Conservatives supported both private enterprise and private property but that first and foremost they were a party of national unity. As such the party abjured all forms of ideology because all ideologies support particular class interests and as such are 'a threat to national unity'.

Up to that point, at least, it can be said that the ideals of an organic society and a unitary welfare state still enjoyed support in some sections of the Conservative Party. In his most recent work, *Dancing with Dogma*, Gilmour reflects on the subsequent triumph of 'new right' ideology and the demise of traditional Conservatism during the Thatcher years.

There may still be dimensions of normative consensus between the neo-liberals and the traditionalists within the Conservative Party. It is, however, the doctrinal divisions between the 'drys' and the 'wets' that are currently most in evidence. At the present time it is the collectivistically minded 'wets' who are most strongly pro-Europe. Nevertheless, it remains to be seen whether these pro-European Conservatives can reconcile the new ideal of 'one Europe' with the older ideal of 'one nation'.

Over time, the Conservative Party ceased to be more or less exclusively identified with landed interests and came to terms with the political, social and economic changes that followed the Industrial Revolution. The party faces challenges of similar magnitude in the immediate future. Traditional Conservatives like Macmillan, Butler and Macleod – were they alive today in the 1990s – would have taken Maastricht and the Social Chapter in their stride. Enoch Powell – one of the last of the *One Nation* authors still living today – looks on the European Union as the negation of everything that traditional Conservatism has always stood for. It is difficult to predict what will happen next. The paradox at the heart of British Conservatism is the manner in which it balances an attachment to tradition with an unrivalled ability to adapt retrospectively to radical change and to make conventional virtues out of brute necessity.

CONCLUSION

Paul Johnson recounts how he was 'once present when a journalist asked Harold Macmillan what was the biggest single factor in shaping his policies as Prime Minister. "Events dear boy, events," said Macmillan cheerfully.' It is this quality of opportunism, combined with an attachment to custom, that makes Conservatism and its approach to social welfare issues such a baffling subject for so many students of social policy, imbued as they are with a belief in the powers of reason and the virtues of rational planning. Insofar as modern Conservatism has affinities with the corporatist approach to social welfare, it accepts the need for a measure of social planning. In default of such a commitment the Conservative search for a measure of national consensus would become a futile enterprise in complex industrial societies.

Traditional Conservatives have no difficulty in conceptualizing statutory social services as practical and effective expressions of an organic model of society. They also accept the need for policy change, as long as it is gradual and evolutionary in character and rests on the broadest possible consensus. In this respect it can be argued that Conservatism in Britain has become a political tradition without a political party. Whether this state of affairs proves to be permanent or temporary remains to be seen. True Conservatives will put their faith in their ability to turn unexpected events to their own best advantage.

GUIDE TO FURTHER READING

Robert Nisbet's essay *Conservatism* (Milton Keynes: Open University Press, 1986) provides a lucid and wide-ranging analysis of the origins of conservative thought and its impact on the development of European sociology. Roger Scruton's *The Meaning of Conservatism* (London: Macmillan, 1984) explores its diverse philosophical qualities in comparison with those of liberalism, socialism and Marxism. Ian Gilmour's *Inside Right* (London: Quartet, 1978) contains clear and useful chapters on some key conservative thinkers and various constitutional themes and issues. Frank O'Gorman's *British Conservatism* (Harlow: Longman, 1986) combines extracts from key texts and commentaries.

Part III of W. H. Greenleaf's second volume of *The British Political Tradition* (London: Routledge, 1988) explores the conservative response to the rise of collectivist ideologies over the past 150 years. Harold Macmillan's *The Middle Way* (London: Macmillan, 1938) sets out a new agenda for modern conservatism as a social-democratic response to the problems of reforming capitalism and defeating socialism. Gilmour's *Dancing with Dogma* (London: Simon and Schuster, 1992) offers a rivetting account of the politics of change in the Conservative Party under Mrs Thatcher's leadership.

Robert Blake's two volumes (*The Conservative Party from Peel to Thatcher*. London: Fontana, 1985) are still, when taken together, the definitive study of the development of the modern Conservative Party. Two recent publications also merit consideration: a lively collection of essays on current policy issues entitled *Conservative Realism*, edited by Kenneth Minogue (London: HarperCollins, 1996); and John Charmley's engaging and perceptive *History of Conservative Politics, 1900–1996* (London: Macmillan, 1996).

tHe socıaL DemocRatıc peRspectıve
mıchaeL suLLıvaN

FABIANISM, ETHICAL SOCIALISM AND SOCIAL DEMOCRACY

Social democracy (or democratic socialism, as its British practitioners sometimes prefer to call it) is often seen as the political fount from which welfare statism sprung. This chapter attempts: to define the nature of early twentieth-century social democracy, which, it argues, gave rise not only to the rise of the Labour Party but also to the specific nature of the welfare state; to describe the nature of post-war social democratic thought and its impact on the development and scope of social policy; and to map out the effect of changing conceptions of social democracy on social policy.

In the UK context, twentieth-century social democracy can be seen as heavily influenced by the development of two strands of thought: Fabianism and ethical socialism. Both Fabianism and ethical socialism influenced the Labour Party in the first half of the century and were significant in providing the ethical and administrative bases for the UK post-war welfare state.

Fabianism's contribution to social democracy

Fabianism's major contributions in the pre-war period were as follows. First, and

in contrast to earlier and later Marxists, Fabians argued that socialism was entirely compatible with political institutions and modes of behaviour which were peculiarly British. Socialism could be and should be achieved through a parliamentary route and, once this had been realized, a politically neutral civil service could be left to administer it. Marx and Marxists had called for the abolition of the capitalist state if socialism was to be achieved. Fabians, on the other hand, saw in socialism an extension of the existing British state (including Parliament, the military and the monarch). Socialism for the Fabians was a sort of collectivism, the rules of which would be guaranteed, and if necessary enforced, by a set of neutral umpires, who would include state functionaries, the law and the royals. In Shaw's words, 'the socialism advocated by the Fabian Society is state socialism exclusively'. Fabian political thought diverged fundamentally from orthodox Marxism in this respect. For Fabians, unlike their Marxist counterparts, the capitalist state was not, in itself, a hindrance to the achievement of socialism. Early Fabians saw it as controlled temporarily by the bourgeoisie but as capable of transformation. The state was, in other words, essentially neutral.

Second, and importantly, Fabianism's faith in the expert administrator as the guarantor of British socialism became a touchstone for British social democracy.

The civil service was to be the guiding hand of socialism, with the elected Parliament acting as a check on its activities. If the Parliament could also be well endowed with experts, then so much the better: 'a body of expert representatives is the only way of coping with expert administrators. The only way to choose expert representatives is popular election, but that is just the worst way to obtain expert administrators' (Fabian Society).

The contribution of Fabianism considered

Fabian thinking, then, might be summarized in the following way. Socialism, or more accurately social democracy, required not that the state be smashed but that it be fashioned into an instrument of social change. This would be possible because the state *per se* was not the creature of any particular social class but the politically neutral administrative arm of government. None the less, the expertise possessed by state personnel made them ideally placed to be guarantors of a socialism won through the ballot box. As we shall see later, Fabian political theory had a not insignificant effect on the Labour Party in the 1940s and 1950s and on its creation and stewardship of welfare statism.

Ethical Socialism: the Heart of Social Reformism

If Fabianism was the *head* of social democracy during this period, then ethical socialism was its *heart*. Ethical socialism is here defined as that strand of political thinking for which the social deprivation experienced by large sections of the working class before the Second World War was seen as reason enough to support a movement for social reform. At the centre of this reform coalition was the Independent Labour Party (ILP; formed in 1893 and later to affiliate to the Labour Party), but its adherents included many individuals driven by a sense of Christian obligation or moral outrage at the appalling conditions of many citizens' lives. Though many so-called ethical socialists were committed, like the ILP, to the collective ownership of the means of production, distribution and exchange, that commitment was often fired by a non-conformist notion of social morality rather than a Marxist passion for class conflict. Thinkers like Tawney, author of the now famous *Religion and the Rise of Capitalism* (1977, first published in 1922), belonged to this grouping. He, like other ethical socialists, was clear that the *raison d'être* of socialism was the achievement of a more equal society. Like many social democrats who followed him, Tawney was concerned not only with the achievement of greater equality but also with the development of a philosophy to underpin this egalitarian drive. For him, as for many social reformers, socialism was also the expression of a Christian or quasi-Christian morality.

In *The Acquisitive Society* (1921), Tawney located the sources of poverty and inequality in the capitalist emphasis on individual rights to the exclusion of individual obligation. Such an emphasis allowed the wealthy to exercise rights under law in order to accrue wealth. Its corollary was that it under-stressed the responsibility persons should feel to act in ways which ensured that the acquisition of wealth for some did not lead to the immiseration of others. Capitalist societies like Britain in the 1920s 'may be called *acquisitive societies* because their whole tendency and interest and preoccupation is to promote the acquisition of wealth'. Driven by the development of an ethical socialist morality which saw the justification for social reform as the abolition of the mean-mindedness of capitalism, Tawney looked for vehicles capable of carrying this morality forward into practical politics. One of these vehicles was Fabian political economy and especially the Webbian formulation of the relationship between the individual and the collective.

The marriage of an ethical socialist morality with Fabian political theory led Tawney to call for a functional society based on the performance of duties rather than the maintenance of rights. This is particularly clear in his *Equality* (1952, originally published in 1931). This book, rightly seen as presenting a philosophy for Labour socialism, mounted a blistering attack on the inequalities seemingly inherent in an unbridled capitalist system, including criticism of the British upper classes for practising a form of class war by their determination to amass wealth through the exploitation of a labouring class. Rather than regard such inequalities as natural or inevitable, Tawney believed them to be grotesque and barbarous. This led him to promote a notion of equality which emphasized equality of esteem and dignity based on common humanity, a definition of equality which allowed for disparities in income and wealth which were not the result of crude exploitation and which placed him at the head of a tradition of thought later expanded by the Labour politician Crosland and the sociologist Marshall.

LABOUR SOCIAL DEMOCRACY: SOCIAL REFORMISM COMES OF AGE?

By 1945, when Labour gained a landslide general election victory, the hostility of the labour movement to state social welfare appears to have evaporated. In part, this appears to have been the result of workers' experience of the protracted slump in the twenties and thirties. During that period, privilege and privation appeared to exist side by side – on the one hand the continued drive for profit by entrepreneurial and corporate capitalists, on the other the crushing poverty for the many of the inter-war years – and as a result the hostility of ordinary people to state intervention to improve living conditions understandably diminished. Trade union opposition to the imposition of a social wage became less strident as many trade union members found themselves without a real wage to be increased by trade union activity. In these circumstances Labour plans like those for a national health service, originating from the Socialist Medical Association in 1930 but becoming party policy by 1934, looked increasingly attractive (see Sullivan, 1992). The call by Keynes, Beveridge and others for a full-employment policy and a welfare state were similarly attractive. Labour's plans during the 1930s to administer a planned economy should it be returned to government and its emerging championing of a welfare state package made it identifiable with the crucial social issues of the day and was responsible, according to one commentator, for it reaching its zenith as a working class party. It was, however, undoubtedly the experience of war which set the seal on Labour as a social reformist party and on social reformism as an electoral advantage.

The influence of social democracy was also no doubt aided by the emphasis during the Second World War on policies, often introduced by Labour ministers in the coalition government, aimed at a rough and ready egalitarianism (for a fuller treatment of this see Sullivan, 1992, chapter 2). What seems incontestable is that the Labour Party had, by the end of the Second World War, come of age as a social reformist party wedded to the practical politics of Fabianism and the political philosophy and morality of ethical socialism.

CITIZENSHIP AND SOCIAL POLICY

Following the establishment of a UK welfare state which was rooted, or so I would argue, in the marriage of inter-war Fabianism and ethical socialism, one might have seen social democracy's influence on social policy as then at its zenith. However, social democracy was to be refined and renewed by the contributions of the academic Marshall and the academic cum politician Crosland. The contributions of these to the redefinition of the citizen marked both a development of social democracy and a set of principles to guide the role of government and state in relation to its role in social policy.

In a seminal article entitled 'Citizenship and social class', first published as his Cambridge inaugural lecture in the late 1940s, Professor T. H. Marshall outlined a model of social policy development, rooted in social rights, which has had considerable influence. The model owes much to Tawney and to the nineteenth-century economist Alfred Marshall's hypothesis that there is a kind of human equality associated with the concept of full membership of a community. Full membership of a community, or society, is – according to the later Marshall – contingent on possession of three sets of citizen rights: civil rights, political rights and social rights. In contemporary society such rights may be defined in the following way:

- *citizen rights* are those rights concerned with individual liberty and include freedom of speech and thought, the right to own private property and the right to justice;
- *political rights* are primarily those rights of participation in the political process of government, either as an elector or as an elected member of an assembly;
- *social rights* cover a whole range of rights, from the right to a modicum of economic security through to the right to share in the heritage and living standards of a civilized society.

State provision of social welfare was perceived by Marshall as part of the package of social rights which are one component of the citizenship rights. The development of a complete bundle of rights which is the property of all social classes is relatively recent. In approximate terms, the formative period for the development of each set of rights can be set in one of the three last centuries. In the eighteenth century, civil rights, especially those of equality before the law, were extended to wider sections of the population than had hitherto been the case. In the nineteenth century and early twentieth century, political rights, previously limited to the aristocracy, were extended first to the middle classes, then to working class men and finally to women. In the twentieth century, social rights, previously available only to the destitute (and then on unfavourable conditions through the operation of the Poor Law), were extended to working people – in the form of selective social welfare provisions – and then, through the creation of a universalist welfare state, to the whole population.

Thus, this approach might be understood as presenting the development of state social welfare as a unilinear and inevitable process. Such an interpretation, however, does this approach less than justice. The roots of citizenship rights are traced back through history and the extension of these rights seen as extensions in the British (social) democratic tradition. However, social rights – including state welfare provision – are seen as having emerged out of a democratic process, ultimately leading to consensus over social and political affairs but which included conflict between classes and genders.

Marshall argues that the movement for equality of political rights, including Chartism in the nineteenth century and suffragism in the early twentieth century, developed from a determination to extend the rights of all citizens beyond equality of civil rights. Similarly, the establishment of universal political rights and enfranchisement, contributing, for example, to the election of working people's representatives to Parliament, aided the struggle for equality of social rights. These social rights, enshrined in welfare state policies, included the right to a modicum of economic security (through the income maintenance system), the right to share in the living standards of a civilized society (through policies of full employment and the health system) and the right to share a common cultural heritage (through the education system).

Although the extension of rights at each stage has been accompanied by political struggle to achieve those rights, the effect has been, at every stage, to mould a new consensus on rights reaching its climax in the extension of social rights. This having been achieved, social rights (education, health and income maintenance rights, for example) advanced the individual's ability to utilize fully his or her civil and political rights.

This citizenship-democracy model was given further substance by the Labour intellectual Anthony Crosland. In his path-breaking work, *The Future of Socialism* (1952), he argued for a refinement of British social democracy which argued for a greater emphasis on the rights of citizens. Eschewing the class-war socialism of inter-war social democracy, he promoted instead the idea of socialism as the guarantor of equality of esteem. In a speech reproduced in a collection of essays published towards the end of his attenuated life, he located the movement for comprehensive secondary education within Marshall's citizenship model.

I believe . . . this represents a strong and irresistible pressure on British society to extend the right of citizenship. Over the past three hundred years these rights have been extended first to personal liberty then to political democracy and later to social welfare. Now they must be further extended to educational equality.

Social democratic views of the state and government are overt in Crosland's analysis. The consensus on rights has roots in a democratic tradition. It may, at times, have been forged out of struggle and conflict but once that consensus had emerged governments inevitably responded to an irresistible groundswell of opinion and the state machinery aided the expansion and implementation of social rights.

Citizenship theory's emphasis on the creation of equality of rights did not, however, imply the creation of material equality through redistributive social and economic policies. On the contrary, Marshall's analysis saw equality of social status as legitimizing economic inequalities. It is, for Marshall, no accident that the growth of citizen rights coincided with the growth of capitalism as an economic system. For economic rights are indispensable in a market economy. This is so because they permit individuals to engage in economic struggle for the maximization of profit through the right to buy, own and sell. Political rights may have redressed some of the power imbalance between the social classes in capitalist society but social rights – by peripherally modifying the pattern of social inequality – had the paradoxical, but utilitarian, effect of making the social class system less vulnerable to change. Social rights accorded community membership to all – and thus made all citizens stakeholders in capitalist society – without effecting any fundamental redistribution in income or wealth. Social welfare raised the level of the lowest (through income maintenance schemes, education, health care systems and the like), but redistribution of resources, where it occurred, was horizontal rather than vertical. In the British welfare state, inequality persisted but the possession by all citizens of a package of social rights created a society in which no *a priori* valuations were made on the basis of social class or social status. For Marshall, then, the aims of social policy and service provision include: the incorporation of all as members of the societal community; the modification of the most excessive and debilitating inequalities of British society; but the legitimization of wider and more fundamental inequalities through this process of incorporation.

Similarly for Crosland, the aims and objectives of welfare state policy were not primarily those of equality through redistribution. For him, social equality, even if desirable, could not be held to be the ultimate purpose of the social services. Rather, the aims were to provide relief of social distress and the correction of social needs. Inequalities would, he believed, be lessened as a result, but the creation of equality was, at most, a subsidiary objective of social democratic social policy. Indeed, in an earlier contribution to the debate on welfare, Crosland made his views on welfare state aims even more explicit:

The object of social services is to provide a cushion of security . . . Once that security has been provided further advances in the national income should normally go to citizens in the form of free income to be spent as they wish and not to be taxed away and then returned in the form of some free service determined by the fiat of the state.

The creation of a welfare state in the 1940s had, in Crosland's view, substantially, if not completely, satisfied the need for universal and full membership of the societal community. The objects of state welfare provision were to cushion insecurity and to ameliorate excessive inequality rather than to promote equality. The idea of state welfare as the shock absorber of inequalities in capitalist society is one which is also found in some of the Marxist views on welfare. The difference is that – while Marshall, Crosland and others see this function as an appropriate one – it formed part of the Marxist critique.

What springs from the pre- and post-war social democratic literature, then, is a set of theoretical perspectives and a practice that served well enough for much of the post-war period. The emergence of a rational/moral consensus led to the development of state social welfare and to the creation of a welfare state. That welfare state aimed at, and to some extent succeeded in, ameliorating social diswelfares and dulling the edges of inequality. It did so by providing hitherto unprovided services and by according a form of non-material equality to citizens. It emerged from a capitalist system which supported – and was supported by – welfare. Social democratic welfare created, in other words, a 'hyphenated society', part capitalist part socialist, or in Harold Macmillan's words, a *middle way* (see chapter II.6). Social democratic, mixed-economy, welfare capitalism appeared to work well enough for thirty or so years (see Sullivan, 1992). But even during this fair-weather period storm clouds were gathering for social democracy.

'LATE TWENTIETH-CENTURY BLUES': SOCIAL DEMOCRACY IN A COLD CLIMATE

The oil-shock economic crises of the 1970s, together with the consequent renewal of neo-liberalism (discussed in chapter II.5), consigned social democracy, and the Labour Party as its political representative, to the back seat for almost two decades (see Sullivan, 1992). During this period Labour moved some way towards a new centre of political gravity which has emerged during and owed much to the Thatcherite policies of the 1980s and 1990s, and this process was completed by the definition of social democracy offered by the Labour leader of the late 1990s, Tony Blair. In the 1990s it seems that Labour has abandoned the ethical socialism of Tawney, the principles of Fabianism and the inclusiveness of citizenship theory.

Social democracy, then, formed the common-sense politics of policy development in social and economic policy for much of the twentieth century. Its heyday was the extended period between the establishment of the welfare state and the global economic crises of the 1970s. Since the late 1970s, aided by the Thatcherite project and Labour's response to it, social democracy has waned in influence. As Labour has moved further towards the centre of UK politics, the philosophies of Fabianism and ethical socialism have been translated into insubstantial icons.

Though social democracy appears far from well in the UK context, its health could not be better in other parts of Europe. Whether avowedly social democratic parties constitute the government (as in Portugal, Greece and Austria) or the parliamentary opposition (as in Germany and France), the politics of interventionism and the ethics of involvement in the lives of ordinary people remain policy commitments. As we move towards the twenty-first century, we may find that re-creating a civilized society will require its rehabilitation in the UK too.

GUIDE TO FURTHER READING

Addison, P. (1975) *The Road to 1945*. London: Quartet. A social and political history of the period and the influences leading to the establishment of the welfare state, including the growth and influence of social democracy.

Addison, P. (1992) *Churchill on the Home Front*. London: Cape. An account of the efforts of the war-time coalition government in relation to social and economic policy which highlights the contribution of Labour ministers and social democratic ideas to the rough and ready egalitarianism of the war years.

Crossman, R. H. S. (ed.) (1952) *New Fabian Essays*. London: Turnstile Press. A collection of essays by post-war Fabians devoted to domestic policy. Many of the essays assume that the establishment of a welfare state had tackled the problem of inequality successfully and that social and economic policy should concentrate on increasing opportunity.

George, V. and Wilding, P. (1985) *Ideology and Social Welfare* (revised edn). London: Routledge & Kegan Paul. A clear, concise and thoughtful delineation of the influence of right- and left-wing philosophies on social policy in the modern period.

Glennerster, H. (1995) *British Social Policy since 1945*. Oxford: Blackwell. A critical history of the welfare state written from a Fabian perspective.

Hennessy, P. (1992) *Never Again*. London: Jonathan Cape. A history of the post-war period in relation to public policy.

Sullivan, M. (1992) *The Politics of Social Policy*. Hemel Hempstead: Harvester Wheatsheaf. A study of consensus politics and social democracy in the post-war period.

Timmins, N. (1995) *The Five Giants: a Biography of the Welfare State*. London: HarperCollins. An extremely well written account of post-war social policy.

II.8

the socialist perspective

norman ginsburg

Essentials

The socialist perspective embraces two assumptions about capitalism or at least the forms of capitalism witnessed hitherto. First, it suggests that capitalist societies do not or cannot meet adequately basic human welfare needs for all their people. Only public services and effective welfare rights, or possibly strictly regulated private services, can provide universal access and democratic accountability. Second, socialists believe that capitalism sustains fundamental social inequalities and divisions, which are both morally unacceptable and economically debilitating. These divisions, particularly class divisions, serve to underpin competitive individualism, most notably in the labour market, and to weaken popular anti-capitalist pressures and movements.

Socialism offers three core principles for the transformation of capitalism:

1 The deployment of the welfare state towards achieving substantial amelioration if not elimination of social inequality.
2 A democratization of the state and civil society, developing popular power.
3 Popular control of the labour market and of big business.

The last is certainly the most controversial principle for socialists and non-socialists alike. For some socialists the socialization of the economy should precede the creation of a socialist welfare state. The focus of this chapter, however, is on socialist analysis of the distribution and consumption of welfare under capitalism and the possibility of its transcendence.

Socialism has the goal of either a radical transformation of capitalism or its transcendence into something quite different. There are widely differing views among socialists about the degree of radical transformation of capitalism required to achieve socialism.

• *Gradualists* believe that socialism can be emergent from the consolidation and radical development of social democracy at national, regional and local levels of government. Perhaps the most widely recognized example of this at a national level is the achievement of Swedish social democracy over the past sixty years. Closer to home, many gradualists would see the pre-1991 National Health Service as an embryonic socialist institution or perhaps the Greater London Council between 1981 and 1986 as a prototype of municipal socialism.
• *Revolutionaries* envisage a politico-economic collapse of capitalism under the weight of its contradictions, with the subsequent construction of a socialist state and society, or perhaps even a new global order if socialism in one

country is a contradiction in terms. The revolutionary moment would initiate a radical break from the capitalist economy and competitive individualism. There are parallels with the anti-capitalist revolutionary processes witnessed, for example, in Russia (1917), China (1948) and Cuba (1958), though few Western socialists today see these revolutions as establishing acceptable forms of socialism.

It has to be recognized right from the start that the very use of the word 'socialism' is extremely problematic for at least two reasons.

1   In Britain the Labour Party has always described itself as socialist and is so described by its opponents. It has embraced many elements of a socialist programme for social policy at certain points in its history. However, in government at both local and national levels it has generally sought a moderate and pragmatic accommodation with capitalism, very much in the postwar continental social democratic tradition. This position has been renewed and modernized under Tony Blair in the mid-1990s. So, in contemporary Britain at least, socialism and social democracy are often used synonymously outside left-wing circles.

2   The word 'socialism' is associated with the Stalinist and Maoist regimes in Eastern Europe, China and beyond. These regimes unquestionably achieved very considerable amelioration of social inequalities and improvements in the meeting of basic needs, compared with the regimes that preceded them. Indeed, their welfare states lent them a certain amount of legitimacy and popular support. They also established state ownership of big business and state control of the labour market, though this hardly amounted to popular control thereof. But they were held in place not by a democratic mandate, but by terror and authoritarianism.

Hence although they described themselves as socialist welfare states and were so described by most outsiders, in fact they embodied forms of authoritarian welfare collectivism which were either very deformed models of socialism or not worthy of the description 'socialist' at all. There are many on the left, particularly in Eastern Europe, who believe that the Stalinist and Maoist experiences have rendered the word socialism valueless. Nevertheless, the idea of socialism remains alive and inspirational for many in the West and beyond.

KEY IDEAS AND CONCEPTS

The first key component of the socialist approach to human welfare is its universalism in two particular senses. Socialists believe that there are universal human welfare needs and that there is a universal societal responsibility for seeing that those basic needs are met. When and where those needs are not met fully, humanity is devalued, human potential is unfulfilled and social conflict is likely to be endemic. Universalism, however, by no means necessarily implies that every individual's needs are the same or that the implementation of the social responsibility for welfare should take the same form for all needs and in all contexts. Universalism does not mean uniformity.

In historical reality the specification of universal welfare needs has been determined pragmatically by social and political movements. Hence during the nineteenth century workers' movements began to demand and become involved in the organization of social insurance against loss of wages due to industrial accidents, old age and sickness. In the twentieth century this was extended to insurance against unemployment, health care costs and other welfare risks. The right to universal, publicly provided education has always been a fundamental socialist principle. More recently, Doyal and Gough (1991) have rigorously analysed the concept of welfare need from a socialist perspective, reinforcing the notion that there are indeed basic and universal human needs.

Many non-socialists would agree with these universalist sentiments, but the second goal of socialism is to achieve *social equality* of outcome in meeting these welfare needs, not just achieving a basic minimum level or developing equal opportunities. The meaning and application of the idea of equality has been widely debated among socialists but, as discussed in chapter II.2, it is rarely taken to mean an absolute uniformity of outcome. Socialists believe that the extent of poverty and of the maldistribution of wealth, income and educational resources is fundamentally unjust, and this also fuels social conflict and crime as well as undermining the economy, not least by the under-utilization of human resources. At the most empirical level, the ideas of equality and inequality are operationalized by analysis of the social distribution of income, wealth, health status, education and other resources, focusing particularly on the negative impact of poverty both on individuals and society. The contribution of social policies to the dramatic growth in poverty and inequality in Britain since 1979 has of course been witnessed with horror by socialists.

Beyond this empirical level, the key parameter of inequality for socialists is class. Capitalist society is inherently divided into classes and the goal of socialism is the achievement of a classless society. It is important to note that ethical socialists such as Tawney were as forthright on this as Marxist socialists. Class position is determined by position in the labour market. In Weberian terms this is linked to occupational status, the working class being blue collar workers and their families. In Marxian terms it is determined by dependency on wages, the working class being those dependent on selling their labour power for subsistence. In practice, socialist analysts sometimes use both concepts of class almost interchangeably, since those in less privileged occupations tend to be those who are most dependent on wages. The core of the working class, skilled and semi-skilled workers organized in trade unions, are the natural constituency for socialism. The class structure has of course never been as clearcut as socialist theory would suggest, and intra-class divisions have often seemed even more politically and socially significant. The class positions of poor people, unemployed people, unpaid carers, professionals and managers, for example, are keenly debated. Be that as it may, socialists are united in seeking to overcome structural class inequalities in meeting welfare needs either by radical social policy reform or by agitating for revolutionary change, or perhaps both.

The historical development of the welfare state, whether it is embryonically socialist or not, is attributed by socialists to the struggle of the labour movement alongside more informal and disorganized working class pressures. Hence the beginnings of the modern welfare state in Germany in the late 1880s were the response of an authoritarian, undemocratic state to acute socialist pressure 'from below'. The modern Swedish welfare state is widely attributed to over sixty years of socialist pressure emanating principally from the labour movement.

Another key element in a socialist approach to social policy is that there must be a firm *public and democratically accountable responsibility* for meeting needs and combatting class inequality with the fullest participation of both users and providers. In effect this normally means guaranteeing welfare rights through legislation and underwriting the costs of welfare provision through redistributive taxation. It should also mean that the delivery of services is subject to regulation and scrutiny by elected representatives of the community served and/or more directly by users themselves. The providers of services, welfare workers, should also be able to participate actively in shaping delivery. For some socialists democratic accountability and universalism can only be assured if welfare benefits and services are delivered by agencies of the state nationally or locally. For others a more pluralist approach to delivery is acceptable provided adequate welfare outcomes are guaranteed by legislation and regulatory supervision of non-statutory providers. These issues are amply illustrated by the history of social housing in Britain.

Council housing developed and managed directly by elected local authorities has been seen by many socialists and non-socialists alike as a socialist or proto-socialist form of delivery. Over the twentieth century council housing has delivered low-cost housing to many millions of working class households, much of it built to reasonable standards and allocated according to need under local democratic supervision. On the other hand, it has also delivered much poor quality accommdation, which has frequently been allocated and managed to reflect prevailing prejudices on class, ethnic, gender and other grounds. Council tenants themselves have had few effective legal powers to challenge their landlord or to participate in management.

Over the past twenty years, the role of providing social housing has been partially transferred to housing associations, which are voluntary, not-for-profit organizations regulated and financed through a central government agency. Housing associations come in diverse forms, including some charities with specialist clienteles, and housing cooperatives developing a particular strand of socialist practice. Apart from more generous public funding and enforced access to private funding, housing associations have the advantages of greater flexibility and less bureaucratism precisely because they are not democratically accountable to their local communities. Housing associations are probably more sensitive to their tenants but formal local accountability is minimal. There are profound differences among socialists about which forms of delivery can best develop socialist outcomes – council housing reflects a collectivist tradition, housing associations a more pluralistic tradition including cooperation.

DIVERSITY OF SOCIALISMS

In discussing key concepts for socialist analysis of social policy here, an attempt has been made to lay out the ideas which are shared across the range of socialist schools of thought. In British discourse, however, it has become the norm to make a clear distinction between 'democratic socialism' (the gradualist tradition) and 'Marxism' (the revolutionary tradition). The juxtaposition of these is in some ways an unfortunate distortion because it suggests that Marxists cannot be democratic socialists and implicitly associates Marxism entirely with anti-democratic, Stalinist ideas. The juxtaposition of gradualism with revolutionism is further problematic because it is possible to combine the two in the belief that a gradual consolidation of socialist forces within capitalism can eventually achieve a wholesale transformation.

Setting aside discussion of the transition to socialism, however, there is in any event much diversity within socialist thinking relevant for social policy, including eco-socialism, communitarian socialism, Christian socialism, libertarian socialism and market socialism. Here there is only room to discuss very briefly three strands of socialist thought which seem to be the most influential currently within the social policy discourse in Britain, namely neo-Marxism, feminist socialism and Fabian socialism.

Neo-Marxism emphasizes the contradictory unity of social welfare under capitalism. On the one hand, it is a response to working class pressures and in some cases hard-fought class struggle. The welfare state relieves some of the pressures and risks borne by the working class in selling their labour power as a commodity, which is their sole access to the means of subsistence. The welfare state therefore brings about the 'decommodification' of the working class, which is a very positive achievement. On the other hand, the welfare state functions in various ways to bolster and renew capitalism.

- First, its very existence makes capitalism seem more humane and acceptable, disguising its underlying brutality. This has been described as the function of legitimation or the reproduction of class relations.
- Second, the welfare state (in theory at least) ensures that a sufficiently educated, healthy and securely housed working population is available in the labour market. This is described as the function of reproduction of labour power.
- Third, the welfare state contributes directly to capital accumulation through its investment in infrastructure – buildings and equipment for schools, hospitals, universities, social housing etc. This is described as the function of reproduction of capital.

The period since the early/mid-1970s in the West is seen by neo-Marxists as one in which the working class has been in retreat as capital has rolled back the achievements of the post-war class compromise. For capital, the costs of the welfare state have outweighed the functional benefits in terms of reproduction and legitimation, and the coercive power of the commodification of labour in the labour market has been reasserted in the form of mass unemployment and a general widening of class inequalities.

Contemporary *socialist feminism* sees patriarchy and capitalism as mutually reinforcing systems of oppression (see also chapter II.9). The post-war welfare state was underpinned by the ideological assumption that people would live in patriarchal families, in which the male

breadwinner would earn a 'family wage' to support a female partner as a dependent unpaid domestic carer and service provider. Women's unpaid work fulfilled the vital functions of the day-to-day reproduction of workers and the unpaid care of children and elderly dependants. The undervaluation, dependence and isolation of women's role in the family contributed to their inferior psychological, cultural and political status. Women also formed part of the industrial reserve army of labour brought into the paid labour force on a temporary or casualized basis when required. Women were thus dependent on their husbands' pensions contributions and were denied access to other benefits in their own right. Strong vestiges from the post-war era remain today, but in recent decades capital has recruited women permanently into paid employment, albeit often still on a casualized or part-time basis. Hence women have increasingly shouldered the dual burden of paid employment while carrying on with the domestic caring role. Further, as pressures on the patriarchal family have intensified, women are increasingly bringing up children unsupported. Socialist feminists have pressed for the development of welfare rights and benefits to relieve women of some of this burden by sharing it with men and the state, thus to enfranchise them fully as citizens. At the core of the socialist feminist tradition are expectations and demands of the welfare state, particularly in the form of affordable child care facilities, reproductive rights, parental leave and support for lone mothers. The pace and extent of reform in these areas has varied enormously among Western European nations over the past twenty years, often reflecting variations in socialist influence.

Fabian socialism can be distinguished from social democracy by its emphasis on a conception of social justice which looks towards the achievement of social equality and the abolition of poverty. Fabians take the firm view that these goals can be fulfilled within capitalism because the social policy measures required to attain them underpin the long-term survival and prosperity of capitalist society. Such measures contribute to economic growth by preventing the wastage of human resources and making efficient use of them; they also underpin social cohesion and foster positive social values of altruism and collective responsibility for human welfare. Fabian socialists, traditionally, have been very sceptical about the ability of private organizations, particularly profit-making ones, to provide fair universal access to welfare benefits and services. For them the welfare state is built around redistributive taxation and universal benefits in partnership with municipal services delivered by competent professionals and administrators, regulated and financed to ensure an acceptable uniformity across the country. In recent decades, particularly in response to the rise of the new right, Fabians have put much more emphasis on a fairer distribution of liberty as well as of resources, with consequently less emphasis on equalizing welfare outcomes.

Hence in contemporary Fabian discussion there is much more emphasis on the empowerment of users and the development of choice through regulated markets or quasi-markets, alongside renewed emphasis on welfare citizenship and legal rights.

CONCLUSION

There is a widespread view that the epoch of socialism is either dead or drawing to a close; and the apparent global triumph of capitalism, the retrenchment of the welfare state and the decline of the labour movement are all symptomatic of this. In fact all these processes make the need for alternative movements and analysis ever more pressing. Socialism still holds out the possibility of social justice, reasonable social equality, popular democracy and popular control of economic resources; and through the promise of a 'welfare state' – or perhaps a more diverse collection of social welfare instruments – socialists seek to extend this appeal to all.

GUIDE TO FURTHER READING

Tawney, R. H. (1931) *Equality*. London: Allen and Unwin, revised edition 1964. A passionate statement of ethical socialist principles of equality, freedom and democracy, developing an eloquent critique of economic privilege, power and class inequality.

Wright, A. (1996) *Socialisms: Old and New*. London: Routledge. A lucid account of the diversity of socialist ideas and debates from their origins to the present day, focusing on the divergences between Marxism and more reformist traditions.

Miliband, R. (1994) *Socialism for a Sceptical Age*. Cambridge: Polity Press. An engaging, non-rhetorical statement of radical, anti-capitalist socialist principles which challenges a wide range of objections to the socialist project.

Harrington, M. (1993) *Socialism: Past and Future*. London: Pluto Press. Originally published in the USA in 1989, it confronts the inadequacies of previous socialisms for the contemporary age, and offers a new synthesis of utopianism and materialism – a visionary gradualism to combat the inequalities and injustices generated by capitalism.

Gough, I. (1979) *The Political Economy of the Welfare State*. London: Macmillan. An accessible and carefully constructed application of neo-Marxist analysis to the political and fiscal crisis of the welfare state, as relevant today as it was in the 1970s.

Doyal, L. and Gough, I. (1991) *A Theory of Human Need*. London: Macmillan. It argues a firm, philosophical case for the existence and specificity of basic human welfare needs which socialist social policy must address, backed by a radical reformist political strategy.

Barrett, M. and McIntosh, M. (1991) *The Anti-social Family*, 2nd edn. London: Verso. A clear, socialist feminist analysis of patriarchal familial ideology and policy, emphasizing how non-conforming 'families' are marginalized, and detailing radical policy changes to reverse this.

Miliband, D. (ed.) (1994) *Reinventing the Left*. Cambridge: Polity Press. A collection of essays and responses, largely from a democratic socialist perspective, covering a wide range of issues relevant to social policy, including gender, race, the future of work, Europe and environmentalism.

feminist perspectives

jane Lewis

Feminist Approaches

Post-war writing on 'the welfare state' made very little mention of women. Richard Titmuss's classic essay on the divisions of social welfare stressed the importance of occupational and fiscal welfare in addition to that provided by the state, but omitted analysis of provision by the voluntary sector and the family, both vital providers of welfare and both historically dominated by women providers. Titmuss, like other post-war commentators, also focused on social class as the most significant variable in the analysis of social welfare, missing gender (as well as race). Yet the post-war settlement in respect of social provision made huge assumptions regarding the roles and behaviour of men and women in society. Policy-makers followed William Beveridge in assuming that adult men would be fully employed, that women would be primarily homemakers and carers, and that marriages would be stable. However, the most significant post-war social trends have been the vast increases in married women's labour market participation, in the divorce rate and in the extra-marital birth rate, all of which have had a disproportionate effect on women.

The first post-war feminist analyses of social policies began to appear in the 1970s. Emanating mainly from socialist feminists, they tended to be critical of the post-war settlement. For example, Elizabeth Wilson's (1977) pioneering study of women and welfare argued that 'social welfare policies amount to no less than the state organization of domestic life' (p. 9). This view was similar to that adopted by some Scandinavian feminists at the time and stressed the patriarchal nature of the post-war welfare state. The Scandinavians stressed the way in which women had become the employees of the welfare state on a huge scale, but found themselves for the most part doing the same kind of jobs that they had traditionally done at home; for example, child care. These jobs remained low paid and low status in the public sector; hence the charge that state patriarchy had replaced private patriarchy. In Britain, it was also stressed that many of the assumptions of the social security system, for example, were traditional. Thus if a woman drawing benefit cohabited with a man it was assumed that he would be supporting her and her benefit was withdrawn. This early feminist analysis attacked the family as the main site of female oppression and also attacked the welfare state for upholding traditional ideas about the roles of men and women within the family.

In some important respects early feminist analysis of the welfare state had much in common with the analysis of the new right that emerged in the early 1980s. Ferdinand Mount, Mrs Thatcher's family policy advisor during the early 1980s, wrote a book praising the family for resisting unwelcome incursions by the state. Mount sought to argue that the family should be left entirely free of state intervention, unless of course it had demonstrably failed in some significant measure, such as child abuse, whereas early feminists had sought more appropriate forms of state intervention. Nevertheless, the analysis of state welfare in terms of 'social control' was similar.

More recent feminist analysis has focused less on whether state intervention is 'good' or 'bad', and rather more on unpacking the complicated relationships between women and welfare systems, and the significance of gender in the analysis of social policies. For it is not possible to reach any easy conclusion as to the effects of social welfare policies on women. If we return briefly to the example of cohabiting women, while state policies enforced traditional assumptions about men's obligation to maintain as soon as a man appears in a household, social security benefits have nevertheless played a significant part in permitting non-traditional, lone mother households to exist autonomously and have thus played a part in permitting the transformation of traditional family forms.

The more recent feminist analysis of social policy has stressed the extent to which gender – the social construction of masculinity and femininity – is important as a variable in the analysis of policies, particularly in respect of their outcomes, and as an explanatory tool in understanding social policies and welfare regimes. Feminist analysis has insisted that the whole fabric of society is gendered. Thus access to income and resources of all kinds – for example, education – is gendered, as are the concepts that are crucial to the study of social policy: need, inequality, dependence, citizenship. Once the persistence of gender divisions is understood, it becomes easier to appreciate the persistence of inequalities. For example, while the occupational structure has changed enormously over the past century, there are still men's jobs and women's jobs. A man's job may become a woman's job, as in the case of librarian or bank clerk, but the gender divisions remain and with them status and pay differentials.

However, it would be a mistake to think that it is possible to identify a single feminist approach to social policy. Feminists have differed both in their theoretical approaches and in the issues they have focused on. Thus liberal feminists have tended to emphasize the importance of rights and equal opportunities and treatment, radical feminists have focused more on male power and on issues such as reproductive technology and domestic violence, and socialist feminists on the relationship between state welfare and capital and its implications for women's position. However, these boxes worked better for the 1970s and 1980s than for the 1990s, and were always much too neat and tidy. More important has been the recent emphasis on 'difference' within feminism and the realization that the interests of women carers may be different from those of women being cared for, as will black women's interests differ from those of white women. In other words, the politics of contested need will be present between different groups of women as well as between women and men. Nevertheless, feminist social policy analysts have evolved their own questions and vocabulary and it is to these that we now turn.

FEMINIST CHALLENGES

Feminists began by challenging mainstream sociological and economic literature that purported to explain women's position, particularly in the family and in employment, the central argument being over the reasons for gendered inequalities in society. Mainstream analysis considered these to be the product of a combination of biology and choice, which in turn rendered them inappropriate targets for social reform. Functional sociologists and neo-classical economists agreed that, given that women wanted children, biology and differential earning power made it rational for husbands and wives to maximize their utilities by husbands becoming the primary earners and wives the primary carers. If they did go out to work, women would therefore choose local part-time work that suited them. The traditional 'male bread-winner model' was thus portrayed as the most efficient and as an essentially harmonious family form.

Feminist questioning of these models focused on both the family and the work-place. Rethinking the family involved first stressing that there was no such thing as 'the family', either in terms of a single family form or in terms of a single experience and understanding on the part of the different family members. As Jessie Bernard pointed out, there were in fact two marriages, his and hers. Male and female interpretations of their position could differ fundamentally. In regard to the economics of the family, Eleanor Rathbone raised the crucial question about the purpose of the wage as early as the 1920s. If the wage was and is a reward for individual effort and merit, how was and is it supposed to provide for dependent wives and children? Feminists have continued to ask awkward questions about the maintenance of family members. Social investigation and policy-makers assumed that money entering the family was shared equally between family members, but feminist investigation has shown unequivocally that this is not the case and that where conflict between the partners becomes violent, women often find themselves better off drawing benefits than relying on their male providers. Thus feminists have questioned both the harmonious working and the efficiency of the male breadwinner model.

They have also questioned whether women's role in reproduction is sufficient to explain their position in the labour force. Such a view minimizes the role played by discrimination. It also ignores conflicting evidence in terms of women's aspirations revealed by the post-1960s dramatic rise in female educational achievement, and the structural constraints experienced by women. Women may choose to have children, but mainstream models also assume that they must necessarily rear them. Questions as to who should care for and maintain children have therefore been central to the feminist analysis of social policies, in particular how far there should be collective provision for children in the form of cash (typically in modern welfare states in the form of child benefits) and care (via daycare and nurseries), and how far individual mothers and fathers should assume responsibility for both cash and care.

ANALYSING WOMEN'S RELATIONSHIP TO THE WELFARE STATE

Insofar as women have entered the traditional social administration texts, they have tended to do so as 'clients' of the welfare state. Feminist analysis has emphasized that women's position in relation to modern welfare states is far more complicated than this. In brief, they should be considered as clients, paid and unpaid providers, and agents.

Those who have charged that women have done disproportionately well out of the welfare state have pointed to the fact that they more often become clients, whether in terms of the number of visits they make to general practitioners, or the amount of benefit they draw, especially as lone mothers and elderly women. But women have also been the main providers of welfare. The vast majority of the increase in post-war employment for married women has been in the service of the welfare state (for example, as health workers and teachers), and women have always provided most of the informal, unpaid welfare within the family.

Women's position as both clients and providers is complicated and is directly related to the unequal gender division of paid and unpaid work in society. Analyses of entitlements to welfare, such as Esping-Andersen's, which examine the conditions under which people are permitted to withdraw from the labour market and thus depend on a strict distinction between work and non-work, cannot encompass the reality of women's existence. The woman who withdraws from the labour market often does so in order to care for children or a dependent adult. She therefore withdraws from paid work in order to engage in unpaid work. So women who are clients of the welfare state are quite likely also to be acting at the same time as unpaid providers of welfare. Similarly, analyses of welfare outcomes that do not take into account women's contribution as unpaid providers will inevitably overestimate what women take out of the system as opposed to what they put in.

Women's agency is also problematic. Seemingly women have had little say in the making of modern welfare states. Recent historical literature has suggested that women may have had more influence when the mixed economy of welfare was tipped more firmly in favour of voluntary and family provision at the turn of the century. Thus in the United States, for example, women's voluntary organizations lobbied successfully for mothers' pensions (an early form of child benefit), protective labour legislation for women workers and maternal and child welfare legislation. Theda Skocpol has suggested that at the beginning of this century the United States set out on the road to becoming a 'maternalist' welfare state in contrast to the 'paternalism' of the European states, which were built up around the concept of social insurance and which in turn relied heavily on the male breadwinner model.

Certainly the relationship between social provision and women's political participation is difficult. T. H. Marshall's idea that states proceeded from the granting of civil rights in the eighteenth century, to the granting of political rights in the nineteenth and to social rights in the twentieth, breaks down completely when women are introduced into the analysis. Women in most Western countries were granted social protection before they were granted the vote, usually in the form of protective labour legislation, which was in turn often designed to reinforce the gender division of labour and to exclude women from certain kinds of employment. The major programmes of modern Western European welfare states were legislated by men and, in the case of social insurance, working as it does through the labour market, primarily for men. However, women have historically played an important role in local politics and in local campaigns around welfare rights and tenants groups, for example. In addition, the fact that women played very little part in the establishment of the programmes of the modern welfare state does not mean that the development of social provision is unimportant in securing women's participation. In the Scandinavian countries, which are acknowledged to have developed the most generous citizenship-based welfare entitlements, women have also succeeded in gaining the greatest formal political representation in Parliament.

THE CONCEPT OF DEPENDENCE

Because of the gendered division of income and work in society and of women's complicated relationship to both work and welfare, the feminist analysis of dependency has been central in exposing the assumptions underlying policy formation. From the policy-making point of view, in both Britain and the United States during the past decade there has been increasing concern about female 'welfare dependency', especially in respect of the growing numbers of lone mother families.

There are three main sources of income for women in modern industrial societies: men, the labour market and the state; although in some countries charity may still play an important part (for example, Italian unmarried mothers must still resort to charity if there is no family support forthcoming). Over the past century, single women without children and married women with children have become increasingly dependent on wages, and single women with children on the state, rather than on male relatives. But because of the gendered division of work, whereby women do a disproportionate amount of the unpaid work, over the life-cycle women will tend to rely on more than one source of income. The woman caring for an elderly relative may become more dependent on state benefits in order to render the person she is caring for more independent. The way in which women 'package income' is therefore likely to be more complicated than it is for men, reflecting the different pattern of their dependencies on the labour market, wages and men.

The assumptions that governments have made about female dependency have historically been simple and in accordance with the male breadwinner model: that adult married women will be dependent on men. Early feminist analysis showed how this assumption had underpinned the post-war settlement in Britain; similar assumptions were a feature of the vast majority of European welfare states. However, different countries have varied in the extent to which they have moved away from this set of assumptions. Sweden and Denmark have moved furthest, to the point at which it is assumed that all adults, male and female, will participate in the labour market, making the dual-earner family the norm. This changed assumption regarding the behaviour of adult women was accompanied by strengthened collective provision in respect of child care, in the form of day care and parental leave insurance. France has attempted to make parallel provision for adult women as mothers and as paid workers, while Germany and Britain have remained relatively strong male breadwinner welfare regimes. In Britain, the state has remained at best neutral, making the division of paid and unpaid work a private matter for individual men and women, whereas the French and Scandinavian governments have attempted in different ways to reconcile paid and unpaid work.

The difficulty and the importance of the ways in which governments have identified adult women as primarily either mothers or workers is shown clearly in the case of lone mothers. In Britain since the Second World War lone mothers with children under sixteen have not been required to make themselves available for employment, whereas in France this applies only to lone mothers with children under three. In the 1990s the pendulum has been swinging back towards treating lone mothers more as workers, and in Britain towards forcing men to maintain their biological children. The point is that within the traditional assumptions regarding female dependence on men, if there is no male breadwinner present, the state has to decide under what conditions it will step in to maintain the woman and her children, or whether it prefers to encourage her to be dependent on wages.

Traditional assumptions regarding female dependence on men, which has been the pattern of dependence preferred by government, have meant that women's substantial contributions to welfare, both informal and formal, have tended to be ignored, together with the entitlements that would have been their due. In addition, there has been a tendency to define women's needs in terms of motherhood as a social function rather than an effort to meet need on an individual basis. Carole Pateman has argued that modern citizenship rights and obligations attach to the individual's capacity for economic independence, which means that the unequal division of work which renders women's position in the labour market marginal also serves to make them second class citizens.

WOMEN'S CLAIMS: EQUALITY OR DIFFERENCE?

Feminist analysis of women's structural position in society and the particulars of their relationship to modern welfare regimes has shown why it is that equal opportunities legislation that focuses heavily on the public world of employment is bound to have at best only moderate success. The gendered divisions of paid and unpaid work and the gendered inequalities that result require much more sophisticated policies. Aiming to treat women the same as men will not do. On the other hand, acknowledging female difference within social policies is likely to reinforce it, as was the case with postwar social security policy which, recognizing the degree to which married women were dependent on men, served to perpetuate it. Feminist analysis has shown that the problem of same or different treatment is a central one for modern social policies.

GUIDE TO FURTHER READING

There are now a range of texts that provide an introduction to feminist approaches to social policy, beginning with Elizabeth Wilson (1977) *Women and the Welfare State*. London: Tavistock. Gillian Pascall (1986) *Social Policy. A Feminist Analysis*. London: Tavistock, is comprehensive, but a little dated. Jennifer Dale and Peggy Foster (1986) *Feminists and State Welfare*. London: Routledge and Kegan Paul, provided more by way of historical background and gave special attention to women in the caring professions. Fiona Williams (1989) *Social Policy: a Critical Introduction*. Cambridge: Polity Press, provides a more sophisticated introduction to feminist theory as it relates to social policy. There are also some books of essays that treat particular themes of importance to the study of women and social policy, e.g. M. Maclean and D. Groves (1991) *Women's Issues in Social Policy*. London: Routledge. Carole Pateman's theoretical work has been extremely influential, see particularly her essay The patriarchal welfare state, in Amy Gutman (ed.) (1988) *Democracy and the Welfare State*. Princeton, NJ: Princeton University Press, pp. 231–60. My own edited volume, *Women and Social Policies in Europe*. Aldershot: Edward Elgar (1993), makes an attempt to analyse women's position in relation to the different kinds of European welfare regimes.

'race' and social welfare

waqar ahmad and gary craig

This chapter summarizes some major conceptual and policy issues in 'race' and social welfare before discussing three specific areas of social policy. Racism in state welfare has a long history. For example, Queen Elizabeth I ordered compulsory repatriation of black people from Britain so that state welfare would be consumed only by white citizens. Williams identifies three important recent historical moments in the relationship between racism and state welfare. These were:

- The importance of the construction of notions of nation, welfare state and citizenship, in the early twentieth century, characterized by increasing exclusion of certain categories of people.
- The significance of the eugenics movement, which constructed certain groups as pathological and to be contained to ensure the greater good of the wider society. Williams (1996) argues that 'discourses involved in this [eugenics] movement were racialized, and ... overlapped with notions of class, gender, disability and sexuality'.
- The post-war period of black immigration encouraged by the state to meet labour shortages, and during which the 'historical legacy of racism reconstituted itself, especially in relation to the pathologization of black family life'. Indeed, the emergence of the welfare state itself was based on fears of the degeneration of the 'British race' and the loss of the empire.

That the state's relationship to racialized minorities remains ambivalent today is therefore not surprising.

This ambivalence is not confined to social policy as *practice*; it is shared by the *academic discipline* of social policy, where it is still not uncommon for mainstream social policy texts to ignore 'race' and racism. This is an odd omission considering that social policy as a discipline is concerned centrally with issues of citizenship rights, welfare, equality, poverty alleviation and social engineering.

RACISM: DEFINITIONS AND THEIR IMPLICATIONS

'Racism' is a messy concept, as it encompasses attitudes, behaviour and outcomes and has been conceptualized in a variety of ways. 'Scientific racism', based on notions of the inherent superiority of certain 'races' over others, is now largely discredited by biologists and social scientists alike. However, versions of it continue to have some popularity. A belief in the natural superiority of some 'races' over others was used to justify slavery and imperialism, and is now being used to argue for the abolition of anti-poverty policies (Fraser,

1995). A particularly popular definition of 'racism' rested on psychological assumptions about an individual being racially prejudiced and having the power to exercise this prejudice to discriminate against people from a different racial group. This psychological approach had great salience in British social policy in the shape of 'multiculturalism' and 'is a central feature of the formation of discourses in education, social work, youth services, counselling, and personal social services' (Mercer, 1986). This conception locates racism in cultural difference: in terms of policy, it can only articulate arguments for tolerance of difference rather than for equality of treatment, resources or outcomes.

An important point in British 'race relations' literature was the publication of *The Empire Strikes Back*, which provided a powerful critique of multiculturalism and psychological approaches to racism. In this the contributors argued for a conceptualization of racism in terms of institutional structures, organizational and professional ideologies and the routine workings of a racist society in which an understanding of imperialism, contemporary relationships between developed and under-developed worlds, and intersections of 'race' and class were vital. Racism is practised by ordinary people in a racist society, and not solely by evil people; combating racism is thus an issue not of changing attitudes or preaching tolerance but of changes in legal and institutional structures, practices and ideologies. Institutions built on white British, Judaeo-Christian values and a racist ideology may well discriminate against individuals and groups of minority ethnic background through the application of routine procedures (residence requirements, ability to speak English, etc.), without the individual functionaries (clerks, administrators etc.) themselves necessarily being racially prejudiced. Anti-racism, the approach to combating inequities built on this notion of racism, emphasized the need to challenge and change structures and procedures – institutional racism rather than individual

prejudice was thus the focus of anti-racist strategies.

In this approach, what was important for minority ethnic communities was their shared experience of racial marginalization and discrimination – leading to the popular adoption of the description 'black' to signify this unity of experience – rather than the discreteness of individual cultures, ethnicities and religions. Anti-racism, in the 1980s, was espoused by a number of 'left' local authorities, including the Greater London Council (GLC), and had salience in social policy areas such as social work and housing. The late 1980s was notable for a backlash against anti-racism, from both within and without the movement. The right criticized it for being politically dangerous and divisive – the tabloid press routinely published stories about the 'excesses' of 'loony left boroughs' as well as of individual activists. Some on the left were concerned about the hardening orthodoxy of the anti-racist movement, which no longer acknowledged difference, or the value of culture, while others questioned its relevance to certain sections of the political black alliance, namely Asian communities. In the late 1980s, questions were also raised about the relevance of anti-racism to struggles around not colour-based racism, but racism articulated increasingly around notions of culture and religion (e.g. in the increasing anti-Muslim sentiments). The abolition of the GLC and political pressure on many of the 'left' boroughs impacted heavily on the viability of anti-racism at the local government level. These and other changes, resulting from the open hostility of a right-wing central government, have left a vacuum where watered-down versions of anti-racism compete for salience with versions of 'ethnic sensitivity'.

CONTROLLING THE 'RACE RELATIONS PROBLEM'

A central plank of British social policy concerns the containment of the 'race relations problem', an important facet of it being repressive and increasingly restrictive immigration control. Punitive immigration control has been justified by both Conservative and Labour governments in terms not just of its importance to the state, but of it being in the interest of minority ethnic communities themselves. Roy Hattersley, when Home Secretary, argued for the necessity of stricter controls if the integration of existing minority ethnic groups was to become a social reality. Mrs Thatcher justified the presumed dangers of continued and large-scale black immigration in terms of the natural resentment, on the part of the white British community, of being 'swamped' by alien cultures, fears which had earlier been aired by others, such as Enoch Powell. Progressively restrictive immigration controls, from the 1960s onwards, were employed through formal legislation as well as administrative techniques such as understaffing in British High Commissions in countries of the 'New Commonwealth', which created long queues of potential entrants. The 1980s saw the informal practice of 'virginity testing' of women from South Asia (based on the racist assumption that genuine applicants would not have engaged in pre-marital sexual activity and hence have unruptured hymens), entering Britain for the purpose of marriage, in ports of entry. The catch-22 of the 'primary purpose rule' (of having to prove that the primary purpose of marriage is not entry into Britain) and discriminatory immigration practices which made entry of men coming to marry women resident in Britain difficult – a practice deemed illegal by the European court – were also introduced in the 1980s. Immigration control for families of people from non-white countries remains punitively restrictive, often keeping families divided across continents and without important kin support.

The state response to the welfare needs of minority communities has been characteristically ambivalent: increasingly restrictive access to state welfare alongside specific funding to local authorities; for example, through Section 11 of the 1966 Local Government Act and various urban programmes to help in the 'integration' of minority communities. The 'twin-track' state response, involving both improved integration, including measures to make racial discrimination illegal, and restrictions on immigration, is evident in the way immigration and race relations legislation has developed in tandem. For example, the 1965 and 1976 Race Relations Acts were each preceded and then followed by Immigration Acts (see Solomos, 1993). Divided families are one consequence of such policies. Even those who possess formal citizenship (characterized by a British passport, voting rights etc.) do not enjoy equality of substantive citizenship (characterized by access to the array of state-funded social welfare) (Ahmad and Husband, 1993), as is discussed in the case studies below. Access to state welfare is also conditioned by continued expectations that minority ethnic communities should prove their deservingness, both literally (see Amin and Oppenheim, 1992) and symbolically (demonstrating loyalty and allegiance to the British way of life, such as by passing the 'cricket test' – Conservative politician Norman Tebbit suggested that when, say, a 'Pakistani immigrant' attended a cricket match between England and Pakistan, the test of Britishness would be which team he cheered for).

CASE STUDIES

Below, we provide case studies of three important policy areas (social security, housing and education) which illustrate some of the ways in which institutional racism limits the access of minority ethnic communities to state welfare.

Social security

What is the problem?

Minority ethnic communities are more likely to experience poverty than the UK population as a whole. This is owing to:

- higher than average unemployment levels (minority ethnic communities are concentrated in inner cities where recession and industrial restructuring have weakened older industrial sectors);
- racism in the selection of people for jobs or redundancy;
- the greater likelihood of low-paid work:
- inadequate health and housing provision;
- restrictions on state financial help for refugees and asylum seekers.

The social security system should maintain adequate income levels, and be a means for identifying minority ethnic communities at greatest risk. In addition, we cannot assume that the minority ethnic community experience of poverty can be extrapolated from that of the population at large. For example, household and age structures of different minority ethnic groups are diverse, and the UK minority ethnic population as a whole is considerably 'younger' than the white population. Given the level of educational qualifications achieved by older members of minority ethnic communities while in the labour market, their shorter UK employment careers and their greater experience of unemployment and low pay, minority ethnic community pensioners are more likely to have both reduced access to occupational pensions and reduced state pensions and other contributory benefit provision. Minority ethnic elders' income is thus generally more dependent on income-replacement (usually means-tested) social security benefits and therefore lower than that of their white counterparts.

Independent research also suggests that the social security system creates further problems for minority ethnic communities. For example, National Association of Citizens Advice Bureaux (NACAB) monitoring of minority ethnic users' experience indicated that direct and indirect racism were common, that 'black clients and clients who speak or write no or little English are not receiving full entitlement

to benefit, and their encounters with the social security system are often distressing and humiliating' (cited in Craig and Rai, 1996, p. 134). Other studies highlight low benefits take-up among minority ethnic communities, resultant on language difficulties, lack of specialist advisors, insufficient awareness and information about sources of help, and cultural and religious factors among the minority ethnic communities themselves. For example, a sense of stigma attached to claiming, among the Bangladeshi and Chinese communities, is based on a belief that those who claim would be looked down on in the community.

The policy response

The social security system cannot identify minority ethnic communities at risk because it has no ethnic monitoring system. Targeted research aimed at exploring the experience of minority ethnic communities is thus difficult to execute and the Department of Social Security provides no 'race'-based analysis of data. Other structural factors which undermine the ability of the social security system to maintain adequate income levels among minority ethnic communities include:

- an emphasis in contributory schemes on non-interruption of contributions, discriminating against those with short or irregular UK working lives;
- their consequent over-reliance on means-tested benefits, notorious for low take-up;
- direct and indirect discrimination against 'people from abroad'.

Following publication of several critical research reports, the Department of Social Security introduced a limited response, including publishing key leaflets in seven other languages, and providing an Urdu/Punjabi helpline, better training for staff in relevant offices, more sensitive publicity and an interpretation/translation service in Bradford. This response failed to address structural processes of discrimination, however. Similarly, in response to NACAB's report, the Department merely commissioned a small-scale investigation into the information needs of minority ethnic communities and established liaison arrangements with NACAB to monitor developments. The Benefits Agency has now committed itself to providing services 'fairly and impartially, never discriminating on any grounds including those of race', but most of the structural issues outlined above have not been addressed. Additionally, most research into the social security system still has no adequate 'race' dimension.

Housing

What is the problem?

Minority ethnic communities are residentially segregated, in terms of regional distribution (being concentrated mainly in South East and North West England and the West Midlands), between urban and rural areas and within urban areas, where the vast majority of minority ethnic communities live. Most white people live in areas with very small minority ethnic populations and about 10 per cent of whites live in urban enumeration districts containing about three-quarters of all minority ethnic communities. Explanations for regional segregation focus particularly on the demand for workers in occupations where there were labour shortages and, within defined urban areas, on the impact of cultural preferences in shaping the concentration of particular minority ethnic communities. This explanation, however, does not clarify why 'they should pursue this in the more run-down segments of the housing stock, rather than in areas where they could secure the symbolic and economic benefits associated with suburban life' (Smith, 1996, p. 37). Minority ethnic communities are most likely to be found in areas which are deprived on many indicators, where housing is older

and of poorer quality and where other services such as education are inadequate. This phenomenon derives from the way the labour market interacts with the housing market.

Because members of minority ethnic communities are more likely to have been working in low-paid, insecure occupations, they have generally had to resort to the poorest forms of housing. A further structural reason for these concentrations, however, lies in the existence of direct individual and indirect structural discrimination in both public and private housing sectors. This has been reflected in policies of direct exclusion, the manipulation of information and opportunities by key housing gatekeepers such as local authority housing managers and private sector estate agents, racist public housing allocation policies and differential access to private housing finance.

The policy response

Addressing racism in housing provision has been complicated by major changes in the housing market, consequent on recent government policy shifts, particularly towards the growth of owner-occupation and (to a lesser extent) of private rented and housing association sectors, and away from direct local authority housing provision. Growth in the small housing association movement offered opportunities for specialist housing provision for minority ethnic communities and in 1986 the Housing Corporation adopted a formal housing strategy for minority ethnic communities. This has led to a larger number of independent associations controlled by minority ethnic communities.

Minority ethnic communities have fared less well in other housing sectors, however. For example, low-income minority ethnic owner-occupiers in disadvantaged urban areas found that a combination of higher repair and maintenance bills, overcrowding and higher loan repayments hindered a general enhancement of their housing status. At the same time, 'right to buy' policies have differentially affected those minority ethnic communities in poorer quality public sector housing to which they had originally been directed on racist grounds. The private rented sector remains a disproportionately significant source of housing for minority ethnic communities but racism in access and allocation continue to be extensive in what is becoming an increasingly deregulated sector.

Education

What is the problem?

Discussion about 'race' and education focuses, as with education more generally, on attempts to identify the factors which affect educational achievement. These have been heightened by claims in some quarters that educational achievement is genetically determined. The minority ethnic community population has a 'younger' demographic profile than the population at large: thus the school population contains proportionately half as many again ethnic minority children as might be expected from the UK population as a whole, and this proportion is continuing to grow. Until 1989, the only source of data on ethnicity and educational attainment was from labour market statistics. These focus on the achievement of formal qualifications but do not 'reflect the educational "value-added" to pupils over the course of their education through a combination of school input and pupil effort' (Law, 1996, p. 171).

Analysis of data suggests that under-achievement is variable between different minority ethnic communities and that this is affected by several factors, including religious, cultural, social or political motivation, broader socio-economic factors, differences in the general quality of schools (including, particularly, the quality of teaching and of school facilities) and racial harassment. Although these factors are not in themselves determined by 'race', there is a strong correlation between low socio-economic status, poor educational provision and 'race', as a result of the kind of structural factors described earlier. The interaction of these factors can be complex: for example, many minority ethnic communities have a higher rate of participation in post-sixteen education than white communities; here, parental motivation appears to be reinforced by a reluctance to enter what may be seen as a racist labour market. However, the rate of minority ethnic communities' admissions to higher education, while again variable between different groups, do not reflect the high level of post-compulsory schooling. Studies suggest that the discretion inherent in admissions procedures often operates in a racist way. Racist assumptions often also underpin the assessment of special needs or the selection of children for exclusion from school.

The policy response

The collection of data from ethnic monitoring has improved at both school and higher education levels since the late 1980s and shows that the gap between minority ethnic pupils and white pupils is narrowing in terms of qualifications, as result of anti-racist policies in a number of policy areas, including housing, health, the labour market and education itself.

However, educational policy developments since 1980 – for example, the growth of local management of schools with devolved (but tight) budgets and the weakened influence of local authority 'race' polices (because of both local management and financial constraints on local government) – mean that there is little impetus for the further enhancement of anti-racist practice within schools. As with housing, minority ethnic groups have reacted in part by developing 'complementary' forms of educational provision such as Saturday schools and autonomous adult education provision. Local proposals for the development of separate educational provision for Muslim children, however, have generally been opposed on the grounds that 'special' provision should not be needed, a particularly ironic response to racism in the general educational system.

GUIDE TO FURTHER READING

Ahmad, W. I. U. and Husband, C. (1993) Religious identity, citizenship and welfare: the case of Muslims in Britain. *American Journal of Islamic Social Science*, 10(2), 217–33. Discusses issues of formal and substantive citizenship with a particular focus on Britain's Muslim communities.

Amin, K. and Oppenheim, C. (1992) *Poverty in Black and White*. London: Child Poverty Action Group/Runnymede Trust. Analyses qualitative and quantitative data on poverty among Black communities; highlights structural factors increasing likelihood of Black communities experiencing poverty.

Centre for Contemporary Cultural Studies (1982) *The Empire Strikes Back: Race and Racism in 70s Britain*. London: Hutchinson. An important critique of multicultural approaches in ethnic relations and state policy.

Craig, G. and Rai, D. K. (1996) Social security, community care – and 'race': the marginal dimension. In W. Ahmad and K. Atkin (eds), *'Race' and Community Care*. Buckingham: Open University Press, pp. 124–43. Reviews poverty and income maintenance research, pointing both to racism in benefit administration and delivery, and to weaknesses in research methodology.

Fraser, S. (ed.) (1995) *The Bell Curve Wars: Race, Intelligence and the Future of America*. New York: Basic Books. Accessible book of essays on the implications of current thinking on the presumed genetic basis of intelligence and inequalities in America.

Law, I. (1996) *Racism, Ethnicity and Social Policy*. Englewood Cliffs, NJ: Prentice Hall. Explores questions of racial equality and ethnicity in relation to most major areas of social welfare provision, in context of review of theoretical and conceptual debates.

Mercer, K. (1986) Racism and transcultural psychiatry. In P. Miller and N. Rose (eds), *The Power of Psychiatry*. Cambridge: Polity Press. Provides an excellent critique of psychological approaches to social policy solutions for minority ethnic communities, using psychiatry as an example.

Rex, J. and Mason, D. (eds) (1984) *Theories of Race and Ethnic Relations*. Cambridge: Cambridge University Press. An important edited text providing an overview of a range of theoretical perspectives on 'race', racism and ethnic relations.

Smith, S. J. (1996) *The Politics of 'Race' and Residence*. Cambridge: Polity Press. Examines racial segregation in Britain, with particular reference to housing, urban and immigration policies: argues for combating racial inequality within a broader strategy for dealing with socio-economic disadvantage.

Solomos, J. (1993) *Race and Racism in Britain*, 2nd edn. London: Macmillan. Accessible introduction to 'race relations'.

Williams, F. (1996) 'Race', welfare and community care: a historical perspective. In W. Ahmad and K. Atkin (eds), *'Race' and Community Care*. Buckingham: Open University Press, pp. 15–28. Provides a useful overview of racism in welfare provision.

II.11

tHe gReeN peRspectIve

mIcHaeL caHILL

THE DEVELOPMENT OF
ENVIRONMENTALISM

In the late 1990s it seems that the Western model of industrialism has conquered the planet: the collapse of communist regimes in Eastern Europe in the late 1980s and the break-up of the Soviet Union removed the last political and economic alternative on the world stage. Yet in this very moment of triumph for capitalist industrialization the environmental damage produced by this economic system is all too plain to see in oil spills, greenhouse gases, the loss of the rain forests, traffic pollution and many other consequences of the industrial way of life.

Over the last quarter of the twentieth century concern for the environment has moved from the province of small uninfluential pressure groups to the agenda of the world's leading nations. Green has become the policy-makers' favourite colour and sustainability is a word never far from their lips. This chapter surveys the rise of green ideas, examines how other political ideologies have responded to them and considers whether it is possible to construct a green social policy.

Widespread interest in the environment can be traced back to the publications of the *Limits to Growth* report in 1971. The authors used various computer models to see how long the world's stocks of basic non-renewables would last given population increases and continuing economic growth. In the same year Friends of the Earth and Greenpeace were formed and began to popularize the environmental message with imaginative and persistent campaigning. Shortly afterwards in 1973 the oil price hike by the Middle East oil producers led to widespread energy saving measures in the Western world, although this was not to endure. An environmental movement began to emerge with a growth in the membership of environmental pressure groups.

However, green (ecology) parties were in their infancy in the 1970s. Green parties gained their electoral success in the 1980s, particularly in West Germany, with *Die Grünen* gaining seats in parliament. The German greens were to popularize many of the green ideas in the 1980s and to gain prominence for green thinking throughout Europe. But it was not so much political parties or pressure groups which spread green ideas – it was the impact of what was happening to nature. In the late 1980s two very serious environmental problems began to emerge: global warming and the discovery of holes in the ozone layer. In the last decade of the century the quickening pace of environmental crisis – particularly the onset of climatic change – has pushed the issue of the environment on to the agenda of the leading industrial countries.

Greens are united in their recognition of the fact that there are natural and social limits to material progress. These have now been reached: the planet is over-populated, the emissions from industrial and transport activity are damaging the biosphere and there is insufficient food to feed the population. The green answer is to call for a reduction in the burden of human activity on the planet and this has profound implications for social policy. How this can be done is at the heart of green arguments and debate. There are a great many ways to classify green thinking. One of the most common is to refer to 'dark' greens and 'light' greens.

'Dark' greens see the survival of nature and the planet as all-important: radical changes need to occur as human beings are but one part of nature, and their activities, particularly in the past two hundred years since the emergence of industrialism, have despoiled the planet and now threaten the existence of other life forms and even the planet itself. Among the most controversial of these are severe curbs on population. Dark ecologists believe that humans, in order to reduce their burden on the planet, need to reduce their consumption patterns. They are at one with supporters of animal rights in calling for an end to the second class treatment of other sentient creatures on the planet. Rather than people from the poor world looking to the rich West for a model, 'dark' greens would have the rich world try to imitate the poor world. Lifestyle change is key to this. People must straight away make changes in their way of life which reduce the damage they cause to the earth. In reply to the charge that this is not terribly attractive to generations reared on consumer products they answer that if people were to give up some of the consumerist lifestyle then they would gain immeasurably. Yet this seems to ignore the fact that many people do gain a sense of their own identity from material possessions. It is important to note that this is a message for the here and now. A sustainable way of life involves reducing one's impact on the environment straight away and not waiting for some future government to legislate.

'Light greens' are reformists: they want to work with the grain of advanced industrial societies and adopt a pragmatic approach. For them, the environmental problems of the world are not too grave or too large to be beyond the powers of science and technology. They believe that it is possible to have continued economic growth yet solve environmental problems. Many think that it is possible to use market mechanisms to correct the environmental imbalances which abound. Cost–benefit analysis would be one way to decide on the degree of environmental protection required. This work involves costs and these can be assigned a monetary value. Equally, it is possible for modern industry to clean up its act and, indeed, the production of technologies to do this will be a highly profitable investment. 'Light green' thinking is not a distinctive ideological position: it prioritizes green issues within existing modes of thinking about the world's political and economic problems.

VARIETIES OF GREEN THOUGHT

Many writers dispute the claim that there can be a distinctive green ideology arguing that many of its key propositions are taken from other traditions of political and social thought. Clearly this is an important and contentious issue, for its resolution will bear upon the viability or otherwise of separate green parties. Let us now summarize some of the positions whose adherents have added the prefix 'eco' to their belief.

- *Eco-socialism* is really only as old as the green movement, although it has to be admitted that many of its decentralist arguments were anticipated by the early socialists a hundred years ago. Eco-socialists link the damage wrought to the biosphere to the organization of economic life under capitalism. They are of the belief that the replacement of this economic system will lead to a society where the profit imperative will not lead to ceaseless encroachment on nature. They do not believe that large-scale production processes must disappear, only that they should be planned and controlled to prevent pollution and waste.

- *Eco-feminism* attributes the environmental problems of our time to the triumph of 'male' values – ambition, struggle for control and independence – over 'feminine' values – nurturing, caring and tending. Naturally there is some considerable doubt as to whether these values can be seen as specifically male or female. All we can say with certainty is that in the history of the modern world one set has been more widespread among men than women and vice versa. Eco-feminists argue that men must become more caring and nurturing and this should be reflected in the world of work, with unpaid, caring work being given a much higher priority by men. Women, for their part, need to take from masculinity the idea of being strong and assertive. In practical terms this might mean much more sharing of the care of children and more sharing of domestic work. In paid work eco-feminists would call for a retreat from a masculine ambience which devalues the emotional life. At the same time it is critical of those feminisms which exalt individual autonomy and self-determination for women for they are merely the female embodiment of consumerist capitalism.
- *Green conservatism*. At first sight it might appear that greens and conservatives were at opposite ends of the political spectrum. But then remember that traditional conservatism in England emphasized the small community and the rural village, and was, on the whole, opposed to urban life. In some ways this made it akin to the

programme of greens today. Dark greens might be said to have some affinities with conservatism. The system of market liberalism is a powerful force which, in moulding and expressing many people's desires for greater wealth, has released enormous energies which endanger the environment. There are many ways in which a politics of 'limits' and restraints on the use of economic and technological power would be close to a traditional conservative position.

What eco-socialism, eco-feminism and green conservatism have in common is that they emphasize certain aspects of their 'parent' ideology in order to reformulate it as a response to the environmental crisis.

THE WELFARE STATE

The role of the state has been crucial in the development of urban industrial societies. It has been a major player in the economy and in many countries led the take-off into industrialization. The welfare state, that creation of the post-1945 world, divides green thinkers and reveals the strands of thought which are present in green movements.

It is fair to say that, on the whole, greens are opposed to the welfare state. Not that they are against the goods which it delivers – free education, free health care, a national minimum – rather that they object to the state delivering these services. However, in many writers this is tempered by the acknowledgement that inequalities in access to services and inequities in distribution are capable of being ameliorated by a state apparatus. Welfare states are welfare bureaucracies and as such become organizations which have the ability to control people's lives, and this tendency has to be resisted. The response of many greens is to argue for a move towards a decentralized welfare system in which there would be less need for welfare, as citizens would be providing these services for themselves and each other. There is a high degree of emphasis on the advantages and positive benefits of mutuality – organizations of like-minded citizens providing services for themselves. Clearly not all welfare state services (for example, health care) could be provided in this way – although, here too, there is a stress on preventative health care which obviates the need for expensive high-tech care.

The welfare state, in most green accounts, would be a local and decentralized welfare state with a high degree of citizen participation and an important role for voluntary organizations. In discussing the future of the welfare state under a green regime one must remain sensitive to the differing Green positions. They stretch from the fundamentalist dark green who would not countenance a welfare state purely because it is a part of the state.

Welfare does not have to be provided by the state; indeed, it will be more spontaneous and appropriate if it is not provided by the state. The neighbourhood, the voluntary organization and what form of local administration is then organized will attend to the welfare needs of the local population. Obviously one of the key problems with this line of argument is that it downplays the role of social justice and disparities in income, and it is unclear in some green accounts whether this is recognized as a problem. Admittedly, structures of welfare can be oppressive, but they are also routine and accessible. This is an important consideration for the weak, vulnerable and isolated who rely on the local welfare state for regular support and assistance. It might also be added that there are some who will find it difficult, whatever the society, to find ready acceptance and help – they might be mentally ill or they might have a disability of some kind – and state services through their employment of professionals aim to integrate such people into the community. The role of the professional is central to the discussion of the place of welfare in a green society. Many greens are

unenthusiastic about welfare state professionals, believing that they have usurped the caring and nurturing which individuals and communities ought to be doing themselves. They feel that they tend to turn their clients into passive consumers of welfare when they should be self-determining individuals.

GREEN POLICIES

Greens argue that the overvaluation of paid work has had destructive consequences for both society and the individual. They were among the early proponents of a basic income (BI) – or citizen's income as it has come to be called – which gives, as a right to all, a weekly income. The intention here is that this will provide some recognition of the worth of unpaid work. There are many variations but the essential thrust is that it would replace all National Insurance benefits, tax allowances and as many means-tested benefits as possible. Such an income has the attraction for greens that it can begin the process of revaluing unpaid work, for those who do unpaid caring work will receive the BI in their own right. It fits in with the green idea that there should and could be more opportunities for local employment, such as workers' cooperatives, and removes some of the disadvantage associated with the low rates of pay often attached to such work. Equally, the income would be paid to those who do voluntary work. Critics of such a scheme point out that it could bear very heavily on the taxpayers who have to fund it, especially the full blown scheme outlined here, although it is crucial of course at what rate the income is paid. The BI has also received a fair amount of criticism for possibly removing the incentive to work, although this is a problem common to all social security provision of a safety net income and is not peculiar to BI. Another telling criticism is that it would require a great deal more centralized and bureaucratic state machinery than is currently available in most accounts of a green society.

In the green society the local economy and society is restored to its place as the centre of people's lives. Another way, therefore, in which greens believe that the volume of unpaid work can be recognized is through the spread of local employment transfer schemes (LETS). These are token economies where people trade their skills with one another and are usually computed on the basis of so many hours worked. The tokens earned, however, remain a local currency and this ensures that the local community benefits from this activity. The advantages of LETS are obvious. They enable a deal of 'economic' activity to go on without the need for conventional employment. They enable those who are poor (that is, without cash income) to obtain goods and services outside of the cash economy.

A central dimension of the green project is to change the way in which people behave, for it is the daily decisions – to drive and not to cycle, to throw litter away and not recycle it, to have a bath rather than a shower – which are accelerating the rate at which the environmental crisis is developing. One obvious way to do this is to change the nature of taxation, away from taxes on individual income towards taxes on polluting activity. These eco-taxes would need to take many forms in order to deal with the various unsustainable

activities prevalent in an advanced economy. A resource depletion tax would try to ensure that a certain resource was only extracted to an agreed level. Pollution taxes could be levied on goods which have deleterious consequences for the environment in order to promote the sale of benign products. In like manner benign goods can be zero rated for some taxes in order to encourage their consumption.

Greens and the Consumer Society

Greens have a distinctive stance in relation to the world of consumer capitalism which most of us inhabit in the advanced industrial societies. Taking as their maxim 'the personal is political', they have a characteristic and radical approach to some of the key issues of the 1990s: consumption, work, caring and transport. In marked contrast to other ideologies, which implicity accept the priorities of consumerism, the greens believe that we should walk and cycle whenever possible, spend more time caring for each other, do less paid work and live much more simply. Many of the implications for social policy have yet to be worked through, but it is crystal clear that this set of beliefs is at odds with consumer societies and offers a clear alternative to them.

Guide to Further Reading

There are some excellent introductions to green ideologies. Andrew Dobson (1995) *Green Political Thought*, 2nd edn. London: Unwin Hyman, is a good starting point, as he covers issues of sustainability and discusses policy implications. Equally useful is Luke Martell (1994) *Ecology and Society*. Cambridge: Polity Press. David Pepper (1996) *Modern Environmentalism: an Introduction*. London: Routledge, is a detailed account of the history and philosophy of the society–nature debate. For a brief guide to the politics of environmentalism in the broadest sense – policy-making, ideologies, parties, pressure groups – consult Robert Garner (1996) *Environmental Politics*. Hemel Hempstead: Prentice Hall/Harvester Wheatsheaf.

For an updating of the *Limits to Growth* argument see Donella Meadows et al. (1992) *Beyond the Limits: Global Collapse or a Sustainable Future*. London: Earthscan. A lucid – but not introductory – guide to environmental economics is Michael Jacobs (1992) *The*

Green Economy. London: Pluto Press. David Pearce achieved a lot of attention with his report for the UK government, which used the techniques of cost–benefit analysis for environmental protection. See David Pearce *et al.* (1989) *Blueprint for a Green Economy*. London: Earthscan. He has continued with this work: the most recent texts are David Pearce (1993) *Blueprint 3: Measuring Sustainable Development*. London: Earthscan, and David Pearce (1995) *Blueprint 4: Capturing Global Environmental Value*. London: Earthscan.

Finally, one needs to go directly to the seminal thinkers in the green movement over the past two decades. Before doing so it would be useful to read Robyn Eckersley (1992) *Environmentalism and Political Theory*. London: UCL Press. Eckersley is a 'dark' green and makes her case within the context established by the key thinkers. The American 'social ecologist' Murray Bookchin has been highly influential with his mix of anarchism and ecology. Among his numerous works one could cite *The Ecology of Freedom*. Palo Alto, CA: Cheshire Books, 1982. Nearer home the Frenchman André Gorz has stimulated a lot of debate, especially among the eco-socialists. His most important work is *Critique of Economic Reason*. London: Verso, 1989.

the social policy context

social policy and economic policy

ian gough

Introduction

Economic policy and the performance of the economy are obviously of tremendous importance for social policy. In recent years the two have become more and more inter-related. But there is still a difference – and social policy continues to play second fiddle. There is much debate about the dividing line between economic and social policy. For some the distinction is one of policy goals; for example, efficiency (economic policy) versus distribution (social policy). For others, it concerns policy area; for example, financial policy versus housing policy. Yet none of these dividing lines is clear. Some social policies, like housing, have implications for the efficiency of the productive economy and almost all economic policies affect the distribution of resources between different groups. Some policy areas, like employment policy, straddle the dividing line between the economic and the social and many commentators regard full employment as an integral part of the post-war welfare state.

Economic policy affects such things as:

- the overall growth of economic output and hence the resources potentially available to pursue social goals;
- the scale of unemployment in society and hence the need for income support;
- the degree of income inequality and the extent of poverty;

- rates of interest and hence the cost of buying a house or of building a hospital;
- the extent of inward and outward investment and hence job opportunities for younger people.

So it affects both the scale of social problems and the ability of social policies to meet them.

On the other hand, social policy impacts on economic policy and performance:

- direct government spending on the main welfare services lays claim to almost two-thirds of total public expenditure and over a quarter of total national output or gross domestic product (GDP) (see box II.12.1);
- taxes and national insurance contributions add to overall labour costs and thus affect firms' ability to compete;
- social benefits like income support and housing benefit can discourage people from seeking work in the formal economy, or from saving;
- on the other hand, education, training and nursery places improve productivity and the ability of the economy to compete in high value-added areas of production.

So social policy reacts back on to the economy in both negative and positive ways.

Figure II.12.1   Welfare spending 1921–91 (Hills, 1993).

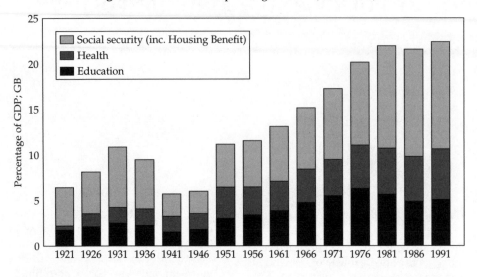

Figure II.12.1 shows that total government spending on the major welfare services grew rapidly in the post-war period as a share of GDP, but then abruptly levelled out from the mid-1970s. Public social expenditure amounts to over one-fifth of total national output. Figure II.12.2 shows that pensions, other social security benefits, health and education each account for a roughly equal share (and this amount excludes tax reliefs for mortgage interest, pensions schemes etc., which were estimated to cost another £15 billion in 1992–3). Yet figure II.12.3 demonstrates that government social spending in Britain claims a lower share of national income than in most other industrialized countries, including all other members of the EU except Portugal.

The rest of this chapter looks at: first, changes in economic policies, mainly in Britain; second, the impact of economic changes and policies on social policy;

Figure II.12.2   Government welfare spending 1992–3, £ million (Hills, 1993).

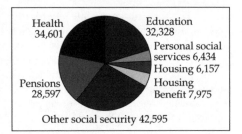

and, third, the impact of social policies on the economy. However, it does not discuss the economics of social policy or the application of economic theory to social problems.

WHAT IS ECONOMIC POLICY?

The very nature and goals of British economic policy underwent a profound change in the late 1970s. Economics is a theory-driven discipline, so that conflicts between economic paradigms are intense, none more so than between Keynesians and monetarists (or 'neo-classicals' or

Figure II.12.3   Government social spending in industrialized countries 1960–89 (Hills, 1993).

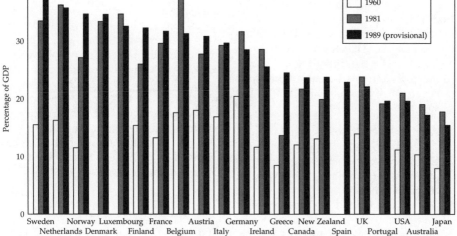

'supply-siders' or 'rational expectationists'). These disputes matter a great deal for actual policy-making, and we can speak of two eras of economic policy: Keynesian from the end of the Second World War to the later 1970s, and monetarist since then.

In the earlier period the classic *goals* of economic policy were usually described as:

- the maintenance of full employment;
- price stability (a low level of inflation);
- equilibrium in the balance of payments;
- a reasonable rate of economic growth.

These objectives are not very precise (what is 'full', 'low', 'reasonable'?) and they have been specified in various ways. Moreover, they frequently conflict and priorities must be made, but none would or could be ignored for long.

The main *instruments* of economic policy were traditionally divided into three.

- Monetary policy. The government (in the UK, the Chancellor of the Exchequer and the Treasury) and the central bank (the Bank of England) try to control either the supply of money and credit or its price – the rate of interest.

- Fiscal policy. This involves control over taxation and public expenditure in order to manage aggregate demand in the economy.
- Regulation and other direct controls. A mix of instruments comprising such things as nationalization, labour market regulation and incomes policies.

There was some link between economic and social policy in this period, though they frequently conflicted, as when the sterling crisis of 1976 led to IMF-dictated cuts in spending programmes. In other European countries the mesh between the two has been closer, as in Sweden's active labour market policies or Germany's vocational training policies.

In the 1970s this older system of economic management began to break down. Partly this was owing to a series of major changes in the global economy. First, the rise of information technology and the service economy was transforming technologies, jobs and skills. Second, the globalization of markets and the end of fixed exchange rates ushered in greater freedom of capital movements; individual governments, like the French in 1981, found that they could not buck the global capital markets. Third, new competitors emerged, particularly the 'tiger economies' of East Asia such as Singapore, Hong Kong, Taiwan and Korea, which undercut many traditional Western industries.

In Britain these shifts coincided with the election of the Thatcher government in 1979, which brought about a sea-change in the goals and instruments of economic policy in the direction of monetarism. The major shifts in *goals* were:

- Giving priority to the fight against inflation and maintaining sound public finance, while rejecting any government responsibility for tackling unemployment.
- A new concern with 'competitiveness' rather than the balance of payments and growth ('No one owes us a living. We must stand on our own two feet').

The new economic policy *instruments* were:

- 'Monetarism'. Originally this meant the pursuit of targets for government borrowing and the money supply; after the Lawson boom and bust the goal has become a stable macroeconomic environment based on low inflation and sound public finance.
- Cutting back the public sector. Spending cuts, privatization and tax cuts became an instrument of economic policy in their own right. The thinking here was that these would boost the 'supply side' of the economy, encouraging flexibility in the labour market and elsewhere. The government failed to reduce the share of state welfare in the economy, but it did prevent it rising at a time of acute unemployment and economic restructuring (see box II.12.1).
- Deregulation. Removing government controls over labour markets and other markets also became an explicit method to enhance economic performance. This has included weakening trades unions and wages councils, privatizing public

utilities, contracting out local authority services and so on.

There is much debate about whether the changing British economic policy in the 1980s was a rational response to the 'globalization' trends noted above, or whether they reflected a distinct ideological and political attack on the old system of political economy (including the old welfare state). The USA and New Zealand apart, it is clear that most Western countries have not pursued such policies to anything like the extent that Britain has. The jury is still out on whether global forces will impose similar economic policies on all countries.

THE IMPACT OF ECONOMIC POLICY ON THE SOCIAL POLICY ENVIRONMENT

What is clear is that these shifts in economic policy have had a profound impact on the environment of social policy. The use of taxes to achieve a more equitable distribution of income was replaced with the pursuit of tax cuts to improve competitiveness. The government, because it rejected Keynes's theories, simply washed its hands of any responsibility to pursue the goal of full employment – unemployment became a 'price worth paying' to get inflation down and to boost British industry. Economic policy became more detached from social policy and in some cases diametrically opposed to it.

To illustrate this let us follow Webb (1995), and trace through the ways that developments in just one part of the economic environment – the labour market – have impinged on social policy in the past two decades. These changes have included:

- The rise of mass unemployment, from 1 million unemployed in 1975 to 2.5 million in 1995.
- Within this total the rise of long-term unemployment, from 0.1 million in 1975 to nearly 1 million in 1995.

- Increasing part-time work: by 1991, 23 per cent of all employees worked part-time (44 per cent in the case of women).
- The decline of the traditional one-worker family, and the rise of two-worker and no-worker families. By 1991–3, only 32 per cent of households had a single worker, 55 per cent had two workers and 13 per cent had no workers. Jobs and unemployment both seem to cluster in families, leading to a growing inequality between 'work-rich' and 'work-poor' households.
- At the same time earnings have become more unequal and low pay more prevalent. The earnings of manual men in the lowest 10 per cent of the labour market fell from 69 per cent of the median in 1978 to 63 per cent in 1993.
- Lastly, more people are working in insecure employment on temporary or casual contracts, or are self-employed.

Taken together, these changes have transformed the environment of social policy. The modern social security system was fashioned in the years following the Second World War, when unemployment was low and stable and when the majority of working-age families had one male breadwinner in a full-time job. One might expect that social policy would gradually adapt to these new requirements, but according to Webb (1995) this has not been the case. A few policy changes have helped to encourage low-paid workers with children to take jobs without harming their standard of living; these include Family Credit and measures to continue with Housing Benefit for up to four weeks after taking a job. But against this must be set, for instance, the general spread of means-tested benefits which, together with family assessment, create perverse incentives not to work (the 'poverty trap' and the 'unemployment trap'). The explanation must be that other goals of economic policy, such as cutting public expenditure, have prevented social policy from adapting to changes in the economic environ-

ment (partly caused by these very changes in economic policy!).

Some have argued that the labour market changes are so far-reaching that a quite different principle must inform future social security: an unconditional 'basic income' or 'citizen's income' paid to all. Others believe that social security should be more closely integrated with work projects and training. But all agree that changes in the labour market have transformed the environment of social policy-making.

THE IMPACT OF SOCIAL POLICY ON THE ECONOMY

What of the reverse relationship – the impact of social policy on economic performance? There has been no shortage of disagreement here ever since the government of Mrs Thatcher claimed that the traditional welfare state was one of the central causes of Britain's economic problems. This view continued in the Major government's refusal to adopt the social provisions of the Maastricht treaty for fear of driving out investment and jobs. Yet others argue that public investment in education and welfare is a precondition for economic success in the modern world. These differences do not necessarily run along party lines; for example, the Conservative Chancellor of the Exchequer, Kenneth Clarke, said in 1994 'A strong welfare state can complement, not hinder, more flexible markets by reducing the fear of change.'

Let me conclude by disentangling some of the issues here, beginning with the anti-welfare state view.

- *Disincentives.* The OECD has stated: 'unemployment insurance and related benefit systems ... have drifted towards quasi-permanent income support in many countries, lowering work incentives'. According to economic theory, high benefit levels will reduce the cost of being without a job and thus prolong periods of unemployment. Minimum wages for particular trades will drive up the wage that people will regard as acceptable and price them out of work. This would suggest that countries with high benefit replacement rates will have higher rates of unemployment, but no clear pattern emerges according to most studies. On the other hand, if the alternative is to replace insurance benefits with means-tested ones, a different disincentive effect appears. In Britain today Income Support is withdrawn pound for pound as earnings rise, i.e. the withdrawal rate is 100 per cent, for Housing Benefit it is 65 per cent and for Family Credit it is 70 per cent. For a couple on Family Credit and Housing Benefit total net income hardly improves whether they work 16 hours or 40 hours a week. Selective, targeted benefits do have clear disincentive effects and thus may create unemployment.

• *Ageing, state pensions and saving.* Most state pension programmes, like Britain's basic pension and SERPS (the State Earnings-Related Pension Scheme), are pay-as-you-go; that is, contributions paid in today finance today's pensions. The World Bank has recently argued that this reduces the savings rate, since people have less incentive to save for their old age, and this in turn weakens investment and thus growth rates. It is better, therefore, to switch to privately funded schemes and confine the state's role to providing a basic pension, possibly means-tested. Others argue that reality does not bear out the theory. Higher savings do not necessarily translate into higher investment (nor higher investment into higher growth). Private pension funds may pursue short-term profit-maximizing strategies which weaken firms' investment. And means-tested pensions will weaken savings still more: why save for your

old age if those who do not will receive a pension anyway?

• *Taxation and disincentives to work and invest.* In box II.12.1 we have noted the large claims made by the welfare state on GDP. All this spending has to be paid for and a principal argument is that the resulting tax levels discourage both work and capital investment. The view that high marginal rates of income tax discourage people from working longer or harder lay behind the drastic cuts in top tax rates in Britain and the switch to indirect taxation through VAT and suchlike. If this was the case, high tax countries should experience lower rates of growth and competitiveness than lower tax ones (like Britain), but the studies undertaken to test this have failed to find a consistent relationship between the two. More important perhaps is the effect of high non-wage labour costs on firms' investment decisions. German firms, it is argued, are forced by these costs to locate new factories over the border in Poland or the Czech Republic, or, if they want to stay in the EU, in Ireland or Britain.

Turning now to pro-welfare state arguments:

• *Social protection and economic flexibility.* Parts of the social security system can enhance flexibility in the labour market and overall economic performance. Unemployment assistance enables people to take longer looking for a new job, which in turn may lead to more effective matching of available skills and jobs. Protection in sickness and maternity assists workers in maintaining links with the workforce. Employment protection may promote commitment to work and raise the productivity of employees. Inadequate social benefits may mean that the unemployed run down their savings and therefore become more dependent and costly to the welfare system when they retire. In these and other ways a well funded income maintenance system can pay for itself in the form of greater productivity.

- *Investing in people.* Much attention has been paid recently to the effects on productivity of an educated workforce. Education and training can teach skills and foster flexible attitudes which encourage individual and collective productivity. Most studies show that public investment in post-school education yields not only a private return in the form of higher earnings but also a social pay-off in the form of faster growth. Britain performs poorly in educating the lower half of the ability range both during and after school, and for some economists this has trapped the country in a 'low skills equilibrium'. Investing in nurseries can also help the economy by enabling women (or men) childminders to return to work.
- *Inequality, crime and the economy.* Countries with weak welfare states, like the USA, exhibit high rates of poverty and crime, and the two features appear to be linked. A rational individual living in a no-hope ghetto may well decide that the benefit–cost ratio of illegal activities exceeds that of legal alternatives. It has been suggested, though there is no hard evidence, that high crime discourages investment. Insur-

ance costs more or is unobtainable, firms must employ large numbers of security personnel and higher grade employees move from the area. In some states of the USA, higher prison and law enforcement costs are directly eating into education budgets. In this way an anti-welfare policy may impose significant costs on the wider economy.

In conclusion, we find arguments for and against the view that social policy harms economic policy. Some policies are clearly harmful, like means-tested benefits with high withdrawal rates or final salary, high-replacement, pay-as-you-go pension systems. Others, like education, training and some income security measures, are clearly helpful. Cross-national studies have found no consistent relationship between high levels of state welfare spending and poor economic performance. Yet there is evidence that countries with less inequality enjoy higher rates of growth.

The task in the years ahead is to design social policies which, while meeting individual needs and pursuing other welfare goals (discussed in earlier chapters in this section), do not harm our ability to compete in an increasingly global capitalist economy. Better still is to develop those welfare policies which, through investing in people and communities, positively help their economies to develop.

GUIDE TO FURTHER READING

Glennerster, H. (1992) *Paying for Welfare: the 1990s.* Hemel Hempstead: Harvester Wheatsheaf. Comprehensive introduction to the financing and planning of social services in modern Britain.

Gough, I. (1996) Social welfare and competitiveness. *New Political Economy,* 1(2), 209–32.

Hills, J. (ed.) (1990) *The State of Welfare: the Welfare State in Britain since 1974.* Oxford: Clarendon Press. Authoritative work on public spending and welfare outcomes in Britain across the major sectors of social policy.

Hills, J. (1993) *The Future of Welfare: a Guide to the Debate.* York: Joseph Rowntree Foundation. Concise and well illustrated guide incorporating material on economic aspects.

Hutton, W. (1995) *The State We're In*. London: Jonathan Cape. Wide-ranging and
   provocative argument linking the British economic system to the decline in our social
   fabric.
Pfaller, A., Gough, I. and Therborn, G. (eds) (1991) *Can the Welfare State Compete? A
   Comparative Study of Five Advanced Capitalist Countries*. London: Macmillan. Studies of
   the interrelation of economic and social policies in five countries including Britain.
Webb, S. (1995) Social security policy in a changing labour market. *Oxford Review of
   Economic Policy*, 11(3), 11–26.

Two journals provide excellent yet readable coverage of economic issues useful to
social policy students: *The Economist* (weekly) and *New Economy* (published four times
a year by the Institute for Public Policy Research).

II.13

social policy: culture and nationhood

fiona williams

INTRODUCTION

An examination of the relationship between social policy and notions of nationhood and nationality involves a critical understanding of the development of welfare in relation to the nation state. In the case of British social policy it requires us to unpack the ideological and material dimensions of 'Britishness' in welfare policy and practice, and how these have changed over time as the meanings and conditions attached to British nationality and culture have themselves changed. In terms of welfare states in general, a range of processes contribute to this relationship:

- the formation and changing organization and conditions of the nation state, systems of indentured labour, systems of migration, colonialism and imperialism;
- the social relations of power engendered by these processes;
- the legacy of ethnic/cultural/religious conflict and relations of domination and subordination (e.g. anti-Semitism);
- the articulation of nation with 'race', ethnicity and culture;
- processes of inclusion and exclusion from the nation state (e.g. citizenship rules of eligibility);
- discourses around nation, 'race', ethnicity, culture and religion (e.g. scientific racism, eugenics, cultural assimilation/pluralism, anti-racism);

- discursive practices (e.g. state, institutional, personal racism);
- forms of mobilization and resistance (e.g. around racism and nationalism) (Williams, 1995, pp. 146–7).

In this chapter I develop the discussion from two key aspects of these processes. The first is the role of social policy in the process of *nation-building* and the development of *national unity*. The second is the relationship between the development of the nation state and the social rights associated with *citizenship*, in particular the processes of inclusion in and exclusion from citizenship. This also involves a reference to the *cultural norms* underpinning welfare practice. In the final section I look briefly at some of the current challenges to traditional notions of culture and nationhood within welfare, including the acknowledgement of *cultural diversity* and the development of *supranational social policy*. Before looking at these specific aspects I contextualize the significance of the nation in a historical analysis of the development of welfare states.

THE HISTORICAL CONTEXT

The period from the 1870s to the 1920s was when most Western industrialized welfare states were established. It is commonly accepted that the context in which the first forms of state collectivism took place was the development of industrial capitalism, combined with a sharpening of class–capital relations; that is, an increasingly organized and enfranchised labour movement. To this picture feminist writers have added the significance of, at the same time, the removal of women, children and older people from paid labour, and the ideological and material drawing of boundaries between the public sphere of paid work and political life and the private sphere of domestic life, along with the mobilization of women's organizations to challenge these processes and to protect their interests within them (see chapter II.9). However, in order to acknowledge the significance of *nation* we need to add a third important process that was taking place at this time as part of the development of the modern nation state: that is, the greater emphasis being placed upon national unity and national identity by the setting of a geographic boundary around an imagined homogeneous cultural, ethnic, racial and linguistic community. This was a period of an increasing '*nation*alization' of society, when the boundaries of nationhood were being given greater economic, social, legal, political and ideological meaning. In other words, the introduction of social rights through social policy reforms took place within a context in which the boundaries of citizenship were becoming more circumscribed (for example, by nationality) and its constituency more complexly differentiated (by class, gender, disability, age and sexuality). The consolidation of national unity and the national ideal was achieved partly through state social reforms around the first forms of collectivism: education, public health, social insurance and, later, maternity provisions. At the same time, the rights and benefits attached to these provisions marked the different degrees of exclusion from and inclusion in the 'nation-welfare state' – a process that has itself been challenged over the century.

Some social policy writers have identified this relationship between nation and welfare as central to an analysis of social policy development. For example, I have argued that over the twentieth century, in different industrialized countries, a variety of welfare settlements emerged from the state's attempt to consolidate changes in the organization, conditions and social relations of power caught up in three interconnected spheres.

- *Work*: the organization and conditions of production.
- *Family*: the organization and conditions of social reproduction.
- *Nation*: the organization and conditions of the nation state.

CITIZENSHIP AND NATIONALITY

One of the ways in which exclusion from the social rights associated with citizenship operated was through the tying of eligibility to those rights to the condition of nationality. So, for example, anyone who had not been both a resident and a British subject for twenty years was not eligible for a pension under the 1908 Pensions Act, and non-British residents who had been living in Britain for less than five years received a lower rate of benefit under the health insurance policies of the 1911 National Insurance Act, even though they paid full contributions. Just as significant was the fact that the context in which these Acts were passed was one which fed easily into the racialization of nationality; that is, that an assumed ethnic or racial difference marked out an individual as alien or non-British. The 1905 Aliens Act marked the introduction of the first immigration controls and, with it, the institutionalization of the 'no recourse to public funds' rule – that any person entering the country who could not support herself or himself without recourse to public funds or welfare provision, or who was homeless within the first twelve months, should be deported – a rule which still exists today and has been tightened up for refugees (see Cohen, 1996).

Campaigns at this time were aimed at Jewish refugees and were supported by all political parties and most labour organizations. They gave rise to and legitimated virulent anti-Semitism and imperialist chauvinism. Moral panic about foreigners provided a stepping stone to link the politics of welfare and nationality to the practices of racism. It became common for people who were assumed to be 'aliens' (that is, who were not white, English-speaking and Christian) to be threatened with deportation if they applied, legitimately, for public funds, or for welfare agencies to be used to police illegal immigrants, or for racialized groups to be treated as scroungers irrespective of their social rights. For example, during growing unemployment in 1919 the Ministry of Labour sent secret instructions to labour exchange managers that black seamen who were eligible for the 'out-of-work-donation' – a relatively generous, non-contributory, non-means-tested benefit – should not be informed of their rights (Fryer, 1984, p. 299). In these ways the formalized condition of nationality was translated into the racialized conditions of eligibility and into a fear of 'aliens' as the bearers of inferior cultures and as welfare 'scroungers'. The use of welfare agencies as internal immigration controls and the perception of racialized groups as scroungers were carried in different ways into the post-war welfare state (see Williams, 1989; Cohen, 1996).

The subsequent history of Commonwealth migration to Britain from the 1950s is an ironic twist in the relationship between citizenship, race, nationality and welfare. In the debates in the late 1940s on the shortage of labour, the recruitment of labour from the Commonwealth (especially the Caribbean and later the Indian subcontinent) was perceived by the government as administratively more straightforward compared with recruitment from Southern Europe precisely because, by virtue of Britain's imperial model of citizenship, these colonized workers were British citizens. However, as British citizens they had access to more than work and residence rights: they had, formally at least, rights to welfare benefits and services. In effect, many of these were denied through the processes of direct or indirect racism. For example, new migrant workers were unable to fulfil residency qualifications for low-cost public housing and were forced into the private sector and into further forms of discrimination. At the same time the very universalism of the welfare state depended upon a restricted notion of the norms of eligibility and need. At its heart was the image of the white male-breadwinner family. Where black migrant workers and their families deviated from this norm, then cultural and material differences were cast in pathological terms. An example of this dynamic was the recruitment of Afro-Caribbean women to work in low-paid jobs with unsocial hours (often in the newly developing welfare services). This meant that children were left behind with relatives until it was possible to bring them over, or if they did migrate, they stepped into a situation where there was little formal provision for the children of working mothers. Either way, their actions challenged the dominant familial ideology of the day, which emphasized the role of women in the home as wives and mothers and warned against the disastrous consequences of mother–child separation. Because of the entrance conditions imposed upon them as migrant workers Afro-Caribbean women were seen to be failing as mothers, especially by welfare professionals. Evidence that emerged by the 1980s showed that disproportionately higher numbers of black children had been taken into care.

It should be noted that the formation of the relationship between the nation state, citizenship and the rights of minority groups took place in different ways with different policy effects in different countries. For example, the German concept of nationhood is based on a restrictive notion of common ethnic descent (*Volk*), whereas in France the concept is more extensive, but assimilationist, based on the acceptance of a common French culture (Brubaker, 1990).

NATION-BUILDING, NATIONAL UNITY AND WELFARE

Richard Titmuss identified war as a spur to social policy reform. Not only, in his view, did war lead to post-war reconstruction ('homes for heroes' was the slogan for public housing development after the First World War) and to improvements in the quality and quantity of the population (the poor state of recruits for the Boer War led to nutritional and health reforms for children), but he also saw the experience of wartime in Britain in the 1940s as providing a national identity and solidarity which overruled existing social divisions and produced 'an enlargement of obligations – an extension of social discipline – to attend to the primary needs of all citizens' (Titmuss, 1963, p. 84). In other words, the egalitarian and solidaristic impulse of wartime was an important generator of a welfare society.

While acknowledging these positive outcomes, it is important to examine a little more critically these meanings of national responsibility and identity and the material and discursive influences upon Britain's role in its foreign and domestic politics. War, in effect, represents only one end of the continuum of an intensified opportunity for a nationalism which operates on different terrain in peacetime. War was not so directly influential, in the 1930s, in the generation of Sweden's welfare state, yet a particular national identity was central to the People's Home in Sweden, as it was called. In Britain there have been a number of shifts in this relationship between nation-building, national unity and welfare over the twentieth century.

The first was in the role of *social imperialism* in the welfare reforms at the beginning of the century. From the 1880s the certainties of the old *laissez-faire* regime were rocked by a number of developments, including the increase in competition to Britain's industrial supremacy abroad, the militant 'new unionism' of workers, the successive slumps and booms of the economy and the international growth of socialist and feminist movements. State collective reform was one way of stabilizing these threats. In the British imperialist context this collectivism was heavily tied to social imperialism. Social imperialism aimed to subordinate class interests to those of nation and empire by suggesting a necessary interdependence between the power and profits of imperialism, national supremacy and welfare reforms, and this was supported by all the main political parties. Thus many trade unionists pressing for welfare reforms did so in the belief that such reforms were the fruits of imperial policy and were necessary to create the national efficiency upon which imperial power depended.

Social imperialist aims were influenced by the scientific and social discourses of Darwinism and the eugenics movement. Darwinism posited the theory of the survival of the fittest, which, when transposed to imperialist social relations, could justify the conquest and domination of the 'uncivilized races' by those at the top of the evolutionary tree – the Anglo-Saxon 'civilized race'. Eugenics was the belief in heredity as the cause of social problems, including physical and mental disabilities, 'feeblemindedness', pauperism, prostitution and alcoholism, which could be eradicated by policies aimed at encouraging the 'fit' to breed and discouraging the 'unfit'. These two theories tied an imperialism abroad to a social imperialism at home. For the working class and others fighting for social reforms there was thus some apparent material and ideological basis for a belief in imperialism and racial supremacy and the jealous guarding of social rights being restricted to British workers.

Two examples of social policies illustrate the complex ways in which improvements for the working class were cast in ways which superimposed the national interest over class or gender interests. They also show an elision between the notions of 'the British' (or, more specifically, 'the English'), the nation and the white 'race'. One example is policies around the regulation and supervision of motherhood which were introduced in the first two decades of the century, e.g. school meals for the needy (1906) and the Maternity and Child Welfare Act (1918). The latter established clinics and health visitors and was accompanied by the emergence of voluntary organizations working to promote and supervise child welfare and domestic hygiene. While these services met women's needs, they also served to consolidate women's place in the home and to tie women's role in the family to the development of 'race' and nation (see Davin, 1978; Williams, 1989). These policies were aimed at increasing the quality of the 'race' to maintain national efficiency and to prevent 'racial decay', and the quantity to sustain imperial defences. A propaganda film made in 1917 to mark National Baby Week started with the slogan 'the Race marches forward on the feet of the children'. Women, as bearers of children and reproducers of culture, formed a real and symbolic link between the racialized ideals of nationhood and nation-building by unifying the nation, populating it and servicing it.

Other policies, however, aimed to deter certain groups from breeding. The 1913 Mental Deficiency Act followed eugenic thinking by implementing the grading and segregating of 'mental defectives' – a category broad enough to encompass unmarried mothers, epileptics, people with mental health problems, petty criminals and people with physical, speech and hearing impairments. These groups were institutionalized in what were called 'colonies', away from both the outside world and the opposite sex.

These ideas about the role of welfare in sustaining Britain's imperial role and racial supremacy shifted after the Second World War. On the one hand, the 1942 Beveridge Report captured once again the white woman's duty: 'housewives as wives and mothers have vital work to do in ensuring the adequate continuance of the British race and British ideals in the world'. On the other hand, the main doctrines of the empire began to fall away. Of power, profits and civilization only civilization remained. The welfare state in Britain became central to the reconstruction of post-war Britain and represented Britain's civilizing mission brought home. This was a civilization of a new order – of social justice and egalitarianism – an order that could replace the old imperial ideal in sustaining cohesion. If national unity and egalitarianism provided the bricks and mortar of the new welfare state, it was migrant workers from the former colonies who also helped to build and service it. Even more ironically, as we have seen, it was these workers and their families who over the post-war period found themselves excluded from these same institutions and began, in response, to challenge the boundaries of citizenship and the cultural norms of policies which had been moulded in earlier decades.

CONTEMPORARY SHIFTS IN NATION AND WELFARE

Up until the Second World War, national unity and British cultural supremacy tied the development of social policy to imperialism abroad. By the Second World War the welfare state became central to post-war national reconstruction. British culture and national unity were used to justify state intervention. By the 1980s the notions of national unity (as well as the traditional family) were used to justify *less* state intervention, but with more central state control. Emphasis was placed upon the family as the transmitter of 'decent' British values and responsible for the morality and discipline of its members. The 1988 Education Act sought to reduce the impact of anti-discriminatory practice in favour of traditional morality and British cultural values. The Act also provided for parents to choose education for their children appropriate to their children's culture. While this could be seen as a shift towards the acknowledgement of cultural diversity, it also represents a form of cultural essentialism where cultures are seen as fixed and unchanging in both form and attachment. In addition, the nationality and immigration laws were further tightened. However, these attempts to reassert and protect the supremacy of British culture should be seen as a defensive response to a wider set of changes: the breaking up and shifting of national boundaries in Eastern Europe and the former Soviet Union; the emergence of supranational political institutions and economic communities (e.g. the European Union, discussed in chapter III.8); the increase in migration movements across the globe; and the rise of transnational identities and movements. While these processes may threaten the viability of a sovereign, territorially bounded, culturally homogeneous nation state, nevertheless their consequences do not necessarily flow in the same direction. A shift to harmonization of European social policies might well offer greater protective employment provisions but only to EU nationals; currently its policies towards migrants and asylum-seekers look set to be more, not less, restrictive. The extent to which a notion of European citizenship is inscribed with exclusions of racialized and ethnicized groups remains to be seen and challenged.

GUIDE TO FURTHER READING

To pursue this subject you need to go beyond the discipline of social policy to work on nation states, nationality and 'race'. However, work which does look at the historical significance of nation both in itself and in relation to family and work in the development of the modern welfare state is Williams, F. (1989) *Social Policy: a Critical Introduction. Issues of Race, Gender and Class.* Cambridge: Polity Press; and Williams, F. (1995) Race/ethnicity, gender and class in welfare states: a framework for comparative analysis. *International Studies in Gender, State and Society,* 2(2), 127–59. A very informative and provocative examination of immigration controls and welfare provision is provided in Cohen, S. (1996) The mighty state of immigration controls. In J. Baldock and M. May (eds), *Social Policy Review 7.* London: Social Policy Association. There is also the classic essay on the relationship between war and welfare in Titmuss, R. (1963) *Essays on 'the Welfare State'.* London: Unwin University Books.

Detailed historical work can be found in Davin, A. (1978) Imperialism and motherhood. *History Workshop Journal,* 5, 9–65; Fryer, P. (1984) *Staying Power: the History of Black People in Britain.* London: Pluto Press; and Brubaker, W. R. (1990) Immigration, citizenship and the nation-state in France and Germany: a comparative historical analysis. *International Sociology,* 5(4), 379–407. The three titles are self-explanatory; these works cover the historical background to the issues raised in the chapter. Finally, for a collection of essays examining some of these issues in contemporary Europe, see Wrench, J. and Solomos, J. (1993) *Racism and Migration in Western Europe.* Oxford: Berg.

II.14

social policy and family policy

jane millar

Families are very much at the centre of contemporary political and policy debate in Britain. Both major political parties claim to have policies that support families, media attention on issues such as working mothers, divorce and teenage motherhood is intense and academic interest in the relationship between family and state has made this a growing area of research and publication. Yet, at the same time, it is also possible to argue that Britain has no family policy at all – if 'family policy' is taken to mean a defined set of goals, pursued by a coherent set of policies, and implemented through an institutional framework of a designated government department. We have no 'Department of the Family'; policies are sometimes contradictory and certainly uncoordinated; there is little agreement over what goals we should be seeking to achieve. On the other hand, however, almost every action that government takes or does not take – whether it be in the fields of social security, taxation, health, education, housing, employment or whatever – has an impact on families and on family life. Family policy, it seems, is nothing and everything at the same time.

This chapter covers three areas. In the first section I consider the family as *context* for social policy. Family change, it is often argued, has upset the assumptions on which the welfare state was built and created new needs that require different policy responses. This section summarizes some of the recent key trends in family formation and structure. The second section considers the question of how far family change can be seen as a *consequence* of social policy and reviews the different views as to what should or could be done about this. The third section examines the different ways in which *family policy*, as a specific area of government activity, has been defined and discusses how the approach in Britain compares with that of other countries.

THE FAMILY AS A CONTEXT FOR POLICY

Much social policy is concerned with families and family life, and in the making of policy certain assumptions must be made about families and family roles. It has often been argued, for example, that the provisions of the post-war British welfare state rested on a very clear model of family life, in which men were full-time workers and women were full-time carers. Men were responsible for supporting their families and they therefore acted as the main point of contact between the family and state financial support. They received tax allowance for their wives and children and most social security benefits were paid to the man, on behalf of the family as a

Table II.14.1   Family formation and family structure in Britain over 25 years

	Early 1970s	Early 1990s
Percentage children born outside marriage	8	33
Percentage single women cohabiting	8 (1979)	23
Median age at first marriage for women/men	21/24	26/28
Number of abortions to single women	63,000	120,000
Total fertility rate (children born per woman)	2.4	1.8
Number of divorces	79,000	175,000
Percentage families headed by lone parents	8	22
Percentage one-person households	18	27
Average household size	3.1	2.4
Percentage mothers employed	49	65

Source: all figures derived from *Social Trends 1995* (London: HMSO, 1995), except cohabitation and mothers' employment from *General Household Survey 1993* (London: HMSO, 1995).

whole. Women were responsible for family care and therefore acted as the main point of contact between the family and state services such as health care, education and social care services. These services provided a back-up to women's caring work, just as benefits provided a back-up to men's earnings. Families were assumed to be stable and long-lasting, and the family roles of men and women were seen as being quite distinct.

It is debatable how far real families ever conformed to this idealized model, even in the 1950s, a decade in which family structures were unusually stable and homogeneous. Families today, however, are much more volatile and heterogeneous. Although the 1960s are often characterized as the 'permissive decade', it was really in the 1970s that patterns of family life in Britain began to change very rapidly. The 1969 Divorce Reform Act, implemented in 1971, made divorce possible for a much wider range of people. Cohabitation also began to rise, as did rates of extra-marital births. Married women started to move into the labour market in significant numbers, usually into part-time jobs. Table II.14.1 summarizes some key features of family formation and structure in the early 1990s and at the start of the 1970s. As can be

seen, there have been some very significant changes over this period. More children are born outside marriage, more couples live together before they marry, first marriage is later, women have fewer children, abortion is more common and there is a much greater risk of divorce. As a consequence there are more lone-parent families, more people live alone and the average household size is smaller. Mothers are now more likely to be employed than not, although much still depends on the age of their children.

Families in the 1990s therefore take a variety of diverse and changing forms. People live alone, have children alone, live with partners, marry, divorce, remarry, have more children – and then they may do it all again. Family patterns also vary by social class, by region, by ethnic group, by income level and so on. Thus to talk about 'the family' is to fail to reflect the range of 'families' that people actually live in. Such diversity, however, poses particular problems for social policy: providing the appropriate support for one type of family may disadvantage another. Or, of more concern to some people, providing support for some types of family may encourage people to behave in particular, and not necessarily welcome, ways.

What Is to Be Done about the Family?

Reactions to family change vary enormously, but can be summarized under three broad headings.

- First, there are the 'family reactionaries', who think the family is disintegrating and who would like to see policy directed towards restoring 'traditional' family patterns.
- Second, there are the 'family pragmatists', who feel that these changes are part of wider trends that cannot be reversed, and therefore policy must adapt and support new family forms.
- Third, there are the 'family libertarians', who positively welcome these changes as a sign of increasing freedom and autonomy for people to live in ways that they choose.

The right-leaning think tank, the Institute of Economic Affairs, has been assiduous in putting forward a 'family reactionary' position. Patricia Morgan's monograph *Farewell to the Family*, published in 1995, brings together all the various threads that make up this argument. She argues that 'since the 1970s, a climate of hostility to the family has provided the general context in which its legal and economic foundations have been easily undermined' (p. 1). Two factors in particular are singled out as the causes of family decline: state welfare policies that have created disincentives to marriage and incentives to lone parenthood; and feminist influences that have marginalized men in the family and encouraged women to seek gratification through paid employment rather than through family life. For Morgan the consequences are already visible and worrying but, she predicts, these will get much worse. Without the traditional family to socialize children, and in particular to provide role models and discipline for young men, delinquency and crime will escalate and society as a whole will be at

risk. To avoid this, social policy should seek positively to support marriage and promote traditional gender roles for men and women.

The pragmatic family view can be found in a variety of accounts, but is well represented through the publications of the left-leaning think tank, the Institute for Public Policy Research. Its 1990 publication *The Family Way*, by Anna Coote, Harriet Harman and Patricia Hewitt, sets this out clearly: 'Long term cross-national trends in the patterns of family life cannot be halted, let alone reversed, by any efforts of government ... the aim should be to ensure that policies are adapted to suit changing practice' (p. 33). The types of policies they propose centre on the goal that men and women should have equal opportunities to be both parents and workers, to be both breadwinners and carers. Ways to reconcile work and family life – schemes of parental leave, state child care provisions or subsidies, equal access to benefits for part-time workers and so on – are at the heart of this. This is also the sort of policy agenda being taken on board in the European Union, where the relationship between employment and family is attracting increasing attention.

The pragmatic approach does welcome family change to some extent, particularly in respect of greater equality between men and women. However, the 'libertarian family' view, in which family change is viewed as positive rather than negative, is most particularly associated with feminism. Many feminist writers have pointed to the 'family' as a site of gender inequality and have analysed the way in which the definition of family as 'private' has obscured, and even legitimated, these inequalities. Changes in the family which have reduced the dependency of women on men have therefore been valued as increasing autonomy and choice for women. However, in this highly politicized debate, 'feminism' is often depicted as 'anti-family' and vice versa: those who are seen as 'anti-family' are labelled 'feminist'. This takes little account of the more complex debates within feminism about the relationship between family and state. And any positive view of family change has also been increasingly crowded out of political and policy debates.

Thirty years ago, the report of the Finer Commission on One-Parent Families (1974) could welcome changing family patterns as a sign of greater freedom of choice, but it is difficult to imagine such views gaining a voice in official publications today. The difficulties that the government faced in 1996 over the reform of divorce law illustrate the way in which more recent debate focuses almost entirely on the negative aspects of family change. One of the aims of the proposed changes was to reduce the conflict surrounding divorce but much of the debate focused on the extent to which it made divorce 'easier', which, for many opponents of the legislation, was self-evidently a bad thing.

One of the most important issues dividing these three points of view is the question of causality, and in particular the extent to which state provisions of welfare have affected family behaviour.

- Do we have more lone parents than most of our European neighbours because state welfare provides them with social security benefits and homes?
- Do we care less about, and less for, our family members because the state will provide for them?
- Do we not marry because there is little financial advantage in doing so?

These are difficult questions to answer. Understanding the *outcomes* of welfare provisions on family circumstances and well-being is complicated but not impossible. We can, for example, examine relative poverty rates, or calculate the level of financial support offered to one family type as compared with another, as in the recent study by Bradshaw et al. of support for children in different countries. But understanding the *consequences* of policy for family behaviour is much more dif-

ficult. There are so many factors involved and our theoretical understanding of the relationship between policy, attitudes and behaviour is very under-developed. However, many of the family trends we see here in Britain are found to a greater or lesser extent throughout the Western industrialized world, despite differences in type, level and nature of welfare provisions. This suggests that our social welfare provisions are unlikely to be the main cause of family change and, if so, changing policy will not reverse these trends.

FAMILY POLICY

As already pointed out, there is no simple way to define family policy. Maximalist definitions include everything that affects families, whether intended or not. Minimalist definitions include only those policies directly targeted on families, with particular goals in mind. The difficulties of defining family policy are discussed by Sheila Kamerman and Alfred Kahn in the introduction to their 1978 collection, *Family Policy: Government and Families in Fourteen Countries*. They start by making a distinction between 'implicit' and 'explicit' family policies.

- Implicit are policies which have consequences for families, although these are not their main target or goal. Their examples are 'industrial locations, decisions about road building, trade and tariff regulations, immigration policy' (p. 3).
- Explicit are areas where families are the object of policy and where particular goals are usually, although not always, specified in advance. Their examples are 'day care, child welfare, family counseling, family planning, income maintenance, some tax benefits, some housing policies' (p. 3).

The terminology of 'explicit' and 'implicit' is perhaps a little misleading, since the notion of implicit can carry with it a suggestion of 'covert' or 'hidden', i.e. that there is a policy agenda that is deliberately being obscured. The terms 'direct' and 'indirect' would express more clearly the notion that families are affected both by policies in particular and by policies in general. Using this terminology, then, three main areas of policy seem to fit under the direct family policy heading.

1 The legal regulation of family behaviour: laws relating to marriage and divorce, to sexual behaviour, to contraception and abortion, to parental rights and duties, to child protection.
2 Policies to support family income: tax allowances, family and child benefits, parental leaves and benefits, enforcement of child support.
3 The provision of services for families: child care provisions, subsidized housing, social services, community care.

In all these areas families are the target of policy and family functioning and well-being will be affected by the nature of the provisions made. And within and across these areas policy goals may overlap, change over time, be articulated more or less clearly and be more or less complementary or contradictory. There is no space here to provide a review of current British policies in these areas (see Fox Harding, 1996; Jones and Millar, 1996). However, under the Conservative governments of the 1980s and 1990s British social policy became increasingly 'targeted' or 'selective' and this is also true for family policy.

There is now less concern with supporting, or intervening in, all families and more concern with particular groups. This is most visible in respect of policies to support family income. For example:

- The universal child benefit (intended for all families) was frozen in value throughout much of the 1980s, while the means-tested benefit family credit (intended for low-income families) was extended in coverage.

- The ongoing focus on reducing public expenditure has also meant that families are expected to do more to support and care for themselves. The very controversial 1991 Child Support Act requires separated and unmarried parents to pay much higher rates of child support but most of the money collected from absent parents is used to offset social security benefit costs.
- Under the 1990 NHS and Community Care Act local authorities must assess the care needs of people requiring services, taking into account the 'informal care' provided usually by family members.
- Despite increased employment rates among mothers, there is limited availability of child-care provisions for young children, and parents must also increasingly meet the costs of their children in higher education. The issue of reconciliation of work and family life, central to family policy in many other countries, is much discussed in the UK but as yet with little by way of positive policies.

The UK approach to issues of family policy does seem to differ from that of many of its European neighbours, although across the industrialized world a range of approaches can be found. At the end of her historical review of the development of family policy in twenty-two industrialized countries, Gauthier identifies four main approaches to family policy.

1 *Pro-family/pro-natalist:* low fertility is a major concern and policies are aimed at encouraging people to have children. This includes polices to help mothers reconcile work and family life, so that employment does not act as a barrier to childbearing. France is the main example here.
2 *Pro-traditional:* the preservation of 'the family' is the main concern. Government takes some responsibility for supporting families, but the most important sources of support

are seen as the families themselves, the communities in which they live, and voluntary and charitable, including church, organizations. Policies support women to stay at home rather than go out to work. Germany is the main example here.

3   *Pro-egalitarian:* the promotion of gender equality is the main concern. Men and women are treated as equal bread-winners and equal carers and policy aims to support dual parent/worker roles. Liberal policies on marriage, divorce and abortion mean that there are few restrictions on how people can choose to organize their family life. Sweden and Denmark are the examples given.

4   *Pro-family but non-interventionist:* the main concern is with families in need. Families are viewed as basically self-sufficient and able to meet their own needs through the private market, with only limited help from the state. There is little by way of support for working parents because it is believed that the market will meet any needs that emerge, as long as it is not hindered by government regulation. The UK and the USA are the examples given of this approach.

Models such as these are, of course, idealized accounts of the rather messier reality in which policies reflect a mixture of objectives and values. But they do highlight the way in which approaches to family policy are closely bound up with approaches to social policy more generally. Family change, alongside employment change, has already put considerable pressure on welfare provisions. And, if current trends continue, the whole question of the boundaries between family and state is likely to become an even more central issue on the future policy agenda.

GUIDE TO FURTHER READING

For statistical data on family trends: *Social Trends* (published annually by HMSO, London) and *Population Trends* (published quarterly by the Office of Population Censuses and Surveys).

Morgan, P. (1995) *Farewell to the Family: Public Policy and Family Breakdown in Britain and the UK.* London: Institute for Economic Affairs. Argues that government activity is destroying the family and promotes a policy agenda to support marriage.

Coote, A., Harman, H. and Hewitt, P. (1990) *The Family Way: a New Approach to Policy Making.* London: Institute for Public Policy Research. Sets out a policy agenda which seeks to accommodate to family change.

Bradshaw, J., Ditch, J., Holmes, H. and Whiteford, P. (1993) *Support for Children: a Comparison of Arrangements in Twenty Countries.* London: HMSO. Interesting both for the methodology used to compare across different countries and for the wealth of information about different systems of support.

Kamerman, S. B. and Kahn, A. J. (eds) (1978) *Family Policy: Government and Families in Fourteen Countries.* New York: Columbia University Press. Something of a classic. The country case studies are perhaps of more historical than contemporary interest, although Hilary Land and Roy Parker provide an excellent analysis of the gendered basis of UK social security and housing policy. The introduction discusses definitions of family policy.

Gauthier, A. H. (1996) *The State and the Family: a Comparative Analysis of Family Policies in Industrialized Countries.* Oxford: Clarendon Press. Wide-ranging over both time and place, and argues that demographic change has been a major factor influencing policy development.

Fox Harding, L. (1996) *Family, State and Social Policy*. London: Macmillan. Good introduction to family policy in the UK.

Jones, H. and Millar, J. (eds) (1996) *The Politics of the Family*. London: Avebury. Drawn from papers given at the 1994 Social Policy Association Annual conference, this collection covers a range of contemporary issues in family policy.

social policy in a shrinking world

bob deacon

The Globalization of Social Policy and the Socialization of Global Politics

In the present phase of world economic development social policy activities traditionally analysed within and undertaken within one country now take on a supranational and transnational character. This is so for several reasons. Economic competition between countries could lead to the economic costs of social protection being shed in order to be more competitive (social dumping) unless there are supranational or global regulations that discourage this. International migratory pressures generate the political logic that there could be income transfers between nations to stave off the political consequences of mass migration. Similarly, common markets in capital and labour between countries give rise to the possibility of supranational authority providing at a supranational level social citizenship rights denied or threatened at national level.

The implications for national, supranational and transnational social policy of this present phase of globalization is an under-theorized and under-researched topic within the subject of social policy. Whereas globalism has received considerable attention recently from scholars

Box II.15.1 Globalization

- Sets welfare states in competition with each other.
- Raises social policy issues to a supranational level.
- Generates a global discourse on the best way to regulate capitalism in the interests of social welfare North and South.

working within the disciplines of political science, sociology, economics and international relations, this has not been the case for social policy. Supranationalism in the context of Europeanization is, of course, an exception. Esping-Andersen has, however, recently reviewed comparative welfare state trends in a global context. The relative decline of the power of national governments in the face of globally mobile capital challenges the traditional frameworks of social policy analysis in a number of ways.

First, it suggests that the *supranational and global actors* need to be given more attention in explanations of changing social policy. Because social policy's analytical frameworks have derived from work on economically privileged North and West welfare states they have tended to downplay the importance of background institutions like the International Monetary Fund

(IMF), the World Bank and the International Labour Organisation (ILO). Now that social policy analysis is encompassing less economically privileged South and East welfare states and because the sustainability of the welfare states of Europe is questioned by global economic competition, this relative neglect of these institutions is no longer justified.

Second, it introduces a new field of enquiry into the subject. This field encompasses what I have called the supranationalization or globalization of social policy instruments, policy and provision. This supranationalization of social policy takes three forms.

- *Supranational regulation* embraces those mechanisms, instruments and policies at a supranational and global level that seek to regulate the terms of trade and the operation of firms in the interests of social protection and welfare objectives. At a global level such instruments and policies are at a primitive level of development. The key issue here is whether the social regulation of capitalism practised by the European Union can and will be elevated to the global playing field.
- *Supranational redistribution* operates between countries. At a subglobal level this operates effectively already within the European Union through the structural and associated funds that ensure a degree of support for poorer regions by richer ones. The valued annual United Nations Human Development Report suggested recently that 'Human society is increasingly taking on a global dimension. Sooner or later it will have to develop the global institutions to match ... a system of progressive income tax [from rich to poor nations] ... a strengthened UN.'
- *Supranational provision* occurs at a level above that of national government. This refers to the embryonic measures so far almost exclusively developed only at the subglobal, especially European, level, whereby people gain an entitlement to a service or are empowered in the field of social citizenship rights by an agency acting at a supranational level. The European Court of Justice in Luxembourg hears cases brought by EU citizens against countries that are perceived as breaking EU law in the social (and other) spheres. The Council of Europe empowers the citizens of member states to take their government to the Strasbourg Court of Human Rights if they believe their rights have been circumscribed. At a global level the only court that exists is the International Court of Justice in the Hague, which is exclusively concerned with war crimes, and not yet accessed by individuals. The United Nations High Commission for Refugees acts in the welfare interests of stateless persons and refugees.

The other side of the coin of the globalization of social policy is the socialization of global politics. In other words, the major agenda issues at intergovernmental meeting are now in essence social (and environmental) ones. For example, the meeting of the Group of Seven (G7) rich industrial nations in April 1996 was divided over a call by the EU to establish minimum global labour standards. Military and security matters have given way to trade and economic matters. The resolution of these issues requires a focus on other social and environmental aspects. The era of global social policy has arrived.

Box II.15.2 Global social policy embraces:

- global social redistribution;
- global social regulation;
- global social provision and/or empowerment.

Welfare States and Global Economic Competition

A vast literature points to the possible problems posed to the social democratic and conservative corporatist welfare states of Europe by the freeing of global regulations on finance capital and the increased free trade negotiated through the General Agreement on Tariffs and Trade (GATT) in the 1970s and 1980s. All concur that the golden age of the Western welfare state was a consequence, in conditions of post-Second World War protected economies, of Keynesian economic management combined with the power of trade unions and social movements to shift resources either from capital to labour or from wages to welfare. Once global movements of capital took place and once governments lost control of investment policies, capital could in principle go 'regime shopping' and engage in 'social dumping', whereby firms leave areas where the taxation (for social purposes) is high.

Three kinds of response to this openness of economies to global trade have been identified by Esping-Andersen. Some social democratic welfare states like Sweden have attempted to maintain the commitment to welfare through job creation in the public sphere, but doubts are increasingly raised about how viable this is as a permanent solution. At the other extreme liberal welfare states have embarked quite enthusiastically on deregulation and wage lowering to attract global investment in lower wage jobs. The USA, which opens its borders to low wage workers from the Third World, has gone furthest down this road. Conservative corporatist regimes like Germany have shed jobs in the less productive sector and have, in effect, gone for a strategy of jobless growth with investment in high productivity firms.

An outcome of the low wage/low unemployment and the high wage/higher unemployment strategy, however, is a dualization of the workforce globally – and often within one country. On the one hand are those still protected in terms of insurance-based benefits and on the other those exposed to a Hobson's choice between low wages or parsimonious means-tested social assistance – at best. This increasing flexibilization of the workforce, the shift towards shedding the low wage periphery, the casualization of work contracts, is generating a challenge to the traditional social security structures and mechanisms that lie at the heart of much of European welfare states. The danger is that the workplace-based social insurance systems, if they can be adapted to new circumstances, become a privileged possession of insiders and that a residualized means-tested assistance becomes the lot of the outsiders.

Because of this, alternative strategies for social policy in the income maintenance field have emerged for serious discussion in recent years. Two examples might be given at this point. One is the citizen's or participation income, which would provide for all a minimum, guaranteed social entitlement. Having dispensed this, governments would then be free to wash their hands of further social obligations in the income maintenance field. Citizens would find what casualized or non-casualized employment they could to supplement this minimum and provide privately for additional benefits in times of sickness and old age. An alternative strategy, but one that is equally far removed from the European employment-based social insurance system, is the provision of tax-based benefits (and services), with better off citizens targeted out via means and asset tests.

Social Policy Concepts in a Global Context

Supranational citizenship

Thinking about the concept of social needs and the concept of social citizenship entitlement in a globalizing world only serves to highlight the double-sidedness of the concept of citizenship. On the one hand, citizenship within the context of democratic capitalist society is about securing rights and entitlements for all within a state. On the other hand, it is about excluding from the benefits of citizenship those outside the state. In the last years of the twentieth century we have seen a simultaneous deepening and strengthening of citizenship rights and entitlements within some states and the tightening of restrictions on migrants to gain access to the citizenship rights of many of those same Northern and Eastern countries.

While these citizenship rights and associated duties were developed historically within capitalist societies within one state, the globalization process is generating the emergence of supranational citizenship entitlements of all three kinds. This process has developed furthest in the European context. The thirty odd member states of the Council of Europe provide for their citizens the right to equal treatment before the Court of Human Rights in Strasbourg with regard to human rights issues. No supranational political and social rights are guaranteed for the citizens of the members states of the Council of Europe, but states are encouraged to ratify the Council's Social Charter, which lays down a range of minimum social rights and entitlements. For the smaller number of states of the EU a plethora of political, civil and social rights now exist and are enshrined in the supranational law of the community. At a global level, the UN Declaration of Human Rights embraces social questions but as yet there is no legal enforcement of these rights in member states of the UN and no individual rights of petition. At the same time there are other ways in which the social aspects of citizenship are, in a piecemeal way, developing an international dimension. Numerous bilateral agreements exist between states regarding the reciprocal recognition of social security and other social rights. At a global level the UN High Commission for Refugees

assumes responsibility for the livelihood of stateless persons.

Justice between states

At one level the transposition of the concepts of equality, rights and social justice from the interpersonal or intergroup to the interstate provides no major conceptual problems. Social policy analysis, thinking globally, would simply join forces with development studies specialists and analyse the extent to which the world was a 'fair' place. Data concerning social inequalities within and between nations are now much more available. We can describe the extent to which the welfare needs of the world's population are increasingly being met but also the extent to which they are being met inequitably both within and across borders.

At another level, however, the issue of transnational justice raises difficult analytical and political questions. The Rawlsian conception of justice appropriate to a capitalist state (whereby that inequality is justified that raises the level of the poorest) becomes problematic at a global level. Equally, the political processes of democratic class struggle within small relatively homogeneous states, which have secured in parts of the North and West a degree of social justice, are not easily replicable on a global terrain. Put simply, how can an alliance be constructed between the poor of the South and the better off poor of the North to struggle to achieve an improvement in the conditions of the poor of the South, without unacceptably undermining the relatively better off poor of the North, and in ways which are economically and ecologically sustainable? By what social and political processes will the uncertain global alliances from below translate into the construction of global political institutions that seek to secure an acceptable measure of global justice? Daunting as this prospect might seem, it is part of the argument of this section that we are already witnessing this process and the progress it is making.

The necessity for the social regulation of free trade

Historically the global issue about efficiency and effectiveness was the demonstrable difference that there was between the economic success of the capitalist West (and the expense of some social security and guarantees for some citizens) and the economic underdevelopment of the 'socialist' East (but with the concommitant provision of social guarantees for all, such as that of employment). The inequalities and insecurities of ideal-type capitalism were argued to be the price to be paid for its economic effectiveness. The economic stagnation of the East was the price to be paid for an imposed egalitarianism. With the collapse of the Cold War the global debate about efficiency, effectiveness and choice becomes the debate about whether unfettered free trade between nations will generate economic and social growth for all or whether, to the contrary, this can only be achieved through socially regulated economic competition. The problem for would-be global policy-makers is that the much vaunted concept of free trade that, under the influence of neo-liberalism, the North and West has come to champion might turn out to be a challenge by the new economies of the South, to the interests of the North. It is the G77 group of Southern nations that is now more clearly acting in favour of free trade, seeing the potential advantage in it for them. It is some of the Northern politicians who are beginning to articulate the case for trade barriers to protect economic and social achievement. Box II.15.3 captures the dilemma and the way in which a solution may be emerging.

Transnationalization of social obligations

Globalization clearly poses the question as to where the limits of altruism to a social

> **Box II.15.3**   World trade and social policy
>
> - The North can accuse the South of social dumping – competing unfairly by denying their workers basic rights and decent social conditions.
> - The South can accuse the North of social protectionism – refusing access to markets to conserve the social welfare privileges of the few.
> - The ILO can not sanction the use of social clauses in world trade because it also represents the South.
> - The World Trade Organization does not (yet?) want to complicate international free trade agreements with social clauses.
> - The global level playing field for social policy within which free trade can take place appears therefore to be set by the World Bank's safety net (social liberalism) strategy.

obligation lie. Can they any longer be regarded as bounded by national frontiers? Equally, in the context of migration and the splitting for long periods of families across borders, do not the associated issues of reciprocal care take on a new dimension? Remittances sent by 'high' wage earning migrants to support poor dependents left behind complicates considerably the assessment of entitlement to assistance of such families.

The globalization process is leading to the further widening of the gender, class and racial division of caring. In the USA and elsewhere, white middle class professional men and women have their caring duties undertaken by black migrant (often illegally migrant) women from the poorer south. These same migrants attempt to feed some of their family left abroad. The issue for global social policy analysts in terms of the gender and racial division of care is therefore how far the process of globalization is exacerbating these inequities in who is cared for by whom. Similarly, how far are transnational movements weakening (or strengthening) reciprocal family obligations and the feelings of altruism that underpin a gift rather than market relationship.

THE SOCIAL POLICY OF GLOBAL AGENCIES

Global social policy was described above as embracing global regulation, redistribution and provision. Equally, it was concerned with the ways in which supranational or global agencies acted in ways to influence the making of national social policy – what kinds of social policy are being prescribed by which agencies for countries to adopt. There are a very large number of agencies using a variety of instruments to push and pull national social policy and practice in often very different directions. An appropriate image would be that of a series of interconnected spiders' webs connecting different departments of government to several different supranational actors exerting different degrees of pull upon policy. Some of these webs would be enormous (the World Bank); some quite tiny (the Council of Europe).

The implicit and explicit social policy prescriptions being articulated by all the main global actors have been discussed elsewhere (see Deacon, 1997). The conclusion of this more detailed analysis is that there is a quite heated contest of ideas taking place within and between these global agencies as to the best future for welfare. This debate sits in the context of the challenge to the traditional workplace-based wage-related social insurance kinds of welfare state typical of Europe. Both within the World Bank and the ILO and elsewhere there are emerging ideas for the future of national social policies that depart from the established patterns of US liberalism, European conservatism and Scandinavian social democracy. The ideas,

discussed above, of on the one hand a citizenship income entitlement and on the other hand a safety net kind of liberalism with a human face (social liberalism), are being articulated within ILO and World Bank circles respectively. Box II.15.4 captures some of the thinking about the future for social policy being expressed in some of the global agency publications. Much more work will be done in the coming years by social policy analysts to refine and develop this initial typological analysis.

THE GLOBAL GOVERNANCE REFORM AGENDA

At one level the global reformist project might be simply expressed as the further development of those systems of *redistribution, regulation* and *provision* just described. A global progressive taxation policy that levied disproportionally from the richer countries to fund social security schemes in the poorer would be an example of the first. An extension of the European social regulation of capitalism project to all of the globe would be an example of the second. The increasing of the powers of supranational courts and the greater empowerment of citizens to use these against governments would be an example of the third. However, the obstacles to the global social reformists' project of seeking to provide, regulate and redistribute at a global level are manifold. An initial shortlist of the most obvious might be national self-interest to which democratic structures are still largely attached, subglobal regional economic trading competition with an associated drive to cost cutting and deregulation, the failure to agree globally on what might constitute global social progress and the very real problems of sustainability.

However, alternative political strategies for global social reformism are being articulated and struggled over. Free trade and the breaking down of trade barriers in the interests of the economic growth of developing countries is a strategy favoured

Box II.15.4 Global social policy discourse

Ideology of welfare	Regime type	Income maintenance	International agency sometimes associated
Existing worlds of welfare			
Burden	Liberalism (USA)	Residual public assistance	International Monetary Fund
Social cohesion	Conservative corporatism (Germany)	Social insurance	European Union International Labour Organisation World Bank (one tendency)
Redistributive commitment	Social democracy (Sweden)	Insurance and citizenship entitlement	—
Future worlds of welfare			
Safety net	Social liberalism	Means- and asset-tested social assistance	World Bank (another tendency)
Citizenship entitlement	Futuristic	Citizen's income	International Labour Organisation (individuals) Council of Europe (individuals)
Welfare failure	Social neglect	Self-reliance	—

by some. The reform of the World Bank and the IMF so that these agencies adopt a more developed strategy of social conditionality in their lending and economic development strategies is another. Social intervention of this kind by supranational agencies to secure poverty programmes, secure human and political rights and protect minorities is a growing phenomenon. Others, not imagining that the world's paramount regulator of global capital can also secure the interests of the world's poor, are adopting the political strategy of the struggle between global agencies. To check the power of the Bank, greater emphasis is being put on the work and power of the UN social agencies, such as the ILO and the World Health Organization (WHO), to help governments to shape social policy. Some argue that the Bank

and Fund should be subject to UN authority. Box II.15.5 captures some of the issues on the current global governance reform agenda.

Box II.15.5 Global governance reform issues

1 Accountability of World Bank and International Monetary Fund.
2 Strengthen role of slimmed down UN in relation to economic and social issues.
3 Social dimension of World Trade Organization.
4 Empowerment of citizens against states through Supranational Courts of Rights

Whether the reforming of the World Bank or the struggle between global agencies is regarded as the most appropriate strategy, both would depend on the development of international social pressure for the global reformist project to succeed.

Whether this will be strengthened in the foreseeable future or whether there will be a collapse into identification with local and ethnic identity is of course a fundamental question upon which any talk of a progressive global social policy depends.

GUIDE TO FURTHER READING

Deacon, B. (1997) *Global Social Policy*. London: Sage. This is the first and only major text that addresses the issue of globalism for students of social policy. It does this by focusing on the role of international organizations such as the World Bank and the ILO in shaping post-communist social policy in Eastern Europe and the former Soviet Union.

Waters, M. (1995) *Globalisation*. London: Routledge. A useful quick guide to the concept of globalization as used by sociologists, political scientists and economists.

Esping-Andersen, G. (1996) *Welfare States in Transition*. London: Sage. A comparative analysis of the contemporary and future changes in welfare states in all the regions of the globe in the context of a globalized economy.

World Bank (1994) *Averting the Old Age Crisis*. Oxford: Oxford University Press. A good and controversial example of the World Bank's interventions in the global discourse about the best future for welfare policy. It stresses the case for only flat rate minimal state pensions and a greater role for the market in funded pension schemes.

International Institute for Labour Studies (1995) *The poverty agenda and the ILO*. Geneva: ILO. A review of the work of the ILO in the business of tackling world poverty. The conclusion poses the dilemma faced by the ILO in only focusing on labour standards when many of the poor are partially employed or unemployed.

United Nations Research Institute for Social Development (UNRISD) (1995) *States of Disarray*. New York: UNRISD. An accessible and challenging introduction to the social effects of globalization. It covers issues of migration, of international crime and of ethnic conflict and war. It calls for the concept of global citizenship to be placed on the agenda.

United Nations Development Programme (UNDP) (1996) *Human Development Report 1996*. Oxford: Oxford University Press. This is an annual review of the welfare of the world's population. A measure of human development based on longevity, educational attainment and access to economic resources is used to compare countries. The report also contributes to the debate on the reform of global governance.

Commission on Global Governance (1995) *Our Global Neighbourhood*. Oxford: Oxford University Press. Written by a global team of respected politicians and experts, the report proposes a reform agenda to create a safer and more equitable world. It stresses the need for shared values, a global civic ethic and enlightened leadership to guide nations in the global neighbourhood.

II.16

SOCIAL POLICY AND
THE POLITICAL PROCESS
MICHAEL HILL

THEORETICAL MODELS OF THE POLITICS OF SOCIAL POLICY

There are two popular images of the politics of social policy, much taught in the past, and still implicit in much talk and journalistic writing. One sees our 'governors' (however defined) as essentially benign problem-solvers, trying to do their best to solve social problems and meet people's (or society's, or the economy's) needs. The other sees those same people as responding to our desires and wishes, and tends to talk about social policy-making as if 'we' are governing ourselves. Clearly there are good reasons why popular and media conceptions of government evolved into a form which assumes that 'democracy' works, and that the things done by our rulers are done either in our best interests or in response to our demands (or both). In mocking this view, here, moreover, I am not trying to attack it as an ideal or aspiration. I am merely suggesting that this is not a very realistic way to explore the politics of social policy.

Instead, I want to offer four alternative models for the analysis of the politics of social policy, all of which make claims to be more realistic, and one of which, furthermore, retains within it some kinds of assertions that the democratic model works. The best simple labels for these models are:

- pluralism;
- elitism;
- economic determinism;
- institutionalism.

These four labels have been chosen to embrace a range of related theories. Alternative labels are on offer. This taxonomy, for instance, does not include Marxism – which may be seen as the major form of economic determinism but also appears in forms very close to elitism. The same may be said of some forms of feminist theory. Another body of theory, used in 'new right' analyses of social policy, is 'public choice'. However, this is a combination of a version of pluralism which stresses the capacity of special interests to make demands for government expenditure with a version of institutionalism which emphasizes public bureaucrats' power as monopoly providers of services. Clearly, realistic models for the examination of the politics of social policy will want to combine the basic approaches discussed here into mixed forms like that. This is a point to which we will return. Meanwhile, let us examine each model in turn.

Pluralism

Pluralism sees decision-making within the state as a product of competition between interests. The simplest way in which that competition may be manifested is through the efforts of the electorate to influence parliamentary decision processes. It has been recognized that this simple model is seldom realized: first, because the process is inevitably mediated through political parties and individual politicians (this is what is described as 'representative government'); second, because much political competition is not direct and does not simply involve parliamentary processes, but is mediated in a variety of ways through pressure groups. Some who have emphasized the latter point talk of 'post-parliamentary democracy'.

Pluralism is seen as offering the nearest we can get to true democracy. Public choice theory sees it providing a distorted political 'market place' in which unrealistic individual demands are made of the kind which would not be made in a true market. Radical critiques suggest that the ideal is undermined by inequalities; we do not compete equally; some interests are much stronger than others.

Elitism

Elitist theory is in many respects the alternative picture of the political process offered by radical critics of pluralism: it asserts that 'the heavenly choir sings with a distinctly upper class voice'. The problem about elitist theory lies in its simplicity. Merely to say that political decision processes are inherently biased and that power is concentrated in the hands of a few does not offer any explanation of why this is the case. This label tends to bring together under a general umbrella a variety of theories about why power is unevenly distributed. Conflicting explanations are on offer, from, at one extreme, psychological or even genetic theories stressing the superiority of elites, to theories which stress the importance of economic inequalities at the other (which come very close to the Marxist theory to be discussed in the next section). Important

perspectives which share much in common with elitism are feminist theories about the way male domination is maintained, and theories which explore the mechanisms racial or national groups use to exercise power. There is also an important vein in elitist theory which stresses the way in which state institutions facilitate the concentration of power.

Economic determinism

Quite the most important form of economic determinist theory is Marxism, which is discussed in some more detail in chapter II.8. In its main forms this theory is not merely saying that power is concentrated in the hands of economic elites but that the logic of the system of production makes this domination inevitable. Social policy decision-making is then seen as subordinate to the requirements of capitalism. Social policy is inevitably limited to a role supporting or helping to legitimize the capitalist order.

Modern Marxist theorists have extensively explored the nature and extent of this determinism, sometimes moving a long way from Marx's original position. But determinism also crops up in non-Marxist forms. One such has been comparative theory, which stresses the commonalities in the forms of social policy development, seeing them as explained by industrialization or urbanization, for example. These have been widely attacked by scholars who have shown how specific political forces seem to have produced varied national responses. However, new forms of determinism keep emerging. To some extent those on the political 'right' who stress the limits to social policy growth in the capitalist economy take very similar stances to Marxist determinists. Emergent theory on the global economy similarly tends to treat the logic of evolving capitalist production processes worldwide as relatively determinist for issues like social policy.

Table II.16.1 Theoretical models of the politics of social policy

Original theory	Development
Pluralism	Consideration of policy networks in and outside the state
Public choice pluralism	Economic theory of bureaucracy
Elitism	Analysis of bureaucratic power
Economic determinism, Marxist version	Exploration of 'relative autonomy of the state'
Other determinist theory	Acceptance of structural constraints within the state

Institutionalism

The last of the models also takes many forms. All of the three previous theoretical approaches tend to take stances on the importance of state institutions themselves. The pluralists tend to treat the state as a neutral body to be influenced. The elitists are interested in the way power outside and inside the state interlocks. The economic determinists see the state as inevitably with limited autonomy. The question is: how much do we need to look inside the state institutions themselves – at how they are structured and organized, at their rule systems (including even constitutions) and standard operating procedures, at the interests of state officials – in order to explain the role of the state in social policy? Such questions are self-evidently pertinent in a society like Britain, where state expenditure is over 40 per cent of gross domestic product and where many are either direct or indirect employees of the state.

All the other theoretical approaches have had to come to terms with this issue; hence, instead of arguing that 'institutionalism' offers a distinctive perspective on its own, it is suggested that the other three theoretical approaches have tended to undergo modification in the way indicated in table II.16.1.

Essentially we see here the various approaches accepting the importance of exploration of interactions and links between state and society. Two approaches of particular importance for social policy, and not fully brought out in table II.16.1, are:

- work on policy communities (seeing, for example, health policy as very influenced by cohesive professional communities running across the conventional state/society boundary);
- work which stresses the way past decisions create structures of constraints and opportunities for future ones (seeing, for example, a social insurance system which gave new advantages to white working class males as a source of blockages to the advancement of the concerns of other groups).

THE POLICY PROCESS

The model of the political process, outlined at the beginning and most closely approximated in the propositions associated with pluralism, sees social policy as *made* by elected representatives, responding to democratic demands, and *implemented* by publicly employed officials who have a duty to translate the general aspirations embodied in policy into detailed practice. The other theories suggest doubts about the extent to which this is the case. Thus they tend to direct attention to interventions which may occur outside the democratic arena. Implicit in their approaches, and particularly in 'institutionalist' theory, is a view that the so-called implementation process may in many respects create policy.

For traditional democratic theory, creative activity during the implementation phase of the policy process represents a threat. It engenders a range of 'top-down' control issues – about the ways in which doctors, teachers, social workers, social security benefit clerks etc. may be made democratically accountable. But the alternative perspectives offered by other theories suggest that it is in many respects more realistic to expect policy to be created within the implementation process and for there to be a complex interaction between the more overt politics of legislation and the more covert politics which follow it. This does not mean that democratic control issues are regarded as irrelevant (though of course that is in many respects the position taken by economic determinism), but that they are more subtle than those embodied in the traditional theory of representative government. This seems particularly important in social policy, where policy goals and policy systems are complex and a great deal of the real politics (in the broadest sense of that term) which influences 'who gets what, when and how' occurs far away from public parliamentary debates.

Clearly here, as throughout any discussion of the politics of social policy, there is a distinction to be made between a realistic analysis of what actually happens and a prescriptive stance on what should happen. A great deal of political activity is directed towards trying to exercise control over a complex process, and legitimized by philosophical propositions about the way the policy system *should* work. The alternative to the theory of representative democracy offered by those who stress the importance of public participation close to the point at which services are delivered is partly grounded upon a recognition of the importance of policy processes occurring at or near to the 'street level'.

THE POLITICAL PROCESS IN BRITAIN

At the moment any account of the politics of social policy in Britain is comparatively simple because of the existence of a unitary system of government. The main forum of party political conflict is in Parliament at Westminster, and the main focus of legislative activity is in ministries located in Whitehall (this reference to the geography of central London emphasizes the point about the centralization of system). There is an important contrast to be made between this centralized politics and the more complex politics of federal systems, and particularly of the United States.

However, there are complexities around the margins of this centralized system, which may well increase. The relationship between the government of the United Kingdom and that of Northern Ireland has moved through various phases since 1922. Scotland and Wales have some separate administrative arrangements from England, though these are linked to London through the absence of either separate Parliaments or separate core executives. That may well change. The European Union has social policies, too, which may challenge British autonomy (discussed in chapter III.8). Again, the present situation is one in which they are of low impact; and the Conservative government's opt-out from the 'social chapter' in the Maastricht Treaty in 1991 was a deliberate effort to try to keep European social policy at bay here. This too may change.

The British system of local government is important for social policy – since much social policy comes wholly or partly within its remit (education, personal social services and housing). However, the dominant model is very much one in which local government's powers derive from central government. Its politics mimic those of Westminster (so much so that the media treat local elections as if they were merely opinion polls for the Parliament). The period of Conservative government from

1979 also saw a very extensive tightening of central powers over local government – above all through the assertion of absolute dominance over finance but also through attacks upon rights to make choices about how services are delivered. These attacks have extended to the encouragement of local service delivery arrangements outside local government, as discussed in chapter III.6. A new government committed to some forms of devolution may reverse this trend, though the salience of social policy issues concerning local government – like selection in education – in national political debate encourage a scepticism about the likelihood of this.

The comments here about the centralization of the political processes apply to party politics and to the creation and design of legislation. But this chapter has suggested that the politics of social policy needs to be conceptualized more widely to take into account what is often called implementation. When we do this the British system is seen to be very much more complex, with its complexity increasing. The central–local relationship described in the last paragraph is one aspect of this complexity. There obviously remain many areas where local politicians and officials can play creative roles in putting central policies in practice.

Rather similar things can be said about the social policy systems over which central government has more obviously direct political control. As discussed in chapter IV.8, the health service is organized through a partially decentralized system of local health authority service 'purchasers' and health service trust or direct practitioner 'providers'. The politics of the area of policy is essentially inter-organizational. The purchaser–provider split initiated after 1990 ostensibly offers a set of market devices in place of inter-organizational relationships; the reality is essentially a system of complex interactions with an intense politics of their own. Furthermore, health politics, in the United Kingdom as elsewhere, is dominated by a series of issues about professional rights, prerogatives and duties, in which bodies like the British Medical Association are key actors.

Until the late 1980s, social security policy in Britain could have been described as very largely policy delivery through a large and complex organization, with its inevitable internal politics (see chapter IV.6). Then the government transformed the system into one in which implementation became the responsibility of a group of agencies, each with a separate contract with the central Department of Social Security. This adds a new complexity to implementation, highlighted by the unhappy history of the Child Support Agency, charged with responsibility to collect financial contributions from absent parents and set goals which it found impossible to achieve. In some respects in this situation a new politics of implementation developed – very like some aspects of central–local government relations – in which an allegedly quasi-independent organization was forced to take the blame for unrealistic politically set goals.

In all sectors, therefore, policy delivery is getting more complex. This is a consequence of the view that social policy implementation should involve many new relationships and partnerships – between central department and agencies, between purchasers and providers – with the implementers being actually (as in social care or social housing) or potentially (in all areas) independent, even profit-making, organizations.

Hence, inasmuch as this chapter has distinguished two kinds of policy process – one up front and parliamentary while the other is much more 'below stage' – we end up having to have regard to two very different political process stories. In Britain the former is much simpler than the other, but given much more attention. The latter is complex and often not readily open to public scrutiny. The public does, however, participate in a variety of ways through pressure groups (including, in particular, employee organizations).

However, these two kinds of 'politics' should not be seen as ultimately separate. There are many issues to consider about how much the former sets the ideological context and the main parameters for the other. Conversely, the latter feeds back issues into the party political and parliamentary system. The extent to which this is the case varies very much from issue to issue – in relation to levels of controversy and the extent to which party politicians choose to make issues their own. The theories outlined in the earlier part of this chapter offer alternative perspectives on the extent to which these linkages can be seen to be democratic, in the pluralist sense, and the extent to which policy agendas are really open to influence.

GUIDE TO FURTHER READING

It is difficult to make wide reading recommendations without taking students deep into the political science literature. On the theoretical models, J. Schwartzmantel (1994) *The State in Contemporary Society*. Hemel Hempstead: Harvester Wheatsheaf, offers a good introduction. A rather more difficult book on the same lines is P. Dunleavy and B. O'Leary (1987) *Theories of the State*. London: Macmillan. The use of the institutional approach is best exemplified by T. Skocpol (1995) *Social Policy in the United States*. Princeton, NJ: Princeton University Press, and D. E. Ashford (1986) *The Emergence of the Welfare States*. Oxford: Blackwell.

M. Hill (1997) *The Policy Process in the Modern State*. Hemel Hempstead: Harvester Wheatsheaf, offers a theoretical exploration of the policy process as a whole.

The importance of relationships between professions and the state has been emphasized. Still the best general work on this is P. Wilding's (1982) now rather dated *Professional Power and Social Welfare*. London: Routledge, but there is a considerable literature on the significance of this for health services. M. Moran and B. Wood (1993) *States, Regulation and the Medical Profession*. Buckingham: Open University Press, offers a comparative account.

On Britain it is difficult to identify anything very specific on the legislative 'politics of policy' other than either general British government textbooks or books like M. Hill (1993) *The Welfare State in Britain*. Aldershot: Edward Elgar, or H. Glennerster (1995) *British Social Policy since 1945*. Oxford: Blackwell, which are concerned to offer up-to-date accounts of the political controversies around social policy. On the other hand, T. Butcher (1995) *Delivering Welfare*. Buckingham: Open University Press, offers a good account of the more complex aspects of the policy implementation process.

part III
the production, organization and consumption of welfare

the production of welfare

III.1

state weLfaRe

NORmaN JOHNSON

Defining Terms

Before we look in more detail at the role
of the state, some consideration must be
given to what is meant by the state in the
context of the production and organization of welfare. The state is an abstraction;
there is nothing one can point to that can
be said to constitute the state, and this
makes an analysis of its involvement in
production and organization something of
a problem.

There are numerous theories of the state.
Dunleavy and O'Leary (1987), for example,
identify five different approaches: pluralism, the new right, elite theory, Marxism
and neo-pluralism. It would not serve the
interests of this chapter to describe and
evaluate these competing perspectives, but
among the characteristics of the modern
state they identify, one is of particular significance for this chapter: 'the state is a
recognizably separate institution or set of
institutions, so differentiated from the rest
of its society as to create identifiable public
and private spheres' (p. 2). Two observations may be made about the 'identifiable
public and private spheres'. The first is that
their relative size will vary from country
to country. Second, the distinction between
public and private is by no means as clear-
cut as the quotation might lead one to
suppose. This is particularly pertinent in
the field of health and welfare, and the
varying and changing interrelationships

between the two are the subject of this and
the next three chapters.

When one is considering the state's
role in the production and organization of
welfare, the simplest strategy is to focus
on the most obvious manifestations of
the state: government and its agencies.
Government is defined widely and includes:

- Central government departments
  (notably the Department of Health,
  the Department of Social Security,
  the Department for Education and
  Employment, the Department of the
  Environment and the Home Office).
- Local authorities.
- A variety of agencies within the National Health Service (NHS): district
  and regional health authorities, health
  commissions, NHS trusts.
- A very large number of semi-
  autonomous executive agencies, which
  may be known as non-departmental
  public bodies (NDPBs), next steps
  agencies or quasi-autonomous non-
  governmental organizations (quangos):
  NHS trusts, the Benefits Agency, the
  Child Support Agency, the Employment Service Agency, the Prison Service Agency, the Housing Corporation,
  police authorities, training and enterprise councils and urban development
  corporations.

The United Kingdom after the Second World War experienced a massive

programme of social legislation covering education, housing, family allowances, national insurance and assistance, children and the NHS (see chapter I.1). This legislation represented an acceptance by the state of a responsibility to protect and promote the welfare of all citizens. It is fair to say, however, that it was designed to provide a national minimum rather than reduce inequalities. One consequence of this legislative activity was a substantial increase in state power and in its pervasiveness in people's lives. During the same period two other developments conspired to increase the role of the state:

- The nationalization of public utilities, which brought major sectors of the economy into public ownership.
- Policies designed to maintain high levels of employment. Beveridge's plan for social security depended on the avoidance of widespread unemployment, and Keynesian economic theories seemed to explain how governments could, by managing aggregate demand, control the level of employment (Timmins, 1996).

The post-war years witnessed a significant increase in the role of the state through nationalization, policies aimed at maintaining high employment levels and the provision of an expanded range of social benefits and services. According to Glennerster (1995), the British welfare state was more highly centralized than many of the systems in the rest of Western Europe. This chapter is concerned mainly with the state's role in the production and organization of welfare, but this has to be seen in the context of the state's other roles and the ideologies underpinning them (Deakin, 1994). Although the issues are discussed mainly in the context of the UK, the role of the state in welfare is a matter of significance internationally (see chapter I.3), and there is much to be gained from a comparative approach (Hill, 1996).

THE MAIN FORMS OF STATE INVOLVEMENT IN WELFARE

There are several ways in which the state can influence welfare provision. First, the government has the capacity to determine overall policy and policies specific to individual services. Crucially, the national government controls expenditure. Second, the state may engage in direct provision of benefits and services. Indeed, this was the usual mode of provision until the 1980s, and even after the changes made in the delivery of welfare, central and local government are still heavily involved in the social security benefits system, the NHS, education and personal social services. Policy changes in the 1980s and 1990s have reduced, but by no means extinguished, direct service provision by the state.

Third, statutory authorities have important planning and supervisory roles in relation to the delivery of welfare. For example, although local authority social services departments are required to make the maximum feasible use of independent providers, they have a responsibility to assess the needs of the local population and to ensure that these are met. They are also required to produce community care plans. In the NHS, parallel functions are performed by district health authorities and health commissions. There are, however, some problems in producing realistic and workable plans which accurately reflect need if responsibility for planning is divorced from direct provision.

Fourth, statutory responsibility for planning implies some obligation to try to ensure that the plans are implemented. This directs attention to the regulatory role of the state in welfare provision. Regulation may be divided into:

- input regulation (deciding who should be allowed to act as providers and what qualifications will be required of the staff they employ);
- process regulation (specifying how a service should be provided);

- output regulation (evaluating the quantity and quality of provision).

Regulation may be strengthened by a formal system of audit or inspection. The system in which statutory purchasers enter into contracts with independent providers involves all three forms of regulation backed up by a variety of inspectorates.

The fifth role for the state is in the area of direct financial assistance, fiscal support and subsidies (discussed in more detail in chapter III.9). Direct financial assistance to providers may take the form of grants (to voluntary agencies, for example) or payment to independent providers for contracted services. Fiscal support takes the form of granting tax relief for certain categories of expenditure or to certain groups of people. The two most extensive of these are the relief on mortgage interest payments to owner occupiers and the relief granted on occupational and private pensions. Tax relief is clearly a form of subsidy, but more direct subsidies are also used. Housing benefit is a good example of a subsidy. Free prescriptions is another.

PRIVATIZATION AND THE CHANGING ROLE OF THE STATE

Privatization in the context of social welfare means a reduction in the role of the state and the transfer of some of its functions to private institutions. The private institutions may be commercial undertakings, voluntary associations or informal networks of families, friends and neighbours.

As already noted, after the war in the UK there was an increase in government intervention on a number of fronts. The welfare mix that emerged was one dominated by the state, which was responsible for policy-making in a national framework and the setting of priorities. In many instances, however, the state was also virtually a monopoly provider. Some of the virtues claimed for state provision stem-

med from the perceived weaknesses of other sources of welfare. It was argued, for example, that the state's superiority over both markets and voluntary organizations lay in its ability to guarantee rights of access and use and to protect and enforce procedural and substantive rights (see chapter II.2). Furthermore, the state's power to levy tax meant that statutory services enjoyed a greater degree of certainty and continuity than either voluntary or commercial services.

The state could more easily secure equality and equity than the market, because it responded to need rather than demand backed up by the ability to pay (see chapter II.1). As sources of welfare, markets were hampered by imperfect knowledge on the part of consumers, and the consumption of health and welfare services was characterized by uncertainty and unpredictability. Furthermore, many consumers did not have unlimited mobility to take advantage of more suitable or cheaper provision elsewhere.

Another set of arguments compared the state and the voluntary sector as potential sources of welfare. Coverage by the state was national, implying more equitable distribution, whereas voluntary sector coverage was uneven. This wider coverage had two further advantages:

- it facilitated planning over a broad area;
- it allowed for economies of scale and the achievement of greater uniformity of provision in mass-produced services such as social security.

Moreover, the voluntary sector was characterized by unclear and multiple accountability: the political accountability typical of public service organizations was absent.

It is not suggested, however, that all of these potential advantages of the state have been realized: that is clearly not the case. Critics of state provision argue that it is too centralized, too bureaucratic and too much dominated by professionals and administrators. These characteristics make statutory services unresponsive to different individual needs and to changing needs. Furthermore, critics argue, after decades of state-dominated provision, Beveridge's five giants of want, disease, ignorance, squalor and idleness have not been overcome.

These anti-state sentiments have been in the ascendancy since the late 1970s, leading to demands for the creation of a mixed economy of welfare in which the state ceased to be a major direct provider of health and welfare services, with greater reliance upon commercial and voluntary sector providers. The basis of the new system is the separation of the purchasing or commissioning of welfare from its provision. The clearest expression of this is to be found in the community care provisions of the National Health Service and Community Care Act of 1990, which took effect in 1993. The local authorities are responsible for assessing the needs of the local population and for drawing up plans to see that needs are met by purchasing services, wherever possible, from independent providers. Contracts are drawn up under which commercial and voluntary sector agencies agree to provide a specified quantity of a particular service for a particular group of clients, meeting certain criteria with regard to mode of delivery and quality. It should be noted that local authorities, while losing their dominant position in direct provision of services, retain, and possibly enlarge, their role in the planning, finance and regulation of provision. The state moves from being a providing state and becomes an enabling or a contracting state. The main idea behind this change was the introduction of competition for contracts among providers and the enlargement of choice for service users. The system introduces market principles into the public sector: such structures are frequently referred to as quasi-markets (Bartlett et al., 1994). The personal social services have been taken as an example, but quasi-markets are also present in different forms in education, health and social housing.

These changes are not restricted to the UK: to different degrees and at different speeds, they are occurring throughout the world. Mixed economies of welfare have become the new orthodoxy, seeming to offer the prospect of a reduced role for the state and the curtailment of public expenditure.

The use of contracts and the introduction of quasi-markets is an attempt to overcome some of the perceived shortcomings of state-provided welfare, especially its alleged bureaucratic rigidities and lack of responsiveness. It may, however, be possible to realize these benefits by improving state provision: two such developments would be greater decentralization and the introduction of more participatory services designed to empower users. Decentralization and user empowerment are key issues in state welfare, and are considered in a little more detail below.

KEY ISSUES AND DEBATES

It may be helpful to identify some of the key issues and debates surrounding the role of the state which will recur at various points in the course of your studies. The issues selected are restricted to those having a significance which goes beyond individual services. It is also important to remember that social policy is never static and that new issues will arise from time to time.

Issue 1: the balance in the welfare mix

The overriding issue is the changing balance in the mixed economy of welfare, and the role of the state within this. There are no right or universal answers. At present in most welfare states there are attempts to reduce the state's role in provision and to rely more heavily on the commercial, voluntary and informal sectors. This raises questions about the relationship of the state to each of these providers. It is clear that the state will retain responsibility for planning and regulation, and that it will have a major role in finance. Attempts to cut public expenditure in all welfare states may lead to an increased use of charges and co-payments. At present the use of contracts for care is well advanced only in the UK and the USA, but there are signs that the practice is spreading to many other countries.

Issue 2: rights

One of the features of the state is its ability to coerce. This can lead to tyranny and totalitarianism, as it did in the former Soviet Union and Eastern Europe after the Second World War. As we have seen, however, the state's power to coerce also makes it the only body that can guarantee civil, political and social rights. Rights to a basic standard of living, education and health care are sometimes described as citizenship rights because they derive from people's status as citizens (Dean, 1996). Citizenship and social rights are, however, contested concepts, and it is clear that citizenship rights are not available to all citizens without regard to race, gender or social class. Deakin (1994) points out that the 'British are subjects, not citizens', and in the absence of a written constitution it is difficult to establish what the rights are and how they are to be enforced (p. 214).

Issue 3: empowerment

One of the criticisms of state welfare is the predominance within it of professionals and bureaucrats, which, it is claimed, renders the services unresponsive to people's expressed needs (see chapter III.5). These features of state welfare have given the impetus, as we have seen, to new non-state forms of service production and delivery.

The transfer of responsibility for the provision of public services to alternative suppliers, however, will not magically produce responsive, user-led services. Furthermore, although the state's role in direct services provision has been curtailed, it remains a major provider. The challenge, irrespective of which sector provides the services, is how to ensure that users have a say, that goes beyond mere consultation, in stating their needs, in deciding what kinds and levels of service best meet those needs and in determining how the services shall be provided and by whom. The involvement of users in policy-making, service provision and even the management of facilities and services all need to be carefully considered. The term 'empowerment' is very much in vogue, but frequently support for it is no more than lip-service, lacking any real substance. The truth is that empowerment is not easily achieved, which is not to say that it should not be attempted (Craig and Mayo, 1995).

Issue 4: regulation

The different forms of regulation (input, process, output and outcome) have already been identified. The most appropriate form of regulation by statutory purchasers/commissioners is a matter for discussion. There has to be some balance between the need for regulation and the need for experimentation and innovation, which requires a degree of independence. What are sometimes forgotten are the financial costs of regulation. To ensure that regulations are complied with requires the providers to provide documentary evidence, and the scrutiny of this evidence by purchasers. Monitoring may be continuous but is much more likely to be intermittent. It cannot be assumed that government agencies have both the resources and the skill for effective monitoring. As services become increasingly fragmented, with a multiplicity of providers, the task of regulating provision becomes more difficult. Decentralization also makes regulation more complex.

Issue 5: decentralization

During the 1980s, as Glennerster (1995) demonstrates, there were two conflicting trends: 'One was the delegation of budgetary control to smaller units: schools, hospitals, housing estates. The other was the stripping of local government of independent powers to tax and run services with a degree of autonomy' (p. 234). Despite the rhetoric of decentralization and rolling back the state, power in the UK became more highly centralized during the 1980s. Other countries' decentralization strategies were somewhat more successful. France, traditionally the most highly centralized country in Europe, began a programme of decentralization in 1982; in Germany the principle of subsidiarity guarantees more power at sub-central levels; and a similar situation prevails in the Netherlands despite recent government attempts to bring a greater degree of integration into the health and welfare system. Decentralization to more local units has also been a major theme in Denmark, Italy, Norway, Sweden and the USA.

Issue 6: equity and equality

Left to themselves, markets and the voluntary sector will not produce equitable outcomes: voluntary organizations are unevenly distributed and markets are little concerned with equity and equality. Furthermore, each individual provider sees only a small segment of the total picture and is concerned only with its own con-

tribution. The state in its role of planner and enabler has greater opportunity to promote equality and equity, particularly because it controls resources. Whether the opportunity is taken will depend on the government's views about the proper pursuits and aims of the welfare state. Is the aim of the welfare state simply to pick up the social casualties, with public services performing a residual role? Or is the welfare state essential to social integration and a society based on justice? If the latter, then decent public services available to all without reference to social class, race, gender or disability have an important role to play.

CONCLUSION

Until comparatively recently, most social policy courses were predominantly concerned with *state* welfare. The worldwide reassessment of the role of the state has meant that more attention is now given to the part played by families, voluntary agencies and commercial enterprises in welfare provision, and this is reflected in the next three chapters. The state, however, remains a major concern in social policy. Although the state's role as a direct provider of welfare may have diminished, its role in policy-making, planning, regulation and finance means that it determines the direction of policy and it fundamentally influences the scale and mode of provision. The environment in which the other sectors operate is an environment created and sustained primarily, though not exclusively, by the state.

GUIDE TO FURTHER READING

An excellent introductory textbook on the nature of the state is Dunleavy, P. and O'Leary, B. (1987) *Theories of the State: The Politics of Liberal Democracy*. London: Macmillan, which identifies and evaluates competing theories of the state. There are several books dealing with social policy from 1945 to the present day. Timmins, N. (1996) *The Five Giants: a Biography of the Welfare State*. London: Fontana Press, is admirably clear and readable, dealing with both personalities and policies. It is particularly strong on the Beveridge Report and its continuing relevance. Another useful book covering the same area is

Glennerster, H. (1995) *British Social Policy since 1945*. Oxford: Blackwell. While neither of these books restricts itself to the role of the state, they accurately reflect the period since the Second World War by making this their main focus. A third book, dealing more with the ideological and political background, is Deakin, N. (1994) *The Politics of Welfare: Continuities and Change*. Hemel Hempstead: Harvester Wheatsheaf. Social policy is becoming increasingly international. A good example of a comparative approach is Hill, M. (1996) *Social Policy: a Comparative Analysis*. Hemel Hempstead: Prentice Hall/Harvester Wheatsheaf, which has a chapter entitled 'Welfare and the state'.

All of the above books address many of the issues identified in the penultimate section of this chapter, but more specialist literature is available. For example, there is a book on quasi-markets: Bartlett, W., Propper, C., Wilson, D. and Le Grand, J. (eds) (1994) *Quasi-markets in the Welfare State*. Bristol: SAUS Publications. The book has a useful chapter on regulation. The issue of empowerment is addressed by Craig, G. and Mayo, M. (eds) (1995) *Community Empowerment: a Reader in Participation and Development*. London: Zed Books. A good book on rights and citizenship is Dean, H. (1996) *Welfare, Law and Citizenship*. Hemel Hempstead: Prentice Hall/Harvester Wheatsheaf.

III.2

pRivate weLfaRe

eDWaRD BRUNSDON

For centuries private welfare has been a feature of the mixed economy of care in Britain. While its magnitude and scope have fluctuated, it has been and remains an important element of provision in health, housing, social security, education and social services. In spite of this, however, it has until recently received scant attention from social policy analysts.

This neglect of private welfare can be explained by the confluence of two factors, the academic interests of social policy analysts and the politics of the post-war period. As discussed in chapter I.1, social policy developed primarily under the guidance of Fabian socialist academics (such as Tawney, Marshall, Titmuss and Townsend) whose main focus was state welfare. Although often critical of provision for particular client groups, in general terms they sought to justify or defend the existence of state-produced, state-delivered, provision as a politically and morally superior way of organizing welfare.

In these same post-war decades, successive Labour and Conservative governments operated with broadly similar Keynesian strategies for managing the economy that included an acceptance of state welfare as the major means of providing accessible services for all the population. Together with the discipline's own concerns, this political agenda pushed private welfare to the periphery. For the majority of academics and politicians there was little

interest in its functioning and development. When it was addressed by analysts, it was primarily used as a negative point of reference in comparisons with state provision.

All this changed in the 1980s. Political interest emerged as successive Conservative governments drew up a new welfare agenda in which more efficient and effective services were sought through the development of welfare markets. These markets grew as governments:

- reduced subsidies (e.g. for prescriptions and council housing);
- reduced direct provision (e.g. free eye checks and dental examinations for adults);
- offered financial inducements to encourage people to purchase welfare services and benefits (as in the case of personal pensions, medical insurance and council houses);
- transferred responsibility for a range of services from the state to employers (e.g. short-term sickness and maternity benefits);
- more recently, directed local authorities to spend 85 per cent of their community care budgets on the purchase of non-statutory services.

As a consequence of these and similar measures, private welfare has expanded dramatically over the past two decades. A range of new businesses, including banks and high-street chain stores, are now competing to provide both alternatives and supplements to state welfare. At the same time, government policy has fostered a climate in which people have become more aware of the need for self-provision.

The response to these developments from social policy analysts was initially slow and focused on the nature and impact of privatization (discussed in chapter III.1). By the early 1990s, however, they had widened their remit, developing research into private welfare consumption, detailed analyses of particular services such as health (Higgins, 1988) and long-term care (Laing, 1993) and assessments of the varying nature of private welfare in different societies (Johnson, 1995) and of the composition and impact of welfare markets (May and Brunsdon, 1996).

This awakening of interest in private welfare is important. But the importance does not simply reside in the fact that a major area of provision has remained under-researched. It is also the case that without an understanding of the funding, operations and services of private welfare organizations, it is difficult to have either a clear conception of past welfare arrangements or a comprehensive picture of the welfare mix engineered over the past two decades. A first stage in that understanding is a consideration of the general nature of private welfare and the issues it generates. This chapter is devoted to these tasks.

PRIVATE WELFARE MARKETS: THE KEY CONSTITUENTS

Private welfare is best understood as *a range of markets trading in welfare products and services*. As with other markets, these involve suppliers and purchasers trading goods and services in diverse institutional conditions. They can be divided into two main types:

- those markets trading in financial services for such products as mortgages,

pensions, health insurance, social care insurance and education plans;
- those trading in welfare services *per se* for schooling, long-term care, hospital provision, community health, home care and housing.

The suppliers to the financial services markets are commercial carriers. They are of two main kinds: provident associations and proprietary businesses. Provident associations are companies (such as Western Provident Association and British United Provident Association – hereafter Bupa) which are limited by guarantee and non-profit distributing. They are exempt from corporation tax and their surpluses over costs become part of the companies' reserves. In contrast, proprietary businesses (such as Lloyds Bank, Virgin and Marks & Spencer) can distribute surpluses over costs to owners or shareholders, and are subject to corporation tax. They, however, find it much easier than the provident associations to raise equity and attract external investment. Both types of supplier sell directly to the public but can also use intermediaries such as brokers.

Apart from 'composite' organizations such as Bupa (that sell both insurance products and health care services), the direct markets in welfare services and products tend to have a different mix of suppliers. Competition to supply can involve multinationals (as in the housing and health care markets), small businesses (as in the long-term care and education markets) and single operators (as in domiciliary and child care). It can also extend to voluntary and statutory agencies competing for custom with their commercial counterparts.

Purchasers within each of these markets can be classified into two main types:

- individuals buying financial products and services for their own present or future consumption;
- 'proxy' buyers (or 'principal agents') purchasing on behalf of present or future 'end-users'.

Traditionally this second grouping comprised individuals buying for their parents, parents purchasing for their children, companies buying for their employees, and trade unions and professional associations buying for their members. Recent government legislation (notably the NHS and Community Care Act 1990) has added NHS trusts, fund-holding general practitioners (GPs) and local authorities purchasing services for different user groups from non-statutory providers. The market for health screening services is a good example of this diversity. Here companies, trade unions, professional associations, GPs and individuals are among those buying services from proprietary and provident commercial health care providers and NHS trusts.

Both buyers and suppliers enter these markets to make gains from their trading. Commercial suppliers, whether individuals or multinational companies, *typically* seek financial gains. Indeed, this has led some policy analysts to characterize private welfare as the 'for profit' sector. Such a representation, however, is both inflexible and misleading. To begin with it cannot be assumed that suppliers always seek profits in the market place. There may well be occasions when, with sufficient financial reserves, they are prepared to trade at a loss in order, say, to capture or secure a section of the market. Second, the notion 'for profit' is a supply-side view of private welfare. It ignores other important features, such as the buyers (and the various gains they anticipate from trading) and many of the institutional features of the markets themselves (such as their size, composition, competition, regulation and more general government intervention).

Buyers and proxy buyers have numerous different grounds for purchasing. For instance, in buying a personal pension people are aiming to enhance their disposable income in retirement. In buying private schooling parents are seeking to enhance their children's life chances. Employers – as the main 'proxy buyer' – have tended

to purchase health and social care services to attract, retain or motivate staff. But they have also used such purchases to reduce absenteeism and, more generally, to maintain employee discipline (May and Brunsdon, 1994). Underwriting these very varied calculations, however, is the anticipation of making gains (financial or otherwise) and getting a return on their 'investments'.

Beyond the sellers and buyers and their myriad calculations are the more general institutional market conditions. It is these features which context the calculations and, when understood as *processes* rather than static conditions, bear witness to the complex formations that constitute private welfare markets. The health insurance market provides a pertinent example.

THE HEALTH INSURANCE MARKET: A CASE STUDY

This market is one in which banks, building societies and insurers compete to supply a range of insurance products to corporate and individual purchasers. These products are then employed to meet the full (or partial) cost of treatment in private hospitals, clinics or NHS pay beds, or to compensate for the loss of income through illness and disability.

Market size

Measured in terms of the number of purchasers, the health insurance market grew from 300,000 subscriptions in 1955 to 3.6 million subscriptions (covering 6.2 million people) by 1996. Within that period, the 1980s saw particularly rapid growth, with subscription levels trebling from 1 to 3 million. Growth in the 1990s has tailed off somewhat, explained by insurance analysts in terms of rising subscription costs and the recession, which has affected company purchases (Association of British Insurers, 1995). Nevertheless, measured in terms of the aggregate premium values, the market is currently worth £1.7 billion and is forecast to grow.

Competition and market composition

Provident associations dominate the health insurance market, accounting for 80 per cent of the premiums (worth £1.34 billion), with two associations – Bupa and Private Patients Plan (PPP) – accounting for 72 per cent. The proprietary carriers hold 20 per cent of the business (in premium income worth £333 million), with the composite insurer Norwich Union (holding 10 per cent of the overall market and 20 per cent of the individual market) being the most successful. This pattern is likely to alter, and quickly, in what is an increasingly competitive market with more than thirty insurers vying for business. The proprietaries are already eroding the providents' dominance. Norwich Union Healthcare has in five years grown to become the third largest operator, Legal & General entered the market in 1996 and PPP (with 27 per cent of the market) announced in February 1996 that it is shedding its provident status to become a limited company in order to raise equity finance and compete more effectively. Partnerships are also emerging. For instance, in March 1996, Barclays Bank announced that Norwich Union would underwrite all the bank's insurance services in a deal worth £100 million, while in June of the same year, the Halifax announced a partnership with Bupa to market health insurance to the society's client base. Foreign companies are also active in this market. The Dutch insurer OHRA entered the British market in 1990, the American company Foundation Health in 1994 and the market is likely to increase as European trade grows.

The products traded

The products traded are varied and inherently complex in medical and insurance terms. It is possible, however, to identify four key health insurance products.

1 *Private medical insurance (PMI)*, which pays for care in private hospitals or NHS pay-bed units should the policy-holder suffer from one or more of a specified list of medical conditions. Although typically limited to elective surgery, some policies also cover outpatient treatment and home nursing. It is by far the most popular form of private health insurance among both corporate and individuals purchasers. Insurance estimates suggest that one in eleven people in the UK are covered by this product.

2 *Permanent health insurance (PHI)* is an income replacement plan designed to replace some or all of the income lost by an individual who is unable to work due to sickness or disability. PHI sales are currently estimated to be in the region of £400 million per annum.

3 *Critical illness insurance (CII)* provides a lump sum payment in the event of a serious illness such as a heart attack, a stroke or cancer (the illnesses covered vary). Sales at present are estimated to be worth approximately £50 million per annum.

4 *Long-term care insurance (LTCI)* is designed to pay for long-term domiciliary or institutional care through either a fixed lump sum or annual payments. LTCI is a recent initiative and has, at present, only 28,000 subscribers. But it is an area in which insurance carriers are planning to expand, particularly in the light of the ageing population and the government's search for new ways of funding long-term care.

The purchasers

Given that the National Health Service offers medical care free at the point of consumption, it is clear that purchasers of private health care cover must see a difference between NHS services and those of private medical establishments. Research into the individual purchase of private health care suggests that people calculate in terms of the perceived quality of medical care and 'hotel' facilities, the individualised nature of care, the speed of access to services and the privacy provided. Employers, the main 'proxy' buyer, purchase some 60 per cent of health insurance subscriptions and do so primarily as a means of attracting, retaining and motivating key staff. Research suggests that: 'among large companies private [health] insurance is . . . the third most valued employee benefit after the pension and company car' (Association of British Insurers, 1995, p. 11).

Regulation and government intervention

The regulation of the health insurance market is currently under review. Traditionally, providers have operated under a liberal regime subject only to the same sales and insolvency regulations as other insurers. While there is therefore some attempt at input (suppliers) and process regulation (sales practices), there has been less concern with regulating output (considered in chapter III.1). Here the general ethos has been one of self-regulation by the industry. This may change in the light of a number of critical reports and pressure to avoid a repeat of the mis-selling of personal pensions that occurred in the late 1980s. The Office of Fair Trading has recently criticized health insurance plans for being difficult to understand and for a tendency to underplay important exclusions by placing them in the small print of policies. It has made a number of recommendations for stronger regulation and in particular for greater consumer protection in the case of LTCI products.

Increased statutory regulation is likely to be contested by the industry and recent government policy suggests that other mechanisms of intervention are more likely to be pursued. Of these the most important are fiscal changes – here, the government

has been ambivalent. It has introduced an Insurance Premium Tax (in October 1994) while allowing tax relief for private health insurance for the over-60s. Indirectly, however, other government policies have contributed to the growth of the private health insurance market through, for example, changes to the public funding of long-term care, hospital and primary provision.

Though trading in a distinctive set of products, the health insurance market exhibits the characteristics and complexity of all welfare markets. Such markets differ in size, product, the nature and range of purchasers and suppliers, levels of competition, and forms of regulation and government intervention. They also change in different ways and at different rates. It is this, above all else, that signifies the complexity of their formation. Any analysis of private welfare must therefore address each market independently while recognizing that they are part of a wider realm and an ever-changing mix of welfare production and consumption.

PRIVATE WELFARE IN A CHANGING WELFARE MIX: ISSUES AND IMPLICATIONS

Policy statements and planned initiatives from both government and opposition parties suggest that private welfare is likely to feature more prominently in the welfare mix of the future. Although growth is likely to be uneven, there is every indication that trading will increase in a range of welfare markets. In the long-term care market, for example, there is likely to be increasing demand for private domiciliary care as well as places in commercial residential and nursing homes. Laing and Buisson (1996) suggest that 38,000 additional beds will be needed over the next five years. Similarly, a number of recent studies point to the likelihood of continued growth in personal pensions, private health care, health insurance, housing and private education from nursery schooling to post-compulsory training. In many of these instances, the main political parties are emphasizing the need for public–private 'partnerships' to meet likely demand.

The increasing significance of private welfare in both funding and delivery poses a number of questions for policy analysts. Some of these are derived from the discipline's Fabian socialist beginnings and question changes in provision and sources of non-state funding from this orthodoxy. Other questions stem from the organization of private welfare itself. In the former grouping are questions emanating from the Fabian conceptions of social justice and universalism (and within this concerns of equality and equity). Can, for instance, the development of private welfare be justified? Is it, as suggested by some proponents, necessary for the continuance of the welfare state or will it undermine it? Will the development of private welfare lead to the erosion of universalism? More specifically, will it lead to growing inequities in the finance and consumption of welfare services? Will those who can afford private welfare opt out of a (declining) state system? Does private welfare complement the state welfare system or does it provide an alternative and conflicting basis? Is the needs led system subjugated by issues of affordability?

What should be clear from this chapter is that any attempt to respond to such questions must involve the initial disaggregation of private welfare into different markets (and a comparable disaggregation of state funding and provision for different services). Neither private welfare nor state welfare is a homogeneous entity and such questions therefore demand both an appreciation of the diverse nature of services and markets and the recognition that the questions *may* generate different responses in different markets and different services.

The second cluster of issues concern private welfare *per se*. One of the more general questions here concerns the explanation of changing welfare markets. For example, how much is the current growth in private welfare due to shifts in government policies, as against the changing calculations of provider organizations and both proxy buyers and end-users? How can the uneven development of welfare markets be explained? Is there consumer pressure for new or different services and benefits and how much of this is stimulated by a perceived decline in statutory provision? There are also questions that should be raised concerning the operation of welfare markets. In a number of observers' eyes, markets are extremely weak at self-regulating and have very little tendency to stability (other than through oligopolistic and monopolistic arrangements). Given this, issues can be raised about *who* is to regulate the markets and *how* are they to be regulated? Will state intervention in the form of increased regulation replace state provision of services or will government expect the professional bodies involved in each market to take on such responsibilities? Again, what if markets fail? Where there is no statutory responsibility, who is going to protect the consumers and how? Will the government subsidize private welfare in order to limit such damaging outcomes or will it devolve these financial responsibilities to local health and social care authorities? It is these clusters of concerns that students are increasingly likely to encounter in their studies of private welfare in the future.

GUIDE TO FURTHER READING

Association of British Insurers (1995) *Risk, Insurance and Welfare*. London: Association of British Insurers. This is a useful text with contributions from a range of academics and insurance analysts who are addressing the changing balance of public provision and private insurance protection in areas such as medical care, long-term care, unemployment, pensions, and sickness and disability.

Higgins, J. (1988) *The Business of Medicine*. London: Macmillan, focuses on the growth of private health care in Britain and provides a good insight into the issues raised for the National Health Service, its patients, providers and consumers.

Johnson, N. (ed.) (1995) *Private Markets in Health and Welfare: an International Perspective*. Oxford/Providence, RI: Berg. This compilation offers illuminating accounts of welfare privatization across nine societies. Each chapter is lucidly written and typically surveys changing provision in health, social care, housing and income maintenance.

Laing and Buisson are independent research consultants who have undertaken a number of surveys of private welfare markets, including long-term care, medical care and medical insurance. Their work contributes a large proportion of the data currently utilized in assessments of these markets. Among their recent publications are: Laing, W. (1993): *Financing Long-term Care: the Crucial Debate*. London: Age Concern; Laing, W. (1996) *Care of Elderly People Survey*. London, Laing & Buisson.

May, M. and Brunsdon, E. (1994) Workplace care in the mixed economy of welfare. In R. Page and J. Baldock (eds), *Social Policy Review 6*. Canterbury: Social Policy Association. This article considers the different forms of workplace care, its utilization by employers and the implications for the mixed economy of care.

May, M. and Brunsdon, E. (1996) Women and private welfare. In C. Hallett (ed.), *Women and Social Policy*. Hemel Hempstead: Harvester Wheatsheaf. This chapter surveys the growth of private welfare and its variable implications for women.

III.3

the voluntary sector

nicholas deakin

Over the past decade, there has been a marked revival of interest in the voluntary sector in the UK, what it is, what it does and its relationship with other sectors – the state, the market and the world of informal care. As a result of this renewed interest there has been substantial debate about:

- the *definition* of the voluntary sector and its activities;
- the *functions* with which it should be entrusted;
- the *terms* on which it should engage with the other sectors, especially the state sector.

The progress of this debate can be traced through a series of reports and inquiries on the role of the sector, extending from the Wolfenden Report of 1978 to, most recently, that of the inquiry set up by the National Council for Voluntary Organisations (NCVO, 1996).

In the course of these discussions the politicians have frequently 'rediscovered' the sector and its potential. There have been many references by successive ministers to the unique qualities of the sector and the various roles which it might perform in future.

Public consciousness of the significance of voluntary action has also been greatly heightened through the promotion of a number of fund-raising events designed to raise money for charities operating in the Third World and the UK, like telethons, concerts, sponsored marathons and 'red nose' days.

Finally, the introduction of the National Lottery in 1995, with its emphasis on raising funds for 'good causes', has greatly enhanced the profile of the sector but also exposed its activities to closer public scrutiny through the media.

BACKGROUND

Until recently, there was a widespread view that the leading role of the voluntary sector in the provision of social welfare had come to an end with the establishment of the welfare state at the end of the Second World War. 'Charity' and 'philanthropy', terms which acquired strong negative associations for many of those at the receiving end of voluntary provision in the Victorian period, could be relegated to the history books, along with the Poor Law that the welfare state displaced.

In fact, the position is more complex. After 1945, voluntary bodies continued to perform a wide variety of functions. Several senior figures in the Labour government of 1945–51 (like the Prime Minister Clement Attlee, and Herbert Morrison) were strong supporters of voluntary action. Nevertheless, voluntary organizations were seen very much as junior partners in the new structure. As we saw in chapter III.1, these reforms transferred and consolidated many functions in health, education and social services under state control.

The steady expansion of the role of the state under both Labour and Conservative governments eventually brought with it disillusionment about the quality and responsiveness of services provided by state bureaucracies (see chapter III.5). New developments on the broader scene – the rise of the women's movement, the impact of immigration from the 'New Commonwealth', a revived interest in community development – began to change the character and composition of the voluntary sector.

During the 1960s and 1970s new organizations appeared (and existing ones were revitalized), concerned with issues like:

* Third World poverty;
* environmental questions;
* local community action;
* provision for excluded groups.

Bodies like MIND, Mencap, Greenpeace, Shelter and the Child Poverty Action Group (CPAG) were founded or refounded during this period.

These changes in the voluntary sector also generated a new style of operation. This meant: more open and democratic internal management; pressure groups using up-to-date campaigning techniques; concern for rights of service users and their involvement as partners. Such developments helped to produce what is sometimes called the *new voluntary sector*. Outside the field of welfare, voluntary action has continued to be the mainstay of a whole range of activities: for example, in sports and recreation, the arts and education.

Over the post-Second World War period as a whole, these developments have helped to produce a voluntary sector which is diverse in its range of activities, complex in its internal relations and constantly evolving, both internally and in its relations with users and other providers of welfare.

THE PRESENT STATE OF THE VOLUNTARY SECTOR

Definitions

The term 'voluntary sector', which is currently (1997) the standard term in general use, is generally not much liked. It is of comparatively recent origin (twenty years) and not employed outside the UK. It tends to be used very loosely. The task of definition is usually approached negatively: thus, the 'sector' covers formally constituted organizations, managed by unpaid committees, that are not part of the state or the market or the informal world of spontaneous or unstructured action (which is discussed in chapter III.4). The term includes organizations with paid staff; they can trade, but not distribute profits. Their objectives are generally taken as being to enhance public benefit. The situation is further complicated by the simultaneous employment of three other terms, which overlap with the notion of a 'voluntary sector' and which are often used in the same context to describe similar activities. These are *charities, community sector* and *volunteers*.

Charities

The term charity has deep roots in English history. The four heads of charity were defined in legislation in 1601: religion, education, the relief of poverty and other purposes beneficial to the whole community. This definition has evolved since then through case law; the terms on which charities operate were most recently reformed by the Charity Act of 1993. Charitable status confers benefits (for example, tax reliefs); it also imposes strict obligations on the trustees of charities.

Charities are regulated by a non-ministerial department, the Charity Commission. The definition of charities encompasses a substantial number of bodies (mostly in the education sector, like the 'public' schools) not customarily thought of as operating in the general public interest, and excludes many that are. The legislation only applies to England and Wales: Scots law is different and the Charity Commission's writ does not run there. Nevertheless, the term 'charities' is frequently employed as a description in debates and discussions as if it covered the British voluntary sector as a whole.

Community sector

This term has come into general use to refer to small groups which operate on a local scale and which are not necessarily formally constituted. These can be distinguished from voluntary organizations by their size and informality, like village hall committees and tenants' associations.

Volunteers

Much discussion about the voluntary sector is conducted on the assumption that those involved in its operations are volunteers. This is not by any means always the case. Volunteers play a very significant part in the operation of a wide range of bodies, including some statutory agencies; but although the sum total of their efforts is substantial it does not by any means encompass the whole of the sector's activities. However, the distinction is often blurred and politicians, in particular, often appear to have difficulty with the distinction between volunteering (by individuals) and voluntary action (by organizations).

Finally, different terms are employed outside the UK to describe the world of voluntary action. In the United States the preferred term is 'third sector', and this is now also sometimes used in the UK. Elsewhere in Europe the term 'associations' is used; this may be significant in future because of moves to evolve a common legal definition identifying the rights and responsibilities of organizations across the European Union as a whole.

Size of the sector

If the definition of the *voluntary sector* given in the first paragraph of this section is used, the best recent estimate of the size of the sector is between 200,000 and 240,000 organisations (Kendall and Knapp, 1996). The Charity Commission maintains a register of charitable bodies; in 1995 there were 170,000 organizations on this register. However, this register only covers England and Wales. If the extent of voluntary action is taken to include the informal *community organizations*, a recent study concludes that there are probably around 1.3 million organizations in the UK. *Volunteering* takes place on a very substantial scale in this country. The National Centre for Volunteering's most recent review of activity (1991) shows that the numbers of those involved in some kind of voluntary activity could be as high as 21 million.

Main areas of activity

The range of activity covered by the voluntary sector is very great. A recent international study of the sector, conducted from Johns Hopkins University in the USA, found that the UK voluntary sector's main areas of action were to be found in the following 'industries': education, social services, culture and recreation, and development and housing. This pattern contrasts quite sharply with the distribution in other countries examined as part of this study. For example, the health sector in the UK is much smaller, mainly as a result of the dominant role played up to now by the NHS in the UK, and the housing section considerably larger (Kendall and Knapp, 1996).

Categories of organization

Another way of distinguishing different parts of the sector is to divide organizations by type (Knight, 1993). They can be split between:

- service providers;
- campaigners;
- 'intermediaries';
- cooperatives and 'mutuals';
- self-help bodies.

Examples of 'service providers' are organizations providing residential care (like homes for old people); 'campaigners' include organizations like Greenpeace and Friends of the Earth; 'intermediaries' are organizations which exist to provide services for other bodies in the sector, like the NCVO; 'self-help bodies' consist of groups of people in similar situations who come together to help each other – the Spastics Society (now Scope) started in this way. Recent evidence suggests that the range of functions being performed in the sector is expanding and that the numbers of individual volunteers are also on the increase (NCVO, 1996).

The resourcing of the voluntary sector

The resources which support the voluntary sector come mainly from the following sources:

- individual giving;
- grants from charitable trusts and foundations;
- donations from the corporate sector;
- support from the state (central and local);
- income generated by voluntary organizations themselves (through investments, trading, charity shops).

In the last year for which we have full data (1991), the total gross income of the sector was estimated by the Central Statistical Office as being £8,427 million and the proportion of funding received from these different sources is shown in table III.3.1. Alongside these financial resources, we need to take into account gifts in kind, including time, in the form of volunteer labour.

Table III.3.1 Percentage of voluntary sector funding received from different sources

Source	Percentage
General public	41
Other charities	8
Corporate sector	9
State (central and local)	24
Internally generated	18

Source: adapted from CAF (1996) *Dimensions of the Voluntary Sector*.

The pattern of individual giving has not changed very much over the past decade, despite the stimulus of the new types of fund-raising events referred to earlier and the introduction of new means of giving, like direct deduction from payrolls, 'affinity cards' which automatically assign a small proportion of sums spent to a specific charity and the 'CAFcard', which facilitates tax-efficient individual giving to charities. The level of individual donations per capita is also quite low compared with some other countries, notably the USA.

State funding, on the other hand, has expanded substantially. Both local and central government fund activities by the voluntary sector: the Home Office, until recently the government department principally concerned, provides substantial block grants for a number of key national organizations. Other government departments support bodies which operate within their departmental area of interest. Most local authorities have a long tradition of supporting their own local voluntary bodies, both by grants to specific organizations to perform particular tasks and by providing support for local coordinating bodies – known as Councils of Voluntary Service (CVSs), or Rural Community Councils (RCCs) in country areas. Latterly, state funding has increasingly come to be provided on different terms, not in the form of grants but through contracts. This development and the reasons for it are explored below.

Table II.3.2 The number and size of NLCB grants by type of work

Type of work	No. of grants	£ million
Health	362	28.8
Development	453	30.0
Advocacy	203	18.3
Social welfare	559	37.7
Training	290	19.0
Housing	60	5.5
Refugees	25	2.4
Sports, arts, conservation	81	3.6
Others	196	13.8
Total	2,229	159.1

Source: from National Lottery Charity Board (1996) *Resource 5*.

A major new source of funding for the sector has been the National Lottery. After the shares of the profits assigned to the operators (Camelot) and taken by the Treasury are deducted the Lottery has generated substantial additional income which is distributed by five appointed boards, covering arts, sports, heritage, the millenium and 'charities'.

Voluntary organizations have benefited from grants made by all these boards; but the main source of funding has been the National Lottery Charities Board (NLCB). This Board had at the time of writing allocated two rounds of grants, totalling over £300 million. In the second round (July 1996) there was particular emphasis on issues of low income and youth; the type of work divided as shown in table III.3.2.

COMMENTARY

The complex problems of defining the voluntary sector and the wide range of activities that it encompasses make it difficult to provide a realistic estimate of the scope of voluntary activity in this society and its impact. However, the importance of voluntary action can be seen in two contrasting ways. First, the growth of activity and increased political visibility of the sector can be emphasized. Attention can be drawn to such factors as:

- the amount of employment generated in the sector;
- the extent of contribution of additional resources;
- the size of membership of voluntary organizations;
- new areas of activity pioneered and an open and 'user-friendly' approach;

There may be as many as a million people now employed in voluntary sector organizations of all kind; estimates of the economic contribution made by the sector's activities run as high as £3 billion. Membership of large organizations like the National Trust now vastly outnumbers that of the political parties, and many important areas of new activity, like action on the environment, the hospice movement or provision for those with HIV/AIDS, have been developed within the voluntary sector. In addition, claims are made for the significance of voluntary action in underpinning the health of civil society through participation in activities that fall between state and market; and reinforcing democracy by encouraging 'active citizenship'.

However, it is important to be wary of indiscriminate 'boosterism'. Analysts point to such problematic issues as:

- the uneven spread of voluntary activity, both geographically and in class terms;
- the difficulty of focusing voluntary action (diversity precludes a 'master plan' and their concern with their independence makes organizations wary of collaboration – hence there is much duplication);
- the problems associated with relying on voluntary action to support minority or unpopular causes.

Some commentators also argue that many of the functions that voluntary organizations are now carrying out can be and are discharged with equal efficiency in the market or even by the state; and many important innovations in policy and practice are not the outcome of voluntary sector initiatives. Furthermore, where voluntary organizations do discharge their tasks efficiently and effectively, they often only do so (it is suggested) by ceasing to operate as traditional voluntary bodies and imitating the style and practice of either statutory bodies or commercial organizations.

RELATIONS WITH THE STATE

The range of activities for which the state is responsible has begun to diminish – a process that began in the middle 1970s and is still continuing. As a result, the boundaries between statutory and voluntary action have shifted and territory once conceded by voluntary organizations is being repossessed. In some ways, this process can be read as a straightforward reversal of past trends; but in other respects the relationship between the two sectors is taking new forms and has a different dynamic. Either way, it is important to set events in the voluntary sector in the context of the wider changes involving the state and the market, considered in chapters III.1 and III.2.

The character of the tasks which voluntary organizations are now being expected to take on derive at least in part from the perception outside the sector of its main strengths. Those most often cited include:

- innovation;
- flexibility;
- lack of bureaucracy.

The voluntary sector is also often seen as possessing particularly important sets of specialist skills and experience. One key example of this is in the personal social services. Here, there has been movement over the course of the period from 1984 towards a 'mixed economy of welfare', in which the local authorities that had previously taken responsibility for all aspects of these services were expected to withdraw to an 'enabling' role. (Similar developments have taken place in other services discussed elsewhere in this book.) The voluntary organizations and for profit agencies which are increasingly expected to perform the function of service delivery do so on the basis of contracts entered into with local authorities. The resulting set of arrangements have become generally known as the 'contract culture', in which the two parties to the contract are the customer (the authority) and the contractor (the agency).

Involvement in the contract culture has been a mixed blessing for voluntary organizations. On the positive side, contracts often provide greater security than the previous pattern of annual grants, which were often not renewed until near (or even after) their date of expiry. Contracts also specify the nature of the task that has to be performed and set up explicit standards by which performance can be judged; this is, potentially at least, helpful to the contracting agency. On the other side, contracting often involves much detailed paper work and requires production of large quantities of information in a form prescribed by the customer. Perhaps more importantly, specifying the nature of the work and ways in which it is to be carried out may sometimes appear to threaten the contracting agency's independence or even compromise its values.

> **Box III.3.1**
>
> Issues in the management and efficiency of voluntary organizations:
> * the governance of voluntary organizations;
> * the situation of users;
> * standards;
> * accountability;
> * regulation;
> * internal management and staff relations.
>
> *Source*: NCVO (1996)

should continue to fund their critics. (The Charity Commission has now provided helpful guidance to organizations which have charitable status and may be concerned about the implications of 'political' campaigning.)

As for democracy, it is reasonable for voluntary organizations to present their activities as an intrinsic part of the democratic process; but if they do so, it is important that they should measure up to democratic standards in their own procedures.

KEY ISSUES AND DEBATES

The revival of voluntary action and the growth of interest in what it can or should achieve has set off a continuing debate among academics and politicians. Among the main issues now being discussed are:

These dangers are by now well known (Gutch, 1992), and the sector has acted to diminish them. Intermediary bodies at both national and local level provide advice and support. Local authorities have shown themselves willing to take account of the special needs of the voluntary organizations with whom they contract.

These developments have also thrown a spotlight on the issue of the management and the efficiency of voluntary organizations in an environment in which they have to compete for contracts with bodies from other sectors. Some of the important issues arising in this area are shown in box III.3.1. This checklist illustrates the competing pressures under which voluntary bodies now have to work. It is important that the quality of what is being provided by the organizations should not be compromised; but there is also a pressing issue of how to maintain the distinctive character of the voluntary sector.

A further issue is the question of the advocacy role of voluntary organizations and the part this plays in the democratic culture, locally and nationally. It is important that voluntary bodies should be able to make the case on behalf of their particular group or interest; but funding bodies also have the right to expect that criticism remains within legitimate limits. If it does not, they may come to wonder why they

* What is the exact nature of the distinctive contribution made by the voluntary sector to society as a whole?
* How can government best help the sector to make a full contribution?
* How many of the tasks until recently performed by the state can the voluntary sector take on without forfeiting its independence?
* Is there a limit to the amount of structuring of its contribution that can take place without damaging the spontaneity and innovation that should characterize the sector's activities?
* How can the voluntary sector best respond to the pressure for users' rights?
* Is it time to reform the law of charities?

Many of these questions have not yet been convincingly answered. But the increased attention that the sector is attracting means that it will need to able to demonstrate convincingly its competence and commitment, often in the face of increased scepticism on the part of the media and the general public.

GUIDE TO FURTHER READING

The best current account of the sector is Kendall, J. and Knapp, M. (1996) *The Voluntary Sector in the UK*. Manchester: Manchester University Press. The volumes edited by Smith, J. D. (1994) *An Introduction to the Voluntary Sector*. London: Routledge, and Knight, B. (1993) *Voluntary Action*. London: Centris, are also helpful. The statistical profile of the sector is covered in the annual repoort produced by the Charities Aid Foundation (CAF) *Dimensions of the Voluntary Sector*. The National Lottery Charities Board produces regular information about the grants it awards. Much important comparative information is contained in Salaman, L. and Anheier, S. (1995) *The Emerging Nonprofit Sector*. Baltimore/London: Johns Hopkins Press. The contract culture is discussed in comparative perspective by Gutch, R. (1992) *Contracting Lessons from the US*. London: NCVO. Future policy for the sector is examined in the report commissioned by NCVO (1996) *Meeting the Challenge of Change*. London: NCVO, which sets out recommendations for action.

the informal sector

clare ungerson

Defining Terms

The term 'informal sector' has only relatively recently entered social policy discussion. The phrase is used to describe an important source of services for people with dependencies. It is often used in conjunction with the idea of 'welfare mix' or the 'mixed economy of welfare': this is taken to mean the combined sources of the state, the voluntary sector, the private for-profit sector and the 'informal sector', all of which provide services for people with dependencies living in their own homes, or, as it is often put, in 'the community'. The term 'informal sector' is best understood in contrast to the 'formal sector'. The *formal sector* consists of *paid* professionals and para-professionals, such as social workers, care managers, district nurses and home carers. Their task is to assess people's needs, using professional and resource driven criteria, and then provide those people directly with services, or else ensure that they are getting what they 'need' from some other source, such as the private, voluntary or informal sectors. (This formal sector is usually called the 'personal social services', which are part of the state sector, but it can also include the voluntary and private for-profit sectors.)

In contrast, the *informal sector* is the term used to describe the essentially *unpaid* provision of services to people with dependencies living in the 'community'. These services are provided by family (or kin),

friends and neighbours. Note that the lack of pay could, in theory, mean that volunteers are included in the informal sector, because they also provide services for free. But the term does *not* normally include volunteers, and this is because the other central feature of the informal sector is that the people who provide the services normally have had a relationship of some kind with the person they are providing services for. It is precisely because of this relationship that they are willing to look after the dependent person. Thus members of the same family may feel they want to look after someone because they love him or her, or they feel that being part of the same family means they are subject to a particular set of moral obligations to care for him or her. Similarly, friends and neighbours may feel they should look after someone because they are fond of him or her, or in return for kindnesses and services that were once provided by the person who needs them now. In short, the informal sector is based on motivation to provide services based on non-monetary 'ties that bind', such as love, duty, shared biography and reciprocity (Finch, 1989).

Claiming and Naming the Informal Sector

The 'informal sector' has only been named as such since the 1970s. Previously, this sector of service provision was widely referred to as 'the family' or 'the community', without any attempt, by policy-makers or policy analysts, to unwrap the constituent parts of those families or communities that provide care, let alone to begin to understand why some people care and others do not. The claiming and naming of the informal sector arose out of 'second wave feminism' – that is, the feminism of the late 1960s and early 1970s – which took as one of its central features the problematization of women's position in the home, and critiqued women's expected role as housewives and servicers of their men and their children (see chapter II.9). It was a short step from the feminist analysis of housework and other forms of domestic labour to an analysis of what feminist policy analysts called 'caring'. Much of the early feminist work on 'care' criticized the British government for encouraging the closure of residential institutions without having regard to who would actually provide the care in the 'community'. As the authors of a classic early article put it: 'Care in the community equals care by the family equals care by women' (Finch and Groves, 1980).

This view of the sexed and gendered assumptions built into policies for community care, and the claiming of what increasingly came to be called 'informal care' as women's work, became very powerful in the 1980s. Not only did it generate feminist-led analysis of the sexism embedded in government policies (Finch and Groves, 1983) and a considerable literature on the sociology of informal care (Lewis and Meredith, 1988; Qureshi and Walker, 1989), but it also formed the basis for a politics of community care and the development of various carers' lobbies, including, and most particularly, the Carers National Association. Feminists argued that community care and care by families were intrinsically exploitative of women. Janet Finch, arguing from an essentially pessimistic perspective about the likelihood of men entering informal care, argued that the only way out was to reintroduce a policy of institutional care, while Gillian Dalley (1988), arguing from a more optimistic perspective and within a utopian tradition, argued that family care should be rejected in favour of new forms of collective and communal care based on libertarian and reciprocal principles.

THE CONVINCING OF GOVERNMENT AND THE GENERATION OF NATIONAL RESEARCH

Policy-makers increasingly listened to these critiques, and, at the same time, were increasingly concerned that, faced with an ageing population and with the majority of women of working age active in the labour market, they would find that the informal sector was simply no longer able to cope with the demands for care. Policy documents began to refer to the need to provide social service support for carers. Government-funded research was also influential. In 1985, and again in 1990, the government annual sample survey of British households (the General Household Survey) decided to count the number of carers nationwide, to find out who they were, what they did and how many hours a week they spent caring. When the results of the 1985 survey were published in 1988, there was some amazement at two features. First, the survey indicated that there were six million carers in Britain, thus demonstrating the enormous importance of the informal sector in sheer numbers. Second, it appeared that there were almost as many men carers as there were women carers: 11 per cent of men were carers, compared to 15 per cent of women.

Immediately researchers began to re-analyse the data, and ferret about within it to find out if, given the apparent number of men carers, the feminists had got it all wrong. Some commentators suggested that the survey questions used to identify 'carers' were likely to underestimate the number of women carers in relation to men because men would more easily identify themselves as doing something special for someone with particular needs, whereas women would simply assume that what they did for others was part of being a 'woman'. Others found, after reanalysing the data, that men and women carers were caring for different kinds of people: men were much more likely to be caring for their wives than for other people, whereas women were almost as likely to be caring for people of a different generation (disabled children or frail elderly people) as they were to be caring for their husbands. As a result, men carers, who were caring for their chronically ill wives, were likely to be older than many women carers. Moreover, when the tasks of caring were reanalysed, it emerged that men and women undertook different kinds of care, with women, much more than men, undertaking the messy and more urgent tasks of care.

Finally, the figure of six million carers came to be refined downwards. While that figure is still frequently used, particularly by organizations wishing to speak up for carers and make claims that their work should be recognized by the politicians, it is now generally acknowledged that the number of people undertaking the really hard and stressful types of care within the British population is currently within the region of 1.3 million. Nevertheless, as the population ages, as residential care becomes increasingly rationed by price and by care managers, and hospitals discharge earlier and earlier, that number is likely to increase – slowly but steadily.

From Feminism to the Mainstream

It is probably the case that second wave feminism's greatest triumph, as far as British social policy is concerned, is the successful identification of informal care as a legitimate issue for public discussion

and as part of the policy agenda. Perhaps the most concrete example of this is the recent history of the payment of a benefit paid to carers of working age – the Invalid Care Allowance – which, when first introduced in 1977, was not available to married women, who, it was argued by the policy-makers, would 'be at home anyway'. This benefit has, since 1987 and a decision of the European Court of Justice, been available to married women carers such that well over 100,000 now receive it. The rhetoric of policy documents has become much more sensitive, at least in theory, to carers' needs. In particular the Griffiths report *Community Care: Agenda for Action*, which laid the basis for the National Health Service and Community Care Act 1990, referred to the need to support informal carers, and the need to integrate them in the 'welfare mix'. The Department of Health has funded much research into carers' needs and their integration in the welfare mix (for example, Twigg and Atkin, 1994). Carers are now legislatively recognized as well: the Carers (Recognition and Services) Act 1995 was introduced as Private Member's legislation but received all-party support as it went through Parliament. As a result, carers have the right to an assessment of their needs when the person they are caring for is assessed by care managers, although the legislation does not give carers any rights to services as such.

Into the 1990s: the Critique of the Feminist Perspective on Informal Care

While feminism has been relatively successful in bringing an issue on to the policy agenda even though it took a considerable time to do so, it would be mistaken to think that feminist analysis has now ceased to develop. Indeed, as one would expect, given what has happened to feminism in relation to all other disciplines, feminist analysis of the informal sector has begun to point up 'difference and diversity' in relation to our understanding of the way in which the informal sector works. Thus Hilary Graham, one of the early writers on informal care from a feminist perspective, has more recently argued that the understanding of the social relations of care should include an analysis of race, disability and sexuality as well as gender. In particular, she suggests that not all care in the home is unpaid, and traditionally it has been undertaken by paid domestic servants, many of whom have been, and continue to be, ethnically distinct from their employers. Sara Arber and Jay Ginn have also argued that the early feminist analysis ignored the fact that many recipients of care are themselves elderly women, and that the feminist analysis overemphasized the dependency and burdensome nature particularly of elderly people. Thus research on the informal sector is increasingly concerned with differences between carers, and work on informal care among ethnic minorities and on the care undertaken by young carers of school age is developing quickly.

Apart from this expansion of a gendered perspective on the informal sector to a perspective that takes account of the diversity of carers, the most important critique of the feminist analysis has come from disabled people. Commentators such as Jenny Morris (1993), who is herself disabled, have argued that the treatment by feminists of the so-called 'cared for' or 'care-recipients' as an undifferentiated, uncharacterized, homogeneous burden is profoundly demeaning to disabled people. Other disabled people, like Lois Keith, have argued that it is wrong to think of all disabled people as in need of care, and that many are carers themselves – of their own children and, if they are heterosexual women, of their men. This literature, coming from the 'disabled lobbies', is gaining a considerable legitimacy, both in government circles, where their views fit well with the current ideas about the need to empower consumers of the 'welfare mix',

and with research funders, who have long sought ways of involving 'the researched' (who, in social policy, are often people with special needs) in research projects (see chapter IV.4). The politics of the informal sector in general, and informal care in particular, have, as a result, become increasingly awkward, with both carers' and disabled lobbies often in opposition to each other, both in terms of debates about the nature and origins of 'dependency' and in terms of arguing where scarce public resources should best be spent – whether emphasis should be put on enabling disabled people to lead independent lives by providing them with suitable and affordable housing and paid for personal assistants, or on supporting their informal carers through social security benefits and social service support designed specifically for those who care.

CURRENT POLICY ISSUES FOR THE INFORMAL SECTOR

As policy makers and analysts would now be the first to acknowledge, the informal sector is the linch pin of the community care reforms put in place under the National Health Service and Community Care Act 1990. This means that policy has to be concerned with the maintenance of the sector, and research has to be funded to discover the conditions under which informal care works best. The central questions are concerned, first, with the supply of informal carers, and, second, with the appropriate forms of support for those carers who have come forward to undertake the tasks of care.

As far as supply is concerned, there are reasons for concern. The increasing 'dependency ratio', the high proportion of women of working age entering paid work, the breakdown of the 'traditional' family which might mean that family obligations to care become far more fluid and negotiable than they have been in the past (who should care for an ex mother-in-law who is the grandmother of your children; do you have a responsibility to care for your ex-wife?): all mean that the traditional sources of supply may falter.

Ways of persuading people to come forward to care move on to the agenda. Various proposals emerge, and their thrust is determined by political stance. For example, should carers be paid to care, as they are in some parts of Europe, notably Finland and Norway? Or should employment generate rights to care leave, so that people in work can take time off to care for sick and dying relatives – as again is the case in many of the Scandinavian countries – without losing employment rights and without becoming dependent on very low rates of social security benefit? Alternative proposals amount to doing nothing and letting developing market relations prevail: if formal care from the public sector becomes heavily targeted such that only a very few with very high dependencies gain access to conventional formal personal social services, and, at the same time, a convincing market develops for residential and domiciliary care, then those with lesser dependencies and with inadequate financial resources to buy in private care will need informal care. The moral pressure for carers to come forward to care in kin networks where there are low financial resources will be considerable. However, there is a middle way between these two scenarios which has recently moved on to the political agenda: proposals for individuals to insure themselves against the costs of long-term care, and thus shift the burden of care away from their current bank balances and their kin networks, are, writing in early 1997,

on the agendas of both the major political parties and the subject of a commission of inquiry mounted by the Joseph Rowntree Foundation.

Once carers have come forward, there are problems about how best to support them in the work that they do. The Carers (Recognition and Services) Act 1995 means that carers have been given a voice to say what they want when they encounter care managers. But what carers want – say, respite care on a regular basis – may at least not be what the person they care for wants, and at most may actually do the disabled person some harm. Other forms of support, such as cash, payable to carers which they can use to buy in support and substitute services as and when they and the person they care for want, may move on to the policy agenda. It is certainly the case that cash is increasingly being inserted into the caring relationship from various state sources, ranging from the Department of Social Security to local authorities. The Community Care (Direct Payments) Act 1996 will make it possible for disabled people aged under 65 to tell their local authority that they would rather have money than services; they will then be responsible for organizing their own care, and paying for their own personal assistants. At present it is proposed that people taking this option will not be allowed to pay their close relatives or people living in the same household (unless they were specifically recruited as live-in personal assistants). It remains to be seen whether, once direct payments are in place, a politics of payment for informal carers, pursued by the Carers National Association, does not gain some purchase in the policy arena.

Guide to Further Reading

An excellent collection of readings on community care brings together excerpts from the work of many of the authors mentioned in this article: Bornat, J. et al. (eds) (1994/ 1997) *Community Care – a Reader*. London: Macmillan/ Open University.

For the early feminist perspective, the following publications are essential reading: Finch, J. and Groves, D. (1980) Community care and the family: a case for equal opportunities? *Journal of Social Policy*, 9(4); Finch, J. and Groves, D. (eds) (1983) *A Labour of Love: Women, Work and Caring*. London: Routledge and Kegan Paul. Lewis, J. and Meredith, B. (1988) *Daughters Who Care: Daughters Caring for Their Mothers at Home*. London: Tavistock; Ungerson, C. (1987) *Policy is Personal: Sex, Gender and Informal Care*. London: Tavistock.

On the caring relationship, and the reasons why carers come forward, see Finch, J. (1989) *Family Obligations and Social Change*. Cambridge: Polity Press; Qureshi, H. and Walker, A. (1989) *The Caring Relationship: Elderly People and Their Families*. London: Macmillan.

For an insight into the early feminist argument about the need to return to collective provision, see: Dalley, G. (1988) *Ideologies of Caring: Rethinking Community and Collectivism*. London: Macmillan.

More recent work that looks at the way carers are integrated (or not) into the welfare mix, is contained in Twigg, J. and Atkin, K. (1994) *Carers Perceived: Policy and Practice in Informal Care*. Buckingham: Open University Press, and the perspective on care developed by disabled people is outlined by Morris, J. (1993) *Independent Lives? Community Care and Disabled People*. London: Macmillan.

the organization of welfare

III.5

managing and delivering welfare

john clarke

This chapter looks at the changing systems of welfare delivery in Britain. It traces a shift from a system in which welfare was mainly organized around two principles: bureaucratic administration and professional intervention. These two principles dominated the provision of welfare by the state between the 1940s and 1980s. By the late 1990s, two distinctive changes were visible. The first, discussed in chapters III.1 to III.4, was a move away from service provision by the state to a more complex set of arrangements involving a greater role for other providers – particularly those in the voluntary and private sectors. The second was an associated shift to structuring welfare provision around managerial principles rather than bureaucracy or professionalism.

WELFARE AND BUREAUCRACY

Bureaucratic administration was central to the development of the welfare state. It was an organizational system that was 'rule bound' – that is, the delivery of welfare services was governed by sets of rules and regulations that could be applied to individual cases. Such a system allowed welfare organizations to deal with a large volume of cases or claims and ensure that they were dealt with in a predictable way. This was particularly significant for the administration of large-scale welfare services, such as income maintenance benefits (Cousins, 1987).

Although bureaucratic administration has been heavily attacked in recent years, its centrality to welfare systems was the result of a number of perceived organizational and social advantages. Organizationally, bureaucratic administration was a highly rationalized system, with the capacity to handle high volumes of demands for welfare benefits and services with efficiency. Its hierarchical structure was intended to ensure that each employee knew his or her task and could refer more complex issues or demands upwards to senior personnel. Accountability also flowed upwards to senior levels of the system and, ultimately, to politicians. Socially, bureaucracies promised impartiality and neutrality in the administration of social welfare. Cases would be dealt with according to the rules, rather than being subject to irrelevant social judgements (or moral desert or worth) or to the personal whims or enthusiasms of the individual dealing with the case. Given the earlier history of social welfare in Britain, this promise of impartial administration was of considerable social significance.

Bureaucratic administration was a widespread organizational principle. In addition to being central to the delivery of welfare services such as income maintenance benefits, it was also the organizational form that predominated in both central and local government in departments with specialized functions (health, education, housing, etc.), each with its administrative hierarchy responsible for the implementation of government policies, rules and regulations. Power in bureaucratic systems was attached to particular places in the hierarchy and was legitimated by reference to administrative policies and the competence needed to apply them.

WELFARE AND PROFESSIONALISM

Nevertheless, not all social welfare was delivered according to these principles. Particularly in areas where needs were seen as complex, the welfare state was also organized around the exercise of professional judgement. This was most obviously the case in relation to health, in which medical professionals and other groups of health workers used expert knowledge to identify symptoms and appropriate treatments. Medical knowledge and power were thus central to the organization of the post-war National Health Service in both hospital settings and general practice. Other areas of welfare provision also rested on professional expertise: education centred on teachers and lecturers; personal social services on social workers and so on. Such groups were both less powerful and more dependent on the state than the medical profession, leading to discussions about whether they were 'real' professions, semi-professions, quasi-professions or mediating professions. These different qualifying terms try to indicate the distinctive character of welfare professionalism in contrast to the model of the traditional or independent professions, such as medicine and the law.

Like bureaucracy, professionalism organizes power in a particular way. Professions stand in a relation of power to users of welfare services (who are dependent on the professional for treatment, access to resources or other forms of intervention).

This power is legitimated by reference to professionals' possession of expert knowledge (gained through training and a qualifying process) which enables them to make judgements that lay knowledge cannot. So we submit ourselves to professional intervention in the belief (or hope) that professionals know best. Professionalism also structures power within organizations, since it involves a demand for autonomy – the space in which professional judgement can be exercised without interference, such as the right for doctors to make clinical decisions, or teachers to control the curriculum (Cousins, 1987).

MANAGERIALISM AND THE CRISIS OF BUREAU-PROFESSIONALISM

Most state welfare organizations in the post-war period combined bureaucratic administration and welfare professionalism, although with different sorts of balances of power between the two axes. The NHS, for example, involved much higher levels of professional power and discretion than social work or teaching, which were more confined by bureaucratic frameworks. In general, though, the welfare state can be seen as having the organizational form of bureau-professionalism (Clarke et al., 1994).

By the 1980s, however, this system of organizing welfare was under attack along a number of different dimensions. One dimension involved a series of challenges to the 'neutrality' of bureau-professionalism. As chapters II.9, II.10 and IV.4 show, social movements taking shape around inequalities of gender, 'race', disability and sexuality challenged not just social policies but also the systems through which these policies were implemented. For example, women's groups challenged the (male) medical control of child birth; black groups challenged definitions of educational failure, the practices of discriminatory policing and the inappropriate judgements of social workers. Disabled people's movements organized to combat the 'disabling' effects of the medical model of disability and the processes of professional power that went with it.

A second dimension concerned the inability of bureau-professional systems to manage the growing demands for cost restraint in public spending from the mid–1970s. The accounting, budgetary and resource control capacity of these systems appeared to give little real management control over the costs of providing welfare and even seemed to be designed to encourage incremental growth in such costs. Administrators and professionals could always find some new activity or project that needed more resources. This was linked to a more systematic critique of bureau-professionalism in 'public choice theory'. This suggested that administrators and professionals had vested interests in maintaining and expanding their 'empires', rather than being disinterested public servants. In addition, the 'monopoly provider' status of state agencies meant that they were insulated from competitive pressures to become more efficient and more responsive to the demands of consumers. Public choice theory asserted the superiority of the market over the state as a mechanism for distributing goods and services.

This was closely associated with new right attacks on the welfare state and shaped many of the reforms of social welfare provision in the late 1980s and 1990s. In particular, it influenced reforms intended to introduce market-like relationships into social welfare (through competition, contracting and a focus on consumer rights). Such changes, it was argued, would simultaneously increase efficiency, create greater choice for service users and break up the old monopoly provider power bases of bureau-professional systems of welfare (Taylor-Gooby and Lawson, 1993; Clarke et al., 1994).

These changes were connected to the shift to managerial forms of organizing

welfare provision. The demand for 'new and better management' was seen as a way of making social welfare organizations more 'businesslike' – managers would carry the drive for greater efficiency and better resource control. They would make welfare organizations more customer-centred and would be a check on the 'empire building' self-interest of bureaucrats and professionals. Such arguments presented management as a set of techniques and technologies which were the best way of running any organization, whether in the private, public or voluntary sectors. However, this neglects issues about managerialism as an ideology and a form of social and organizational power (Pollitt, 1993). Managerialism involves a claim to organizational power that challenges the discretion of other groups (whether workers, professionals or bureaucrats) in the name of managers needing the 'freedom to manage'. The result was a series of complex power struggles *within* social welfare organizations for control of resources, decision-making and agenda setting power (Clarke and Newman, 1997).

CONTRACTS AND CUSTOMERS

The changing system of welfare provision was marked by the introduction of market mechanisms in a variety of forms. These are discussed more fully in part IV but the NHS was restructured around a split between purchasers and providers. District health authorities (DHAs) and fund-holding general practitioners (GPs) purchased health care on behalf of patients from competing providers (hospitals and other services). In community care, local authority social services departments assessed needs and purchased services to make up 'packages of care' from competing provider organizations based in the public, private and voluntary sectors (as well as 'primary carers' among family and friends).

In other welfare fields, slightly different varieties of market mechanisms were introduced. In education, for example, both schools and universities were invited to compete for 'customers' and for the resources that were attached to the number of customers they won. Different again was the requirement that local authorities and other organizations 'contracted out' the provision of ancillary and some professional services, inviting tenders from organizations to deliver these services.

Such changes were intended to promote a number of positive developments. The dominant one was the creation of 'efficiency gains', as competition between providers would tend to drive down the overall cost of services. Although evidence suggests that contracting in this way did drive down the costs of services, other costs created by the new systems need to be offset against such gains. There were 'transition costs', involved in establishing the new systems and 'transaction costs' of running and managing a more dispersed set of organizations: writing, tendering for and monitoring contracts, for example (see Walsh, 1995). Other costs were 'externalized' by subcontracting to cheaper sources of labour (in the private and voluntary sectors) or by requiring families to provide more 'free' caring work.

Second, the introduction of market-limiting relationships was intended to promote greater consumer choice in the use of services. The evidence on this front is also equivocal. The power of users to exercise choice was mediated in a number of ways. For example, in relation to schooling, parental choice over their child's schooling was constrained by the ability of schools to limit entry and exercise some degree of choice over the children they were willing to accept. In health care, patient choice was mediated by the purchasing decisions being made by GPs and DHAs – unless patients had the resources to buy into the expanding private sector. In social care, packages of care were put together by local authority 'care managers' rather than the direct user of services. The dominant trend was thus towards what might be called

'proxy customers' – agents acting on behalf of the user.

Finally, the introduction of market relations was intended to make welfare organizations more business-like. However, the operation of these markets was heavily constrained by central government limitations – about funding, policy and the range of activities that organizations could be 'in the business of'. Funding constraints played a particularly important role, in that organizations were as threatened by winning too much business as they were by winning too little. As a result, many welfare organizations found themselves preoccupied by managing demand rather than winning business, since new demand would be a drain on limited resources.

COMPETITION AND COOPERATION

Nevertheless, the changes did promote a more competitive set of relationships between organizations providing social welfare. Some of this took the form of enforced competition between public organizations within a field of social welfare (schools and universities within education; hospital trusts within health care and so on). But the changes also promoted greater competition across sectors – with expanded roles for private and voluntary sector providers competing for contracts, particularly in social care. The field of relationships between organizations thus became structured around competition and increasingly managed through contracts.

This pattern of competitive relationships involved different forms of competition. In some cases, it was direct competition for 'customers', especially for what might be called 'funded customers' – those who could be translated into funds provided by central government. In other settings, it was competition for contracts from purchasing agencies. Even where direct competition like this did not exist, central government introduced a competitive range of performance measurements with published results (school league tables, police efficiency, hospital mortality rates and so on). Such competitive evaluation was intended to drive up the overall standards of 'performance'.

The decentralization of resources and management discretion that accompanied these marketizing reforms created a series of problems about the 'boundaries' between different organizations and services. As each organization was encouraged to define its 'core business', so there was an increasing number of boundary disputes about who 'owned' needs and resources. One particular focus of such disputes was the separation between health and social care – particularly the long-term care needs of the elderly. Health organizations were increasingly concerned to define such needs as 'social care' matters (thus moving them from their budgets to those of social services), while social services were equally concerned to define them as 'health care' needs (see chapter IV.3). Inter-agency cooperation was, in many respects, increasingly problematic in a field of relationships dominated by competition, contracting and the 'ownership' of budgets and resources. And as the number of different organizations involved in providing welfare increased, so did the number of boundaries around which such disputes could take place.

KEEPING CONTROL: INSPECTION, REGULATION AND AUDIT

Given the greater complexity created by decentralization, competition and contracting, questions of how the new system of welfare provision is to be integrated and controlled have taken on greater importance. The old hierarchical systems of bureaucratic administration with their principles of instructions being passed downwards while reports and information flows back to the top are no longer appro-

priate. They have been replaced by a number of different forms of control.

The decentralization of managerial autonomy to individual organizations (and thus the responsibility for delivering welfare services) is tempered by a high level of centralization of power in central government. This power focuses most obviously on policy formation and resource control, particularly financial resources. Within such limits, organizations are (at least nominally) 'set free' to 'go about their business'. However, this mixture of centralization and decentralization has been supplemented by the development of an array of evaluative systems. These originally centred on issues of financial management – whether organizations could prove that they were being responsible in the management of public funds. The Audit Commission was created in 1983 to monitor the financial processes and controls of local authorities and the NHS, with the purpose of ensuring that they delivered the 'three Es': economy, efficiency and effectiveness. Subsequently, evaluation has expanded to a wider concern with organizational performance – assessing the effectiveness, quality and standards of welfare organization. In many areas, this has led inspectorates, the Audit Commission and other 'quangos' into the business of organizational design – advising or telling organizations how to manage themselves.

These issues of control are also reflected in the problems of subcontracting service provision at a local level. Contracting has proved to be a problematic process for both purchaser and provider organizations, particularly where what are being contracted for are complex service processes. Such services are difficult to specify adequately in contractual terms – particularly in relation to desired outcomes, rather than quantitative levels of provision. One response to this has been the expansion of monitoring and inspection functions to evaluate provider performance. A second has been to develop processes that enable service users (or customers) to complain about standards of provision. A third has been to look beyond simple contracting to building longer-term collaborative relationships which both imply and create 'trust' (Walsh, 1995). As Walsh has suggested, the contracting model implies the absence of trust and incurs increasing costs of contracting and evaluation. Contracting also produces problems about accountability in complex and 'arm's length' sets of relationships between central government, local government and sub-contracted agencies. It has also had impacts on 'provider organizations', especially in the voluntary sector, requiring them to become 'more businesslike' too, with consequences for both their internal management processes and their traditional roles of lobbying and advocacy.

DISPERSED WELFARE PROVISION AND MANAGERIALISM

What is difficult to know is what all this complex of changes in the delivery of welfare adds up to. This problem can be indicated by the diversity of terms used to describe these new forms. Have we arrived at a new *mixed economy of care*, characterized by a reduction in the state's role and the growth of other 'sectors'? Has welfare become *marketized* or even *quasi-marketized*? Do we now have an enabling state whose role is to set free individuals, families, communities and multiple providers to create social welfare? Is this a *contracting state* – both shrinking and resorting to contractual mechanisms to secure services for welfare users? Or is it an *evaluative state* developing new processes to scrutinize the performance of agencies and organizations involved in delivering welfare? This diversity of terms indicates the scale of the problem of defining the new welfare order. In my view, the new arrangements are best understood as a 'managerial state' (Clarke and Newman, 1997). Managerialism is central to both the ideology and the practice of the new arrangements. It provides the organizing principle that attempts to hold together the dispersal of power, responsibilities, resources and tasks between organizations. It promises that 'better management' will ensure efficient running, effective co-ordination, greater customer satisfaction and the delivery of more for less in the battle to control public spending on welfare in the face of rising public demand. However, its effect has been to shift the dilemmas and tensions of providing welfare into new forms and new settings rather than overcoming them.

GUIDE TO FURTHER READING

Butcher, T. (1995) *Delivering Welfare*. Buckingham: Open University Press, provides an account of the main features of the shift from old to new principles for organizing welfare services.

Clarke, J., Cochrane, A. and McLaughlin, E. (eds) (1994) *Managing Social Policy*. London: Sage, examines the impact of managerialism on the welfare state in general and its implications.

Clarke, J. and Newman, J. (1997) *The Managerial State*. London: Sage, extends some of the arguments of Clarke, Cochrane and McLaughlin in examining the role and consequences of managerialism in the restructuring of the British welfare state.

Cousins, C. (1987) *Controlling Welfare*. Hemel Hempstead: Harvester Wheatsheaf, provides a sociological analysis of the organizing principles of social welfare, focusing on bureaucracy and professions and their changing place in the welfare state.

Flynn, N. (1990) *Public Sector Management*. Hemel Hempstead: Harvester Wheatsheaf, is a lucid introduction to the conditions and problems of managing in the public sector.

Le Grand, J. and Bartlett, W. (eds) (1993) *Quasi-markets and Social Policy*. London: Macmillan, explores the theory and practice of market relations in social welfare.

Pollitt, C. (1993) *Managerialism and the Public Services*. Oxford: Blackwell, is a pioneering study of the application of managerial ideology and practice to the public sector in the USA and the UK.

Taylor-Gooby, P. and Lawson, R. (eds) (1993) *Markets and Managers*. Buckingham: Open University Press, is a collection which examines the restructuring of public services around both market relations and managerial principles.

Walsh, K. (1995) *Public Services and Market Mechanisms*. London: Macmillan, examines the impact of contracting on the organization and delivery of public services.

III.6

central–Local Relations

allan cochrane

As other chapters make clear, the state has never been the sole (or even most important) provider of welfare for most people. Some commentators have tried to capture the complexity of relations which characterise welfare provision in the UK by talking of mixed economies of care. Others use terms such as welfare regime. Although this chapter focuses on aspects of welfare which are directly associated with the state, it highlights the internally differentiated nature of that state. The British welfare state is not a homogeneous entity. This chapter explores the relationships between some of its different elements and is specifically concerned with the relationships between local and central government.

In recent years the British state seems to have been subject to a relentless process of centralization. Not only has local government faced a series of reorganizations imposed from above, but (following the poll tax debacle of the late 1980s) councils have found their capacity to raise tax income on their own account substantially reduced. As chapter III.9 notes, over 80 per cent of local authority income is now derived from central government grant of one sort or another. At the same time rules and regulations about how councils may operate have become tighter. A wide range of activities, previously handled in-house, now have to be put out to competitive tender. Any possibility of significant investment in new social housing has been removed, while council houses have been offered for sale to sitting tenants. A national curriculum has been introduced and schools have been given the right to opt out of local authority control. Social services departments are increasingly constrained by a plethora of guidelines and the requirement to work in partnership with other agencies, such as health authorities and the police, as well as voluntary sector and private providers.

All this, it seems, simply confirms the subsidiary position of local government within the British political system. Unlike many other European countries, there are no constitutional guarantees of autonomy for local authorities in Britain. In principle, all political power is delegated from above, usually through parliamentary legislation. So, it might be concluded, central–local relations don't really matter. Whatever the centre wants it can get. In practice, however, such a conclusion would be misleading. Central initiatives can rarely be imposed by edict from above, and local authorities continue to develop their own policy initiatives in unexpected ways. A focus on central–local relations makes it easier to understand the emergence of social policy as it is experienced, rather than the way it appears in White Papers, guidance notes or the policy statements of government departments.

DIVISIONS OF LABOUR

The British welfare state is divided along functional lines. Different central government departments have responsibilities for its different elements. Despite their changing names over time, and mergers and demergers between them, responsibility for social security, education and training, housing, urban policy, health, community care and children's services are shared between a number of departments (see Butcher, T., 1995, *Delivering Welfare. The Governance of the Social Services in the 1980s*. Buckingham: Open University Press, chapter. 2). Increasingly, too, a number of specialist (semi-autonomous) agencies have been allocated responsibility for specific aspects of provision. These currently include the National Health Service, the Benefits Agency and the Child Support Agency, as well as a range of regulatory agencies such as OFSTED (Office for Standards in Education), the Social Services Inspectorate and even the Audit Commission. Already, it will be apparent, therefore, that the relations between these bodies are likely to be important in influencing social policy outcomes. Questions are bound to arise about the extent to which they follow similar approaches to the tasks which they have been set. It is not always clear that they do. The resources which each is allocated may vary according to their success (or the success of the ministers who speak for them) in the internal battles over budgets. Even if the overall ethos of a government is one which stresses financial prudence (or the 'rolling back of the state' which was said to characterize the Thatcher governments of the 1980s), each agency and department is likely to find itself arguing that its own budget deserves to be protected.

The complexity of relations within the welfare state is reinforced when the functional divisions are in turn overlaid by divisions of responsibility according to spatial scale. Such divisions even have an expression within 'central' government. As chapter III.7 shows, the Northern Ireland Office, the Scottish Office and the Welsh Office operate in ways which cut across the other functional divisions – with some agencies and departments (such as the National Health Service) operating across the UK and others being incorporated within the territorially based departments.

These spatial divisions of labour, however, find their strongest expression in the allocation of responsibility for delivering (or ensuring the delivery of) many welfare services to local authorities of one sort or another. In principle it is relatively easy to identify which council is responsible for overseeing the delivery of which service. Each local government textbook has a chart showing who does what at the time of its publication, although there is always a danger that as soon as they have been pinned down the precise allocation will change again. Currently, Northern Ireland has its own quite distinctive arrangements, which allocate little responsibility to elected councils, but instead largely work through appointed boards. By contrast, Scotland and Wales have one principal layer of local government in the form of district councils, which have responsibility for most of the traditional functions of local government, including social services, housing, planning and education. In England matters are rather more complicated, with five distinct types of local government (in addition to parishes). There are metropolitan district councils in the big urban agglomerations (West Midlands, Greater Manchester, South and West Yorkshire, Merseyside, Tyne and Wear), while Greater London is divided into a series of London boroughs (such as Lambeth, Richmond upon Thames, Tower Hamlets and Westminster), and some urban areas in other parts of the country (including Milton Keynes, Luton and Southampton) are governed by unitary district councils. The creation of these councils followed a review of local government in England's counties outside the metropolitan areas in the early 1990s.

Only some councils in the counties were given unitary status, and the changes were introduced on a piecemeal and gradual basis. These unitary district councils have similar responsibilities to the districts in Scotland and Wales. Elsewhere, and outside these areas, county councils (such as Buckinghamshire, Derbyshire and North-amptonshire) share responsibility with district councils. These counties look after education and social services, while the districts within them are responsible for housing and development control. In England, the nature of your local government will depend on where you live.

Alongside elected local government there is also an extensive array of unelected local agencies which have responsibility for specific aspects of welfare provision (and are increasingly helping to define what is meant by welfare in the UK). So, for example, within the National Health Service local hospital trusts and health authorities, as well as GP fundholders, all have some role in determining what is available; in the field of education, further education colleges are now run as independent agencies, and the local management of schools has become more important, even for those which are not grant maintained; Training and Enterprise Councils and Local Enterprise Companies have been given the responsibility for managing the government's training budgets. *Ad hoc* agencies associated with specific government initiatives have also been important, whether in the form of urban development corporations or partnerships associated with a range of urban regeneration schemes (including City Challenge and the Single Regeneration Budget).

DUAL STATE OR UNITARY STATE?

There have been many attempts to explain the division of labour which has emerged between levels of government. One approach (e.g. Saunders, 1994) has suggested that there is a 'dual state'. This argument contrasts national and local politics and identifies functional divisions between different levels of the state. The national level is said to be mainly concerned with issues relating to production and the economy, with any bargaining taking place between major interests, such as the representatives of capital and labour. By contrast, it is argued, the local state concerns itself principally with issues of social consumption (that is, largely welfare issues), and is more open, more pluralist and less corporatist than the national state. Because the local state is not responsible for the issues which are of central concern to business (and which are dealt with at national level), there is said to be space for initiative which can be utilized by locally based groups. The approach implies that at national level structural factors effectively determine political decision-making, while at local level diverse political interest groups have a more or less direct influence on policy-making, through a sort of 'imperfect pluralism'.

The dual state thesis helpfully highlights some of the divisions which exist, and identifies some of the roots of conflict between central and local government. The central state is responsible for the overall management of public spending, but decisions on the levels and nature of that spending are often made at local level. The tensions between central and local government can be seen as part of a battle for control over state expenditure. They can also be seen as a continuing battle over political direction, since the greater openness of local government may sometimes allow councils directly to challenge unpopular governments over key issues of their policy. In the mid-1980s councils such as the Greater London Council saw themselves as developing high-profile alternatives to the policies of the Thatcher government, which had a very strong national agenda of its own. Not surprisingly, perhaps, one consequence of the local challenge was that the Greater London Council and the other metropolitan county councils were simply abolished in 1986.

Although it is useful in highlighting some of the pressures and tensions, however, the dual state thesis cannot be used as a universal template. It takes aspects of the existing division of labour for granted and assumes that there is some functional reason for them. Unfortunately, the actual division of labour is rather more complex than the theory seems to allow (e.g. Dunleavy, 1994). Some key aspects of social consumption, such as the National Health Service, have been handled through national agencies through most of the period since 1945, while others (such as education) have been handled quite differently in other European countries (for example, as a regional responsibility in Germany and a national responsibility in France). Other key aspects of welfare are barely considered by dual state theorists because they fit uneasily with the argument. So, for example, over the past fifty years, the prime responsibility for income maintenance through social security payments has been handled through a national system, although before that the operation of the poor law was a local responsibility.

The importance of the politics of production at local level also fits uneasily with the model. The reshaping of Britain's main urban centres in the 1950s and 1960s (with new road networks, city centre redevelopment and the building of industrial estates) was in large part the product of local rather than central government initiative. The increased profile of local economic development on the local government agenda since the early 1980s has been widely noted, and has been accompanied by the emergence of new corporate style public–private partnerships and agencies such as Training and Enterprise Councils and Local Enterprise Companies at local level. In other words, any belief that there is some straightforward structural basis for the division of labour between central and local government is mistaken.

NETWORKS AND RELATIONS

It is increasingly apparent that what are rather misleadingly called central–local relations are instead characterized by complex cross-cutting networks, which help to constitute the welfare state as a set of relationships rather than a unitary and undifferentiated entity, in what Bob Jessop (*State Theory. Putting Capitalist States in Their Place.* Cambridge: Polity, 1990) calls an 'institutional ensemble'. One problem with the assumptions underpinning popular conceptions of central–local relations is (as Rhodes, 1988, argues) that there is no single 'central' government, at least in the sense that some agency at the centre can pull a decision-making lever and expect its ambitions to be realized throughout the system. Central government is, as suggested above, itself divided on functional lines. And within the different departments there are likely to be further divisions (in the case of the Department of Health, for example, between those concerned principally with the health service and those concerned with the personal social services, as well as between those concerned with community care and those concerned with children's services). Each of these 'multiple centres' will be part of its own 'policy network' which brings together those working in the field: politicians, professionals and civil servants, those operating in unelected agencies, as well as those working for local government. There is, Rhodes suggests, little coordination between these policy networks, even if there is coordination within them.

This makes the imagery of central control difficult to sustain, despite the emergence of the array of new controls discussed in chapter III.5. Policy networks are service based and cut across hierarchies (being represented at different levels of government) within what Rhodes calls a 'differentiated polity'. Each side of the network is dependent on the other: at local level officers are dependent for finance from the centre, and at national level civil servants (and ministers) are dependent on local officers for implementation. In the case of community care following the National Health Service and Community Care Act 1990, for example, the implementation of the policy has been highly dependent on local initiative, as social services departments have attempted to redefine their roles within the new context (see Wistow et al., 1994).

At central level, departments (or parts of departments) may also act as representatives of those they manage. So, for example, the government may be arguing strongly for reductions in spending as part of an overall economic programme, while at the same time, civil servants within the Department for Education and Employment, or the Department of Health, are arguing with their counterparts at local level for increased spending on particular schemes. In England, the Department of the Environment is in a particularly uncertain position. In arguments with the Treasury, it is likely to support more spending in the areas for which it is responsible through local government, yet in its relations with local government it acts as the policer of budgets – indeed, it effectively plays the Treasury role. And matters are made still more complex because, even in this context of departmental pressure for retrenchment, some parts of the department – those responsible for housing, planning and other spending areas – may also be encouraging increased spending.

If one important aspect of this is the acknowledgement that the centre cannot be seen as a homogeneous category, a second is that the same applies to local government. At one level that may not be very surprising – after all, one of the claims made by the defenders of local government is precisely that there may be significant variation in the policies adopted by different councils. And, of course, the emergence of more locally based agencies might also be expected to encourage policy variation between places. Perhaps what is more surprising – given the variation one might

expect – is how similar councils are in the ways in which they operate. The point being made here, therefore, is not so much that there is variation between places, but rather that there are significant divisions between professional and other groups *within* local authorities. These reflect the extent to which those groups and the institutional arrangements which follow from them fit into wider national (and sometimes even international) networks.

CONCLUSION

One of the tensions within central–local relations in Britain is that those at the 'centre' often appear to believe that they can direct a system which is highly differentiated and is characterized by extensive negotiation through networks of professional and bureaucratic politics. But this tension is exacerbated by the way in which apparently functional divisions of labour are mapped on to democratic structures, which have a clear territorial dimension. Although many local political institutions are now run by unelected boards, it is the existence of elected local government which gives councillors and officers their own locally based political legitimacy. The local welfare state is not just the product of devolved administrative responsibility from the centre. On the contrary, it has emerged from a historical process of claim and counter-claim, of continuing contestation. The particular division of labour between different levels of government in the UK reflects the ways in which the welfare state has developed since the middle of the nineteenth century. Most of the activities which we currently understand as constituting the welfare state began as locally based initiatives. The poor law was operated by local boards, as was education. Public health provision emerged from local networks linking state, charities and private interests. Through the first half of the twentieth century, local governments took the initiative in developing welfare services across the board, from housing to education, health to children's services.

Only after 1945 was it taken for granted that some activities and services would best be handled at national level. But the nationalization of some activities was accompanied by a massive expansion of others, as local budgets increased and a local welfare state emerged with responsibilities for a massively expanded programme of social housing, a growing personal social services sector and a major commitment to state education. The incorporation of this local welfare state into the existing democratic structures of local government has helped to guarantee a continuing process of conflict as attempts have been made to control and restructure the welfare state since the mid-1970s. But the survival of local forms of political legitimacy has been an important element in ensuring that conflicts between central and local government are not always resolved in favour of the centre, even if the presumption is that they often will be.

This helps to explain some of the difficulties which central government has had in reducing spending dramatically, or savagely cutting back the state. Certainly there have been cuts and pressures to cut back further, but the scale of it has been less significant than the political rhetoric has suggested. The dramatic failure to impose a new system of local taxation in the form of the community charge or poll tax at the end of the 1980s (which brought in its wake a change of Prime Minister, if not of government) is only the highest profile example of the difficulties involved. Even where the overall direction of change can be identified with some confidence, the differentiated nature of the welfare state, with its overlapping policy networks cutting across levels of responsibility, means that the outcomes of specific policy initiatives are likely to be unpredictable.

GUIDE TO FURTHER READING

This chapter has concentrated largely on debates around the issue of central–local relations. It has not looked specifically at the operation of local government. There are several books which provide useful introductions to the local government system in the UK, although most of them in practice principally draw on examples from England. These include Byrne, T. (1992) *Local Government in Britain*. Harmondsworth: Penguin, which is regularly updated. Wilson, D. and Game, C. (1994) *Local Government in the United Kingdom*. London: Macmillan, is very comprehensive and makes rather more of an attempt to cover arrangements outside England, although some of the structures outlined have now been overtaken by events.

The most comprehensive discussion of central–local relations in Britain remains Rhodes, R. A. W. (1988) *Beyond Westminster and Whitehall: Sub-central Governments of Britain*. London: Unwin Hyman. In this book Rhodes focuses on the decentralized structures of central departments, the nationalized industries and *ad hoc* bodies or quangos as well as elected local governments, arguing that answering the question 'who gets what public services when and how?' requires an analysis of sub-central governments as the deliverers of services as well as the complexity of relationships between them and with the central institutions of the state. The dual state thesis is well summarized in two chapters in Boddy, M. and Fudge, C. (eds) (1994) *Local Socialism? Labour Councils and New Left Alternatives*. London: Macmillan. The first of these chapters is by P. Saunders, and is entitled 'Rethinking local politics', and the second is by P. Dunleavy and entitled 'The limits to local government'.

Cochrane, A. (1993) *Whatever Happened to Local Government?* Buckingham: Open University Press, reviews the recent experience of local government, showing how it has changed and been restructured within a wider state system over the past thirty or forty years. It sets out to explore the wider systems of local politics, extending beyond elected local government into the emerging networks of unelected local governance. The future of local government continues to be a subject of much debate. Contributions which are worth following up include: Davis, H. et al. (1996) *Enabling or Disabling Local Government.* Buckingham: Open University Press, and Burns, D., Hambleton, R. and Hoggett, P. (1994) *The Politics of Decentralisation. Revitalising Local Democracy.* London: Macmillan. Butler, D., Adonis, A. and Travers, T. (1995) analyse the politics underlying the introduction of the poll tax in *Failure in British Government: the Politics of the Poll Tax.* Oxford: Oxford University Press. It makes a good story.

There often seems to be a division between discussions of local government and its reorganization and debates about the reshaping of Britain's welfare state. Two books by G. Wistow and his colleagues which look at the impact of legislative change on social care at local level help to bridge this gap. These are Wistow, G., Knapp, M., Hardy, B. and Allen, C. (1994) *Social Care in a Mixed Economy.* Buckingham: Open University Press, and Wistow, G., Knapp, M., Hardy, B., Forder, J., Kendall, J. and Manning, R. (1996) *Social Care Markets. Progress and Prospects.* Buckingham: Open University Press. They explore the emergence of what might be called local mixed economies of care in the context of nationally driven restructuring.

III.7

SOCIAL POLICY WITHIN THE UNITED KINGDOM

RICHARD PARRY

The United Kingdom is a strongly unitary state and lacks a clear concept of regional differences in social policy in terms of formation, implementation and content. The main source of difference is the status of Scotland, Wales and Northern Ireland within the United Kingdom, enjoying nationhood but not statehood. As the British political system becomes more interested in European-level policy it risks neglecting these differences and failing to learn from experiences of policy-making they embody.

This chapter seeks to provide a guide to the range and type of country-specific social policy legislation in England, Scotland, Wales and Northern Ireland; the powers and responsibilities of the separate social policy agencies in the latter three nations and the English regions; and the major policy initiatives at sub-national level. It concludes by asking whether anyone cares, or should care, about the differences that are revealed.

THE PROBLEM OF ENGLISH DOMINANCE

The starting point is the dominance of England in the United Kingdom. It accounts for nearly 85 per cent of the population and London, its capital, is the centre of political, governmental, cultural and media activity. This dominance, so taken for granted in Britain, is not inevit-able. Many countries, most notably Germany, have a spread of regional centres. In the United States the levels of unemployment and health benefits vary among the states. In Germany all of education is run at the *Land* level and social care services vary according to municipality. Italy, Spain and to some extent France have been developing regional government in recent years. There is a general uniformity of social security benefits in these countries, but the systems have a less concentrated administration than does Britain's. Only Britain carries through the concept of uniformity and standardization so far (for example, there are no official figures on inflation at below the United Kingdom level, partly to avoid debates about differential upratings of benefit). Britain has a lesser sense of federal political structure, in which policies may be pursued at the sub-national level, than any country of comparable size.

There is, though, a counterbalance to the dominance of England in the separate historical tradition and political profile of Scotland, Wales and Northern Ireland. Scotland was independent until 1707 and the Act of Union preserved its legal system, Presbyterian Church and local government. It had stronger traditions in education and medicine than did England, and became a United Kingdom leader in these fields. Wales was never a defined independent state but its linguistic and religious pattern was clearly different. Ireland had a separate

Table III.7.1 Who runs United Kingdom social policy

Health	Scottish Office Department of Health NHS Management Executive for Scotland 15 Health boards 47 NHS trusts	Welsh Office Health Department 5 Health authorities 29 NHS trusts	Department of Health and Social Services (NI) 4 Health and Social Services Boards 15 Health and Social Services trusts	Department of Health NHS Executive and 8 regional offices 90 Health authorities 433 NHS trusts
Education	Scottish Office Education and Industry Department (grants to further education colleges) 32 local authorities Scottish Higher Education Funding Council 2 grant-maintained schools	Welsh Office Education Department 22 local authorities Further Education Funding Council for Wales Higher Education Funding Council for Wales 16 grant-maintained schools	Department of Education for Northern Ireland (grants to higher and further education) 5 Education and Library Boards	Department for Education and Employment Local authorities Higher Education Funding Council for England Further Education Funding Council 1032 grant-maintained schools
Housing	Scottish Homes 32 local authorities Housing associations	Housing for Wales (Tai Cymru) 22 local authorities Housing associations	Northern Ireland Housing Executive Housing associations	Local authorities Housing Corporation Housing associations
Training	Scottish Enterprise, Highlands and Islands Enterprise 22 local enterprise companies	7 Training and Enterprise Councils	Training and Employment Agency (NI)	74 Training and Enterprise Councils

Source: compiled mainly from *Departmental Reports* (1996) London: HMSO (Cm 3210–3216).

Parliament until 1801, then united with Great Britain but split in 1922 into an independent country (later the Republic of Ireland) and the six counties of Northern Ireland, which remained in the United Kingdom but were given a local Parliament. This was suspended in 1972 but the attempts to resuscitate it in some form in 1973, 1982 and 1996 express the determination of the British political system to treat Northern Ireland separately. In a host of cultural and social forms, the patriotic identity of the non-English nations is asserted and cherished.

Where does this leave social policy? The main issues are money and politics rather than need or the nature of services. Most social policies involve the transfer of cash or the provision of human services like health or education. If separate systems at sub-national level are less good than the norm they will not be politically attractive, but if they are better and more expensive national governments may not be happy to finance them. Politically, the need for separate political management of Scotland, Wales and Northern Ireland is widely, if sometimes grudgingly, conceded, but Conservatives especially have wished to promote uniform policies. Therefore, there is a tension in United Kingdom social policy between tolerating and resisting differences.

Nation-specific Social Policy Legislation

The legislative framework for social policy is generally the same for social security throughout the United Kingdom (Northern Ireland has different original legislation but has had strict parity of structure and rates). Education and housing legislation is largely the same in England and Wales but different in Scotland and Northern Ireland (especially in the structure of school examinations in Scotland and denominational education in Northern Ireland). These latter two nations also had a distinct tradition in health, but Scotland especially has converged with the English norm. While Scotland had a separate Act in 1946 to found the National Health Service (actually passed before the English one), it was included in the National Health Service and Community Care Act 1991 which launched the 'new NHS' and has embraced NHS trusts and GP fundholding, though at a somewhat reluctant and slower pace.

In explaining this pattern, we need to distinguish the protocol of legislating separately for the four nations from the substance of policy difference. There has been resistance to bolting on Scottish sections to English Bills, because they will lack proper consideration through the separate parliamentary channels (the Scottish Grand Committee, consisting of all its MPs, and the Select Committee on Scottish Affairs). There are similar committees for Wales but here the main social legislation tends to be incorporated with that of England. Whatever the legislative mechanism, a Conservative government strongly committed to a unitary United Kingdom has found it difficult to justify distinctive policies that stem from a different approach to the issue rather than the circumstances of the nation. What we end up with are similar policies (on, for instance, GP fundholding, assisted places in schools, the financing of housing associations and the organization of training) with different administrative rules that tend to be more cautious than the English norm and steer more closely to the previous socialized pattern.

The Role of the Territorial Departments

The administration of social policy in the four nations of the United Kingdom is summarized in table III.7.1. Outside England, the systems tend to be similar but miniaturized, with boards and authorities covering smaller populations. An essential role is played by the Scottish, Welsh and

Northern Ireland Offices not just as a mechanism for administration but as a repository of symbolic identity in the nations. Ministers in the territorial departments run a network of consultation and implementation that runs on different channels to the Whitehall-centred ones and impresses upon them the distinctiveness of their nations (even on Conservative Secretaries of State for Wales, five out of six of whom have sat for English constituencies). Many services are run through appointed bodies which draw on small pools of competent and politically acceptable people (in Wales, for instance, the Secretary of State makes 366 appointments to heath bodies alone).

The offices are very different in history and character. The Scottish Office is venerable (1885), patriotic (nearly exclusively Scottish in birth and education among ministers and senior officials) and federal in character, being divided into five departments (reorganized in 1995): Agriculture, Environment and Fisheries; Development; Education and Industry; Health; and Home. The Office administers very little itself (notably prisons and student grants) and is essentially a lobbyist for Scottish interests within the Cabinet system and a mover of money (to local authorities, health boards and housing agencies and in the form of industrial and agricultural subsidies). During the 1980s it and its ministers were associated with a sense of resistance to 'Thatcherite' social legislation and some health and education changes were delayed. There are, for example only two grant-maintained schools in Scotland; GP fundholding is less advanced (covering a quarter of patients rather than the half in England and Wales); and school testing is less mandatory. Michael Forsyth, Secretary of State from 1995, is more right wing and politically adroit than his predecessors, and has avoided controversy in social policy while carrying forward choice-based ideas like nursery vouchers.

The Welsh Office is much younger, dating only from 1964, since when it has acquired health, education, social services and housing, but within a policy framework little different from that in England. Wales's small scale allows close monitoring of policy and implementation, especially in health. Just as in Scotland, Secretaries of State have been charged with the political management of a nation long unsympathetic to the Conservatives. Peter Walker, Secretary of State from 1987 to 1990, was notable as a political heavyweight with a taste for intervention. A later incumbent, John Redwood (1993–5), was aggressively Anglocentric and free market; after his unsuccessful challenge to John Major's leadership the post was used for the second time (after David Hunt) as an entry route into the Cabinet for an up-and-coming politician, the Yorkshireman William Hague.

Northern Ireland's social policy still reflects the legacy of the devolved government which operated from Stormont between 1921 and 1972. The Northern Ireland Civil Service is separate, and there are Departments of Economic Development (which runs training), Education, Environment, and Health and Social Services supervised by junior ministers of the Northern Ireland Office. The Stormont government maintained religiously discriminatory features in education and housing while seeking parity with mainland standards in health and social security. Later policies have emphasized equal opportunities (with explicit legislation against religious discrimination) and left a relatively benign and well resourced climate for social policy, with minimal direct political input. The economic and security context of policy has left politicians disinclined to attack the welfare state. School education retains selectivity on academic grounds in a way not found in the rest of the United Kingdom.

Local government in the three nations is much more neatly organized than it is in England (see chapter III.6), reflecting the strength of the territorial departments in moulding the systems. In 1996, local government in Scotland and Wales was reorganized from two-tier (regions or counties and districts) to single-tier (32 and 22 authorities). Northern Ireland has had 26 districts since 1973 but with all important social functions administered by appointed bodies (Education and Libraries Boards, Health and Social Services Boards (uniquely in the United Kingdom uniting health and social work) and the Northern Ireland Housing Executive). England, by contrast, has an evolving patchwork quilt of two-tier county and districts in most areas, broken up by most-purpose metropolitan boroughs and single-tier unitary authorities in major urban centres (from 1997) and former counties judged not to have built a strong local identity. Management of local expenditure outside England is easier because of the smaller number of local authorities, their closer relations to central government departments and the higher level of central financial support.

TERRITORIAL ORGANIZATION OF SOCIAL POLICY IN ENGLAND

It is impossible to run the social policies of 50 million people from a central department, but government in England sometimes gives a good impression of trying. Social security is run by civil service agencies (the largest of which is the 67,000 staff Benefits Agency) on an all-Britain basis; Northern Ireland has a separate Social Security Agency. Local offices are linked to a computer network and have lost most discretion on benefit levels; major benefits like pensions are run Britain-wide from centralized offices. The corporate identity of the agencies is reinforcing their national 'branding', like the retail stores and banks their style and culture is seeking to emulate.

The regional tier of government in England is weak, but the central government outposts have been consolidated into 'Government Offices for the Regions' (responsible for industry, employment, training, transport and the environment), which have a potentially higher profile and advocacy role. Health, in contrast, has been deregionalized. In 1996 the former regional health authorities were merged into the former NHS Management Executive to form the NHS Executive, based in Leeds and whose staff are civil servants, with eight regional offices. This model is being followed in the Funding Agency for Schools, which channels funds to the 1000 grant-maintained schools. Higher and further education have separate England-wide funding bodies. Outside the formal public sector altogether are Training and Enterprise Councils and housing associations, again with long lines of control.

Pressures for elected regional government in England are weak, with even the Labour Party highly cautious in comparison with its enthusiasm for Scottish and Welsh devolution. Instead, we have a pattern of smaller than ever operating entities on the ground tied by long lines of control to Whitehall. The system generally works, but the temptation is to interpose control centres (like the NHS Executive offices) which serve as emissaries of the centre rather than any kind of local democratic representative. This is an expression of the Conservative conviction that once the right answer is found (like community care, market-testing and self-government of schools) it is the right answer for everywhere and is not to be denied by the intervention of local politicians. In Scotland, Wales and Northern Ireland the national institutions provide a pause for adaptation; in England there is no such provision.

NEEDS AND RESOURCES AT SUB-NATIONAL LEVEL

The United Kingdom's social policy has been underwritten by an implicit north-west to south-east gradient – that Scotland, Wales, Northern Ireland and Northern England were relatively deprived and so could claim additional resources to deal with their problems. The spending relativities remain (table III.7.2) but the justification for them is less certain since the

Richard Parry

Table III.7.2 Spending per head on social policy 1993–4 (index, UK = 100)

	Total social	Social security	Health and personal social services	Education	Housing
Northern Ireland	117	110	111	138	164
Scotland	115	104	122	129	143
Wales	112	115	110	99	151
North West	108	114	99	100	117
North	106	116	98	95	72
South East	101	100	101	98	122
Yorkshire & Humberside	99	102	97	97	78
West Midlands	96	100	90	95	68
South West	93	99	92	87	34
East Midlands	91	94	89	94	60
East Anglia	89	93	88	88	43
UK ave (£)	2886	1473	740	585	88

Note: the 12 per cent of social spending in England which cannot be allocated between regions has been apportioned in the same ratio as that which can.

Source: calculated from HM Treasury, *Public Expenditure Statistical Analysis 1996–97*. London: HMSO (Cm 3201, 1996) tables 7.5 and 7.9.

recession of the early 1990s, which undermined the prosperity of the Midlands and South of England.

On relative need, in the 1960s Scotland, Wales and Northern Ireland had weaknesses on unemployment and wealth; since then unemployment rates in Britain have converged, and Scotland has nearly caught up with England in personal incomes per head (Wales and Northern Ireland remain over 10 per cent behind). On some measures, there are points of weakness: large parts of Scotland and Wales qualify for help from European Union Structural Funds because of the decline in smokestack industries like coal and steel, urban multiple deprivation or rural deprivation. The

Highlands and Islands, and Merseyside in England, have recently joined Northern Ireland in qualifying for 'Objective 1' status because of their low income per head. But because house prices are lower and public sector health and education better serviced, the non-English nations may feel better off and rank high in subjective quality-of-life indices.

This provides the backdrop to the position on relative public spending (table III.7.2). Data are not complete but they reveal that Northern Ireland, Scotland and Wales (in that order) receive more social expenditure per head than does any region of England: 17, 15 and 12 per cent more than the average. Social security does not have different policies. Public housing expenditure is now so small (3 per cent of the total in table III.7.2) that the wide variations, attributable to different tenure structures, are no longer of great significance; one-third of Scottish dwellings are still owned by local authorities, twice the level in England and Wales, but general rent subsidies have been nearly eliminated in recent years. More important is the advantage in health and education, especially in Scotland, which is more structural in nature and does raise issues for expenditure management. A Needs Assessment Study in 1979 confirmed that provision to Scotland ran ahead of need, and it has been the subject of defensive action by the Scottish Office over the years (the Welsh Office has less of an advantage but tends to make common cause with the Scots). For long, statistics of regional English differences were unavailable, but they now show a range from 89 to 108 per cent of the United Kingdom average, with the North and North West gaining in social security but not other services and the South East doing relatively well.

What has changed is that the differentials are beginning to look less and less acceptable to the Treasury. In 1992 it forced a change in the formula used for apportioning expenditure to the territories: put simply, this changes in relation to changes in corresponding English expenditure and is made available as a block to the Secretaries of State. This avoids constant haggling over items and is meant to converge expenditure over time. In practice the differentials are not moving much and they are no longer underwritten by palpable economic disadvantage.

FLEXIBLE INITIATIVES AT SUB-NATIONAL LEVEL

The justification for devolution is that it allows for flexibility and experimentation. Certainly the centralization of policy change, with its massive reorganizations (health, education, local government structure and finance) proceeding in one step throughout the country, risks a centralization of error.

We must distinguish distinctiveness where the policy is different from that where the administrative machine works better. The former happens rarely and steadily less frequently. In 1968 the Scottish system of children's hearings (non-judicial disposals of the cases of children in trouble) was implemented through the definition of a policy area as social work rather than law and order. Scottish school examinations remain quite different, with broadly based highers rather than more specialized A levels. From 1998 the 'higher still' proposals will integrate post-16 academic and vocational qualifications. The Welsh language is promoted in Welsh schools more than ever before, even in nearly exclusively English-speaking areas. These sorts of differences might be seen as barriers to mobility in the internal labour market but they have resisted Conservative thoughts of uniformity.

On the administrative side, much depends on the scale of the problems and the personal interest of ministers and officials. An often-cited example is the All-Wales Strategy for Mental Handicap (1983), which pioneered de-institutionalization; it was facilitated by the Welsh Office's ability to, in effect, run the health service. It stands in contrast to the more cautious approach to community care in Scotland, which has some very distinct and largely self-contained administrative and professional complexes in education, medicine and justice. The speed and nature of response to drug addictions and AIDS in Scotland has been facilitated by local responsibility. Housing has strong national bodies (Scottish Homes and Tai Cymru) able to mobilize housing associations. Industrial development and training has had a much stronger and better resourced administrative impetus in the territories than in

England. The flexibility of policy in the territories should not be exaggerated, but the existence of their administrative apparatus is a clear advantage when compared to the English regions.

Conclusion: the Stability and Acceptability of Variations

The United Kingdom's social policy is a top-down system with a few variations added on, but seldom the subject of political debate. Social policy specialists, committed to a notion of general upward harmonization of provision, have avoided the political dimension, which has involved relatively kind treatment of Scotland, Wales and Northern Ireland. Party consensus on this approach is weakening. Conservatives are increasingly strongly inclined towards a notion of an all-in United Kingdom with common patterns of provision except where circumstances are objectively different. Labour proposes a democratic underwriting of differences through a Scottish Parliament, a Welsh Assembly and perhaps, down the line, English regional assemblies. Either way, the issues look set to move up the political agenda.

Guide to Further Reading

Good textbooks on this topic are scarce. A pioneering study was Williamson, A. and Room, G. (eds) (1983) *Health and Welfare States of Britain*. London: Heinemann, which has the right focus but is now out of date. English, J. (ed.) (1988) *Social Services in Scotland*. Edinburgh: Scottish Academic Press, is more recent and has a lot of information. Hunter, D. and Wistow, G. (1987) *Community Care in Britain: Variations on a Theme*. London: King Edward's Hospital Fund, shows how policy can develop in different ways within a policy framework. Journals like the quarterly *Scottish Affairs* and the annual *Contemporary Wales* are very useful. The annual Departmental Reports of the Scottish, Welsh and Northern Ireland Offices are good sources of statistics and policy detail. Wilson, D. and Game, C. (1994) *Local Government in the United Kingdom*. London: Macmillan, is a very useful handbook which takes account of the variations in Scotland, Wales and Northern Ireland, and Midwinter, A. (1995) *Local Government in Scotland*. London: Macmillan, assesses the reorganized system. Tindale, S. (ed.) (1996) *The State and the Nations: the Politics of Devolution*. London: Institute for Public Policy Research, sets up a debate that may well become crucial.

III.8

eUROPeaN aND sUPRaNatIONaL DIMeNsIONs

LINDa HaNtRaIS

Britain was not one of the six founding member states of the European Economic Community (EEC) when it was established in 1957 with the signing of the Treaty of Rome. Following accession in 1973, the United Kingdom opposed Community action in the social policy area and was the only member state not to sign the 1989 Community Charter of the Fundamental Social Rights of Workers. Its opposition led to the chapter on social affairs being relegated to a Protocol and Agreement on Social Policy, which were appended to the Maastricht Treaty on European Union when it came into force in 1993. The UK has also sought to impede the progress of legislation on workers' rights, including proposals for improving part-time working conditions and introducing parental leave, on the grounds that they would impinge on national sovereignty and adversely affect employment.

This chapter looks at the way in which the social policy remit of the European Union has emerged and developed both prior to and since British membership. The European social policy formation and implementation processes are examined in an overview of the main policy-making bodies, the instruments available to them and the areas of intervention in which they have been most active. The chapter goes on to identify some of the key debates surrounding the European social dimension, before commenting briefly on the linkages between European and other supranational agencies engaged in social policy formation (see also chapter II.15).

THE DEVELOPMENT OF THE UNION'S SOCIAL POLICY REMIT

Although, as its name implied, the EEC was essentially an economic community, from the outset it was attributed a social policy remit. Articles 117–128 of the Treaty of Rome, which dealt with social policy, advocated close cooperation between member states, particularly in matters relating to training, employment, working conditions, social security and collective bargaining. They also stated the need to observe the equal pay principle and make provision for the harmonization of social security measures to accommodate migrant workers. Specific arrangements were to be made for operating a European Social Fund (ESF) to assist in the employment and re-employment of workers and to encourage geographical and occupational mobility.

In the post-war context of rapid economic growth, the underlying objectives of European social policy were to avoid any distortion of competition and to promote free movement of labour within the Community. Since the welfare systems of the founder member states (Belgium, France, the Federal Republic of Germany, Italy, Luxembourg and the Netherlands) were based largely on the insurance principle, which depended on contributions from employers and employees, it was feared that unfair competition might arise if some countries levied higher social charges on employment, leading to social dumping as companies relocated to areas with lower labour costs. The expectation was that the functioning of the common market, in conjunction with the Treaty's rules preventing unfair competition, would automatically result in social development, so that the Community would not need to interfere directly with redistributive benefits. By the mid-1970s, economic growth was slowing down following the oil crises, and the belief in automatic social harmonization was being called into question. A more active approach to social reform was therefore required. A 1974 resolution from the Council of Ministers on a social action programme proposed that the Community should work to develop objectives for national social policies but without seeking to standardize solutions to social problems and without removing responsibility for social policy from member states.

Despite attempts to give a higher profile to social policy in the 1980s, the principle established in the social action programme set the tone for social legislation in subsequent years. The 1980s were marked by pressures to develop a 'social space', which the Commission President, Jacques Delors, saw as the natural complement to the completion of the internal market. Delors advocated a social dialogue between trade unions and employers (the social partners) as a means of reaching agreement over objectives and establishing a minimum platform of guaranteed social (implying workers' employment related) rights, which could then be applied by individual member states with a view to stimulating convergence.

The problem of agreeing even a minimum level of protection for workers was apparent in the negotiations leading up to the Community Charter of the Fundamental Social Rights of Workers, which did not have force of law and was couched in non-specific terms. The action programmes for implementing the Charter continued to recognize the importance of observing national diversity, and the Maastricht Treaty formalized the principle of subsidiarity, which means that the Union is empowered to act only if its aims can be more effectively achieved at European than at national level. Since decisions about social policy frequently concern individuals or families, it can be argued that they are best taken at a local level remote from European institutions. Accordingly, opportunities for concerted action among nations are minimal.

Membership of the European Union (EU) has taken place in four successive waves, each making harmonization, or even convergence, of social policy provisions more difficult to achieve. As mentioned above, the social protection systems of the six original EEC member states can be considered as variants of what has come to be known as the Bismarckian or continental model of welfare, based on the employment-insurance principle. The new members (the United Kingdom, Denmark and Ireland), which joined the Community in the 1970s, subscribed to social protection systems funded from taxation and aimed at universal flat-rate coverage. The southern member states (Greece, Portugal and Spain), which joined in the early 1980s, had less developed welfare systems, whereas the Nordic states (Finland and Sweden), which took up membership in 1995, shared features with Denmark, and Austria was closer to the German pattern. While the goal of harmonizing social protection would seem to have become more pressing with the move towards the Single European Market (SEM) and economic and monetary union, doubts have increasingly been expressed about the feasibility and desirability of attempts at European level to harmonize such different welfare systems. There is, however, evidence to suggest that some convergence may be occurring as a result of the common trend towards retrenchment of welfare, made necessary by economic recession, and the shift towards mixed systems of welfare.

SOCIAL POLICY-MAKING PROCESSES IN THE EU

Despite the relatively limited social policy remit of the European Union, after fifty years of operation, the European Union has developed what can be described as a multi-tiered system of governance (Leibfried and Pierson, 1995). The decision-making, legislative and implementation procedures of the Union depend upon a number of institutions, with their own functions and operating mechanisms, but often in competition with one another.

The Council of Europe is the main governing body representing national interests and responsible for taking decisions on laws to be applied throughout the Union. All the heads of government meet twice a year to determine policy directions. The UK, like France, Germany and Italy, has a block of ten votes. The presidency of the Council rotates between member states every six months, providing the opportunity for national governments to set the policy agenda. The Single European Act (SEA) of 1986 introduced qualified majority voting in the areas of health and safety at work, working conditions, information and consultation of workers, equality between men and women and the integration of persons excluded from the labour market, with the aim of facilitating the passage of contentious legislation.

The Commission formally initiates, implements and monitors European legislation. Commissioners are political appointments but are expected to act independently of national interests. The UK has two members, as do the other larger member states. The directorates general are responsible for preparing proposals and working documents for consideration by the Council of Ministers and, therefore, play an important

part in setting the Union's policy agenda. For example, the Commission's 1995 White Paper on European Social Policy established a framework for Union action through to the twenty-first century.

The European Court of Justice (ECJ), which sits in Luxembourg, is the Union's legal voice and the guardian of treaties and implementing legislation. Its thirteen judges are appointed by the governments of member states for six-year terms of office. Its main tasks are to ensure that legal instruments adopted at European and national level are compatible with European law. Through its interpretation of legislation, it has built up a substantial and influential body of case law in the social area.

The European Parliament is directly elected by citizens of member states. The Parliament has budgetary and supervisory powers. It cannot initiate bills, but it can decline to take up a position on a Commission proposal and require the Commission to answer its questions. MEPs form political rather than national blocks. Their powers were increased by the SEA, which introduced a new cooperation procedure, allowing a second reading stage in the legislative process and making for closer collaboration with the Commission.

The Union's legal sources include primary legislation in the form of treaties and secondary legislation ranging from regulations, directives and decisions, which are its most binding instruments, to recommendations, resolutions and opinions, which are advisory, or communications and memoranda, which are used to signal initial thinking on an issue. Relatively few regulations have been introduced in the social field, with the exception of freedom of movement of workers and the Structural Funds. Directives, which lay down objectives for legislation but leave individual states to select the most suitable form of implementation, have been used to considerable effect in the areas of equal treatment and health and safety at work. Recommendations have played an important role in developing a framework for concerted action and convergence in the social policy field.

The Union has established a broad array of multilayered and fragmented policy-making institutions and instruments, which are often in competition with national systems. European policy-making is, therefore, subject to a complex process of negotiation and compromise, involving vested interests and trade-offs. While the progress of the social dimension has undoubtedly been slowed down by internal wrangling, the Union has gradually extended its area of competence and authority.

EU Social Policy Intervention

From the 1970s, Community programmes were initiated in the areas of education and training, health and safety at work, workers' and women's rights and poverty; many of them funded by the ESF. The Commission also set up a number of networks and observatories to stimulate action and monitor progress in the social field.

Rather than seeking to change national systems, action in the area of education and training focused initially on comparing the content and level of qualifications across the Community in an attempt to reach agreement over transferability from one member state to another. General directives were issued on the mutual recognition of the equivalence of diplomas. From the mid-1970s, initiatives were taken at European level, through a series of action programmes, to develop vocational training, encourage mobility among students and young workers and stimulate cooperation between education and industry.

Several articles in the EEC Treaty were devoted to the improvement of living and working conditions as a means of equalizing opportunities and promoting mobility. Particular attention has been paid to health and safety at work, resulting in a large body of binding legislation. The introduction of qualified majority voting in this area has meant that the health and safety banner has been used to initiate directives designed not only to ensure the protection of workers against dangerous products and other industrial hazards but also to control the organization of working time, to protect pregnant women and to take forward wider issues concerning public health.

In line with the priority given at European level to employment policy and working conditions, the Commission has been concerned to legislate and set up action programmes to protect women as workers rather than as citizens. Directives on equal opportunities in respect of equal pay for work of equal value, equal treatment and employment-related social insurance rights have sought to redress the balance for economically active women. Increasingly, attention has been paid to measures designed to help to reconcile occupational and family life, although legislation in this area has been opposed by some member states – notably the UK and Denmark – who are wary of the possible impact on employment practices and equal opportunities.

In a context where greater life expectancy has been accompanied by heavy demands on health and care services, member states have become increasingly concerned, individually and collectively, about the effects of population ageing on social protection systems. The Commission has monitored provision for older and disabled people, particularly with regard to maintenance and caring, arrangements for transferring the rights of mobile workers and pensioners and the overall impact of policy on living standards.

In the 1970s, the impact of economic recession, rising unemployment and demographic ageing moved on to the policy agenda, while the prospect of greater freedom of movement heightened concern about welfare tourism and the exporting of poverty from one member state to another, on the grounds that unemployed workers and their families might seek to move to states with more generous provision. The Commission has funded a series of action programmes to combat poverty and social exclusion, and the Structural Funds have been deployed to underpin regional policy by tackling the sources of economic disparities.

The Commission's objective of removing barriers to the free movement of labour has served to justify policies for coordinating social protection systems, mutual recognition of qualifications, the general improvement of living and working conditions and directives on equality of access to social benefits and measures to combat poverty. Despite the considerable body of legislation in this area, information about intra-European mobility suggests that migration between member states has remained relatively low. Progressively, more attention has been paid to the problems arising from third country immigration and the challenges it poses for coordinating national policies.

While doubts may be expressed about the coherence of the Union's social policy remit, these examples illustrate how the Union's institutions have developed a wide-ranging competence in social affairs, with the result that they have become a major, if disputed, social policy actor.

KEY ISSUES IN EUROPEAN SOCIAL POLICY ANALYSIS

By the mid-1990s, the Commission had formally recognized that member states should remain responsible for their own systems of social protection, but, as in the original Treaty of Rome, it was again advocating closer cooperation with a view to identifying possible common solutions. The debates of the 1970s and 1980s over such fundamental issues as whether or not the Community should have a social dimension seemed to have lost their salience in the face of pressing social problems requiring a common response.

Although EU member states may not be able to reach agreement over the extent of the involvement of the Union in the social policy area or the form it should take, they do seem to agree broadly about the major social problems they are confronting as they prepare for the twenty-first century (see also chapter I.3). Demographic trends in combination with technological and structural change, the prospects for further enlargement of the Union to the countries of Central and Eastern Europe, and the extension of its sphere of influence have created new pressures on welfare systems. Member states are seeking innovative ways of dealing with high unemployment, instability of employment and income, growing female economic activity rates, long-term dependency of older people and the changing structure of households, while struggling to contain the costs of providing high-quality services.

These changes have called into question the principles on which national social security systems were founded. EU member states are concerned to ensure the financial viability of social protection, while safeguarding employment and avoiding the development of a dependency culture. Population ageing has raised questions about the conditions governing retirement age and pension rights, while also exacerbating the problems of making provision for health and caring. Different mixes of solutions have been tried: from greater targeting of benefits, the tightening of eligibility criteria and emphasis on active measures to get people into work and off benefits, to the introduction of new social insurance schemes to cover long-term care and the privatization of services.

EUROPEAN AND SUPRANATIONAL AGENCIES

Despite the blocking tactics of some member states, a considerable body of legislation and practice – *acquis communautaire* – has been put in place, requiring compliance from national governments and constraining their domain of action. At the same time, the changes brought about by the SEA and the Maastricht Treaty, the British opt-out over the Social Protocol and the shift towards less binding forms of legislation in the social field have tended to result in standards being set that can realistically be achieved by the least advanced countries – the lowest common denominator – and have left individual member states with greater discretion in the way they implement policy.

The examples used in this chapter to illustrate the Union's social policy competence suggest that the policy-making process is dependent upon the ability of a plurality of national and supranational actors to cooperate in setting objectives, initiating, enacting and implementing legislation. The sharing of responsibility distinguishes European structures from those of most international organizations. As in federal states, the Union has to steer a difficult path in acting for the greater good of its member states, which is itself not easy to identify, while not encroaching too far into national sovereignty or infringing the principle of subsidiarity. A delicate balance has to be struck in accommodating the interests of the different tiers of the Union's institutions, some of which are protecting and promoting national causes (Council of Ministers and Parliament, national governments), while others are expected to act independently of governments (Commission and ECJ). Consequently, the Union has still not secured full legitimacy as a supranational authority in the social policy field, whereas the competence of member states has undoubtedly been eroded.

GUIDE TO FURTHER READING

The European Commission's annual reports on *Social Protection in Europe*. Luxembourg: Office for Official Publications of the European Communities, provide commentary on the progress made towards achieving common objectives for national systems of social protection. Detailed information about the operation of national social security arrangements is contained in the annual reports produced by the Commission and MISSOC, *Social Protection in the Member States of the Union*. Luxembourg: Office for Official Publications of the European Communities.

The development of the social dimension of the Union, its role in setting a European-wide social policy agenda and the impact of its policies at national level are examined by Hantrais, L. (1995) *Social Policy in the European Union*. London and New York: Macmillan. The author analyses the central concepts associated with European social policy-making, covering education and training, the improvement of living and working conditions, provision for families and women, older and disabled people, and policies to combat social exclusion and encourage mobility. The collection by Leibfried, S. and Pierson, P. (eds) (1995) *European Social Policy: between Fragmentation and Integration*. Washington, DC: The Brookings Institute, looks at the impact of European integration on social policy-making. The contributors describe the multi-tiered structure that has developed in the social policy field, examining industrial relations, the Structural Funds, gender, the Common Agricultural Policy and migration, and draw comparisons with Canada and the United States. The collection by George, V. and Taylor-Gooby, P. (eds) (1996) *European Welfare Policy: Squaring the Welfare Circle*. London: Macmillan, investigates how seven EU member states, representing different policy traditions, are responding to the crisis in welfare provision. The emphasis is on employment in the contributions to Gold, M. (ed.) (1993) *The Social Dimension: Employment Policy in the European Community*. London: Macmillan, including employment protection and promotion, and the social dialogue.

the consumption of welfare

paying for welfare

howard glennerster

Who Pays Matters

None of the ideals discussed by earlier contributors to this volume are attainable unless the means to achieve them are paid for by someone. Meeting socially defined needs, equality of access to basic services by all members of society, individual responsibility for the care and education of those in one's own family – all these goals have to be paid for, one way or another. One of the reasons why the state has continued to play a large role in providing services like education and health, despite concerns about taxation and people's desire to buy services for themselves, is the sheer cost to families of meeting school or hospital bills at those times in their lives when these burdens are greatest. So, despite the high-minded ideals of all the various advocates of change, the hard realities of how you pay for them drive much of practical social policy.

Moreover, if you, as a graduate of social policy, go out into the world to work in a human service agency, the first thing you will become aware of is the budget limit and the means by which that agency is funded. It is crucial to be able to put these facts into a wider context. How do schools get their cash, or hospitals or social service organizations? Your working life will not make much sense unless you can answer these questions.

What Are We Paying for?

Previous authors have discussed what social policy means in general terms. For our purposes we define it as the allocation of scarce resources necessary to human existence. We are not concerned with the economics of video recorders – at least not yet! The notion of what is a basic necessity changes over time and between societies. We are concerned with minimum food requirements, shelter, education, health care and the care of those who can no longer look after themselves because of old age or infirmity. There is no intrinsic reason why any of these services should not be purchased by individuals for themselves, if they had the money. All are by the rich. Many economists argue that the state should confine itself to giving poor people enough money to exist and get out of the business of providing services. That case was made in a highly influential book many years ago by Milton Friedman (1962). There are, however, some basic characteristics of many human services which mean that they are not well suited to individual purchases in the market place. A clean and healthy environment cannot be bought across the counter. We cannot buy clean air in bottles and consume it as a private product. If the air is clean it will be enjoyed by the whole population of our own and other countries. This 'non-excludability' is a characteristic

Figure III.9.1   Incomes by age as affected by 1991 tax and social security systems in Great Britain (Hills, 1993).

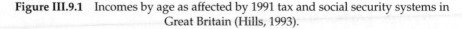

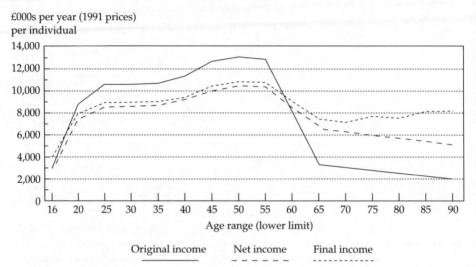

£000s per year (1991 prices) per individual

Age range (lower limit)

Original income   Net income   Final income

of what economists call a public or a social good. Where goods and services are like this we say that markets fail. Nevertheless, such goods are not free. We pay for the cost of clean air regulations in the prices of the goods produced in factories that have to install filters and burn smokeless fuels.

While some aspects of social policy concern the production of social goods like clean air, others do not. We may be able to buy medical care or education yet we may tend to make inefficient choices as private consumers. The information we need to buy our own medical care efficiently is not readily available to most of us. There is an imbalance of information between seller and buyer. We may have to rely on a doctor to advise our buying. Economists call this a problem of information failure. Market failure and information failure between them explain why, in most of the world, many human services are provided and paid for, not through ordinary private markets but through collective means of funding – taxes, insurance contributions and the like. Paying for them is a problem for other reasons. The things we need, like education for our children, a new home

for the family, health care and pensions, cannot be financed very readily at exactly the time we want them. When we are ill we have little, or possibly no, income to pay high health care fees. Education and housing are very expensive and demand payment early in a family's existence before it has had time to amass sufficient savings. Only if the family has very rich parents or a secure inheritance will banks lend you the money to pay the bills now and let you repay later. So the market may make it possible for some families to borrow now to pay later for expensive necessities but will not do so for most people. Part of what social policy is doing, therefore, is to shift the time at which people pay for the services they need from periods when they cannot pay to times when they can. Social policy is acting like a lifetime savings bank. This is illustrated in figure III.9.1.

The unbroken line shows the average incomes individuals would earn at each age through their lives assuming the world were frozen in 1991 terms. Net income is the income of individuals after income taxes are taken off. The final income line includes all individuals' income after tax

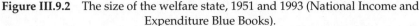

Figure III.9.2   The size of the welfare state, 1951 and 1993 (National Income and Expenditure Blue Books).

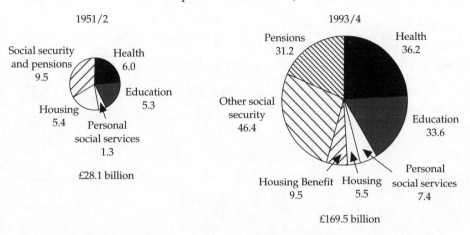

The sums are in billions of pounds expressed in 1993/4 prices on a UK basis

and the value of benefits received from the state, not just in cash but including the value of services in kind like health and personal social services. We can see very clearly from this figure how taxes are creamed off during working life to pay for the heavy costs of old age. In addition, those of us with higher lifetime incomes are paying for the services given to the lifetime poor, but it turns out that this is far less important than the lifetime redistribution from us when young to us when old (Falkingham and Hills, 1995). There is another way of looking at the question of what we are paying for. The total social policy budget funded by taxation is spent in ways you can see in figure III.9.2. Pensions and other social security payments constitute nearly half of the total. Education and health each make up about a fifth of the total and housing and the personal social services make up the remainder.

WHO PAYS?

Despite the natural focus on public tax financed social services in this volume, many of the human services included in

social policy's remit are, as discussed in chapter III.2, paid for directly out of individuals' own earnings now or by private borrowing or through private insurance policies. In addition to this form of private welfare, firms may provide their employees with pension schemes or health care. Titmuss called this occupational welfare. Hills (1995) recently calculated how much of the total costs of welfare were paid for in these different ways. It was the first time since Titmuss's early work that the national accounts had been recalculated to cover this range of funding sources. It turns out that roughly half of all the nation's income is spent on the broad purposes of providing human services – the long-term care of dependent elderly, health, education, pensions and housing. Even this does not cover items not included in the nation's accounts: the care provided by the family for its own members discussed in chapter III.4, for example. Of that vast total spent on human services, 40 per cent is paid for through the private market. That figure varies enormously between services. Roughly 60 per cent of the costs of housing are paid directly by individuals for themselves, but only 11 per cent of education and a similar share of health costs.

Figure III.9.3 The flow of funds.

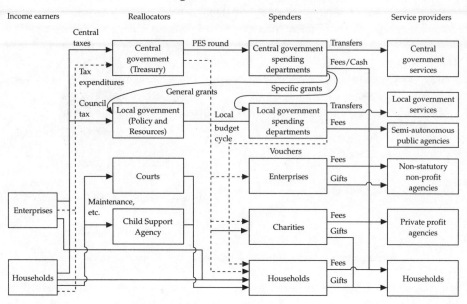

This leaves a very large sum – nearly £200 billion in 1996 – to be paid for out of taxes of one kind or another. Unusually among advanced industrialized countries, the United Kingdom relies overwhelmingly on taxes raised by the national government to pay for its social services. Less than 5 per cent is paid for out of taxes raised by local government – the council tax. Health and social security are directly provided by central government agencies in one form or another. But housing, education and the personal social services are not and there therefore has to be a complex system of grants that rechannels the taxes raised by central government to pay local councils to provide them.

A diagrammatic representation of this flow of money is to be found in figure III.9.3. On the far left of the figure are the originators of income and wealth – households and firms. Central government taxes these individuals either directly by taking a proportion of their incomes in income tax and corporation tax or through indirect taxes on goods and services. Value added tax is an example. In addition, government may tax some individuals less heavily to encourage a particular form of saving for retirement, house purchase or giving to charity. This has the effect of encouraging households to do their own saving for retirement or house purchase but it costs the government money in lost revenue. Economists call these flows tax *expenditures*.

Her Majesty's Treasury is the central government department responsible for advising the Cabinet how much the economy can afford to spend on public programmes and it masterminds the complex round of negotiations between the spending departments that determine how much is to be available to, for example, the health service or universities in the next year. This annual cycle is called the public expenditure survey round (PES for short). Under changes introduced by the Conservative government in the 1990s this set of decisions about spending coincide with the government's decisions about taxation and both are announced in the presentation of the new Unified Budget to Parliament by the Chancellor of the Exchequer at the end of November. This timing may, or may not, change if another government is elected. The process is unlikely to change in any major way. It determines how much grant local authorities and the National Health Service will receive.

Local councils get their largest income from a general or untied grant which they can spend on any of their services. They also receive some specific grants which are tied to particular smaller services. What they are permitted to raise additionally from the council tax is heavily constrained by government rules – 'capping limits'. Central government also allocates money to local health authorities and does so on the basis of a population-based formula which gives an area more money if it has more elderly or ill or poor people, because they use health services more.

Once these local agencies receive their money they then allocate it out to increasingly autonomous units like schools or hospital trusts. Schools compete for students and are paid for each one they attract. Hospital trusts compete for patients and are paid for those they treat. Social services departments pay their own old people's homes or voluntary agencies or sometimes profit agencies to provide services for the old or the disabled.

Vouchers and Quasi-vouchers

So far we have described the way grants are allocated to local authorities and then on to bodies like schools and hospitals. Some economists argue that these institutions will only work efficiently if they are forced to compete for custom and that public money for education should therefore be given, not to institutions like schools, but to individuals and families in the form of a voucher that can be cashed in at the school of their choice, public or private. The Conservative government is introducing such a voucher scheme for nursery education in 1997. One of the arguments for such a change is that state primary and

nursery schools have proved very reluctant to adapt their opening hours and facilities for the convenience of working mothers. Private nurseries have. If state schools are forced to compete they will, it is argued, adapt to the needs of working mothers. On the other hand, competition for paying customers may lead to schools competing for the richer parents and result in class segregation. I have reviewed the case for vouchers more widely elsewhere (Glennerster, 1996). It is important to recognize that giving state schools, or GPs, money on the basis of the number of children or patients they attract is already a form of voucher – a 'quasi-voucher' system – and we have moved some way to such a system in the 1990s in the UK.

Court-based Welfare

Alongside the tax-based systems of welfare run other systems of redistribution to families in need. One of the most controversial is the system of court-based support for divorced or separated wives provided in theory by ex-husbands. This operates alongside the social security system, which has to come into play when this court-enforced system fails. As the Finer Committee pointed out two decades ago, this dual system of support works very poorly. Government has changed its attitude to such cases over the years (as discussed in chapter IV.5) and the Child Support Agency now seeks to recover money from fathers who are deemed responsible for the children they have fathered.

Giving

Individuals give large sums of money and time to voluntary organizations, and statutory ones too, helping to visit old people or run youth clubs. Giving cash attracts tax relief but giving time does not. In his classic study of blood doning,

Titmuss (1970) showed how giving blood to the National Blood Transfusion Service without compensation was not only a tangible example of individuals contributing to a larger social whole and enriching that society in the process, but also turned out to be a more efficient process because donors had no incentive to lie about their medical history. This might make them carriers of infected blood, and where poor people were paid to give their blood they had an incentive to lie about their medical history. Feminist writers (discussed in chapters II.9 and III.4) have made us much more aware of the scale of giving that takes place within the family when women, and to a lesser extent men, undertake caring tasks. The personal social services budget would need to double if we were to pay women for these duties, represented by the line in figure III.9.3 that runs from households to households.

RATIONING

We have seen that the Treasury essentially sets the limits to public spending on the social services, under political direction of course! The result is that the supply of these services is fixed by political decisions. Yet these services are free, or at least partly free. Price cannot rise to levels that will equate demand with supply. The result is that service providers have to take some action to set priorities and ration care. As

is also discussed in chapter III.10, this may take the form of rules and entitlement to benefit, or judgements made by professional staff working to fixed budgets. The budgets they get may be the result of an explicit priority decision that that part of the service receive a given sum for that year, but exactly which patient or class of patient gets the service will usually depend on judgements made by professional staff in the front line. Rationing of scarce social policy resources thus takes place in a whole range of decisions, that descend from fairly explicit judgements made by Cabinet about what each service shall receive, through more explicit allocations on a formula basis to areas and, indeed, institutions like schools. But these are followed by front line and less explicit judgements about which child in a class or which social work client gets most of the worker's attention. You might like to discuss how we should make decisions to limit what we spend on health and who should be given priority. Should those who smoke and endanger their own health be supported by the rest of us when they become ill? Should we leave all these difficult decisions to doctors? You could also discuss the fundamental question addressed by John Hills (1993): can we afford the welfare state? These are some of the most difficult questions we face as a society. The responses to them are equally complex and varied, as the rest of this volume shows.

GUIDE TO FURTHER READING

Glennerster, H. (1997) *Paying for Welfare: towards 2000*. Hemel Hempstead: Harvester Wheatsheaf. Written because there was nothing else to teach from, this text summarizes the economic theoretical literature in simple terms about market and government failure and quasi-markets. It then describes the process of Treasury control and the finance of local government, with a separate chapter on the finance of each of the main services. It ends by asking: can we afford the welfare state?

Glennerster, H. (1996) Vouchers and quasi-vouchers in education. In M. May, E. Brunsdon and G. Craig (eds), *Social Policy Review 8*. London: Social Policy Association.

Hills, J. (1993) *The Future of Welfare*. York: Rowntree Foundation. This colourful volume, with charts and diagrams, presents the range of arguments about whether we can or cannot afford to sustain the present levels of spending and how to pay for it in a very readable way.

Hills, J. (1995) Funding the welfare state. *Oxford Review of Economic Policy*, 11(3), 27–43.

Thain, C. and Wright, M. (1995) *Treasury and Whitehall: the Planning and Control of Public Expenditure 1973–1993*. Oxford: Oxford University Press. For those who need a detailed account of the way the Treasury has controlled public spending in the Thatcher period.

Friedman, M. (1962) *Capitalism and Freedom*. Chicago: University of Chicago Press. A hugely influential book in which can be found most of the ideas of the Thatcher period in social policy. Makes the case for minimal government intervention, vouchers and student loans.

Falkingham, J. and Hills, J. (1995) *The Dynamics of Welfare*. Hemel Hempstead: Harvester Wheatsheaf. Shows how and why the welfare state redistributes income through the lifetime.

Foster, P. (1983) *Access to Welfare*. London: Macmillan. Summarizes the work on rationing, especially at the front line, well and simply.

Titmuss, R. M. T. (1970) *The Gift Relationship*. London: Allen & Unwin. Titmuss's last work, in which he takes the doning of blood as a parable for the virtues of giving in modern societies.

PRINCIPLES of welfARE

RUTH LISTER

INTRODUCTION

Definitions of social policy tend to centre on human welfare and on the societal institutions designed to promote it. A critical question both for social policy and for individuals and groups is how resources, limited by economic and political constraints, are allocated so as best to promote welfare and meet human needs. In other words, social policy is partly about how resources are rationed. This chapter discusses the key competing principles which govern this rationing process and thereby the rules determining the access of individuals and groups to welfare.

It begins by introducing some of the principal concepts upon which the chapter will draw, within the framework of different approaches to meeting need. The second section focuses more explicitly on the key principles governing access to welfare and their implications, drawing mainly on social security benefits as illustration. These principles are set out in diagrammatic form in box III.10.1. The chapter concludes by exploring some of the ways in which welfare might be enhanced through the promotion of citizenship and welfare rights.

DIFFERENT APPROACHES TO MEETING NEED

A primary criterion for assessing the different principles governing access to wel-

Box III.10.1. Access to welfare: interpretations of need

Need	
Broad	Narrow
Citizenship/ universality	Residual/means-tested/selectivity
Rights	Discretion

fare is whether the rules derived from them are successful in ensuring that people's needs are met. The concept of *need* was discussed in chapter II.1. It is by no means straightforward when applied to the question of access to welfare.

On the one hand it is invoked to justify an approach to social welfare which is *rights*-based and which is founded on the principle of *social citizenship*. As is further discussed in chapter II.2, in this formulation the principle of need is counterposed to that of the market. The principle of social citizenship overrides (at least in theory, even if not always in practice) that of the market, in that it is argued that every member of society has a right to be able to participate fully in that society. This right has to be underwritten by the state so as to ensure that people are not totally reliant on the labour market to meet their needs. Social rights are necessary to enable people to exercise their political and legal rights.

For example, without a home, it is very difficult to get on the electoral register, never mind receive a polling card. And although in theory we are all equal before the law, in practice some are more equal than others, so that without assistance through the legal aid and advice scheme or from a law or advice centre, poor people's access to the law is effectively blocked. Nor can people be expected to fulfil their responsibilities to the wider community as citizens if that wider community is not prepared to ensure that their needs are met.

The principle of citizenship is also about equality of status. Consequently, those subscribing to it argue that everyone should have access to the same set of rights, the principle of *universality*, instead of dividing off the poor from the rest of society through the application of *selective* mechanisms, such as means-testing, which promote *residual* welfare.

Yet proponents of such selective mechanisms also appeal to the concept of need to justify their position. When resources are limited, the argument goes, they should be targeted upon those who really need them. Means-testing, whereby assistance is limited to those whose resources fall below a certain level, is the most common means of *targeting*, particularly in social security schemes. The use of *discretion*, whereby officials or professionals decide what an applicant needs and what she can have instead of the applicant being able to claim on the basis of predetermined rights, is another approach, more common in the provision of services such as housing and community care. This individualized approach, it is contended, is more likely to ensure that the individual's 'true' needs will be met than one based on rigid rules. The disadvantages of such selective approaches are explored below.

In practice, the distinction between rights and discretion in meeting needs is not as clear-cut as this discussion might imply. On the one hand, officials often have to exercise judgement or discretion in applying the rules governing rights; on the other,

discretion is frequently exercised on the basis of (non-legally binding) guidelines set down by central or local government. Nevertheless, as the basis for organizing access to welfare they represent two very different approaches. Together with the citizenship versus residual welfare models (discussed in chapter I.3), these distinctions have implications for the welfare achieved by individuals and social groups, which are explored in the next section.

ACCESS TO WELFARE

Immigration and Residence Status

First, we need to take a step back and consider what for newcomers to a country is the first gateway to access to welfare: rules which include or exclude people on the basis of their immigration or residence status. As chapter II.13 also shows, one way in which nation states can limit the resources devoted to welfare is to limit the access of non-nationals both through restrictive immigration and asylum laws and through circumscribing access to welfare for those immigrants and asylum-seekers allowed into the country. Here citizenship is being used as a tool of exclusion rather than inclusion, overriding rather than underpinning the basic principle of meeting need.

Many Western countries are now using both immigration and welfare laws to exclude 'outsiders' from their welfare benefits and services. Behind the ramparts of 'Fortress Europe', tougher laws are being enacted to exclude immigrants and asylum-seekers. In the UK, access to welfare is being tied ever more tightly to immigration or residence status, thereby making it more difficult for immigrants and asylum-seekers to receive financial or housing assistance from the state. This then has consequences for minority ethnic group 'insiders', who are frequently subjected to passport-checking when claiming

Box III.10.2 Principles of access to welfare

Residence/immigration status

	Rights	Discretion
Citizenship	Residual/selective/ charity/ means-tested	*State*
		need/desert; professional interpretation of need for services; social fund
Unconditional, e.g. child benefit, citizen's income	Conditional/ social insurance	

welfare; some can be deterred from claiming altogether for fear that their own immigration status might be jeopardized or to avoid such racist practices.

Discretion

The potential for racist or other prejudiced attitudes leading to discriminatory decision-making by those controlling access to welfare is one of the chief arguments against the discretionary approach. Its roots lie in charity, where access to welfare was as likely to be governed as much by considerations of merit or deservingness as of need. It was partly in reaction to this that a number of rights to welfare were enshrined in the post-war welfare state. Nevertheless, discretion continued to play a role.

In the British social security system, the extent of this role in the safety-net social assistance scheme was a major focus of debate in the 1960s and 1970s. Much of the criticism of the scheme was directed to its continued heavy reliance on discretion, which was seen as acting as a rationing system which put too much power in the hands of individual officials, leaving claimants uncertain as to what they might get and without any rights to back up a claim for help. Gradually, the scope of discretion was reduced, but one of the most controversial aspects of the reform of social security in the mid-1980s was its revival in the form of the social fund – a cash-limited fund paying out mainly loans to meet one-off needs such as furniture and bedding. Discretion was reintroduced explicitly as a rationing mechanism to reduce expenditure on such one-off payments. The social fund is an example of how discretion can be managed on the basis of detailed official guidelines, without giving claimants themselves any rights.

Discretion plays a more prominent role in the social assistance schemes of many other European countries and in the UK in the service sector. Even if a right to a service exists, it is harder to specify how that right should be met by the statutory authorities and professional interpretations of need come to the fore, again in the context of the rationing of limited resources.

Thus, for example, the right to health care, enshrined in the British National Health Service, does not constitute a right to any treatment a user might demand; her right to treatment will be interpreted according to health professionals' assessment of her need.

In the field of community care, local authorities have a duty to assess the needs of disabled people, and more recently of carers, but they can then exercise their discretion as to whether and how they meet any needs that may have been identified. The exact boundaries between discretion and rights are, however, rather hazy here, as in a few cases the legislation has been used to require a local authority to provide a service once a need has been established. The problem is that, as long as local authorities' own resources are so limited, the temptation will be not to identify the need in the first place, so that discretion again comes into play as a rationing device (see too chapter III.9). The power that the discretionary approach gives to professionals has been challenged by the disabled people's movement, a development addressed in more detail in chapter IV.4. Instead of having to rely on professional assessments of their needs, some disabled people are framing their demands in the language of citizenship rights.

Rights

The advantage of the rights-based approach to welfare is that it gives greater power to users by providing them with (more or less) clear, enforceable entitlements. Provided she meets the criteria of entitlement, the claimant can refer to legal rules in support of her claim. Not all rights claims are, however, rooted in the principle of citizenship. As box III.10.2 indicates, rights too can be selective and the citizenship principle itself can be interpreted to embrace both unconditional and conditional forms of welfare.

RESIDUAL SELECTIVITY

The case for selective means-tested welfare – that it targets help on those in greatest need – has long been the subject of controversy. Critics point to the significant minorities who fail to claim the means-tested benefits for which they are eligible: in 1993/4, it is officially estimated that in the UK between £1.56 and £3.18 billion was unclaimed. The reasons are varied but include the sheer complexity of the benefits and the claiming process. Minority ethnic groups are particularly likely to underclaim. Similarly, there is evidence that as local authorities apply charges and means tests to more services, some people prefer to do without.

Means tests are also criticized for trapping people in poverty, as an increase in income reduces their benefit, and for penalizing savings. They do not provide people with genuine security, as changes in circumstances can affect entitlement. They also tend to disadvantage women in couples and to reinforce their economy dependency on male partners. Entitlement is calculated on the basis of a couple's joint income. This means that where, as is frequently the case, income is not shared fairly within a family, means tests may be failing to target help on women within families who need it, with potential consequences for the welfare of children. Moreover, because of the strict rules limiting earnings while one is claiming income support (the safety-net benefit for those not in full-time work), it is not worth the wives of unemployed claimants doing paid work.

Claiming a means-tested benefit means admitting to the label of poverty, which can still be experienced as stigmatizing. One of the dangers of a residual welfare system, it is argued, is that benefits and services confined to the poor can all too easily become poor benefits and services, as the rest of society no longer has an interest in ensuring their adequacy and quality. The United States is cited as an example. Thus, when access to welfare is confined to the poor it contravenes the principle of common citizenship.

CITIZENSHIP: CONDITIONAL AND UNCONDITIONAL

In the British social security system, social insurance is often held up as exemplifying the principle of common citizenship. Here, access to welfare depends primarily on having paid contributions of a specified value while in work and, in the case of the unemployed, on being available for and actively seeking work. However, it is, some would maintain, a conditional and limited form of citizenship which is promoted by the current social insurance scheme. Instead of overriding the market as a mechanism for distributing income, it mirrors market principles by confining entitlement to those with an adequate labour market record and, through earnings-related pensions, perpetuating inequalities in earning power. The conditional nature of the social insurance (and social assistance) system is being intensified through increasingly tough rules enforcing the obligation to seek and take work. The whole issue of the proper balance between rights and obligations has become an increasingly central one in debates about welfare.

Because the rules governing access to social insurance are based on male employment patterns, women, in particular, are the losers. Nearly two million women are excluded from the system altogether because their earnings are too low to bring them into the social insurance system. Immigrants too are disadvantaged.

Totally universal, unconditional, citizenship benefits are rare. The closest approximation in the British social security system is child benefit, which is paid for virtually every child in the country. There are a number of other benefits which are paid to people in specific categories, such as

carers and disabled people, without either contribution or means test. However, they tend to be less generous than their contributory equivalents.

The social security systems of different countries combine the principles of access to welfare in different combinations, although generally with one predominating. Thus, for instance, as noted in chapter I.3, the citizenship approach is associated with Scandinavia; the residual with the United States; and the conditional social insurance with Germany. The UK more than most is a hybrid but is moving increasingly down the road of residual welfare. The citizenship principle does, though, still operate in the National Health Service. However, as discussed above, it is difficult to operationalize in specific terms what is a generalized right to health care, free at the point of use.

THE ENHANCEMENT OF WELFARE

The weaknesses in current welfare arrangements have prompted a range of proposals for improvement. These can be divided into substantive and procedural or process reforms.

Substantive reforms

One area of substantive reform proposals aims at shifting the balance of social security entitlement from residual to citizenship based principles of access. One example is the recasting of social insurance so that it excludes fewer people and in particular better reflects women's employment patterns. Another is the idea of a citizen's income under which every individual would receive a tax-free benefit without any conditions attached. Access would be on the basis of citizenship rights alone. More narrowly, the replacement of the social fund with a system of clear rights to extra help, underpinned by a discretionary fall-back system, would enhance claimants' rights without losing the advantages of an element of discretion in the meeting of unusual needs.

The development of substantive rights to services is more difficult. One approach has been to suggest, as a first step, a framework of broad constitutional rights, partly building on the existing European Social Charter of the Council of Europe. This would provide rights to services at a generalized level, expressed as duties pertaining to government. Specific legislation would then need to develop more specific enforceable rights within such a framework.

Procedural or process reforms

It is easier to envisage how procedural reforms might improve access to welfare services. The Conservative government under John Major adopted such an approach in its Citizen's Charter. However, this has been criticized as representing the principles of consumerism rather than citizenship, as the individual citizen's *qua* customer's rights are limited to the provision of information, the expression of choice and compensation claims for public services which do not meet Charter standards.

A more citizenship-oriented notion of procedural rights has been promoted by the Institute of Public Policy Research (see Coote, 1992). Procedural rights to welfare focus on the processes through which substantive rights can be secured, on how people are treated and the manner in which decisions are taken. An important element of procedural rights is enforceability. To access and enforce rights people must have information about them and often need advice and assistance in negotiating with welfare institutions and taking cases to tribunals or, less frequently, the courts. Access to such information, advice and

advocacy has itself been referred to as a right of citizenship by the National Consumer Council. This right is promoted by a range of agencies, such as law and advice centres and local authority and voluntary sector welfare rights specialists, which require better and more stable funding than they enjoy at present.

This right is also promoted by self-help groups, where users help each other without having to rely on professionals. The principle of citizenship is taken still further in the growing demands for user or citizen involvement in service development. The case is made on the grounds that welfare will be enhanced both by the greater democratic accountability of welfare institutions and by the empowerment of users. Thus, in incorporating a more dynamic and active conception of citizenship, which treats people as active agents rather than as the passive recipients of rights, the principle of citizenship is promoted in terms of both outcomes and process. The principle of user involvement is now recognized in community care law, although in practice it still has some way to go to avoid criticisms of tokenism.

CONCLUSION

This chapter has emphasized the importance of the principles which govern access to welfare resources, highlighting the processes of rationing involved and the ways in which different principles affect marginalized groups such as women, members of minority ethnic communities and disabled people. In considering approaches to the enhancement of welfare, it has focused on those which promote citizenship as opposed to residual selectivity. It has also underlined the significance of issues of process: procedural rights which assist people in claiming and enforcing substantive rights to welfare and user involvement in the development of welfare.

Guide to Further Reading

Amin, K. with Oppenheim, C. (1992) *Poverty in Black and White*. London: CPAG Ltd/ Runneymede Trust. Chapters 5 and 9 explain some of the ways in which immigration and social security laws impede the access of minority ethnic groups to welfare.

Coote, A. (ed.) (1992) *The Welfare of Citizens*. London: IPPR/Rivers Oram Press. An exploration of the ways in which substantive and procedural social citizenship rights can be developed, particularly in relation to service provision.

Croft, S. and Beresford, P. (1992) The politics of participation. *Critical Social Policy*, 35, 20–44. An introduction to ideas about user involvement.

Dean, H. (1996) *Welfare, Law and Citizenship*. London: Prentice Hall/Harvester Wheatsheaf. A discussion of many of the ideas raised in this chapter through an exploration of welfare rights and social legislation in historical, comparative and critical contexts.

Hallett, C. (1996) *Women and Social Policy: an Introduction*. Hemel Hempstead: Harvester Wheatsheaf. An overview of the ways in which women are often disadvantaged by the principles governing access to welfare.

Lister, R. (1990) *The Exclusive Society: Citizenship and the Poor*. London: Child Poverty Action Group. A critical examination of citizenship and the ways in which disadvantaged groups are currently excluded from full citizenship.

Lister, R. (1993) Welfare rights and the constitution. In A. Barnett, C. Ellis and P. Hirst (eds), *Welfare Rights and the Constitution*. Cambridge: Polity Press. A brief overview of approaches to the development of social rights.

Oliver, M. (1996) *Understanding Disability. From Theory to Practice*. Basingstoke: Macmillan. A discussion of a number of the principles discussed in this chapter from the perspective of disabled people.

III.11

the DISTRIBUTION of welFaRe

JOHN HiLLs

INTRODUCTION

Distribution is a central issue in the appraisal of social policies; for some, it is *the* central issue. Much of the justification advanced for social policy is in terms of distribution: 'without a National Health Service providing free medical care the poor could not afford treatment'; or 'the primary aim of social security is preventing poverty'.

Most of this chapter is about the distributional effects of government spending on welfare services. However, redistribution – and its measurement – are not only issues for government. A major recent social policy development was the Child Support Act. Under this, the state attempts to enforce payments by absent parents (generally fathers) to parents 'with care' (usually mothers). These payments are important distributionally, but outside the 'welfare state'.

Whether redistribution is occurring can depend on the point of analysis. Under private insurance for, say, burglaries, a large number of people make annual payments (insurance premiums) to an insurance company, but only a small number receive payouts from the company. After the event (*ex post*) there is redistribution from the (fortunate) many to the (unfortunate) few. But, looking at the position in advance (*ex ante*), not knowing who is going to be burgled, all pay in a premium

equalling their risk of being burgled, multiplied by the size of the payout if this happens (plus the insurance company's costs and profits). In 'actuarial' terms there is no redistribution – people have arranged a certain small loss (the premium) rather than the risk of a much larger loss (being burgled without insurance).

If you look at pension schemes over a single year, some people pay in contributions, while others receive pensions. On this 'snapshot', there is apparently redistribution from the former to the latter. But with a longer time horizon, today's pensioners simply get back what they paid in earlier. Redistribution is across their own life cycles, rather than between different people.

Assessing redistribution depends on the aims against which you want to measure services, and the picture obtained depends on decisions like the time period used. The next section discusses the first of these issues, the aims of welfare services. The subsequent sections discuss the conceptual issues raised in trying to measure distributional effects, illustrate some of the empirical findings on different bases and discuss their implications.

AIMS OF WELFARE SERVICES

As previous chapters have shown, there is little consensus on the aims of social policy or of government intervention to provide or finance welfare services. For some, the primary aim of welfare services is redistribution from rich to poor. Whether the welfare state is successful therefore depends on which income groups benefit: do the rich use the NHS more than the poor, and are social security benefits 'targeted' on those with the lowest incomes ?

For others, this is only a part of the welfare state's rationale. Depending on political perspective, other aims will be more important. Some of the main aims advanced and their implications for assessing distributional effects are as follows:

1 *Vertical redistribution.* If the aim is redistribution from rich to poor, the crucial question is which income groups benefit. Since welfare services do not come from thin air, the important question may be which are the *net gainers* and *net losers*, after taking account of who pays the taxes which finance welfare provision.

2 *Horizontal redistribution on the basis of needs.* For many, relative incomes are not the only reason for receiving services. The NHS is there for people with particular medical needs: it should achieve 'horizontal redistribution' between people with similar incomes, but different medical needs.

3 *Redistribution between different groups.* An aim might be redistribution between social groups defined other than by income; for instance, favouring particular groups to offset disadvantages elsewhere in the economy. Or the system might be intended to be non-discriminatory between groups. Either way, we may need to analyse distribution by dimensions such as social class, gender, ethnicity, age or age cohort (generation), rather than just income.

4 *Insurance.* Much of the welfare state is insurance against adversity. People 'pay in' through tax or national insurance contributions, but in return, if they are the ones who become ill or unemployed, the system is there to protect them. It does not make sense just to look at which individual happens to receive an expensive heart bypass operation this year and present him or her as the main 'gainer' from the system. All benefit to the extent that they face a risk of needing such an operation. The system is best appraised in actuarial terms; that is, in terms of the extent someone would expect to benefit on average.

5 *Efficiency justifications.* An extensive literature discusses how universal, compulsory and possibly state-provided systems can be cheaper or more efficient than the market left to itself for some activities, particularly core welfare services like health care, unemployment insurance and education. Where this is the motivation for state provision one might not expect to see any redistribution between income or other groups. Services might be appraised according to the 'benefit principle' – how much do people receive in relation to what they pay? – and the absence of net redistribution would not be a sign of failure.

6 *Life cycle smoothing.* Most welfare services are unevenly spread over the life cycle. Education goes disproportionately to the young; health care and pensions to the old; while the taxes which finance them come mostly from the working generation. A snapshot picture of redistribution may be misleading – it would be better to compare how much people get out of the system over their whole lives, and how much they pay in.

7 *Compensating for 'family failure'.* Many parents do, of course, meet their children's needs, and many higher earning husbands share their cash incomes equally with their lower earning wives. But in other families this is not so – family members may not share equally in its income. Where policies are aimed at countering this kind of problem it

may not be enough to evaluate simply in terms of distribution between families, we may also need to look at distribution between individuals; that is, within families as well.

8 *External benefits.* Finally some, services may be justified by 'external' or 'spill-over' benefits beyond those to the direct beneficiary. Promoting the education of even the relatively affluent may be in society's interests, if this produces a more dynamic economy for all. Appraisal of who gains ought to take account of such benefits (although in practice this is hard).

The relative importance given to each aim thus affects not only the interpretation placed on particular findings, but also the appropriate kind of analysis.

CONCEPTUAL ISSUES

As will already be clear, there is no single measure of how welfare services are distributed. It depends on precisely what is measured, and apparently technical choices can make a great difference to the findings.

The counterfactual

To answer 'how are welfare services distributed?', you have to add 'compared to what?' What is the 'counterfactual' situation with which you are comparing reality? A particular group may receive state medical services worth £500 per year. In one sense, this is the amount they benefit by. But if the medical services did not exist, what else would be different? Government spending might be lower, and hence tax bills, including their own. The net benefit, allowing for taxes, might be much less than £500 per year.

Knock-on effects may go further. In an economy with lower taxes, many other things might be different. At the same time, without the NHS, people would

make other arrangements: private medical insurance, for instance. The money paid for that would not be available for other spending, with further knock-on effects through the economy. Britain without the NHS would differ in all sorts of ways from Britain with it, and strictly it is this hypothetical alternative country we ought to compare with to measure the impact of the NHS. In practice, this is very difficult – which limits the conclusiveness of most empirical studies.

Incidence

Closely related is the question of 'incidence': who *really* benefits from a service? Do children benefit from free education, or their parents who would otherwise have paid school fees? Are tenants of subsidized housing the true beneficiaries of the subsidies, or can employers attract labour to the area at lower wages than they would otherwise have to pay? In each case different assumptions about who really gains may be plausible and affect the findings.

Valuation

To look at the combined effects of different services, their values have to be added up in some way, most conveniently by putting a money value on them. But to do this requires a price for the services received. This is fine for cash benefits, but not for benefits which come as services 'in kind', like the NHS or education. To know how much someone benefits from a service, you want to know how much it is worth *to them* – but you cannot usually observe this. Most studies use the *cost* to the state of providing the service. But 'value' and 'cost' are not necessarily the same. It may *cost* a great deal to provide people with a particular service, but if offered the choice they might prefer a smaller cash sum to spend how they like: the cost is higher than its value to the recipients.

Distribution between which groups?

Comparing groups arranged according to some income measure is of obvious interest, but so may be looking at distribution between social classes, age groups, men and women or ethnic groups. A related issue is the 'unit of analysis': households, families or individuals? A larger unit makes some things easier: we do not have to worry about how income is shared within the family or household. But it may mask what we are interested in: for instance, distribution between men and women. It may also affect how we classify different beneficiaries. The official Central Statistical Office results described below examine the distribution of welfare benefits between *households*. In this analysis a family with four children 'scores' the same as a single pensioner living alone – the situation of six people is given the same weight as that of one person. Weighting each person equally may affect the picture.

Distribution of what?

Depending on the question, the definition of what is being examined will vary: for instance,

1 Gross public spending.
2 Net public spending after allowing for taxes financing services.
3 Gross public spending in relation to need.

These can give apparently conflicting answers. NHS spending may be concentrated on the poor, but this may reflect their poor health. Allowing for differences in sickness rates, the distribution of NHS care in relation to need may not favour the poor after all.

Similarly, the gross benefits from a service may appear 'pro-rich'; that is, its absolute value to high income households exceeds that to low income households, say by 50 per cent. But if the tax which pays for the service is twice as much for rich households, the *combination* of the service and the tax may still be *redistributive*, in that the poorer households are net gainers and the richer ones net losers.

Time period

In a single week fewer people will receive a service than over a year. As services vary across the life cycle, a single year snapshot will differ from the picture across a whole lifetime. But available data relate to short time periods: there are no surveys tracking use of welfare services throughout people's whole lives. To answer questions about lifetime distribution requires hypothetical models – the results from which depend greatly on the assumptions fed into them.

Data problems

Finally, research in this area is based on sample surveys: whole population surveys like the Census do not ask the questions about incomes and service use required. Even the sample surveys may not be very specific, asking, for instance, whether someone has visited a GP recently, but not how long the consultation lasted, whether any expensive tests were done and so on. Results assume that GP visits are worth the same to all patients. But this may gloss over the point at issue: if GPs spend longer on appointments with middle class patients – and are more likely to send them for further treatment – the distribution of medical services may be 'pro-rich', even if the number of GP consultations is constant between income groups.

SOME EMPIRICAL RESULTS

This section illustrates some of these issues by considering findings from recent empirical analysis, contrasting the gross distribution of welfare services with that of the taxes required to pay for them, and showing the differences which result from switching from a 'snapshot' to a 'lifetime' perspective.

Figure III.11.1 Welfare benefits by income group 1994–5 (derived from CSO, 1995).

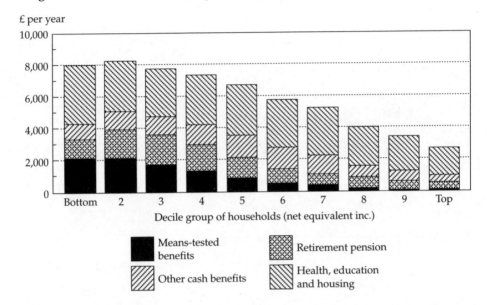

£ per year

Decile group of households (net equivalent inc.)

■ Means-tested benefits

▨ Other cash benefits

▧ Retirement pension

▨ Health, education and housing

Cross-sectional redistribution

Figure III.11.1 shows official (CSO, 1995) estimates of the average benefits in cash and kind from welfare services received by households in different income groups in 1994–5. Households are arranged in order of 'equivalent disposable income' (that is, income including cash benefits but after direct taxes like income tax, and allowing for the greater needs of bigger households). The poorest 'decile group' (tenth) is on the left, the richest on the right.

On average, households with the bottom half of incomes received 2.4 times as much from cash benefits as those with the top half. Means-tested benefits like Income Support and Housing Benefit are most concentrated on the poorest, but even 'universal' benefits like the retirement pension are worth more to lower than to higher income households.

The figure also shows estimates of the combined value of benefits in kind from the NHS, state education and housing subsidies. Evandrou et al. (1993) suggest that such figures can be qualified on various

grounds, such as the omission of the benefits of higher education for students living away from home (which tends to understate benefits to high-income households), or the way in which housing subsidies are calculated (which tends to understate benefits to low-income households). However, even with such adjustments, the general picture is similar: benefits in kind are less concentrated on the poor than cash benefits, but households at the bottom of the distribution receive considerably more than those at the top. On the CSO's estimates, benefits in kind were worth an average of £3700 for the poorest tenth of households in 1994–5, but only £1700 for the richest tenth. On these estimates, the absolute value of welfare benefits is greatest for low-income households, and much lower than average for high-income families. Taxation, by contrast, is greater in absolute terms for those with higher incomes (although it is not necessarily a greater proportion of income).

Most welfare spending is financed from general taxation, so it is hard to be precise about *which* taxes are paying for welfare: if state education was abolished, would it

Figure III.11.2 Benefits and allocated taxes by income group (derived from CSO, 1995).

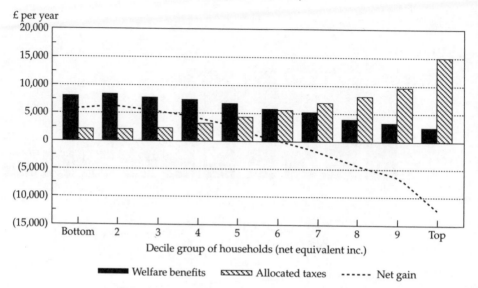

be income tax or VAT which would fall? Figure III.11.2 compares the total of welfare benefits given in the previous figure with the CSO's estimates of the impact of national insurance contributions and an equal proportion of each other tax to cover the remainder of welfare spending. For the bottom five-tenths of the distribution, benefits are higher than taxes and the figures suggest a net gain; for those in the top four groups – particularly the top two-tenths – taxes are higher, suggesting a net loss.

These results suggest that on a cross-sectional basis, the combination of welfare services and, on plausible assumptions, their financing is significantly redistributive from high- to low-income groups (although they say nothing about the scale of such gains in relation to 'need', such as for medical care).

Life cycle redistribution

The picture looks rather different over a lifetime. As discussed above, actually measuring 'lifetime' impacts of benefits and taxes is not straightforward. The findings

in figure III.11.3 are drawn from a computer simulation model of 4000 hypothetical life histories (see Falkingham and Hills, 1995). The model builds up the effects of the tax and welfare systems on a wide range of individuals on the assumption that the systems remain in a 'steady state' for their whole lives. Its results therefore illustrate the lifetime effects of today's systems, not a forecast of the combined effects of different systems which may apply in future.

The top panel gives a 'lifetime' analogue of the cross-sectional picture in figure III.11.1. The bars show total lifetime benefits from social security, education and the NHS going to each group of model individuals, ordered by their average *lifetime* living standards, with the 'lifetime poorest' on the left. The 'lifetime poorest' receive somewhat more than the 'lifetime richest', but the striking feature is that the overall distribution of gross benefits is much flatter than on an annual basis. Regardless of lifetime income, *gross* receipts look much the same.

Over their lives people both receive benefits and pay taxes. Those with higher

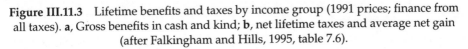

Figure III.11.3   Lifetime benefits and taxes by income group (1991 prices; finance from all taxes). **a**, Gross benefits in cash and kind; **b**, net lifetime taxes and average net gain (after Falkingham and Hills, 1995, table 7.6).

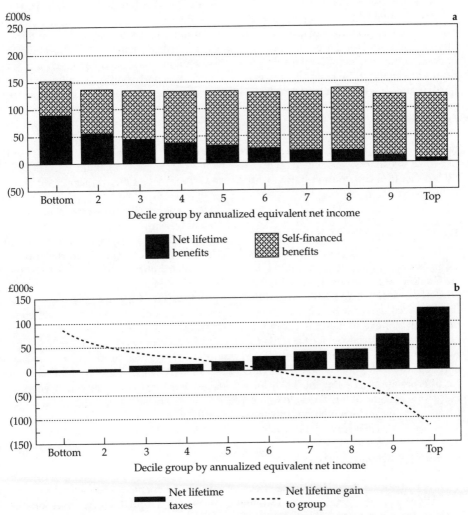

lifetime incomes pay much more tax than those with low incomes. In effect, people finance some of the benefits they receive through their *own* lifetime tax payments. However, some people do not pay enough lifetime tax to pay for all of their benefits; they receive 'net lifetime benefits' from the system. These net lifetime benefits are paid for by others who pay more than enough tax to finance their own benefits; they pay 'net lifetime taxes' into the system.

The bars in the top panel of figure III.11.3 are therefore divided between 'net' and 'self-financed' benefits, the latter being a rising proportion moving up through the income groups. The bars in the lower panel show where the net lifetime taxes are coming from. Net lifetime taxes also rise moving up through the income groups. Finally, the line in the lower panel – analogous to that in figure III.11.2 – shows the net gain or loss from the system to each lifetime income group as a whole. The bottom five groups are net gainers on average; the sixth group breaks even; the top four groups are net losers.

Thus, even on a lifetime perspective, the system does appear to redistribute from 'lifetime rich' to 'lifetime poor' (and also, importantly, from men to women, when the results are analysed by gender). However, the diagram suggests that *most* benefits are self-financed over people's lifetimes, rather than being paid for by others (see also chapter III.9). On these results, nearly three-quarters of what the welfare state does is like a 'savings bank', and only a quarter is 'Robin Hood' redistribution between different people.

IMPLICATIONS

In his book *The Strategy of Equality*, Julian Le Grand (1982) reaches the striking conclusion that 'Almost all public expenditure on the social services benefits the better off to a greater extent than the poor.' If so, a large part of social policy has failed in what many would see as one of its main aims. However, this conclusion needs careful interpretation (see Powell, 1995, for a discussion of some of the issues). It follows from an analysis which includes transport subsidies as a social service, but excludes

social security (half of all welfare spending). It looks at gross benefits and their distribution between socio-economic and income groups, but does not look at who pays for these services through taxation. For some services the analysis is in terms of the distribution of gross benefits between households unadjusted for need, but for others the conclusion only follows if one looks at the distribution of services in relation to need, notably of health care in relation to the reported health status of different groups (and analysis of more recent data than the 1972 figures used by Le Grand, such as that by O'Donnell and Propper, 1991, reaches different conclusions).

How welfare services are distributed has a major bearing on whether we judge them successful. But such judgements rest on a particular series of choices in the way in which distribution is analysed. Alternative ways of looking at the problem – including the kinds of results presented in the previous section – can give a very different impression, suggesting that it is highly unlikely that the poor would be better off and the rich worse off if welfare services were swept away. These are fundamental issues, but ones where care is needed in how they are analysed, and in defining exactly what question is being answered by that analysis.

GUIDE TO FURTHER READING

Central Statistical Office (1995) The effects of taxes and benefits on household income, 1994/95. *Economic Trends*, 506, December, 21–59. This annual article gives official estimates of the distributional effect of taxation and of a large part of public spending, including social security and welfare services.

Evandrou, M., Falkingham, J., Hills, J. and Le Grand, J. (1993) Welfare benefits in kind and income distribution. *Fiscal Studies*, 14(1), 57–76. This article reports research using an alternative data source to test the robustness of the CSO's findings on the distribution of welfare services in kind.

Evandrou, M., Falkingham, J., Le Grand, J. and Winter, D. (1992) Equity in health and social care. *Journal of Social Policy*, 21(4), 489–523. This article presents the results of an econometric study of who uses health and personal social services, examining differences between income groups and genders and other determinants of service use.

Falkingham, J. and Hills, J. (eds) (1995) *The Dynamic of Welfare: the Welfare State and the Life Cycle*. Hemel Hempstead: Prentice Hall/ Harvester Wheatsheaf. This book looks at the impact of the welfare state taking a life cycle perspective using a variety of approaches, including presenting results from a computer simulation model, LIFEMOD.

Goodin, R.E. and Le Grand, J. (1987) *Not only the Poor: the Middle Classes and the Welfare State*. London: Allen and Unwin. This book presents evidence from a variety of sources, covering both Australia and Britain, in support of the 'middle class capture' thesis about the benefits from welfare spending.

Le Grand, J. (1982) *The Strategy of Equality*. London: George Allen & Unwin. This book advances the proposition that welfare services disproportionately benefit the 'middle class', examining health care, education, housing and transport.

O'Donnell, O. and Propper, C. (1991) Equity and the distribution of NHS resources. *Journal of Health Economics*, 10, 1–19. This study looks at more recent data than used in Le Grand's original study, and presents alternative ways of analysing the data, leading the authors to conclude that health spending in the UK is generally distributed in accordance with need.

Powell, M. (1995) The strategy of equality revisited. *Journal of Social Policy*, 24(2), 163–85. This article, followed by a reply by Le Grand, critically examines the evidence and conclusions presented in Le Grand's 1982 study.

part IV
issues in social policy

social policy and particular groups

CHILDREN

CHRISTINE HALLETT

Children and young people, defined here as those aged under 18, comprise 23 per cent of the UK population. They are key consumers of social policy. In health care, for example, children (together with older people) consume greater amounts of health care per capita than those in middle age. Despite the recent growth in higher, further and continuing education, the education budget is largely devoted to schooling for children and young people and very substantial sums are spent on child-related income transfers in the social security system through family credit, income support etc. However, for the purposes of this chapter, the topic is rather more narrowly defined to encompass those services for children provided by the personal social services.

CHILD WELFARE SERVICES

Child welfare or child care services are provided by local authority social services departments or social work departments in Scotland (see chapter IV.11 for more discussion of social services). Prior to the establishment of social services departments in 1971, services for children were provided since 1948 by separate children's departments. The focus of work was, and remains, on children who are troubled or troublesome, in need of care and protection by virtue of adjudged deficiencies in the quality of parenting in their own homes or who, as young offenders, are in trouble with the law. The main focus of provision was, and remains, substitute care, provided in children's homes, foster homes or through adoption, day care in local authority nurseries or family centres or, more commonly, services provided to children in their own homes by social workers.

The personal social services are a residual service, consuming a much smaller proportion of social welfare spending than, for example, education, the national health service or social security. Within the personal social services budget a relatively small proportion (23 per cent) of expenditure is devoted to services for children and families, as is shown in table IV.1.1.

As is shown in table IV.1.2, the main items of spending are on substitute care for children no longer living in their own homes (40 per cent on residential care and 22 per cent on foster home placements). Day care comprises 16 per cent of spending and preventive and supportive services only 10 per cent.

CHILDREN LOOKED AFTER BY LOCAL AUTHORITIES

An important trend in child welfare in recent years has been the fall in the number of children in care. With the implementation in 1991 of the Children Act 1989 the

Table IV.1.1　Net expenditure on personal social services by client groups 1994–5[a]

	£ (thousands)	%
Children and families	1,564,210	23
Elderly people	3,441,343	51
People with physical or sensory disability	502,132	7
People with learning disabilities	946,665	14
People with mental health needs	316,580	5
Total	6,770,930	100

[a]Including management and support services.

Source: CIPFA (1996) Personal Social Services Statistics 1994–95 Actuals (England & Wales).

Table IV.1.2　Components of net personal social services expenditure on children and families[a]

	£ (thousands)	%
Residential care	536,318	40
Foster placements	297,030	22
Day care	214,520	16
Intermediate treatment, preventive and supportive services	160,090	12
Other	142,966	10
Total	1,350,924	100

[a]Including management and support services.

Source: CIPFA (1996) Personal Social Services Statistics 1994–95 Actuals (England & Wales).

terminology changed from children 'in care' to children 'looked after' by local authorities. This inelegant phrase was designed to emphasize continuing parental responsibility for children whom the local authority was 'looking after', and to avoid the stigma said to be associated with being a child in care. (Similar changes are incorporated in the Children (Scotland) Act 1995.) Under the Children Act 1989 a child is looked after by a local authority if he or she is placed in its care by a court order or provided with accommodation on a voluntary basis. In 1995 (on the census date of 31 March), 49,000 children were looked after by local authorities, 55 per cent as a result of court orders. Sixty-five per cent of looked after children lived in foster

homes. This reflected a significant change on three dimensions from the position obtaining earlier.

First, the numbers in care had fallen by almost half from over 900,000 in the late 1970s to over 69,000 in 1985, over 59,000 in 1991 and 49,000 in 1995. In Scotland, figures published in 1996 showed that the numbers in care fell from 15,500 in 1983 to 12,370 in 1993. Second, the proportion of those in care in community placements in foster care had risen from 50 per cent in 1985 to 65 per cent in 1995. Third, the proportion in residential accommodation (children's homes) had fallen to 17 per cent by comparison with 26 per cent in 1985 and 43 per cent in 1975. A similar decrease to 17 per cent in 1993 from 26 per cent in

1985 occurred in Scotland. These trends reflected changes in public policy and professional practice, including a recognition of the potentially harmful consequences for children's identity and development of living in residential care, including the actual harms directly inflicted on some children through physical or sexual abuse while in care and the escalating costs of institutional provision.

THE SWINGING PENDULUM OF CHILD WELFARE

Child welfare policy involves striking a balance between the responsibilities and rights of parents, the rights and needs of children and the role of the state and other service providers. The point at which the balance is struck is not fixed. It varies over time, affected, *inter alia*, by changes in the political economy of welfare and in professional practice and buffeted by key public events, scandals and tragedies. Legislative reform in child welfare testifies to the changing balance in particular epochs. Policies for children's welfare are affected by the models or ideologies of child welfare which prevail and, in particular, by the assumptions about the needs, capacities and rights of children, the right of parents and the role of the state on which they are based. Fox Harding (1991) has identified four such value positions as follows:

- *laissez-faire* and patriarchy;
- state paternalism and child protection;
- defence of the birth family and parents' rights;
- children's rights and child liberation.

The first of Fox Harding's value positions, *laissez-faire* and patriarchy, has its origins in late eighteenth- and nineteenth-century ideas about a limited role for the state, the supremacy of markets and the defence of individual freedom from coercion and state intervention. These ideas have seen a resurgence in the twentieth century with the rise of new right or neo-liberal ideologies associated with free-market economics. In child welfare, the policy consequences are a limited, residual role for the state, and an emphasis on patriarchal power and on the sanctity of the family as a private sphere. Such ideas have influenced recent child welfare legislation in the UK in the Children Act 1989 in England and Wales, and the Children (Scotland) Act 1995, in emphasizing, for example, parental responsibility for the upbringing of children and the presumption of 'no order', that is the requirement that the courts should not make an order unless they consider that it is better for the child than making no order at all.

In the second value position, state paternalism and child protection, there is an emphasis on the capacity of the state to act as the protector of children, with a duty to intervene decisively and authoritatively when required. There is a proactive child rescue role for the state, which is required to make speedy decisions to secure alternative care when parenting fails, epitomized by the permanency planning movement in the USA and Europe in the 1970s and 1980s. This relies on a confidence in the state's capacity to act benignly and to provide good substitute quality care.

In the third value position, the defence of the birth family and parents' rights, a role for the state in supporting kinship and birth rights is envisaged. There is an emphasis on parents' need for help and support to bolster their capacity to care, coupled with an acknowledgement that poverty and deprivation are important in affecting the quality of parenting. There is evidence of the influence of such a view in the Children Act 1989 and the Children (Scotland) Act 1995; for example, in the provision of family support services provided in partnership with parents for children in need.

Finally, the children's rights and child liberation approach is founded on a libertarian position in respect of children. Proponents of these views argue for children's rights to self-determination – for example, to leave home – to an independent income and to freedom from coercion and interference by adults. They suggest that children have far greater capacities than are assumed in current paternalistic and authoritarian child welfare policies. The full-blown liberationist perspective is not evident in existing child care systems, and it may be argued that such views both overestimate the capacity of young children and potentially deny protection to the vulnerable. None the less, a greater emphasis on children's rights has been an important factor in shaping policies and practice in child welfare in recent years, as discussed below.

THE CHANGING STATUS OF CHILDHOOD

Complex and wide-ranging changes in the status of children in recent years have made some impact on policy and practice in child welfare services. They include, first, at a socio-cultural level, an increasing trend (reflected in developments in the sociology of childhood) towards viewing children as 'actors' in their own right, engaged in constructing their own lives rather than simply being 'passively' acted upon by others. Second, there has been a growing awareness of the autonomy of family members, particularly women and children, as individuals rather than as the property of the (male) head of the household. The emphasis on individualism and the disaggregation of the family unit was boosted by the emergence of domestic violence and child abuse as issues of public policy from the 1960s onwards. The public revelation of the family as a site of conflict and violence along the axes of gender and generation, between men and women and between adults and children, highlighted differential power within the family unit and the identification of the needs and rights of individual family members, particularly women and children. Third,

changes in the political economy of welfare and notably the transformation (rhetorically, at least) of service users from clients to consumers have been important. Despite their limited economic resources, the importance of children (or those who purchase on their behalf) as consumers (for example of clothes, toys and popular culture) is well recognized by those who produce, advertise and market commercial goods. In child welfare, there has been some limited recognition of children as service users whose views and preferences have some importance.

THE UN CONVENTION ON THE RIGHTS OF THE CHILD

Globally, the changes sketched above were influential in the UN Convention on the Rights of the Child, adopted in 1989 and ratified by the UK government in 1991. The Convention expresses key values about children's status and their rights, without discrimination, to protection and participation, particularly in articles 2, 3, 6 and 12 (reproduced in box IV.1.1.) These principles are reflected in the key legislative reforms in children's services, the Children Act 1989 and the Children (Scotland) Act 1995, notably in the emphasis on the paramountcy of the welfare of the child and in the statutory requirements to ascertain the views of children and take them into account in decision-making.

THE RISE (AND FALL?) OF CHILD PROTECTION

Undoubtedly the most significant development in child care policy in Britain over the past twenty-five years has been the preoccupation with child abuse. An excellent account of the processes by which child abuse came to be identified in the UK as a social problem in the late 1960s and early 1970s rather than merely a private trouble has been given by Parton

Box IV.1.1 UN Convention on the Rights of the Child: key components

Article 2.1
States parties shall respect and ensure the rights set forth in the present conventions to each child within their jurisdiction without discrimination of any kind, irrespective of the child's or his or her parent's or legal guardian's race, colour, sex, language, religious, political or other opinion, national ethnic or social origin, property, disability or other status.

Article 3.1
In all actions concerning children, whether undertaken by public or private social welfare institutions, courts of law, administrative authorities or legislative bodies, the best interests of the child shall be a primary consideration.

Article 6.2
States parties shall ensure to the maximum extent possible the survival and development of the child.

Article 12.1
States parties shall assure to the child who is capable of forming his or her own views freely in all matters affecting the child, the views of the child be given due weight, in accordance with the age and maturity of the child.

(1985), with respect to the physical injury of children. The roles played by the key interest groups (such as the medical profession and voluntary child care agencies) in identifying and publicizing the problem and campaigning for a place on the public policy agenda are highlighted. Particular attention is paid to the changing political economy, which, Parton suggests, was particularly propitious at this time for the 'rediscovery' as a social problem of something which had existed for centuries.

While comparable processes were taking place elsewhere in Europe, following developments in the USA, Britain was unusual in having a succession of highly publicized inquiries into child abuse tragedies. The first in this epoch was the case of Maria Colwell, who died in 1973 as a result of injuries inflicted in her home while under the supervision of social workers. Over forty inquiries have since taken place, some, such as the Jasmine Beckford and Kimberley Carlisle inquiries, into cases of death following physical injury; others, notably the Cleveland and Orkney inquiries into situations involving multiple children alleged to have been the subject of over-zealous intervention by social workers and others, following suspicions of sexual abuse. These inquiries have had a powerful impact upon public perceptions and professional practice, and have shaped the policy response in the UK to the problem of child abuse. In particular, they have led to the promulgation of extensive procedural guidance at central and local levels to social welfare and other agencies designed to avoid repetition of tragedy and scandal.

One result is that, within child care services, cases of child abuse have received high priority, pushing down the agenda other child care services, including preventive work with children and families. High priority has been given in social work to the initial investigation of cases of child abuse and to establishing 'case status', in particular whether the child's name should be entered on the child protection registers – local lists of children deemed to have been abused (or to be at risk of significant harm) and for whom an inter-agency child protection plan is required.

There are four main categories of child abuse which preoccupy the child welfare services in the UK. These are physical injury, neglect, sexual abuse and emotional abuse. The local child protection registers in England contained almost 35,000 children and young people on 31 March 1995, a rate of 32 children per 10,000 of the population under eighteen. These figures were similar to those in 1994 but lower than the peak of 45,300 in 1991. Approximately 40 per cent of registrations concerned risk of physical injury, 30 per cent neglect and 24 per cent sexual abuse. In Scotland, the number of registrations was some 2600 children in 1994, a rate of 23 children per 10,000 of the population under 18.

The activities of investigation, holding multidisciplinary case conferences to decide on registration and plans, monitoring and review have consumed very considerable (although largely unquantified) proportions of the resources available for child welfare. In the 1990s, concerns were raised about the efficacy of the system. Several related studies commissioned by the Department of Health and summarized in the document *Child Protection: Messages from Research* (Department of Health, 1995), together with the Audit Commission report *Seen but Not Heard* (1994), suggested that the child protection system was poorly focused, drawing too many children and families into the net of child protection investigations, only a small proportion of whom proceeded to registration and thus to receipt of a child protection service, despite the fact that in many cases significant needs for welfare services (apart from child protection) were identified. These studies also revealed that children and parents who were the subject of child protection investigations often perceived them to be unwelcome and coercive. The studies also found the system to be front-loaded, with the greatest interagency effort focused upon the early stages of case identification and investigation; fewer resources were devoted to delivering effective help to children and parents in the longer-term.

A consequence of these developments is a current emphasis on redressing the balance between child protection and child welfare, with the aim of focusing more broadly on meeting the needs of children and their parents (rather than on the identification of specific injuries or other forms of abuse) and on working in partnership with children and parents. Whether this can be achieved without significant additional resources is, as yet, unclear.

GUIDE TO FURTHER READING

Several books provide accounts of child welfare services in the post-Second World War period, covering the establishment of children's departments in the 1940s and subsequent developments, including: M. Heywood (1978) *Children in Care*, 3rd edn. London: Routledge and Kegan Paul; J. Packman (1981) *The Child's Generation*, 2nd edn. Oxford: Blackwell. L. Fox Harding (1991) *Perspectives in Child Care Policy*. Harlow: Longman, presents the four value positions in child care discussed in the chapter and identifies key authors associated with the perspectives. In two subsequent articles in the *Journal of Social Welfare and Family Law* in 1991 (33, 179–93; 34, 299–316), she applies the perspectives to the Children Act 1989, the major child care law reform of recent decades. B. Franklin (ed.) (1986) *The Rights of Children*. Oxford: Blackwell, is a useful overview of the topic.

The literature on child abuse and child protection is voluminous. N. Parton (1985) *The Politics of Child Abuse*. Basingstoke: Macmillan, recounts how child (physical) abuse came to be established as a significant social problem in the UK from the late 1960s onwards. O. Stevenson (ed.) (1989) *Child Abuse: Public Policy and Professional Practice*. Hemel Hempstead: Harvester Wheatsheaf, contains, *inter alia*, chapters on the frequency of child abuse (Birchall), child abuse inquiries and public policy (Hallett) and reflections on social work practice (Stevenson). The 1995 publication *Child Protection: Messages from*

Research. London: HMSO, reviews and gives the references for twenty studies completed as part of the Department of Health's programme of research into child protection, covering, *inter alia*, definitions of abuse, the effects of the child protection process on children and families, and the effects and effectiveness of intervention. It is a useful source book.

IV.2

young people

bob coles

'Youth' has been identified with 'social problems' throughout the centuries, and the late 1990s are no exception. In 1995, the UK had more than a million young people unemployed, young people figured prominently among the homeless and estimates suggested that the public and private annual cost of youth crime might be as high as £14 billion. The UK also has a teenage pregnancy rate twice that of Germany, three times that of France and ten times that of Switzerland. One in five children truant from school and a larger proportion of 15–16 year olds have either experimented with illegal drugs or use them regularly. These are the headlines which continue to proclaim 'youth' as wheeling out of control, feckless, predatory and consummatory; simultaneously both victims and villains of social change.

This chapter reviews the social policies espoused by a number of different government departments and welfare institutions dealing with young people. Sometimes policies have shifted, and on occasions oscillated, wildly. Approaches to young offenders, for instance, have changed from introducing 'short, sharp shocks', through a period of realization that 'prisons are expensive ways of making bad people worse' and back to the reintroduction of severe regimes through 'boot camps'. Health promotion interventions have sought to frighten young people with icebergs (to warn them of the dangers of unprotected sex), or with images of wizened, decrepit drug addicts skulking in doorways. Both have failed to match the realities experienced by young people and have proved to be expensively ineffective. Frequently, it is only glamorous youth or dramatic policy interventions which grab the headlines. Yet, as this chapter will show, it is more often the more mundane policy interventions and assumptions which have transformed young people's lives. The chapter will illustrate this through focusing especially upon changes in post-16 education and training and the youth labour market. Here, as we will see, policy interventions driven by youth unemployment have produced a generation disillusioned with training initiatives, yet willingly turning to a longer period in education instead. The chapter will document how the combination of social policy initiatives in training *and* young people's responses to changed opportunities have fundamentally reshaped the nature of youth. The chapter also describes areas which have proved to be beyond the control of social policy interventions – changes in family structures and family relationships. It will examine the impact of extended periods of family dependency on young people's lives. In the final section it will consider the plight of the most vulnerable of young people who are in public care. This group is chosen to illustrate that it is particularly when public welfare and social policy are at their most responsible for young people that they prove most damaging. Indeed, it is this group which, for understandable reasons, becomes the fodder for newspaper headlines about abuse and victimization, as well as concerning unemployment, homelessness, early parenting, criminal activity and imprisonment. The analysis of this group is used to advance a more general case for a more effective and holistic approach to youth policy.

'Youth' is often defined as a phase in the life course between childhood and adulthood. This begs the crucial questions about when childhood ends and adulthood begins. There are many different legally based definitions of 'adulthood'. For instance, young people may be held to be criminally responsible for their actions after the age of ten in England and Wales. Yet the arbitrary nature of this age-related definition is shown by the fact that, in Scotland, the age of criminal responsibility is eight, in Switzerland seven, whereas in Spain and Belgium it is 16 and 18 respectively. By contrast, social security legislation in the UK determines that a person is not entitled to income support at the adult rate until the age of 25. Rights and responsibilities, then, are granted at a variety of different ages. This chapter will not, however, focus on the complexities of rights and responsibilities as enshrined in the law. Rather, it will illustrate how 'youth' is a social, cultural and economic construct. It will show how 'youth' is constructed by the complex interplay of policy-makers, those responsible for the implementation of social policy *and* young people and their parents making active 'choices' in the changing opportunity structures they see around them.

Social scientists often define youth as a set of interrelated 'transitions', a series of status sequences through which young people pass. Attention has focused on three main transitions: leaving full-time education and eventually entering the labour market, or the school-to-work transition;

attaining (relative) independence of families of origin (including the beginning of new family formations), or the domestic transition; and moving away from the parental home, sometimes initially involving temporary transitional accommodation, or the housing transition. In 'traditional transitions', which were commonplace until the mid-1970s, young people would leave school at minimum school-leaving age and obtain employment. They would save while living in the parental home, form partnerships, get engaged and then maried, and on marriage, move to their own home and start a family. Such traditional transitions are now rare. In what follows, the nature of the three transitions, together with the ways in which they are related, will be examined in order to explore the new patterns which are emerging. The chapter will also explore the ways in which they have been affected by policy interventions.

THE SOCIAL AND ECONOMIC RECONSTRUCTION OF THE SCHOOL-TO-WORK TRANSITION

In the mid-1970s in Britain, nearly two-thirds of young people left school at the end of the year when they reached minimum school-leaving age and got a job. Only around one in eight went on to university at the age of 18. By the mid-1990s, in most parts of the country, eight out ten young people stay on in full-time education after the age of 16 and nearly one in three go into higher education at 18. This extension of full-time education has not been simple, straightforward or unilinear in its development. Indeed, increases in staying-on rates have only come about in the wake of more than a decade of widespread concern about youth unemployment and disillusionment with repeated attempts to develop schemes of youth training.

In 1978, in response to rising youth unemployment among early school leavers, the first of a number of training schemes (YOP) was developed. This comprised a six-month scheme of work experience, structured skills training and social and life skills, largely designed for early, un-qualified school leavers. When YOP did not stem the rising tide of youth unemployment it was followed by more schemes of greater length, recruiting an increasing number of the age cohort. By 1986, the Youth Training Scheme (YTS) lasted for 24 months and catered for over a quarter of 16–18 year olds. By the mid-1980s, those undertaking YTS also included a significant proportion of young people who already had a number of formal qualifications, who joined because there were even fewer jobs for school leavers. The impact of the expansion of youth training was to produce a collapse in the unsubsidized youth labour market, including the old trade apprenticeships. It 'remedied' the supply of youth labour while doing nothing to increase labour demand. Youth unemployment was not eradicated and, for many trainees, unemployment had merely been delayed. In 1988, following the implementation of the 1986 Social Security Act, young people not in full-time education and without a job were denied access to Income Support before the age of 18 on the grounds that the government 'guaranteed' a place of youth training for all school leavers. This was an attempt to make it more difficult to avoid the choice between further education, employment or training. There was a failure to recognize that, for the most vulnerable young people, none of these options was a realistic possibility. The result was an intensification of poverty among the most vulnerable rather than a policing of the wilfully idle. In 1994, there were 140,000 applications from 16 year olds for Severe Hardship Payments, an emergency (and inadequate) replacement for Income Support.

A new training scheme 'Youth Training' (YT) was introduced in the 1990s but, by then, the image of youth training was one of poor quality, 'slave labour', with little prospect of secure employment at the end. YT was refocused and repackaged, but this did little to make it attractive. Further, by the 1990s many of the (often unrecognized) benefits of educational reform had also come to fruition, including new forms of assessment under GCSE. This resulted in significant increase in the proportion of young people gaining success in 16-plus examinations. Following the implementation of the 1988 Education Reform Act, school and colleges had a financial incentive to keep young people in education for longer. With pressure on school budgets now delegated to individual schools, keeping ten extra young people in year 12 at school more than paid for the salary of a member of staff. More young people were qualified to stay on and schools and colleges were, therefore, eager and willing to take them. All potential leavers saw as an alternative to staying on at school was a discredited training system. Clearly, this has extended the period of time taken for the school-to-work transition. Further, the meaning of 'youth' has been transformed by *both* social policy directed changes in the structure of opportunities for young people *and* shifting patterns of choice. Thus, training measures have largely been unsuccessful, either in stemming the increase in youth unemployment or in producing high-quality training. Instead, they destroyed the youth labour market and led more young people to choose to stay on at school and college for longer.

There is some debate about the net impact of these changes in education, training and the youth labour market on the reproduction of social inequalities. Some argue they have had little effect, and use the concept of 'youth trajectory' to signify the degree to which, despite the 'mirage' of changing opportunities and choices, the eventual outcome of young people's school-to-work transitions are highly predictable. Although young people are faced by a huge and complex array of different choices at the age of 16, and despite many schools, colleges and employers espousing equal opportunity policies, career choice patterns remain remarkably 'segmented', with young men and young women from different ethnic groups and class backgrounds locked into a limited range of real choices. Some of those most likely to experience poor outcomes are those from (particularly Afro-Caribbean) ethnic minority backgrounds. In one study in Liverpool, for instance, black 18–19 year olds were more than twice as likely as their white counterparts to be unemployed, a pattern which was not explainable by differences in educational qualifications. This suggests a pattern of racial inequality in the labour market which is confirmed by national labour force surveys. Other groups twice as likely to become unemployed are young people with disabilities and those experiencing some form of special educational needs. Those with physical or learning disabilities do stay on in some form of education beyond minimum school-leaving age and may be offered some form of sheltered training opportunities. But the severely disabled are likely never to obtain employment. Some attempt is being made in the 1990s to involve them and a number of welfare professionals in 'transition planning'. But for this group the transition is not so much a transition to work, but to other forms of social activity and training for independent living.

DOMESTIC AND HOUSING TRANSITIONS

The domestic and housing transitions are closely interwoven and will be dealt with together. Family policy is a complex area, containing a mixture of state support in the bringing up of children, a reluctance to intervene in private affairs (hence a move towards 'no fault' divorce) together with a recognition that, in extreme cases, the state must intervene 'in the best interests of the child'. Much recent family 'policy' has, however, arrived by default –

it has been influenced by policy thinking but it is difficult to see how that the actual effect produced matches that which was planned.

Patterns of leaving home and family formation in the 1990s are now very different from the 'traditional transitions' of the 1970s, mainly as a result of changes in the labour market and cultural changes in the ways in which marriage and parenting are approached. More than 80 per cent of females and 60 per cent of males born in the late 1940s were married by the age of 25. In the 1990s, marriage and parenting take place much later than in previous decades, and cohabiting before marriage is now the norm rather than the exception. By 1990, fewer than 50 per cent of female and 30 per cent of male 25 year olds were married. The average age at which young women have their first child has also risen from 24 in 1971 to 27.5 by the 1991 census. Changing patterns of partnering, marriage and family formation have also, therefore, extended the period of 'youth'. Extended education has also resulted in an extension of family dependency (especially financial dependency). Young people are dependent on their families for longer and start families of their own later in life.

A significant area of concern is the ability of different family forms to cope with the increasing demands being made of them. The number of lone parent families has more than doubled between 1971 and 1991 (see chapter IV.5 for more discussion of this), and since the 1960s there has been a quadrupling of divorces, and a threefold increase in remarriages. By the end of the century fewer than half of all 16 year olds will be living in families with both their biological parents. Some evidence suggests that young women living in reconstituted families (where at least one parent is not biologically related) find family dependency especially difficult to cope with, and many may leave both school and home at the earliest opportunity, even though this may result in unemployment or homelessness. Whereas runaway children have been a concern of children's agencies for some time, 'throw-away' young people have been a growing concern of the 1990s, where families have proved unable (or unwilling) to cope with the pressures and demands extended youth transitions make upon them.

Despite rises in the age of first entry to the full-time labour market, marriage and parenting, leaving the parental home by the late teens is widespread. However, this often involves leaving home and return-ing on several different occasions. Youth transitions are often seen as means through which young people move from a status of dependency to a status in which they are (relatively) independent of their family in terms of their ability to provide econom-ically, socially and emotionally for them-selves. Clearly, complete 'independence' is rarely either desired or desirable and young people remain dependent upon their families in many and diverse ways, long after they can be considered to be adult. Paradoxically, it is the most vul-nerable of young people who are required to move to 'independent living' at an early age, with, in many cases, little by way of welfare support.

VULNERABLE YOUTH

One area of growing concern is with the care of young people outside of biological families. The number of children brought up in public care, whether it be foster care or in children's homes, declined through-out the 1980s and 1990s. Those who are 'looked after' by local authorities are highly likely to come from the most deprived social and economic backgrounds, three and a half times more likely to be living in overcrowded accommodation and eight times more likely to be living with a single adult rather than two parents. More than 60 per cent of those in care are over the age of ten, with 70 per cent of those in residential care over the age of 13. A number of enquiries and research reports have indicated that, rather than receiv-ing effective and compensatory welfare support, young people in care are sub-ject to abuse, denied their rights and hugely disadvantaged in attempting youth transitions. Many young people in care experience 'placement breakdowns' and are moved repeatedly from one placement to another and, as a consequence, from school to school. As many as a quarter do not attend school regularly or have been excluded from school between the ages of 14 and 16. As a result, the vast majority of young people in care have a very poor education, obtain no formal qualifications before they leave school and are highly likely to experience unemployment. Yet, at the same time that they are also expected to compete against the odds in the shrun-ken youth labour market, care leavers are expected to prepare themselves for inde-pendent living, much of this in hostels or bed and breakfast accommodation. Unable to cope, many become homeless as well as unemployed. One study of the young homeless reported that one in four of those 'sleeping rough' had been in a children's home and a further one in ten had been in foster care.

In the face of poor labour market pro-spects, many vulnerable young people concentrate upon more viable alternat-ives. Nearly half of the young women in one study were reported to have become parents within two years of leaving care. Others, particularly young men, become involved in crime. A survey of the prison population indicates that as many as one-third of prisoners had been in care. Those brought up in care, therefore, while repres-enting only a tiny proportion (less than 1 per cent) of each cohort attempting the precarious transitions of youth, are among the most highly vulnerable to experience 'fractured transitions'. They leave school without being able to find a job. They leave 'home' without secure alternative accom-modation, and they are cut free of family, surrogate family or other forms of social support.

YOUTH POLICY AND THE WELFARE OUTCOMES OF YOUTH TRANSITIONS

'Fractured youth transitions' are the most obvious negative outcome for young people of rapid social and economic change. As we have seen, they are, unfortunately, also the outcome of social policy interventions. Unemployment is socially and psychologically debilitating, injurious of physical and mental health, and a key aspect of social exclusion which traps people into poverty. Young people have proved to be particularly vulnerable to periods of both unemployment and homelessness. In the absence of 'legitimate' careers, many young people have turned to alternatives involving crime.

Much social policy directed at youth has focused on the symptoms rather than the causes of the difficulties they face. There has been a failure to recognize that, if the three main youth transitions are indeed closely interrelated, then there must be a holistic approach to youth policy rather than a piecemeal approach to separate problems. The needs of young people in terms of education, training, employment, housing and family (and surrogate family) support must be addressed together and a coherent approach to youth policy developed across different government departments. Without a coordination of effort between different ministries of state, the social problems of youth will only be displaced from one area to another. The costs of policy failures are huge and no longer affordable. Unfortunately, policy failures can be counted, not only in terms of the costs of crime and long-term welfare dependency, but in frustrated ambitions, suicides, lost opportunities and wasted lives.

GUIDE TO FURTHER READING

While there are numerous books on 'youth', few texts until recently have attempted to provide a coherent framework for the discussion of 'youth policy'. The following two books usefully complement each other. The second more specifically reviews 'vulnerable youth': 'looked after' in care, young people with disabilities and those involved in crime.

Jones, G. and Wallace, C. (1992) *Youth, Family and Citizenship*. Milton Keynes: Open University Press.
Coles, B. (1995) *Youth and Social Policy: Youth Citizenship and Young Careers*. London: UCL Press.

More common have been research and textbooks which cover specific aspects of youth transitions.

Roberts, K. (1995) *Youth and Employment in Modern Britain*. Oxford: Oxford University Press, provides a readable and comprehensive account of the development of unemployment and training measures in the past few decades and a review of our understanding of the youth labour market.
Jones, G. (1995) *Leaving Home*. Buckingham: Open University Press, is largely based upon her own research in Scotland but is a good introduction to an increasingly important topic.
Brannen, J. et al. (1994) *Young People, Health and Family Life*. Buckingham: Open University Press, is again based upon a specific research project but provides valuable insight into family relationships around health issues.

Finally there are useful studies of particular groups or categories of young people.

Biehal, N. et al. (1995) *Moving on: Young People and Leaving Care Schemes*. London: HMSO, is a study of young people 'looked after' by local authorities, leaving care and leaving care schemes.

Wilkinson, C. (1995) *The Drop out Society*. Leicester: Youth Work Press, more generally reviews the social problems faced by the most vulnerable.

oLdeR peopLe

aLaN waLkeR

Older people have <u>always been a major focus for social policy</u> and, because the <u>UK is an ageing society</u>, their importance to the subject is likely to increase further. Like other modern welfare systems, the British welfare state originated in pension provision for older people and today this group are the <u>main users</u> of the health and social services and the <u>main recipients</u> of social security spending. Compared with unemployed people and lone parents, older people are often viewed as a group that is 'deserving' of social policy and, especially, social security. Indeed, it is sometimes said that the <u>true test of a civilized society is how it treats its older and vulnerable groups.</u> Despite this group's position as one of the most deserving of welfare, students of social policy will be aware that there are <u>many negative images of old age.</u> In common with other Western societies, Britain is a country in which age discrimination, or ageism, is widespread. Many cultural images of older people emphasize passivity and decrepitude; for example, W. B. Yeats, 'When you are old and grey and full of sleep, and nodding by the fire . . .'. Television stereotypes older people in a variety of ways – kindly grandparents, mad aunts and burdensome parents – many of which suggest detachment from mainstream society and, often, an association between old age and ill health. This age discrimination, both visible and invisible, has important policy implications and

these have not received the same sustained attention as those arising from sex and race discrimination. Therefore, in this brief overview of key social policy issues affecting older people, I will focus on age discrimination, particularly its impact on the <u>labour market</u>. The two other key issues dealt with here are <u>pensions</u> and <u>social care</u>. Unfortunately, there is not space to pursue the many other important policy issues surrounding older people, but the guide at the end of this chapter provides the basis for further reading. I start with an outline of the population in question.

WHO ARE 'OLDER PEOPLE'?

Before the advent of public pension systems, workers relied on the benevolence of their employers to provide occupational pensions and, in <u>the late nineteenth century, it was common for people to work until their health failed rather than there being a fixed retirement age.</u> (This is a situation that pertains today in much of the underdeveloped world.) As in most Western countries, it was the British civil service that was the first major occupational group to secure the provision of pensions from their employers, and they adopted a retirement age of 70. This was the age used, for both men and women, when the first state pension was introduced in 1908, and it was reduced to 65 in

Table IV.3.1　Age groups as a proportion of total UK population (percentages)

Ages	1995	2000	2010	2020	2040
0–19	25.3	25.4	23.8	22.3	21.1
20–49	43.3	42.0	41.0	37.5	35.4
50–64	15.6	17.1	19.0	21.3	18.3
65–79	11.7	11.5	11.8	14.3	17.8
80+	4.0	4.0	4.3	4.7	7.4
65+	15.7	15.6	16.2	19.0	25.2
All ages	100	100	100	100	100

Source: Government Actuary's mid-1994 based principal projections.

1925. In 1940, the pension age for women was cut to 60. The universalization of public pensions, following the recommendations of the Beveridge Report, maintained the differential pension ages (65 for men and 60 for women). These were quickly adopted by employers as retirement ages – even though Beveridge had intended that people would work beyond the designated ages and earn additional pensions for doing so – and, in effect, they became the basic thresholds of old age for men and women. Thus, for much of the post-war period old age in Britain has been defined statistically as those over the state pension ages or those aged 65 and over. In the November 1993 Budget the government announced that the state pension age will be equalized at 65 and that, to protect the expectations of women aged 44 and over, this will be phased in over ten years commencing in 2010.

Table IV.3.1 shows the proportion of the total population made up by different age groups, and the expected expansion in the numbers of older people over the next four decades. As can be seen, population ageing consists of a shrinkage in the proportion of younger people coupled with a rise in the proportion of older ones. The two socio-demographic factors underlying this development are falling fertility rates and increasing longevity. The trend is a long-term one: at the turn of the century those

aged 65 and over comprised just 4.7 per cent of the population and those aged 80 and over a tiny 0.3 per cent. In all there are some 9.2 million people aged 65 and over (more than ten million when women aged 60–64 are included), a figure that is projected to rise to 14.9 million in 2040.

Hidden within the figures shown in table IV.3.1 is one of the most important features of the older population – its gender distribution. At successively older ages the proportion of women increasingly outstrips that of men: 49 per cent of those aged 0–19 are women, for the 20–64 age group it is 50 per cent, for the 65–79 group the figure is 56 per cent and for those aged 80 and over it is 70 per cent. The main reason for this is that female life expectancy (at birth) exceeds the male rate by 5.2 years and, although male life expectancy is projected to improve over the next forty-five years, so will women's. Therefore, by the year 2040 the differential will still be around five years (78.6 years for men and 83.6 years for men, compared with 74.2 and 79.4 respectively today). Largely because of different life expectancies, the majority of men aged 75 and over are married (62 per cent) whereas the majority of women of that age are widowed (64 per cent). Among black and minority ethnic groups the proportion of older people currently is much smaller than that of the white population – only 6 per cent aged

60 and over – though the figure for all ethnic groups mirrors that of the white group.

Of course, population ageing is a sign of social and economic development, including the role of social policies in combating many of the diseases that cut short people's lives in previous centuries. However, the growing numbers of older people are not always viewed in such a positive light. For example, it has become common for economists, international economic agencies (such as the IMF and OECD) and some politicians to refer to the growing 'burden' that this represents, and to go on to suggest that the pension and health care costs associated with population ageing are unsustainable. In the USA, this pessimistic perspective took an extreme form in the 1980s, when war between the generations was predicted (Walker, 1996). What is lacking from most of these gloomy accounts is any evidence: they usually consist of projections and predictions which assume that policies remain stable while demography advances. What is overlooked is that 'old age' was defined (or in sociological terms 'socially constructed') in precise age categories by social policy (i.e. pension policy) and, therefore, it can be redefined as circumstances change. Indeed, this is happening in Britain to some extent, by the raising of the female pension age, and in several other European Union (EU) countries such as Germany and Italy. It is worth noting, though, that even without this change and assuming that pensions are raised along with overall living standards (which goes beyond current policy), the net effect of population ageing on the public finance over the next fifty years would be around 5 per cent of GDP – 'no more than the recent increase related to recession over the past *three* years' (Hills, 1993, p.14).

Older people themselves do not readily conform to their caricature as passive burdens. Surveys in Britain and other EU countries show a very different picture: the majority remain active, often making important contributions within families (for example, to child care), and reject discriminatory labels such as 'the elderly' in favour of more active ones such as older people or senior citizens (Walker and Maltby, 1996). Older people favour inclusion in society rather than the exclusion that sometimes afflicts them.

AGE DISCRIMINATION IN THE LABOUR MARKET

One of the main sources of exclusion is the labour market. I have already noted the conflation of retirement with pension ages. In practice, older people, particularly older men, have been used as a kind of reserve army of labour – encouraged to stay in employment at times of labour shortage (as in the late 1940s and early 1950s) and quickly jettisoned when demand contracts (as in the mid-1970s). Mindful of the decline in the numbers of young people entering employment and the cost of pensions, the government is currently running campaigns to try to persuade employers to recruit or retain older workers. This is an uphill task because, as table IV.3.2 shows, the horses have bolted. It is now only a minority of men that 'retire' in the conventional sense of leaving work on or close to their sixty-fifth birthday. The majority leave employment at earlier ages and reach the statutory pension age in a variety of non-employed statuses, such as unemployment, long-term sickness or disability and early retirement.

The dramatic growth of early retirement, or early labour force exit, since the mid-1970s has contributed to a redefinition of older people into two groups instead of one. The 'third age' covers those aged 50–74 and the 'fourth age' comprises those aged 75 and over. This distinction is sometimes used to imply that the former 'young old' are active while the latter 'old old' are passive but, as indicated later in this chapter, this is grossly misleading.

Table IV.3.2 Labour force participation of older men and women in Britain 1951–94

	1951	1961	1971	1975	1981	1985	1990	1994
Men								
55–59	95.0	97.1	95.3	93.0	89.4	82.0	81.0	76.1
60–64	87.7	91.0	86.6	82.3	69.3	54.4	54.4	51.2
65+	31.1	25.0	23.5	19.2	10.3	8.2	8.6	7.5
Women								
55–59	29.1	39.2	50.9	52.4	53.4	52.1	54.9	55.7
60–64	14.1	19.7	28.8	28.6	23.3	18.9	22.7	25.6
65+	4.1	4.6	6.3	4.9	3.7	3.0	3.3	3.2

Sources: 1951–71, Census of Population for England and Wales and for Scotland; 1975–94, Department of Employment, *Gazette* (various); UK Labour Force Survey.

The main factors explaining the growth of early exit among British men are demand-related, particularly the recessions of the mid-1970s and early 1980s (Phillipson and Walker, 1986; Laczko and Phillipson, 1991). For many older workers the loss of a job in their fifties or even late forties means that they may never re-enter employment. This can have severe consequences for the individuals concerned and their families, including, most importantly, the necessity of living on a low income or in poverty for a long period before receiving a pension. It also means that the skills possessed by many older workers are lost forever. For the government it means not only lost revenue but also increased benefit payments.

Recent research has shown that people aged 50 to 60 face considerable discrimination from employers. For example, age restrictions in job advertisements are a common barrier to employment. Employers often restrict access to training programmes to workers under the age of 50. Yet when employers are asked to rank the most important factors discouraging the recruitment of older workers, 'lack of appropriate skills' comes top. There is, it seems, a sort of self-fulfilling prophecy at work here. Many employers have been shown to hold stereotypical attitudes towards older workers; for example,

that they are hard to train, are too cautious, cannot adapt to new technology and are inflexible. Such prejudices are not supported by research evidence, but they continue to exert a powerful influence over the life chances of people in their third age. Such discriminatory attitudes not only offend social justice but are increasingly at odds with Britain's ageing society and ageing workforce (by the year 2005 the majority of people in the labour market will be over 40). The British government has chosen to try to combat them by educating employers about the value of recruiting and retaining older workers. In contrast to the passive, non-interventionist, approach of the UK government the USA has had anti-age discrimination legislation for more than a decade. The Dutch government has recently committed itself to outlawing unnecessary age barriers in job advertisements and the British Labour Party has promised to introduce anti-age discrimination legislation.

PENSIONS AND POVERTY IN OLD AGE

Pensions are one of the central social policy issues, but they are also one of the most contentious because of their sheer scale and their escalating cost in an ageing society. The basic national insurance pension alone costs £28.8 billion per annum (1994–5) and the total public expenditure on pensions approaches the amounts spent on health and education. Social security is by far the largest single expenditure programme, and over half of it is devoted to older people. By the year 2000, public pension spending is expected to exceed £40 billion.

Despite the scale of public spending there is still a close association between low incomes and poverty and old age. Beveridge had intended that the national insurance (NI) pension would overcome poverty in old age, or the giant of 'want' as he put it. However, older people formed the largest group among the poor for most of the post-war period, being exceeded by the unemployed in the early 1980s as unemployment spiralled and as the government began a long series of reductions in unemployment benefits (see Phillipson and Walker, 1986). When it came to establishing the level of the NI pension this was set below that of national assistance (now income support), which meant that receipt of the pension alone was not sufficient to lift older people above the official poverty line. Occupational pensions have raised the living standards of many pensioners, particularly couples, and the government has reduced the benefits of unemployed people more drastically than those of pensioners. None the less, older people still form one of the largest groups living in poverty in the UK, and they are more likely to be poor than older people in other comparable EU countries (Walker and Maltby, 1996). In 1992/3 (the latest available statistics) households where the head or spouse were aged 60 or over comprised 23 per cent of the poor (defined by the government as living below 50 per cent of average income after housing costs) and the unemployed represented 22 per cent. One third of older people, some 3.3 million people, live in poverty by this definition. Older people form a smaller proportion of the very poorest (the bottom 10 per cent)

than do the unemployed (10 per cent compared with 33 per cent for the latter). Indeed, the impact of government policy on the unemployed and the relative rise in the living standards of older people can be seen by the fact that, in 1979, they comprised 16 per cent of the bottom 10 per cent, while pensioners made up 33 per cent.

The introduction of public pensions, which started in 1908 and were made universal forty years later following the recommendations of the Beveridge Report, served a number of functions. Most importantly, of course, they provided a secure income for those who did not have access to occupational pensions or whose employers had summarily dismissed them on grounds of age. At the same time, the introduction of state pensions was of crucial importance in the creation of mass retirement, which allowed employers to terminate working lives and to spread the cost of doing so over the whole population of working age. Although Beveridge had intended that a fund would be built up from the payments of contributions by employers and employees, the post-war Labour government decided to introduce the NI pension at once and the result is that the NI pension is financed on a pay-as-you-go (PAYG) basis. This means that the NI contributions of those in employment go to pay the pensions of those in retirement. In effect there is a social contract between the generations: those in retirement paid taxes and contributions to fund the pensions of the previous generation in the expectation that the succeeding generations would do the same for them. Other important elements of state welfare provision, such as the NHS and social services, are financed on a similar basis.

Unfortunately, the PAYG system is vulnerable to political interference and when the social contract was instigated those involved did not envisage that a future government would drastically rewrite the rules. This is what happened, in effect, in the 1980s. The Thatcher government was intent on cutting public expenditure and, because of the scale of pension spending, this was a prime target. Thus, in 1980, the government altered the uprating link for the NI pension from earnings to prices. The cumulative effect of this seemingly innocuous cut has been to reduce the value of the single person's pension by £22.55 a week (at April 1996 benefit levels) and, for a couple, the reduction is £35.95 a week. The reductions represent more than one-third of the value of the existing pension levels. Then, in 1986, the government cut in half the value of the State Earnings Related Pension (SERP), which was introduced with all-party support in 1978 and was due to reach full maturity in 1988. The reduction in the SERP scheme affects women in particular because the relatively generous credits for periods spent out of employment, (for example, in child rearing) have been curtailed. These cuts have had a deterrent effect on younger generations – undermining their confidence in the state pension system and encouraging them to invest in private pensions. It is a salutary fact that, if present trends continue, the NI pension will be worth less than 10 per cent of average earnings in 2020. As well as deterrence, the government's policy has consisted of positive inducements for younger people to opt out of the state sector and into the private one. These have taken the form of generous NI contribution rebates and tax reliefs, costing more than £16 billion. The result is that some six million contributors have been enticed from the SERP scheme into personal pension plans. Now only 17 per cent of the workforce are left in the SERP scheme. However, it is estimated that because of the mis-selling of personal pensions, as many as two million people would have been better off staying in the state scheme.

At the time of writing the future of state pensions is in doubt. The SERP scheme was intended to abolish poverty in old age but it and the basic NI pension have been residualized. The main alternative, personal pensions, depend on investments and therefore their outcome is uncertain.

Moreover, they are of little use to part-time workers, mostly women, and those in various forms of discontinuous employment. The impact of this policy change on the contract between the generations has not been considered publicly. Most importantly, it is likely that poverty will continue to be a feature of old age in the UK for the foreseeable future.

LONG-TERM CARE

It is commonly assumed that older people, particularly those in their fourth age, are physically dependent. In fact, the vast majority of older people are active and able to look after themselves without assistance from others. Even among the very old the bulk of care is self-provided. Among people aged eighty and over only 15 per cent are resident in care homes, nursing homes or hospitals, and for those aged ninety and over the proportion is 36 per cent. However, as these figures suggest, there is an association between advanced old age and disability and, because women live longer than men, they are more likely than men to be disabled. The numbers of women aged eighty and over resident in homes and hospitals is nearly five times that of men.

For most of the post-war period the policy favoured by successive governments has been community care. In reality this has meant that families have been by far the main source of care for disabled older people and others needing support. Social policy researchers have demonstrated that 'family' care usually means care by female kin, although in couples care by older male spouses is not uncommon. However, the socio-demographic changes referred to earlier are placing the family-based system of care under increasing strain. For example, smaller family size means fewer relatives to share care between. Greater longevity means that some caring relations across the generations are being extended, which may create strains on both sides. Increased female participation in the labour market imposes additional responsibilities on women. We do not yet have a clear picture of the impact of divorce on patterns of family care. Because of these changes and the growth in need associated with population ageing, there is a widening 'care gap' between the need for care among older people and the supply of both family care and formal care from the public, private and voluntary sectors.

The government's response in the 1980s to this growth in demand was to depart from the previous consensus on community care services being centred on local authority social services departments and to encourage the expansion of the private sector. This was achieved by means of social security subsidies for older people living on income support to enter private homes, while holding down expenditure on public services. The result was a huge rise in the numbers of older people entering private residential homes. The numbers nearly doubled between 1979 and 1984, and by 1994 had increased fivefold. Unfortunately, this policy conflicted with the government's desire to restrict public spending (the social security budget for board and lodging payments rose from £10 million in 1978 to over £2000 million in 1993). As a result measures were introduced, under the NHS and Community Care Act 1990, to curtail these escalating costs and to recast the role of local authorities as purchasers of services from the private and voluntary sectors instead of direct providers. At the same time, financial restrictions in the health service have led to a clearer line being drawn between health and social care, with the result that health authorities are reducing the numbers of long-stay beds for older people and expecting the social care system to take over responsibility for those former patients.

Thus, although additional resources were allocated to local authorities for the implementation of the 1990 Act, they are insufficient to keep pace with rising needs and there is an urgent need for a radical reappraisal of long-term care policy. At the time of writing, the Conservative government was in the process of taking limited action to protect the assets of older people entering private homes (it is estimated that some 40,000 people are being forced to sell their homes each year); while the Labour Opposition promised a Royal Commission if it were elected. Meanwhile, Germany has recently extended its pension system to include insurance for long-term care needs.

CONCLUSION

As will be apparent from this brief introduction, social policy towards older people in the UK is in a state of flux. This is partly because the foundations on which public support for old age were built in the immediate post-war period are being undermined by changes in the labour market and in the life course. But there is also an institutional and ideological reluctance to come to terms with the reality of an ageing society. Some other EU countries are making this transition much more smoothly.

GUIDE TO FURTHER READING

Phillipson, C. and Walker, A. (eds) (1986) *Ageing and Social Policy*. Aldershot: Gower. A general introduction to the main policy issues related to older people.

Bond, J., Coleman, P. and Peace, S. (eds) (1993) *Ageing in Society*. London: Sage. A general introduction to the field of social gerontology.

McEwan, E. (ed.) (1990) *Age: the Unrecognised Discrimination*. London: Age Concern. Deals with different aspects of age discrimination.

Hills, J. (1993) *The Future of Welfare: a Guide to the Debate*. York: Joseph Rowntree Foundation. Very accessible account of the public expenditure and taxation issues surrounding the welfare state.

Walker, A. (ed.) (1996) *The New Generational Contract*. London: UCL Press. Covers both macro and micro issues with regard to relations between the generations.

Walker, A. and Maltby, T. (1996) *Ageing Europe*. Buckingham: Open University Press. Comparative analysis of ageing and social policy in different EU countries.

Laczko, F. and Phillipson, C. (1991) *Changing Work and Retirement*. Buckingham: Open University Press. Covers the main issues concerning employment.

Arber, S. and Ginn, J. (eds) (1995) *Connecting Gender and Ageing*. Buckingham: Open University Press. Readings on the important issue of the gendered nature of old age.

IV.4

DISABLED PEOPLE
mike oliver

THE CONTEXT AND EXPLANATIONS

The evidence that disabled people experience severe economic deprivation and social disadvantage is overwhelming and no longer in dispute, whether it be from the government's own commissioned research, from research institutes, academics or disabled people themselves. For example, after over a century of state-provided education, disabled children and young people are still not entitled to the same kind of schooling as their able-bodied peers, nor do they leave with equivalent qualifications. The majority of British schools, colleges and universities remain unprepared to accommodate disabled students within a mainstream setting. Thus, many young disabled people have little choice but to accept a particular form of segregated 'special' education which is both educationally and socially divisive, and fails to provide them with the necessary skills for adult living.

Similarly, since the end of the Second World War at least, disabled people have consistently experienced higher rates of unemployment than the rest of the population, not because they are unable to work but because of the discriminatory behaviour of employers in failing even to attempt to meet their legal obligations under the quota system and the lack of political will to insist upon its enforcement. As a result,

currently, disabled people are more likely to be out of work than non-disabled people, they are out of work longer than other unemployed workers and when they do find work it is more often than not low-paid, low-status work with poor working conditions.

The majority of disabled people and their families, therefore, are forced into depending on welfare benefits in order to survive. Further, the present disability benefit system does not even cover impairment-related costs and effectively discourages many of those who struggle for autonomy and financial independence. Dependence is the inevitable result and this is compounded by the present system of health and welfare services, most of which are dominated by the interests of the professionals who run them and the traditional assumption that disabled people are incapable of running their own lives.

What is at issue is why this should be so, the role of welfare in compounding or alleviating this situation and what can be done about it. I would argue that there can only be two possible explanations for the appalling economic and social circumstances under which the vast majority of disabled people are forced to live; one, that disability has such a traumatic physical and psychological effect on individuals that they cannot ensure a reasonable quality of life for themselves by their own efforts; the other, that the economic and social barriers that disabled people face are so pervasive that they are prevented from ensuring themselves a reasonable quality of life by their own efforts.

The former has become known as the individual model of disability and is underpinned by personal tragedy theory. It has been under severe attack in recent years from a variety of sources, to the point that it is now generally recognized that it is an inadequate basis for developing a proper understanding of disability. The latter has become known as the social model of disability, and has shifted the focus away from impaired individuals and on to restrictive environments and disabling barriers. This has received acceptance to such an extent that it has almost become the new orthodoxy.

THE CLASSIC WELFARE STATE

The project to establish a welfare state which would provide 'cradle to grave' security for all its members has failed disabled people, as I have already suggested. This failure can be traced back almost to the foundations of the welfare state during the Second World War and the subsequent legislation that laid the foundations of the welfare state as we know it today.

The first Act of Parliament to treat disabled people as a single group was the Disabled Persons (Employment) Act 1944, which attempted to secure employment rights for disabled people. Further, the Education Act 1944, underpinned by an egalitarian ideology, specified that disabled children should be educated alongside their peers in primary and secondary education. The National Assistance Act 1948 laid a duty on local authorities to arrange a variety of services for disabled people, in both the community and institutions. The National Health Service Act 1948 also provided hospital-based treatment and long-term care for disabled people.

It soon became clear that implementation of the Disabled Persons (Employment) Act was more concerned with not upsetting employers than ensuring that disabled people seeking employment were treated fairly. The Education Act became the legal mechanism for the establishment of a huge infrastructure of segregated special education based around eleven medical categories. The National Assistance Act allowed, but did not require, local authorities to provide services and the choice for many disabled people was survive without assistance or go into residential care. The National Health Service Act offered little beyond acute treatment and long-term care usually meant living on a geriatric ward even if you weren't old.

Since the late 1950s there has been a concerted attempt by successive governments to reduce the numbers of people living in segregated institutions of one kind or another. The shift towards community-based services took a decisive turn in the early 1960s, when the government announced its intention to reduce the number of beds in mental hospitals by half. The rhetoric of community care continued to obscure the reality that for many previously incarcerated people, living in the community bestowed no more rights other than perhaps to starve, freeze or die alone.

By the late 1960s, attempts were being made to rationalize the chaos that was the reality of community care. The Chronically Sick and Disabled Persons Act 1970 was supposed to be the vehicle for this rationalization. It was even heralded at one point by two non-disabled commentators as a 'Charter (of rights) for the disabled', but the reality was that it was merely an extension of the needs-based welfare provision of the National Assistance Act.

The only two extra duties were to be imposed on local authorities: the duty to compile a register and the duty to publicize services. The former produced little information of value and the latter was widely ignored. The services listed under section 2 only needed to be provided where it was 'practical and reasonable' to do so, and for most local authorities it wasn't, so they didn't.

Despite the rhetoric of integration, community care and rights which emerged in the 1980s, neither the Education Act 1981 nor the Disabled Persons (Services, Consultation and Representation) Act 1986 has significantly improved the quality of welfare services available to disabled people. The evidence for this continuing failure has been provided by officially commissioned government research showing the extent of poverty and unemployment among disabled people; studies by independent research institutes showing that disabled people are 'last on the list' as far as welfare services are concerned; academics who show that services to enable disabled people to live in the community are poor; and disabled people who condemn health authorities and social service departments that fail to provide them with a satisfactory quality of life.

What has become more contentious in recent years is the issue of statutory entitlements. It is certainly true that despite the establishment of a comprehensive legal framework for the provision of services to disabled people, these services somehow do not get delivered. The main reasons for this are: first, services have come to be provided on the basis of professional definitions of need; second, governments of all political persuasion have resisted pressure to force local authorities to meet their statutory obligations; third, those services that have been provided have locked disabled people into dependency upon them.

RETHINKING COMMUNTY CARE

The problems with welfare services were not unique to disabled people and prompted a major review of the welfare state in the mid-1980s. Beginning with a damning report on community care from the Audit Commission (1986), the Griffiths Report (1988) followed in 1990 and, after much delay, this was incorporated into a White Paper, *Caring for People*. After a very short consultation period the White Paper was incorporated into the National Health Service and Community Care Act 1990.

Central to the new legislation was a new managerial strategy for providing services which was to be supplemented by a market strategy that involved stimulating the private and voluntary sectors to act as providers of services, and the statutory authorities to act as enablers and purchasers of services rather than sole providers. By opting for this combination of market and managerial strategies, the government hoped that the problems of professional dominance and dependency creation would be addressed. However, such hopes were soon dashed, from the point of view of disabled people at least. Davis (in Swain et al., 1993) comments on the continuing dominance of professionals over service delivery: 'At this juncture, our lives are substantially still in their hands. They still determine most decisions and their practical outcomes.'

While it is too early to be definitive about the ways in which the restructuring is working, it has to be said that the early signs are not hopeful. There is little evidence that disabled people are being involved in the planning and delivery of services in the way that legislation requires. Nor is there much evidence that local authority assessment procedures adequately reflect the legal requirement to place individual needs at the centre of the reforms. Finally, studies that have recently been carried out are not optimistic that the existing reforms are enough, and unless further changes are made, as far as disabled people are concerned, 'their opportunities to be independent citizens will disappear' (Morris, 1993).

The new reforms do not change the balance of power between professional and service user. It is now the care manager who assesses the needs of the service user. Users do now have rights to see and even contribute to their care plans, but they have no greater rights to service and still no access to legally enforceable grievance procedures. Although the quote below was written before the recent legislation, the situation described by Cohen (1985) remains unchanged: 'much the same groups of experts are doing much the same business as usual. The basic rituals incorporated into the move to the mind – taking case histories, writing social enquiry reports, constructing files, organising case conferences – are still being enacted.' In the post-1990 world, the same people, albeit with different jobs titles and perhaps in plusher buildings, are doing the same things to disabled people although they may now be called 'doing a needs led assessment' or 'producing a care plan'.

Davis (1990) is clear that the newly emerging profession of care management will not provide the necessary structural reforms:

it is simply not enough for brokers, care managers or any other agent to potter about in the existing mish-mash of inappropriate and inadequate services, with a view to helping individual disabled people to piece together some kind of survival plan for existing in a hostile world. We have been there too long.

So the welfare state has not ensured the rights and entitlements of disabled people in the past; nor does the current restructuring appear likely to change this. Services as they are currently being provided are unlikely to satisfy disabled people, and fall short of the demands made by disabled people from all over Europe when they met at a conference in Strasbourg to discuss their own struggles for independent living.

We demand social welfare systems that include personal assistance services that are consumer controlled and which allow various models of independent living for disabled people, regardless of their disability and income. We demand social welfare legislation which recognises these services as basic civil rights and which provide necessary appeal procedures. (Press Release, European Network on Independent Living, 1989)

RECONCEPTUALIZING THE PROBLEM: FROM NEEDS TO RIGHTS

It is not denied any longer that the systematic deprivation and disadvantage that disabled people experience is caused by restrictive environments and disabling barriers. The point at issue here is what should be done about it. Until recently, successive governments have taken the view that the way to deal with this is through the provision of professional services aimed at meeting individual needs, coupled with a strategy aimed at persuading the rest of society to remove their disabling barriers, and to change their restrictive environments. As a former Minister for Disabled People put it: 'Nor would I deny that discrimination exists – of course it does. We have to battle against it, but, rather than legislating, the most constructive and productive way forward is through raising awareness in the community as a whole' (Hansard, 1991, 1150).

As I have already argued, professionalized service provision within a needs-based system of welfare has added to existing forms of discrimination and, in addition, has created new forms of its own, including the provision of stigmatized segregated services such as day care and the development of professional assessments and practices based upon invasions of privacy, as well as creating a language of paternalism which can only enhance discriminatory practices.

On top of that, policies of persuasion have turned out to be bankrupt, as the cost of implementing them grows, while at the same time disabled children are still directed into segregated special schools, the number of disabled people who are unemployed increases and the number of disabled people living in poverty continues to expand. That this unacceptable situation is owing to disabling barriers rather than personal limitations is now clear; it is also clear that previous attempts to dismantle these barriers have been based on incorrect understandings of the real nature of discrimination. Discrimination does not exist in the prejudiced attitudes of individuals but in the institutionalized practices of society.

This new understanding of the real nature of the problem involves the idea of institutional discrimination which can be described in the following ways. First, institutional discrimination is evident when the policies and activities of public or private organizations, social groups and all other organizational forms result in unequal treatment or unequal outcomes between disabled and non-disabled people. Second, institutional discrimination is embedded in the work of welfare institutions when they deny disabled people the right to live autonomously, through failure to meet their statutory obligations in terms of service provision, through their differential implementation of legislative and advisory codes, through interference in the privacy of disabled people and through the provision of inappropriate and segregative services.

Given this proviso, it is none the less the right to appropriate welfare services to meet their own self-defined needs that disabled people are demanding, not to have their needs defined and met by others.

disabled people themselves are demanding a new emphasis on civil rights, equal opportunities and citizenship. They see institutional discrimination as the main disability they face, and are lobbying for new equal rights legislation to outlaw discrimination on the grounds of disability. The first priority is equal access to basic essentials such as an adequate income, housing, access to employment, to public transport, to education and to the ordinary facilities of everyday life. (Doyle and Harding, in Coote, 1992)

CONCLUSION

It is clear we have seen a significant shift in the discourses about disability, building upon the insights of the social model of disability. Issues of discrimination and civil rights are now on the political agenda and have become part of the welfare discourse. One commentator suggests that disabled people are 'seeking a model of welfare built not on need and philanthropy, but on equal citizenship as a means of self determination' (Coote, 1992).

The government itself recognized that these shifting discourses needed a more appropriate political response and passed the Disability Discrimination Act 1995. Whether this represented a significant shifting from seeing disability as an issue of managed care to seeing it as one of civil rights is, however, open to doubt. Certainly its failure to make the Act comprehensive and its unwillingness to provide an enforcement commission leave this open to doubt.

GUIDE TO FURTHER READING

Barnes, C. (1991) *Discrimination and Disabled People in Britain*. London: Hurst and Co. Develops the concept of institutional discrimination and uses published evidence to describe its nature and extent.

Barnes, C. and Mercer, G. (eds) (1996) *Exploring the Divide: Illness and Disability*. Leeds The Disability Press. Explores the experience of disability in the context of medicine and health.

Barton, L. (eds) (1996) *Disability and Society: Emerging Issues and Insights*. London Longman. A series of essays written from sociological viewpoints.

Campbell, J. and Oliver, M. (1996) *Disability Politics: Understanding Our Past, Changing Our Future*. London: Routledge. Charts the rise of the disability movement and includes material on its relation to the welfare state.

Cohen, S. (1985) *Visions of Social Control*. Cambridge: Polity Press.

Coote, A. (ed.) (1992) *The Welfare of Citizens: Developing New Social Rights*. London: Rivers Oram Press.

Davis, K. (1990) Old medicine is still no cure. *Community Care*, 8 September, 14.

French, S. (ed.) (1994) *On Equal Terms: Working with Disabled People*. London: Butterworth Heinemann. A comprehensive set of issues are covered, including policy as well as practice.

Hales, G. (ed.) (1995) *Beyond Disability: towards an Enabling Society*. London: Sage. Discusses services for disabled people in the context of personal experiences of impairment.

Morris, J. (1993) *Independent Lives? Community Care and Disabled People*. Basingstoke: Macmillan. Good policy discussions on independent living and community care.

Oliver, M. (1990) *The Politics of Disablement*. Basingstoke: Macmillan. Describes the emergence of capitalism and the rise of the welfare state for disabled people.

Oliver, M. (1996) *Understanding Disability: from Theory to Practice*. Basingstoke: Macmillan. A series of essays, many of which are about social policy and disability.

Swain, J., Finkelstein, V., French, S. and Oliver, M. (1993) *Disabling Barriers – Enabling Environments*. London: Sage. Useful discussion of policy debates which incorporate the views of disabled people.

Zarb, G. (ed.) (1995) *Removing Disabling Barriers*. London: Policy Studies Institute. A collection of papers on policy themes.

Copies of the international journal *Disability and Society* (formerly *Disability, Handicap and Society*) are also useful.

IV.5

Lone parents

Jonathan Bradshaw

Introduction

Changes taking place in family form pose new challenges to social policy. One of the most dramatic of these changes has been the increase in the prevalence of lone parent families during the past three decades. (The words single parent families and one parent families are also widely used to describe these families, but lone parents and lone parent families are preferred, despite their slightly emotive ring, in order to avoid confusion with one category of lone parents – single lone parents – and the difficulties of using 'one parenthood' and 'one parents'.) The rapid increase in the proportion of families with children headed by a lone parent has in recent years been evinced as evidence of: a breakdown of traditional family form; the collapse of the role of husband and father; an example of the underclass; a cause of a culture of dependency; a reason for the UK no longer being able to afford the welfare state; an example of how the welfare state has undermined the social structure; and an important reason for youth crime, indiscipline, poor educational attainment and many other ills of modern society. Indeed, for the student of social policy the vilification, indeed sometimes moral panic, about lone parents by politicians, some academic commentators, the media and others has come so thick and fast that it has been hard to keep pace. It has to be admitted that many of the claims made about lone parents have yet to be investigated adequately empirically. Nevertheless, the subject of social policy has made a substantial contribution to what we do know. The purpose of this chapter is to show how social policy approaches the topic and what we have discovered.

A change as rapid as this presents the institutions of the welfare state with remarkable challenges, and there are fascinating opportunities to observe, and, indeed, to influence how those institutions adapt or fail to adapt to demographic change, how policy is made and the extent to which the state can or should attempt to influence or engineer changes in family form or in the behaviour of lone parent families. So though we may be concerned with the plight of lone parents, as students of social policy we recognize that the social policy context of lone parenthood is a rich arena for understanding the subject as a whole.

The Demography of Lone Parents

In the UK a lone parent is now commonly defined as:

> a parent who is not living as a married or cohabiting couple, may or may not be living with others (friends or parents), living with at least one of her or his

children under 16 years or under 19 years and in full-time education.

However, definitions will vary according to purpose – benefit assessment, taxation, research surveys, the census and so on. It is important to be sensitive to these, particularly when making comparisons btween countries.

Although they are lumped together in popular discussion, lone parent families are far from being a homogeneous group. At the moment only about 10 per cent of lone parent families are headed by men. Lone fathers tend to be older, have older children, are more likely than lone mothers to be in employment and about half of them are widowers. The largest group of lone mothers are the previously married; that is, women who are divorced, separated or widowed. They tend to be older than other lone mother families and have older and more children. The most rapidly growing group of lone mother families is single, never married, lone mothers but increasingly there are two rather distinct groups among them. There are those who have never had a living together relationship with the father of their child. These tend to be younger (47 per cent of single lone mothers are teenagers when their child is born) and their children are young. The other half of single lone mothers are in fact more like divorced mothers, in that they became lone mothers as a result of cohabitation breakdown – they and often their child or children have lived together with the father. At the moment, official statistics do not distinguish between these two groups of single lone mothers, but we know from birth registration data that about half of all births outside marriage are registered by both parents at the same address.

These differences in the characteristics of lone parents are important in thinking about social policy in relation to them. But there are also other important factors to take into account. These are summarized in box IV.5.1.

Box IV.5.1 Lone parenthood

- Being a lone parent is, for most, only a temporary experience. Most lone mothers and fathers repartner – creating step families.
- Some lone parents experience more than one episode of lone parenthood and experience more than one type of lone parenthood.
- Lone parent families are becoming increasingly spatially segregated, concentrated in urban and inner-city areas. But lone parents in rural areas may also have special problems.
- There is a much higher prevalence of lone parent families among Afro-Caribbean families but a lower proportion among Asian families.
- Lone mother families are concentrated in social housing – indeed, one of the consequences of relationship breakdowns is for lone mothers and their children to move down the housing ladder and at worst to experience homelessness.

THE PROBLEMS OF LONE PARENTS

Why are lone parents the focus of social or collective concern rather than just a private matter? There are three main reasons.

Dependency

Lone parenthood almost invariably results in a period of dependency on state benefits. Just over two-thirds of lone parent families are dependent on Income Support and over 80 per cent are supported by Income Support, Housing Benefit or Family Credit. This dependency on benefits costs a great deal of money: in 1994/5 benefit expenditure on lone parents was expected to be £9.1 billion, compared to £4 billion in 1989/90. Cash benefits are not the only resource costs of lone parenthood. For example, it has been estimated that an extra 800,000 dwellings are needed at any one time as a result of lone parenthood, and most of these are needed in the social sector.

Poverty

A corollary of dependence on means-tested benefits, but also associated with low earnings power and inadequate child care, is the high prevalence of poverty among lone parents. There is evidence from the work of Millar (1989) that lone parents on social assistance (Income Support) are particularly hard pressed, not least because they are dependent for longer periods than married couples with children. Lone parents and their children make up a substantial proportion of the poor. In 1992/3, 58 per cent of lone parent families were living in poverty (with incomes below 50 per cent of average after housing costs), and although they represent only 7 per cent of the population as a whole, they formed 17 per cent of the bottom quintile (20 per cent) of the income distribution after housing costs (DSS, 1995). The prevalence of poverty among lone parent families in Britain is high compared with other countries (Bradshaw et al., 1996).

The impact on children

Associated with this poverty is a general belief that divorce, and living in a lone parent family, is bad for children. Evidence on this needs to be interpreted with great care, not least because quite a lot of it is not very soundly based. The better evidence also relies to a considerable extent on the outcomes for children experiencing lone parenthood in the 1960s and 1970s, when it was much more unusual and therefore possibly more stigmatizing. Much

---

> **Box IV.5.2**   Possible objectives of policy for lone parents
>
> - Maintain an adequate living standard for lone parents and their children.
> - Enable lone parents to support their children and to do so without work if they want to.
> - Meet lone parents' special and extra needs.
> - Reduce dependence on benefits.
> - Enable lone parents to work outside the home if they want to.
> - Discourage the breakdown of marriage and cohabitation and births outside marriage.
> - Make sure that the absent parents contribute to the costs of their families.
> - Maintain equity with married/ cohabiting couples.
> - Reinforce the institution of marriage.
> - Encourage repartnering.

of the evidence quoted uses American sources, where lone parenthood is more closely associated with race than it is in the UK. It is also very difficult to separate the influences of living in a lone parent family (and the associated deprivations) from the affects of unhappy family life prior to breakdown. The evidence has been reviewed by Burghes (1994).

THE OBJECTIVES OF POLICY FOR LONE PARENTS

What might the objectives of social policy be for lone parent families? Box IV.5.2 presents a selection of possible objectives in no particular order. Of course many of these objectives either compete or are not easy to reconcile in practice. No government has tackled the task of clarifying which should have precedence, and how policy should be adapted to pursue that objective. There has been a tendency in official pronouncements to emphasize that policy is neutral – neutral with respect to the treatment of different family forms and neutral with respect to the employment of lone parents. Policy has inevitably been preoccupied with cost. A Cabinet Briefing Paper on lone parents leaked to the *Guardian* in September 1993 stated:

We have assumed that the primary objective of any measures taken will be to reduce the burden on public expenditure caused by lone parent families, and that measures should therefore be directed towards discouraging lone parenthood and other ways of reducing public expenditure which do not harm the interests of the children of lone parents.

Over time it is possible to discern a shift in the emphasis given to the different objectives of policy in respect of lone parents.

MEETING THE EXTRA COSTS OF LONE PARENTS

To take one example, following the report of the Finer Committee on one parent families in 1970, a number of changes were made to the tax and benefit system which sought to recognize the extra costs of bringing up a child alone. Thus, One Parent Benefit was introduced as an addition to Child Benefit for the first child in a lone parent family. A Tapered Earnings Disregard (a proportion of part-time earnings not taken into account in the means test) was introduced into Supplementary Benefit to encourage and enable lone parents to supplement their benefit income with part-time earnings. When Income Support was introduced in 1988, there was a lone parent premium in the scales of benefit which also had its equivalent in Housing Benefit. In the income tax system, lone parents were treated no less generously than couples, in that they were entitled to an allowance equivalent to the

married couples allowance. In the Family Credit means test, the income of lone parents was assessed in exactly the same way as that of couples.

Now it appears that this recognition of the extra needs of lone parents may be changing. The Tapered Earnings Disregard was abolished when Income Support started in 1988. In the 1996 uprating of benefits, One Parent Benefit and the Lone Parent Premium in Income Support were frozen, and the Secretary of State for Social Security has since taken powers to alter the relative value of benefits in the future.

THE EMPLOYMENT OF LONE PARENTS

Another example of a possibly less neutral stance in policy towards lone parents concerns employment. In many other countries, lone parents are expected to seek employment when their youngest child is three years old (Bradshaw et al., 1996). In the UK, lone parents are entitled to Income Support until their youngest child is 16. This rule exists because of the strongly held view of some that it is in the interests of lone parent families, at least for a time after the birth of a child outside marriage, or after the breakdown of a marriage or cohabitation, that the lone parent should not be encouraged or made to take paid work. At other times it might be in the interests of the lone parent, her children and the community that she is not required to combine paid work and caring responsibilities. Further, it may be better for children for their mother to be at home, especially following a period of disruption in their lives. Yet the influence of these ideas on policy may be losing ground. This is partly due to the fact that while the proportion of married women in employment continues to increase rapidly, the proportion of lone mothers in employment has been static or declining in recent years. Further, compared to other countries the proportion of lone mothers in employment in the UK is low (41 per cent in 1990/2 compared, for example, with 82 per cent in France, 70 per cent in Sweden and 60 per cent in the USA). Further, in most other countries most lone mothers working tend to work full-time, while in the UK they tend to work part-time. There is also evidence that, although employment is not a guarantee against poverty, in all countries including the UK the prevalence of poverty among lone mothers is much lower if they are in employment (Bradshaw et al., 1996).

While there has been no change in the entitlement rules governing the child age limit in Income Support (perhaps because it would increase the unemployment count), there have been a number of changes in recent times which indicate a less neutral position towards lone mothers employment. These are summarized in box IV.5.3. There is evidence that some of these changes have had a small impact. For example, by 1995, 100,000 lone parents were working 16–24 hours per week and receiving Family Credit, and 18,000 were utilizing the child care disregard in Family Credit. However, there are still over one million lone parents receiving Income Support.

What other measures might be employed to increase the proportion of lone mothers in employment? These can be divided into push factors and pull factors.

Push factors

1 Require that lone parents actively seek work before their youngest child is 16, perhaps when they go to school at five or secondary school at 11. It might be necessary to allow a period of, say, up to two years for those who become lone parents when their youngest child is older than this, in order for them to have a chance to overcome the disruption in their lives.

2 Increase the skills and earning potential of lone parents by specially targeted

---

Box IV.5.3 Changes to benefits which affect lone mothers' employment

- The replacement of Family Income Supplement by more generous Family Credit in 1988. The hours rule was also reduced from 24 to 16.
- One of the explicit objectives of the Child Support Act 1991 was to encourage the employment of lone parents. It sought to achieve this by not taking into account some child support in the means test for Family Credit taking into account all child support in Income Support.
- In 1995, a child care disregard (an allowance of some child care costs) was introduced into Family Credit and improved in value in 1996.
- A Back to Work Bonus designed to encourage lone parents and others on Income Support who are able to work part-time to increase their hours to 16, come off Income Support and receive half of their part-time earnings up to £1000 as a bonus tax-free. A similar Child Maintenance Bonus was introduced from April 1997.
- A limited scheme for nursery vouchers is being tested in three areas.
- There have been other modest changes, such as an expansion in holiday child care, pilot schemes introducing case-workers to help lone parents in local Benefits Agency offices and special efforts in some local training agencies.
- Cuts in the real level of the premium on top of Income Support which goes to lone parents.

---

education or training schemes. For example, at one time there was an Employment Training Scheme which paid up to

£50 per week in child care costs for six months for participating lone parents. The scheme appears to have been more or less brought to a halt when Training and Enterprise Councils took over.

3 Reduce the real level of Income Support paid to lone parents. This is the policy that was pursued in the 1996 uprating, despite the evidence discussed earlier that lone parents are already very hard pressed.

Pull factors

1 Improve the in-work incomes of lone parents. This might be achieved in a variety of ways.

- A minimum wage could increase earnings. However, because of the low income thresholds for tax and national insurance contributions and the loss of means tested benefits (Housing Benefit and Family Credit), the improvement in net income would not be great.
- Increase Child Benefit (expensive) or One Parent Benefit (less expensive but raises equity issues with married couples).
- Increase the value of Family Credit.
- One of the main financial disincentives to entering employment is the treatment of housing costs in the benefit system. While on Income Support rents and council tax are paid in full, as is mortgage interest after six months. When in employment, tenants are in principle eligible for Housing Benefit, though in practice most of those receiving Family Credit are lifted out of eligibility. Mortgagees, who are increasingly prevalent among lone parents, receive no help at all. Thus, there are very sharp increases in housing costs for both tenants and owner occupiers when moving off Income Support into employment. The solutions to this include the lowering of real rents by increasing subsidies to enable lower rents in social housing, a lowering of

the taper in Housing Benefit and the introduction of a mortgage benefit scheme.

2 Introduce an effective child maintenance regime. The Child Support Act, despite having been subject to repeated scrutiny by official bodies, two amending Acts and many operational changes, is still failing to deliver on its objectives, causing hideous disruption to people's lives. It is also subject to widespread collusion, and is very expensive to administer (Clarke et al., 1996). It is widely considered to have been a major disaster in policy-making, and therefore it is a lesson for future attempts by central government to intervene in this sensitive area of people's lives. One proposal for reform is that the adjudication functions of the Child Support Agency (CSA) might be returned to the courts or to a conciliation service, while payment and enforcement remain the responsibility of the CSA. However, for maintenance to be a solid support for employment it needs, as already happens in many European countries, to be guaranteed or underwritten by the state; that is, paid to the lone parent whether or not the absent parent makes payments.

3 Child care is probably at the heart of this matter. Without good quality, flexible and affordable child care, including holiday and after-school care, it is unlikely to be possible to make an impact on lone parents' employment. Compared with most other countries, the provision of pre-school child care in the UK is abysmal. Those lone mothers who do work in the UK either work full-time and for a wage that enables them to employ a child-minder, or part-time, relying entirely on family or other informal support. The most prevalent patterns of child care in other countries are heavily subsidized provision in nurseries or, increasingly, subsidized and supervised family day care. As 50 per cent of three and four year olds are already in nursery classes in the UK (though with wide geographical variations and mostly part-time),

schools may offer the best way of developing provision in those years. The government's nursery voucher scheme, in 1997
in an experimental phase, is restricted to
four year olds, is insufficient in value to
cover full-time care, requires parental top-
up and redistributes resources from good
statutory provision to less good statutory
and private provision. The most prevalent
form of full-time child care for the under-
threes is child minders – unsubsidized,
under-regulated and with cause for serious
anxieties about quality. To improve this
provision requires a major investment of
public resources in vouchers, tax relief or
direct or indirect subsidies through the
benefit system or the expansion or public
nursery facilities.

CONCLUSION

In only a very short period, social policy for lone parents has moved from the
doldrums to the forefront of the political agenda. However, policy-making remains tentative and incremental, seemingly
bewildered by the speed and nature of the
changes. Balancing the needs of lone parents, and particularly their children, with
other objectives of policy has not proven
easy. The result is high levels of poverty
and dependence on benefits, certainly compared to other countries grappling with
the same changes. This is an arena where
the balance between individual and collective solutions to social problems is still to
be settled.

GUIDE FOR FURTHER READING

The best source on the demography of lone parents is the quarterly journal, *Population Trends* which publishes regular articles summarizing the most recent data on family patterns: see, for example, Haskey, J. (1994) Estimated numbers of lone parent families and their prevalence in Great Britain in 1991. *Population Trends, 78*. London: HMSO.

The most comprehensive study of lone parent families in the UK is Bradshaw, J. and Millar, J. (1991) *Lone Parent Families in the UK*, DSS Research Report no. 6. London: HMSO. Since then the Policy Studies Institute has been undertaking a rolling series of surveys of lone parents. The latest is Ford, R. et al. (1995) *Changes in Lone Parenthood 1989–1993*, DSS Research report series 40. London: HMSO.

The best study of the living standards of lone parents is Millar, J. (1989) *Poverty and the Lone Parent Family: the Challenge to Social Policy*. Aldershot: Avebury. In Department of Social Security (1995) *Households below Average Incomes; a Statistical Analysis 1979–1992/93*. London: HMSO, there are up-to-date data on poverty among lone parents.

The publications of the Family Policy Studies Centre are the best source of up-to-date research and policy commentary on lone parents. Recent publications include Burghes, L. and Brown, M. (1995) *Single Lone Mothers: Problems, Prospects and Policies*. London: Family Policy Studies Centre; Bradshaw, J. et al. (1996) *The Employment of Lone Parents: a Comparison of Policy in 20 Countries*. London: Family Policy Studies Centre; Burghes, L. (1993) *One Parent Families, Policy Options for the 1990s*. York: Joseph Rowntree Foundation; Burghes, L. (1994) *Lone Parenthood and Family Disruption: the Outcomes for Children*. London: Family Policy Studies Centre; Utting, D. (1995) *Family and Parenthood: Supporting Families, Preventing Breakdown*. York: Joseph Rowntree Foundation; Clarke, K. et al. (1996) *Small Change: the Impact of the Child Support Act on Lone Mothers and Children*. London: Family Policy Studies Centre.

Finally, the National Council for One Parent Families publishes a series of guides on policies for lone parents; for example, National Council for One Parent Families (1996) *Benefits/Tax Information*. London: NCOPF.

service-based issues

IV.6

INCOME PROTECTION AND SOCIAL SECURITY

JOHN DITCH

The very term 'social security' is full of ambiguity and means different things to different people in different places. In the 1990s in the USA, social security usually refers to retirement pensions; in the UK, on the other hand, social security includes all cash benefits (over thirty) which are transferred via the state. In continental Europe the term 'social security' is used much less frequently, the term 'social protection' (deemed to include cash benefits and health care) being preferred. However, it is possible to identify a surprisingly similar set of principles and values which underpin the development and delivery of social security benefits. But the circumstances under which financial support is provided to those in need, the conditions of eligibility, modes of financing, the value of payments and the length of time for which they may be paid vary from country to country. The word 'social' reflects the societal context and the presumption of reciprocity and obligation which exist between people (sometimes in their role as workers and sometimes as citizens); 'security' reflects the support and protection which is provided against the expected (having children or being old) or unexpected (sudden death of a breadwinner, unemployment or ill health). This chapter will concentrate on the British social security system and will describe some of its key features, the policy objectives and principles that are served and the

developing challenges to social security as we approach a new millennium. The chapter concludes by reviewing the contemporary debate about future options for social security.

The British social security system has its origins in the Poor Law arrangements, which were extended, reformed and complemented during the nineteenth and early twentieth centuries by state-facilitated insurance-based schemes. The defining document in the history of British social security is the Beveridge Report of 1942, which simultaneously provided a rationale for state intervention and a template for future provision. For the past fifty years this report has been the benchmark against which social security provision and analytical reviews have been compared. With the benefit of hindsight the flaws and deficiencies of the Beveridge paradigm can be clearly seen: these have been elaborated *ad nauseam*. Beveridge embodied the virtues, values and assumptions of his time. He expected the majority of men to spend most of their active lives in paid employment and therefore in a position to make regular social/national insurance contributions. Conversely, he presumed that most women would get married, have children and not work outside the home. Beveridge could not have foreseen the changes which were to happen: the failure of governments to maintain full employment; the rising levels of female economic activity; the

Table IV.6.1. A typology of social security

Type	Form	Example
Contributory	Social insurance	Retirement Pension
Means-tested	Social assistance	Income Support
Categorical	Neither means nor contribution tested	Child Benefit
Occupational	Based on employment record/status	Statutory Sick Pay
Discretionary	Based on rules and judgements	Social Fund

growth in self-employment, part-time and insecure employment; the challenges faced by families as a result of the increase in separation, divorce and lone parenthood; the increase in life expectancy and the decline in the birth rate. Taken together, these changes to the social, economic and demographic fabric of the country were to put great pressure on the social security system. For the past twenty-five years policy-makers have been trying to adapt the social security system to these new circumstances. Surprisingly, however, the Beveridge report retains a relevance: its clear articulation of values and principles remains a benchmark for thinking and practice in social security provision.

CLASSIFYING SOCIAL SECURITY

The British system of social security has grown piecemeal in the post-war years. Despite periodic attempts to simplify the structure and reduce the number of benefits, there remain over thirty and these can be assigned to one of five categories (Table IV.6.1.). Fundamental to the Beveridge paradigm, and reflected in the title of his famous report (Social Insurance and Allied Services), are contributory benefits. First introduced in the UK in the first decade of the century, contributory benefits (which include Retirement Pension, Unemployment Benefit, Sickness Benefit and Widow's Benefit) are paid for by National Insurance contributions made by both employers and employees. Entitlement is established when sufficient contributions

to the National Insurance Fund have been made. The scope of these benefits has been contracting over the past two decades.

Of growing importance are the means-tested benefits. Conceived by Beveridge as residual benefits for those without, or who exhausted entitlement to, insurance (contributory) benefits, they are paid to individuals (and their dependants) when their income and assets fall below a prescribed amount, which varies according to family needs and circumstances. The most significant benefit of this kind in the UK is Income Support (previously known as Supplementary Benefit and before that National Assistance). Income Support is for claimants who have no (or very little) employment and no other source of income. Family Credit (formerly Family Income Supplement) is paid to families (with dependent children) who are working for low wages. Other benefits of this kind include Housing Benefit, Council Tax Benefit and Disability Working Allowance. In addition to the basic benefits, recipients are entitled to a range of 'passported' benefits, such as free prescriptions. Means-tested benefits are more expensive than other benefits to administer and are associated with stigma and low take-up (a situation where people who are entitled to a benefit do not claim it).

Categorical benefits are neither means-tested nor contribution-based, but are paid, in specified circumstances, to particular groups of people. An example is Child Benefit, which is paid for all children living in the UK if they are under 16 and to unmarried young people under 19 if they are still at school or college. Other categorical benefits include Disability Living Allowance and Invalid Care Allowance.

Occupational benefits are dependent upon employment history. Some are at the discretion of employers and most usually take the form of occupational pensions funds: the contributions (from employees and employers) are invested and are paid, in the form of a pension, when the individual retires. There are two statutory schemes which are now administered by employers. These are Statutory Sick Pay and Statutory Maternity Pay, and they are only available to employees who meet specified qualifying conditions.

Discretionary benefits play a small but important part in social security. The Social Fund, established in the late 1980s, provides assistance (in the form of either a grant or a loan) to claimants (usually on Income Support) who have urgent or exceptional needs. There is no right to a Social Fund payment and the amount of money available is limited, so DSS officials have to decide who should get a grant/loan and who should not. This is one of the most controversial areas of the whole social security system.

The traditional distinction has been between selective (means-tested) and universal (non means-tested) benefits. Such an approach is too simplistic. There are no truly universal benefits: Child Benefit is directed at families with dependent children; Retirement Pensions go to older people. All benefits, in one way or another, have some regard to need, circumstances, contributions history or current resources. Similarly, it is possible to target benefits without testing income. For example, age, disability or parenthood may be the key condition to trigger entitlement.

Social security policies exist to satisfy any number of objectives: they will vary through time, across countries and between client/claimant groups. It should not be surprising that many objectives are implicit rather than explicit and that on occasions they are in contradiction with one another.

Five general objectives for social security can be identified.

1 To meet immediate financial need following an unexpected event, such as the death of a breadwinner, redundancy or industrial injury.
2 To meet the (additional) costs associated with disability or care. Examples include the Disability Living Allowance, Severe Disablement Allowance and Attendance Allowance.
3 To support the family as a social unit: historically this has been based on traditional patterns of a nuclear family but now support (indeed, additional support) is given to a variety of family forms. A typical example is Child Benefit or One Parent Benefit.
4 To prevent or alleviate poverty. In the absence of social security provision many millions of individuals and families would be without visible means of support and would be in poverty. However, it is unclear that social assistance benefits remove claimants from the experience of deprivation. There is great uncertainty about how poverty is to be defined and how benefit levels are to be set in relation to various definitions of adequacy.
5 To redistribute resources. Clearly this is inherent in any social security system: but from whom and to whom? Various dimensions exist; from young to old, over the life cycle; from rich to poor, between income groups; from those without children to those with children; from able-bodied to disabled. The distribution and redistribution of resources, at the very heart of social policy, can only be understood in relation to the wider contexts of employment, taxation and public expenditure.

Having identified the structure and purpose of social security benefits, it is also necessary to specify some principles in relation to its provision. Six key conditions need to be met in an ideal-type system.

1 Benefits need to be *adequate*: but for what? How can adequacy be defined? This is an issue which is both technically and methodologically complex and politically sensitive. What (whose?) standards are to be applied? What is to be the unit for assessment and payment? Should it be the individual, the family or the household?

2 Social security systems should be *comprehensive*: in addition to entitlement based on contributions and category there is a need for a wider safety-net benefit. The greater the reliance placed on safety-net benefits, the higher the probability that there will be extensive experience of stigma and consequent low take-up.

3 There is a need for *consistency* at two levels. First, structural compatibility with other state provided sub-systems of the social policy framework, including health, housing, employment and criminal justice. Second, there is a need to ensure that individuals with like circumstances are dealt with in similar ways: social security schemes should be regulated and rule bound. Schemes with minimum levels of officer discretion are more likely to be successful in this respect. On the other hand, social security systems should adapt and be sympathetic to the circumstances of claimants rather than requiring claimants to adapt to the imperatives of social security provision.

4 *Simplicity* should be a watch word in social security. Benefits should be easy to claim and easy to administer; both claimants and staff should find them easy to understand. Complexity adds to administrative costs, increases the risk of error, stimulates/masks fraud and undermines effective take-up by eligible applicants.

5 On the other hand, benefits should be *flexible* and responsive to the changing circumstances of claimants and the expectations of the wider society. Some benefits, like Income Support, require claimants to inform the DSS immediately of significant changes in their lives: these include getting a job, moving home, having a baby, increasing the hours of part-time work. In the light of the reported changes in circumstances the level of benefit paid will either increase or decrease according to the new level of assessed need. On the other hand, some benefits, such as Family Credit, assess a claimants's circumstances every six months and determine a level of benefit which remains fixed, irrespective of changes in circumstances, until the next formal assessment. Each approach has its merits.

6 All social security benefits, and benefit delivery arrangements, should be *non-discriminatory*. There should be no distinction in treatment on the basis of gender, race, religion, age, disability or sexual orientation.

Social security in the UK is big business. The total expenditure on social security was of the order of £95 billion in 1996/7; the DSS employs a total of 85,000 staff in headquarters and six executive agencies; administrative costs amount to over £4 billion per year. Resources for the social security programme come from two principal sources: for contributory benefits from the National Insurance Fund financed (primarily) from employers' and employees' National Insurance contributions; for non-contributory benefits from resources voted by Parliament from general taxation, which now provides over a half of total programme income. At any one moment there are over 10 million older people in receipt of a retirement pension, almost 7 million families (12.6 million children) in receipt of Child Benefit and 5.8 million in receipt of Income Support. Social security is much more important for those at the bottom of the income distribution than it is for those at the top: cash benefits represent 75 per cent of the gross income of the poorest tenth, but less than 2 per cent for the richest tenth. One in seven of the UK's population is dependent on Income Support.

One of the key areas for debate and controversy in recent years has concerned the growth in expenditure on social security. The DSS is inclined to point out that since 1949–50 expenditure on social security has increased from £597 million to £85 billion in 1994/5; allowing for inflation, an eightfold increase in real terms. Most expenditure is demand-led and the only parts of the budget which are 'capped' relate to the discretionary Social Fund, Independent Living Fund and grants to Motability (an independent charitable organization which helps people with disabilities to obtain vehicles on favourable terms using the higher rate of Disability Living Allowance mobility component). In 1993, the DSS predicted that expenditure on benefits would increase at the rate of 3.3 per cent per year (excluding the effects of unemployment) until the end of the century. The DSS's strategy has been to contain this increase to within 2 per cent per annum: transferring responsibility for income protection back to individuals, employers and the wider private sector. This perspective sees the welfare state as being in crisis, with costs tending to be out of control, driven ever upwards by a so-called 'demographic timebomb' and social trends. But these figures have been challenged: although there clearly are upward pressures associated with demographic ageing and its implications for the costs of care and the adequacy of pensions, the predicted costs are likely to be no greater than the costs of the recession which has affected the whole of the Western economy for the past decade or more. Moreover, levels of UK spending on social security, expressed as a proportion of GDP, are in the middle of the range for European Union countries.

It would be unwise to ignore the management and administrative changes which have occurred within the Department of Social Security over the past decade. First, there was the separation of social security from its historic link to health, and then the establishment of six separate executive agencies within the DSS, covering a variety of functional areas, including contributions, payments, information technology, child support and war pensions. There is greater emphasis on the quality of service provided to claimants (or customers as they are now known): many benefit offices have been refitted and performance measures are now commonplace. Even the most cynical of observers acknowledge the improvements that have been made. On the other hand, this concentration on structure and process has arguably diverted attention away from more fundamental matters: the growth in means-tested benefits, the sheer number of people wholly dependent on social security and the (in)adequacy of the benefit levels. A case of old wine in new bottles.

With the establishment of agencies within the DSS and the implementation of programmes of so-called 'new public management', there is a clear statement of the more specific aims of the DSS provided in the department's annual report. Within this context there has been a shift in tone and context. The primary aim is declared as being 'to support Ministers in the development and implementation of the social security programme designed to provide a fair and efficient system of help for beneficiaries and other social security customers while ensuring the best possible value for money for the tax payer.' The emphasis is upon process conditions and performance rather than outcomes achieved. For example, in addition to providing a service which is 'professional, efficient, responsive and fair', importance is attached to the quality of information provided, adjudication standards, minimizing fraud and abuse and promoting staff development.

These generic objectives have been refined in the past two decades by both Labour and Conservative governments. In the mid-1970s the Labour government aimed to end dependence on means-tested benefits, to pay benefits on an indexed basis and to promote equality of entitlement between men and women. By the mid-1980s the Conservative government had shifted focus: benefits should meet genuine need; social security expenditure should be consistent with the overall objectives for the economy and compatible with the needs of the market; social security should be simpler to understand and easier to administer. The thrust of these changes is caught in the following government statement: 'While it is one of the functions of the social security system to help those who are unemployed, it is self-defeating if it creates barriers to the creation of jobs, to job mobility or to people rejoining the labour force. Clearly such obstacles exist if people believe themselves to be better off out of work than in.' In other words, replacement rates should be reduced and more benefits should be means-tested.

Clearly, the world is not as it was when Beveridge wrote his report: labour markets have changed, family forms have adapted and evolved, social roles and attitudes have (arguably) matured. Most countries, and the UK is no exception, have experienced a dislocation between socio-economic realities and policy frameworks. But it is misplaced to construct debates around the future of social security in terms of *crisis*: adaptation and adjustment are the requirements for a developing social policy. At the macro level, the challenge will be to reconcile the need for a just social security system on the one hand with the wider interests of the economy and taxpayers on the other; at the micro level the social security system must be more sensitive and effective in its capacity to reconcile family structures with employment preferences and practices. In order to adjust to these new circumstances there are many proposals for the reform of social security: they vary from incremental refinements to a particular benefit to 'big-bang' transformations involving the integration of tax and benefit systems. The

government, the opposition, the European Commission and independent think-tanks and charities have all contributed to the debate. Recent changes to the British system include the introduction of a new Incapacity Benefit, with tougher medical assessment for applicants, and a Jobseekers Allowance, with more rigorous job-search requirements. A common thread running through several initiatives has been a commitment to reduce the barriers to employment: these have included the provision of enhanced incentives to work; minimizing risks when moving into employment and encouraging employers to provide low-paid employment. However, possibly more radical reforms include moves to encourage individual assessment (and payment) of benefit and the introduction of a basic income/citizens' income. The individualization of benefit would be consistent with the general trend towards minimizing presumed dependency of one person on another. This is a laudable principle, and one strongly advanced by the European Union, but the day-to-day realities of living and working arrangements are such that if implemented it would risk increased vulnerability and poverty for some categories of women. Moreover, there is significant evidence that 'derived rights' (entitlements based on the contribution records of husbands) are very popular. A more practical difficulty relates to the resulting need for more (and not less) means-testing in order to establish eligibility. On the other hand, the basic income proposals would involve the payment of a flat-rate benefit to all citizens irrespective of status, family structure, employment or means. In a fully developed form all other benefits would be abolished and the cost would be met from general taxation. But the basic payment would be of only limited value and supplements would be required to meet full living costs and special circumstances, including disability and old age. The practical difficulties involved in implementation, together with the anticipated overall cost, keep this proposal at the level of theory.

Social security policy is central to social and public policy for three reasons: first, because it represents a third of all government expenditure; second, because at any one time approximately one-third of the population will be in receipt of one social security benefit or another; third, because the values and principles of allocations are contentious and the very stuff of politics. The future of social security will remain a primary concern to public and politicians alike: it is most unlikely, however, that consensus will ever be achieved.

GUIDE TO FURTHER READING

For such an important subject there is a shortage of sound, accessible and up-to-date material. For a general introduction and overview see Ditch, J. S. (ed.) (1997) *Poverty and Social Security: Issues and Research*. Englewood Cliffs, NJ: Prentice Hall. Michael Hill's (1990) *Social Security Policy in Britain*. Aldershot: Edward Elgar, is a good introductory text but tending to be a little dated. Paul Spicker's (1993) *Poverty and Social Security*. London: Routledge, is characteristically iconoclastic but very readable. Sally Baldwin and Jane Falkingham (eds) (1994) *Social Security and Social Change*. Hemel Hempstead: Harvester Wheatsheaf, is very good on the limitations of and challenges to the Beveridge paradigm.

Official publications are essential reading for students of social security: *The Social Security Departmental Report: the Government's Expenditure Plans* is published annually and is invaluable as a source of information. Similarly, but with a critical edge, the annual reports of the Social Security Advisory Committee should not be missed. The DSS has its own Research Report series (now over 40 volumes), in which the results of independently conducted research are published: for detailed and rigorous reviews of many aspects of social security in practice they are invaluable. The DSS has also published *The Growth of Social Security* (HMSO, 1993) and *Containing the Cost of Social Security – the International Context* (HMSO, 1993). The House of Commons Select Committee on Social Security publishes very useful reports, as does the National Audit Office.

For an international perspective starting points are the ILO's (both 1984) *Introduction to Social Security* and *Into the Twenty-First Century: the Development of Social Security*: both are thoughtful and comprehensive. For a historical perspective on the Beveridge–Bismarck paradigms see: Hills, J, Ditch, J. and Glennerster, H. (eds) (1994) *Beveridge and Social Security: an International Retrospective*. Oxford: Clarendon Press. The European Commission publishes (every two years) *Social Protection in Europe*, a comprehensive overview of trends and policies.

For a more critical perspective see publications of the CPAG; Walker, C. (1993) *Managing Poverty: the Limits of Social Assistance*. London: Routledge; and Hill, J. (1993) *The Future of Welfare: a Guide to the Debate*. York: JRF.

IV.7

employment

alan deacon

Employment policies are central to the concerns of social policy. For millions of people work is not only their major – or sole – source of income, but it is also the basis of their social standing and of their self-respect. Those who are excluded from paid employment may experience not only poverty but demoralization and a loss of self-worth. Such exclusion, of course, is much more likely to be experienced by some groups in the population than by others. Unemployment is also linked to a range of other social problems. Whatever the precise patterns of causality, it is undeniable that communities in which unemployment is high are also disproportionately affected by ill-health, crime and family breakdown.

Unemployment is also very costly for governments. It increases expenditure on social security benefits and reduces the income from taxes and national insurance contributions. Indeed, those who planned and introduced the classic welfare state of the 1940s were adamant that it could only be afforded if unemployment remained low.

For all their significance, however, employment policies figure relatively little in most social policy courses. Much attention is paid to the problems generated by a high rate of unemployment, but less to the policies and measures which could be adopted to reduce that rate in the first place. The obvious reason for this is that unemployment is seen as a problem of economics rather than of social policy. This means that the employment measures and services which are discussed in this chapter are generally regarded as instruments of economic policy rather than as social services. Such a distinction, however, makes less and less sense as the provision of employment measures becomes increasingly linked to that of education and training and to the administration of social security benefits.

There is, however, a further reason for the relative neglect of employment measures. Quite simply, they are a muddle. There has been a proliferation of schemes, programmes, projects and other initiatives, offering different opportunities and with different names, eligibility criteria and administrative structures. The outcome has been described by one commentator as 'a veritable alphabet soup of initials' (Whiteside, 1995, p. 66). More fundamentally, the muddle reflects a lack of clarity on the part of both the government and its critics as to the purpose and objectives of many of these measures.

The first task, therefore, is to provide an overview of the different types of employment measures and services. There then follows a brief discussion of the issues which will have to be resolved if they are to make a more effective contribution to the reduction of unemployment in Britain.

EMPLOYMENT MEASURES AND SERVICES

The first step is to distinguish between projects and schemes which are provided just for the unemployed, and so-called comprehensive manpower policies which are concerned with the skills and capacities of the labour force as a whole. As Timmins notes, there has been a growing tendency for politicians in particular to confuse the two, and to talk continually of 'a new if not always closely defined construct "education'n'training"' (Timmins, 1995, p. 486). The extent to which Britain has developed a comprehensive policy is an important question, but it is not one which can be considered here. Instead, the focus of this chapter is upon measures which are specifically for the unemployed.

Measures for the unemployed can be divided into five broad categories.

- *Placement and related services.* The basic function of the placement services is to put people who are looking for work in touch with employers who have vacancies. In practice, however, very many employers prefer to recruit staff through advertisements in newspapers or private employment agencies. This means that the Job Centres run by the Employment Service are notified of only one-third of all vacancies, and these are often for less skilled and poorly paid jobs. Similarly, the placement services are available to anyone who is looking for a job, but the majority of those using the Job Centres are people claiming unemployment benefits.
- *'Back to work' plans and Restart interviews.* Claimants registering for benefit are required to draw up a 'back to work' plan which sets out the steps they will take to find a job. Their progress is reviewed if they remain out of work after three months and if they are still unemployed after six months they will be required to attend a Restart interview. This involves a scrutiny of their efforts thus far and may lead to a referral to one or more projects or schemes. Two of these projects are particularly significant. Jobclubs provide practical advice on job seeking and the free use of telephones and stationery, and the Job Interview Guarantee scheme offers training in self-presentation and a guarantee of an interview with an employer who has a suitable vacancy. The Restart interviews continue at six-monthly intervals for as long as benefit is claimed. In addition, a claimant who remains unemployed for a long period will be required to accept some of the 'opportunities' which he or she is offered or be disqualified from benefit. It will be seen later that this element of compulsion has become increasingly important and controversial in recent years.
- *Job creation schemes.* Since the mid-1970s there have been a succession of schemes which have provided temporary work for particular groups of unemployed people. The most significant of these was the Community Programme (CP), which ran from 1982 to 1988. The CP provided up to 300,000 jobs a year, although the great majority were part-time and none lasted longer than twelve months. Those working on the CP were paid 'the rate for the job', but participants in other schemes have received a weekly allowance on top of their normal benefits. Two problems in particular have always dogged such job creation schemes. The first is the difficulty of identifying work which is 'of benefit to the community' but which would not otherwise be undertaken. The second – and more serious – is the lack of a training component, which has led to frequent criticisms that the schemes offer only 'dead end jobs', at the end of which participants simply return to unemployment.
- *Training and work experience programmes.* The criticisms made of job creation

schemes have led to a shift in emphasis towards programmes which combine work experience with some measure of training. This is currently the aim of Training for Work (TFW), which in 1994/5 provided around 270,000 places for people who had been unemployed for more than six months. (It should be noted that people with disabilities have immediate access to this and many other schemes.) It is estimated that around 200,000 people a year will obtain a National Vocational Qualification through TFW. The places are provided by local employers, voluntary bodies, local colleges and commercial training organizations on contract to local Training and Enterprise Councils (TECs) in England and Wales and Local Enterprise Councils (LECs) in Scotland. The TECs and LECs are employer-led bodies which were established in 1990/1 with a broad remit to 'promote more effective training by employers and individuals', although subsequent restrictions on their funding have meant that the activities of the TECs and LECs have focused more and more upon schemes for the unemployed.

- *Job subsidies.* The aim of these schemes is to encourage employers to take on people who have been out of work for a long time through the payment of a wage subsidy. Under the Workstart pilot, for example, employers receive £60 a week for six months and then £30 a week for a further six months for each recruit who had been unemployed for more than two years. The scheme is very small in scale – the original pilot provided only 1500 places – but proposals to expand such subsidies figure prominently in debates as to future policy.

Employment Measures in Context

Before we discuss the policy issues which arise in respect of employment measures, there are two points which should be made about the context in which they operate.

The objectives of employment measures

The first point is that measures such as Restart or work experience schemes are trying to achieve two objectives which may not be compatible. They are seeking to be of benefit to the substantial majority of the unemployed who are anxious to find work while at the same trying to prevent the abuse of the social security system by a minority who are not looking for a job or who are working while claiming benefit. This ambiguity is reflected in a memorandum submitted to the Employment Committee of the House of Commons by the Department of Employment. This said that the requirement that the long-term unemployed attend a Restart course 'acts as a deterrent to those who are claiming fraudulently, or who are not genuinely seeking work. For genuine claimants – the majority – participation in the courses is of benefit in looking for work' (Employment Committee, 1994, p. 5).

This ambiguity, however, is only one manifestation of a broader and long-standing tension between the objectives of the Employment Service as a placing agency and its role in the administration of unemployment benefits. It has a clear responsibility to submit to employers those best qualified for the jobs available, but these are unlikely to be the people whose attitudes to work it is most anxious to test. More broadly, it would meet the immediate needs of employers most effectively by focusing its activities upon those who has just become unemployed and are more likely to be 'job ready' than the long-term unemployed. It is the latter group, however, who need more assistance in finding work. Hence the dilemma for the Employment Service: giving priority to the short-term unemployed risks being accused of abandoning those who most need help;

giving priority to the long-term unemployed risks alienating the employers upon whose cooperation it depends.

It is perhaps not surprising then that, in Whiteside's phrase, 'there has been a tendency for official programmes to fall heavily between two stools' (1995, p. 63). Indeed, the fact that the same agency is responsible for both placement work and registration for benefit is seen by many commentators as the major cause of Britain's failure to develop a comprehensive manpower policy. An attempt was made to develop a comprehensive policy in the 1970s, with the creation of Job Centres which were separate from the benefit offices. This attempt was soon abandoned, however, in the face of rising unemployment (King, 1995).

Unemployment: stocks and flows

The second point to make about the context in which employment measures operate concerns the difficult but very important distinction between the *flow* of people on to and off the unemployment register and the *stock* of people who are unemployed at any one time. There is not a static, standing army of unemployed. In the twelve months to October 1994, for example, 3.9 million people came on to the register and 4.2 million people moved off it. The net reduction of 300,000 was thus the relatively small difference between two very large flows. What this means is that the majority of people who become unemployed find another job quite quickly. Using data for 1993/4, for example, the Department of Employment estimates that 50 per cent will return to work within three months, 67 per cent within six months and 84 per cent within a year. In other words, 16 per cent of those becoming unemployed are likely to remain out of work a year later. Those who do become long-term unemployed, however, find it increasingly difficult to get back into

work. This is partly because the experience of unemployment erodes people's skills and motivation and partly because employers are reluctant to engage someone who does not have a recent work record. The outcome, then, is a division between a group who may remain on benefit for several years and a larger group who are moving on and off benefit. Moreover, because the former group remain on benefit for longer periods they form a higher proportion of those unemployed at any one time – the *stock* – than they do of those who become unemployed during a year – the *flow*. It is important to recognize that some of those who move off benefit quickly may be moving to temporary or very insecure jobs, and so are likely to become unemployed again. Nevertheless, the crucial point here is that it is the group of long-term claimants who are the focus of current debates about the effectiveness and legitimacy of employment measures.

THE POLICY ISSUES

Employment measures have recently been at the forefront of the debate about whether or not it is feasible to reduce substantially the current levels of long-term unemployment. Richard Layard, for example, argues that the state should guarantee that anyone out of work for twelve months would be offered temporary work for at least six months. In return the claimant should 'accept one of a few reasonable offers' or lose his or her right to benefit (Employment Committee, 1994, p. 21). The scheme would be funded by the state paying to the employer the money which would otherwise have been drawn in benefits. A similar scheme has been developed by Dennis Snower and the Conservative MP Sir Ralph Howell, while others have placed the emphasis upon an expansion of work experience and training programmes (Employment Committee, 1994, 1995, 1996). In early 1996, the Labour Party produced a plan for education and training for young people, under which benefit would be withdrawn from those who refused to participate.

What all these schemes have in common is the notion of mutual obligations: that of the state to provide work or training and that of the individual to take advantage of the opportunity this creates. There are, therefore, two questions which arise immediately: can such schemes work, and, if so, is the element of compulsion reasonable?

The effectiveness of employment measures

Critics of such schemes argue that they will not create jobs on anything like the scale envisaged by Professors Layard or Snower, and that the jobs which are created will prove to be extremely costly for the taxpayer. This is because some of the people employed would have found a job anyway – the problem of *deadweight* – and because in many cases workers who benefit from the subsidy will get jobs at the expense of others who are thereby made unemployed in their place – the problem of *substitution*. This second criticism can also be levelled at schemes such as Restart, which are often accused of simply 'shuffling the pack' rather than reducing the overall level of unemployment.

In response, Layard and Snower argue that their proposals would give the long-term unemployed some work experience and that this will make them much more attractive to employers. This in turn will increase the effective supply of labour within the economy and thereby improve the trade-off between unemployment and inflation. In an earlier book Layard and Philpott (1991, p. 13) insisted that there 'is not a predetermined pool of jobs. If we can improve the supply of labour we can have new jobs without inflation rising.' The Conservative government remained sceptical, however, and continued to argue that better results would be obtained from its policy of combining training, assistance

with job search and measures to ensure that unemployed people made greater efforts to find work for themselves (Employment Committee, 1996).

The principle of conditionality

There is, however, one important element of common ground in the above debate. This is the principle of conditionality – the idea that an individual's entitlement to benefit should depend upon whether or not he or she is willing to take temporary work, attend a Restart course or meet some other condition imposed by the government. Other commentators, however, are highly critical of the principle of conditionality.

The case *against* conditional benefits rests on the proposition that unemployment is a structural problem, beyond the control of the individual. Making benefits conditional upon behaviour, however, suggests that the claimant would have found work if he or she had tried harder, and this is manifestly unjust when the jobs are simply not there. If good jobs or training schemes are available, then the unemployed will take them anyway. Conversely, it is often counter-productive to force someone to attend a course which he or she considers to be unsuitable or even pointless – a view expressed strongly by some who have experience of providing courses (Employment Committee, 1995, p. 97).

The case *for* conditional benefits is usually advanced on one or both of two grounds. The first is deterrence: that it prevents the abuse of benefits. The second is a more moralistic argument: that because the effect of prolonged joblessness is to demotivate claimants, it is reasonable to require them to take steps which are to their long-term benefit but which they would not otherwise take. This argument is not new – it was advanced by William Beveridge in 1942 to support the imposition of a training condition – but it has been strengthened in recent years by evidence of the social isolation of the long-term unemployed and by evidence that the Restart programme may have had some positive effects (White and Lakey, 1992).

CONCLUSION

Employment measures of the type discussed in this chapter are likely to become increasingly important in academic and political debates about unemployment.

This is simply because current economic thinking offers few alternative remedies. The conventional wisdom is now that the pressures of worldwide competition are such that a British government of any party can achieve little through fiscal or monetary policy. Instead, the focus must be upon reforms to education and the labour market which will enhance international competitiveness. In such a context, the purpose and efficacy of employment measures and their interaction with the benefits system will remain crucial issues for social policy.

GUIDE TO FURTHER READING

Brown, J. (1990) *Victims or Villains? Social Security Benefits in Unemployment.* York: Joseph Rowntree Memorial Trust. Provides a clear account of the development of employment measures to 1990.

Deacon, A. (1994) Justifying workfare: the historical context of the debate. In M. White (ed.), *Unemployment and Public Policy in a Changing Labour Market.* London: Policy Studies Institute. Discusses the different arguments which have been put forward to justify conditionality.

Employment Committee (1994, 1995, 1996) *Second Report: the Right to Work/Workfare.* Report and Minutes of Evidence HC 31 Session 1994–5 and HC 82 Session 1995–6. An invaluable source for the debate about the feasibility of job guarantee schemes and about conditionality. Also provides a summary of the measures in operation in 1994–5.

King, D. S. (1995) *Actively Seeking Work?* London and Chicago: University of Chicago Press. A political history of the development of employment measures in Britain and the USA. Highly critical of conditionality.

Layard, R. and Philpott, J. (1991) *Stopping Unemployment.* London: Employment Policy Institute. Argues that long-term unemployment can be virtually eliminated by an extension of employment measures and that entitlement to benefit should be conditional upon such measures.

Timmins, N. (1995) *The Five Giants: a Biography of the Welfare State.* London: HarperCollins. A very readable history of social policy since 1945, and particularly good on the Thatcher years.

White, M. and Lakey, J. (1992) *The Restart Effect.* London: Policy Studies Institute. Discusses the effectiveness of Restart and similar schemes.

Whiteside, N. (1995) Employment policy: a chronicle of decline? In D. Gladstone (ed.), *British Social Welfare.* London: UCL Press. Discusses employment measures in the context of wider economic policies.

IV.8

HEALTH CARE

JUDITH ALLSOP

INTRODUCTION

Why does health matter? A World Bank report, *Investing in Health* (1993), which reviewed health policies worldwide, commented on the aims of health policy thus:

Good health, as people know from their own experience, is a crucial part of well-being, but spending on health can also be justified on purely economic grounds. Improved health contributes to economic growth in four ways: it reduces production losses caused by worker illness; it permits the use of natural resources [hitherto] inaccessible because of disease; it increases the enrolment of children in school and makes them better able to learn; and it frees for alternative uses resources that would otherwise have been spent on treating illness. (p. 17)

The quotation neatly sums up why societies, whether developing or developed, are concerned with policies for health. In broad terms, countries face similar issues. A balance must be struck between preventing ill-health and curing illness. In developed economies particularly, demand for health care tends to outstrip ability to pay irrespective of the method of funding, so mechanisms are required to contain costs. Primary care often requires specific initiatives to develop as hospitals tend to attract resources. Yet changes in health systems are often difficult to achieve, as recent struggles over health policy reforms in France, Holland, Sweden, the UK and the USA show. Powerful political interests can skew the way policies are implemented or even block policy change altogether.

In this chapter, the focus is on health care in Britain and on how health care has been studied within the area of social policy. Two broad approaches or traditions can be identified. The first concentrates on analysing issues which will contribute to the formation of policies *for* health. The approach is essentially rationalist. The view is that health policy should be based on knowledge about the health status of the population, patterns of ill-health and how effectively health needs are being met through the services provided. A second tradition centres on the analysis *of* policy. The focus here is on the policies of governments or international bodies. In Britain, the study of the health policy tends to be a study of the National Health Service (NHS), which from 1948 has provided health care free at the point of service for the whole population.

ANALYSIS FOR POLICY

Health care needs

In order to provide health services which are appropriate, it is important to know about the patterns of health and illness. Social policy analysts have made a major contribution to investigating the causes of illness and death and, in particular, the inequalities in health status between different groups in different regions of the country. Social divisions such as age, class, ethnic group and gender are associated with differences in the length of life, the causes of death as well as differential death and illness rates. For example, some of the most important empirical studies on health care have shown that there is a strong association between poverty and ill-health and that people from lower social groups have mortality rates about three times higher than the highest social groups. Moreover, it has recently been demonstrated that in Britain, the differential in health status between the better off and the poor is increasing in parallel with widening income differentials.

The question of why some people are healthy and others are not has been the subject of considerable debate which crosses disciplines. Some scholars have researched the relationship between poor material conditions and ill-health. Others have found that individual lifestyles, such as smoking, excessive alcohol consumption, poor diets and lack of exercise, lead to ill health. However, geneticists point out that family history also plays a part in increasing susceptibility to certain diseases. In fact, although the social patterning of illness is clear, the linkage between various causal factors for particular individuals is not, and neither are the policy implications. Causal factors are likely to be cumulative over the lifespan and where, and how, to intervene to improve individual health or that of communities has been a matter for debate which draws on value assumptions as well as research findings.

Who provides health care and how is it distributed?

Health care can be divided into acute, caring and preventive services and the division of labour between those who provide these services is also a topic for study. A distinction can be made between the informal sector in health care where care is given without pay, and the formal sector of paid health workers. Most day-to-day health work is carried out within families, particularly by women acting as health educators and who give care and support to those who are ill or frail. The formal sector is made up of a wide range of health professionals and other ancillary workers, and there is a lack of recognition of the informal sector, particularly in relation to community care – yet the NHS could not function without the unpaid labour.

Within the formal sector, medical professionals have traditionally played a dominant role in influencing the context and content of health work. In Britain, there are divisions within medicine between general practitioners, hospital doctors and public health doctors which have their origins in the nineteenth century and which affect the pattern of health services today, as do the divisions between different types of health worker. Over the past decade, managers, nurses and other health workers as well as consumer and patient groups have presented various forms of challenge to the medical profession.

How services have been distributed also forms part of the study of health care. While, in principle, the NHS provides equality of access, universal coverage and comprehensive care irrespective of social position, whether services actually go to those most in need is a matter for research and debate. Some argue that there is an inverse care law and that the already disadvantaged receive worse services. Others have shown that, particularly in relation to acute care, there is equality of access for those who are ill, irrespective of social position. A number of empirical studies have been undertaken on this topic.

ANALYSIS OF POLICY

Maintaining health

A distinction can be made between policies which aim to maintain health and those which aim to restore health. Until relatively recently, British health policy has been almost completely dominated by issues concerned with restoring health through treating ill people. This may be explained by the fact that people's expectations for what health care can do are high – medical science can now do a great deal more to prolong life and relieve suffering. However, a further factor may be that, once established, the institutions to treat illness act as a powerful magnet to attract resources.

Recently, more emphasis has been placed on policies to maintain health and prevent illness. In theory, much illness is preventable and, furthermore, Britain now has very high rates of heart disease and certain cancers compared to her European neighbours. How to develop healthy public policy has become a more important issue. The current strategy has been to set targets for reducing death rates, introduce screening programmes for the early detection of symptoms and promote health education. However, there is a fundamental difference between those with individualistic political values who favour strategies to educate and change individual behaviour and collectivists who prefer regulatory approaches which reduce risk for populations and equalize access to good living conditions.

Restoring health

The treatment of illness and supporting the sick through the provision of health services has been central to government health policy in Britain. Since the 1940s, issues of funding health care and obtaining value for money have tended to dominate. In common with many other developed countries, the UK has an ageing population. Very elderly people are an increasing proportion of the population and elderly people are heavy users of health services. For this reason, and because medical knowledge, techniques and therapies have continued to develop, demand for health care has grown and governments have been faced with dilemmas about how to pay for health care. In 1995, approximately £37.5 billion was spent annually, or around 6 per cent of GDP. In the NHS, resource policies have been pursued with more rigour than service policies. Resource policies have aimed to limit the global sum allocated to the NHS, to distribute funds equitably to local level authorities on the basis of population and to achieve value for money and efficiency savings. The implementation of service policies for community and primary care have been less strongly pursued.

Funding health care

Health care may be funded through private insurance, a national insurance scheme, directly from taxation or through a combination of these. The various methods have advantages and disadvantages. In Britain, public spending on health is predominant. About 15 per cent of spending on health is private, among the lowest in the OECD countries, while 85 per cent comes from the public purse. In the mid-1990s, about 12 per cent of the population had private health insurance. Within the NHS, 80 per cent of spending comes from taxes, 15 per cent from national insurance contributions and 5 per cent from direct payments. The main feature of a tax-based system is that governments can control the overall allocations to the NHS effectively. However, supply has not met the demand for health care and various forms of rationing, such as long waiting lists, have led to public concern about underspending. Private insurance has grown as a consequence. In the 1980s and 1990s Conservative governments, for both political and administrative reasons, have eschewed radical changes in NHS funding, issuing instead directives to increase efficiency. The 1990 NHS reforms, the strengthening of management and the encouragement of private sector are part of this endeavour.

The health service reforms

In 1990, the NHS and Community Care Act introduced changes based on ideas which have been termed the 'new public management' and had already been introduced in other public services. Common features have been identified as:

- a devolution of responsibility from central government towards lower level agencies;
- strict budgetary limits on expenditure at all levels with incentives to collaborate with the private sector;
- the introduction of an element of competition between providers and the encouragement of enterprise;
- the concentration on core services and the privatization of support services;
- the strengthening of the management function and the introduction of performance incentives, performance measures and quality standards;
- more user/consumer information and choice.

Following the 1990 Act, a split was introduced between the functions of purchasing health services and providing them. On the purchaser side, a smaller number of larger health authorities have budgets to buy services for their population. They must draw up service contracts to meet health needs. In addition, general practitioners (GPs) may also purchase services for their practice patients if they are fundholders. Because budgets are limited, purchasers must determine priorities and therefore decide *not* to fund some health care. On the provider side, a variety of NHS hospital, community and ambulance trusts, as well as private sector agencies, tender for contracts and GPs continue to provide primary care under contract. The financial viability of trusts depends upon their ability to gain contracts, and there may be an element of competition depending on local circumstances. The theory is that these changes will encourage trusts to provide cost-effective services.

The health service reforms have strengthened the management function in the NHS. The 1983 NHS Management Inquiry chaired by Sir Roy Griffiths had introduced general management within the service. At the centre, the NHS Executive ensures that government policy is implemented, while within the lower level authorities and trusts, a chief executive replaced the teams of professionals and administrators. Since the reforms, managers are expected to have business plans, to cost and price health care interventions and to control clinical activity within planned levels. Relationships based on trust have been replaced by those based on contract.

An aspect of cost-effectiveness has been the shift towards the evaluation of clinical procedures and their effectiveness. Many medical procedures are carried out because the condition of the patient requires urgent action rather than because they are known to be beneficial. Considerable variations in practice occur and costs can vary widely. Methodologies for establishing good practice and guidelines have developed. As a consequence, there is considerable pressure on health agencies and professionals to adopt tried and proven treatments. The process is reinforced by clinical audit. Professionals review each other's practice to improve the quality of care. Evidence-based medicine will provide purchasers with a mechanism to establish what health care is the 'best buy'. However, ways of involving health care users in the process are in their infancy.

In summary, the health reforms were intended to bring financial discipline and parsimony into NHS care. Responsibility for deciding on health services has been devolved to the local level, and an element of competition has been introduced within a still largely monopolistic public service. However, the other side of the market is consumer demand. Although it has been part of government policy to empower the health care user, in practice there is little direct choice for patients within the NHS.

GP fundholders and purchasing authorities act as proxies for patients. Furthermore, decisions by health authorities have become even less visible, as there are weak mechanisms through which the views of patients, groups or communities can be represented. Government strategies for user involvement have been to set standards, to improve systems for the redress of grievances and to exhort health agencies to increase the amount of information available and to consult with user groups. The Patient's Charter, initially distributed to every household, outlines patients' rights within the NHS and gives targets for operational standards.

It is not yet known whether the health reforms will lead to a more cost-effective use of resources; whether the quality of care will be higher; whether the services which patients want will be available; whether access to services will be equitable between different groups; and whether those who can afford it will opt out of the NHS. Empirical studies of the impact of the health reforms have been limited so far, but evaluations of the changes will be a vital aspect of the future study of health care.

POLICIES FOR PRIMARY CARE

The improvement of primary care has been a focus of recent policy. The World Health Organization has promoted good first line care as the key feature of community development, and countries with well developed primary care systems tend to have lower overall health care costs. Although, in the British NHS, most people register with a GP who provides a first diagnosis and only refers where necessary, there has been a relative policy neglect of primary care, and a drift towards hospital-based treatment. The health reforms have strengthened the position of GPs in relation to the hospital by encouraging them to develop their facilities at practice level, to undertake more preventive health checks

and to purchase secondary care from hospitals and community nursing services for their patients. GPs who hold funds for purchasing have seen their powers in relation to hospital doctors enhanced through contracting, and they can also purchase community nursing services. Various pilot schemes have been set up to evaluate locality-based purchasing, where groups of GPs combine to contract for a range of services. Such schemes may eventually extend to cover the social care provided by local authorities. However, new forms of management will need to develop. Collaboration between authorities across health and social care has so far proved difficult to achieve.

THE POLITICS OF THE NHS

The development and implementation of health policy and the barriers to change have also been the subject of study by social policy analysts. A political analysis based on the identification of structured interests and their power to shape the policy process has been a dominant approach. Governments and their agents, managers, with their definition of the public interest, are taken as one group. The health professions, particularly the medical profession, are a second. Their interest is to maintain clinical control over their own work. The third group is the health care users. Their concern is the treatment of their own ill-health, that of their family and the services available to them in the community. Government and the medical profession have been taken as the dominant interest groups. Until recently, it has been argued that there have been separate spheres of influence. While governments hold the purse strings, doctors have had autonomy to practise based on expertise. They are able to determine what is health and disease (cultural autonomy) and the content of medical work (clinical autonomy), and to influence the context in which medicine is practised (social autonomy). The health reforms have changed the context of medical work and some have argued that medical dominance is waning in the face of a managerial and consumer challenge. Conversely, others have suggested that the claim to expertise ensures that medical hegemony remains intact. The context of practice may have changed but doctors still determine the content of medical work, and their dominance is simply taking a different form.

CONCLUSION

To conclude this brief account, I suggest that the major policy issues over the next decade will be a search for appropriate policies to maintain health. There will be political differences in approach between the left, who favour the reduction of inequalities in life chances, and the right, who emphasize changing individual behaviour. There will also be differences in approach over the degree and scope of regulatory controls. Whatever the approach, evaluations of the effectiveness of public health interventions will be necessary. It is likely that governments will continue to promote primary health care, although whether this will reduce the demand for hospital care is doubtful. If the NHS remains tax-funded, then debates about priorities and which services to fund will be a major issue for local health authorities, as will the assessment of good quality, effective treatments.

Ways must be found of involving local communities in the process.

In Britain, adherence to a tax-funded NHS and popular support for this has led to a greater political consensus in health than in other areas of social policy. However, greater divergence could occur over the next decade. On the supply side, a movement to the right could bring greater private sector involvement in financing hospital care, while limits on funding NHS services would lead to an increased take-up of private insurance to offset the actual or perceived inadequacies of the NHS on the demand side. Policies of the left, if principles of equitable outcome were followed, could focus on dealing with inequalities in health status. Social policies concerned with narrowing income differentials and providing access to good housing would follow, as health status is associated with income and other material conditions. Greater regulation to control the factors which cause ill-health could also be introduced.

For policy analysts, a major challenge is to assess the effects of the health reforms in relation to the criteria of equity, comprehensiveness and choice, as well as efficiency. For those with an interest in power relations and the role of the expert in contemporary society, whether clinician or scientist, the interrelationship between medicine and management is a topic of enduring fascination.

GUIDE TO FURTHER READING

Students of social policy should be aware that present policy is strongly influenced by the past. Thane, P. (1982) provides a history of health and welfare in Britain in *The Foundations of the Welfare State*. Harlow: Longman. The patterns of inequalities in health are well reviewed by Whitehead, M. (1992) *Inequalities in Health*, 2nd edn. Harmondsworth: Penguin; and Blaxter, M. (1990) *Health and Lifestyles*. London: Tavistock/Routledge. In an edited series of essays, *The Sociology of Health Promotion*. London: Routledge, Bunton, R., Nettleton, S. and Burrows, R. (1995) critique policies to prevent ill health.

There is a wide range of primary sources, such as government reports, White Papers and circulars. These should be read alongside critical commentaries, as they represent particular views of problms. Of particular importance in understanding contemporary health policy are *Working for Patients* (Secretary of State for Health, HMSO, London, 1989) and *The Health of the Nation* (Department of Health, HMSO, London, 1992). Selected official statistics on government expenditure on health services and the activity of service providers, such as hospitals and general practitioners, as well as on death rates (mortality) and sickness (morbidity) are published annually in *Social Trends* (Central Statistical Office, HMSO, London).

Appelby, J. (1992) provides a useful text: *Financing Health Care in the 1990s*. Buckingham: Open University Press. Allsop, J. (1995) *Health Policy and the NHS: towards 2000*, 2nd edn. Harlow: Longman; Ham, C. (1992) *Health Policy in Britain*, 3rd edn. London: Macmillan; Klein, R. (1995) *The New Politics of the NHS*, 3rd edn. Harlow: Longman, provide overviews of health policy. An evaluation of the health care reforms is available in Robinson, R. and LeGrand, J. (1994) *Evaluating the Health Care Reform*. London: King's Fund Institute.

Priorities for health policy are discussed in World Bank (1993) *Investing in Health*. Geneva: World Bank. OECD (1992) *The Reform of Health Care: a Comparative Analysis of Seven OECD Countries*. Paris: OECD, provides an account of how different countries deal with similar problems. Moran, M. and Wood, B. (1993) *States, Regulation and the Medical Profession*. Buckingham: Open University Press, compare health systems.

eDucaTIon

mIRIam DavID

INTRODUCTION

This chapter is about the present state of policy on education in Britain, mainly in England and Wales, since the Scottish system is somewhat different in both policy development and administration, the latter often having been the test ground for policy developments later introduced in England and Wales. The context of current political and economic orthodoxies around choice, consumerism, diversity and markets, and the complementary arguments about standards and quality assurance, is the setting for the discussion. The main focus is on compulsory education, or rather education for five to sixteen year olds, but reference is also made to further and higher education, and early childhood education, particularly that for children below five, the age of compulsory schooling. The key characteristic of education policy in the present climate is diversity, and it is difficult at the present juncture to describe what used to be called the education 'system'. However, another essential characteristic of education policy is that of central control of standards, within which markets are able to flourish.

CONTEXTUAL ISSUES

All countries now have an education system and policies for educational develop-ments, especially around education and/or training for particular forms of employment. In the advanced industrial societies, such as Britain, the educational system is highly developed and complex, and subject to regular changes to maintain competitiveness. The need to maintain and enhance international competitiveness has been one of the main reasons for educational policy developments in all industrial societies in the past two decades. There have been similar developments to those in Britain in countries such as the USA, Canada, Australia and New Zealand, and many of the European nations (David, 1993; Centre for Educational Research and Innovation, 1994). However, the form and content of the changes have differed in terms of the political complexion of the government and its values.

None of the policy developments in Britain over the past twenty years have had issues of equality of opportunity, in terms of class, disability, gender, race/ethnicity or sexuality, uppermost or explicitly on the agenda. The concern has been more with efficiency, value for money and the development of performance standards and quality-assurance rather than questions in particular of gender equality. Nevertheless, it is possible to trace changes with respect to such issues as equality of opportunity and part of this chapter will attempt this. On the other hand, the explicit goal of education policy, as with other areas of social provision, has been to put the consumer or user of education centre stage. Thus, with respect to compulsory education and early childhood education, parents (rather than children themselves) have assumed a far greater prominence than hitherto, particularly with respect to school choice and power over educational decision-making.

This chapter will also attempt to consider the ways in which policies on education have increased the role of parent as the consumer in a range of contexts, including the marketing of educational institutions. This period of policy development has been called that of the ideology of parentocracy to signal the pre-eminent position of parents afforded by the Conservative government, by contrast with previous Labour and Conservative administrations, who were committed to the 'ideology of meritocracy'. In this latter notion academic ability and merit rather than parental backgrounds of privilege or poverty were the determining factor in educational decisions (David, 1993). The term 'meritocracy' was originally coined by Michael, now Lord, Young of Dartington in 1956 in his book entitled *The Rise of the Meritocracy*, in which he satirized attempts to transform our education system from one based upon social and economic advantage to one based entirely upon academic merit. Nevertheless, the enduring feature of the post-war period to 1980 was the 'bipartisan' consensus around equality of educational opportunity as a goal and principle.

THE ERA 1988: A NEW ERA?

The defining policy on education in England and Wales at present is the 1988 Education Reform Act, known by its initials as the ERA. The then Secretary of State for Education, Kenneth Baker, deliberately chose to put in the term 'reform' in order that the initials would signal a new era, borrowing the idea of education reform from the USA, where it had already entered into common usage as a substitute for education policy. In the USA there was also a commitment to re-establish notions of educational excellence, and the Conservative government in Britain aimed to emulate the American example (David, 1993). The first key feature of the ERA was that it was innovative in legislating on both compulsory and further and higher education, which no single piece of British educational legislation had captured before. Second, it sought to create a variety of essentially autonomous educational institutions, separate from and independent of local government and run largely as business concerns. Third, however, the Act also set in place, also as a unique landmark, a national curriculum, with associated schemes of testing and assessment, for compulsory education. In this respect, the ERA differentiated between compulsory and post-compulsory education, since with respect to the latter no national curriculum was developed, although new forms of vocational qualifications were developed for parts of further education. Many commentators on the ERA have mentioned, with respect to schooling, the balance between central control, particularly through the National Curriculum, and market forces, through the creation of a range of different types of school – from City Technology Colleges (CTCs) to grant-maintained schools (GMS) to traditional county and/or voluntary aided schools with the freedom to develop their own budgets, through local management of schools (LMS) (David, 1993).

A central aim of the ERA was to create a variety of schools within the state system of education, run by local education authorities (LEAs) or LEAs in association with religious bodies, or schools which had opted out of LEA control and obtained grants from central government, making them GMS and also CTCs. Schools remaining within the LEA sphere of control not only were afforded LMS but also had to operate a new system of open enrolment, ensuring that parents who opted for the school were allowed a place for their child, up to the limit of physical capacity, rather than an arbitrary limit set by the LEA, as previously imposed by the 1980 Education Act for England and Wales. In Scotland, no such arbitrary limits had ever been set, thus setting the scene for the testing of legislation in Scotland.

Open enrolment had been a commitment in the Conservative Party's 1987 general election manifesto which spelled out the basic political thinking behind the idea of an education market and parental choice:

Schools will be required to enrol up to the school's agreed physical capacity instead of artificially restricting pupil numbers, as can happen today. Popular schools, which have earned parental support by offering good education, will then be able to expand beyond present physical numbers. These steps will compel schools to respond to the views of parents.

In other words, the aim was to ensure that parents chose a school to meet their defined needs for their child, rather than decisions on educational appropriateness being made by educational administrators in LEAs. The official view taken was that unpopular schools (in terms of parental choice) would then go out of business. On the other hand, the range of independent schools was also allowed growth and development at various levels of the 'system'. Moreover, academic selection and single sex schooling were also allowed further unfettered development, such that parents as the consumers of education would have a variety of schools from which to choose. Gewirtz et al. argue that:

The education market (like all markets) is intended to be driven by self-interest: first, the self-interest of parents, as consumers, choosing schools that will provide the maximum advantage to their children; second, the self interest of schools or their senior managers, as producers, in making policy decisions that are based upon ensuring that their institutions thrive, or at least survive, in the marketplace. The

demand for school places is inelastic, that is, the number of potential students is fixed. Where there are surplus places, the result is meant to be competition, emulation and rivalry: survival can only be ensured by attracting consumers away from other schools. (Gewirtz et al., 1995, p. 2)

In the early 1980s, a system of grants for children of parents of modest means had been introduced as the Assisted Places Scheme, to enable able children to attend a wide range of independent secondary schools, if they passed the academic entrance examination. This aimed to extend access to academic educational opportunities for a small group of able children from economically disadvantaged backgrounds. However, the scheme did not meet the needs of the most disadvantaged, since 40 per cent of the children were from single parent families in which the mother had high educational achievements, a group called 'the sunken middle class' (Edwards et al., 1989).

EXPANDING PARENTAL CHOICE AND EDUCATION MARKETS

However, the system created by the ERA was not as robust as had been anticipated and further measures were needed to strengthen particular objectives and parts of the system. Indeed, the balance between central control and market forces remained in place for three years until after Mrs Thatcher left office. John Major, as Prime Minister, was more committed to the user perspective and signalled this through the Citizen's Charter published in 1991. One of the first documents to take this forward was the Parent's Charter, entitled *You and Your Child's Education*, first published in 1991 and revised in 1994. In particular, this afforded parents rights to choose and complain about the service they received for their child. It also set down parental responsibilities: 'You have a duty to ensure that your child gets an education – and you can choose the school that you would like your child to go to. Your choice is wider as a result of recent changes.' (This was changed in the 1994 version back to the language of the early 1980s, i.e. 'You can say which school you would prefer your child to go to'.)

In addition, further legislation was introduced to strengthen aspects of choice and diversity rather than central control, tilting the balance in the direction of consumerism rather than central direction. At the same time, however, national performance standards were being developed and a new system of quality control introduced to ensure minimum standards. For example, the 1992 Education (Schools) Act created the Office for Standards in Education (OFSTED), having abolished Her Majesty's Inspectors of Schools (HMI), and a system of regular and routine statutory reviews of school practice, and it legislated for the publication of annual performance league tables, particularly of school examination results. This latter was largely with the aim of providing the information on which parents could make informed choices of their child's schooling.

In the summer of 1992, a White Paper entitled *Choice and Diversity: a New Framework for Schools* (Cm 2021) set out the measures to be taken to enlarge upon the provisions of the 1988 ERA. These were then incorporated into the 1993 Education Act, which established a Funding Agency for Schools (FAS) for the funding of grant-maintained schools and those LEAs where the majority of schools had opted out of local authority control. Since 1993 further accretions to educational policy have been tried, namely the pressure to ensure that all voluntary aided schools become grant-maintained, and the allowing of forms of selection for schools, particularly grant-maintained schools. By the end of 1995, it could be argued that education had become fully marketized, although there was no one general education market in operation in England. 'Education markets are localised and need to be analysed and understood in terms of a set of complex dynamics which mediate and contextualize the impact and effects of the Government's policy' (Gewirtz et al., p. 3).

There are now a range of different types of school in any one area – from county-maintained and voluntary-aided schools, to grant-maintained and CTCs, to private and independent schools. In some areas this variety exists for early childhood education as well as for primary and secondary schooling, whereas in others the diversity only pertains at secondary school level. In the case of secondary schooling there is also diversity with respect to single sex and coeducational schooling, both within and across types of school, and in some areas now there is quite a dramatic return to selective secondary schooling, whether private GMS or county grammar schools. In some recent research, however, little evidence of parental preference for selective education within the state system was found, although there is considerable evidence to suggest that parents who opt for private education do so on the grounds of academic selection. Moreover, the performance league tables have not contributed greatly to the information on which parents make decisions about secondary schools, many commenting on how difficult it was to make sense of them (David et al., 1994).

The move to formalize information about the quality and standards of schooling has, nevertheless, been extremely useful as a basis for examining trends and patterns in educational provision. In particular, it has been important for identifying trends in examination performance, despite the fact that no one official database exists at present. In another study, for the Equal Opportunities Commission, gender entry and examination performance patterns over a ten year period (1984–94) were mapped and identified, demonstrating that there had been an overall improvement in educational standards. For GCSE, there had been a general closing of the gender gap in entry and performance, although boys still retained their edge in technology, and girls theirs in English and social studies. In GCE A levels, however, boys still retained their advantage in terms of science subjects (chemistry especially), but girls closed the gender gap, particularly in English and modern foreign languages (Arnot et al., 1996).

The study also looked at schools' and LEAs' perspectives on the impact of educational reforms on gender equality in schools. Primary and secondary schools varied in their views of the impact of the reforms in their schools, although all in the sample had become more involved in equal opportunities policy-making in the period since the ERA than before it. The developments in examination performance bear witness to the hard work and success of schools in coping with relatively constant change in the past ten years. Both schools and LEAs painted different pictures of their relative roles and monitoring activities. For the most part LEAs had been extremely supportive of schools in equal opportunities policy developments but now feel heavily constrained in the support they may be able to offer. Schools, and secondary schools in particular, felt that certain reforms had been beneficial, especially those to do with curricular developments and testing, including especially the Technical and Vocational Educational Initiative (TVEI), whereas organizational changes, such as LMS, had detracted from their abilities to develop. OFSTED inspections, with their equal opportunities criteria, were seen, especially by the case study LEAs, to be particularly important. On the other hand, there was found to be a persistence of male cultures with respect to management in schools, but, by contrast, 'a gender-fair culture' with respect to the treatment of pupils and their attitudes towards gender equality.

Gewirtz and her colleagues also found diversity in the impact of policy developments, and they argue that there are now locally specific circumstances for the marketization of schools:

We would argue, however, with respect to education, that although the pre-1988 English education system was far from perfectly comprehensive, many schools were able to maintain relatively mixed intakes and to develop, often in conjunction with the LEAs, policies and strategies designed to promote equal opportunity for students on the basis of class, 'race', gender and ability ... Our evidence suggests that the processes of the English market seem to be halting and reversing such developments and contributing to a process of 'decomprehensivization' ...

Effectively, the market system of education and the concomitant processes of decomprehensivization mean that resources are flowing from those children with greatest need to those with least need. Thus we are seeing a growing inequality of access to the quality of provision necessary for children to succeed educationally ... our research also indicates that the English market fails the desert-based equity test ... because success in the marketplace is not primarily a function of family motivation but rather parental skill, social and material advantages, the perceived raw-score potential of the child, and to some extent, pure chance. (Gewirtz et al., 1995, pp. 188–9)

CHOICE, DIVERSITY AND EDUCATION MARKETS IN PRE- AND POST-SCHOOL EDUCATION

It is important also to note that these changes are not only pertinent to schools but have been affecting other levels of the education system too. In particular, the introduction of the market mechanism has been seen, in early childhood education, through the pilot project to introduce education vouchers. In further and higher education, there have been a myriad of changes, through the funding mechanisms such as the Further Education Funding Council (FEFC) and the Higher Education Funding Councils (HEFC), through institutional autonomy, which has turned the majority of higher education institutions into universities, and through developments in terms of managerialism. Here of particular note for higher education is the introduction of forms of quality assurance through, for instance, quality audit, teaching quality assessment and the research assessment exercises. All of these moves have led to increased institutional competitiveness and rivalry within and between groups of higher education institutions (HEIs). What had been created by the end of 1995 was a relatively 'mass' system of higher education, with relatively equal numbers of men and women as students but unevenly distributed in terms of institutions and full- and part-time study. For example, the majority of women students are mature, and are to be found on part-time courses in the new rather than the traditional universities. Similarly there has been a growth in the numbers of ethnic minority students participating in higher education, but their distribution across the sector is also very uneven. In both cases staffing does not reflect student participation, a measure of what has been called 'the glass ceiling'.

In conclusion, it can be argued that markets now predominate in education at all levels, leading to considerable amounts of inequity of access and outcome, despite the fact that such developments have allowed for the growth of a mass system of further and higher education, and longer attendance of pupils in school. These latter trends, however, may have more to do with labour market circumstances than with the provisions of education *tout court*.

GUIDE TO FURTHER READING

The subject of education policy is of concern not only to social policy analysts but also to students of sociology and educational studies. Some of the material cited in the text has been written by sociologists of education rather than social policy experts and is concerned particularly with the analysis of education as a field, with a particular research focus, i.e.

Arnot, M., David, M. E. and Weiner, G. (1996) *Educational Reforms and Gender Equality in Schools*. Manchester: Equal Opportunities Commission, Research Series No. 10.

David, M. E., West, A. and Ribbens, J. (1994) *Mother's Intuition? Choosing Secondary Schools*. London: The Falmer Press.

Edwards, T., Fitz, J. and Whitty, G. (1989) *The State and Private Education: an Evaluation of the Assisted Places Scheme*. Basingstoke: The Falmer Press.

Gewirtz, S., Ball, S. J. and Bowe, R. (1995) *Markets, Choice and Equity in Education*. Buckingham: Open University Press.

There are also several texts which explore policy changes in an international context, a key one here being Centre for Educational Research and Innovation (1994) *School: a Matter of Choice*. Paris: OECD.

A book which explores changes in social and educational policy (across the levels of education) and sets the international and social context for such developments is David, M. E. (1993) *Parents, Gender and Education Reform*. Cambridge: Polity Press.

There are also government publications which provide useful reading, in particular here the White Paper *Choice and Diversity: A New Framework for Schools*. London: HMSO, Cm 2021.

Numerous journals may be looked at for commentaries on education, the key ones being *The Journal of Educational Policy, British Educational Research Journal, British Journal of Sociology of Education, Gender and Education* and *The Journal of Social Policy*.

IV.10

HOUSING

aLan MuRIe

INTRODUCTION

Housing has formed a central part in debates about social problems and social policy. Images of affluence and deprivation, status and social standing, and issues of segregation and stigmatization, social exclusion and community integration are all strongly associated with housing. At the same time, housing forms the focus for family life. It is the place of residence, the home and place for homemaking, and can represent a significant source and store of wealth.

Housing involves the market, the state and the voluntary sector and processes of production, exchange, ownership and control. Unlike some areas of social policy, housing has never been a state monopoly, but there have been dramatic shifts in policy and the role of the state. Private ownership and provision has remained dominant throughout, but the form of provision has changed. The private sector is involved in the production of state housing and the state is involved in the regulation and financing of private housing.

In Britain responses to the housing problems of the present century involved a significant role for the state. Council housing has been important in the general improvement of housing conditions and had a marked impact on cities and towns. As policy has changed in recent years, the role of local government and local control over housing has declined. There has been significant centralization of policy. At the same time privatization has reduced the direct influence of the state over the housing sector.

THE HISTORICAL LEGACY

Accounts of the development of modern housing policy in Britain refer to the problems of nineteenth-century industrialization. They refer to reforms designed to control threats to the health of the whole population. Public health measures introduced in a market dominated by private landlordism had an impact upon the poor quality of the built environment but also made private investment in housing less attractive than in other sectors of the economy. The attempts to meet housing needs through philanthropic effort were insufficient, and before the outbreak of the First World War there was pressure to develop a new housing policy. There were proposals to introduce subsidies to enable local authorities to build affordable housing for working class families. The effects of the First World War, including rent controls introduced to prevent exploitation of the wartime situation, and the post-war pledge to provide homes fit for heroes, added to the case for a new policy. Against this background the key development in state housing policy was the introduction, in 1919, of Exchequer subsidies for council housing. From this date, and for the next sixty years, local authorities developed a key role in the provision of council housing. At the same time the private rented sector declined and private provision switched towards individual home ownership – initially among the more affluent sections of the community. The long-term decline of private renting was speeded by the reintroduction of rent control during the Second World War and by the process of slum clearance. Furthermore, as more affluent groups (influenced by a favourable financial environment) moved into home ownership, and as a high quality council rented sector developed, the rent levels that people were able and prepared to pay for properties which were not subject to rent control were not sufficient to make investment in rented housing an attractive option.

In the period 1919–79 local authority housing and owner occupation grew alongside one another. Following 1979, the restrictions on local authority house building combined with policies to sell council housing meant that the owner-occupied sector alone was a sector of expansion. The modernization of housing tenure led to a significant improvement in house conditions. New building, slum clearance and house improvement, combined with changes in household composition and affluence, created a very different housing environment.

KEY PHASES OF POLICY

In the period since 1919 there have been a number of different periods of policy. Continuities in policy were broken by the Second World War with limited new building and the destruction of housing. In the period immediately following 1945 the emphasis upon the production of state housing was greater than at any other stage. Leaving aside this period, govern-

ments consistently encouraged home ownership and largely neglected private renting. Policies towards council housing were less consistent. In both the inter-war years and the post-war period policy shifted between general needs building and slum clearance rehousing. The high-quality, high-cost council housing built immediately after 1945 was associated with meeting general needs. The subsequent phases of policy included periods with an emphasis upon slum clearance rehousing and periods in which the council house building programme had a more limited role alongside house improvement programmes. In the period since 1979, the government's view has not favoured significant new building by local authorities and in the period after 1988 housing associations were the preferred vehicle for new social rented housing. The council housing stock declined in size as a result of the sale of properties, both to individual tenants and to alternative landlords in the form of housing associations. Some local authorities have transferred the whole of their housing stock to new housing associations and the fragmentation of control has increased, with the strategic or enabling role of local government replacing its role as direct provider.

In the more recent phases of policy, attitudes have been influenced by the view that the housing problem had largely been solved. The key agenda was no longer about providing housing and improving the quality of the housing stock but was on meeting aspirations about ownership and control. This focus fitted strongly with the Conservative Party's adoption of the idea of a property owning democracy and with the dominant concerns about reducing taxation and public expenditure in the period after 1976. Housing proved a valuable resource to Chancellors of the Exchequer. Not only could public expenditure on the formal housing programme be cut and the housing programme contribute in this way to Treasury objectives but the privatization of council housing

Table IV.10.1   Housing tenure in Great Britain, 1914–94 (percentages of all households)

	Public rented	Owner-occupied	Private rented[a]
1914	–	10	90
1945	12	26	62
1951	18	29	53
1961	27	43	31
1969	30	49	21
1971	31	53	17
1979	32	54	14
1984	27	60	13
1989	23	65	12
1994	20	67	14

[a]Including housing associations. Before 1988 housing associations were regarded as part of the public sector but a new financial regime involving greater use of private finance was introduced in 1988, and following that associations have been regarded as part of the private sector. They currently provide 4 per cent of the dwelling stock.

Sources: Malpass and Murie (1994) and *Housing and Construction Statistics*.

could actually yield cash receipts which more actively helped in achieving these objectives. In terms of the generation of capital receipts, the sale of council houses has proved the single most significant part of government's privatization programme since 1979.

TENURE CHANGES

The policy developments described above have been associated with significant changes in tenure (table IV.10.1). Britain has moved from a nation of private tenants to a nation of home owners, with a transitional period in between in which a much more mixed tenure structure existed. These national figures obscure enormous local differences, with some localities dominated by public provision and others with little alternative to home ownership.

As tenures have grown or declined, so their nature and characteristics have changed. The private rented sector has become a dilapidated sector housing a residual population of elderly long-term tenants and a more mixed, transient population using other parts of the stock. The home ownership sector and the council housing sector, which both developed in the 1920s catering for young families, have changed and diverged. The home ownership sector remains one which caters significantly for the most affluent sections of the population but has become differentiated. It also includes groups of very poor households, including the elderly and those who have experienced unemployment or other crises. It is also a sector which is marked by enormous differences in value and desirability – from luxurious rural and suburban mansions to inner-city housing, ill maintained before transfer from private landlords and ill maintained subsequently. The council housing sector now caters more exclusively for low-income groups. However, they are no longer predominantly families with children as they were in the early years of the tenure. Instead they include elderly persons, young lone parent households and those with long-term illnesses and disabilities. This pattern of change has been referred to as the residualization of council housing – the tendency for the poorest sections of the population to become more concentrated in council housing. It applies to the council sector as a whole but is most marked in certain parts of it. The rationing of access and the allocation of council housing have tended to leave those with least bargaining power in the worst or the least desirable housing.

The home ownership sector, in the post-war years until 1990, was increasingly associated with accumulation. Rising property prices meant that some owner occupiers' wealth increased significantly. This situation has changed since 1990. House prices fell in real terms and a considerable number of households were left with negative equity – the value of their property had fallen and was not sufficient to cover the outstanding mortgage.

For council tenants Right to Buy has formed an important route enabling transfer of some two million dwellings out of a total of 6.5 million to home ownership on favourable terms, and accessing the advantages of home ownership to that group. In some cases this has also meant exposing council tenants to disadvantages associated with home ownership.

HOMELESSNESS

Debates about changes in tenure and the tenure structure focus upon households in housing. However, a key element of the debate about housing policy has always related to those who are not in housing or are in inadequate housing. In Britain the term 'homelessness' is usually associated with a legislative category which does not include all of those who are inadequately housed and in that sense are without an adequate home. At the same time it includes more than simply those who are without a roof over their heads. Research on homelessness in Britain has always identified the key role of the housing market in determining homelessness and the

risks faced by ordinary families of becoming homeless because of the operation of that market.

The statistics on homelessness which relate to the legislative category 'the homeless' have shown a considerable increase in homelessness since the late 1970s. It is generally accepted that this is associated with changes in the housing market and shortages of both social rented housing and affordable private rented housing. At the same time the pattern has been exacerbated by demographic trends, changes in the benefit system and changes in employment. Greater social inequality has resulted in a greater number of people being exposed to homelessness in Britain.

HOUSING IN THE WELFARE STATE

Tenure restructuring in Britain has been associated with changes in the system of housing finance, taxation and subsidy. Rent control represented a form of subsidy to private tenants, protecting them from market prices. Subsidized council housing has involved a redistributive transfer in favour of the council tenant. The various fiscal and other supports to home ownership have involved transfers favouring the home owner. These have included tax reliefs for mortgage interest payments and capital gains. Mortgage interest tax relief has involved very large sums of money, especially in periods of high house prices and high interest rates, and in general these have tended to benefit better off households paying higher rates of tax and with larger mortgages. Only in the 1990s have changes in the system of tax relief moderated this regressive pattern.

The social division of welfare in relation to housing has not only benefited affluent groups, and the pattern of benefit in kind which council tenants have received in the form of subsidized high-quality housing has been a significant part of the redistributive structure of the welfare state. Through the 1980s the financing of council housing has changed, rents have been increased towards market levels and the system of finance has shifted from the general Exchequer subsidy system, which originated in 1919 and applied to the tenure as a whole, towards individual means-tested housing benefit. Assistance with housing costs in the council housing, housing association and private rented sectors is now provided through the social security system. Council tenants as a group no longer receive subsidy. Indeed, their rents are such as to enable a cross-subsidy towards those who are on housing benefit. In England the poorest tenants are subsidized by fellow tenants. Some owner-occupiers who are on income support also qualify for social security assistance, but through a different regime. Housing finance remains partitioned, with different arrangements for different tenures, and a unified system of housing finance that is tenure-neutral has not been developed.

REGENERATION AND MANAGEMENT

Council housing, when it was built, represented high-standard, desirable housing which was in high demand from households. This was particularly true of the majority of council housing, which was traditionally built houses with gardens. In some cases estates had a poor reputation from the outset and in some phases of building, especially associated with slum clearance, the quality of housing was not so high and the reputation of areas was damaged from the outset. The short-lived period in which highrise flats were favoured as a result of government subsidy structures and the enthusiasm of professionals in local government also left an undesirable legacy in many areas. These parts of the council housing stock (and some areas outside the council sector) have increasingly become places of last resort. The concentrations of deprived households

in these areas have become more apparent and problems of crime, drug abuse, unemployment and low social esteem have increased.

Difficult to let, difficult to manage and difficult to live in estates have been the subject of important policy initiatives. These have involved local management, attempts to involve tenants in the management of areas and increased investment in dwellings, services and infrastructure. These interventions have generally had at least a short-lived positive effect but do not solve problems of deprivation, segregation and stigmatization. As social inequality has increased in Britain, so the pressures on these areas have become greater and management initiatives have been overwhelmed by changes in the economy and housing finance. The poverty trap and rising unemployment have made it more difficult for lower-income households to change their circumstances and to escape from these areas.

In this context the emphasis in policy has shifted from management initiatives towards more holistic local regeneration policies with a strong emphasis on employment, education and training. Housing problems have become inextricably bound up with problems in the economy. The problems of lower-income households are not just housing problems but are affected by limited access to jobs and other services. Housing activity is a significant part of economic activity and has a major role in regeneration.

THE CONTEMPORARY HOUSING SITUATION

In the mid-1970s it was widely argued that housing problems had been generally solved and what remained were specific, local problems which needed targeted interventions. By the mid-1990s it is difficult to retain this view of housing problems. Issues of homelessness and deprived council estates figure prominently in general images of social malaise. Social segregation and differentiation in cities is more striking than in the past and there is increasing reference to problems of racial segregation, urban crime, an underclass and patterns of inequality which are dysfunctional socially and economically. New problems are apparent in the owner-occupied sector. These are associated with the larger number of older and low-income households in the sector unable to maintain their dwellings adequately. It is also associated with the state of the market in the mid-1990s and a period in which house prices have not increased, transaction levels have been low and mortgage arrears, repossessions and negative equity have emerged. The home ownership sector can no longer be regarded as one which solves housing problems, but contains its own share of housing problems.

House condition problems have become more apparent in the local authority and the owner-occupied sectors as these age and as problems of underinvestment become marked. With the continuing high level of dilapidation in the private rented sector, it is arguable that the need for clearance and replacement has re-emerged in Britain. With increased social inequality, shortages of affordable rented housing have become more apparent. There is a new concern about the interaction between housing and health, housing and crime and housing and family life. Problems which were assumed to have been dealt with by the 1960s are re-emerging on the agenda of the 1990s.

The deregulation of private renting and changes in the housing association sector have resulted in higher rents and fewer rights. Rooflessness and rough sleeping in British cities is apparent on a scale that is unprecedented in the post-war period. While the language of policy has increasingly been about choice and empowerment, the reality for at least a substantial minority of households has been of less choice and less control. Choices between tenures exist for some households but for others there is no choice between dwellings, let alone tenures. While the housing situation has improved for the majority of households, there are significant and growing problems within the sector. At the same time, housing policy has moved from a dominant and prominent position in the welfare state to a peripheral one. There is no longer a major programme of intervention in the housing sector designed to build high-quality housing for general household needs or for lower-income households, and the governance of housing is increasingly fragmented. The emphasis in policy has shifted towards relying upon the private market to make provision and providing means-tested social security support to enable people to meet the costs of housing. This recipe has not been working effectively and generates significant problems in relation to the poverty trap and work incentives.

The challenge for policy-makers is to reconstruct housing policy in a different social, economic and political context. Global issues and the competitiveness of economies prohibit the level of public sector borrowing or taxation which would be required to go back to large-scale public investment. One option is to change the definitions of public expenditure and another is to transfer the ownership of housing to new organizations (local housing companies with some local authority involvement) outside the public sector and public expenditure definitions. However, there are problems with these approaches and in any event they do not address the problems of local economic regeneration, the poverty trap and work incentives. The search for effective regeneration strategies is made more difficult by a housing finance system which is dependent on means testing. A return to some element of bricks and mortar subsidy in order to reduce the severity of the poverty trap would seem to be one component in a framework which could enable regeneration to be achieved.

The economic and other factors which are increasing social exclusion and segregation and affecting housing should not be underestimated. Policies which will avoid a continuing residualization and differentiation require new thinking about organizational structures, tenure relationships and systems of subsidy. Most of all they will need to be developed in conjunction with changes in the wider welfare state. The view that housing policy alone can remedy problems in the housing sector is untenable. At the same time, review and reform of housing policy is an essential ingredient in strategies to reduce social problems relating to incomes, employment, health, social order and the family.

GUIDE TO FURTHER READING

Contemporary housing policy issues are fully discussed in the journals *Housing, Housing Review, Inside Housing* and *Roof*. These provide journalistic articles, facts and figures and short critical articles on key issues. The leading academic journal in the field is *Housing Studies*. Key texts include:

Malpass, P. and Murie, A. (1994) *Housing Policy and Practice*, 4th edn. London: Macmillan. A general introduction to housing policy in the UK with chapters on the historical development, the administrative and financial frameworks, the context for policy and key issues affecting the making, implementation and evaluation of housing policy.

Burnett, J. (1985) *A Social History of Housing 1815–1985*, 2nd edn. Newton Abbott: David and Charles. An introduction to the history of housing and the social context for changes in housing provision.

Malpass, P. (1990) *Reshaping Housing Policy*. London: Routledge. An account of the development of housing policy with a particular emphasis on the key issues of rents and central–local relations.

Gibb, K. and Munro, M. (1991) *Housing Finance in the UK: an Introduction*. London: Macmillan. A clearly written description of the key policies and mechanisms of housing finance in the UK.

Hills, J. (1990) *Unravelling Housing Finance*. Oxford: Clarendon Press. A critical and analytic discussion of housing finance focusing on issues of efficiency and equity and with an important discussion of policy implications.

Malpass, P. and Means, R. (1993) *Implementing Housing Policy*. Buckingham: Open University Press. A collection of papers on different aspects of the implementation of housing policy, focusing on implementation issues following new housing legislation in 1988.

Forrest, R., Murie, A. and Williams, P. (1990) *Home Ownership: Differentiation and Fragmentation*. London: Unwin Hyman. A broad discussion of the development of the home ownership sector and policies to encourage home ownership but emphasizing increasing variation within the sector.

Forrest, R. and Murie, A. (1990) *Selling The Welfare State*, 2nd edn. London: Croom Helm. Research-based account of the origins, details and consequences of policies for the sale of council housing in the UK.

Cole, I. and Furbey, R. (1993) *The Eclipse of Council Housing*. London: Routledge. Wide ranging discussion of the growth and decline of council housing and key policy issues related to that tenure.

Up-to-date statistics are found in *Housing and Construction Statistics* (London: HMSO) and in the annual reports of the key government departments: the Department of the Environment, the Northern Ireland Office, the Scottish and the Welsh Offices.

the personal social services and community care

JOHN BaLDOCK

THE 'FIFTH SOCIAL SERVICE'

The personal social services are one of the oldest but also usually one of the smallest parts of modern welfare states. They can trace their origins to pre-industrial forms of alms- and care-giving, often organized by the church and religious orders. In the United Kingdom, by the end of the Second World War a substantial proportion of these activities had been taken over by the state. None the less, even in the mid-1990s, public expenditure on what are called the personal social services is only a fraction of that spent on other major areas of state welfare. In the financial year April 1995 to March 1996, for the whole of the United Kingdom, some £9 billion was spent by government on these services, mainly by local authorities. While this is a great deal of money, about £166 per head of population, it is small compared with expenditure on education (£640), health (£709) or social security (£1666).

There is a residual quality to the personal social services. Their responsibilities can sometimes appear to be a ragbag of disparate social rescue activities that are left over by the other parts of the welfare system. They have been called 'the fifth social service': seen as last not only in terms of size but also in terms of resort; the service people turn to when all else has failed. Yet it is this residual quality that makes them perhaps the most com-

plex and fascinating of the social services. In order to understand the personal social services one has to come to grips with many of the key issues of social policy: the technical problems to do with organization, effectiveness and efficiency; and the moral and political dilemmas to do with need and entitlement, rationing and fairness, dependency and autonomy. These are also essentially the most human of the public services; concerned with how individuals cope with a great variety of difficulties that life can throw at them. They may sometimes have to function as the nearest thing to a public substitute for the family. The personal social services lie at the heart of what we, as citizens, can do and are prepared to do to help each other, and ourselves, in adversity.

RESPONSIBILITIES AND ORGANIZATION

In industrial societies the main functions associated with the personal social services are: the care and protection of children who are at risk of harm or neglect or whose behaviour is beyond the sole control of their families; helping to organize and sometimes provide care and support for elderly people and others whose disabilities or illnesses mean they cannot manage on their own (these can include the younger physically disabled, people suffering from a mental illness, people with learning difficulties and people with chronic illness like AIDS/HIV); supporting those who have been excluded by the wider society, such as the homeless, travellers, migrants and refugees. The help that is offered to these people is often called social work, and social workers are at the centre of the public image of the personal social services. However, in the United Kingdom, for example, in 1995 social workers accounted for only 14 per cent of the employees of the local authority social services; there is much other work carried out by residential and daycare staff (45 per cent) and by domiciliary workers (25 per cent) who provide help in people's homes.

The particular ways in which these functions are financed, organized and delivered vary considerably between even quite similar industrial nations, such as those of the European Union. There are also wide regional and local variations within countries. For example, in Britain levels of expenditure vary substantially between authorities, as do the mix of services they provide. One's chances of obtaining social services help can depend very much upon where one lives and whether the local authority has developed the sort of service one wants. This chapter concentrates on the personal social services in the United Kingdom. While the details may be different in other industrial societies, the essential choices and problems are fairly universal.

In the United Kingdom the term 'the personal social services' is generally used to refer to the work of local authority social services departments in England and Wales, of social work departments in Scotand and, in Northern Ireland, of social services staff within the health and social service boards. However, when the term first came into common usage in the second half of the 1960s, it was commonly extended to include a much wider range of provision by voluntary, charitable and private organizations that in some way

sought to help people at the level of the individual or family. Thus, for example, the work of the clergy, of the NSPCC (National Society for the Prevention of Cruelty to Children), of probation officers, of Relate (marriage guidance counsellors), to name of few of the huge variety of occupations and organizations that provide personal help, have all at times been considered a part of 'the personal social services'.

A MARGINAL AND RESIDUAL SERVICE

In principle the personal social services might become involved in almost any aspect of our lives from birth to death; in practice most people, even those with substantial social needs, will go through life with little or no contact with their local social services authority. This is because a key characteristic that marks out the public personal social services and makes them essentially different to the education or the health services, for example, is that they provide or are responsible for only a small part of personal social care in our society. Whereas the vast majority of people will turn to the NHS when they are ill and to state education for their children's schooling, it is not the case that most children with special social or physical needs, or most elderly people who need care, will receive help from their local social services department.

For example, in Britain at any one time a local social services department will be working with: a third of those over 85; less than 4 per cent of children in families living on benefit; less than 2 per cent of children with physical disabilities; and less than 10 per cent of those who are mentally ill and living in the community. This is not necessarily to say that the others either want help or are not getting it, but simply to emphasize that the public social services provide only a fraction of the social care needed or given. Most social care is provided by the family and, to a lesser extent, by friends and neighbours. Much of the most intensive caring, of frail elderly people, for example, is done by women.

This fact, that the state-funded personal social services provide for only a fraction of each of the wide variety of need groups they are charged with helping, is central to most of the key debates and issues which surround their work. It has meant that the services have always been open to criticisms that what they are doing is partial, arbitrary, ineffective and ripe for review and change. An extreme example of this occured in the late 1970s, when social workers in the London Borough of Camden were on strike for nearly six months. Some commentators argued that that there was no evidence of increased social casualties or that the community could not cope on its own – though this argument tended to ignore the fact that the absence of social workers meant there was less likelihood of harm coming to light.

The marginal character of the local social services departments also means that in almost all their work success does not depend entirely or even mostly on what they achieve. In order to achieve their goals they must usually work with a wide range of other services and agencies: other statutory services such as general practitioners, hospital specialists, community nurses, housing and education departments as well as other members of families, neighbours, volunteers and voluntary organizations, the churches and increasingly private, profit-seeking care agencies.

A History of Frequent Reorganizations but Steady Growth

Since their creation in their modern form after 1945, the British local authority social services have been subject to frequent and radical reorganizations. This does not reflect a high political profile and public interest but rather its opposite. Because the users of social services are a transient sample of the poorest and least powerful, politicians, once in government, have felt relatively free to impose new structures or models of working which reflect their particular perceptions of the problems and their solutions.

The public personal social services emerged from the whirlwind of post-1945 welfare legislation largely in the form of two distinct local authority deparments: the specialist children's departments and the health and welfare departments, which dealt with adult users. In 1971 these were amalgamated, following recommendations of the Seebohm Report, within a single, generic social services department whose object was initially to provide one source of help – 'a single door' – to which all citizens in social need could turn. This was to be a bold and ambitious solution to the residual quality of the services, gradually turning them into a source of help that would be used by all classes – the social service equivalent of the NHS.

Only three years later, the 1974 reorganization of local government created a fresh round of new, often larger social services departments. In the late 1970s and early 1980s some departments further restructured themselves, devolving as much responsibility as possible to neighbourhood teams which would seek to redress their marginality by integrating their work into the life of local communities. This approach was reflected in the 1982 Barclay Report on the role and tasks of social workers which recognized that, given their limited resources, public personal social services could not hope to provide directly for growing social need and should concentrate on 'enabling' communities to provide and develop their own support systems. Quite how this was to happen remained vague until in the the late 1980s the Conservative governments led by Mrs Thatcher succeeded in developing a radical conception of social services as a part of a wider, mixed economy of welfare.

In the mid-1990s social services departments are experiencing yet another round of reorganization with the creation of new unitary local government authorities following the work of the Local Government Commission in England and the even more radical changes legislated for Scotland and Wales. On 1 April 1996 Scotland replaced its 12 regional councils, each of which had a social work department, with 32 new unitary authorities. In Wales the eight counties together with their social services departments were abolished to create 22 new unitary authorities. In England the reorganization has been less comprehensive, most of the counties surviving and losing only parts of their territory to the 47 unitary authorities being created between 1996 and 1998, mainly in highly urbanized areas. It is not clear yet whether the unitary authorities will harm or benefit social services in the longer run. In the short term the changes are clearly disruptive coming so soon after the introduction of the sweeping community care and children's legislation described in the rest of this chapter. In some cases the opportunity has been taken to amalgamate social and housing services into one department. In practice this could bring benefits, since housing problems are central to the difficulties of many social service users, but some social workers fear a downgrading of their influence in the new authorities, particularly as some of them will not be headed by directors from a personal social service background.

In the first five years after 1971 the new Seebohm departments grew fast, sometimes by more than 10 per cent a year. However, over the longer term, constraints on public expenditure from the mid-1970s have meant that service provision was never able to do more than match the growth of numbers in the relevant user groups, particularly of elderly and disabled people living in the community

rather than in institutions. None the less, the overall picture of the post-war growth of the personal social services, measured in both money and staff numbers, has been of steady growth, continuing through the 1980s and 1990s and averaging some 2–3 per cent a year in real terms. While there have been exceptions in some years and in some authorities (sharp cuts in real expenditure are not unknown), this is a record unmatched by any other of the major social services.

THE COMMUNITY CARE REVOLUTION

Since 1979 the Conservative governments of Mrs Thatcher and John Major have enacted more than fifty pieces of legislation that have greatly changed and added to the responsibilities of the local authority personal social services. The most important are the National Health Service and Community Care Act 1990 and the Children Act 1989. These have been followed and supplemented by a great deal of supporting legislation and policy guidance in the form of letters and circulars issued by the Department of Health and its equivalents within the Welsh and Scottish Offices and the Northern Ireland Executive. Many of these new policies and systems came into effect in the five years from April 1991 and even in official documents they are frequently described as amounting to 'a revolution' and 'a sea change in the planning and delivery of services'. As a result, in recent years, social services departments have been preoccupied with issues of organization and management. Many staff have found themselves in new posts and with responsibilities that require them to change established work practices and sometimes strongly held professional values.

The policies that are driving these changes are often portrayed as distinctly a product of the Conservative right and their preference for private provision and market mechanisms. However, at the core of the recent reforms are two ideas which are as old as social work itself: that care in the community is to be preferred to care in institutions; and that prevention is better social work than rescuing social casualties. The idea of community care has been a central post-war theme, to be found, irrespective of the government in power, in almost all the major inquiries and reports of the past forty years. It essentially means that public support should not take place in institutions such as children's homes, special schools and communities, or in residential and nursing homes and longstay hospitals, but rather that, whenever possible, care should be encouraged in people's own homes, or in foster homes, and that support should be family- and community-based. Similarly, the principle of prevention, particularly in social work with children and their families, is to be found at the heart of all the key post-war legislation, in particular the Children's and Young Persons' Acts of the 1960s, which emphasized preventing the need for children to come into local authority care (see chapter IV.1 for more discussion of this).

'New Managerialism'

What is radical and different about recent policy is the ways in which the public personal social services are expected to achieve these established goals. They are to be primarily concerned not with service provision but with the management of care and sometimes with its purchase: that is, the assessment of need and then referral to the most appropriate services, who will often be private and voluntary providers. Social services departments are rapidly cutting down on direct provision, becoming, in the language of the time, 'minority providers within a mixed economy of independent care agencies'.

Where social service departments do continue to provide the resources for care

it is now commonly on the basis of a means test. Whereas in the 1960s the goal of the social work profession, set out in the Seebohm Report, was that the personal social services should become a system of universal, tax-funded provision, today only the very poorest are likely to have their care paid for. Many more users are finding that they are being asked to pay for some or all of the services they are assessed as needing. As a result, issues to do with the organization and fairness of fees and charges have become important.

At the same time, a more managerial role in reviewing the outcomes of care and in monitoring and inspecting the quality of provision by others is being developed. While this managerialist approach marks a break with more traditional social work values – social workers are often heard to complain they did not join the profession to do paperwork – it does promise to make the service more accountable. There is now a great deal more public information available about the personal social services. Departments are required by law to publish a 'Community Care Charter' which must indicate, among other things, how users and carers can complain and how quickly they must receive a response. Each authority must produce an annual 'community care plan', indicating the levels of needs in its community and how it intends to meet them. The authority must be able to show that it has formally consulted users and taken their views into account in drawing up the plan. Many departments are also producing 'children's services plans' on the same basis.

Much of the activity of departments is monitored by the Department of Health's Social Service Inspectorate and its equivalents within the Welsh and Scottish Offices and in Northern Ireland. Many of their publications are free and report on inspections by teams which include lay members of the public and service users. These inspections tackle and report on consumer issues which have traditionally received little more than lip-service, such as equal opportunities and sensitivity to issues of gender and ethnicity. In 1996 the Inspectorate began an ambitious series of inspections which seek to discover and measure the outcomes for users. Clearly, while the huge increase in information does not guarantee better services, it does in principle make them more accountable and open to scrutiny.

THE CONSUMER EXPERIENCE OF COMMUNITY CARE

In the case of children and younger adults with physical disabilities, learning difficulties or who suffer from mental illness, community care has become a reality in the limited sense that hardly any of these groups are now living in the large, impersonal and often isolated institutions that could still be found well into the 1970s. What is less clear is that the families and informal carers who now provide most care are getting adequate support. For example, services for children and families consume more than half of social worker time and nearly 30 per cent of departmental resources. This is very expensive work, since the number of children involved at any one time in the United Kingdom is less than 100,000, about 60 per cent of whom will be in foster homes, 16 per cent in children's homes (run by the local authorities or by voluntary bodies or profit-seeking firms) and the remainder at home.

However, the second core goal, that of prevention, remains elusive. The central aim of the Children Act 1989 was that social workers should work in partnership with families, proactively providing preventive services on the basis of needs and individual care plans, rather than responding mainly when some emergency or risk arises. The Social Services Inspectorate has published a series of reports which show that while progress has been made, most resources are still going on children on Child Protection Registers (about 50 per cent of cases), and cases where no immediate risk is expected are rarely, and usually inadequately, reviewed.

For the elderly, who are the fastest growing category of people who need care, deinstitutionalization has been less successful. The longstay geriatric wards in NHS hospitals have all but disappeared, but the proportion of people over 75 who are in residential care or nursing homes has not fallen during the past two decades. However, the withdrawal of the social services departments from direct provision is taking place quickly. Fewer than 25 per cent of the 400,000 institutional places for the elderly in the UK in 1996 were publicly provided; private and voluntary provision now predominates. The same is happening in the case of domiciliary services. By September 1995 the independent sector (voluntary and for-profit organisations) provided 30 per cent of local authority purchases of homecare help and government policy intended this figure to rise to over 80 per cent.

Services are also more tightly targeted on those elderly people judged to have the greatest needs. The 1990 Community Care Act requires authorities to carry out needs-based assessments and these, though very time-consuming, have led to sharp reductions in the numbers of people who are then defined as eligible for local authority funded help. The number of households receiving homecare fell by over 5 per cent in 1995. This is part of a trend that has led, in some parts of the country, to the withdrawal of domiciliary services from people who had got used to receiving them. A number of legal test cases have followed and the grounds upon which local authorities may effectively change assessments and withdraw services remain uncertain until the issue is resolved by the House of Lords.

As in the case of children's services, the Social Service Inspectorate has been monitoring the effects on users of the changes in community care. In 1995 it reported the result of inspections in six local authorities, which showed that, while most users appeared reasonably satisfied, many of the problems the new assessment-based system was designed to remedy continued: users did not feel involved in their assessments; there was little monitoring of provision by private suppliers; and co-ordination between social services and the NHS, particularly over hospital discharges, remained haphazard.

CONCLUSION

The publicly funded personal social services consume only slightly more than 1 per cent of the national product. At any one time they impinge little on the lives of the vast majority of the population. Yet they are utterly relevant to the lives of the poorest and most disadvantaged in our society: vulnerable children, disabled adults and frail old people. During the 1990s the financing and delivery of these services is being radically transformed, in ways that people will not appreciate until they find they need them. The changes are bold and risky and they raise many of the difficult moral and technical questions that are central to the study of social policy.

GUIDE TO FURTHER READING

The pace of change means that textbooks are too quickly out of date. A regular reading of the weekly professional journal *Community Care* (Reed Business Publishing) is the best way of keeping up. The annual reports of the Chief Inspector of Social Services provide a comprehensive review and a rich source of references, but beware of the failure ever to mention poverty: Department of Health (1996) *Progress through Change. The Fifth Annual Report.* London: HMSO. Eileen Younghusband (1981) *The Newest Profession: a Short History of Social Work.* London: IPC Business Press, remains a classic history; and Maureen Oswin (1971) *The Empty Hours: a Study of the Week-end Life of Handicapped Children in Institutions.* London: Allen Lane Penguin Press, is a moving account of an institutional world that is fortunately gone. Nigel Parton (1991) *Governing the Family: Child Care, Child Protection and the State.* Basingstoke: Macmillan, is balanced, interesting and well written. For a reasonably optimistic account of the new community care there is Jane Lewis and Howard Glennerster (1996) *Implementing the New Community Care.* Buckingham: Open University Press, while Roger Hadley and Roger Clough (1996) *Care in Chaos: Frustration and Challenge in Community Care.* London: Cassell, presents a much less positive view. For a European perspective, Brian Munday and Peter Ely (1996) *Social Care in Europe.* Hemel Hempstead: Prentice Hall, is an excellent guide. Well informed fictional accounts are a good way of getting a feel of what social work is about. Margaret Forster (1992) *The Battle for Christabel.* Harmondsworth: Penguin Books, and (1990) *Have the Men Had Enough.* Harmondsworth: Penguin Books, are moving and beautifully written.

part v
resources

stuDyING socIaL poLIcy

V.1

DOING PROJECTS IN SOCIAL POLICY
HARTLEY DEAN

'Project' is an overworked word. It can be used to describe the simplest learning exercise or as a metaphor for the greatest of human achievements. Yet whenever the word is used, it refers to some kind of active process; to something that is performed or 'done'. This chapter is about the kind of projects which social policy students might be expected to do in order to develop and demonstrate their investigative skills; in order that they should be not the passive recipients of other people's knowledge, but the active creators of their own.

As a social policy student you might be asked to prepare and present a case study as part of the assessment within a particular module or unit; to undertake a systematic literature review as the basis for an extended essay; or to research and write a substantial dissertation as part of your degree. In this chapter we shall first discuss the essential activity – research – that is involved in doing all kinds of project. We shall then be concerned with choosing project topics, with the kind of approaches (or 'methodologies') you might use, the kind of techniques (or 'methods') which might be appropriate and the special ethical considerations which sometimes apply when you are investigating matters of social policy. Finally, we shall consider issues to do with writing up and presenting project findings.

WHAT IS RESEARCH?

Some of the projects undertaken by social policy sudents involve observations, questionnaires, interviews, statistical analysis: these are the sort of technical processes which are often associated with the term 'research'. Certainly, most social policy students will at some point in their studies receive some formal training in technical research methods, and this chapter is partly intended to give you some idea of what to expect in this connection. However, it is important to emphasize that doing projects can also involve modes of inquiry and independent study which will carry you no further than the library and your own desk. Although distinctions may be drawn between 'theorizing' and 'research', any theorist of social policy must first find out about the origins, the substance and the impact of social policy, even if to do so he or she has to draw on and interpret work done by other people.

The research that is required for doing projects in social policy involves finding things out and then drawing conclusions. It entails some kind of synthesis by the student between information or 'facts' on the one hand and ideas or 'theory' on the other – that is how knowledge is produced. There is no reason why students, through their projects, should not only find out things for themselves but also make their

---

Box V.1.1

Type of project	Examples
Illustrative case study	A presentation to demonstrate how the concept of 'market-ization' might help to understand recent developments in: (a) the health service; (b) the personal social services; (c) education; (d) housing; or (e) the social security system.
Extended essay	An assignment which investigates the likely outcome for a particular group of some current legislative proposal, such as:

- the impact of changes in criteria for 'continuing care' upon full time carers;
- the effects of changes in social security rules on asylum seekers;
- the consequences which the introduction of a minimum wage might have for families on low incomes.

Dissertation project	A project based on a small-scale local investigation, but which might address the social policy implications of:

- the provision of housing for disabled people in a particular local ward;
- the physical security of women in a particular block of flats;
- the accessibility of leisure facilities to a particular minority ethnic community;
- the career destinations of 'middle' and 'working' class children from a particular local school.

---

own original contributions to knowledge, or their own recommendations for changes in policy. Box V.1.1 gives some examples of the sorts of inquiry students might typically undertake as projects. However, it illustrates no more than a tiny selection of the topics which might be appropriate, depending on your particular programme of study.

CHOOSING PROJECT TOPICS

For some sorts of small-scale project you may be assigned a specific subject for investigation, but for most substantial project assignments or dissertations the first thing you will have to decide is what you want to study. Three things are important.

- First, choose a topic which interests you. Your project may involve many hours of work and you will need to sustain your commitment to it.
- Second, your topic must be clearly focused. You will note from the selection of topics in box V.1.1 that they are all quite specific: they are addressed not to a general subject area, but to a particular question or problem. Some projects may be designed specifically to test a hypothesis or proposition. Others may set out to evaluate or explore the outcomes or the likely outcomes of specific policies or policy proposals. Students often start by saying, for example, 'I'd like to do something around homelessness', but they must then frame the particular question

about homelessness and housing policy which they will set out to answer.

- Third, the topic must be 'doable'. Although a project, especially a dissertation, may represent a substantial piece of work for you as a student, it will necessarily be conducted on a relatively small scale. It must be realistically planned and take account of the time, the resources and the opportunities which are available to you.

Additionally, you will need to take account of any specific guidelines which your institution provides and the advice of your project supervisor.

METHODOLOGY

When you choose your topic, you will also have to decide upon the conceptual approach, or 'methodology', which you will adopt. Methodology concerns the relationship between your theoretical stance and the manner in which you carry out your investigation. Students of social policy are introduced to questions of methodology in a variety of ways: sometimes formally as part of a research methods module or unit; sometimes in the course of studying the philosophy of social science. Most projects in social policy do not fit neatly into any one methodological category or 'paradigm', but generally speaking you will need to be aware of three broad schools of thought.

- First, there are 'hard' or empiricist approaches. All project work involves the use of empirical evidence, but what is called empiri*cism* is an approach to evidence that is aligned to the conventions associated with the natural sciences. It is concerned to explain external realities from an objective standpoint. It tends to deal in processes of quantitative measurement.
- Second, there are 'soft' or interpretive approaches. In fact, these are no less rigorous in their use of evidence than empiricist approaches, but interpret-

ivism is a stance which characterizes a major strand within the *social* sciences. It is concerned to understand the nature or meaning of the social world from the subjective standpoint of the people involved. It tends to deal in processes of qualitative observation.

- Third, there are critical approaches. Any theoretical stance can result in criticisms of social policy, but a critical approach to the use of evidence is one that is grounded in the analysis of social conflict or relationships of power (for example, Marxism, feminism, antiracism or such movements as poststructuralism). A critical approach may draw on elements of either or both the other approaches insofar as they help to explain or understand social policy, but it is sceptical of empiricism and interpretivism because they do not *necessarily* question the underlying basis of the status quo.

Many projects in social policy are 'applied' rather than 'theoretical', and you may find it difficult to be explicit about the nature of your chosen methodology. It is none the less important that you should understand that no research activity can be free from the conceptual assumptions and values which you yourself bring to the project.

METHODS AND PROJECT DESIGN

Having determined what you will investigate and from what kind of perspective you will need to design your project. If your project is an assessed case study or extended essay then your principal method is likely to be a literature review. All social policy students will learn the skills required for undertaking literature reviews, including, for example, the use of computerized literature searches and citation indices. Reviewing and interpeting the existing literature on a subject is an essential form of research activity in its own right. In fact, almost any project is likely to incorporate

---

Box V.1.2

Data gathering method	Examples
Secondary source methods	
	• Documentary/archive research
	• Secondary data-set analysis
Survey methods	
	• Questionnaires
	• Structured interviews
	• Telephone surveys
Discursive methods	
	• In-depth interviews
	• Focus group discussions
	• Life histories
	• Diaries
Observational methods	
	• Non-participant observation
	• Participative/ethnographic observation
	• Action research

---

a literature review as part of an investigation: this is necessary not only to familiarize yourself with the conceptual, historical and factual background to a subject, but because projects similar or identical to your own may already have been undertaken and the findings published.

If your project extends beyond a literature review, you will need to choose methods for gathering and analysing 'data'. The term data can apply to any kind of information resulting from counting, measuring or observing. Data can exist or be recorded in quantitative or numerical form on the one hand, or qualitative or discursive (i.e. written or spoken) form on the other. Box V.1.2 lists the principal means by which data might be gathered for a project. A project may employ data gathered using several different methods.

Once gathered, data must be analysed. The patterns and relationships within quantitative data may be analysed using statistical techniques, ranging from the simple to the highly complex. The handling of quantitative data has been revolutionized by the development of specialized computer software which makes even quite sophisticated statistical manipulation relatively straightforward, and all social policy

students will have an opportunity to learn about this. Qualitative data may be analysed either by coding them in ways which make it possible to apply quantitative techniques, or by a variety of inductive techniques for interpeting the content and the themes which occur within discursive material. There has been an upsurge of interest in qualitative data analysis in recent years, including the use not only of conventional interview transcripts and observational reports, but of audio- and video-recordings and the development of computer software packages for the analysis of textual material.

ETHICS

Projects in social policy are ultimately concerned with people and the things which affect their lives. Social policy itself is often concerned with specially vulnerable people. All social research involves ethical considerations and the sort of projects which social policy students undertake will sometimes raise particular issues, especially if you should seek direct access to the users or potential users of welfare services.

Many academic institutions have ethical guidelines or codes of practice which staff and students are required to follow, and some even have ethics committees to which project proposals must be submitted for approval. Some kinds of project may in any event require ethical clearance from other bodies: for example, any project which involves the collection of data from or about patients of the National Health Service must be considered by a local research ethics committee. Whether or not they are directly constrained, all students undertaking projects should take account of their ethical responsibilities. They are responsible to their fellow students and the institution at which they study – whose interests could be damaged if, for example, insensitive inquiries of local welfare agencies should sour future relations. Students must also be responsible for their own welfare and should not place themselves in dangerous situations. However, the most important area of responsibility lies in relation to research 'subjects': the people that your project is about.

This particularly applies if your research subjects participate directly by answering questionnaires, taking part in interviews or allowing themselves to be observed. It is essential, except in the most exceptional circumstances, that their participation should be on the basis of their informed consent. Not only should they agree to take part, but you should ensure that they understand the nature and purposes of your project. It will often be important in such circumstances to undertake to protect the confidentiality of people or organizations taking part; and to make sure that you do not (even inadvertently) pass on information about them which they would wish to be kept confidential, or disclose their identity in any report or publication if they should wish to remain anonymous.

At a more general level, you should be prepared to reflect on the nature of your responsibilities as a student/investigator to the people or group you are studying. For example, could the way in which you interact with, investigate or report on disabled people, asylum-seekers or 'the poor' have any adverse consequences, even at the level of perpetuating or reinforcing pejorative stereotypes? Projects which adopt an explicitly critical approach (in the sense outlined above) might imply a very particular ethical agenda. For example, some feminist methodologies seek as a matter of principle to eschew the traditional hierarchical relationship between researcher and researched in favour of a democratic and participatory relationship between the researcher and the women in whose lives she seeks to share.

THE PRESENTATION OF FINDINGS

The purpose of any project is fulfilled by writing it up or presenting it. There is no point in undertaking any sort of research activity unless you disseminate the findings. What is more, the skills involved in presenting findings are among the most important you will learn. They are skills required well beyond the boundaries of academia. At both a national and a local level the politicians who make social policy, the officials who interpret it and the agencies (public, voluntary and private) who deliver welfare services all require clear, concise and relevant information and commentary.

Students are likely to receive specific guidelines from their institutions and/ or detailed advice from their tutors/ supervisors about the writing of project reports. In general, however, the report (whether it is presented orally or in writing) should be structured so as to provide a narrative. It should:

- explain how you first identified and defined the question or problem which the project addresses;
- set out the conceptual or theoretical framework you decided to use and why;

- outline the background provided by your literature review, the issues raised and any conclusions you may have drawn from the literature or from other secondary sources.

If your project entailed an original empirical investigation, it should:

- describe the research design and method(s) used, and the way you analysed the resulting data;
- explain any limitations or contraints to which the project was subject, and the implications these might have for the reliability or validity of the findings;
- set out and discuss your findings;
- provide conclusions and, if appropriate, recommendations for action.

You will normally be expected to add a summary of the key points.

CONCLUSION

The opportunity to undertake projects represents an important part of a social policy degree. The value of doing projects in social policy lies in the experience it offers in independent study, the application of theory to 'real world' situations, the use of research methods, the development of skills of analysis, presentation and report writing. Projects put the student 'in the driving seat'. Social policy is full of controversies – about oppression, disadvantage and who gets what in a 'welfare state'. It is through projects that you may be able to explore the issues which excite or matter most to you, and in the manner best suited to your own aptitudes.

ACKNOWLEDGEMENT

The author is grateful to John Paley for helpful suggestions upon an earlier draft of this chapter.

GUIDE TO FURTHER READING

There is a vast and ever expanding literature on research methods, although little of it is aimed specifically at social policy students. None the less, an appropriate introductory guide is: Bell, J. (1993) *Doing Your Research Project: a Guide for First-time Researchers in Education and Social Science*, 2nd edn. Buckingham: Open University Press.

For an excellent introduction to wider issues in social research see: May, T. (1993) *Social Research: Issues, Methods and Process*. Buckingham: Open University Press.

Alternatively, for a comprehensive 'one-stop' textbook see: Robson, C. (1993) *Real World Research: a Resource for Social Scientists and Practitioner Researchers*. Oxford: Blackwell.

Although it is in certain details rather dated now, the following still represents a stimulating collection of essays for anyone interested in social policy research: Bell, C. and Roberts, H. (eds) (1984) *Social Researching: Politics, Problems, Practice*. London: Routledge & Kegan Paul.

A contemporary discussion of research ethics that is focused on social policy can be found in: Dean, H. (ed.) (1996) *Ethics and Social Policy Research*. Luton: University of Luton Press/Social Policy Association.

Finally, two books examining different aspects of data analysis: Bryman, A. and Cramer, D. (1990) *Quantitative Data Analysis for Social Scientists*. London: Routledge; Dey, I. (1993) *Qualitative Data Analysis: a User-friendly Guide for Social Scientists*. London: Routledge.

fieLDworK pLacement
aND tHe sociaL poLicy curricuLum
DuNcaN scott

Students who have undertaken field-work placements as an integral part of their undergraduate social policy degree typically conclude that: 'I have learned more than I ever dreamed was possible in such a short period' and 'The field-work experience was a life-changing one for me. It put all my values and assumptions into question' (Joan and Jean in Burnham et al., 1993, p. 13). Yet, even while such positive experiences can be duplicated across a wide range of higher education institutions, there are signs that the commitment of social policy courses to fieldwork, as a central part of the under-graduate curriculum, is at best uneven and at worst in retreat.

This chapter will identify what is involved in fieldwork placements, and why students should be encouraged to undertake them; it will conclude by briefly considering the prospects for the further development of social policy fieldwork approaches in higher education.

What Is Fieldwork?

Popular perceptions

A quick look through the pages of 1996 university undergraduate handbooks provides a number of very common pictures. We see geography students sitting on the cliffs at Charmouth in Dorset (Oxford University), on boulders half way up a mountain in North Wales (Nottingham) or on a lava flow in Hawaii (Leeds). Similar pictures on the same theme portray archae-ology students at an Iron Age burial site in Hampshire or human sciences students finding out about traditional medicine in Kenya (both Oxford).

Most of these pictures are about organ-ized visits to study the physical environ-ment – and they are popular with the editors of handbooks because the images convey a sense of the exciting possibilities awaiting the hopeful sixth former. More careful examination of the handbook might reveal a wide range of 'visiting' – from the language student who may spend up to a year in France, Germany or Spain, to the anthropologist off to Western Ireland or Africa, or the planning student fresh from a project in a suburban housing estate. In different ways all these forms of outreach demonstrate a belief in the importance of direct contact between the student and what he or she is studying. It is argued that greater closeness, even in some cases the development of social relationships, can lead to a deeper form of learning. The textbook is helpful up to a point; things become 'real' when they are observed, touched and related to.

Social policy fieldwork

Social policy fieldwork takes place within a 'family' of academic disciplines or areas

Figure V.2.1   The organization of fieldwork.

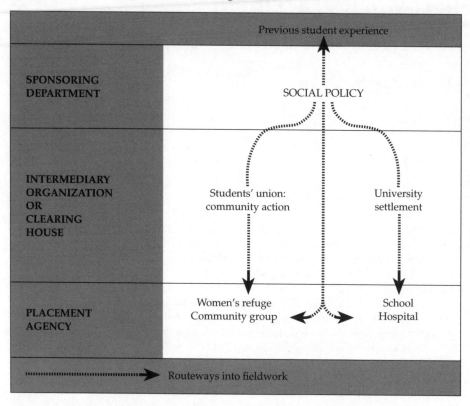

of study (e.g. sociology, anthropology), often in collaboration with 'cousins' involved in professional training (e.g. social work). Figure V.2.1 attempts to illustrate this and to connect the departmental 'sponsor' of fieldwork with the intermediary agencies or clearing houses and the actual organizational placements. The broken lines indicate different routeways to a placement, i.e. a student may be placed directly with an agency, or be helped to locate one through the students' union or university settlement. Some older students use previous experience (e.g. work as a care assistant) instead of undertaking a new placement, perhaps because existing family commitments make this difficult.

The early development of social policy fieldwork often took place via university settlements; in 1901 the Manchester settle-

ment's annual report celebrated the fact that 'the Settlement is slowly if surely acquiring the character of a bureau of social information' (Rose and Woods, 1995, p. 77). A typical example of how students used the strategic location of the settlement to improve their own academic skills while producing something of use to local people is illustrated in figure V.2.2.

Reports by social policy fieldworkers were, however, not greeted with universal enthusiasm, as some people resented the 'snoopers' from the university; a Manchester councillor pleaded with his colleagues, in a 1935 housing debate, 'for God's sake, not to give room to those self-appointed investigators who went about dissecting and vivisecting the lives of the working class' (Rose and Woods, 1995, p. 82). These are continuing ethical and

Figure V.2.2 Manchester University Settlement Survey (Rose and Woods, 1995, p. 78).

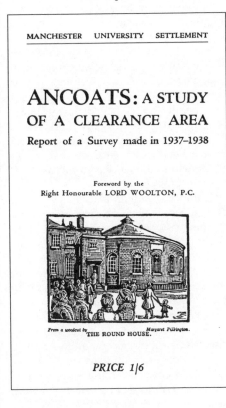

MANCHESTER   UNIVERSITY   SETTLEMENT

ANCOATS: A STUDY OF A CLEARANCE AREA

Report of a Survey made in 1937–1938

Foreword by the
Right Honourable LORD WOOLTON, P.C.

From a woodcut by THE ROUND HOUSE. *Margaret Pilkington.*

PRICE 1/6

in the 1990s: 'What justification was there for "letting loose" naive and green students like me in welfare settings where there are people whose permission is not even sought? What are the benefits to placement agencies who allow students to go in?' (Bridget, 17 November 1995).

WHY DO SOCIAL POLICY FIELDWORK?

There are three overlapping arguments in favour of doing social policy fieldwork, and these are summarized in table V.2.1. All social policy fieldwork placements emphasize the centrality of finding out about social policy issues in society (level III), very often simultaneously reflecting on the processes whereby this finding out (or research) takes place. In some instances, there is also an emphasis on what are called 'transferable skills'; for example, a student may learn from participation in a group how to make decisions, work in a team and communicate. These skills are not specific to the particular social policy context, they can be transferred into settings such as a bank, factory or town hall (see level II in table V.2.1).

Inevitably, the process of entering what is often a completely new social world leads to new relationships. Although these are rarely more than temporary and superficial they can be the means through which a student learns to cope in a crisis, handle a conflict or work through personal uncertainties, fears and prejudices (e.g.

political concerns; if social policy fieldwork placements are constructed so as to allow students greater experiences of social needs and responses, a number of questions are raised. A social policy student summed up her experiences of a four-week placement

Table V.2.1 Educational purposes in social policy

Purpose: 'knowledge about . . .'	Learning focus	Learning outcome
I Self	*through* relationships	personal growth
II Group	*from* relationships	team-building communication skills
III Society	*about* relationships	policy/practice knowledge

about working with people with learning disabilities, ex-offenders, drug addicts, the mentally ill and so on). (See level I in table V.2.1.)

How a particular individual student combines these three purposes will depend on the circumstances of the placement and on his or her overall career direction. For example, he or she may intend to use the fieldwork as preparation either for further professional training or as the first piece of in-depth academic work which could, eventually, lead to more intensive postgraduate study. In the first example social work is a common career destination, but there are also parallel moves into teaching, housing, planning, youth work, welfare rights and paid work in voluntary agencies (e.g. work with the elderly, children and families).

A second response may involve a dissertation which grows out of the initial fieldwork placement. A student may revisit a women's refuge or a special school, and gather information about its policies and practices; this will usually form the basis of several linked chapters containing between 10,000 and 15,000 words. For undergraduates this is often the largest piece of written work they produce, and may give them confidence to undertake more advanced and intensive fieldwork at postgraduate level, as part of masters and doctoral programmes.

What Is Involved in a Fieldwork Placement?

Practical matters

A placement may take place at the same time as coursework (e.g. every Wednesday for one or two terms) or in a block of time (e.g. four weeks in the vacation). When students are involved in exchange schemes with European universities they may spend a term or more away from their 'home base'. In a few cases a field-

work placement may occupy 30 weeks and therefore constitute an extra year in the undergraduate degree programme.

Students may be placed within walking distance of their parental home, close to their termtime address or half the way around the world. Most are in Britain – popular examples include community centres, luncheon clubs for older people, schools for children with disabilities, residential units for ex-offenders, the homeless, refugees, the mentally ill etc. Exotic examples include a kibbutz in Israel, orphanages in Romania, summer camps in Lithuania and the USA as well as development projects in the Third World.

The most common placements outside Britain are within the European Union Erasmus/Socrates programme. Students (individually or in small groups) exchange with their peers in EU member states; the period of study in the new institution replaces, for assessment purposes, the comparable time in their home university. While away from Britain the social policy student need not undertake a specific fieldwork placement, although visits to social policy institutions (schools, hospitals, prisons, hostels for refugees etc.) are often arranged. In a sense the whole exchange is like a 'giant' piece of fieldwork in which an individual can learn more about himself or herself and her or his skills in group situations, and deepen a comparative understanding of different policy environments.

The 'official' reasons for Socrates are that it will encourage the development of intellectual, cultural and linguistic skills and provide students with a valuable addition to their employability factor. It is becoming clear that some prospective employers consider time spent on exchanges as an indicator of individual initiative and of someone likely to be more enthusiastic and knowledgeable about Europe.

Students talk of the 'hassles' involved in preparing for all fieldwork and particularly the EU exchanges: extra costs, covering for accommodation left behind, learning enough of a new language, settling in, a different social life, administrative confusions and so on. A consistent majority come back with a greater understanding of themselves and of a wide spectrum of new knowledge about other countries. They talk incessantly of their experiences and show off their souvenir T-shirts. All in all they tend to support the idea of being 'somewhere else' long enough to notice and understand difference.

Academic matters

The location, status and significance of fieldwork in the undergraduate curriculum varies in three main respects:

1 Is it integrated or marginal? Do the weeks of fieldwork really connect in a direct way with substantial blocks of classroom teaching, or are they handled briefly and separately in the 'cracks' between the basic building bricks of the courses?
2 Is the fieldwork assessed or not? Do the reports really count towards the final degree classification?
3 Is the fieldwork compulsory or voluntary? Does the department expect you to make all the effort, or leave it to individual enthusiasms?

Whatever the departmental significance of fieldwork, its essential characteristics remain the same; it is about processes of individual (sometimes small group) interaction whereby the student seeks to understand the everyday life of individuals, groups and organizations by entering their social worlds or 'fields', and trying as much as is possible to see things from their point of view. Figure V.2.3 represents two related dimensions of this process: the fieldwork student is 'climbing into the picture', but the drawing alerts us to possible ways in which the social characteristics (e.g. age, gender, class, race), first of the student and second of those already

in the field, will interrupt or shape subsequent relationships. Just how far the figure in the suit will really learn to see things from the perspective of the young workers in overalls is uncertain. All that is clear is that some social differences are likely to play a crucial role in the placement process.

Students who are asked to undertake 'projects', usually of a research-based kind, are less likely to engage in such social interactions; their task is primarily to observe, interview and record information. In some contrast, the fieldwork placement often hinges on the fact that 'Once some sort of relation has been created, the character of that particular relationship determines what sorts of experience and hence what kinds of experiential and intuitive insights the fieldworkers will gain' (Emerson in Bailey, 1996, p. 64).

Some university departments view fieldwork placements in a fairly narrow way; they take the view that a young, inexperienced student 'should try to fit in with whatever they do' (Social Policy Placement Guidelines, 1995–6, X University). At the level of being polite they are absolutely right – the student is a guest and should not consciously create disturbances in her or his host agency. On the other hand, fitting in need not preclude other emotional and intellectual experiences. For a variety of reasons – the personal character of the student, the key individuals in the placement agency and the events which unfold during the fieldwork – an individual may react to the social field in more complex ways. For example, a trio of female students in an orphanage found the behaviour of key people 'irritating', 'puzzling', even 'objectionable'. They found themselves getting frustrated and angry and subsequently (back at university) reflected on different possible explanations for these responses. They concluded that some of the difficulties had been triggered by clashes of personalities (including theirs), but that others reflected on the way the orphanages were organized, and the

level of social policy provision for children in the society as a whole. Instead of fitting in mentally and intellectually (to match their general and necessary politeness), they had learnt how to explore both their feelings and their analytic abilities. In short, they had learnt from their experiences about themselves, groups and institutions.

Fieldwork as art?

Because the student can't prepare for all eventualities, she or he must accept and creatively explore uncertainties when they arise. The report which emerges from such experiences can be more than a cold recitation of data gathering. Indeed, there are some commentators who argue that fieldwork accounts must be more than 'efficient', 'systematic' or 'scientific'. They would argue that fieldwork touches 'art' to the extent that the student can discover in 'personal experience an account that offers to a discerning audience a level of insight and understanding into human social life that exceeds whatever might be achieved through attention solely to gathering and reporting data' (Wolcott, 1995, p. 251).

If the student who interviews a young single mother in depressing circumstances is moved to anger and tears, she or he may search for ways to provide a degree of detail about the physical and emotional context – to convey the depth of the experience, to treat the person as more than another specimen to be put into a glass case. All of this raises ethical and political questions which must always be thought through. For example, what should one do if the woman appears to be an inconsistently competent mother, even when all her circumstances are considered? Again, what should be done if it is clear that a local authority social worker makes half-hearted attempts to contact the mother, or deliberately overlooks the complex family dynamics in order to 'manage' her or his case-load?

For the moment it is worth emphasizing that fieldwork is not just about 'mindwork', it is also about close observation and above all about emotions and sensitivities; the poet and the novelist can help in this regard. Seamus Heaney talks of how he:

could see the vaccination mark
stretched on your upper arm, and smell the coal smell
of the train that comes between us, a slow goods
(Heaney, 1979, p. 52)

He is reminding us not just of the creative power of poetry but also of the contribution of careful fine-grained observation, and of all the senses which can contribute to a more complete picture.

Finally, the novelist can reveal to us that fieldwork need not be all earnest soul-searching, that there may be moments, even whole periods of days and weeks, of enjoyment and fun. Dr Robyn Penrose, temporary lecturer in English at 'Rummidge' university, provides more than a wry smile for the reader as she struggles to make sense of her fieldwork placement at Pringle's engineering works (Lodge, 1989). We are presented with page after page of comic episodes neatly interwoven with more serious asides about the social distance between the ivory tower and the factory. Robyn's journey – from very reluctant fieldworker to defender of greater connections between the two institutions – can be ours; and we can laugh along the way!

FIELDWORK IN HIGHER EDUCATION: CONTINUITIES AND CONTRADICTIONS

Most social policy departments do not regard a compulsory formally assessed fieldwork placement as a necessary and integral part of their core curriculum. Yet, at the same time, they encourage the development of project work, organize European exchanges and practise an everyday, anecdotal form of fieldwork in the various ways in which lecturers intersperse 'tales from their domestic and neighbourhood lives' in their lectures. In other parts of the university, a wide range of departments will be sending out nurses to learn about localities, trainee teachers into classrooms, geographers to map housing estates and hillsides, planners to build models of new towns and so on. Over in the students' union, various societies will be organizing community action projects, helping in literacy schemes, environmental work and a multitude more.

Universities clearly encourage a loose form of fieldwork right across the campus. The big question is whether the processes of fieldwork are sufficiently anchored in the intellectual heartland of the curriculum, and not just mere decorations around its edge. Where the emphasis is on training, e.g. education and social work, integration is strongest.

Social policy academics have not yet developed a strong consensus for or against fieldwork. Individual departments seem to be more or less committed because of significant 'champions', i.e. individual staff who are strongly committed to the idea and have been around long enough to obtain and safeguard a place for fieldwork in the curriculum. Those who have abandoned fieldwork frequently talk about 'dwindling resources' without revealing how little placements actually cost, and with negligible attention to its academic benefits.

Meanwhile, across higher education, governments through the 1980s and 1990s have cried out for 'relevance'. This is a code word for making what students learn more exactly what commerce and industry require – a giant kind of 'fitting-in'. At least two processes may be taking place at more or less the same time, but for very

different reasons. First, some social policy departments may be abandoning a strong commitment to fieldwork, because they perceive this to be a vital resource saving move, and because it will allegedly allow students to spend more time with more theoretical material. Second, other social policy departments may be promoting narrow forms of 'relevance', whereby students complete practical tasks for placement institutions ranging from businesses to hospitals to community centres.

Both tendencies have put forward strong arguments for their positions. The worry remains that if 'theory' is held to lie outside fieldwork then placements will become increasingly practical; 'relevance' will be similarly defined. Social policy can rediscover fieldwork as an intellectually legitimate activity and thereby guard against narrowness. It can redefine relevance and argue that fieldwork is one way in which students can be encouraged to develop a more confident self-knowledge and critical non-conformity. There are still examples upon which it can draw for sustenance. One of these has been termed 'critical adult education' – a tradition that seems to link personal growth with analyses of contemporary social problems. This tradition goes back to the beginning of the industrial revolution, when welfare explorers raised questions about inequality and poverty, violence and unaccountable economic and political systems, and suggested new possibilities of a more just kind.

No doubt personal growth and a critical engagement with social need can be developed in the library. The challenge from fieldwork is to make connections, to help students to learn how social policy isn't just observing and writing about the world, but trying to change it, and themselves in the same process; they have to begin somewhere.

Guide to Further Reading

The foundations of social policy fieldwork were laid down by those men and women in the nineteenth century who set out to record the size and shape of human need.

They charted the living conditions of poor factory workers huddled together in sub-standard housing, and pressured politicians for reform. Towards the end of the nine-teenth century many universities established 'settlements' from which fieldwork was undertaken. M. E. Rose and A. Woods (1995) *The Round House: a Hundred Years of the Manchester University Settlement*. Manchester: University of Manchester, provides a well illustrated introduction to the fieldwork tradition from the 1890s to the present day.

A student interested in social policy fieldwork and its place in the curriculum could begin from V. Burnham et al. (1993) *Enterprising Fieldwork: a Guide to Fieldwork Learning*. Manchester: School of Social Policy, University of Manchester. This is a gentle intro-duction to all the processes of an undergraduate placement.

When a wider view is needed, books seem to operate on two, often disconnected, levels. First, there are the 'how to do it' accounts, such as Carol A. Bailey (1996) *A Guide to Field Research*. Newbury Park, CA: Pine Forge Press. This is particularly useful because it regards ethical questions as central; the student is urged to consider how and why she engages with social groups in the field. Another 'how to do it', but at a more sophisticated and literary level, is Harry F. Wolcott (1995) *The Art of Fieldwork*. Walnut Creek, CA: Altamira. Wolcott is an American anthropologist who sets out to show how fieldwork is more than a narrow mechanistic activity.

The second level of writing attempts to identify how the fieldwork tradition in social policy is more than the choices made by its teachers in specific departments: there are sets of wider structural influences derived from the interests of governments and industrialists.

My essay 'Nice (field) work': field-based approaches in social policy and the significance of enterprise in higher education. In John Baldock and Margaret May (eds) (1995), *Social Policy Review 7*. London: Social Policy Association, pp. 272–98 attempts to make wider connections. A good example of a short chapter that pulls together the historical legacy of fieldwork, and contemporary developments in the way it is being developed, is provided by Katherine Hughes (1995) Really useful knowledge: adult learning and the Ruskin Learning Project. In Marjorie Mayo and Jane Thompson (eds), *Adult Learning Critical Intelligence and Social Change*. Washington, DC: National Institute of Adult and Continuing Education, pp. 97–110.

Finally, when students are even half persuaded that fieldwork can and should be both creative and fun, they could read one of Seamus Heaney's (1979) poems in *Field Work*. London: Faber and Faber, or David Lodge (1989) *Nice Work*. Harmondsworth: Penguin.

Learning resources

V.3

a guide to the literature

robert m. page

When 'asked by a colleague in another subject to recommend some books for his teenage son, who was considering studying social administration', Gilbert Smith (1985, p. 260) suggested that it would be 'best to look at a few good research reports'. Although the reading of such reports has much to commend it, prospective students should also consult some of the accessible and informative textbooks and monographs in this area of academic enquiry. Indeed, the dramatic growth of such texts in recent years has ensured that it is no longer appropriate to regard the subject as dull or, worse, 'boring' (Taylor-Gooby, 1978). Although the future of the welfare state is now more uncertain than it was even twenty years ago, the academic study of social policy and administration continues to thrive, develop and adapt.

In this chapter an attempt will be made to identify some of the key texts which have been published in the field of social policy, predominantly in the post-1945 period. Naturally, any choice of this kind is likely to be as contentious as selecting the greatest players who have worn the colours of one's favourite football club or nominating the dozen best post-war British novels. The selection of texts, which is guided partly by discussions in other parts of the companion, is divided into four sections: classics, pathbreakers, overviews and introductory texts.

CLASSICS

My classic selections will probably prove to be the least controversial: two books by Richard Titmuss (the leading figure in post-war British social administration) and one each from R. H. Tawney and T. H. Marshall.

Richard Titmuss (1950)
Problems of Social Policy

Problems of Social Policy was one of the officially commissioned civilian war histories. Titmuss avoided the danger of producing a dry overgeneralized account of wartime developments, preferring instead to capture the social impact of total war on the civilian population by means of what he termed 'selective illustration' (p. ix). In concentrating on a narrow range of issues – evacuation, hospital services and the care afforded to homeless people – Titmuss brought to life the complexities of policy-making, the adaptability and general goodwill of the civilian population and the positive role of collective action. This book compels the reader to wrestle with the difficulties of constructing social policy and provides the finest illustration of Titmuss's problem-oriented approach to the subject.

Richard Titmuss (1970)
The Gift Relationship

In *The Gift Relationship*, Titmuss sought, through a case study of blood doning, to persuade his readers that collectivist welfare could 'help to actualize the social and moral potentialities of all citizens' (p. 238). Resisting the temptation to make exaggerated claims about the altruism of the British public, Titmuss was nevertheless able to show how the establishment of a social institution such as the National Health Service could create the social cohesion necessary for displays of effective forms of selflessness. The book's continued relevance for social policy was recently underlined by Colin Ward (1996), who confessed that he had 'dismissed' this volume when it was first published but now regards it as invaluable not least because of the way it highlights the rapidity with which 'market ideology has been transferred from economic theory to social policy' (p. 35).

R. H. Tawney (1931) *Equality*

Equality has proved to be one of the most influential texts for successive generations of social policy scholars. Tawney stresses the equal worth of all citizens and calls for the creation of a community which 'uses its material resources to promote the dignity and refinement of the individual human beings who comprise it' (p. 103). *Equality* is firmly underpinned by Tawney's Christian socialist beliefs and the contemporary reader is likely to find much of interest here in terms of the continuing debate about rights and obligations.

T. H. Marshall (1950)
Citizenship and Social Class

The work of T. H. Marshall remains important for the student of social policy, largely because of his seminal work on the notion of citizenship. In *Citizenship and Social Class*, Marshall charts the evolution of citizenship rights over the centuries (legal rights, eighteenth century; political rights, nineteenth century; social rights, twentieth century). In reading *Citizenship and Social Class* (Marshall and Bottomore, 1992), students will also be able to observe the development of Marshall's ideas concerning the possibility of forging a society in which both a modified capitalism and a collectivist form of welfare can coexist – a perspective which has been termed a 'middle way' approach to social policy (Pinker, 1995).

PATHBREAKERS

The pathbreaker category presents more difficulties in terms of selection because of the differing interests of many scholars and commentators in the field. Impact and breadth are two of the central criteria influencing the choice of titles here.

Brian Abel-Smith and Peter Townsend (1965)
The Poor and the Poorest

Although recently adjudged 'unreadable' by Frank Field (1996), *The Poor and the Poorest* had a major impact on the postwar poverty debate in Britain, promoting as it did the importance of relative conceptions of poverty and highlighting the need for continued focus on the living conditions of poorer citizens – a task which has been so successfully taken up by the Child Poverty Action Group in recent decades. This publication was one of an excellent series of occasional papers on social administration, many of which are of continuing relevance.

Robert Pinker (1971) *Social Theory and Social Policy*

One of the major criticisms of post-1945 social policy and administration was its limited theoretical underpinning. In *Social Theory and Social Policy*, Robert Pinker reviews the historic roots of social administration and examines the insights which sociological theory can bring to the subject. Pinker's discussion of stigma, exchange, selectivity, universalism, self-interest and altruism continue to stimulate and enlighten. Indeed, the richness of the material encourages one to return to this volume again and again.

Vic George and Paul Wilding (1976) *Ideology and Social Welfare*

Ideology and Social Welfare has proved to be one of the most influential books in terms of challenging the implicit functionalism of what Wilding (1983) has termed 'traditional' social administration. In the first edition of this book the authors compare and contrast the values, approach to society, attitudes to government and the welfare state of the anti-collectivists, the reluctant collectivists, the Fabian socialists and the Marxists in an attempt to demonstrate the essentially contested nature of social policy. This book has stimulated a lively debate in this area and has gone through countless reprints and editions, most recently as *Welfare and Ideology* (in which six distinctive perspectives – new right, middle way, democratic socialist, Marxist, feminist and green – are featured). One of the great strengths of this book is the clarity of the writing (which is also a feature of the work of Ramesh Mishra and Norman Johnson). This has helped to ensure its continued popularity with students.

Ian Gough (1979) *The Political Economy of the Welfare State*

This book remains one of the most significant contributions to the study of the modern welfare state. Using insights from economics, sociology and political science, Gough (acknowledging his academic debt to James O'Connor: see O'Connor, 1973; Gough, 1995) provides an authoritative account of the contradictory nature of the welfare state within advanced capitalist societies (i.e. the way in which state welfare can simultaneously serve to aid capital accumulation while also providing social benefits for those in need). The great strength of this book is the way it encourages students to consider the interrelationship between economic and social policy and gauge the relevance of Marxist or neo-Marxist approaches to welfare.

Charles Murray (1984) *Losing Ground*

Another significant event of the past two decades or so has been the resurgence of anti-collectivist thought (which is now commonly referred to as the new right perspective). This has led to renewed interest in the work of luminaries such as Hayek (1944, 1960) and Friedman (1962). Although Charles Murray tends to focus on policy issues in the USA, his influence in the UK should not be underestimated (Murray, 1990). In *Losing Ground* Murray employs a heady mix of argument, evidence and persuasion to suggest that government welfare interventions have exacerbated rather than improved the situation of the disadvantaged. Murray's ideas have been well received in new right circles and have underpinned a number of Conservative government welfare 'initiatives' in the 1980s and 1990s, especially in the field of social security.

Julian Le Grand (1982) *The Strategy of Equality*

The Strategy of Equality provides a detailed review of the failure of the post-1945 welfare state to reduce inequalities (in terms of spending, use, costs or outcomes) in the areas of health care, education, housing and transport. Le Grand concludes that only a fundamental attack on the deep rooted 'ideology of inequality' which legitimates vast disparities in income will resolve this dilemma. This book presents a real challenge to welfare redistributionists and has helped to focus attention on alternative welfare strategies (see Le Grand, 1989, 1993).

Ramesh Mishra (1984)
The Welfare State in Crisis

In this volume Mishra reviews some of the main factors (most notably faltering economic performance) which have undermined the welfare state in the 1970s and 1980s and considers the response to the 'crisis of legitimacy' from a new right, Marxist, corporatist and social democratic perspective. Mishra suggests that the adoption of the voluntary corporatist strategy pursued in Austria and Sweden – in which the economic, industrial and public sectors are intertwined – provides the best means of preserving the welfare state. The value of a book of this kind is the interest it has generated in transnational welfare trends and the refinement of analytical perspectives (see also Mishra, 1990, 1995).

Gillian Pascall (1986) *Social Policy: a Feminist Analysis*

One of the most significant developments in the social policy literature over the past 25 years has been the way in which feminist ideas have moved from the periphery into the mainstream (Wilson, 1977; Finch and Groves, 1983). Gillian Pascall's book (a fully revised edition of which was published by Routledge in the latter part of 1996 – *Social Policy: a New Feminist Analysis*) is a fine example of feminist scholarship in this field, drawing as it does upon a wide range of evidence

in order to illustrate the importance of considering the 'reproductive' rather than merely the 'productive' sphere of social and economic life. The book highlights the need to examine the ways in which social policy may constrain as well as enhance the life chances of women.

Michael Cahill (1994)
The New Social Policy

Given the lack of clearly delineated disciplinary boundaries in social policy and administration, efforts continue to be made to recast the focus of the subject. One of the most influential recent attempts in this regard has come from Michael Cahill, who contends that key aspects of modern life – communicating, viewing, travelling, shopping, working and playing – merit far greater attention by the social policy community, not least because of the emergence of new inequalities in an increasingly consumerist society. Importantly, Cahill also focuses on the issue of sustainability, which lies at the heart of various 'green' welfare strategies.

Will Hutton (1995)
The State We're In

Although Will Hutton does not write from a specifically social policy perspective, his wide-ranging review of the economic, social and political malaise affecting late twentieth-century Britain provides a refreshing account of a centre left strategy for the millennium which is firmly underpinned by a neo-Keynesian economic strategy. Hutton is most persuasive when analysing what has gone wrong with British society and the types of change which could remedy the situation. A more detailed political strategy for achieving change requires further elaboration. The great value of this volume is the inspiration it provides for those seeking imaginative and plausible alternatives to neo-liberal welfare strategies (See also in relation to this topic the reports of the Commission on Social Justice, 1994; the Commission on Wealth Creation and Social Cohesion, 1995.)

OVERVIEWS

Eight volumes have been selected for the overview section.

Pat Thane (1982) *Foundations of the British Welfare State*

Some familiarity with historical welfare developments is vital for any contemporary student of social policy, not least because it provides an invaluable context to contemporary issues and debates (Gilbert, 1970; Fraser, 1984). In this volume Thane traces key welfare developments from 1870 to the early 1950s in the areas of social security, health, unemployment, education and housing in a lively and imaginative way. A key feature of the book is the way in which the evolution of social policy is linked to broader economic and political questions both at home and abroad.

Rodney Lowe (1993) *The Welfare State in Britain Since 1945*

Written by a historian who has shown a commendable willingness to engage in cross-disciplinary dialogue, *The Welfare State since 1945* provides an outstanding overview of the welfare state during its 'classic' period (1945–75). The main section of the book is devoted to a detailed service by service review in which Lowe's sure-footed command of his subject matter is always in evidence. The book also contains a review of some of the definitional issues surrounding the welfare state, and a discussion of 'pragmatic' (democratic socialist, new right) and 'general' (pluralism, feminism and marxism) welfare strategies. Lowe contends that the welfare state has had

some marked success in the post-war period and remains confident of its longer-term survival.

Nicholas Deakin (1994) *The Politics of Welfare* (first published in 1987)

In this volume Nicholas Deakin details the background of the post-war welfare 'consensus' as a prelude to a thoughtful review and assessment of the welfare policies of successive Conservative administrations between 1979 and 1992. One of Deakin's great strengths is his ability to capture the cut and thrust of the social policy debate at party political, governmental and administrative levels. Moreover, Deakin (like Robert Pinker and Richard Silburn) is one of the most stylish writers in the field. Indeed, his elegant use of gardening imagery (of which Titmuss would undoubtedly have approved: Abel-Smith, 1973) at the end of this volume can justly be compared to the sight of former Manchester City footballer Neil Young ghosting past defenders on a windswept afternoon at Maine Road.

Norman Ginsburg (1992) *Divisions of Welfare*

The limited attention paid to welfare developments in other nations was one of the weaknesses of 'traditional' social administration. However, the pioneering work of scholars such as Barbara Rodgers and Peter Kaim-Caudle among others has begun to bear fruit. There are now a growing number of lively internationally focused texts and publications (Clasen and Freeman, 1994; Brunsdon and May, 1995; Deacon et al., 1992; Cochrane and Clarke, 1993; Gould, 1993; Esping-Andersen, 1990, 1996) which have captured the imagination of students. *Divisions of Welfare* is an excellent example of this genre. After reviewing some of the fundamental concerns in analysing and comparing welfare, Ginsburg turns his attention to ideology, expenditure trends, social security, health care, family, gender and race issues in Sweden, Germany, the United States and Great Britain. The tight analytical framework employed throughout makes this an extremely accessible and stimulating book.

Howard Glennerster (1992) *Paying for Welfare: the 1990s*

An understanding of the economic dimensions of welfare remains extremely important for students of social policy. Although many students are willing to grapple with this topic, they often find much of the specialist economic literature unintelligible. Glennerster's text provides a useful starting place for the social policy student, providing as it does clear summaries of underlying theories and concepts, the role of central and local government and the diverse revenue sources. There are also individual chapters on the health service, the personal social services, education, housing and social security, as well as a thoughtful concluding chapter on the issue of affordability.

John Hills (1993) *The Future of Welfare: a Guide to the Debate*

Students of social policy will also find the work of John Hills extremely useful as they try to grapple with the complexities of such topics as tax and benefits (Hills, 1988), housing finance (Hills, 1991) and the distribution of income and wealth (Joseph Rowntree Foundation, 1995). The erudition and demystification which John Hills brings to complex topics is now legendary. This publication provides a first rate example of the Hills approach – a wealth of data presented in a user-friendly way with careful explanation and judicious discussion.

Fiona Williams (1989) *Social Policy: a Critical Introduction*

Although this book could form part of an introductory reading list, it is often best appreciated by second or third year undergraduate students. Responding to some of the deficiencies in 'mainstream' theorizing about the welfare state, Fiona Williams argues for primacy to be given to race, gender and class factors in assessing the development of social policy – an approach which alerts students to the importance of racism, patriarchy and materialism. The success of this book is reflected in part by the way in which the key dimensions addressed by Williams (especially race and racism) have become the subject of increased discussion in the social policy literature.

Norman Johnson (1987) *The Welfare State in Transition*

The fact that discussions of state-provided welfare have figured so prominently in the social policy literature has tended to lead to a neglect of non-state provision. However, the fact that the legitimacy of the welfare state has now come under threat, not least from those who have expressed an ideological preference for pluralist forms of provision, has led to a renewal of interest in the informal, voluntary and commercial sectors. In *The Welfare State in Transition* Johnson provides a concise and informative overview of the informal, voluntary and commercial welfare sectors in Britain and abroad. As well as being an accessible guide to the various welfare sectors, this book provides a critical introduction to the 'welfare pluralist' perspective.

INTRODUCTORY TEXTS

In the selection of introductory texts emphasis has been given to books which are suitable for anyone with an interest in but little or no background knowledge of the subject.

Anne Digby (1989)
British Welfare Policy

Written by a historian, this book (which is currently out of print) provides a concise introduction to key themes in the subject, highlighting as it does the evolution of the welfare state in the Victorian and Edwardian era; the emergence of the 'classic' welfare state; developments in the voluntary, informal, commercial and occupational welfare sectors; the challenge to state welfare in the 1980s; and the importance of an international welfare perspective.

Nicholas Timmins (1995)
The Five Giants

Given the sheer magnitude of this book it may prove necessary to coax the more faint-hearted scholar to sample the delights contained within. Here is a book brimming with information, ideas and anecdotes which can be read from cover to cover or dipped into when the mood suits. If you are new to the subject Timmins is as good a place to start as any. If this volume does not inspire you it is unlikely that social policy will prove to be the course for you.

Paul Spicker (1995)
Social Policy: Themes and Perspectives

Peter Alcock (1996)
Social Policy in Britain: Themes and Issues

My final two selections have a more conventional introductory feel, not least in terms of their breadth of coverage. These books contain a wealth of valuable

information on issues such as the nature of the discipline, the organization and delivery of services, the policy process, ideologies and international comparisons. The book by Spicker also contains some useful study tips in the appendix and a glossary.

In addition to the *Social Policy Review*, which is published annually by the Social Policy Association, students should also consult specialist journals, newspapers and periodicals.

JOURNALS

All of the following journals are worth consulting, though, as the titles suggest, their focus varies. In all of these journals you will find some articles which provide broad overviews and others which focus in detail on a particular area of policy.

Journal of Social Policy
Critical Social Policy
Social Policy & Administration
Journal of European Social Policy
20th Century British History
Policy and Politics
Public Administration
The Political Quarterly

NEWSPAPERS

Given the rapid changes in social policy it is vital to read newspapers, which will keep you abreast of welfare developments. The following broadsheet papers provide useful information.

The Guardian
The Observer
The Independent
The Independent on Sunday
The Times
The Sunday Times

It is also informative to look at the portrayal of social policy issues in the popular or tabloid press.

PERIODICALS

A number of weekly or monthly magazines also devote space to social policy issues. *New Statesman and Society* and *The Spectator* tend to carry shorter articles, while *Prospect* and *The Economist* provide more in-depth analysis.

BIBLIOGRAPHY

Abel-Smith, B. (1973) Richard Morris Titmuss. *Journal of Social Policy*, 2(3), July.
Abel-Smith, B. and Townsend, P. (1965) *The Poor and the Poorest*. Occasional Paper on Social Administration, No. 17. London: Bell.
Alcock, P. (1996) *Social Policy in Britain: Themes and Issues*. London: Macmillan.
Brunsdon, E. and May, M. (eds) (1995) *Swedish Welfare: Policy and Provision*. London: SPA.
Cahill, M. (1994) *The New Social Policy*. Oxford: Blackwell.
Clasen, J. and Freeman, R. (eds) (1994) *Social Policy in Germany*. Hemel Hempstead: Harvester Wheatsheaf.
Cochrane, A. and Clarke, J. (eds) (1993) *Comparing Welfare States: Britain in International Context*. London: Sage.
Commission on Social Justice (1994) *Social Justice*. London: Vintage.
Commission on Wealth Creation and Social Cohesion (1995) *Report on Wealth Creation and Social Cohesion in a Free Society*. London: Commission on Wealth Creation and Social Cohesion.
Deacon, B. et al. (1992) *The New Eastern Europe*. London: Sage.
Deakin, N. (1994) *The Politics of Welfare*. Hemel Hempstead: Harvester Wheatsheaf.
Digby, A. (1989) *British Welfare Policy: Workhouse to Welfare*. London: Faber & Faber.
Esping-Andersen, G. (1990) *The Three Worlds of Welfare Capitalism*. Cambridge: Polity Press.
Esping-Andersen, G. (ed.) (1996) *Welfare States in Transition*. London: Sage.
Field, F. (1996) Obituary of Brian Abel Smith. *The Guardian*, 9 April.
Finch, J. and Groves, D. (eds) (1983) *A Labour of Love: Women, Work and Caring*. London: Routledge and Kegan Paul.
Fraser, D. (1984) *The Evolution of the British Welfare State*, 2nd edn. London: Macmillan.
Friedman, M. (1962) *Capitalism and Freedom*. Chicago: University of Chicago Press.
George, V. and Page, R. (eds) (1995) *Modern Thinkers on Welfare*. Hemel Hempstead: Prentice Hall/Harvester Wheatsheaf.
George, V. and Wilding, P. (1976) *Ideology and Social Welfare*. London: Routledge and Kegan Paul. Most recently published as George, V. and Wilding, P. (1994) *Welfare and Ideology*. Hemel Hempstead: Harvester Wheatsheaf.
Gilbert, B. B. (1970) *British Social Policy 1914–1939*. London: Batsford.
Ginsburg, N. (1992) *Divisions of Welfare*. London: Sage.
Glennerster, H. (1992) *Paying for Welfare the 1990s*. Hemel Hempstead: Harvester Wheatsheaf.
Gough, I. (1979) *The Political Economy of the Welfare State*. London: Macmillan.
Gough, I. (1995) O'Connor. In V. George and R. Page (eds), *op. cit.*, chapter 12.
Gould, A. (1993) *Capitalist Welfare Systems: a Comparison of Japan, Britain and Sweden*. London: Longman.
Hayek, F. A. (1944) *The Road to Serfdom*. London: Routledge & Kegan Paul.
Hayek, F. A. (1960) *The Constitution of Liberty*. London: Routledge & Kegan Paul.
Hills, J. (1988) *Changing Tax: How the Tax System Works and How to Change It*. London: CPAG.

Hills, J. (1991) *Unravelling Housing Finance: Subsidies, Benefits and Taxation*. Oxford: Clarendon.
Hills, J. (1993) *The Future of Welfare*. York: Joseph Rowntree Foundation.
Hutton, W. (1995) *The State We're In*. London: Jonathan Cape.
Johnson, N. (1987) *The Welfare State in Transition*. Brighton: Wheatsheaf.
Joseph Rowntree Foundation (1995) *Inquiry into Income and Wealth*, 2 vols. York: Joseph Rowntree Foundation.
Le Grand, J. (1982) *The Strategy of Equality*. London: Allen & Unwin.
Le Grand, J. (1989) Markets, welfare, and equality. In J. Le Grand and S. Estrin (eds), *Market Socialism*. Oxford: Clarendon, chapter 8.
Le Grand, J. (1993) Paying for or providing welfare. In N. Deakin and R. Page (eds), *The Costs of Welfare*. Aldershot: Avebury, chapter 5.
Lowe, R. (1993) *The Welfare State in Britain since 1945*. London: Macmillan.
Marshall, T. H. and Bottomore, T. (1992) *Citizenship and Social Class*. London: Pluto.
Mishra, R. (1984) *The Welfare State in Crisis*. Brighton: Wheatsheaf.
Mishra, R. (1990) *The Welfare State in Capitalist Society*. London: Harvester Wheatsheaf.
Mishra, R. (1995) Social policy after socialism. In J. Baldock and M. May (eds), *Social Policy Review 7*. Canterbury: Social Policy Association, chapter 3.
Murray, C. (1984) *Losing Ground*. New York: Basic Books.
Murray, C. (1990) *The Emerging British Underclass*. London: IEA.
O'Connor, J. (1973) *The Fiscal Crisis of the State*. New York: St Martin's Press.
Pascall, G. (1986) *Social Policy: a Feminist Analysis*. London: Tavistock.
Pinker, R. A. (1971) *Social Theory and Social Policy*. London: Heinemann.
Pinker, R. A. (1995) T. H. Marshall. In V. George and R. Page (eds), *op. cit.*, chapter 6.
Smith, G. (1985) Review essay: dimensions of the 'crisis' in social administration. *Sociology of Health and Illness*, 7(2), 260–8.
Spicker, P. (1995) *Social Policy: Themes and Approaches*. Hemel Hempstead: Prentice Hall/Harvester Wheatsheaf.
Taylor-Gooby, P. (1978) The boring crisis of social administration. *Times Higher Education Supplement*, 3 February, p. 17.
Tawney, R. H. (1931) *Equality*. London: Allen & Unwin.
Thane, P. (1982) *The Foundations of the British Welfare State*. London: Longman.
Timmins, N. (1995) *The Five Giants*. London: HarperCollins.
Titmuss, R. M. (1950) *Problems of Social Policy*. London: HMSO and Longman, Green and Co.
Titmuss, R. M. (1970) *The Gift Relationship*. London: Allen & Unwin.
Ward, C. (1996) Fringe benefits. *New Statesman & Society*, 8 March.
Wilding, P. (1983) The evolution of social administration. In P. Bean and S. MacPherson (eds), *Approaches to Welfare*. London: Routledge & Kegan Paul, chapter 1.
Williams, F. (1989) *Social Policy: a Critical Introduction*. Cambridge: Polity Press.
Wilson, E. (1977) *Women and the Welfare State*. London: Tavistock.

V.4

Data Sources in the UK: National, Central and Local Government

Fran Wasoff

Evidence, and the critical use of evidence, is central to the study of social policy. As a student of social policy you need to know how evidence informs social policy and be able to use and draw on evidence yourself to develop your own critical appraisal of social policies. Government, because of its responsibilities and resources, is one of the most important sources of empirical data for the study and practice of social policy. In addition, there are other sources of data at a national level that are important resources for understanding social policy and its effects. This chapter is an introduction to the main sources of empirical data produced by central government and other producers of data at a national level on social policy issues in the UK. In this chapter we look at:

- the main sources of data from government for the study of social policy;
- their nature, scope, advantages and limitations;
- how you can gain access to data sources in print and electronically;
- pointers to further information about these data sources.

The main sources of data at a national level are national data-sets and statistical publications of government departments.

National Data Sources: Data-sets

What is a data-set?

A data-set is a collection of observations, measurements or variables from a study of a set of individuals (people or other units, such as households or houses, called *cases*), and contains all the variables measured for those cases. The most typical data-set has data collected from a survey. A data-set consists of not only the set of measurements for variables for each case, but also a list of the names and definitions of the variables and the values they can take (this is called a codebook), so that the measurements can be understood and interpreted. National data-sets are important for the study of social policy since they typically contain information about a very large number of cases that, as a group, are representative of the nation as a whole, because the cases that are studied (the sample) are chosen by random sampling methods that ensure that the sample closely approximates, or is similar to, the entire population from which it was chosen (Robson, 1993).

Box V.4.1   National data-sets used in social policy

Census-based data-sets
Census of Population
1991 Census Samples of Anonymised Records (SARs)
Longitudinal Study (LS)
Continuous or recurrent cross-sectional surveys
General Household Survey (GHS)
Family Expenditure Survey (FES)
Quarterly Labour Force Survey (LFS)
New Earnings Survey (NES)
Family Resources Survey
Census of Employment
Longitudinal surveys or panel studies
Longitudinal Study (LS)
British Household Panel Survey (BHPS)
National Child Development Study (NCDS)
Quarterly Labour Force Survey (panel study element)
Other surveys of government departments and non-government bodies
Households below Average Income Dataset, 1961–1991 (HBAI)
British Social Attitudes Survey (BSAS) [SCPR]
National Child Development Study (NCDS)
British Household Panel Survey (BHPS)

Who produces national data-sets?

Government surveys produce most of the significant national data-sets. Survey information is used by government to help to inform the making and evaluation of policy. They are also important sources of evidence for the social policy academic community. Many government surveys are conducted by the Office for National Statistics (ONS), which is part of the Government Statistical Service. The ONS is both a government agency and a government department, and is independent of other government departments. It was formed in 1996 by merging the OPCS (Office of Population Censuses and Surveys) and the CSO (Central Statistical Office). It is responsible for collecting and disseminating UK statistics, and co-ordinates a wide range of economic and social statistics collected by government. In addition, government departments sometimes conduct their own surveys, and produce and report their own statistics.

National data-sets commonly used in social policy are also produced by other, non-governmental, bodies, often with government support, such as the Economic and Social Research Council (ESRC), Social and Community Planning Research (SCPR), the Institute for Fiscal Studies (IFS) and the Social Statistics Research Unit (SSRU) at City University.

What are the most commonly used national data-sets?

Since social policy is a broad-based and multidisciplinary area of study, it draws on a wide range of data sources. In this chapter, we will look at some that are commonly used. National data-sets have several research designs: census, continuous or recurrent cross-sectional surveys (a 'snapshot' in which each set of respondents is studied once at about the same time), one-off national surveys and longitudinal surveys or panel studies (where data are collected from the same group of people more than once in order to study changes over time).

Census of Population

The British Census of Population is conducted every ten years. It is a cross-sectional 'snapshot' that contains information about every household and every individual in Great Britain. There is no sampling for the census, since it attempts to collect information from *every* household; each household is legally obliged to fill in a census return. The census contains information about household characteristics, such as housing tenure, house type and number of rooms, and family composition. It also has information about all people in the household, such as their ages, sex, social class, marital status, economic activity, ethnic origin (as the respondent defines it), occupation and educational qualifications. (It does not have information about household or individuals' incomes.) It gives the most accurate count of population size (of people and households) for national and local areas. Like most government statistics, the results are published as tables of aggregate data, i.e. the individual cases are grouped together, and reported as a group; it is not possible to recover the individual observation or case. Census information is available not only at national level, but also at sub-national levels, such as regions, or even smaller geographic units. Small area statistics or local base statistics can be used for local analyses, e.g. for local government areas. Census statistics are published as printed reports and as statistical abstracts, both available from reference libraries. A further feature of census data is that for the non-specialist user there is access only to those tables that ONS/OPCS has chosen to publish, and this may not meet all needs. But in the 1991 census, a further important

resource became available that goes a long way to dealing with this limitation.

1991 Census Sample of Anonymized Records (SARs)

Census data can now be used for data analysis tailored to the researcher's individual requirements and objectives. Samples of anonymized records (SARs), also called census microdata, are subsets of census data available on a 'case by case' basis, but are 'anonymized'; that is, they contain no names, addresses or any other information that would allow individuals or households to be identified. (This ensures that the census requirement for confidentiality and security of data is respected.) There are two types of SARs: household and individual. The household SAR is a 1 per cent sample of households and the individuals in each of these households. It has information about household characteristics, such as housing tenure and number of rooms, as well as information about each person in the household and how he or she is related to the head of the household. The individual SARs are a 2 per cent sample of individuals in households and communal establishments, containing over one million cases and information about age, sex, social class, ethnicity, economic activity and housing circumstances. SARs are useful for studying patterns not only at a national level, but also at sub-national level, e.g. regional level. The development of the SARs was jointly sponsored by OPCS and ESRC and is available as a resource to the academic community. Further information about SARs can be obtained from the Census Microdata Unit, University of Manchester, Manchester M13 9PL.

Recurrent or continuous surveys

The ONS conducts a number of recurrent or continuous surveys which are cross-sectional surveys, repeated in approximately similar form annually or at other intervals. (They are called *continuous* surveys because, as they are so large, the work on them is carried out continuously, like painting the Forth Bridge in the past (it is not now painted continuously!). When work on one survey is completed, the next one begins.) Two important surveys of this type for students of social policy are the General Household Survey and the Family Expenditure Survey.

General Household Survey (GHS)

The General Household Survey (GHS) is an annual multi-purpose survey, providing national (Great Britain) information on, for example, housing and consumer durables, household composition, social class, employment, income (individual and household), education, health and social services, transport, population and social security. It is a nationally representative continuous survey based on a sample of the general population resident in private, non-institutional households (it does not collect information from people living in institutions or in Northern Ireland). Information is collected by face-to-face interviews with all household members for about 18,000 individuals and 9700 households, chosen as a stratified random sample; thus it cannot be used for analysis of sub-national areas.

Family Expenditure Survey (FES)

The Family Expenditure Survey (FES) is an annual UK multi-purpose survey of about 10,000 households (approximately 1 in 2000 of all UK households chosen as a stratified sample). It is nationally representative, but not appropriate for sub-national analyses. Data are collected by face-to-face interviews and from expenditure diaries kept by respondents for two weeks. It has information about household and individuals' incomes and expenditure, including some recurrent payments (such as rent, fuel bills, telephone bills and hire purchase payments). The survey is used to calculate the UK Retail Price Index (RPI), but is also used more generally by government and academic researchers where detailed data are needed about income and expenditure at the household, tax unit and individual levels.

Labour Force Survey

The Quarterly Labour Force Survey has been conducted by the Department of Employment since 1973 (known formerly as the Labour Force Survey). Its scope has expanded steadily. It became an annual survey in 1983 and in 1992, when the sample size was boosted, coverage was extended to Northern Ireland, residents in NHS hospital accommodation and students in halls of residences; at the same time the results were published quarterly. It is a national survey with individual and household level data about the labour market and is used by government (e.g. the Departments of Employment and Social Security and the Home Office) in the making of social and economic policy; for example, to decide on the allocation of the EU Social Fund. It contains information about household and family structure, basic housing information, education and economic activity. Data from the survey are available for national and local government areas. It has cross-sectional and panel study elements and consists of a quarterly survey conducted in the UK throughout the year, in which each individual sampled is interviewed (personally and by telephone) five times at quarterly intervals, producing about 15,000 responding households in every quarter, 'boosted' by a larger survey for the spring quarter. As a result, there are interview data from over 44,000 households in Great Britain and over 4000 households in Northern Ireland.

New Earnings Survey

The New Earnings Survey is an annual survey, conducted since 1970 by the Department of Employment, of earnings of employees in Great Britain (a similar survey is carried out for Northern Ireland). Information about earnings is collected from employers in a 1 per cent random sample of employees paying income tax by PAYE. There is information about earnings by industry, occupation and national collective agreement.

Family Resources Survey

The Family Resources Survey is a nearly national survey (of private households in Great Britain south of the Caledonian Canal) of about 25,000 households, carried out by ONS/OPCS and Social and Community Planning Research (SCPR) for the Department of Social Security. Data are collected by personal interview and there is information about household characteristics, household income (including welfare benefits and unearned income), assets, pensions and savings, housing costs, consumer durables, child care arrangements and costs, carers and disability. Information about individuals includes employment status and ethnic origin. The purpose of this survey is to provide the DSS with data to monitor and evaluate policy, to forecast benefit expenditure and to contribute to other analyses, such as 'households below average income'.

Census of Employment

This bi-annual survey, carried out since 1971, describes the level and distribution of employment in Great Britain. It contains data on the number of jobs by local area, sex and full- and part-time work. A separate Census of Employment is conducted for Northern Ireland, and these data are combined with the Census of Employment to produce UK figures. This survey has a large sample size; it is either a full census of about 1.25 million businesses or a sample survey of about 300,000 businesses. In 1995, it was replaced by the Annual Employment Survey of about 130,000 businesses.

Longitudinal studies

The Longitudinal Study (LS)

The Longitudinal Study is based on census data and traces individuals from one census to subsequent ones. A 1 per cent sample of individuals (about 500,000 people) chosen from the 1971 census was followed to the 1981 and 1991 censuses. A similar sample was chosen from the 1981 census and traced forward. The Longitudinal Study links the returns by those individuals across censuses; this allows comparison of snapshots at ten-year intervals.

British Household Panel Survey

The British Household Panel Survey is a nationally representative (Great Britain), large-scale (over 16,000 cases), longitudinal study sponsored by the ESRC, managed by the ESRC Research Centre on Micro-Social Change and carried out by National Opinion Polls (NOP). It aims to enhance our understanding of social and economic change at the individual and household level likely to occur up to and beyond the year 2000. It consists of annual surveys, beginning in 1991, following the *same* respondents over time, with data from personal and telephone interviews and self-completed questionnaires. The survey includes individual and household-level information about social structure and social and political attitudes, household organization, labour market behaviour, income and wealth, housing, health and education. It has been used to study how households change; for example, housing mobility and the distribution of resources within households (Buck et al., 1994).

The National Child Development Study (NCDS)

The National Child Development Study is a large, nationally representative longitudinal study of all the children born in Great Britain during one week in March 1958. It has charted the lives of about 17,000 people from early childhood to the age of 33 in order to enhance our knowledge of the influences on human physical, educational and social development over the whole lifespan. This birth cohort has been studied on five occasions, or 'sweeps': at ages 7, 11, 16, 23 and 33. For the first three NCDS surveys, information was obtained from parents (who were interviewed by health visitors), head-teachers and class teachers (who completed questionnaires), the schools health service (who carried out medical examinations) and the children themselves (who completed tests of ability and, latterly, questionnaires). In the 1981 and 1991 surveys information was obtained from the cohort members by interviewers and self-completion questionnaires. The 1991 survey also collected information from husbands, wives, cohabitees and some children of cohort members.

The study was conducted by the Social Statistics Research Unit, City University, with support from many bodies, primarily the Economic and Social Research Council, but also including the Departments of Health, Social Security, Employment, Education and Science, Environment, the Training Agency and the Health and Safety Executive, and voluntary organizations, such as the National Children's Bureau.

Other surveys of government departments and non-government bodies

Households below Average Income Data-set, 1961–1991 (HBAI)

This data-set is obtained from the Family Expenditure Survey, from which a second-ary analysis (Hakim, 1982; Dale et al., 1988) of a subset of data is carried out. It describes household incomes and charac-teristics of nationally representative sam-ples for the period 1961–91, which can be used as the basis for analysing trends in poverty, inequality and real living stand-ards in the UK over thirty years. It was carried out by the Institute for Fiscal Studies (IFS), with input from the Depart-ment of Employment and the CSO, and support from the Joseph Rowntree Founda-tion. It uses the same methodology as used by the Department of Social Security to produce its households below average income statistics. There is information about household income (before and after housing costs, and by source of income), household and benefit unit characteristics (e.g. region and housing tenure, economic status, number of children, type of benefit received).

Ad Hoc and other cross-sectional surveys

There are many other important sources of national data for social policy from ad hoc surveys, which are single, one-off surveys carried out for a particular pur-pose, though they are often valuable for secondary analysis. They are carried out by a government department or by a non-government organization, with support coming from both public and private sources.

GETTING ACCESS TO SURVEY DATA

Data are available from printed sources and, increasingly, from electronic sources.

Print access

Information derived from data-sets is typically published as tables of aggregate data; and in the case of continuous sur-veys, publication is periodic (e.g. every year or every quarter). Check the reference library in your university or college. A particularly useful source of data in social policy is the annual periodical *Social Trends* (see below).

Electronic access

Data are increasingly available electronically, either as aggregated data in tables and charts or as the data-set itself. Some data are available on the World Wide Web (see chapter V.7).

Doing your own secondary data analysis with national data-sets

You may wish to have access to the data-set itself in order to learn research methods or to carry out your own research or in-depth project. Data are increasingly available in computer-readable form, in a variety of formats, to conform to different software packages. Access to national data-sets, while a valuable development for the research community, nevertheless requires a considerable level of computer literacy, since users may need to be familiar with various statistical and data management software, different computer operating systems and a variety of file transfer techniques across a network. A considerable investment of time and money may be required to learn the various software packages and to obtain the codebooks and questionnaires in order to use a data-set intelligently. Registration and an undertaking to use the data responsibly are normally conditions for obtaining access to a data-set. Some data-sets have been adapted as teaching data-sets; these also require registration, but this is usually integral to the course in which they are used.

How to find out more about data-sets

There is a great deal more to learn about national data-sets. There are a few refer-

ences at the end of this chapter where you can start. In addition, some of the producers of national data-sets also produce newsletters and bulletins to keep users up to date, such as the *ESRC Data Archive Newsletter*, the *General Household Survey Newsletter* (published by the ESRC Data Archive twice a year) and the *MIDAS Newsletter*. The Department of Employment, which is responsible for the Quarterly Labour Force Survey, issues two publications (with a subscription fee): the *Labour Force Survey Rapid Release* (LFSRR) for quick access to findings of each quarter's survey and the *Labour Force Survey Quarterly Bulletin* (LFSQB) for full results. Some publications are free; others are available by subscription. If you have access to the Internet or World Wide Web you can find out more if you visit appropriate web sites. For more information about connecting to web sites using the Internet, see chapter V.7.

CENTRAL GOVERNMENT STATISTICAL DATA SOURCES

There are numerous statistical data sources collected and published by government bodies, available from many reference and university libraries, that inform the study of social policy. These are produced by government primarily to meet the needs of is own policy-makers and those who monitor social policies, but they are also rich sources of evidence for students and the academic community. The data are usually presented as tables or graphically. The range is extensive; below some commonly used publications are listed. The ONS/CSO publishes a comprehensive reference, *Guide to Official Statistics*, with information about where to find more. It is organized by subject area and includes population, education, labour market, health and social care, income and living standards, crime and justice, housing, environment and the economy. It also produces a free publication listing all statistical publications and electronic data sources produced by government departments and agencies: *Government Statistics – a Brief Guide to Sources*.

Publications of the ONS/CSO

Social Trends is an annual publication of the ONS/CSO which is a particularly useful multi-purpose source that presents statistics collected by many government departments to give a statistical snapshot of society today, and how it is changing. Information is presented in user-friendly form variously as text, tables, charts and graphs. It is also available electronically on CD-ROM. It draws together data from a wide range of other government statistical sources. Each chapter focuses on a different social policy area, such as population, households and families, education, employment, income and wealth, health, social protection, crime and justice, housing, environment, transport and leisure.

Key Data: UK Social and Economic Statistics is another annual multi-purpose statistical publication of the ONS/CSO that contains basic statistics in the main economic and social areas. Tables are taken from other publications, usually of the ONS.

Regional Trends (ONS/CSO; annual) provides a wide range of regional demographic, social and economic statistics, presented by regional profile, topic, areas, counties and districts.

Population Trends (ONS/OPCS; annual) publishes articles on a wide range of population and health subjects and contains vital statistics summaries.

Annual Abstract of Statistics (ONS/CSO; annual) publishes in a single volume statistics on population, vital statistics (births, marriages, deaths), social services, social security, the National Health Service, law enforcement, education, employment, national income and expenditure, personal income and wealth, and central and local government finance.

Public and tax expenditure

Every year the government produces a series of publications about its expenditure plans for the following two years; the most recent is entitled *The Government's Expenditure Plans 1996/97 to 1998/99*. These are annual departmental reports published as parliamentary papers referenced with command numbers. There are separate publications by each government department, published as a series in March, with each report containing the department's own expenditure plans as well as useful information about users, programmes, plans for the future and operations. Most relevant for social policy are the reports of the Department for Education and Employment, Department of Health, Department of Social Security, Department of the Environment, the Home Office and Charity Commission, the Lord Chancellor's Department and the Scottish, Welsh and Northern Ireland Offices. Also in this series is *Public Expenditure Statistical Analyses 1996/97*, an overview of central and local government expenditure and trends in public expenditure. Other useful publications are *Inland Revenue Statistics* (Inland Revenue) and *Government Finance Statistics Yearbook*.

STATISTICAL INFORMATION ABOUT LOCAL GOVERNMENT

Some statistical information about local government is collected by local authorities but compiled and published centrally, such as: *Local Government Trends* (Chartered Institute of Public Finance and Accountancy); *Local Government Financial Statistics England* (Department of Environment); *Scottish Local Government Financial Statistics* (the Scottish Office).

There is also information about individual local authorities in publications on housing and education. Local authorities collect information about performance

---

Box V.4.2   Statistical publications of other central government departments

Education
Education Statistics for the United Kingdom
Schools' Census (for England) (also Schools' Census Wales and Schools' Census
    Scotland)
Employment
Labour Market Trends (incorporating *Employment Gazette*)
Health
Health and Personal Social Services Statistics for England
Health and Personal Social Services Statistics for Wales
Scottish Health Statistics
Housing
Housing and Construction Statistics (England and Wales)
Housing Revenue Account Statistics
House Condition Survey (Department of the Environment)
Scottish Office Statistical Bulletin (Housing Series)
Justice
Criminal Statistics England and Wales
Judicial Statistics England and Wales
Civil Judicial Statistics Scotland
Home Office Statistical Bulletin
British Crime Survey
Social security
Social Security Statistics (Department of Social Security)

---

indicators in social services, education and housing, which is collated and published in December by the Audit Commission for England and Wales and the Accounts Commission for Scotland. In addition, local authorities themselves collect and publish statistics about their own areas in relation to particular local authority operations, such as services for children, housing plans with statistical information and plans for care in the community. These publications vary; sometimes they form part of authorities' annual reports to local government committees. Check with the individual authority to see what is available. Further information about local government can be obtained from: the Convention of Scottish Local Authorities (COSLA), Rosebery Terrace, 9 Haymarket Terrace, Edinburgh EH12 5XZ; the Local Government Association (for English and Welsh local authorities from April 1997), Local Government Information Unit, 1–5 Bath Street, London EC1V 9QQ; and the Scottish Local Government Information Unit (SLGIU), Baltic Chambers, 50 Wellington Street, Glasgow G2 6HJ.

GUIDE TO FURTHER READING

Buck, N., Gershuny, J., Rose, D. and Scott, J. (eds) (1994) *Changing Households: the BHPS 1990 to 1992*. Colchester: ESRC Research Centre on Micro-Social Change (this is a full guide to the BHPS).

Dale, A. and Marsh, C. (1993) *The 1991 Census User's Guide*. London: HMSO (for further information about the Census, SARs, the Longitudinal Study).

Dale, A., Arber, S. and Proctor, M. (1988) *Doing Secondary Analysis*. London: Unwin Hyman (a user-friendly handbook for carrying out data analysis on large government survey data).

Department of Social Security (1995) *Family Resources Survey Statistics Great Britain 1993/94*. London: HMSO (a full guide to the survey).

Ferri, E. (ed.) (1993) *Life at 33: the Fifth Follow-up of the National Child Development Study*. London: National Children's Bureau (this volume describes the Fifth NCDS carried out in 1991 and its preliminary findings).

Hakim, C. (1982) *Secondary Analysis in Social Research*. London: George Allen & Unwin (this is a textbook about data analysis on existing data-sets).

Labour Force Survey Rapid Release (LFSRR) (ONS) provides quick access to findings of each Quarterly Labour Force Survey. *The Labour Force Survey Quarterly Bulletin* (LFSQB) (ONS) contains a fuller account of the findings of each Quarterly Labour Force Survey. Results also appear in *Labour Market Trends*, published monthly by HMSO.

Office for National Statistics, *Family Spending*. London: HMSO (the annual report of the Family Expenditure Survey).

Office of Population Censuses and Surveys Social Survey Division (1996) *Living in Britain: Results from the 1994 General Household Survey*. London: HMSO.

ONS/OPCS, Social Survey Division (every year from 1972) *General Household Survey*. London: HMSO (this is the annual guide to the GHS and its key findings).

Office for National Statistics, *Government Statistics – a Brief Guide to Sources*, available from the Library, ONS, Cardiff Road, Newport NP9 1XG (tel. 01633 812973). This is a free publication listing all statistical publications and electronic data sources produced by government departments and agencies.

Office for National Statistics (1996) *Guide to Official Statistics: 1996 Edition*. London: HMSO (this is an easy-to-use and comprehensive reference to statistical publications and electronic data sources produced by government departments and agencies).

Robson, C. (1993) *Real World Research*. Oxford: Blackwell (a clear and comprehensive textbook of research methods for social scientists).

V.5

OTHER SOURCES of UK DATA
fRAN BENNETT

INTRODUCTION

This chapter provides an introduction to the main sources of information on social policy issues produced by organizations in the UK other than central and local government and commercial publishers. Its main focus is on publications from voluntary organizations, although 'think-tanks', foundations and some private sector sources are also mentioned. Its focus is primarily on organizations themselves, rather than on particular books or reports, since many such publications quickly go out of print. Certain key texts are noted, however, as well as some annually updated guides and regular journals.

This introduction outlines problems in gaining access to publications from such sources. The next section gives an overview of available information, reviewing some of its strengths and weaknesses and indicating how to use it. There is then a round-up of sources of information crossing different social policy areas. The final section describes the main sources of information in specific subject areas.

There are several reasons why social policy students may be unaware of the information produced by non-academic, non-governmental sources. Unless individual academics have personal links with voluntary organizations, such publications may not appear on reading lists or in academic libraries. Some voluntary organizations, who see themselves primarily as pressure groups, may claim that 'spreading the message' is a high priority, but may focus more on policy-makers and the media than students. Some voluntary organizations, who see themselves primarily as service providers, have only recently begun to put priority on reporting on their work for a wider audience, and may have underdeveloped marketing and distribution systems.

All these factors mean that advance planning is essential. Public libraries or bookshops are likely to stock only the major texts from bigger organizations, and then only those published in book format. However, voluntary organizations willingly send out copies of their latest publications lists, and the academic library can then be asked to order the relevant publications, or subscribe to a journal. Another useful source of information on recent reports from non-governmental sources in twelve different areas of social policy is the 'Social policy digest' in the *Journal of Social Policy*, the quarterly journal of the Social Policy Association published by Cambridge University Press.

Students can write to voluntary organizations themselves. But these groups are usually very hard-pressed, and may receive hundreds of such requests. The more specific a request is, the more likely it is to get a quick reply – perhaps a summary of a publication, sent out free of charge. Orders for books may take several weeks, and payment may have to be sent with the order. It is possible to visit some organizations' headquarters to buy their publications, but most are located in central London. Finally, voluntary organizations are slowly exploiting the potential of the Internet, but most have not progressed far enough for people to access publications in this way.

OVERVIEW OF AVAILABLE INFORMATION

Material from sources outside academia and government has a crucial contribution to make to the social policy debate. But it has both strengths and weaknesses. Compared with academic publications, it is likely to be much more up-to-date, and so can take account of the most recent policy shifts. But most voluntary organizations' resources do not stretch to funding large quantitative studies – although a critique of existing data is common. Their material will be particularly valuable for its in-depth policy analysis, qualitative research findings and communication of the 'user's' perspective. It may not display much awareness of ongoing academic debates, even within its own policy area.

Most information from voluntary organizations or the private sector will be practical rather than theoretical in orientation. It is likely to focus on specific policy issues, rather than to give an overview of current developments or a historical perspective. This is worth remembering when deciding whether to try to obtain such material for a project or essay.

A publication will also have been written with a particular purpose in view. A pressure group may want to persuade the government for or against a certain policy. A private sector organization may want to sell more of a particular product, such as a type of insurance policy. It could be argued, however, that any written product always contains its own agenda; some are merely more open about this than others.

SOURCES OF INFORMATION WHICH CROSSES DIFFERENT POLICY AREAS

Think-tanks

'Think-tanks' are usually small, policy-oriented organizations which hope to influence governments, opinion-formers, the media and the public. They are often overtly or covertly linked to particular political parties or ideologies. Their main method of communication is usually the written word – via journals, pamphlets and books – although some may also organize seminars or conferences and other activities.

The think-tanks which contribute most to social policy debates probably include:

- the Health and Welfare Unit of the *Institute of Economic Affairs* (2 Lord North Street, London SW1P 3LB), which proclaims its political independence, but which many commentators place on the right of the political spectrum, with an emphasis on market solutions to welfare problems;
- the *Social Market Foundation* (20 Queen Anne's Gate, London SW1H 9AA), often identified in the past with the Social Democratic Party, and interested in exploring the 'social market' approach;
- the *Fabian Society* (11 Dartmouth Street, London SW1H 9BN), set up by Sidney and Beatrice Webb, among others, in 1884, and linked to the Labour Party;
- the *Institute for Public Policy Research* (30/32 Southampton Street, London WC2E 7RA), which was 'established ... to provide an alternative to the free market think tanks', and is seen as left of centre; it serviced the Commission on Social Justice, linked to but independent of the Labour Party;
- *Demos* (9 Bridewell Place, London EC4V 6AP), which is less easy to classify in terms of traditional political labels.

Three other think-tanks, the *Adam Smith Institute*, the *Social Affairs Unit* and the *Centre for Policy Studies* – also normally placed on the right of the political spectrum – have also contributed many pamphlets to the social policy debate.

Think-tanks vary in size and the strength of their support; but some may consist only of a group of research associates loosely connected with the organization, and a part-time administrator to send out publications. They also vary in the quality and depth of their analysis; but their publications will usually contain strong views and policy prescriptions.

The *Radical Statistics Group* (c/o London Hazards Centre, 3rd Floor, Headland House, 308 Interchange Studios, Dalby Street, London NW5 3NQ) is a group of statisticians and researchers committed to demystifying statistics and concerned about the lack of community control over their use. Recent journal articles have examined Census figures, unemployment statistics and health and education data.

Two other important organizations often thought of as research institutes rather than think-tanks are:

- the *Institute for Fiscal Studies* (7 Ridgmount Street, London WC1E 7AE), which concentrates on economic, public finance and tax issues, and is known for quantitative research;
- the *Policy Studies Institute* (100 Park Village East, London NW1 3SR), which conducts research on a wide variety of social policy issues, often, but not always, commissioned by government departments.

Foundations

Foundations are usually grant-giving bodies. They commission research or policy analysis directly, or wait for requests for research funding (or both). They may fund a programme of work in a specific area, or set up an inquiry to investigate an issue.

Two of the best known foundations in the social policy area are:

- the *Nuffield Foundation* (28 Bedford Square, London WC1B 3EG), whose interests include education (in its broadest sense) and medicine;
- the *Joseph Rowntree Foundation* (The Homestead, 40 Water End, York YO3 6LP), whose main interest is in the underlying causes of poverty, but which works on housing, disability and community care, the family and parenthood, volunteering, and income and wealth distribution, among other issues.

The Joseph Rowntree Foundation publishes useful summaries (often called 'Findings') of the results from many of the research projects it funds. Individual copies may be available free of charge. The full reports are published by the Foundation or another publisher. A key social policy text from the Foundation is: J. Hills with the LSE Welfare State Programme (1993) *The Future of Welfare: a Guide to the Debate*. York: Joseph Rowntree Foundation. This analysis examines critically the assertion that the welfare state is in crisis, and analyses options for change in social security, health, education and social services.

Government-funded bodies

Some of the key government-funded bodies with broad-ranging responsibilities in the social policy field are:

- the *National Consumer Council* (20 Grosvenor Gardens, London SW1W 0DH), which describes itself as 'the independent voice of the consumer', and has a special focus on low-income consumers;
- the *Equal Opportunities Commission* (Overseas House, Quay Street, Manchester M3 3HN), which examines inequality between men and women, and can support legal test cases or undertake investigations into particular organizations' practices;

- the *Commission for Racial Equality* (Elliot House, 10/12 Allington Street, London SW1E 5EH), which monitors racial discrimination and the position of minority ethnic groups in UK society.

Each has its own publications programme.

The *National Association of Citizens Advice Bureaux* (115–123 Pentonville Road, London N1 9LZ) is also largely government-funded. There is a Citizens Advice Bureau in most towns, providing free advice and information on a wide range of topics. NACAB produces 'evidence reports' on a variety of social policy issues on the basis of individual cases.

SOURCES OF INFORMATION ON SPECIFIC SOCIAL POLICY ISSUES

Poverty and income distribution

Probably the most valuable up-to-date source of information on poverty and inequality in the UK is the report of the Joseph Rowntree Foundation's *Inquiry into Income and Wealth*, which draws together and analyss the findings from a large body of specially commissioned research and other evidence (a summary is available). The first volume gives an overview and policy recommendations; the second gives more details of the research:

- Barclay, P. (1995) *Joseph Rowntree Foundation Inquiry into Income and Wealth*, Volume 1. York: JRF.
- Hills, J. (1995) *Joseph Rowntree Foundation Inquiry into Income and Wealth*, Volume 2. York: JRF.

Relevant research findings, summaries of current debates and an analysis of the impact of poverty on different groups are drawn together by the Child Poverty Action Group: Oppenheim, C. and Harker, L. (1996) *Poverty: the Facts*, 3rd edn. London: CPAG Ltd (from CPAG Ltd, 4th Floor, 1–5 Bath Street, London EC1V 9PY). This

key text covers a much broader field than child poverty. It is updated every few years. CPAG Ltd also publishes a journal, *Poverty*, three times a year, containing new data, as well as news and feature articles.

Although the Commission on Social Justice covered a much wider area, it was often seen as concentrating on income inequality and redistribution. A summary is available from the Institute for Public Policy Research, as well as a series of pamphlets published by the Commission. The two initial reports were: Commission on Social Justice (1993) *Social Justice in a Changing World*; and *The Justice Gap*. London: Institute for Public Policy Research. But the full report was published commercially: The Report of the Commission on Social Justice (1994) *Social Justice: Strategies for National Renewal*. London: Vintage.

Community 'empowerment' strategies to combat poverty and disadvantage are also crucial. The *Community Development Foundation* (60 Highbury Grove, London N5 2AG) produces many reports about area regeneration and community development work.

Social security and income protection

The *Social Security Advisory Committee* is the government-appointed watchdog for the social security system. It publishes annual reviews of its work, and commissions research or investigates policy issues itself, producing readable reports published by HMSO.

Several voluntary organizations publish annually updated handbooks on the social security benefits system:

- the *National Welfare Benefits Handbook* and the *Rights Guide to Non-Means-Tested Benefits*, published by CPAG Ltd, cover the whole benefits system;
- the *Disability Rights Handbook*, covering benefits for disabled people, is published by the Disability Alliance Educational and Research Association

(1st Floor East, Universal House, 88–94 Wentworth Street, London E1 7SA);
- *Your Rights* is published by Age Concern England, Astral House, 1268 London Road, London SW16 4EJ, and covers benefits for older people.

These books are usually published in April each year. Changes in the benefits system during the year are covered in articles in the organizations' journals.

Key texts reviewing and commenting on possible policy changes in the social security system include several of the pamphlets from the Commission on Social Justice, and two booklets from CPAG Ltd (the subsidiary of the Child Poverty Action Group). From the private sector, a series of essays about the potential and pitfalls of private insurance to protect income was commissioned and published by the insurance industry: Association of British Insurers (1995) *Risk, Insurance and Welfare: the Changing Balance between State and Private Provision*. London: ABI.

The National Association of Pension Funds, which brings together occupational pension scheme providers, serviced an inquiry into the future of pension provision: (1995) *Pensions: 2000 and Beyond – Report of the Retirement Income Inquiry*, Volumes I and II (from Shelwing Ltd, Folkestone, CT20 2BL)

Health and health care

A useful source of information and views on services can often be obtained from service providers, the trade unions and professional associations. In health, the *British Medical Association* and the *British Medical Journal* have regularly commented on both the state of health of the population and the government's policies: (1993) *The Health of the Nation: the BMJ View*. London: British Medical Journal (this publication comments on the Department of Health White Paper of 1992).

A key foundation in the health field is the *King's Fund*, whose publications can

be obtained from King's Fund Publishing, 11–13 Cavendish Square, London W1M 0AN. *The Public Health Alliance* (BVSC, 138 Digbeth, Birmingham B5 2DR) publishes more practical material focusing on strategies to promote health.

Education

It is more difficult to point to key texts in education, since it spans such a broad area. *The Advisory Centre for Education* (1b Aberedeen Studios, 22–24 Highbury Grove, London N5 2DQ) produces handbooks about the current education system for parents, governors and schools. A study examining the impact of the recent education reforms on children of low-income families is: Smith, T. and Noble, M. (1995) *Education Divides: Poverty and Schooling in the 1990s*. London: CPAG Ltd.

Local Schools Information (1–5 Bath Street, London EC1V 9QQ) produces information about the local management of schools. The *Campaign for State Education* (158 Durham Road, London SW20 0DE) produces briefings which focus on current concerns in education, as well as information leaflets, booklets and a bulletin.

Housing

A valuable round-up of issues in housing policy is given in the second and final report of the Joseph Rowntree Foundation's Inquiry, chaired by the Duke of Edinburgh. More specific issues about housing finance were investigated by John Hills:

- JRF (1991) *Inquiry into British Housing*, Second Report. York: Joseph Rowntree Foundation.
- Hills, J. (1991) *Thirty-nine Steps to Housing Finance Reform*. York: Joseph Rowntree Foundation.

The major pressure group working on homelessness and housing issues is *Shelter* (88 Old Street, London EC1V 9HU), which produces regular publications analysing homelessness figures and commenting on government policy proposals. More specialized groups, such as CHAR (5–15 Cromer Street, London WC1H 8LS), concentrate on more specific issues – in this case, single people's housing needs.

Various organizations corresponding to the different sectors of the housing market produce reports analysing issues relevant to their own sector. The publications of the *National Federation of Housing Associations* (175 Gray's Inn Road, London WC1 8UP) are often relevant to social housing as a whole.

Personal social services

Organizations representing the interests of particular groups (such as *Age Concern England* and *Disability Alliance*) often deal with issues about service provision as well as income. There are also many organizations that focus on specific disabilities. The *Carers' National Association* (20–25 Glasshouse Yard, London EC1A 4JS) produces reports about informal care. (For children and social services, see 'Children and the family' below.)

There is a strong movement towards organisations *of*, rather than *for*, service users. One such body is the *British Council of Organisations of Disabled People* (Litchurch Plaza, 5 Litchurch Lane, Derby DE24 8AA), which groups together many organizations run by disabled people themselves. A *Citizens' Commission on the Future of the Welfare State* (Tempo House, 15 Falcon Road, London SW11 2PJ) has also been set up, to 'offer welfare state service users a real opportunity to say what kind of welfare state they would like to see'. It is to produce a report about its findings.

Law and the offender

There is a plethora of groups working on criminal justice and penal affairs issues. Fortunately, they publish many of their reports under a joint imprint: the *Penal*

Affairs Consortium (169 Clapham Road, London SW9 0PU). The *National Association of Probation Officers* and the *Association of Chief Probation Officers* also have a tradition of commissioning research and publishing policy analysis.

If the law itself is regarded as a social policy issue, the *Legal Action Group* (242 Pentonville Road, London N1 9UN) is a key organization. It publishes policy comment on issues such as proposals to reform legal aid.

Unemployment and the labour market

Key organizations in this field include:

- The *Unemployment Unit* and its sister organization *Youthaid* (322 St John Street, London EC1V 4NT), which produce an alternative unemployment count, and are experts in government training and work schemes. Their journal is *Working Brief*, and they publish guides to benefits and training for the unemployed.

- The *Employment Policy Institute* (Southbank House, Black Prince Road, London SE1 7SJ), which analyses government employment policies and proposes reforms.

- The *Low Pay Unit* (27/29 Amwell Street, London EC1R 1UN), which as its name suggests focuses on low pay, and proposes a statutory minimum wage as the main policy solution. It has a journal, *The New Review*, and policy publications. There are also several independent regional Low Pay Units.

The Joseph Rowntree Foundation is currently organizing a programme of research on the future of work, which will be reporting in 1997. The churches have also set up a joint inquiry into unemployment, also due to report in 1997: *Churches Enquiry into Unemployment and the Future of Work*, Christchurch Industrial Centre, 27 Blackfriars Road, London SE1 8NY.

'Race' and gender

As mentioned above, the Commission for Racial Equality and the Equal Opportunities Commission publish material on 'race' and gender respectively. One of the pamphlets written for the Commission on Social Justice discussed the complexities of racial discrimination: Modood, T. (1994) *Racial Equality: Colour, Culture and Justice*. London: Commission on Social Justice, Institute for Public Policy Research.

A key text on the experience of poverty among minority ethnic groups is: Amin, K. with Oppenheim, C. (1992) *Poverty in Black and White: Deprivation and Ethnic Minorities*. London: CPAG Ltd, in association with Runnymede Trust.

Material on refugee and asylum issues is published by the *Joint Council for the Welfare of Immigrants* (115 Old Street, London EC1V 9JR).

There is no one voluntary organization with a brief to look at all aspects of gender inequality, although many different groups exist which publish material on the impact of specific policies on women.

Children and the family

The major voluntary organization producing briefings and publications on families and family policy is the *Family Policy Studies Centre* (231 Baker Street, London NW1 6XE).

More specialist organisations publish material about specific types of family – such as the *National Council for One Parent Families* (255 Kentish Town Road, London NW5 2LX).

There are so many children's charities that it is not possible to list them all. Most produce some publications – on family centres, juvenile justice, child abuse, child poverty and other social policies affecting children. The relevant umbrella organization is the *National Council of Voluntary Child Care Organisations* (Unit 4, Pride Court, 80–82 White Lion Street, London N1 9PF). The key research organization is the *National Children's Bureau* (8 Wakley Street, London EC1V 7QE).

The voluntary sector

The central texts on issues relating to voluntary organizations themselves are probably published by the umbrella body, the *National Council for Voluntary Organisations* (NCVO, Regent's Wharf, 8 All Saints Street, London N1 9RL). It has equivalent bodies in Northern Ireland and Scotland. The NCVO may also be a good starting point to find out what voluntary organizations are operating in the policy area that students are interested in.

CONCLUSION

Publications from outside the academic and government mainstream are usually up-to-date and user-friendly. They are often written by people who are grappling with practical policy issues every day. They can contribute significantly to the study of social policy. If this chapter has helped to overcome their main drawback – that they are too often ignored as a source of added value for students – it will have performed a useful function.

V.6

eUROPeaN aND iNTernationaL Data soURCes

DeBORaH maBBett

INTRODUCTION

This chapter reviews data sources which give information on more than one country. A number of resources have been developed to facilitate international comparative analysis. Some areas of social policy have proved more susceptible to comparison than others, and this is reflected in the data available. Furthermore, while it is possible to use international data sources to extract data for a single country, it is important to be aware of the pitfalls of doing this. International data sources facilitate comparison by overriding the specific institutional features of each country; if undertaking a single country study, the researcher should usually grapple with these institutional specifics. National data are more fruitful for a researcher wanting to understand the peculiarities of one country's social policy environment.

AREAS COVERED BY EUROPEAN AND INTERNATIONAL DATA SOURCES

An important issue in the comparison of social policies is whether the comparison is to be confined to the welfare state, which means focusing on government expenditure, mandatory measures and the administration of programmes by public institutions. The idea of a 'mixed economy of welfare' has propelled some researchers towards a broader approach, in which the analysis extends to non-state provision of goods and services and their impact on welfare (see Higgins, 1986). The choice depends on the questions the researcher wants to answer. There are reasons to focus on the measures that governments have taken, while acknowledging that these measures will not provide a complete explanation of welfare outcomes. From the perspective of data availability, there is a wide range of material on welfare outcomes, a certain amount on government measures and rather little on non-state structures and provision. To some extent, this bias towards state action is deliberate. For example, the International Labour Organization (ILO) definition of social security acknowledges explicitly that it is concerned with state activity. 'The system must have been set up by legislation which attributes specified individual rights to, or which imposes specified obligations on, a public, semi-public or autonomous body' (ILO, 1996, p. 3). One consequence is that legal obligations imposed upon employers (e.g. to pay sick pay in the early weeks of illness) are not included if they are met by direct relationship between the employer and the beneficiary and there is no 'mediating' public or autonomous institution taking contributions and paying benefits. The bias towards information on state activity is partly for a very practical reason: many data-sets rely on reports provided by government officials and information generated by government reporting structures. The absence of a mediating institution also means the absence of a data collection point. One implication of this is that privatization of provision can mean that data are also privatized. For example, accounting and consultancy firms collect information on legislation on employee benefits (including sick pay, pension contributions, etc.) which they sell to multinational employers (e.g. the Europe Benefits Report produced by Watson Wyatt DataServices). The cost of these reports is prohibitive for most researchers.

EUROPEAN AND INTERNATIONAL ORGANIZATIONS AND THEIR OUTLOOK

International organizations collect data for reasons which reflect their underlying concerns and motivations. They search for commonalities, similarities and patterns of dissemination across countries, and are prone to find them when others might be more impressed by differences and divergences.

The United Nations

Organizations of the United Nations have endeavoured to establish 'social indicators' which provide systematic and comparable measures of welfare outcomes, on a par with well established economic indicators. With a few exceptions (notably in social security), UN publications do not provide much insight into the detail of government programmes and social policy interventions. Often the data collected by UN organizations are intended to publicize the extent of social inequality between First and Third World countries, and to help to justify expenditure on UN projects and programmes to improve health, education

and welfare outcomes. The UN organizations aim to present data on all member countries, but the researcher soon finds that the comprehensive coverage of the table formats is marred by a large number of missing observations. None the less, UN organizations are the best sources for readily accessible information outside the European Union (EU) and Organisation for Economic Cooperation and Development (OECD) countries (see box V.6.1).

The Organisation for Economic Cooperation and Development

The OECD comprises all the EU member states and other developed European countries (Switzerland, Norway, Iceland), along with Turkey. In addition, the USA, Canada, Japan, Australia and New Zealand are members.

The OECD exists to promote 'economic cooperation', and its offices in Paris originally provided a forum for ministerial-level discussion on trade and economic policy. Social policy appeared on the agenda largely because of its macroeconomic implications: there is a lot of emphasis in OECD publications on the pressures for growth in health expenditure and pension costs, and on the fiscal effects of unemployment. Other social concerns common to member states have also come on to the agenda in recent years; for example, the OECD publishes extensively in the areas of transport and environmental policy.

As is shown in box V.6.2, the OECD is a repository for vast amounts of data. While some statistics are published regularly, in other cases the OECD's collection effort is related to the production of major reports, often for high-level government meetings and conferences. The fact that the OECD's work is very much oriented towards the production of policy advice for member countries is both a strength and a weakness for its use in comparative research. It is a strength insofar as a lot of

---

Box V.6.1 Organizations of the United Nations and associated international bodies

The Department for Economic and Social Information and Policy Analysis publishes population information and projections, including a *Demographic Yearbook*.

The United Nations Educational, Scientific and Cultural Organisation (UNESCO) statistical yearbook includes measures of education expenditure as a percentage of gross domestic product (GDP) and government expenditure, numbers of teachers and pupils and illiteracy rates. More context is given in UNESCO's *World Education Report*, but the data are less timely.

The World Health Organisation (WHO) maintains a data-set on a range of socio-economic and health indicators from life expectancy, fertility and infant mortality to information on health care provision and health institutions. These data are published in the *World Health Statistics Annual*, and data can also be obtained on disk direct from WHO.

ILO: In addition to its reports on *The Cost of Social Security*, the ILO publishes a *Yearbook of Labour Statistics*, containing data on employment, wages, prices, industrial injuries, strikes etc.

The International Social Security Association (ISSA) publishes the *International Social Security Review*, which contains, in addition to academic articles, notes and reports on social security developments in its 130 member countries.

The *World Bank* publishes a *Social Indicators of Development* yearbook, which includes some social data from other UN organizations, along with Bank material from national reports. A particular focus of World Bank work on social indicators has been the measurement of poverty, although the data available on poverty are limited to 25 countries in the 1995 edition.

---

information is reported about policy initiatives in member states, and statistics are often presented in a way which serves to highlight their policy implications. However, it is a weakness in that the OECD's world view is imposed on the information in a somewhat relentless, and at times tedious, way. A key part of this world view is that countries can import and export policies with very little modification for country-specific conditions.

The European Union

DG V

The Directorate-General for Employment, Industrial Relations and Social Affairs (DG V) has initiated a number of projects to report on developments in social protec-

tion in member states and present data about them. MISSOC (Mutual Information System on Social Protection in the Community) is an information system based on rapporteurs from the member countries. MISSOC publishes quarterly information updates (*MISSOC-Info*). A similar system of quarterly reports exists for employment policies (MISEP, Mutual Information System on Employment Policies; SYSDEM, European System for Documentation on Employment) and industrial relations (EURi, European Observatory on Industrial Relations). Reports from MISSOC, MISEP, SYSDEM and EURi are available in an indexed collection on CD-ROM, called SociBase. MISSOC also produces an annual report on *Social Protection in the Member States of the European Union*, which is summarized in table V.6.1.

Box V.6.2 The OECD

The OECD makes some data-sets available on disk, notably *OECD Health Data* (Poullier, 1993). Provision of data has recently been expanded with the development of the SOCX database, which provides information on expenditure on pensions, health care, education, housing, employment programmes, sickness and maternity benefits and other programmes. Information on variables other than expenditure (numbers of beneficiaries, levels of benefits) remains rather partial (see Butare, 1994, pp. 13–15 for further explanation).

Some idea of the data held can be got from OECD social policy publications (a major recent report is *New Orientations for Social Policy* (1994)). The presentations of data in these reports are accompanied by extensive analytical discussions and secondary analysis of the statistics to generate research findings.

Regularly published OECD statistical bulletins include *Employment Outlook, Labour Force Statistics, National Accounts* and *The Tax/Benefit Position of Production Workers*. These are good sources for data on economic growth rates, unemployment, labour force participation, wage levels, taxation and disposable income, birthrates and population projections, dependency ratios, and government expenditure and its components (health, pensions etc.). Data from *The Tax/Benefit Position of Production Workers* are often used in studies comparing replacement ratios (ratios of benefit levels to in-work income).

National accounts are an important source of economic data (data on GDP, consumption, investment etc.). International comparability is achieved by common use of the UN System of National Accounts (UN SNA). However, the usefulness of national accounts for social policy research is rather limited. Social policy interventions are defined in very particular ways for compatibility with the overall SNA context. Thus, a variety of pension arrangements are separately accounted for under 'pension funds and other financial institutions', while some sick pay comes under 'wages and salaries' and social security benefits not provided on an insurance basis may find their way into 'general public services'.

Eurostat

The work of Eurostat, the statistical office of the European Union, sometimes has an explicitly agenda-setting aspect, linking in to attempts by the Commission to persuade member governments to adopt 'harmonized' policies or to agree on the establishment or continuation of Union-level programmes. The presentation of statistics is accompanied by observations about the accelerating pace of integration and convergence – although sometimes the statisticians are forced to concede that 'the scale of the problems of economic and social convergence is apparent' (*A Social Portrait of Europe*, 1992, p. 85).

One area in which the political dimension of European statistics has been vividly brought out is in the measurement of poverty. The Commission's interest in poverty measurement stems from its remit to ameliorate the economic and social costs arising from the creation of the single market. In *Poverty in Figures: Europe in the Early 1980s*, findings are presented on the incidence of poverty using expenditure data from family budget surveys. Two thresholds (40 and 50 per cent of mean expenditure) and two reference societies (the member states separately and the Community as a whole) are reported on. Despite this eclectic approach, Eurostat's work on poverty and social exclusion has

Table V.6.1 MISSOC comparative tables

Organization of social protection	Charts giving an overview of government administration of social security, health, family affairs, housing and labour
Financing of social protection	Financing principle, contribution rates and public authorities' contributions by ESSPROS[a] functional classification
Health care	Law (name and date), beneficiaries covered, conditions, organization of doctors and hospitals, benefits provided, charges levied

Cash benefits
ESSPROS functional classification:
  Sickness
  Maternity
  Invalidity
  Old age
  Survivors
  Employment injuries and occupational
    diseases
  Family benefits
  Unemployment
  Guaranteeing sufficient resources
	Law, coverage, conditions, duration and amount of benefits, taxation of benefits for each functional classification
	Additional information on particular benefits where relevant, including:
	• accumulation (other benefits payable in conjunction, particularly with invalidity benefits);
	• risks covered, prevention and rehabilitation (invalidity and employment injury);
	• adjustment (indexation), early retirement, deferment (old age);
	• single parent allowances (family benefits).

[a]ESSPROS: European system of integrated social protection statistics.

been subject to criticism from the UK Government (e.g. *Sigma*, Special Issue on Statistics and the Social Dimension, May/ June 1992, p. 10).

Eurostat publishes *Social Protection Expenditure and Receipts* annually but with a considerable lag (four to five years). The main tables report expenditure by ESSPROS function (see table V.6.1 for a list). Expenditure is reported in national currency, national currency at constant prices, ECU and purchasing power standard units. It is not easy to relate the Eurostat expenditure data to national source data, although Eurostat has published a series of digests, organized by function, which explain which benefits have been included under which heading for each country. Eurostat expenditure estimates also depart significantly from those reported in the ILO study, *The Cost of Social Security*. While Eurostat put total UK benefit expenditure in 1986 at just under £90 billion, the ILO reported a figure of £72.5 billion. (The UK government's public expenditure estimates put spending on health and personal social services at under £21 billion in the year to March 1986, and social security at £43 billion, leaving a considerable shortfall against both estimates.) The introduction to the ILO's publication discusses the reasons for the discrepancy against Eurostat. At the very least, the divergences in the estimates mean that only data from the same source can be compared; more realistically, they suggest that a diligent researcher will have to spend some time uncovering the basis of the figures and ensuring that it is appropriate to the research objectives.

OTHER OFFICIAL DATA SOURCES

A number of regional international associations publish data relevant to social policy (for example, there are associations of the Nordic countries and the Latin American countries). The United States also puts resources into international data collection. For example, the Center for International Research at the US Bureau of the Census maintains a database on the ageing of the world's population. A major and well established exercise in describing social security schemes is the US Social Security Administration's (SSA's) publication *Social Security Programs Throughout the World*. The SSA's publication follows a strict format, presenting an identical matrix for each country, in which the columns are types of benefit (old age/invalidity/death, sickness and maternity, work injury, unemployment, family allowances) and each row describes specified characteristics of the benefit (first law, current law, coverage (residents, employed etc.), source of funds, qualifying conditions, benefit level etc.). The coverage of countries is impressive – 145 were included in 1989 – but the usefulness of the findings is limited by the restrictions of the format.

DATA HELD BY ACADEMIC INSTITUTIONS

The past three decades have seen a number of major comparative projects on the welfare state established, and the host institutions have established data-sets to support these projects. For example, the data for *State, Economy, and Society in Western Europe 1815–1975* (assembled by a team led by Peter Flora) are held at the Mannheim Centre for European Social Research (MZES), along with the data for a subsequent project on the Western European welfare states since the Second World War. Similarly, the data used by Esping-Andersen in *The Three Worlds of Welfare Capitalism* was drawn from a larger project based around a comparative data-set at the Swedish National Institute for Social Research. Access to these 'project' data-sets usually involves establishing a collaborative working relationship with a partner at the host institution, or attending the institution as a research student.

One important data-set which has more flexible access arrangements is the Luxembourg Income Study (LIS). LIS is an international cooperative venture to assemble micro-data files from participating countries' household surveys, achieve some consistency between the coding of the surveys, and make the data available to interested researchers. LIS has expanded steadily since its establishment in 1983 and now includes surveys from 25 countries. Recently, labour force surveys have begun to be assembled on the same cooperative basis in the Luxembourg Employment Study (LES). Introductory user packages are available, and there is an abundance of research literature based on LIS data (e.g. Smeeding et al., 1990). The availability of micro-data has facilitated new comparative work on the distribution of income, poverty and the impact of benefits on inequality. Familiarity with handling survey micro-data is necessary to use LIS and LES. Problems of setting up and coding, familiar to users of national micro-data-sets, mean that the data are at least five years old by the time they become available. None the less, LIS and LES offer great opportunities to apply sophisticated statistical techniques to international comparative work.

CONCLUSION

International comparative analysis of social policy is an expanding field. There are several motives or dynamics behind this expansion: increased social integration in the case of the EU, the possibilities for transferring policy innovations between countries, a desire to understand the social policies of economic competitors or the search for evidence for critiques of national social policy. In the abundance of international comparative data is the basis for much interesting and insightful research, but there are also plenty of possibilities for meaningless comparison, and many traps for the unwary.

GUIDE TO FURTHER READING

Butare, T. (1994) *Social Security Quantitative Data: an Inventory of Existing Databases*, Occasional Papers on Social Security. Geneva: International Social Security Association. A survey with contact addresses encompassing social security data-sets held at academic research institutes as well as those maintained by national public authorities and international organizations.

Higgins, J. (1986) Comparative social policy. *Quarterly Journal of Social Affairs*, 2(3), 221–42. An overview and critique of different methodological approaches to comparative social policy.

ILO (1996) *The Cost of Social Security. Fourteenth International Inquiry, 1987–1989*. Geneva: ILO. Presents data on state social security schemes for 105 countries, based on responses to a questionnaire by national authorities.

Poullier, J.-P. (1993) *OECD Health Systems*, 2 Volumes, Health Policy Studies No. 3, Paris: OECD. A comprehensive presentation of OECD health data, with commentary.

Smeeding, T., Rainwater, L. and O'Higgins, M. (1990) *Poverty, Inequality and Income Distribution in a Comparative Perspective*. Hemel Hempstead: Harvester Wheatsheaf. A compilation of studies using LIS which gives insights into the research questions which can be examined using micro-data and the methodological issues which arise.

V.7

THE ROLE OF COMPUTERS IN SOCIAL POLICY

MILLSOM HENRY

INTRODUCTION

The aim of this chapter is to outline the range of technological resources on offer and to assess their potential benefits for the student of social policy. No attempt is made to provide a fully exhaustive list of all resources or a step-by-step guide to how to use computers. Instead, this chapter will highlight where students of social policy can utilize the range of generic and subject-specific resources (from word-processing programs, databases, spread-sheets, quantitative and qualitative data analysis programs, simulation packages, CD-ROMs to the varying forms of electronic communication) to explore, in a much more interactive and intuitive way, the heterogeneous nature of social policy.

BACKGROUND

Owing primarily to a combination of factors, namely the expansion of the higher education sector, the advancements in technology and the desire to match the needs of industry with education, institutions of higher education have begun to revise/update teaching methods by embracing new technology. As a direct result, students not only need to become proficient in particular subject areas, but also need to develop a set of transferable skills which will increase their overall market potential. In this regard, the ability

to use a range of technological tools and resources has become important.

COMPUTERS IN SOCIAL POLICY

Since the late 1970s, there has been a significant shift away from the use of large mainframe computers to personal computers. This shift led to the development of generic software programs such as word-processing packages, spreadsheets, and databases. As a result, the ability to type, edit, search, manipulate, save and print text, data and figures easily and quickly has led to improvements in basic information technology (IT) skills among the general population and, arguably, has encouraged the wider access to and the dissemination of knowledge.

Unfortunately, within higher education, a number of subject areas, such as social policy, have not been able to harness the new technologies as effectively as other disciplines, and this has led to some inequalities in terms of the availability of technological resources, knowledge and skills. The tendency has been to use computers in social policy (and the social sciences generally) for mainly quantitative data analysis. While this is an important area for social policy, it has reinforced some of the prevailing and marginalizing attitudes about the use of computers. It is not at all surprising, then, that there are still no customized undergraduate social policy modules/programs which are used across institutions in the UK compared to the disciplines of mathematics or modern languages. The reasons for this are complex:

1 The historical image of computing.
2 The pedagogical differences between the life and social sciences.
3 The lack of financial resources and time constraints.
4 Ineffective skills training of social policy staff in higher education.

The overriding effect had meant that there has been hardly any exposure for students to the direct application of technology in social policy.

More recently, new developments in technological expertise have led to the growth of computer-assisted learning programs which embrace some of the key features of the social sciences, namely the analysis of text, images and behavioural patterns: for example, qualitative data analysis programs which code and analyse textual information; simulation programs which facilitate urban planning and population projections; and decision-making systems which allow the user to take part in scenarios and make judgements accordingly. These new developments are welcomed, as they point to a future which may well redress the balance between discipline areas and offer the student of social policy more innovative ways to understand how social policy is created, developed and maintained. Clearly, though, it is the wider use of a range of local, national and global resources in electronic formats which offers the student of social policy more. In particular, access to on-line data services, the use of CD-ROM technology and the Internet show the way to the greater exploitation of and access to information.

ON-LINE DATA SERVICES

One of the key skills in social policy is the ability to find, search and analyse information from a number of different sources, formats, organizations and countries. Developments in technology have meant that it is now possible to get direct access to databases and data archives from the desktop via a computer modem, rather than manually through a library/ organization. This means that the student of social policy can now explore a vast array of local, national and global information with relative ease and with little, if any cost.

There are two main types of on-line data services in the social sciences

1 Databases of textual information.
2 Sets of archived numerical data.

Both types of service offer the student of social policy an opportunity to keep up to date with a wider range of information and to manipulate real-life data in a convenient manner. For example, BIDS (Bath Information and Data Services) houses the main social science citation index, which allows users to search references from papers in over 7000 journals, and BUBL (the Bulletin Board for Libraries) provides access to a large number of resources, both generic and of direct interest to students of social policy.

The main repositories for the social scientific data in the UK are the ESRC Data Archive based at the University of Essex and the University of Manchester Computing Centre. The ESRC Data Archive provides on-line access to a searchable catalogue (BIRON, Bibliographical Information Retrieval On-line) of over 5000 data-sets, and MIDAS (the Manchester Information Datasets and Associated Services) Centre provides direct on-line access to data-sets such as the Census, the British Social Attitudes Survey, the Labour Force Survey, the General Household Survey and the British Crime Survey. The number of data-sets and archives are increasing all the time and students should be aware of the many European, North American and Australasian data services, such as the SSDA (Social Science Data Archive) based in Australia, the DDA (Danish Data Archives), the Social Sciences Data Archive at Hebrew University, the ICPSR (Inter-university Consortium for Political and Social Research) at Michigan and IASSIST (International Association for Social Science Information Service and Technology. In essence, then, these services provide students of social policy with access to information which would have previously been either too expensive or too cumbersome to get hold of. Details of these services can be found from the ESRC Data Archive Web site listed below. For further information about other useful data-sets and archives in social policy, see chapter V.4.

CD-ROMs (compact disk-read only memory)

CD-ROM technology has enabled large amounts of text, data, graphics and sound to be stored and read directly into a computer. This information can then be used to carry out general or specific searches very quickly. The ability to use CD-ROMs in this way allows the user to view and query data from a number of government surveys and data-sets in a less time-consuming manner. For example, the following are now available on CD-ROM: the British Social Attitudes Surveys from 1983 through 1989; the British Election Studies Information System (BESIS), a compilation on CD-ROM of data and documentation from British general elections from 1964 to 1992; and Sociofile, which lists all abstracts of social science journals from 1974. In addition, many national/international newspapers and magazines are storing material on CD-ROM; for example, *The Times* and the *Guardian*. For instance, it is possible now to look at shifts in social policy much more readily by searching through the *Guardian/ The Times* CD-ROM for stories relating to, say, the government's changing policy on the Poll Tax. The ability to exploit these

secondary sources of information in this versatile manner provides an invaluable set of resources to students. CD-ROMs can also be customized (for a small fee) at the ESRC Data Archive to include a selection of relevant data-sets and information which would provide students with a valuable resource for project work and would also enable material to be added again and again. There may well be a time when students will be able to submit their entire degree work on CD-ROM!

Electronic mail and conferencing

Electronic forms of communication are a cheap, fast, flexible and sophisticated way of communicating locally and globally. As a starting point, students should first consult their local computing centre/library and consult relevant impartial advice from magazines such as the *Which Guides to Computing*, but here are a few useful starting points.

All UK institutions of higher education are linked to JANET (Joint Academic NETwork), and the most useful generic gateway is provided by NISS (National Information on Software and Systems), based at the University of Bath. The typical format of an e-mail address is:

nameofsite@server.domain.country

e.g.

gateway@niss.ac.uk

If an e-mail message is sent to this address, a list of help messages and details of the services available via e-mail, gopher or the World Wide Web will be sent to the user. For example, NISS maintains a comprehensive list on a number of resources in the education sector, such as details about all aspects of information technology, including: a glossary to explain some of the jargon associated with technology, such as gopher or ftp; news and current affairs; the latest information on academic prices of software and hardware; and notices about jobs and research. A good training guide to the many services available electronically is provided on- and off-line by Netskills, a centre based at the University of Newcastle. Students should send an e-mail message with the following text:

help

to:

netskills@mailbase.ac.uk

Electronic news/discussion groups essentially offers students a chance to send comments/queries electronically to a group of people on a specific topic-based list. Electronic conferencing usually refers to a specific event, just like a traditional conference, but here users can engage in debate in 'real' and 'virtual' time. In a field like social policy, access to this global network of people and information is invaluable. To join an electronic discussion group or an electronic conference, students still need a username and password. The main UK discussion list system, Mailbase, is housed at the University of Newcastle. You simply need to send an e-mail message with the single word:

help

to:

mailbase@mailbase.ac.uk

Thereafter, you will receive full details of discussions groups according to subject area, access to past discussions, details of membership and who owns/looks after the list. There is a discussion group set up by the Social Policy Association and students can join by sending an e-mail message with the text:

join social-policy firstname lastname

to:

social-policy-request@mailbase.ac.uk

One good thing about electronic forms of communication is that there are no formalities, there are some guidelines for good manners (netiquette), but there is no need to address users with 'Dear Prof/ Dr' etc., so you could be sending messages and getting responses from the expert in social policy or another student as far afield as New Zealand!

The Internet and World Wide Web

Essentially, the Internet is a global system of networks, a world wide web which expands every day. Consequently, efforts to update sites/addresses regularly are not always easy. No one owns or controls the Internet: it relies on the goodwill of many in the academic, commercial and public arena. Access to the Internet simply requires a good computer and a modem. Information on the web is viewed/read through a 'browser'; the most common are Netscape, Mosaic and Microsoft Internet Explorer. These browsers enable the user to view/read the divergent multimedia formats of text, graphics, animation, pictures, video and sound from a particular site/address. The typical format of a web site address is:

http://webpages.nameofsite.domain. country/file

e.g.

http://www.stir.ac.uk/socinfo

The Web provides a way in which users can utilize all the technologies of computing, namely CD-ROMs, e-mail and other forms of computer-mediated communication, free (at point of use) and at a time that is convenient. Information on the Web is stored as a hypertext document, which simply means that some parts of the text point and lead the viewer/reader to more data/information by a click of the mouse. As there are so many sites of information, it is often difficult to know where to start and easy to get lost.

However, there are a number of useful tools to help the user to navigate and search through the information, some of which are useful, others less so. One of the most sophisticated generic search engines at the moment is called Alta Vista and can be found at:

http://www.altavista.com/

Currently, Alta Vista can handle simple or more complex queries across over 30 million Web pages. The speed and accuracy of the returns are impressive. For example, if you want to find out any information on the 'Jobseekers Allowance', you would simply type:

jobseekers+allowance

in the blank box on Alta Vista, then click the mouse on the 'submit' button. Alta Vista goes off and searches the Web for the information. Usually the first twenty returns are the most relevant. The returns will point to more information available via another Web site or as a text document. This is an easy and fairly comprehensive way of using the Internet.

For the student of social policy, there are also a number of excellent subject-specific gateways which act as useful filters to social scientific information, such as political parties, pressure groups, local and national governments, ministerial offices, official publications, national and internal newspapers and journals. These are strongly recommended.

Gateways

Social Science Information Gateway (SOSIG): http://www.sosig.bris.ac.uk/

The SOSIG gateway provides links to over 1000 UK and worldwide social science resources by classification and offers a good search facility across its site.

The ESRC Data Archive Web Site: http://dawww.essex.ac.uk/

The ESRC Data Archive is based at University of Essex and houses the largest collection of accessible computer-readable data in the social sciences and humanities in the United Kingdom. It is a national resource centre, disseminating data throughout the United Kingdom and, by arrangement with other national archives, internationally. Founded in 1967, it now houses approximately seven thousand data-sets of interest to researchers in all sectors and from many different disciplines. In addition, the Web site contains a useful facility which allows users to search comparatively through a number of archives using key words.

QUALIDATA: http://www.essex.ac.uk:80/qualidata

QUALIDATA is funded as a Resource Centre by the ESRC and University of Essex and is located within the Department of Sociology at the University of Essex. Its key objective is to improve access to qualitative data and to promote the secondary use of such data.

New United Kingdom Official Publications On-line (NUKOP): http://www.soton.ac.uk/~nukop/

New United Kingdom Official Publications On-line houses data drawn from the extensive Ford Collection of British Official Publications at Southampton University, including most items published by HMSO. The information is kept in a database which contains references to over 4300 records, including Acts of Parliament, Departmental Publications, Green Paper, House of Commons and House of Lords Bills, papers, library research papers and Standing Committee reports.

UK Government Home Page (CCTA): http://www.open.gov.uk/

The CCTA Web site is located in Norwich (UK) at the headquarters of CCTA (the Central Computer and Telecommunications Agency). CCTA is an Executive Agency of the Office of Public Service. This Web server holds information from over one hundred central government departments, executive agencies, police forces and local authorities. In addition, an index of other central and local government sites can be found through its central search service.

SocInfo, CTI Centre for Sociology, Politics and Social Policy: http://www.stir.ac.uk/socinfo/

The SocInfo Centre aims to encourage academics in sociology, politics and social policy to use the range of new technologies effectively in the teaching and learning process. The site points to a number of useful resources in social policy as well as to areas which focus on technology. It also has a good search facility linked to Alta Vista.

Political Science Association: http://www.lgu.ac.uk/psa/

The Political Science Association Web site refers to an extensive list of resources that are of interest to social policy students, from local to international governments, policy, pressure groups and politicians.

These World Wide Web sites are just a few of the good starting points for students of social policy, as they provide useful gateways to information and data, which in turn should lead to more exploratory forms of learning. In particular, the emphasis within social policy on comparative forms of analysis and the multifaceted nature of public policy lend themselves well to the use of global information that is available on the Internet. Students should therefore be encouraged to take the plunge and use the Web to browse independently as well as to search for a specific range of resources. The key is to learn by doing and the Web is the ideal mechanism to permit this. As users become more and more confident with the technology and as more information is placed on the Internet, further developments in the way social policy is taught in higher education will be made. The goal of students and teachers alike must be to ensure that the technology remains the tool, not the driving force, of the subject.

CONCLUSION

The improvements in the range of technological resources over the past five years offer the student of social policy more choice, flexibility and opportunity to develop a useful set of transferable skills and to understand more about the multifaceted nature of social policy. The potential benefits to students are therefore wide-ranging.

In addition, advancements in technology should be regarded as a legitimate area of concern to students of social policy. However, relatively little has been done to raise the specific and complex issues of access, accountability, confidentiality and ethics in these new forms of technology, and it may be that such debates will only become more prominent as the subject improves its own levels of IT literacy. In this regard, students of today may well help to shape the public and social policy of tomorrow.

Guide to Further Reading

Booth, P. (1989) *An Introduction to Human–Computer Interaction*. London: Lawrence Erlbaum. This book offers a good introduction to the issues surrounding all forms of human–computer interaction and is useful in both a theoretical and a practical sense.

Fielding, N. and Lee, R. (eds) (1991) *Using Computers in Qualitative Research*. London: Sage. This edited book has become a classic text as a basic guide to using computers for qualitative data analysis. It outlines some of the current programs and provides a useful glossary of key terms.

Glastonbury, B. and LaMendola, W. (1992) *Integrity of Intelligence – a Bill for the Information Age*. London: Macmillan. This book is a must for students, as it offers a comprehensive outline of the main issues to do with computers and society. Attention is paid to the design of computers, programs, access to technology and equal opportunities, and a model Bill of Rights for the technological age is developed.

Henry, M. S. and Rafferty, J. (1995) Equality and CAL in higher education. *Journal of Computer-Assisted Learning*, 11, 72–8. This article looks more closely at the issues to do with the development of computer-assisted learning in relation to its effect on different groups in society.

Henry, M. S. (1996) Using computers in sociology. In J. Gubbay and C. Middleton (eds), *A Companion to Sociology*. Oxford: Blackwell. This provides a useful contrast to the chapter on using computers in social policy and should be referred to, as there are overlaps between the discipline areas.

Henry, M. S. (ed.) (1996) *Using Technology Effectively in the Social Sciences*. London: Taylor and Francis. This edited book is based on a selection of papers presented at the 1995 International Technology and Education in the Social Sciences (TESS) conference in Stirling. The book examines four main stages in the development of computer-assisted learning in the social sciences, namely development, implementation, assessment and evaluation. It also refers to a wide range of resources available in the social sciences.

Henry, M. S. (ed.) (1997) *Computers for Sociology and Political Science Students*. Oxford: Blackwell. This edited book consists of a selection of papers by expert academics in the fields of sociology and political science about the use of technology.

Lee, R. (ed.) (1995) *Information Technology for the Social Scientist*. London: UCL Press. This book offers some practical hints and reviews about the use of IT in the social sciences.

Macarov, D. (ed.) (1990) Computers in the social services: papers from a consultation. *International Journal of Sociology and Social Policy*, 10(4/5/6). This volume is useful as it summarizes some of the main issues involved in the use of IT in public policy organizations.

McCartan, A. (ed.) (1991) *Computer Literacy for Every Graduate: Strategies and Challenges for the Early Nineties*. Oxford: CTISS Publications. This report focuses on the needs of students in relation to IT based on a national survey, and advocates a number of areas for change.

part VI
careers in social policy

VI.1

CAREERS AND SOCIAL POLICY GRADUATES IN THE UK

EITHNE MCLAUGHLIN

INTRODUCTION

Graduates, like most other people, face a less predictable and more rapidly changing labour market than ever before. The end of a 'job for life' means that people have to think harder about the kinds of jobs they want to do, in both the short and long term, and career planning and job search skills have become more important. This chapter is intended to contribute to the career planning which students should begin during their time as undergraduates. It is, of course, only a supplement to the activities and resources offered by university careers services. The focus is on employment opportunities in the UK, but for those interested in pursuing careers in other European countries, there are special guides, such as that by Hempshell (1994), available.

Attending a university for three years represents a major investment of effort and time by students, their families and the government through financial support. To maximize the benefits of what you are offered and acquire through your degree studies requires: an understanding of what might be available in the labour market, including an awareness of the skills employers want; an analysis of, and reflection on, your own skills. A common problem is that students underestimate the skills they have acquired through their degree studies and part-time work, voluntary

work and other life experiences. Most university careers services will offer individual help to assist students in identifying these.

The next two sections provide information on the labour market prospects of new graduates, and the following two discuss the kinds of jobs social policy graduates may want to plan for. Throughout, you will find sample job advertisements for the various types of jobs discussed in the final section.

WHAT ARE YOUR CHANCES OF GETTING A JOB?

Since the 1970s, graduate employment has fluctuated considerably. The low point of 40 per cent in permanent employment six months after graduation was in 1991/2, since when the proportion has again risen (*IES Graduate Annual Review*). Unemployment rates six months after graduation averaged only 7 per cent over the 25 year period 1969–94, and varied from a low of 2.9 per cent in 1972/3 to a high of 12.5 per cent in 1981–3, dropping again to 11.5 per cent in 1993. Figure VI.1.1 summarizes the pattern of new graduate activity between 1969 and 1994.

Most of the changes in new graduate employment and unemployment rates over time are due to changes in the economy generally. However, access to higher education also expanded considerably during

Figure VI.1.1   Destinations of established universities' first degree graduates
1969–94 (*IES Annual Graduate Review 1995–96*, Institute for Employment Studies,
Brighton, 1996, figure 3.5).

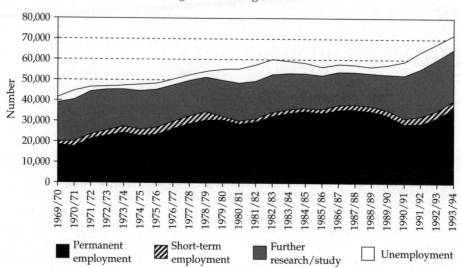

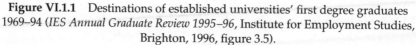

the 1980s and early 1990s, so that the supply of graduates on to the labour market
recently has been quite high. The UK supply of new graduates, at 20 out of 100
people of expected graduation age remains,
however, lower than in Japan (23), Denmark (22) and the USA (25) (*IES Graduate
Annual Review*). The increasing supply
has also been offset to some degree by two
trends: first, a higher level of recruitment
of graduates into 'traditional' graduate
jobs; second, a broadening of the range of
jobs into which graduates are recruited.
By the mid-1990s, this meant that the rise
in vacancies for graduates was greater than
the rise in the numbers of new graduates.
Some graduates, of course, are more successful than others – those with first or
upper second class degrees are more successful in obtaining employment, going on
to further study and avoiding early unemployment. The probability of obtaining employment, especially employment which
utilizes your social policy degree content,
can also be improved by obtaining a higher
degree.

It is probably at least two years after
graduation before graduates who have not

elected for further study have settled into
whatever kind of job they are likely to
remain in for some time, and obviously
longer still for those who choose further
study. The statistics reported annually,
however, are 'first destination statistics' –
the activities of new graduates six months
after graduation – which have been collected by UK universities for some time.
These statistics are obviously limited and
have become less reliable as the labour
market becomes more fragmented and less
secure. In the 1990s, the recruitment of
graduates with one or two years of employment experience is four times the size
of that of new graduates (Rigg et al., 1990,
p. 12). However, there have been very few
longer-term studies of graduate employment. One study which followed three
years of graduating students from a single
university showed that you should not be
'put off' by initial difficulties in establishing
a career:

*One year after graduation, unemployment rates had
dropped for all three years output, to ten per cent on
average [from an initial rate of 15 per cent] ...
three years after graduation, 72 per cent of the 1991*

Table VI.1.1 The effect of subject taken for first degree in 1993: destinations of graduates, six months after graduation (percentages)

	Unemployment	Employment[a]	Further study	Other[b]
Biological Sciences	11.7	38.9	37.3	12.1
Veterinary science, agriculture & related	10.3	59.1	18.0	12.6
Physical sciences	13.5	36.3	40.6	9.6
Mathematical sciences	13.6	51.6	22.5	12.3
Engineering & technology	12.4	47.9	18.1	21.6
Architecture & related	11.5	57.8	13.6	17.1
Social sciences	10.5	38.0	36.1	15.4
Business & financial studies	10.1	60.2	9.6	20.1
Librarianship & information science	14.3	56.7	15.2	13.8
Languages & related	10.8	37.9	32.1	19.3
Humanities	13.5	39.6	34.8	12.1
Creative arts	15.7	51.0	4.0	29.3

Notes:
[a] UK employment only; short-term and permanent employment. [b] Includes overseas students who have returned home, employment outside the UK, those without employment not seeking it nor engaged in further study. Source: 'first destination statistics'.

Source: derived from figure 3.20, Court et al. (1996, p. 37).

cohort were in permanent employment, considerably higher than the 41 per cent recorded at the six month stage. Two out of three of those who had been unemployed initially were in employment three years after they had graduated. (Connor and Pollard, 1995, p. x)

DOES THE SUBJECT OF YOUR DEGREE MATTER?

Graduate unemployment rates vary less than most people believe between the sciences, social sciences and arts – in the 1990s they were all between 10.3 and 15.7 per cent (excluding subjects like medicine, where entrance numbers are tightly regulated in line with expected demand). The pattern in 1993, shown in table VI.1.1 was fairly typical of the decade from 1986 to 1995. The unemployment rate for physical and mathematical sciences and engineering graduates in 1993 was higher than for social sciences graduates. In the case of the physical sciences, this was not because a higher proportion of social science than physical science graduates 'escaped' unemployment by undertaking further study.

One of the reasons why subject of degree does not matter as much as most people think is that about half of all graduates are recruited to jobs because they have a degree, not because of the subject the degree is in. This is even higher in some sectors, such as finance (75 per cent) and general management (89 per cent) (Rigg et al., 1990, p. 20). Employers recruiting into these 'generalist' jobs repeatedly stress that it is the personal qualities of candidates, such as good communication skills, literacy, numeracy, motivation and the ability to work in groups/teams, that are the dominant factors in recruitment (Pearson and Pike, 1989). Since 1990, such 'generalist' graduate jobs have grown in importance; for example, in financial management and/ or advice, public relations management, journalism and advertising.

Eithne McLaughlin

Table VI.1.2 Destinations six months after graduation, social policy and social sciences students, first half of the 1990s, in each of ten universities (percentages)

	Social policy, single/ major only					Social policy with other social science subjects				
	A	B	C	D	E	F	G	H	I	J
Employment	48	33	40	40	75	28	36	34	37	52
Unemployment	0	11	17	24	–	22	20	7	11	9
Further study/training	12	43	23	17	8	28	11	16	39	16
Other	0	6	4	5	–	0	11	0	7	4
Unknown	40	7	16	14	–	22	22	43	5	19

Notes: as for table VI.1.1.

National data from the annual survey of graduate destinations, as in table VI.1.1, divides subjects into broad groups such as 'the sciences' and 'the social sciences'. It is not possible to state the employment rate of social policy graduates specifically. However, as a result of the introduction of a national system of teaching quality assessment, most university departments are beginning to collate information on the destinations of their own recent graduates. These documents can usually be obtained from the departments concerned and tend to draw on the (limited) data provided by their graduates for the national destinations survey discussed above. Three factors have to be borne in mind when looking at such data:

- whether the data relate to graduates who took social policy alone (that is, single honours social policy) or whether it was combined with other subjects;
- regional labour market conditions;
- the proportion of graduates whose destinations are unknown.

Ten university departments offered information covering the early to mid–1990s for use in this *Companion* and this is shown in table VI.1.2. Employment rates at the six-month point after graduation varied from a third (33 per cent) to three-quarters (75 per cent) and those for further study or training varied from just one in twelve (8 per cent) to just over two in five (43 per cent). Only five of the ten universities were able to disaggregate social policy students from other social sciences students. These are universities A to E in the table. Among these five, employment rates varied from 75 to 33 per cent. The latter, lowest figure, however, occurred in the region with the highest unemployment in the UK, and a region where the majority of students at the university concerned are residents of that region. The high variations in response rates, together with the impact of regional labour market circumstances, means that it would be unwise for students to assume that if their department's employment rates are lower than the national average, their degree course is not 'worth as much' as others, or not offering them the right opportunities to acquire skills.

There is some evidence, both in table VI.1.2 and elsewhere, to suggest that single or major honours social policy graduates fare better than other social science graduates. More of the latter, for instance, apply for funding from the ESRC to undertake PhD study, suggesting that the new graduate labour market for social policy students may be healthier than for others. This is probably not surprising given the kinds of subject-related jobs available to social sciences graduates, profiled below, and examples of which are given in the boxed sample job advertisements you can see throughout this chapter.

PREPARING FOR THE WORLD OF WORK

The kinds of jobs to which new graduates in the first year or two after graduation are likely to be recruited are often called 'entry level jobs'. 'Second step' jobs are those to which graduates may move after they have acquired some experience – perhaps two to five years after graduation. In the final part of this section, and in the next, the focus is on the kinds of skills required for the entry and second level jobs that social policy graduates may wish to apply for which utilize the subject-specific content of their degrees. First, however, this section turns to the kinds of personal qualities and skills which all employers want, whether for generalist or subject-specific jobs: communication and interpersonal skills.

Communication skills

Employers expect graduates to be both fluent and accurate writers. Punctuation, spelling, grammar, sentence and paragraph construction, and structuring of written work, should be taken seriously. Employers seeking references from staff in higher education institutions often ask for comments on communication skills. If you are unclear or unsure how to improve your writing skills, try to obtain specific examples from your tutors of what you have done wrong and what would 'make it right'.

Just as important as written communication skills are oral skills. Seminars and tutorials are the traditional ways in higher education for students to practise and develop their oral skills. Learning to make succinct, effective comments on other people's contributions to discussions, and learning how to make a persuasive argument of your own, through participation in seminars and tutorials, are just as important as the content of your studies for your future employment chances. Developing your oral communication skills will improve your interview performance and so help your to get a job, but it will also improve your performance (in meetings, for example) once you are in a job, and therefore improve your chances of getting promotion or permanent employment within an organization.

Assignments and assessment based on formal oral presentations of a piece of work are particularly valuable, as they offer the opportunity to learn how to structure a presentation, how to get the right blend of information versus interpretation and argument, how to use overhead projectors, flipcharts and handouts. Some job interviews require a short presentation, and most of the jobs described in the next section involve making presentations either within the organization concerned or to other people on behalf of the organization employing you.

Work placements, voluntary work and participation in student clubs and societies also offer opportunities for improving both oral communication skills and interpersonal skills.

Interpersonal skills

Working with other people on a group project involves learning to identify the chain of tasks involved, negotiating responsibilities for specific tasks, providing mutual support but also direction, if required, in order to secure completion of tasks by those concerned, and diplomacy. All these skills are required in almost any work setting, yet they are not skills you can acquire when working in the traditional way in higher education; that is, on your own on an essay. Working in a group takes time and skill and it is because of the importance of these kinds of skills that employers look favourably upon people with existing employment experience.

Analytical and research skills

Many jobs which utilize the content of a social policy degree require research skills, as this comment from the ex-head of research in a local authority underlines:

I was involved in recruiting to . . . posts in research and for functions in the Chief Executive's Dept . . . Social policy graduates came through strongly, although only if they had a good research training (not just for the research jobs – such training was useful for corporate policy jobs too) . . . the health authority [also] recruited social policy graduates to research posts. So in my experience there are career opportunities in local government and health authority research, and local government corporate policy planning and performance review posts . . . I saw some of the social policy graduates that were appointed make quite rapid career advances. (Tim Blackman, personal communication)

Research methods courses are not generally the most popular of courses among students, and many teaching staff regard methods teaching as the most difficult form of teaching. An appreciation of the vocational importance of methods courses may help to make them more palatable! Research skills in the academic sense, however, need to be complemented, as you will see from the sample advertisements included here, by the general skills discussed above and familiarity with personal computers. Utilize whatever opportunities your university or department provides for learning word-processing and preferably the use of spreadsheets on personal computers.

What seems to new graduates to be a vicious circle – 'I can't get experience without a job, I can't get a job without experience' – can, then, be overcome in a variety of ways. First, maximize the opportunities there are within your degree studies for acquiring employment-relevant skills. Second, analyse your degree studies, vacation work, part-time work and/or voluntary work activities in terms of the skills they have allowed you to develop, or required you to exercise, and learn how to convey these in your curriculum vitae, application forms and interviews. Most university careers services offer sessions on how to write a good curriculum vitae and it is wise to take up such offers. Finally, use the first year after graduation productively, even if you have not obtained a job – do not allow initial difficulties to deter you.

'SOCIAL POLICY' JOBS

Excluding jobs that do not benefit from, or require, a social policy background, most entry and second level jobs fall into one of six main areas of activity.

Housing provision

Job titles in this area are varied and include support worker, housing assistant, housing officer and housing manager. The sectors involved are also diverse – there are a substantial number of posts with housing associations (see box VI.1.1), some in other voluntary sector organizations, some in local council Housing Departments, and occasionally some in the private sector.

Box VI.1.1

Housing Association Support Coordinator

The Support Coordinator will provide intensive housing management and support to single vulnerable tenants, assist in the assessment, resettlement, planning and monitoring of a caseload of individuals, ensuring access to and coordination of community services.

Requirements: experience of individual care/ support planning systems; excellent communication and interpersonal skills; generic experience of the needs of single vulnerable people particularly in the field of mental health; experience of working in the public or voluntary sectors; sound knowledge of the welfare benefits system.

Box VI.1.2

> ## (Voluntary organization)
> ## Carers and Primary Health Care Worker
>
> The person appointed will work with GPs and Primary Health Care Teams to promote the needs of carers.
>
> *Requirements: skills in training and organizing events; understanding of the pressures on primary health care teams.*

Box VI.1.3

> ## Health Trust
> ## Mental Health Act Officer
>
> To ensure the Trust's mental health hospitals perform their duties under the Act, administer the Act within the Trust, manage appeals, provide advice on all aspects of the 1983 Mental Health Act to professionals, patients, relatives, and carers.
>
> Requirements: detailed knowledge and understanding of the legislation, sound administration skills, ability to communicate effectively at all levels.

Care and support services

As with housing provision, the development of the mixed economy of welfare has meant that care and support services are now often provided by voluntary organizations (see, for example, box VI.1.2) as well as the traditional public sector organizations. The latter include local council social services departments and the probation service. Job titles in the voluntary sector include day care worker, community care worker, care supervisor and care worker, some of which may also be used in local council social services alongside the more traditional social worker or social work assistant. While most 'care and support' services posts require completion of an appropriate vocational qualification, such as the CQSW, on top of a first degree, not all do.

The health service

Following the 1990–3 NHS reforms, health care is provided by hospital trusts and family doctors, and planning and commissioning functions are undertaken by health authorities. Posts such as NHS management trainee or hospital administrator are located in trusts, while policy and planning posts (see 'Policy' jobs below) as well as general administrative posts tend to be more frequent in health authorities (see box VI.1.3, however, as an example of a post combining policy and practice in a trust).

Information/advice work

Social policy study obviously equips graduates to enter posts which involve obtaining and giving information and advice on social security, social services provision and housing, though most advice workers are also expected to be competent in relation to employment rights. Most advice posts are in the voluntary sector (where the largest organization is the network of Citizens Advice Bureaux). Job titles include advisor, housing advisor, community care advisor and outreach worker. Most posts require previous experience, but CABs offer a formal volunteering programme, involving high quality training, and sufficient experience on an unpaid volunteer basis will usually be accepted as equivalent to paid experience (see boxes VI.1.4 and VI.1.5). Some local councils, particularly as part of local socio-economic regeneration programmes in specific disadvantaged localities, may also employ advisors and the titles for these posts in recent years have included outreach workers, project workers and welfare workers. There may

Box VI.1.4

Citizens Advice Bureau

wishes to appoint a

Mental Health Advice Worker

This post, funded by X Health Authority, will provide advice services with a focus on welfare benefits to people with serious mental illness.

Requirements: one year's experience, paid or unpaid, of advising clients and carrying out casework, including welfare benefits, and an awareness of issues affecting people with mental health problems.

Box VI.1.5

Independent Advice Centre General Advice Worker

To provide advice and assistance to clients, undertake in-depth case work and participate in social policy work.

Requirements: one year's advice experience, paid or unpaid, in housing, immigration, welfare rights, employment, or debt.

Box VI.1.6

(National charity, regional office)
Social Policy Officer

To develop the organization's social policy work, undertake effective and efficient research, write papers, and represent the organization to policy-makers in the statutory sector.

Requirements: two years' relevant experience of policy development.

Box VI.1.7

(Voluntary sector organization)
Research & Development Worker

A research and development worker is required to research social policy issues and develop ideas for projects from that research.

Requirements: knowledge of research methodology; knowledge of computer-based information systems.

also be advice posts in private sector financial services organizations (for example, debt advice).

Policy and corporate planning

As noted above, these are posts in local councils, non-departmental public bodies (or 'quangos') and the voluntary sector which involve knowledge of central government legislation in a particular area, the ability to analyse and assess the implications of legislation and accompanying regulations and guidance, for local practice and opportunities for development of services, and the ability to obtain and understand monitoring and evaluation of information and statistics. Job titles include, for example, social policy officer (see box VI.1.6) and development officer (box VI.1.7) in charitable organizations, and assistant policy planner in chief executives' offices within local councils. There can be an overlap between jobs in this area and those in the next (see, for example, box VI.1.8).

Box VI.1.8

City Council
Chief Executive's
Department

Research Analyst

The person appointed will join the research team of the policy unit in the Chief Executive's Office. The research team supports the development of corporate strategies and policy, planning of council services, and prepares bids for additional funding.

Requirements: two years' experience of conducting applied research, expertise in manipulating computerised information and an ability to evaluate the policy implications of research for the council.

Box VI.1.10

(Central Government
Department)
Research Officers

To carry out research, manage and commission research from universities and other centres, compile and analyse statistics.

Requirements: clear interest in the development of social policy, thorough knowledge of research methodologies, research work experience and/or postgraduate study and/or the collection, analysis and presentation of statistics on social or economic issues, effective interpersonal and communication skills, strong powers of analysis, numeracy, appreciation of the use of computers.

Box VI.1.9

City Council, Housing Department

Research Officer

This post involves informing the corporate housing strategy, providing management information for senior managers and elected members, responsibility for a range of research projects including the coordination and presentation of surveys; interrogation, maintenance and refinement of information systems about housing issues, policy and development.

Requirements: thorough understanding of housing issues; clear understanding of research methods and statistical analysis.

---

dents appreciate. It is not only academics in universities who engage in research. Voluntary/charitable organizations as well as non-departmental public bodies employ research assistants or research officers, as do local councils and central government departments (see boxes VI.1.9 and VI.1.10). In both the voluntary and university sectors, research assistant or research officer posts are often fixed-term (most often one or two years duration). This is sometimes called 'contract research', and to pursue a career in this area will usually involve a high degree of geographical mobility. For these posts, research skills are obviously necessary and a taught masters programme or PhD study will provide an advantage. PhD study is now almost certainly necessary for appointment to lectureships in universities, where academic social research is combined with teaching (see below).

Research

Opportunities to pursue a career in social research are probably more varied and numerous than most undergraduate stu-

Teaching

Further and community education

The development of BTec and NVQs in social policy related fields in further education, together with an expansion in the community education field, has created new opportunities for teaching social policy. For those interested in such teaching, it is not essential to have a postgraduate certificate in education (whereas it is for teaching in secondary and primary schools). Full-time posts in colleges of education (or the adult/continuing education departments of universities) are scarce but most colleges recruit part-time lecturing staff annually and/or have lists of people willing to be called upon. Advertisements are usually in August and September. It is also possible to approach colleges in your area, and declare an interest in offering part-time teaching. In the field of community education, there are well known organizations such as the Workers Educational Association, as well as lesser known community organizations, which offer classes in community centres and may be interested in an offer from you of part-time teaching in social policy/social welfare subjects.

Higher education

As noted above, to obtain a lectureship in a social policy department in a university, you will be expected to have obtained at least a master's degree by research and more likely to have completed, or be near to completion of, a PhD. In addition, towards the end of postgraduate study, you should have sought publication of some of your work in academic outlets, such as academic journals. The numbers of candidates for social policy posts are much smaller than in other social science disciplines, such as sociology or politics. The prospects of an academic appointment following postgraduate study are, therefore, quite good, especially given that there will be a high number of retirements in the universities in the next decade.

Conclusions

The evidence suggests that prospects for social policy graduates are healthy. But obtaining a good class of degree, and utilizing opportunities for developing oral and written communication skills, interpersonal skills and research skills are all important elements in success. In addition, it is important to begin reflecting on your skills and experiences early in your undergraduate career. Good career planning and strong presentation of your skills and experience on paper (for example, in CVs) are essential.

The first year after graduation for those without either a job or further study can be used well by engaging in voluntary work, preferably in organizations offering good training to volunteers, and by investigating options for the future. 'Generalist' jobs also provide opportunities for the development of personal skills which can be used to acquire a more subject-specific job later.

Sources of Information and Useful Addresses

Annual publications

Association of Graduate Careers Advisory Services (AGCAS), *What Do Graduates Do?* A CRAC publication. Cambridge: Hobsons.
Association of Graduate Recruiters, *Graduate Salaries and Vacancies*. Cambridge: AGR.
Institute of Employment Studies, *The IES Annual Graduate Review*. Brighton: IES.
60,000 Graduate Jobs and Courses. A CRAC publication. Cambridge: Hobsons.

Other

Hempshell, M. (1994) *How to Get a Job in Europe: a Guide to Employment Opportunities and Contacts*. Plymouth: How To Books.

Web Sites

Several university career services place their vacancy information, profiles of key occupations and postgraduate opportunities on Web pages. Start browsing by locating: *Prospects Web: http://www.prospects.csu.man.ac.uk* Some of the larger graduate recruiters also have, or may have in the future, Web sites. Try *Price Jamieson: http:// www.pricejsam.com*, or *Unixis Solutions:http://www.unis.com* and find other related sites from there.

Organization addresses

Association of Graduate Careers Advisory Services (AGCAS), c/o Careers Advisory Services (CAS), University of Warwick, Senate House, Coventry CV4 7AL. Tel: 01203 523498.
Association of Graduate Recruiters (AGR), Sheraton House, Castle Park, Cambridge CB3 OAX. Tel: 01223 356720.
Institute for Employment Studies, Mantell Building, University of Sussex, Brighton BN1 9RF. Tel: 01273 686751.

Guide to Further Reading

Connor, H. and Pollard, E. (1995) *What do Graduates Really Do?* Brighton: IES.
Court, G., Jagger, N. and Connor, H. (1996) *The IES Graduate Review, 1995–6*. Brighton: IES.
Pearson, R. and Pike, G. (1989) *The Graduate Labour Market in the 1990s*. Brighton: IES.
Rigg, M., Elias, P., White, M. and Johnson, S. (1990) *An Overview of the Demand for Graduates*. London: HMSO.

V1.2

postgraduate and further training opportunities
francesca peroni

You have your degree in social policy: what next? One possibility, and an increasingly popular one, is postgraduate study. In recent years over a quarter of all new graduates have undertaken further study: among the courses taken are those in social policy or social policy related areas. If you are thinking about the postgraduate option useful questions to consider are: What is involved? Where can I study? What about funding? How do I apply? What does the further study lead to?

What Is Involved?

Postgraduate study comes in a variety of forms, but essentially involves either a research degree (PhD or MPhil) or a taught course (usually a diploma or masters). Both may be studied on a full- or part-time basis. The choice between a taught course or a research degree is likely to be influenced by your reasons for undertaking further study. You may wish to study an aspect of social policy in more depth, or use a taught course to broaden your knowledge base before specializing further. Alternatively, you may want to add a professional qualification in a related area, like social work, housing management or health service management, to your degree. Postgraduate study can also be used to change direction by means of a conversion course. Social policy graduates have used such

courses to move into areas like law, information technology or management training. Opportunities at postgraduate level for those with a first degree in social policy are vast.

If you are choosing the research route what is involved? A social policy PhD undertaken in Britain is usually assessed entirely on the basis of an extensive thesis submitted towards the end of three years of full-time or a longer period of part-time study. The thesis would be expected to push forward significantly the knowledge base of the particular social policy topic. Before embarking on the research for the thesis a research student will spend part of the first year on various courses designed to provide a good understanding of appropriate methods and procedures. The methods component is a compulsory element in most programmes (and is essential for Economic and Social Research Council (ESRC) funding). An MPhil programme is essentially similar to a PhD programme but its shorter timescale limits what can be covered in the thesis, and there is not the same emphasis on an original piece of research. Often students are initially registered for an MPhil and then transfer to a PhD after their first year of study if their progress and the review of their proposal are satisfactory.

There is a large and growing variety of taught courses, particularly taught masters. It is impossible to describe briefly the full range of opportunities, as what is available at this level is rapidly changing and evolving. Universities, in order to compete in the masters' market, are generally becoming more flexible in what they provide and are devising new programmes to appeal to specific client groups. Taught masters programmes are now studied not only by the traditional one-year full-time route but also through a variety of part-time day and evening modes (with or without a residential component). Increasingly these programmes operate on a credit accumulation basis, enabling study to be paced over a variable time period according to students' other commitments. Typically, the first six to nine months of the masters is taken up with advanced courses which utilize some combination of lectures, seminars and/or groupwork. These classes are assessed by examination or coursework, and a satisfactory performance is usually required before the postgraduate is allowed to proceed to a dissertation or other form of project work in the final three to six months of the programme. Generally diplomas take less time: most full-time postgraduate diplomas consist of taught courses and examinations over a period of nine months. Usually they are vocational and may be essential requirements if you are thinking of a career in law or of teaching in a state school. A postgraduate diploma can also act as an initial step to a higher degree for those not meeting the full entrance requirements.

When asked to make comparisons with their undergraduate experience, most postgraduates point out the potential for feeling isolated. Research students who are working on their own for much of the time are more likely to experience this problem, but taught postgraduates who move to a different university are not immune, especially if class sizes are small and interaction with other courses is minimal. The advice that postgraduates give is to make the most of opportunities for contact with others by taking part in postgraduate seminars and events in your department and by joining your university's postgraduate society. Another useful tip is to join the Social Policy Association, which has special rates for postgraduate members, who are encouraged to participate in study groups and conferences.

Probably the factor which will have most impact on your experience of postgraduate life is your relationship with your main supervisor. In the past students tended to be assigned to a single supervisor but increasingly departments are appointing supervisory teams that can offer a range of perspectives or expertise to the postgraduate. Having a team of supervisors also provides an 'escape route' where there is a clash between a postgraduate and a main supervisor. While acknowledging that postgraduate study can be more lonely than the more structured life of an undergraduate, these same students put far more stress on the positive features. Further study provides the opportunity of delving more deeply into those aspects of social policy that you most enjoy, and if you are doing a PhD you can contribute in an original way to the development of your topic. Further study is also likely to find you engaged in challenging debates with your supervisor, with other postgraduates and with visiting speakers at staff/postgraduate seminars.

WHERE TO STUDY

Once you have decided on what to study and the mode of study you need to think carefully about where to study. It is an important decision, so check out all relevant courses and institutions with scrupulous care. Ask questions about main areas of research, potential supervisors, facilities for postgraduates, funding and completion rates. The location of potential supervisors may influence decisions about where to study, or availability of funding may be the determining factor. Decisions also have to be made about whether to stay in familiar surroundings. There are advantages in staying on at your undergraduate institution, as you know the ropes, particularly if your course is only for a year. The advantage of going elsewhere is to gain experience of different ways of conceptualizing and dealing with your subject. Another point to consider is whether you want to study in a small or large department or in a graduate school, all of which have their attractions. Your choice maybe more limited if you are tied to a certain geographical area because of employment or family commitments or for financial reasons. Economic pressures mean that more students wishing to proceed to a higher degree are taking the part-time route in their local area. At first sight it may appear that the particular course you are looking for is not available locally, but check this out carefully, as similar courses can be provided under a variety of headings. The broad social science base of your social policy degree could enable you to take a postgraduate qualification in a range of disciplines.

POSTGRADUATE STUDY OVERSEAS

If you are not tied to a particular locality another option you might consider is post-graduate study overseas. Opportunities exist worldwide, but language and cultural barriers often limit where students go. The most popular destinations are North America and Australasia, although an increasing number of graduates are taking courses in EU countries. Countries you might consider are Sweden and the Netherlands, where social policy can be studied in English. If you are contemplating the overseas option it is important to recognize where systems differ. An important difference is the time it generally takes to complete a PhD in North America. In Canada and the United States postgraduate degrees include both coursework and thesis components. In most American universities students are usually required to complete a masters degree before proceeding to a doctoral programme, and it is likely to take

at least five years to complete the two degrees. In contrast, a UK student with a three-year honours degree can go straight into a PhD in New Zealand if he or she has the funding. Another point to note is that the label 'social policy' may not be used. Topics we study as part of social policy are often studied under the umbrella of other disciplines in much of Europe and North America. In the USA, postgraduate courses on social welfare, social problems, family studies, women's studies, health administration and policy, policy analysis and public policy are among the many programmes that have a familiar ring.

HOW TO APPLY

If you are contemplating postgraduate study you should act early. Investigating options before your final year could prove invaluable later. Early action is particularly crucial if you are planning to study overseas. You need to allow time to investigate options thoroughly and to arrange to take any graduate admission tests that are required. It can take months to organize and obtain the results for tests for North American universities, while some scholarships are likely to have closing dates early in your final undergraduate year. Even if you are staying on in the UK, early investigation of possible options can enable you to use summer vacations to gain relevant experience in paid or voluntary work, which will strengthen your postgraduate application. The peak time for applications in the UK is November to March, and securing a place early leaves more time to apply for funding, but if places are available and you are self-funding applications can be made until the start of the course.

The advice is to start searching for information early, but where do you look? A university or college careers service is likely to hold a range of publications on postgraduate study or be able to give you advice on where to obtain them locally.

The Students' Guide to Graduate Studies (POSTGRAD) is a useful reference source for options in the UK. Information on postgraduate study in the Commonwealth can be obtained from the Commonwealth University Yearbook. Graduate Programs in the Humanities and Social Sciences (Peterson) is a useful source for study in the United States. Information on how the system works and on possible options in Europe can be found in the Guide to Postgraduate Study in Europe (FEDORA, 1995). The various guides and directories provide much useful information but should be treated with caution, as contributing departments are often expected to buy space in them and not all departments choose to be included, so it is wise to consult other sources as well. The education and cultural department of particular embassies or high commissions provide another source of information on study overseas. Newspapers and journals are an additional source of information on postgraduate courses and research opportunities in the UK. A regular look at the Times Higher Education Supplement, the Guardian, The Independent and the New Statesman could prove informative. Also use the Internet: most universities have a Web page. Another place to look for up-to-date information is your departmental noticeboard. Yet a further source, and probably the most useful starting point, is to talk to a member of staff in your undergraduate department, particularly someone who is knowledgeable about the topic you are interested in. He or she will be able to give you advice about which departments and individuals have strong reputations in particular fields of study. Or if you are unsure about the range of social policy opportunities open to you with a social policy degree, again the possibilities can be explored with your undergraduate tutor.

With a few exceptions there is no formal clearing system for postgraduate study and no standardized application form or closing date. The exceptions include social work, law and teaching. For the vast majority of higher degrees, once you have identified courses of potential interest, the onus is on you to make enquiries of and to apply directly to relevant institutions. When filling in application forms think carefully about your reasons for applying for a particular course; stress relevant parts of your first degree, including a specialized option or dissertation. If you are hoping to do a research degree you will probably be asked to outline a proposal. This needs to be properly researched and fully referenced, a task which is likely to be easier if an informal approach is made to a potential department or supervisor prior to making a formal application. When making your application you will be asked for academic references: select referees who know your work well. When applying for study overseas you need to ensure that all the appropriate documentation is sent with the application.

WHAT ABOUT FUNDING?

The cost of postgraduate study with fees and maintenance can run into thousands, but funding for such study is hard to find. The ESRC funds research and courses in social policy and related areas, but the awards are very competitive and even a first class degree does not guarantee funding. The ESRC allocates almost all of its advance course awards through a quota system. In 1996, new training guidelines were introduced which indicate that about 60 per cent of research studentships will be tied to nine broad themes around which the ESRC now organizes its research. A number of these themes cover topics of interest to social policy graduates. The research training awards do not have to be geared to the themes. ESRC awards cover both fees and a maintenance grant, and there is an additional allowance for study-related travel.

There are other sources of finance beyond the research council awards. Some universities offer scholarships and bursaries to outstanding candidates. Universities also advertise research assistantships, which provide the opportunity for registering for a higher degree. In specific circumstances the European social fund also provides quotas for certain courses. Vocational courses like social work have a limited quota of awards for which applicants can be nominated, while teacher training receives automatic awards. Local authorities can provide another source for vocational courses like youth work, but in practice very few funds are available.

Charities and trusts also provide some funding but again should not be relied on as they often make only a small contribution. Some students are sponsored by employers, especially for vocationally oriented courses, but many finance themselves. Some self-financing students take out career development loans for vocational courses, others undertake postgraduate study alongside paid employment, yet others work for a period to fund a full-time course later. The funding climate is harsh but remember that some funding is available for almost all kinds of courses and someone has to get it.

Postgraduate study overseas is expensive but some UK students obtain grants or scholarships from a range of sources, including international organizations, bilateral agreements or host institutions. Commonwealth scholarships are a valued source of support for students applying to Australia, New Zealand or Canada, while there are a range of scholarships for postgraduate study in the United States, including the annual Fulbright Awards. Teaching assistantships are another source of funding in North American universities.

WHAT DOES FURTHER STUDY LEAD TO?

On past performance the House of Commons and the House of Lords are possibilities. A recent Secretary of State for Health and a spokesperson for the opposition in the Lords are among a number of people in Parliament who have undertaken a postgraduate qualification or research in a social policy related area. There has also been a history of those active in social policy research acting as government advisors or consultants. What are the more regular destinations?

Students with a vocationally oriented or specialist qualification tend to take up posts in the area of their postgraduate studies, whether this is in health service or housing management, social work, probation, voluntary sector studies, social planning in developing countries, public sector management, personnel management, criminal justice policy or a range of other possibilities. Many students may already work in a relevant area before taking a course and return to their old job or the same sector with enhanced skills and a broader knowledge base.

Broader postgraduate courses in social policy have led to varied destinations. They have provided a step to research degrees and acted as a conversion course for those wanting to move into social policy related work. They have also enabled those working in specialist areas to shift direction. Thus nurses and those employed in the voluntary sector or housing have used their postgraduate qualification to move into more policy- or planning-oriented jobs in their field.

Students armed with a research degree in social policy have often taken up academic posts, in this country or abroad, either as lecturers or as researchers. The prospects of using a PhD in social policy for entry into a university career look good as we move towards the next century. Many of the staff appointed during the expansionary years of the 1960s and early 1970s will be reaching retirement over the next ten years or so, opening up opportunities for well qualified postgraduates. Posts in government research departments have been another destination for students with PhDs or MPhils in social policy.

What this chapter has illustrated is the diverse range of experiences and opportunities open for those undertaking postgraduate study in social policy related areas. If you select the postgraduate route at the end of your study you will have acquired or enhanced a range of abilities, including the ability to undertake an independent project to evaluate and synthesize findings. This expertise will enable you to follow a wide range of exciting destinations.

USEFUL SOURCES OF INFORMATION

Awards for Postgraduate Study at Commonwealth Universities. London: The Association of Commonwealth Universities.
Commonwealth Universities Yearbook. London: The Association of Commonwealth Universities.
European Education Yearbook. Kent: Nexus Business Communications Limited.
FEDORA (1995) *Guide to Postgraduate Study in Europe*. Free University of Brussels: Forum Européenne de l'Orientation.
Graduate Programs in the Humanities and Social Sciences. Princeton, NJ: Peterson's Guides.
POSTGRAD, the Students' Guide to Graduate Studies. London: Hobsons for CRAC.
The Edition X11 Guide to Postgraduate Arts, Humanities and Social Sciences Studies in Europe. London: Edition Twelve Limited.
Postgraduate Study and Research in the UK. Manchester: CSU for AGCAS.

Except where a date is given the guides listed above are published annually or regularly updated.

SOURCES OF FURTHER INFORMATION

Economic and Social Research Council (ESRC), Postgraduate Training Division, Polaris House, North Star Avenue, Swindon SN2 1UJ.
The Association of Commonwealth Universities, John Foster House, 36 Gordon Square, London WC1 OPE.
The Fulbright Commission, 62 Doughty Street, London WC1N 2LS.

A source of information for overseas students applying to British universities is *POSTGRAD, the Students' Guide*. This not only provides a comprehensive list of courses offered but also contains a useful article on 'preparing to study in the UK' (pp. 65 and 67).

gLossaRy of key teRms

This glossary is intended for newcomers to social policy, and provides an introduction to key concepts and technical terms with which readers may not be familiar. Many of these notions have been employed in different ways in the literature. For the most part, however, we have tried to remain true to their common usage.

Words in *italics* which form part of the definition of each term are detailed elsewhere in the glossary.

Accountability: ensuring service *providers* are responsible to *purchasers*, users and the wider society through a variety of politically representative structures and/or managerial *quality assurance* and *redress* procedures.

Action research: research undertaken to inform decision-making and improve programme delivery or the situation of a particular group or area.

Active Citizenship: an approach to voluntary service which emphasizes people's social responsibilities and, in particular, the duty of the more affluent to support and participate in charitable and voluntary activities (chapter III.3).

Active labour market policies: policies whereby the government takes responsibility for countering unemployment through job-creation schemes. This type of intervention is often associated with Scandinavian welfare systems (chapters II.12, III.8, IV.7).

Adverse selection: occurs when buyers or suppliers possess characteristics that may adversely affect the provision of a benefit or a service that are known to them but concealed from the other party in the transaction.

Advocacy: representing and promoting the needs and views of individuals or groups.

Altruism: acting in the interests of others or the wider 'common good' (chapters II.4, II.15, III.3, III.4).

Audit Commission: a *quango* established in 1983 with a remit to monitor the efficiency and effectiveness of statutory health and social care providers and to advise on ways of improving their performance.

Basic income: an individualized form of income maintenance aimed to provide all citizens with a guaranteed minimum which could be 'topped up' through earnings or savings (chapters II.11, II.12, II.15, III.10, IV.6).

Bureaucracy: The hierarchical structuring of organizations in which staff are placed in different ranks with defined authority and responsibilities and where activities are based on codified rules and procedures (chapter III.5).

Bureau-professionalism: The organizational form characteristic of public welfare agencies, based on combining bureaucratic structures and processes with the exercise of professional discretion by specialist staff and care practitioners (chapter III.5).

Care management: the process of assessing and meeting a service user's needs advocated in the 1990 NHS and Community Care Act. It includes the activities of finding, referral and screening; assessing need; care planning and service packaging; monitoring and re-assessment (chapters III.4, IV.3, V.1).

Care manager: the individual responsible for constructing and monitoring care packages or care plans. In some authorities posts are restricted to qualified social workers, but they can include other practitioners, such as home care organizers, occupational therapists or health authority staff (chapters III.1, IV.3, IV.11).

Carer: an individual providing unpaid physical care and personal assistance for one or more individuals (chapters III.4, IV.11).

Care plan: see *Care manager* (chapters IV.3, IV.11).

Categorical benefits: income support schemes aimed to meet the needs of specified groups and which are neither means-tested nor contribution-tested (chapter IV.9).

Charities: voluntary organizations recognized as meeting or promoting one of four objectives: religion, education, the relief of poverty or other purposes beneficial to the whole community (chapters II.5, III.3).

Child Support Agency: established under the 1991 Child Support Act to determine and collect financial contributions from absent parents (chapters II.14, II.16, IV.5, IV.6).

Citizen's Charter: an initiative involving the setting of targets for public services, entitling consumers to information and more effective complaint and redress procedures (chapters III.10, IV.9).

Citizen's income: see *Basic income* (chapters II.11, II.12, II.15, III.10).

Citizenship: membership of a particular political community or nation state which brings both rights (often distinguished as civil, political and *social rights*) and responsibilities (chapters I.1, I.3, II.2, II.9, II.13, II.15, III.1, III.10).

Clinical audits: the process whereby members of the medical profession review each other's practice with a view to improving quality (chapter IV.8).

Collectivism: advocates the pooling of society's resources to meet specific welfare needs and enhance equality (chapters I.1, I.3, II.5).

Community: a widely used but complex and emotive concept with a multiplicity of meanings. For some it refers to a defined locality or geographical area; for others a local social system or set of relationships centred in a particular locality; more broadly it denotes a sense of common identity based on shared interests or experiences which are not necessarily geographically based (chapters II.9, III.4, IV.3, IV.11).

Community care: the provision of support in their own homes for those unable to care for themselves (chapters II.9, III.4, IV.3, IV.11).

Community care plan: under the 1990 NHS and Community Care Act, local authorities are obliged to produce annual statements of their assessments of local need and strategies for meeting them. In preparing their plans they are required to consult user and carer groups, health and housing services and the independent sector (chapter IV.3).

Conditional benefits: forms of income maintenance and welfare services where entitlement and continued support are dependent on reciprocal action by the claimant; for instance, basing unemployment benefit on claimants' participation in work training (chapters III.10, IV.7).

Contingency benefits: forms of income support aimed to meet specified social circumstances (chapter IV.9).

Contract: a legally binding agreement between two parties (or legal entities).

Contract culture: the dual process whereby government grants – the traditional means of funding voluntary organizations – is giving way to contracts and the delivery of welfare services is being transferred from public providers to voluntary and other organizations (chapters III.3, IV.8, IV.11).

Contracting state: a form of government advocated particularly by some *neo-liberals* in which public services are only supplied under *contract* by a range of non-statutory agencies (chapters III.1, III.5).

Corporatism: a mode of political and economic decision-making based on consultation and negotiation between the state and leading organizational representatives of employers and unions.

Cost–benefit analysis: an accountancy device for aiding decision-making through weighing up the financial advantages and disadvantages of a particular policy or action.

Cream-skimming: describes the tendency for providers to focus on profitable or easy forms of care and treatment while avoiding costly and/or problematic cases.

Culture of dependency: a term used by those who argue that people have become over-reliant on state support and 'disabled' from providing for themselves (chapters II.14, III.5, IV.4, IV.5, IV.10).

Decentralization: the process whereby welfare benefits and services are devolved from central government to smaller localized units or to authorities and agencies deemed closer to citizens and users (chapters II.11, III.1, III.5, III.6, III.8).

Decommodification: a concept developed by G. Esping-Andersen to refer to the extent to which individuals or households can uphold a socially acceptable standard of living independently of market participation (chapters I.3, II.2, III.10).

Dependency: a state of reliance on state benefits or, alternatively, the reliance on welfare agencies or *carers* for help in meeting personal needs (chapters II.9, III.4, IV.3, IV.4, IV.5, IV.11).

Dependency ratio: the population who are not economically active as a proportion of those who are in employment.

Dependent population: individuals who are not in paid employment.

Deregulation: the removal or reduction of government controls over product, housing and labour markets and the activities of market participants (chapters II.12, IV.10).

Desert: the notion that some attribute or activity warrants social support in the form of benefits or services (chapters II.2, II.4, III.10, III.11, IV.6).

Disregard: the amount of an individual's earnings or assets which is ignored in determining benefit entitlements.

Divisions of welfare (the social division of welfare): the notion first developed by Richard Titmuss that welfare benefits and services could be provided in functionally equivalent modes with differing distributional consequences. He distinguished three such modes: state welfare, *fiscal welfare* and *occupational welfare* (chapters II.8, III.1, III.2, III.3, III.9).

Domiciliary care: the provision of health and care services in an individual's home.

Earnings-related: contributions or benefits which vary with an individual's current or previous earnings.

Eco-feminism: views environmental damage as the product of the dominance of 'male' values and behaviour (chapter II.11).

Eco-socialism: attributes the damage to the biosphere to the organization of economic life under capitalism (chapter II.11).

Eco-taxes: forms of taxation on polluting activities (chapter II.11).

Effectiveness: a measure of desired outcomes; the extent to which benefits and services are delivered to target populations (chapter II.15).

Efficiency: the production of welfare units at the minimum cost per unit. An efficient service would thus be one where it is impossible to reduce costs without reducing either the quantity or the quality of provision (chapters II.3, II.12, II.15, III.9, IV.8).

Egalitarianism: A central principle of socialist conceptions of welfare which seeks to treat different groups in equal terms, whether this is a matter of 'equality of opportunity' or access to services or 'equality of outcome' (chapters II.2, II.4, III.9, III.10, III.11).

Empowerment: the processes involving users in identifying needs, engaging in policymaking, service planning, management and assessment and having more direct control over service provision (chapters II.8, II.15, III.1, IV.8, IV.11).

Enabling: the processes whereby statutory welfare agencies, rather than providing services, organize and manage the provision purchased from voluntary organizations and commercial bodies and offered by local support networks (chapters IV.8, IV.10, IV.11).

End-user: individuals receiving benefits or services which have been purchased or arranged by others, including employers, relatives, care agencies and general practitioners (chapters III.1, III.2, IV.8, IV.11).

Equality of opportunity: policies aimed to give individuals an equal starting point in an unequal society (chapters II.2, II.8, III.8, IV.9).

Equality of outcome: an aspiration of egalitarian policies which aim to place individuals in positions of equal value (chapters II.2, III.8).

Equity: the provision of benefits or services on the basis of need rather than the ability to pay (chapters I.1, II.1, II.2, III.10, III.11).

Eugenics movement: the belief expressed by a number of early twentieth-century social commentators that social problems were often the product of hereditary factors which could be eradicated by policies to reduce the fertility rates of the 'unfit' (chapter II.13).

European Charter of the Fundamental Social Rights of Workers: a declaration of principles signed in 1989 by 11 of the then 12 member states of the European Community concerning basic standards of living and working conditions for workers (chapter III.8).

European Social Fund: established under the 1957 Treaty of Rome to assist in the employment and redeployment of workers displaced by economic and technological change (chapter III.8).

Evaluative research: research undertaken to test or assess the effectiveness of a particular benefit scheme or service.

Fabianism: one of the founding left-wing intellectual traditions in social policy analysis, named after the Roman general Fabius, and based on the belief that the goals of social justice and social equality can be achieved on a gradualist basis through the management of a capitalist economy (chapters I.1, II.8).

Family wage: the assumption, implicit in much post-war welfare legislation and fiscal policy, that people would live in families supported by a male breadwinner whose earnings would enable the wife to undertake unpaid caring and domestic responsibilities in the home (chapters II.8, II.9).

Feminism: a term embracing a wide range of perspectives which share the aim of promoting women's equality with men in all areas of life (chapters II.9, II.13, II.14, III.4, III.5, IV.9).

Fiscal welfare: the allocation of welfare support and benefits through the tax system (chapters III.9, III.11).

Flat-rate: contributions or benefits paid at a fixed rate unrelated to an individual's past earnings.

Friendly society: a mutual insurance organization owned by its members.

Funded schemes: income maintenance and other schemes organized on the basis of using contributions to build up an independent fund from which benefits can then be paid to members.

Gatekeepers: those engaged in the provision of benefits or services who determine access to those benefits or services.

Gender: denotes the social construction of femininity and masculinity and expectations about the characteristics and behaviour appropriate for men and women (chapters II.9, II.13, II.14, III.4, IV.4, IV.9).

Globalization: the development of worldwide economic, political, social or cultural interdependencies in which developments and decision-making in one part of the world are likely to have repercussions in other localities (chapters I.3, II.12, II.15).

Green Paper: a consultative document produced by UK governments which interested groups and the wider public are invited to comment on as a prelude to the publication of proposals for legislation.

Gross domestic product (GDP): the value of all goods and services produced by UK residents in the UK (chapters I.2, II.12).

Gross national product (GNP): the value of all goods and services produced by UK residents including resources and investments held abroad.

Harmonization: the promotion of greater coordination and affinity between the social policies of European Union member states (chapters II.13, III.8).

Horizontal redistribution: redistributing resources between individuals with similar resources but different needs (chapter III.11).

Housing associations: charities, cooperatives and other *NGOs* responsible for the provision of social housing (chapters II.8, III.3, IV.10).

Ideology: a set of shared beliefs or understandings of reality which serve both as a basis for action and the means of legitimizing outcomes to actions (chapters I.1, II.2, II.13, II.14, III.5).

Income-Smoothing: the redistribution of resources across an individual's life-cycle (chapter III.11).

Independent sector: a term used in many official documents to distinguish non-statutory from statutory welfare, and encompassing both commercial enterprises and voluntary organizations (chapters III.1, IV.6).

Institutional discrimination: evidenced when the policies, activities or practices of organizations or groups result in the unequal treatment of individuals (chapters II.9, IV.2, IV.3, IV.5).

Internal markets: the creation of competition within public services between *purchaser* units and *provider* units (chapters III.5, IV.7, IV.8).

Inverse care law: the extent to which the most disadvantaged or needy individuals/groups/areas receive the least welfare provision (chapters III.10, III.11, IV.5, IV.8, IV.9).

Laissez-faire: the belief that if left alone and not subjected to government intervention, the market is the best distributor of goods and services (chapters II.5, II.13, IV.1).

Libertarian: theories which advocate minimalist government, freedom based on property rights and a free market (chapter IV.1).

Local employment transfer schemes (LETS): economies where people trade skills with one another and are paid in the form of tokens whose value is typically calculated on the basis of the hours worked. The tokens are then exchanged locally for other goods and services (chapter II.11).

Male breadwinner model: a welfare system or welfare arrangements which assume that adult married women and their children will be dependent on men through the operation of the *family wage* (chapters II.9, II.13, III.4, IV.4, IV.11).

Maintenance payment: the sum payable by an absent parent to support his or her children and, in some instances, the other parent.

Managerialism/new managerialism: see *New public management*.

Marginal benefit: used to describe the increase in benefits (outcomes) acquired from increasing inputs by specified units (chapter II.3).

Marginal cost: used to describe the increase in costs generated by increasing output by specified units (chapter II.3).

Marginal tax: the amount of tax paid on an extra unit of income.

Marginal utility: used to refer to the extra value generated by an increase in the consumption of a product or service (chapters II.3, II.6).

Marketization: the establishment of market processes (particularly competition) in the funding and distribution of public services (chapters III.1, IV.3, IV.9, IV.10, IV.11).

Means test: a mechanism widely used in social security systems for limiting the receipt of benefits or services to those whose income and/or assets fall below a specified amount (chapters II.12, IV.11).

Mixed economy of welfare: describes the different combinations of commercial, statutory, voluntary and informal welfare that pertain in a society (chapters III.1, III.3).

Monetarism: an economic policy based on the theory that the supply of money can be varied to control aggregate effective demand and inflation (chapter II.12).

Moral hazard: the situation in which an insured individual can adversely effect the liability of an insurance carrier without its knowledge by engaging in risky or damaging behaviour.

Mutual aid association: organizations such as building societies, *friendly societies* and insurance associations which are owned by and provide financial assistance or other forms of support for their members (chapters II.5, II.6, II.11).

National efficiency: a concept developed in the early twentieth century to denote the links between the country's military and productive capacity and the health of the population (chapter II.13).

Needs-led assessment: the provision of social care based on needs identified by a *care manager* in consultation with the potential service user and, where appropriate, the main *carer* (chapters III.4, IV.3, IV.11).

Neo-classical economic theory: see *Neo-liberal.*

Neo-conservatism: a strand of *new right* thinking which emphasizes the centrality of authority, the family and family-related values and the demoralizing effects of extensive state welfare.

Neo-liberalism: an intellectual tradition which favours a competitive market economy and, correlatively, opposes economic systems planned and directed by the state. It maintains that a market economy supported by the rule of law is the best guarantor of freedom, morality and prosperity (chapters II.3, II.5, II.6, IV.1).

New managerialism: see *New public management.*

New public management: the importation of the practices and *ideology* of commercial management into state welfare services (chapters III.1, IV.3, IV.6, IV.8, IV.9, IV.11).

New right: the *ideologies* associated with the Thatcher governments and, more recently, factions of the Conservative Party. *Neo-liberalism* and *neo-conservatism* are two important elements in this stance (chapters II.6, III.1, III.5, IV.1).

Non-government organizations (NGOs): agencies such as *voluntary organizations, charities* and mutual aid associations that are constitutionally distinct from government, though they may subsidized or regulated by the state or provide welfare services under *contract* (chapters II.1, II.11).

Occupational welfare: benefits and services provided through the workplace, either by the employer or by work-based organizations such as unions and *professional associations* (chapters III.2, III.9, IV.6).

Opportunity cost: denotes the ways in which making choices in conditions of scarcity involves a cost, the cost being the value of whatever has to be given up; the opportunity cost of any action is thus the best alternative forgone (chapters II.3, III.9).

Paternalism: perceives society in hierarchical terms, wherein each level has clear reciprocal obligations and the more powerful and affluent a duty to provide for the less well off (chapters II.4, II.6, III.3).

Paternalistic: as above, but also used pejoratively to criticize service providers for disregarding users' views in policy-making and service delivery.

Patient's Charter: details the service standards and redress systems available to NHS patients; see *Citizen's Charter* (chapter IV.8).

Patriarchy: the dominance of men over women or the structures and practices through which men dominate women.

Pay-as-you-go: state pensions (and health care) schemes paid out of current revenues rather than from a funded scheme (chapters II.12, III.9, III.11, IV.6).

Personal social services: refers to the work of local authority social service departments in England and Wales, and social work departments in Scotland and Northern Ireland. In Northern Ireland it also refers to the work of social services staff within the health and social services boards.

Pluralism: a set of political theories which sees power as diffused between diverse interest groups and decision-making as the product of competition and negotiation between them (chapters II.16, II.17).

Poverty trap: a situation where an employed individual gaining an increase in wages may be worse off as a consequence of the combined effects of benefit losses and taxation (chapters II.12, III.10, IV.10).

Privatization: the replacement or reduction of one or more of the three traditional forms of state welfare: direct provision, subsidies and regulation (chapters II.5, II.12, IV.10).

Procedural rights: entitlements to specified forms of service delivery and forms of redress (chapters III.10, IV.3).

Profession(s): a term used in many ways, but generally to describe occupations which claim a specific expertise requiring specialist training and qualification, and whose representative bodies (professional associations) control entry and codes of behaviour (chapters II.8, II.11, II.16, III.5, IV.3).

Professionalization: processes through which members of an occupation build up control over its practice through laying claim to particular expertise, and restricting access through establishing entry, training and qualifying criteria.

Proxy-customer: an individual such as a *care manager* or general practitioner who purchases care for someone else (the *end-user*).

Public choice theory: an approach to welfare based on the application of economic analysis and methods (chapter II.16).

Public expenditure: the amount spent on all public services by central and local government, financed by taxation and public borrowing, over a particular time period (usually a year) (chapters I.3, II.12, III.9, III.11).

Public sector borrowing requirement (PSBR): the total sum that has to be borrowed by the government to meet the gap between tax receipts and the level of public spending.

Purchaser–provider split: the division of state welfare agencies into separate units, one charged with service delivery, the other with commissioning and buying services on behalf of users (chapters II.16, III.5, IV.8, IV.11).

Quality assurance: a planned system of activities and procedures designed to ensure that services or products satisfy agreed standards within agreed resources and time scales (chapters III.5, IV.8, IV.9, IV.11).

Quangos: quasi non-governmental organizations; bodies responsible for managing public services and whose members are appointed and financed by the government but are nominally independent.

Quasi-market(s): the simulation of market conditions in public welfare services by introducing competition between *providers* and choice for *purchasers* (chapters II.8, II.16, III.1, III.5, IV.8, IV.11).

Racism (direct/indirect): a form of discrimination in which individuals are differentiated on the basis of physical, religious or cultural characteristics and practices (chapters II.10, II.13).

Reciprocity: the notion that the receipt of a benefit or service entails some form of return to the provider.

Redress: securing remedial action in the event of poor quality or inappropriate service delivery.

Regulation: government setting and enforcement of standards for the conduct, production, delivery and, in some instances, outcomes of welfare benefits and services (chapters II.5, II.6, III.1, III.2).

Residual/ization: the restriction of state welfare to minimal benefits and services (chapters I.3, III.10, IV.10, IV.11).

Selectivism: limiting of benefits and welfare services to specified individuals or groups on the basis of *means-testing* (chapters II.14, III.10, IV.6).

Social assistance: forms of income support/benefits, usually *means-tested*, which are not contingent on claimants' contributions but are funded out of general taxation.

Social division of welfare: see *Division of welfare*.

Social dumping: the relocation of firms (especially transnational corporations) from countries with high taxation and welfare benefits to those with lower 'social overheads' (chapters II.15, III.8).

Social fund: a cash-limited form of means-tested social assistance providing loans and grants to meet one-off or 'exceptional' needs (chapters III.10, IV.6).

Social insurance: a form of funding state welfare benefits and services through specified contributions paid into an insurance fund which entitles the contributee to support without a test of means or need. Contributions are usually compulsory and based on labour market participation. The individual's contribution may be supported by employer's contributions and/or a subvention from the state (chapters II.9, III.10).

Social rights: in a narrow sense this notion refers to an individual's legal entitlements; in a broader sense it is a socially constructed claim to perceived entitlements, e.g. the 'right to work' (chapters II.2, II.8, III.1, III.10, IV.2).

Social tourism: the movement of claimants from one part of a country to another or from one country to another in order to gain higher benefits or service provision.

Stakeholders: social or organizational arrangements in which the 'stakes' held by all participants are recognized in terms of both their responsibilities and entitlements (chapter II.2).

Substantive rights: legally enforceable entitlements to particular benefits or services (chapter III.10).

Subsidiarity: the principle that welfare support should be provided in the first instance by agencies closest to the users (chapters III.1, III.8).

Take-up: the proportion of those eligible for a particular benefit or service who receive it.

Targeting: *concentrating* welfare benefits and services on particular groups or categories, usually those who are construed or perceived as being in greatest 'need'; *means-testing* is the most common means of targeting (chapters II.12, II.14, III.10).

Tax expenditures: the cost of the amount of tax forgone by the government through the provision of *tax relief* or *fiscal welfare* in the form of special allowances, exemptions, exclusions, credits, preferential rates and deductions for individuals or organizations (chapters II.11, III.1).

Tax relief: allowances to individuals and organizations which reduce their overall tax liability and in effect subsidize the purchase of those goods and services wholly or partially exempt from taxation (chapters II.11, III.1).

Territorial justice: the extent to which different geographical areas receive equal coverage and treatment from state welfare services.

Total quality management: a form of work organization which centres on engaging all employees in securing 'consumer satisfaction' and seeking continuous improvements in the processes of service delivery and the quality of the products or services offered.

Transaction costs: the cost of the administrative overheads arising from the drafting, negotiation, monitoring and enforcement of *contracts* and contractual arrangements.

Unemployment trap: a situation faced particularly by those in low-waged occupations in which an individual/household is no better off (or worse off) in work than when claiming unemployment and related benefits as a result of the combined effects of loss of benefits and taxation (chapter II.12).

Underclass: commonly used to delineate those at the bottom (or outside) of the social hierarchy. Some characterize this group in terms of a lifestyle and value system which is held to be different from that of the wider society; others emphasize the processes which marginalize those at the lower end of society (chapters IV.5, IV.10).

Universalism: the provision of welfare services and benefits to all citizens. In socialist thinking this reflects the belief that there are universal human welfare needs and that there is a universal societal responsibility for meeting them (chapters II.8, III.10, III.11, IV.8).

Utility: used to denote the satisfaction or value derived by an individual from the consumption of a product or service; utility is usually seen as being expressed when an individual chooses one good or service in preference to another.

Vertical redistribution: the redistribution of resources from more affluent to less affluent groups or individuals.

Voluntary organizations: organizations which can be distinguished from statutory and commercial welfare providers by their overall mission and non-profit-distributing characteristics (chapters II.11, III.3).

Welfare mix: see *Mixed economy of welfare.*

Welfare pluralism: used descriptively to denote the production and consumption of welfare through both statutory and non-statutory means; also used prescriptively by those who favour a *mixed economy of welfare* (part III).

Welfare rights: see *Social rights.*

Welfare rights advisors: those who provide information and guidance about benefit and service entitlements to claimants and potential users.

White Paper: a UK central government document setting out the government's legislative proposals.

Workfare: schemes developed originally in the United States which make the receipt of unemployment benefit conditional on the claimant undertaking training or preparation for work (chapter IV.7).

appendix: the social policy association (spa)

The SPA is the professional association for academics, researchers and students in social policy and administration. As an academic association in the social science field, it is a member of the Association of Learned Societies in the Social Sciences (ALSISS), and it has close collaborative links with other professional associations in cognate fields, such as the British Sociological Association (BSA) and the Political Studies Association (PSA).

The SPA is a membership organization and membership is open to all students, teachers and others working in the social policy field. All members pay an annual fee and in return receive a range of membership services including:

- a regular, and popular, newsletter;
- free subscription to the leading social policy journal, the *Journal of Social Policy*;
- a small grants scheme to support the setting up of seminars and conferences for members;
- subgroups for postgraduate students, women members and comparative policy analysis;
- an Annual Conference held in July each year at an academic institution in the UK;
- an annual review of developments in the field, *Social Policy Review*.

The cost of membership varies with income across a number of broad bands, and membership is also open to corporate bodies such as research institutes. The majority of members of the SPA live and work in the United Kingdom, but the Association also has active members all over the world, including in particular Europe, North America, the Far East and Australia. The Association is also developing formal links with partner organizations in other European countries in order to develop further comparative work within the discipline.

The Association is managed by an Executive Committee comprised of members elected at the Annual Conference, with members serving on the committee for periods of three years at a time. In addition there are officers – a Chair, Secretary and Treasurer – also elected and serving on a three-year basis. Students of social policy are encouraged to join the Association and to contact staff members in their departments, schools or faculties. The SPA can be contacted through the Secretary, who currently is:

Caroline Glendinning
NPCRDC
5th Floor, Williamson Building
University of Manchester
Oxford Road
Manchester M13 9PL

Name index

Abel-Smith, Brian   336, 339
Acton, J.   57
Ahmad, W. I. U.   93
Alcock, Peter   341
Amin, K.   93
Arber, Sara   172
Arnot, M.   297
Association of British Insurers   156, 158
Atkin, K.   171
Atkinson, P.   328
Attlee, Clement   8, 161

Bailey, Carol A.   327
Baker, Kenneth   294
Baldwin, Peter   52–3
Barclay, P.   357
Bartlett, W.   150
Becker, G. S.   50, 60–1
Bernard, Jessie   87
Beveridge, William   8, 9, 52, 73, 85, 253, 284
Blackstone, William   58
Blair, Tony   76, 79
Booth, Charles   8
Bosanquet, Bernard and Helen   8
Bottomore, T.   336
Bradshaw, J.   124, 265, 266, 267
Brunsdon, E.   156, 339
Buck, N.   348
Burghes, L.   265
Burke, Edmund   65–6
Burnham, V.   323
Butler, R. A. B.   10, 69

Cahill, Michael   338
Centre for Contemporary Cultural Studies   92
Centre for Educational Research and
    Innovation   293

Chamberlain, Joseph   66–7
Clarke, J.   178, 179, 182, 339
Clarke, K.   268
Clarke, Kenneth   111
Clasen, J.   339
Cochrane, A.   339
Cohen, S.   117, 260
Connor, H.   379
Coote, A.   123, 219, 261
Cousins, C.   177, 178
Craig, G.   94, 151
Crosland, Anthony   40, 73, 74,
    75–6

Dale, A.   349
Dalley, Gillian   170
David, M. E.   293, 294, 296
Davin, A.   119
Davis, K.   259, 260
Dawkins, Richard   53
Deacon, B.   133, 339
Deakin, N.   148, 151, 339
Dean, H.   37, 41, 151
Delors, Jacques   200
Digby, Anne   341
Disraeli, Benjamin   66
Doyal, L.   34, 38, 39, 80
DSS   265
Dunleavy, P.   147, 187

Edwards, T.   295
Elizabeth I, Queen   91
Employment Committee (1994)   282, 283
Employment Committee (1996)   284
Esping-Andersen, G.   24–5, 88, 128, 130, 339,
    366
Evandrou, M.   225

Falkingham, J. 209, 226, 227
Field, Frank 336
Finch, J. 51, 169, 170, 338
Folbre, Nancy 50
Forsyth, Michael 194
Fox Harding, L. 125
Fraser, D. 339
Fraser, S. 91
Freeman, R. 339
Friedman, M. and R. 61
Friedman, Milton 207

Gauthier, A. H. 125
George, V. 37, 38, 40, 337
Gewirtz, S. 295, 296, 297
Gilbert, B. B. 339
Gilmour, Ian 68
Ginn, Jay 172
Ginsburg, Norman 339–40
Glennerster, H. 148, 152, 211, 340
Gough, I. 34, 38, 39, 80, 337
Gould, A. 339
Graham, Hilary 172
Griffiths, Roy 289
Groves, D. 170, 338
Gutch, R. 167

Hague, William 194
Hakim, C. 349
Hammersley, M. 328
Hantrais, L. 23
Harman, Harriet 123
Harris, Jose 52
Hattersley, Roy 93
Haworth, A. 59
Hayek, F. A. von 10, 58, 61
Heaney, Seamus 329
Heath, Edward 68
Hempshell, M. 377
Hewitt, Patricia 123
Higgins, J. 361
Hill, M. 148
Hills, John 108, 109, 208, 209, 211, 226, 227,
251, 340, 356, 357, 358
Hogg, Quintin (Lord Hailsham) 67–8
Husband, C. 93
Hutton, Will 338–9

IES Graduate Annual Review 377, 378

Jessop, Bob 187
Johnson, Norman 340
Johnson, Paul 69
Jones, H. 125
Joseph Rowntree Foundation 340

Kahn, Alfred 124
Kaim-Caudle, Peter 339
Kamerman, Sheila 124
Keith, Lois 172
Kendall, J. 163
King, D. S. 283
King, Martin Luther 61
Knapp, M. 163
Knight, B. 163

Laczko, F. 252
Laing, W. 158
Lakey, J. 285
Land, Hilary 51
Law, I. 96
Lawson, R. 179
Layard, Richard 283, 284
Le Grand, Julian 228, 337–8
Lebeaux, C. N. 23
Lewis, J. 170
Lodge, David 329
Louis XIV, King of France 57
Lowe, Rodney 339

MacLeod, Ian 68, 69
Macmillan, Harold 67, 68, 69, 76
Major, John 219, 295
Maltby, T. 251, 253
Mangen, S. 23
Marshall, Alfred 74
Marshall, T. H. 8, 38, 73, 74, 75, 88,
336
Marx, Karl 71, 80
Mason, Jennifer 51
Maude, Angus 69
May, M. 156, 339
Mayo, M. 151
Mercer, K. 92
Meredith, B. 170
Midgley, Mary 50
Millar, J. 125, 265
Mills, C. Wright 34
Mishra, Ramesh 338
Morgan, Patricia 123
Morris, J. 172, 259
Morrison, Herbert 161
Mount, Ferdinand 85–6
Murray, Charles 337
Myrdal, Alva 51

National Council for Voluntary Organisations
161, 164
Newman, J. 179, 182
Noble, M. 358
Nozick, R. 39–40

Oakeshott, Michael 58–9
O'Connor, James 337
O'Donnell, O. 228
O'Leary, B. 147
O'Neill, John 49
Oppenheim, C. 93

Page, R. 37, 38, 40
Parton, N. 238–9
Pascall, Gillian 338
Pateman, Carole 89
Pearson, R. 379
Penrose, Robyn 329
Phillipson, C. 252, 253
Philpott, J. 284
Piachaud, D. 34
Pike, G. 379
Pinker, Robert 52, 54, 336–7
Plant, R. 39, 40
Pollard, E. 379
Pollitt, C. 179
Popper, Karl 58
Poullier, J.-P. 364
Powell, Enoch 68, 69, 93
Powell, M. 228
Propper, C. 228

Qureshi, H. 170

Rai, D. K. 94
Rathbone, Eleanor 87
Rawls, John 40, 131
Redwood, John 194
Rhodes, R. A. W. 187
Rigg, M. 378, 379
Robson, C. 344
Rodgers, Barbara 339
Rose, Hilary 51
Rose, M. E. 324, 325
Rowntree, Joseph 8
Rowntree, Seebohm 16

Saunders, P. 186
Shaw, George Bernard 71

Skocpol, Theda 88
Smeeding, T. 366
Smith, Adam 49–50, 59–60, 62
Smith, Gilbert 335
Smith, S. J. 95
Smith, T. 358
Snower, Dennis 283, 284
Solomos, J. 93
Spicker, Paul 341
Sullivan, M. 73, 76
Swain, J. 259

Tawney, R. H. 8, 72–3, 80, 336
Taylor-Gooby, P. 37, 39, 41, 179, 335
Thane, Pat 339
Thatcher, Margaret 11, 50, 53, 61, 65, 68, 85, 93, 110, 111, 186–7, 253–4, 309
Timmins, N. 148, 341
Titmuss, R. M. T. 8, 24, 52, 85, 118, 209, 211, 335–6
Townsend, Peter 8, 9, 336
Twigg, J. 171

Walker, A. 170, 251, 252, 253
Walsh, K. 180, 182
Walker, Peter 194
Ward, Colin 336
Webb, S. 110, 111
Webb, Sydney and Beatrice 8
Weber, Max 38, 80
White, M. 285
Whiteside, N. 280, 283
Wilding, Paul 337
Wilenski, H. L. 23
Williams, F. 91, 115, 117, 119, 340
Wilson, E. 85, 338
Wilson, Harold 40
Wistow, G. 188
Wolcott, Hary F. 329
Woods, A. 324, 325

Young, Michael 294

subject index

absolute monarchy 57, 58
abuse: children 238–40; of social security 282, 284; young people 243
accountability 80–1, 139, 177, 310, 395
Adam Smith Institute 356
Advisory Centre for Education 358
ageing of population 249, 250–1, 366
Aliens Act (1905) 116–17
All-Wales Strategy for Mental Handicap 197
Alta Vista 372
altruism 49–54, 209, 222, 395
Annual Employment Survey 348
Assisted Places Scheme 295
association, corporate/civil 58–9
Association of Chief Probation Officers 359
Audit Commission 181, 185, 240, 259, 395

Back to Work 267, 281
Barclay Report (1982) 308
basic income: see citizen's income
Bath Information and Data Services 369
benefit types: categorical 274–5; discretionary 275; index-based 278; means-tested 215, 217, 274; national insurance funded 10; occupational 275; passported 274; tax-based 130; universal 275
benefits: conditionality 274, 275, 284–5, 396; cuts 253; dependency 88–90, 172–3, 242, 245–6, 257–8, 264–5; egalitarianism 37–8; feminism 25–6; income groups 225, 226, 227–8, 357; lone mothers 267, 268; principles 275–6; self-financing 228; stigma 274; take-up 94, 217, 274; targeting 215; value 225; see also child benefit; entitlement
Benefits Agency 95, 185, 195
Beveridge Report (1942) 119, 148, 250, 273–4

blood donors 52, 211–12, 336
Britain: England's dominance 191, 193; European Union 199, 200; housing tenure 301–2; political process 139–41; social policy departments 192; see also individual countries
British Council of Organisations of Disabled People 359
British Election Studies Information System 370
British Household Panel Survey 348
British Medical Association 140, 358
British Social Attitudes Surveys 370
Bulletin Board for Libraries 369
Bupa 157

Campaign for State Education 358
campaigners 164
capitalism 10–11, 71, 72, 78–9, 82
care: carers 171, 173; feminism 212; gendered roles 26, 171, 254; informal sector 125, 170–1; jobs in 383; for older people 254–5; value 51; vocation 51; see also community care
care managers 180, 260
Carers (Recognition and Services) Act (1995) 171, 173
Carers National Association 170, 176, 359
case study 317, 318
CD-ROMs 370
Census of Employment 348
Census Microdata Unit 346
Census of Population 346
Census Sample of Anonymized Records (SARs) 346
Central Statistical Office 224, 345, 350–1
Centre for Contemporary Cultural Studies 92

Centre for Policy Studies 356
CHAR 359
charities 161, 162–3, 164, 360, 396
Charity Act (1993) 162
Charity Commission 162–3, 167
Charity Organisation Society 8
child abuse 238–40
child benefit 87, 88, 125, 218, 266, 268, 274–5, 276
child care 82, 87, 125, 267–9
Child Maintenance Bonus 267
Child Poverty Action Group 336, 357, 358, 360
child protection 238–40, 311
Child Support Act (1991) 51, 125, 221, 267, 268
Child Support Agency 140, 185, 211, 268, 396
children: charities 360; health care 235; lone parents 265; looked after by local authorities 235–7; National Child Development Study 349; rights 237–8; status 238; welfare 38, 235, 237–8
Children (Scotland) Act (1995) 236, 237, 238
Children Act (1989) 235–6, 237, 238, 309, 311
Children's and Young Persons' Acts (1960s) 310
Chronically Sick and Disabled Persons Act (1970) 258–9
Churches Enquiry into Unemployment and the Future of Work 359
citation index 369
Citizens Advice Bureaux 357, 383–4
Citizen's Charter 219, 295, 396
Citizens' Commission of the Future of the Welfare State 359
citizen's income 101–2, 111, 130, 133, 218, 278–9, 396
citizenship 73–6, 396; active 42, 165, 395; conditions 218; exclusion 91, 115, 116; nationality 116–18; rights 74, 131, 151, 214–15, 217–18; supranational 130–1
City Technology Colleges 294
civil service 72, 188, 249
class 80, 81–2
clean air regulations, costs 208
cohabitation 85, 86, 122, 245
collectivism 51–3, 59, 67, 72, 115–16, 396
command economies 47–8
Commentaries on the Laws of England (Blackstone) 58
Commission for Racial Equality 357, 360
Commission on Social Justice 37, 41, 357, 360
communication skills 381

community 59, 60, 163, 396
community care 309–10, 396; consumer experience 311–12; disabled people 217, 258–60; informal sector 169–70; older people 254–5
Community Care (Direct Payments) Act (1996) 173
Community Charter of the Fundamental Social Rights of Workers (1989) 199, 200
Community Development Foundation 357
Community Programmes 281
competition: choice 47; conservatism 66; global 130; health care 180–1, 289; markets 61, 62; welfare 150, 155, 157
computers 368–9, 371, 372–3
conditionality 284–5
confidentiality 321
conservatism: competition 66; and Enlightenment 64–5; green 100; modern 65–7; and neo-liberalism 68–9; reactionaries 64; social reform 67–8; welfare regime 25
Conservatives: Citizen's Charter 219, 295; health care 288; lack of egalitarianism 40–1; lone parents 266; market forces 11, 154–5; personal social services 309–10; targeting 125, 215; welfare 32–3, 65, 154–5
consumerism 44–5, 50, 99, 102
contracts 150, 166, 179–80, 396
Convention of Scottish Local Authorities 352
cooperation 31, 180–1
corporatism 58–9, 397
Council of Europe 129, 131, 201
council housing 10, 81, 299–302; allocation 39; deprivation 303–4; lone parents 264; post-war 118; regeneration/management 303; Right to Buy 302; *see also* housing; housing policy
Council of Ministers 201
Councils of Voluntary Service 164
crime 113, 123, 242, 246, 247
criminal justice, information sources 359
criminal responsibility 243
culture 23, 92, 115, 120
customers 179–80

Darwinism 118
data: academic sources 366; analysis 320, 368–9; computer use 368–9, 371, 372–3; evidence 344; gathering 320; international 361–2, 363–6; national 344–9; non-academic/non-governmental 354–5; on-line 369–72; from surveys 349–50

data archives 369
data-sets 344, 345–6, 350
databases 369–70
DDA (Danish Data Archives) 370
de-institutionalization 197
decentralization 152, 397
decommodification 24–5, 82, 397
degrees, postgraduate 388–9
democracy, neo-liberal 60
democratic socialism 71, 81
demographic trends 16, 202, 203, 249, 250
Demos 355
Denmark, family policy 126
Department for Economic and Social
  Information and Policy Analysis 363
Department of Employment, Labour Force
  Survey 347
Department of Health, *Child Protection:
  Messages from Research* 240
Department of Social Security 94–5, 140,
  276–7
dependency 397; disabled people 257–8;
  lone parents 88–90, 124, 264–5; and
  responsibility 172–3; young people 242,
  245–6
Directorate-General for Employment 363
Disability Discrimination Act (1995) 261
disabled people: community care 217,
  258–60; dependency 257–8; discrimination
  257–8, 260–1; education 257–8; informal
  care analysis 172; service provision 259,
  260; unemployment 245, 257–8; welfare
  state 258–9
Disabled Persons (Employment) Act (1944) 258
Disabled Persons (Services, Consultation and
  Representation) Act (1986) 259
discretion 215, 216–17
dissertation 317, 318, 326
distribution of services 107, 221, 223, 224–8
divorce 16, 35, 124, 245
Divorce Reform Act (1969) 122
domestic transition 243, 245–6
drugs, illegal 242

earnings: age-related 208–9; equal pay 199;
  inequalities 111; minimum wage 112,
  268; and unemployment 130; *see also*
  income groups
eco-feminism 100, 397
eco-socialism 99–100, 397
ecology parties 98–9
economic determinism 137, 138
economics: choice 43–4, 47–8; efficiency
  44–8; information failure 208; social
  policy 43–4, 107–8, 109, 111–13, 362–3

education 9–10, 79–80, 293–4; Assisted
  Places Scheme 295; budget 235; choice
  180, 294, 295–7; contracts 180;
  decomprehensivization 297; disabled
  people 257–8; England 293–8; equality
  293–4; ethnic minority communities 95,
  96–7; extension 243–5; gender 86, 87,
  296–7; information sources 358; Ireland
  192, 193; jobs in 385–6; market forces
  294–7; pre-/post-school 297; Scotland
  192, 193, 194, 293, 295; statistics 352; for
  workforce 113; *see also* higher education
Education (Schools) Act (1992) 296
Education Act (1944) 258
Education Act (1981) 259
Education Act (1988) 120
Education Act (1993) 296
Education Act for England and Wales (1980)
  295
Education Reform Act (1988) 244, 294
effectiveness 46, 132, 397
efficiency 44–8, 107, 132, 180, 222, 397
egalitarianism 37–8, 119, 398
elderly: *see* older people
elitism 137, 138
e-mail 370–1
empiricism 319
employers, as proxy buyers 156, 158
employment: economic policy 107, 109;
  gendered 86; graduates 377–8, 380–1;
  lone parents 266–9; self-employment 111;
  statistics 348, 352
Employment Committee (1994) 282
employment policies 10, 73, 148, 280, 282–5
Employment Policy Institute 359
Employment Service 282–3
Employment Training Scheme, child care
  costs 267–8
empowerment 151, 398
England: education 293–8; local government
  185, 195; Local Government Commission
  309; social policy organization 192, 195
Enlightenment 64–5
entitlement: analysis 88; conditionality 274,
  275, 284–5; desert-based 39; equality 278;
  statutory 259
environmental cleanliness 99, 207–8
environmentalism 98–9, 100–2
Equal Opportunities Commission 296, 356,
  360
equality: earnings 199; education 293–4;
  entitlement 278; opportunity 37–8, 40–1,
  202, 293, 398; outcome 37–8, 40–1, 80, 398;
  welfare 76, 152
equity 46–7, 152, 398

Erasmus programme 326
ESRC (Economic and Social Research
Council) 348, 388, 391
ESRC Data Archive 369, 372
essay, extended 317, 318
essentialism, cultural 120
ethical socialism 72–3
ethics, social policy 320–1, 324–5, 329
ethnic minority communities 92, 93–7, 117,
217, 245, 298; *see also* race
eugenics 53, 91, 118–19, 398
EURi 363
Europe Benefits Report 362
European Commission 21, 201, 202–3
European Court of Human Rights 129, 131
European Court of Justice 129, 171, 201
European Economic Community 199
European Parliament 201
European Social Fund 199, 202, 398
European Union: autonomy 139; data
sources 363–6; equality of opportunity
202; fieldwork placements 326–7;
harmonization 12, 120, 200–1, 364;
poverty 202–3; Social Chapter/Charter
131, 139; social policy 21, 129, 199–203,
347; social work 307; welfare models 200
European Union Structural Funds 196
Eurostat 364–6
experience, direct 18, 34

Fabian Society 8, 9, 355
Fabianism 71–2, 82–3, 154, 398
family: care, gendered 254; diversity 117,
122, 245; failure 222; female oppression
85; feminism 123–4; health care 287;
income sharing 87, 222–3, 398; as
institution 49, 51–2; legality 125; male
breadwinner model 87, 117, 121–2;
obligations 51; relationships 50–1;
socialization of children 120, 123;
structure 16, 111, 122, 123–4, 263; support
125, 308; welfare 31–2, 275
Family Credit 111, 112, 125, 264, 266, 267,
268, 274, 276
Family Expenditure Survey 347, 349
family policy 119, 121–6, 245, 360
Family Policy Studies Centre 360
Family Resources Survey 348
feminism 86, 338, 398; benefits 25–6; care
212; elitism 137, 138; family 123–4;
gendering of welfare 11, 25, 254; informal
care 170, 171–2; second wave 170, 171;
socialist 82, 85, 86; welfare state 85–6
fieldwork 323–5; higher education 329–30;
placements 326–9

Finer Commission, One-Parent Families
(1974) 124, 266
fiscal policy 109, 149, 398
foundations 356
France 64, 118, 125, 267
free trade 132, 133–4
friendly societies 32
Friends of the Earth 98
Funding Agency for Schools 296
Further Education Funding Council 297

GATT 130
GCSE 244
gender 86, 399; care 254; carers 26, 171;
education 86, 87, 296–7; employment 86;
information sources 360; labour division
88; lone parents 264; welfare 11, 25–6,
254
General Household Survey 170–1, 347
general practitioners, fundholding 156, 289,
290
Germany 80, 98, 117–18, 126, 130, 152
globalization 21–2, 109–10, 128–30, 133, 134,
399
government: centralization 184; labour
division 185–7; market economies 48;
power 57; statistics 350–1; welfare
departments 147; *see also* local
government; state
government-funded bodies 356–7
graduates 377–8, 379, 380
Greater London Council 78, 92, 186–7
green policies 98–9, 100–2
Greenpeace 98
Griffiths Report 171, 259

health 286–8, 291
health care: children 235; competition
180–1, 289; deregionalized 195; family
287; funding 288–9; information sources
358; jobs in 383; needs 286–7; patient
choice 180; policy analysis 287–90;
preventative 101, 156; primary care 286,
290; private sectors 291; provision 140,
188, 287, 288–9; rights 140, 217; statistics
352; women 287; *see also* National Health
Service
health insurance market 156–8
health promotions 242
Health and Welfare Unit, Institute of
Economic Affairs 355
higher education 298, 329–30, 386
Higher Education Funding Council 297
home ownership 300, 301–2, 303, 304
homelessness 215, 242, 246, 264, 302, 303–4

hospitals 61, 67; *see also* National Health Service
households 16; *see also* family
Households below Average Income Data-set 349
housing: information sources 358–9; jobs in 382; low-income groups 301–2; organizations 197–8, 304; private rented sector 299–300, 301, 302, 304; racism 95–6, 117; social exclusion 305; statistics 352; subsidies 302; *see also* council housing; home ownership
housing associations 81, 399
Housing Benefit 111, 112, 264, 266
Housing Corporation 95
housing policy 16, 299–301
housing transition 243, 245–6
human capital 50
human nature 49–50, 60

IASSIST (International Association for Social Science Information Service and Technology) 370
ICPSR (Interuniversity Consortium for Political and Social Research) 370
immigration 91, 117, 215–16
Immigration Acts 93
impartiality 177
imperialism 66–7
Incapacity Benefit 278
income groups, benefits 225, 226, 227–8, 357
income protection 357–8
Income Support 274; and earning 112, 268; lone parents 264, 265, 266, 267, 268; statistics 276; youth 243, 244
income tax 61, 208–9, 266
Independent Labour Party 72
Independent Living Fund 277
individual 38, 41, 62, 72
individualism 40, 51, 59
inequality: earnings 111; health status 286–7; racial 94, 245; redistribution 75
inflation 109, 110
informal sector 64–5, 125, 169–73, 308
information/advice work 383–4
information failure 208
information technology 109, 368–9; *see also* data
Institute of Economic Affairs 58, 123, 355
Institute for Fiscal Studies 356
Institute for Public Policy Research 123, 219, 355, 357
institutions 18, 24, 31, 52, 92–7, 117, 149
insurance: health 156–8; private 288, 358; redistribution 53, 221–2; social 39, 79, 218

Insurance Premium Tax 158
International Court of Justice, Hague 129
International Labour Organisation 129, 132, 133, 361, 363, 365–6
International Monetary Fund 128–9, 134
International Social Security Association 363
Internet 350, 371
interpersonal skills 381
intervention: social 134, 138–9; state 119–20, 273–4
Invalid Care Allowance 171
investing in people 113
Ireland, Northern: education 192, 193; government 185, 194; social policy 192, 196–7; Social Security Agency 195; status 139, 191, 193

JANET 370
job advertisement samples 382–6
Job Centres 281, 283
job creation 281
Job Interview Guarantee scheme 281
job subsidies 282
Jobclubs 281
jobs, social policy degrees 377–9, 382–6; entry level/second step 381; personal qualities 379; skills needed 380–2
Jobseekers Allowance 278
Joint Council for the Welfare of Immigrants 360
Joseph Rowntree Foundation 173, 356, 357, 358, 359
justice 131–2, 352; *see also* social justice

Keynesian policy 73, 108–9
King's Fund 358

labour 39–40, 82, 91
labour division 31, 88, 185–7
Labour Force Survey 347
labour market: age discrimination 251–2; class 80; deregulated 110; female participation 85, 122, 255; graduates 377; information sources 359
Labour Party 8, 71, 72; education and training 283–4; NHS 73; political shift 76; Scottish independence 198; socialism 79; welfare state 9, 32, 73
laissez-faire 59, 237, 399
law 58, 60; *see also* legislation
Legal Action Group 359
legal aid 215
legislation: child welfare 237; personal social services 309–10; social policy 193; social security 243

LETS (local employment transfer schemes)
    102, 399
liberalism 8, 25, 59
liberty 58–9, 61
life expectancy 250
lifestyle change 99, 102, 287
Limits to Growth report 98
local authorities: capping limits 211;
    children looked after 235–7; community
    care 217, 259–60; hospitals 67; NHS and
    Community Care Act 125, 150, 188, 255,
    311; social services 309; welfare 150
local education authorities 294–5
Local Enterprise Companies 186
Local Enterprise Councils 282
local government 139–40, 184; England
    185–7, 195; Scotland 139, 185–7, 194–5;
    statistics 351–2; Wales 185–7, 194–5;
    welfare 188–9
Local Government Association 352
Local Schools Information 358
London boroughs 185
London School of Economics 8–9
lone parents 265–6; Conservatives 266;
    council housing 264; demography 263–4;
    employment 266–9; family 263; fathers
    264; minimum wage 268; mothers 89,
    264, 267; poverty 265; welfare dependency
    88–90, 124, 264–5
Longitudinal Study 348
Low Pay Unit 359
Luxembourg Employment Study 366
Luxembourg Income Study 366

Maastricht Treaty 111, 139, 199, 200
male breadwinner model of family 87, 117,
    121–2, 399
managerialism 178–9, 182, 310–11, 399
Mannheim Centre for European Social
    Research 366
manpower policies 281
Maoist regimes 79
marginal utility, diminishing 44–5, 64,
    399–400
market forces 11, 50, 61, 62, 154–6, 157,
    294–7, 400
Marxism 10, 81, 137, 337
Maternity and Child Welfare Act (1918) 119
means-testing 215, 217, 274, 400
Mental Deficiency Act (1913) 119
meritocracy 40, 294
metropolitan district councils 185
MIDAS (Manchester Information Datasets
    and Associated Services) 369
migrant workers 130, 132–3

minimum wage 112, 268
MISEP 363
MISSOC 363, 365
monarchy, absolute 57, 58
monetarists 108–9, 110, 400
Motability 277
mutual aid 65, 101, 400
mutual associations 32, 400

nation-building 118–19
National Assistance Act (1948) 258
National Association of Citizens Advice
    Bureaux 94, 95, 357
National Association of Pension Funds 358
National Association of Probation Officers
    359
National Baby Week 119
National Centre for Volunteering 163
National Child Development Study 349
National Children's Bureau 360
National Consumer Council 219, 356
National Council for One Parent Families
    360
National Council of Voluntary Child Care
    Organisations 360
National Council for Voluntary Organisations
    360
national curriculum 294
National Federation of Housing Associations
    359
National Health Service: Beveridge 9;
    Labour Party 73; politics 290–1; reforms
    61, 179, 185, 288–90; regulation 181–2;
    socialism 78; trusts 156, 186
National Health Service Act (1948) 258
National Health Service and Community
    Care Act (1990); community care 259, 309;
    informal care 125, 171, 172; local
    authorities 125, 150, 188, 255, 311; NHS
    Trusts 156, 186; responsibility 289
National Health Service Executive 195
National Health Service Management Inquiry
    (1983) 289
National Insurance Act (1911) 116
National Insurance Fund 276
National Lottery 161, 165
National Opinion Polls 348
National Vocational Qualifications 282
nationalization 148
nationhood 115, 118–19
needs 23, 33–4; approaches 214–15; budget
    limits 207; measured 36; redistribution
    222; and rights 260–1
Needs Assessment Study (1979) 197
negative income tax 61

neo-Keynesianism 338–9
neo-liberalism 57–8, 60–2, 68–9, 132, 400
neo-Marxism 81–2
Netherlands 152, 390
Netskills 371
New Earnings Survey 348
new left 10
new radicals 11
new right 10–11, 68, 85–6, 136, 179, 237, 337, 400
New United Kingdom Official Publications 372
NISS 370–1
non-governmental organizations 32, 400
Northern Ireland office 194
Nozick, R. 39–40
Nuffield Foundation 356
nursery education vouchers 211, 267, 269, 297

obligations: collective 51–3; family 51; moral 169; social 132–3; of unemployed 284
occupational benefits 275, 400
Office of Fair Trading 158
Office for National Statistics 345, 346–7, 348, 350–1
Office of Population Censuses and Surveys 345
Office for Standards in Education 296, 297
older people 249–51; care 16, 254–5; gender distribution 250; labour market 251–2; poverty 252–4; race distribution 250–1; social security subsidies 255; support services 39
on-line data services 369–72
opportunity cost 43–4, 400
oral skills 381
Organisation for Economic Cooperation and Development 362–3, 364

parents: age at first baby 245; as consumers 156, 294; responsibility 236, 237; rights 237; school choice 180, 294, 295–7; *see also* lone parents
Parent's Charter 295–6
part-time work 111, 122
paternalism 65, 66, 237, 401
patient choice 180
Patient's Charter 290, 401
patriarchy 82, 85–6, 237, 401
Penal Affairs Consortium 359
pensions: ethnic minority communities 94; information sources 358; occupational 253; personal 254; and poverty 252–4;

redistribution 221; as social contract 253–4; state 15, 112; women 251
Pensions Act (1908) 116
personal social services 166, 169, 401; expenditure 236; information sources 359; legislation 309–10; managerialism 310–11; organizations 307; reorganization 308–9; residual 235, 306–8; responsibilities 306–7; users 308
pluralism 136–7, 138, 340, 401
policy and corporate planning, jobs 384–5
Policy Studies Institute 356
political process, Britain 138–41
political rights 74–5, 214–15
Political Science Association 373
Poor Law 8, 66, 67, 74, 188, 273
population ageing 249, 250–1, 366
postgraduate study 388–9; application 390–1; funding 391–2; location 389–90; outcomes 392–3; supervision 389
poverty 8; alleviation 275; Conservative government 35; crime 113; ethnic minority communities 93–4; European Union 202–3; information sources 336, 357; lone parents 265, 267; measurements 34, 80; older people 252–4; race 360; young people 244
poverty trap 111, 217, 303, 304, 401
primary care 286, 290
Private Patients Plan 157
private welfare 154–6, 158–9
privatization 61, 149–50, 401
production 45, 46
professionalism 101, 178–9, 401
project 317, 318–22
Protestantism 57
provident associations 157
Public Assistance 67
public choice theory 136, 137, 179, 401
public expenditure 401; cost restraint 179; cuts 110, 125; distribution 224; rationing 212; statistics 108, 351; survey 210
Public Health Alliance 358
public housing: *see* council housing
public/private spheres 102, 116, 147
public utilities 148

QUALIDATA 372
quasi-vouchers 211

race: lone parents 264; nationality 116–18; older people 250–1; unemployment 245; welfare 11, 91–2, 216–17; *see also* ethnic minority communities
Race Relations Acts (1965, 1976) 93

racism 360, 402; access to welfare 11, 91–2, 216–17; housing 95–6, 117; institutional 92–7, 117; social security 93–5
Radical Statistics Group 356
reciprocity 49, 50, 51, 402
redistribution: altruism 53, 209, 222; benefits 275; cross-sectional 225–6; global taxation 133–5; insurance 221; life cycles 221, 222, 226–8; by need 222; supranational 129; welfare 338
refugees 117
regulation: economic policy 109; free trade 132, 133–4; global 133–5; health insurance 158; by state 148–9; supranational 129; welfare 151, 181–2
regulatory agencies 185
remarriage 245
research 317–18; analytical skills 382; methods courses 382, 388; opportunities 385
residence status 215–16
residualism 402; personal social services 235, 306–8; welfare 24, 215, 217–18
resources: allocation 49, 195–7, 207, 214; rationing 212; redistribution 75; welfare 39–40
responsibility 41, 236, 237, 243, 289, 306–7
Restart interviews 281, 282, 284
Retail Price Index 347
retirement 249–50, 251–2
rights 38–9, 41, 214–15; children 237–8; citizenship 74, 131, 151, 214–15, 217–18; civil 74; derived 278; health care 140, 217; legal 214, 215; needs 260–1; parents 237; social 38–9, 74, 75, 199, 214; state 151; women 88
Rome, Treaty of 199, 203
rough sleeping 304

SARs 346
Scandinavia 85, 88
school-to-work transition 243–5
schools 294, 296; see also education
scientific racism 91–2
Scotland 139; charities 163; children looked after by local authorities 236–7; children's hearings 197; education 192, 193, 194, 293, 295; local government 185, 194–5, 352; social policy 192, 196–7; social service departments 309; status 191
Scottish Local Government Information Unit 352
Scottish Office 193–4
Seebohm Report 308, 309, 310
segregation 95, 257–8

self-employment 111
self-help bodies 164, 219
self-interest 49, 62
self-reliance 53–4
selfishness 49, 53, 59–60
SERP (State Earnings Related Pension) 254
service providers 164
service users 259–60
Severe Hardship Payments 244
Shelter 358–9
Single European Act (1986) 201
single parenthood: see lone parents
skill levels 113
social action 7, 200
Social Affairs Unit 356
Social Chapter, Maastricht Treaty 139
Social Charter, Council of Europe 131
Social and Community Planning Research 348
social control 86
social democracy 25, 71, 73, 76–7, 78
social dumping 128, 130, 132
social fund 216, 275, 277
social housing: see council housing
social indicators, UN 362, 363
social insurance 39, 79, 218
social justice 39–40, 41, 82–3, 119, 159
Social Market Foundation 355
social policy 7–12, 14, 17–19, 31, 91; citizenship 73–6; comparisons 20–2, 196; economic concepts 43–4; and economic policy 107–8, 109, 111–13, 362–3; ethics 320–1, 324–5, 329; European Union 21, 129, 199–203, 347; Fabianism 154; fieldwork 323–6; institutions 18; jobs in 377, 382–6; legislation 193; as lifetime savings bank 208; lone parents 265–6; politics 136–8; resource allocation 195–7; targeting 125; world trade 132
Social Policy Association 371, 389, 404
social policy books: classics 335–6; introductory texts 340–1; overviews 339–40; pathbreakers 336–9
social policy journals 341
social policy newspapers 341
social policy periodicals 342
social problems 16–17, 34–5, 280
social protection 112–13, 132, 273
social reformism 67–8, 73
social science citation index 369
Social Science Information Gateway 372
social security 275; abuse 282, 284; Beveridge plan 148, 273–4; classified 274–9; country comparisons 218; expenditure 253, 276; from National

Insurance contributions 274; information sources 357–8; International Labour Organisation 361; legislation 243; older people 253; patriarchy 85–6; racism 93–5; statistics 352; training 111
Social Security Act (1986) 244
Social Security Advisory Committee 357
Social Service Inspectorate 310–12
social welfare: *see* welfare
social work 307; *see also* personal social services
social workers 179, 307, 308
socialism 78–81; accountability 80–1; democratic 71; diversity 81–3; ecological 99–100; ethical 72–3; Western 58
socialist feminism 82, 85, 86
SociBase 363
society: corporate/civil association 58–9; nationalized 116; organic model 64, 65, 66; Thatcher 53, 65
SocInfo centre 373
sociobiology 53–4
Sociofile 370
Socrates programme 326
solidarity 53
special educational needs 245
SSDA (Social Science Data Archive) 369–70
stakeholders 41
Stalinism 79
state 147; bureaucracy 162, 395; centralization 184; care of citizens 20–1; dual/unitary 186–7; employment policies 10, 73, 148, 280, 282–5; and individual 38; intervention 119–20, 273–4; networks/relations 187–8; rights 151; voluntary sector 149–50, 166–7; welfare cuts 188; *see also* government
state benefits: *see* benefits
state welfare: *see* welfare
Statutory Maternity Pay 275
Statutory Sick Pay 275
stereotypes, in research 321
stigma 24, 94, 217, 260, 274
subsidiarity 152, 200, 204, 402
subsidies 149, 302
Supplementary Benefit 266
supranational agencies 21–2, 203–4
surveys, recurrent/continuous 346–7
Sweden: family policy 126; job creation 130; lone parent employment 267; postgraduate study 390; social democracy 78; welfare 80, 118
Swedish National Institute for Social Research 366
SYSDEM 363

Tapered Earnings Disregard 266
Tariff Reform League 66–7
tax relief 108, 149
taxation: and benefits 130; cuts 110; as disincentive 112; expenditure 210, 351, 402; fiscal policies 109; green policies 102; income tax 61, 208–9, 266; indirect 112; social services 209–11; welfare spending 225–6
teaching jobs 385–6
Technical and Vocational Educational Initiative 297
Thatcher, Margaret: family policy 85; GLC 186–7; health reforms 61; immigration 93; Maastricht Treaty 111; markets 50; monetarism 110; new right 11, 68; pensions 253–4; social services 309; society 53, 65
think-tanks 355
trade unions 118
training 111, 244, 281–2
Training and Enterprise Councils 186, 282
Training for Work 282
truancy 242

UK Government Home Page 373
unemployed 281–2, 284, 285; unemployment 359; disabled people 245, 257–8; earnings 130; ethnic minority communities 94, 245; graduates 377–9; and inflation 110; long-term 16–17, 285; mass 110–11; older people 252; social problems 280; stocks and flows 283; substitution 284; young people 242, 243–4, 246, 247
Unemployment Unit 359
unitary authorities 309
unitary district councils 185–6
United Nations 362, 363, 364
United Nations Convention on the Rights of the Child 238, 239
United Nations Declaration of Human Rights 131
United Nations High Commission for Refugees 129, 131
United Nations Human Development Report 129
universalism 79–81, 159, 215, 250, 275, 403
USA 88, 126, 130, 267
US Bureau of the Census 366
US Social Security Administration 366
utility maximizing 60, 61, 403

valuation, services 223
value 35, 51, 223, 225
VAT 112, 210

virginity testing 93
voluntary sector 167, 360, 403; citizen's
  income 101; organizations 163–4, 354–5;
  range 165–6; resourcing 164–5; and state
  149–50, 166–7; welfare 161–5
volunteers 163
vouchers 211, 267, 269, 297

wages: *see* earnings
Wales 139; Assembly 198; education
  293–8; language 197; local government
  185, 194–5; social policy 192, 196–7; social
  service departments 309; status 191
Watson Wyatt DataServices 362
welfare 18, 221–3; access to 215–17;
  bureaucracy 177–8; children 38, 235,
  237–8; classified regimes 20–2, 23–5;
  competition 130, 150, 155, 157;
  Conservatives 32–3, 65, 154–5; as
  consumption good 33; contracts 179–80;
  cuts 188; as disincentive 111–12;
  enhancement 218–19; equality 76, 152;
  expenditure 108, 225–6; family 31–2, 275;
  gendered 11, 25–6, 254; institutions 52;
  Labour Party 9, 32; managerialism
  178–9, 182, 310–11; patriarchy 85;
  pluralism 340; professionalism 101,
  178–9; race 11, 91–2, 216–17; reforms
  218–19; regulation 151, 181–2; residual
  24, 215, 217–18; resources 39–40; rights-
  based 38–9, 214; self-provision 155;
  social control 86; social 31–2, 74, 112–13;
  state/private 49, 51–2, 147–50; traditions
  65; universalism 79–81; voluntary sector
  161–5
welfare benefits: *see* benefits
welfare market 154–6, 157

welfare mix 12, 150–1, 169, 172, 361, 403
welfare state 9–10, 258–9; capitalism 82;
  comparisons 128–9, 200; development
  80; environmentalism 100–1; feminism
  85–6; historical context 115–16; housing
  302–3; labour division 185–6; Labour
  government 9, 32, 73; 1951/1993
  compared 209; women 87–90
Welsh Office 193–4
Whigs 65
Wolfenden Report 161
women: Afro-Caribbean 117; altruism 50–1,
  53–4; dependency 88–90, 217; domestic
  role 85, 119, 122; health care 287;
  informal social services 308; in labour
  market 85, 122, 255; motherhood 89–90;
  nation-building 119; paid/unpaid work
  82, 88, 89, 122, 170; pensions 251; rights
  88; and welfare state 87–90
work: casualization 130; paid/unpaid 82,
  88, 89, 101, 122, 170; part-time 111, 122;
  see also employment
work experience 281–2
Workers Educational Association 386
Workstart 282
World Bank 112, 129, 132, 133, 134, 286, 363
World Health Organisation 290, 363
World Trade Organization 132
World Wide Web 350, 371, 387

young offenders 242
young people: in care 242–3, 246; outside of
  biological families 246; poverty 244;
  pregnancies 242; social problems 242–3;
  training schemes 244; transitions 243–6,
  247; unemployment 242, 243–4, 246, 247
Youthaid 359